T0202653

Lecture Notes in Computer Science 14253

Founding Editors

Gerhard Goos
Juris Hartmanis

The series Lecture Notes in Computer Science (LNCS), including its subseries Lecture Notes in Artificial Intelligence (LNAI) and Lecture Notes in Bioinformatics (LNBI), has established itself as a medium for the publication of new developments in computer science and information technology research, teaching, and education.

LNCS enjoys close cooperation with the computer science R & D community, the series counts many renowned academics among its volume editors and paper authors, and collaborates with prestigious societies. Its mission is to serve this international community by providing an invaluable service, mainly focused on the publication of conference and workshop proceedings and postproceedings. LNCS commenced publication in 1973.

Henrik I. Christensen · Peter Corke ·
Renaud Detry · Jean-Baptiste Weibel ·
Markus Vincze

Editors

Computer Vision Systems

14th International Conference, ICVS 2023
Vienna, Austria, September 27–29, 2023
Proceedings

 Springer

Editors
Henrik I. Christensen (ID)
UC San Diego
La Jolla, CA, USA

Peter Corke (ID)
Queensland University of Technology
Brisbane, QLD, Australia

Renaud Detry (ID)
KU Leuven
Leuven, Belgium

Jean-Baptiste Weibel (ID)
TU Wien
Vienna, Austria

Markus Vincze (ID)
TU Wien
Vienna, Austria

ISSN 0302-9743   ISSN 1611-3349 (electronic)
Lecture Notes in Computer Science
ISBN 978-3-031-44136-3   ISBN 978-3-031-44137-0 (eBook)
https://doi.org/10.1007/978-3-031-44137-0

This Springer imprint is published by the registered company Springer Nature Switzerland AG
The registered company address is: Gewerbestrasse 11, 6330 Cham, Switzerland

Paper in this product is recyclable.

Preface

In order to imbue future intelligent machines with the capacity to comprehend their environment in a manner akin to human perception, it is crucial to equip them with the ability to "see." Vision is a fundamental and central human sense, as it facilitates seamless interaction with the surroundings. Over recent decades, advances in various research domains have significantly propelled computer vision systems, enhancing their capacity to interpret the world and thus enabling support for sophisticated machines. Nonetheless, existing artificial vision systems still confront limitations in their ability to operate in unconstrained, real-life environments and adapt to novel situations. Consequently, the principal mission of the International Conference on Computer Vision Systems (ICVS) to address and overcome these challenges is as relevant as ever.

The 14th edition of ICVS was held during September 27–29th, 2023, in the city of Vienna, Austria. Past editions had taken the conference to different countries across multiple continents and brought together researchers from all around the world. In 2023, ICVS remained vibrantly international with authors coming from 21 countries.

ICVS 2023 received 74 submissions, out of which 37 were accepted as oral presentations at the main conference. Each paper was double-blindly reviewed by at least two members of the Program Committee or external reviewers. The authors of accepted submissions were then asked to submit their final versions, taking into consideration the comments and suggestions in the reviews. The best paper of the conference was selected by the general and program chairs, after suggestions from the Program Committee were made. Accepted papers cover a broad spectrum of issues falling under the wide scope of computer vision in real-world applications, including among others vision systems for robotics, agriculture, medicine and industry. In this volume, the papers are organized into the following sections: Humans and Hands, Medical and Health Care, Farming and Forestry, Automation and Manufacturing, Mobile Robotics and Autonomous Systems, and Performance and Robustness.

The technical program of ICVS 2023 was enhanced with three invited speakers. First, Jeremy L. Wyatt (Amazon / University of Birmingham) described in his talk challenging robotic manipulation problems faced by Amazon in terms of scale, item variability and process variability. He proceeded to talk about the visual perception, grasp learning, failure detection, continual learning and automated A/B testing that were used to deploy hundreds of robots that pick millions of packages every day. The second invited speaker, Martin Humenberger (NAVER Labs) shared NAVER Labs' experience of deploying more than 100 robots in their headquarters in Seoul, South Korea to fulfill a variety of delivery tasks every day. Through that process, new connections between the digital and the physical world are created through AI and robotics. Finally, the third invited speaker, Timothy Patten (Abyss Solutions / University of Technology Sydney) explored in his talk the diverse challenges of data capture in remote marine environments. He then proceeded to discuss the technology and methods for operationalizing machine learning algorithms for defect detection across various applications.

The conference also hosted two workshops, which were organized in conjunction with the main conference. The "Industrial Computer Vision Systems" workshop was organized by Doris Antensteiner, Roberto Mecca, Petra Gospodnetic, Gernot Stübl, Luigi Di Stefano, Alfred Marcel Bruckstein, Fotios Logothetis and Roberto Cipolla. It discussed the challenges of technologies such as robotic vision, inline inspection, bin picking, real-time vision, cognitive vision systems, human-robot interaction, performance evaluations, vision system architectures and feedback loops and how they differ from everyday computer vision tasks. The workshop "Computer Vision Systems for Agricultural and Precision Farming" was organized by Dimitrios Giakoumis, Ioannis Mariolis and Dimitrios Tzovaras. This workshop engaged the current research on the complexity and variability of natural scenes, the occlusion and deformation of objects of interest, illumination and weather changes, the limited computational resources and power supply of robots, and the ethical and social implications of robot deployment that are central issues of computer vision systems for agriculture.

We wish to thank the Automation and Control Institute of TU Wien for institutional support. We express our sincere thanks to all the people who contributed to the organization and success of ICVS 2023; in particular, the members of the Program Committee, external reviewers, invited speakers, workshop organizers, as well as all the authors who submitted their works to and presented them at ICVS 2023. Finally, we thank Springer for publishing the proceedings in the Lecture Notes in Computer Science series.

September 2023

Henrik I. Christensen
Peter Corke
Renaud Detry
Jean-Baptiste Weibel
Markus Vincze

Organization

General Chair

Jean-Baptiste Weibel   TU Wien, Austria

Program Committee Chairs

Henrik I. Christensen   University of California San Diego, USA
Peter Corke   Queensland University of Technology, Australia
Renaud Detry   KU Leuven, Belgium

Steering Committee

Doris Antensteiner   Austrian Institute of Technology, Austria
Dominik Bauer   Columbia University, USA
Timothy Patten   University of Technology Sydney, Australia
Stefan Thalhammer   TU Wien, Austria
Markus Vincze   TU Wien, Austria
Ehsan Yaghoubi   Universität Hamburg, Germany

Program Committee

Antonis Argyros   University of Crete, Greece
William Beksi   University of Texas at Arlington, USA
Richard Bormann   Fraunhofer IPA, Germany
Alessandro Carfì   University of Genoa, Italy
Mohamed Chaabane   University of Louisville, USA
Dimitrios Chrysostomou   Aalborg University, Denmark
Grzegorz Cielniak   University of Lincoln, UK
Donald Dansereau   University of Sydney, Australia
Diego Faria   University of Hertfordshire, UK
Qichen Fu   Apple, USA
Dimitris Giakoumis   Centre for Research and Technology Hellas, Greece
Marc Hanheide   University of Lincoln, UK

Danish Khan	University of Sydney, Australia
Walter G. Kropatsch	TU Wien, Austria
Revant Kumar	Apple, USA
Mikko Lauri	Universität Hamburg, Germany
Vincent Lepetit	ENPC ParisTech, France
Elisa Maiettini	Istituto Italiano di Tecnologia, Italy
Lazaros Nalpantidis	Technical University of Denmark, Denmark
Lorenzo Natale	Istituto Italiano di Tecnologia, Italy
Anh Nguyen	University of Liverpool, UK
George Nikolakopoulos	Luleå University of Technology, Sweden
Giulia Pasquale	Istituto Italiano di Tecnologia, Italy
Kebin Peng	University of Texas at San Antonio, USA
Ioannis Pratikakis	Democritus University of Thrace, Greece
Alberto Pretto	University of Padua, Italy
Peter Riegler-Nurscher	Josephinum Research, Austria
Stefano Rosa	Istituto Italiano di Tecnologia, Italy
Peter M. Roth	TU Graz, Austria
Martin Rudorfer	Aston University, UK
Gernot Stübl	Profactor, Austria
Anirudh Topiwala	Aurora Innovation, USA
Ivan Vidović	FERIT Osijek, Croatia
Christian Wilms	Universität Hamburg, Germany
Zhi Yan	University of Technology of Belfort-Montbéliard, France

Contents

Performance and Robustness

Humans and Hands

Tracking and Identification of Ice Hockey Players

Qiao Chen$^{(\boxtimes)}$ and Charalambos Poullis

Immersive and Creative Technologies Lab, Concordia University, Montreal, Canada
cq.jocelyn@gmail.com, charalambos@poullis.org

Abstract. Due to the rapid movement of players, ice hockey is a high-speed sport that poses significant challenges for player tracking. In this paper, we present a comprehensive framework for player identification and tracking in ice hockey games, utilising deep neural networks trained on actual gameplay data. Player detection, identification, and tracking are the three main components of our architecture. The player detection component detects individuals in an image sequence using a region proposal technique. The player identification component makes use of a text detector model that performs character recognition on regions containing text detected by a scene text recognition model, enabling us to resolve ambiguities caused by players from the same squad having similar appearances. After identifying the players, a visual multi-object tracking model is used to track their movements throughout the game.

Experiments conducted with data collected from actual ice hockey games demonstrate the viability of our proposed framework for tracking and identifying players in real-world settings. Our framework achieves an average precision (AP) of 67.3 and a Multiple Object Tracking Accuracy (MOTA) of 80.2 for player detection and tracking, respectively. In addition, our team identification and player number identification accuracy is 82.39% and 87.19%, respectively. Overall, our framework is a significant advancement in the field of player tracking and identification in ice hockey, utilising cutting-edge deep learning techniques to achieve high accuracy and robustness in the face of complex and fast-paced gameplay. Our framework has the potential to be applied in a variety of applications, including sports analysis, player tracking, and team performance evaluation. Further enhancements can be made to address the challenges posed by complex and cluttered environments and enhance the system's precision.

Keywords: Object tracking · Text recognition · Player tagging

1 Introduction

The computer vision community is becoming increasingly interested in automated sports video analysis because it can provide insights into the game plan

H. I. Christensen et al. (Eds.): ICVS 2023, LNCS 14253, pp. 3–16, 2023.
https://doi.org/10.1007/978-3-031-44137-0_1

decision-making process, aid coaching decisions, and make the game more exciting for spectators. Nevertheless, player tracking and identification in fast-paced sports, such as ice hockey, is difficult due to the rapid movement of players and the puck, as well as the occlusions and complex motion of the players. This paper proposes a player tracking and identification system for fast-paced sports based on deep neural networks and demonstrates its applicability to ice hockey in order to address this challenge. The proposed system is comprised of three major elements: object detection, text detection and recognition, and player tracking.

The Faster R-CNN object detector is initially trained to recognise people in each video frame. To determine the jersey number of each player, we detect the region of the jersey number on the back of the player jerseys using a scene text recognition model [2] and fine-tune the CRAFT text detector [3]. The combination of object detection and text detection provides a more precise and reliable method for identifying players. Tracking multiple players is difficult due to the similar appearance of players on the same team, as well as the occlusions and complex motion of the players, which increase the difficulty. To address this challenge, we employ the Neural Solver Mot [6], a framework for visual multi-object tracking that can track multiple objects in video sequences using rudimentary data association and state estimation techniques.

We evaluated our proposed system using real-world data and obtained an 80.2 Multiple Object Tracking Accuracy (MOTA) score, which is superior to existing state-of-the-art methods. Moreover, we propose a practical method of transfer learning and fine-tuning a text detection model on player jersey numbers that achieves an accuracy of 87.19%. Our contributions consist of a comprehensive framework for player tracking and identification in ice hockey, which can provide valuable insights into the game plan decision-making process, and a practical method of transfer learning and refining a text detection model for player jersey numbers.

2   Related Work

2.1   Dataset

State-of-the-art techniques for player tracking, such as [8] and [35], have achieved impressive results using broadcast National Hockey League (NHL) videos. However, publicly available benchmark datasets that provide identification information for the teams and players are currently lacking. In this paper, we address this issue by using the McGill Hockey Player Tracking Dataset (MHPTD) [38], which is a publicly available dataset that consists of NHL broadcasting videos taken by the primary game camera. We use the MHPTD dataset and augment it with player identification jersey number labels to provide a publicly available benchmark dataset that enables accurate player tracking and identification in ice hockey videos. This will facilitate further research and development in this important area of sports video analysis.

2.2   Player Detection

The foundation of the majority of player detection algorithms has been the Viola-Jones Object Detection Framework [36] and Histograms of Oriented Gradients for Human Detection (HOG) [10]. These methods relied on hand-crafted features and segmentation and recognition of players. However, modern deep learning-based algorithms have eliminated the majority of the drawbacks of these early attempts at human recognition [25,31]. AlexNet [17], which won the Imagenet Large Scale Visual Recognition Challenge (ILSVRC) [30], marked the beginning of deep neural networks. Since then, owing to the continual improvement and advancements in hardware and convolutional neural network methodology, numerous new robust solutions have been developed to address the challenges in sports videos. Today, object detection heavily relies on deep neural networks such as YOLO [26], or part-based approaches [32], which provide superior performance in terms of missed, false, duplicate, and unreliable detection boundaries. Chan et al. suggested a residual network (ResNet) [14] as the CNN base with recurrent long short-term memory (LSTM) [15] for player identification. Vats et al. [35] introduced a temporal 1D CNN with no other specialized networks for processing temporal information. Region-based Convolutional Neural Networks (R-CNN) [13], Fast R-CNN [12], and Faster R-CNN [27], which are considered to be state-of-the-art deep learning visual object detection algorithms, might be the most effective and widely used approach to object detection.

In our work, we utilize the Faster R-CNN [27] algorithm due to its rapid convergence when generating detection proposals. The Faster R-CNN algorithm consists of two parts: a region proposal network (RPN) and a region-based convolutional neural network (RCNN). The RPN generates a set of object proposals by sliding a small network over the convolutional feature map output by the backbone network. The RCNN then refines the proposals and performs classification. This two-stage approach allows the Faster R-CNN to achieve high accuracy while still being computationally efficient. In summary, while early player detection algorithms relied on hand-crafted features and segmentation and recognition of players, modern deep learning-based algorithms have significantly improved the accuracy of player detection in sports videos. Today, object detection heavily relies on deep neural networks such as Faster R-CNN [27], which allows for accurate and efficient player detection.

2.3   Player Tracking

Tracking-by-detection multi-object tracking frameworks such as SORT [5] and Deep SORT [37] have gained attention as they can track multiple objects in video sequences using rudimentary data association and state estimation approaches. The trackers compare detections using various measures such as features, Kalman filter, and person re-identification (ReID). SIFT [21], SURF [4], and ORB [29] are the most popular descriptors for feature extraction and matching in object tracking systems. ORB is frequently used for tracking, mapping, and relocalization due to its quick feature extraction and tolerance to picture rotation and noise. Kalman filter [16] is widely used to track moving objects by estimating their velocity and acceleration based on their locations. The primary function of the Kalman filter is to associate detections with trajectories [5,37,39]. In recent years, unscented Kalman filtering techniques have also been employed to track multiple moving objects with occlusion [9]. Another approach to tracking-by-detection is person re-identification (ReID), which is the process of identifying people across several images. For detection and ReID, ice hockey player tracking approaches such as [7] employ hand-crafted features. Ahmed et al. [1] present a method of learning features and accompanying similarity metrics for person re-identification. If the images contain the same person, the network returns either a similarity score between the images or a classification of the images as identical. Neural Solver Mot [6] is a recent work that jointly learns features over the global graph of the entire set of detections and predicts final solutions. Our tracking system leverages the Neural Solver Mot [6] and employs ReID measures instead of face recognition and number detection since faces and jersey numbers are not always visible to the primary camera during sporting events.

2.4 Number Recognition

Jersey number recognition algorithms can be classified into two categories: OCR-based methods and CNN-based methods. OCR-based methods, such as those presented in [22] and [24], use hand-crafted features to localize the text or number regions on the player uniform and then pass the segmented regions to an OCR module for recognition of the text or number. These methods have been used for a long time but have been outperformed by CNN-based models, which have shown superior results in terms of number recognition, as reported in [11,23] and [33]. However, CNN-based models have the disadvantage of being limited to the training set. Typically, jersey number detection follows a localization and recognition step. After character cells are detected, the recognition proceeds by first recognizing each word and then resolving ambiguous cases. Classes that share at least one digit are susceptible to erroneous recognition. To address this problem, digit-wise techniques presented by Li et al. [18] and Gerke et al. [11] have been proposed. These techniques fuse with the spatial transformer network (STN) to improve recognition. Jersey number recognition is difficult due to variations in player poses and viewpoints. To overcome this challenge, CRAFT [3], a scene text detection method, has shown promising results in challenging scenes with arbitrarily-oriented, curved, or deformed texts. In our work, we fine-tune the CRAFT text detector for jersey number recognition, which achieved an accuracy of 87.19%.

3   System Overview

The proposed solution for player identification consists of four steps: player detection, player tracking, team identification, and jersey number recognition. The first step involves using the region proposals generated by Faster R-CNN to detect players in each frame of the video sequence. These detections are then used to track the players throughout the image sequence using similarity metrics for person re-identification. This produces a set of tracklets that describe the motion path of each player in the video. The next step involves identifying the team for each player in the tracklets. This is done by extracting the dominant color from the region containing the player and using it to classify the team to which the player belongs. Finally, for each player tracklet, the system identifies the jersey number of the player. This is accomplished using the CRAFT scene text detection method to recognize the digits on the back of the player's jersey. Figure 1 provides an overview of the proposed system's pipeline, depicting how the different components work together to achieve player tracking and identification. In the following sections, each component of the system is described in more detail.

Fig. 1. Overview of player tracking and identification system.

3.1 Player Detection

The first stage of the proposed pipeline is player detection, which is performed on a sequence of images obtained by converting a video of an ice hockey game. The detection process begins with preliminary person detection since players are instances of the class person. Subsequently, all further processing is performed solely on the regions where a human is detected. Several deep learning-based frameworks such as YOLO [26] and Faster R-CNN [27] have been used for accurate object identification. For this purpose, we used the Faster R-CNN Inception-V2-COCO model due to its higher performance. This model has been trained on 91 categories of objects from the Common Objects in Context (COCO) dataset [20]. Faster R-CNN produces plausible bounding boxes from an image using convolutional feature maps, which are region-based detectors. The Region Proposal Network (RPN) classifier is then applied, which simultaneously regresses region boundaries and objectness scores at each point on proposed regions/bounding boxes. RPNs can accurately predict region proposals with varying scales and aspect ratios. Finally, post-processing techniques such as non-maximum suppression are used to refine the bounding boxes, eliminate duplicate detections, and re-score the bounding boxes depending on other objects in the scene, after the region has been predicted. The Faster-RCNN loss function can be expressed as follows:

$$L(\mathcal{P}i, b_i) = \frac{1}{S_c} \sum iL_c(\mathcal{P}i, Gp_i) + w \times \frac{1}{S_r} \sum i\mathcal{P}_iL_r(B_i, Gb_i) \qquad (1)$$

where i is the index of an anchor in a batch and $\mathcal{P}_i$ is the probability of anchor i being an object. b_i is a vector representing the coordinates of the predicted bounding box. S_c and S_r are the normalization mini-batch size of classification and regression, respectively. L_c and L_r are the classification and regression loss, respectively. The ground-truth label Gp_i is 1 if the anchor is positive and is 0 if the anchor is negative. B_i is a vector representing the coordinates bounding box, and Gb_i is that of the ground-truth box. The two terms are weighted by a balancing parameter w.

3.2   Player Tracking

After detecting players in the first step, the second step of the proposed pipeline is individual player tracking. For this, the Neural Solver Mot [6] is used on the ice hockey dataset as the tracker to generate player tracklets. However, since perfect detection is challenging, errors in detection need to be considered using person re-identification (ReID) metrics. In multiple object tracking (MOT) techniques, external ReID databases are commonly incorporated. The network used in this step is pre-trained on three publicly available datasets for the ReIdentification (ReID) task: Market1501 [40], CUHK03 [19], and DukeMTMC [28].

In the player tracking step, the pseudocode checks whether the detection has the same trajectory and is temporally consecutive. If these conditions are met, a node v is added to the graph G. The set of edges E is then formed by connecting each pair of detections in separate frames. The evaluation of each tracklet is based on a fractional solution $\hat{F}$, which is determined by a similarity metric. If the similarity is greater than or equal to a threshold τ_θ, a tracklet is generated for that player. Finally, the output of this step is a set of tracklets T' that describes the motion path of each player in the image sequence.

3.3   Player Identification

Players are identified by their jersey numbers. Recognizing jersey numbers is challenging since jerseys are deformable objects that can appear somewhat distorted in the image. Moreover, there is great variation in the players' poses and camera view angles, which has a significant impact on the projected area and perceived font of jersey numbers.

Number/Text Detection. Following the extraction of the tracklets for each player, the jersey number is identified. We apply a scene text detection algorithm [3] to each image in a player's tracklet, in order to localize the jersey number region. The model architecture has a VGG-16 backbone network [34]

Algorithm 1: Player Tracking

Input : Player Detections
$P = \{p_1, ..., p_n\}$
MOT Graph $G = (V, E)$,
Fractional solution $\hat{F}$
Output: set of *tracklets* $T' = \{T_1, . . . , T_m\}$ $e = 0$ for all e in
$G = (V, E)$ #Initialization
for $p_i \in P$ **do**
   node v represents p_i, $v \in V$
   if p_i *has the same trajectory T*
   & *is temporally consecutive*
   then
     | $e = 1$ in $G = (V, E)$
   else
     | $e = 0$ in $G = (V, E)$
end
for $\{(e_1, e_2), ..., (e_{n_{i-1}}, e_{n_i})\} \in E$ **do**
   if $\hat{F}_{(e_{n_{i-1}}, e_{n_i})} \geq \tau_\theta$ **then**
     | $T_i = 1$, $T_i \in \{T_1, ..., T_m\}$
   end
   else
     | $T_i = 0$
   end
end

The pseudocode for player tracking is given in Algorithm 1. The input consists of a collection of player detections $P = p_1, \ldots, p_n$, where n is the total number of objects across all frames. Each detection is represented by $p_i = (a_i, c_i, t_i)$, where a_i denotes the raw pixels of the bounding box, c_i includes its 2D image coordinates, and t_i its timestamp. A tracklet is defined as a collection of time-ordered object detections $T_i = p_{i_1}, \ldots, p_{i_{n_i}}$, where n_i is the number of detections that comprise the trajectory i. The objective of MOT is to identify the set of tracklets $T' = T_1, \ldots, T_m$, which provides the best explanation for the observations O. This problem can be modelled as an undirected graph $G = (V, E)$, where $V = 1, \ldots, n$, $E \subset V \times V$, and each node $i \in V$ represents a unique detection $p_i \in O$. The set of edges E is formed so that each pair of detections, i.e., nodes, in separate frames is connected, thus enabling the recovery of tracklets with missed detections.

and is supervised to localize character regions and connect the regions from the bottom up. Using the pretrained CRAFT model [3], we identify texts of diverse horizontal, curved and arbitrary orientations. The model generates two-channel score maps: a region score for each character's location and an affinity score for associating characters to instances. The loss function L is defined as follows:

$$L = \sum_i [S_r(i) - S'_r(i)]^2_2 + \sum_i [S_a(i) - S'_a(i)]^2_2 \qquad (2)$$

where $S'_r(i)$ and $S'_a(i)$ indicate region score and affinity map of the ground truth respectively, and $S_r(i)$ and $S_a(i)$ indicate the predicted region score and affinity score, respectively. We further improve the robustness by extending it with a post-processing step that filters out text instances that are unlikely to be a jersey number based on the aspect ratio of the detected region.

Table 1. Comparison of different approaches for multiple object tracking in a video clip.

Method	MOTA↑	IDF1↑	MT↑	FP↓	FN↓
SORT [5]	55.1	76.3	404	615	1296
Deep SORT [37]	56.3	77.1	435	487	968
MOT Neural Solver [6]	67.3	80.2	656	422	917

Number Identification. All number-detected regions are further processed for (i) team identification and (ii) number identification to identify each player's tracklets.

- **Team identification.** In team identification, the aim is to separate the detected jersey numbers into two groups corresponding to the two teams playing in the video. This is necessary because in some cases, two players may have identical jersey numbers. To achieve this, the input patches are binarized and the dominant color of each patch is analyzed. Patches with a dark foreground color on a bright background are classified as white team jerseys, while patches with a bright foreground color on a dark background are classified as black team jerseys. If a team roster is available, the process also eliminates false detections by removing jersey numbers that do not exist in the team roster.
- **Number identification.** The second step, number identification, involves recognizing the jersey numbers for each player. This is achieved through a pre-trained model for TPS-ResNet-BiLSTM-Atten text recognition, which is a four-stage framework for scene text recognition. This model is capable of recognizing the jersey number as a whole, which is essential for identifying multiple-digit jersey numbers taken from non-frontal, distorted views.
The approach of Baek et al. [2] describes two types of implementations for the text recognition model: Connectionist Temporal Classification (CTC) and Attention mechanism (Attn). CTC involves computing the conditional probability by summing the probabilities that are mapped onto the label sequence, as in Eq. 3:

$$P(S_l|S_i) = \sum_{\pi:M(\pi)=S_l} P(\pi|S_i) \tag{3}$$

where S_l is the label sequence, S_i is input sequence and $P(\pi|H)$ is the probability of observing either a character or a blank at a point in time, and M is the mapping of π onto S_l. The Attn approach uses an LSTM attention decoder to predict the output at each time step, using trainable parameters, context vectors, and hidden states from the LSTM decoder as follows,

$$O_t = softmax(W_0 h_t + p_0) \tag{4}$$
$$h_t = LSTM(O_{t-1}, c_t, h_{t-1}) \tag{5}$$

where W_0, p_0 are the trainable parameters, c_t is a context vector, and h_t, h_{t-1} represent the decoder LSTM hidden states at time steps t and $t-1$, respectively.

4   Results

4.1   Dataset

The most relevant state-of-the-art methods to our tracking system are [35] and [8], however direct comparison is not possible because the authors do not provide their datasets. Thus, we report on the MHPTD dataset [38], a publicly available dataset which consists of 25 NHL gameplay video clips of resolution 1280 × 720 pixels. Each clip consists of a single shot of the gameplay from the overhead camera position comprised of a sequence of frames that run continuously without a cut scene or camera view change. The clips have mixed frame rates, including both 60 and 30 frames per second, which are standard NHL broadcast video frame rates available on the market. To facilitate the evaluation of the player tracking and identification, we augment the ground truth tracking information provided by MHPTD with manually labeled tracking IDs containing the jersey number and team label.

(a)   (b)   (c)

Fig. 2. (a) A visual comparison of output player tracklets using YOLO_v3 model (top-row) and Faster-RCNN model (bottom-row). (b) Comparison of Text Detection without(top row) or with(bottom row) fine-tuning. (c) Some failed detections, typically occurring when there are complex backgrounds such as banner advertisements which may contain text, player collisions and occlusions, low contrast, and contours resulting from stripes and other logos on the players' jerseys.

4.2   Player Tracking

A Faster-RCNN network [27] pre-trained on the COCO dataset [20] is utilised for player detection. We compared two different object detectors for player detection, the detector presented in Faster-RCNN [27] and the one in YOLO_v3 [26], respectively. There can be erroneous detections owing to misclassification, occlusions, and the presence of the audience, but the majority of them can be filtered with the *tracklets* length and patch size. Figure 2a depicts an example of a *tracklet*, a sequence of images of a tracked player, with YOLO_v3 in the top row, and Faster-RCNN in the bottom row. The Faster-RCNN model recognizes a more comprehensive player zone. For the test videos, the object detector of Faster-RCNN achieves an average precision (AP) of 66.8, whereas YOLO_v3 achieves an average precision (AP) of 53.32. We tested three cutting-edge tracking algorithms on a dataset of hockey players, and used Multiple Object Tracking Accuracy (MOTA) and IDF1 Score (IDF1) as the main evaluation metrics. The authors also mention a third metric, Mostly Tracked (MT) trajectories, which

refers to the trajectory coverage. The study reports the results of the evaluation in Table 1. According to the results, the MOT Neural Solver tracking model
with person re-identification (reID) re-trained on the hockey dataset achieved
the best tracking performance. The reported average for MOTA was 56.3, and
the average for IDF1 was 60.67, according to the authors. However, based on
the experiments conducted in the study, the MOT Neural Resolver algorithm
achieved the highest average MOTA and IDF1 scores on the test videos, which
were 67.3 and 80.2, respectively.

4.3   Player Identification

Text Detection. We adjust the pretrained weights of the CRAFT detector
to the ice hockey dataset by performing fine-tuning. The fine-tuning process
involved training the model for 30 epochs using a learning rate of $3.2e - 5$,
with 500 images from the dataset used for this purpose. The remaining subsets
were used for testing and validation. During training, the authors performed
image augmentation techniques, such as affine transformation, Gaussian blur,
and modulation of the color channels, on both the original player images and
the corresponding bounding boxes of the jersey number regions. This helped to
improve the robustness of the model to variations in the input images.

Figure 2b provides an example of text detection using the fine-tuned CRAFT
detector on the ice hockey dataset. The authors report that fine-tuning the
pretrained model on the ice hockey dataset resulted in enhanced detection of
jersey number regions, which is important for identifying players in the video.

However, the authors also note that there were some unsuccessful detections, which typically occurred in the presence of complicated backdrops such as
banner advertisements containing text, player collisions and occlusions, low contrast, and contours arising from stripes and other logos on the players' jerseys.
Figure 2c provides examples of such failed detections.

Team Identification. Using the text region recognised for each player, we
binarize and convert the image to black and white. This step simplifies the image
and helps to identify the dominant colors in the image. Next, the dominant patch
color is identified. If the text is white on a dark backdrop, then the dominant
color in the patch will be dark, and the player is assigned to the home team. If
the text is black on a bright background, then the dominant color in the patch
will be bright, and the player is assigned to the visiting team. This process is
based on the assumption that each team has a distinct color for their jerseys
and that the numbers on their jerseys are a contrasting colour. The proposed
technique achieved an accuracy of 82.39% in classifying teams based on the color
of their jerseys. However, the authors note that some inaccuracies were observed,
primarily due to officials being misidentified as players, and colors with poor
contrast leading to erroneous detections. Misidentifying officials as players is a
common challenge in sports analysis, as officials often wear uniforms that are
similar to those of the players. This can lead to inaccurate results if not properly

accounted for in the algorithm. Poor contrast between the color of the jerseys and the background can also affect the accuracy of the algorithm by making it difficult to detect the colors of the jerseys accurately.

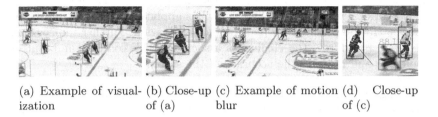

(a) Example of visualization (b) Close-up of (a) (c) Example of motion blur (d)   Close-up of (c)

Fig. 3. Visualization of the output of the tracking system. If a player is tracked, a random coloured bounding box is drawn, and the jersey number label and the identified team are annotated above the box.

Jersey Number Identification. For jersey number recognition, we use the pre-trained text recognition model TPS-ResNet-BiLSTM-Atten [2]. This model uses an attention mechanism to handle problematic situations such as jersey numbers that share at least one digit, variations in player position, and shifts in camera perspective. The tracking result includes 459 player tracklets extracted from 15,083 player photos, along with the jersey number bounding box annotation and a per-player class. For each player's tracklet, the jersey number label with the most votes is assigned. The recognition accuracy of the jersey numbers is reported to be 87.19%. The authors provide an example of the output of their system in Fig. 3, where team and player jersey number identification are overlaid on the input video. If a player is tracked, a bounding box of a random color is generated, and the jersey number label and team are marked above the box. However, the authors note that some unrecognised poses within the same tracklet may be assigned the jersey number label from other frames within the same tracklet, as player tracking does not use jersey number information.

5 Conclusion

We presented a complete framework for player tracking and identification in ice hockey that exploits the high performance of deep learning neural networks. The framework consists of three main components, namely player detection, player tracking, and player identification. We extended the publicly available dataset called MHPTD with jersey number and team information and conducted experiments to evaluate the performance of the proposed framework. The results of the experiments show that the average precision (AP) for player detection using the method is 67.3, the Multiple Object Tracking Accuracy (MOTA) for player tracking is 80.2, and the accuracies for team identification and player number identification are 82.39% and 87.19%, respectively. Our framework can track multiple players simultaneously in fast-paced games such as ice hockey and that its performance is equivalent to that of cutting-edge player tracking and identification systems. Overall, our results suggest that the proposed framework is effective in tracking and identifying players in ice hockey games using deep learning neural networks. This can be useful for various applications such as sports analysis, player tracking, and team performance evaluation. Further improvements can be made to address the challenges associated with complex and cluttered environments and improve the accuracy of the system.

Acknowledgements. This research is based upon work supported by the Natural Sciences and Engineering Research Council of Canada Grants No. RGPIN-2021-03479 (Discovery Grant) and ALLRP 571887-21 (Alliance). Special thanks to Livebarn Inc. for their support.

References

1. Ahmed, E., Jones, M., Marks, T.K.: An improved deep learning architecture for person re-identification. In: Proceedings of the IEEE Conference on Computer Vision and Pattern Recognition, pp. 3908–3916 (2015)
2. Baek, J., et al.: What is wrong with scene text recognition model comparisons? dataset and model analysis. In: Proceedings of the IEEE/CVF International Conference on Computer Vision, pp. 4715–4723 (2019)
3. Baek, Y., Lee, B., Han, D., Yun, S., Lee, H.: Character region awareness for text detection. In: Proceedings of the IEEE/CVF Conference on Computer Vision and Pattern Recognition, pp. 9365–9374 (2019)
4. Bay, H., Tuytelaars, T., Van Gool, L.: SURF: speeded up robust features. In: Leonardis, A., Bischof, H., Pinz, A. (eds.) ECCV 2006. LNCS, vol. 3951, pp. 404–417. Springer, Heidelberg (2006). https://doi.org/10.1007/11744023_32
5. Bewley, A., Ge, Z., Ott, L., Ramos, F., Upcroft, B.: Simple online and realtime tracking. In: 2016 IEEE International Conference on Image Processing (ICIP), pp. 3464–3468. IEEE (2016)
6. Brasó, G., Leal-Taixé, L.: Learning a neural solver for multiple object tracking. In: Proceedings of the IEEE/CVF Conference on Computer Vision and Pattern Recognition, pp. 6247–6257 (2020)
7. Cai, Y., de Freitas, N., Little, J.J.: Robust visual tracking for multiple targets. In: Leonardis, A., Bischof, H., Pinz, A. (eds.) ECCV 2006. LNCS, vol. 3954, pp. 107–118. Springer, Heidelberg (2006). https://doi.org/10.1007/11744085_9
8. Chan, A., Levine, M.D., Javan, M.: Player identification in hockey broadcast videos. Expert Syst. Appl. **165**, 113891 (2021)
9. Chen, X., Wang, X., Xuan, J.: Tracking multiple moving objects using unscented kalman filtering techniques. arXiv preprint arXiv:1802.01235 (2018)
10. Dalal, N., Triggs, B.: Histograms of oriented gradients for human detection. In: 2005 IEEE Computer Society Conference on Computer Vision and Pattern Recognition (CVPR 2005), vol. 1, pp. 886–893. IEEE (2005)
11. Gerke, S., Muller, K., Schafer, R.: Soccer jersey number recognition using convolutional neural networks. In: Proceedings of the IEEE International Conference on Computer Vision Workshops, pp. 17–24 (2015)

12. Girshick, R.: Fast R-CNN. In: Proceedings of the IEEE International Conference on Computer Vision, pp. 1440–1448 (2015)
13. Girshick, R., Donahue, J., Darrell, T., Malik, J.: Rich feature hierarchies for accurate object detection and semantic segmentation. In: Proceedings of the IEEE Conference on Computer Vision and Pattern Recognition, pp. 580–587 (2014)
14. He, K., Zhang, X., Ren, S., Sun, J.: Deep residual learning for image recognition. In: Proceedings of the IEEE Conference on Computer Vision and Pattern Recognition, pp. 770–778 (2016)
15. Hochreiter, S., Schmidhuber, J.: Long short-term memory. Neural Comput. 9(8), 1735–1780 (1997)
16. Kalman, R.E.: A new approach to linear filtering and prediction problems (1960)
17. Krizhevsky, A., Sutskever, I., Hinton, G.E.: Imagenet classification with deep convolutional neural networks. In: Advances in Neural Information Processing Systems, vol. 25 (2012)
18. Li, G., Xu, S., Liu, X., Li, L., Wang, C.: Jersey number recognition with semi-supervised spatial transformer network. In: Proceedings of the IEEE Conference on Computer Vision and Pattern Recognition Workshops, pp. 1783–1790 (2018)
19. Li, W., Zhao, R., Xiao, T., Wang, X.: DeepREID: deep filter pairing neural network for person re-identification. In: Proceedings of the IEEE Conference on Computer Vision and Pattern Recognition, pp. 152–159 (2014)
20. Lin, T.-Y., et al.: Microsoft COCO: common objects in context. In: Fleet, D., Pajdla, T., Schiele, B., Tuytelaars, T. (eds.) ECCV 2014. LNCS, vol. 8693, pp. 740–755. Springer, Cham (2014). https://doi.org/10.1007/978-3-319-10602-1_48
21. Lowe, D.G.: Distinctive image features from scale-invariant keypoints. Int. J. Comput. Vision 60(2), 91–110 (2004)
22. Lu, C.W., Lin, C.Y., Hsu, C.Y., Weng, M.F., Kang, L.W., Liao, H.Y.M.: Identification and tracking of players in sport videos. In: Proceedings of the Fifth International Conference on Internet Multimedia Computing and Service, pp. 113–116 (2013)
23. Lyu, P., Liao, M., Yao, C., Wu, W., Bai, X.: Mask textspotter: an end-to-end trainable neural network for spotting text with arbitrary shapes. In: Proceedings of the European Conference on Computer Vision (ECCV), pp. 67–83 (2018)
24. Messelodi, S., Modena, C.: Scene text recognition and tracking to identify athletes in sport videos. Multimedia Tools Appl. 63, 1–25 (2012). https://doi.org/10.1007/s11042-011-0878-y
25. Okuma, K., Taleghani, A., de Freitas, N., Little, J.J., Lowe, D.G.: A boosted particle filter: multitarget detection and tracking. In: Pajdla, T., Matas, J. (eds.) ECCV 2004. LNCS, vol. 3021, pp. 28–39. Springer, Heidelberg (2004). https://doi.org/10.1007/978-3-540-24670-1_3
26. Redmon, J., Divvala, S., Girshick, R., Farhadi, A.: You only look once: Unified, real-time object detection. In: Proceedings of the IEEE Conference on Computer Vision and Pattern Recognition, pp. 779–788 (2016)
27. Ren, S., He, K., Girshick, R., Sun, J.: Faster R-CNN: towards real-time object detection with region proposal networks. In: Advances in Neural Information Processing Systems, vol. 28 (2015)
28. Ristani, E., Solera, F., Zou, R., Cucchiara, R., Tomasi, C.: Performance measures and a data set for multi-target, multi-camera tracking. In: Hua, G., Jégou, H. (eds.) ECCV 2016. LNCS, vol. 9914, pp. 17–35. Springer, Cham (2016). https://doi.org/10.1007/978-3-319-48881-3_2

29. Rublee, E., Rabaud, V., Konolige, K., Bradski, G.: ORB: an efficient alternative to SIFT or SURF. In: 2011 International Conference on Computer Vision, pp. 2564–2571. IEEE (2011)
30. Russakovsky, O., et al.: ImageNet large scale visual recognition challenge. Int. J. Comput. Vis. (IJCV) **115**, 211–252 (2012)
31. Šaric, M., Dujmic, H., Papic, V., Rožic, N.: Player number localization and recognition in soccer video using HSV color space and internal contours. Int. J. Electr. Comput. Eng. **2**(7), 1408–1412 (2008)
32. Senocak, A., Oh, T.H., Kim, J., So Kweon, I.: Part-based player identification using deep convolutional representation and multi-scale pooling. In: Proceedings of the IEEE Conference on Computer Vision and Pattern Recognition Workshops, pp. 1732–1739 (2018)
33. Shi, B., Bai, X., Yao, C.: An end-to-end trainable neural network for image-based sequence recognition and its application to scene text recognition. IEEE Trans. Pattern Anal. Mach. Intell. **39**(11), 2298–2304 (2016)
34. Simonyan, K., Zisserman, A.: Very deep convolutional networks for large-scale image recognition. arXiv preprint arXiv:1409.1556 (2014)
35. Vats, K., Walters, P., Fani, M., Clausi, D.A., Zelek, J.: Player tracking and identification in ice hockey. arXiv preprint arXiv:2110.03090 (2021)
36. Viola, P., Jones, M.: Rapid object detection using a boosted cascade of simple features. In: Proceedings of the 2001 IEEE Computer Society Conference on Computer Vision and Pattern Recognition. CVPR 2001, vol. 1, pp. I-I. Ieee (2001)
37. Wojke, N., Bewley, A., Paulus, D.: Simple online and realtime tracking with a deep association metric. In: 2017 IEEE international Conference on Image Processing (ICIP), pp. 3645–3649. IEEE (2017)
38. Zhao, Y., Zihui Li, K.C.: A method for tracking hockey players by exploiting multiple detections and omni-scale appearance features. Project Report (2020)
39. Zhang, Y., Wang, C., Wang, X., Zeng, W., Liu, W.: Fairmot: on the fairness of detection and re-identification in multiple object tracking. Int. J. Comput. Vision **129**(11), 3069–3087 (2021)
40. Zheng, L., Shen, L., Tian, L., Wang, S., Wang, J., Tian, Q.: Scalable person re-identification: A benchmark. In: Proceedings of the IEEE International Conference on Computer Vision, pp. 1116–1124 (2015)

Dedicated Encoding-Streams Based Spatio-Temporal Framework for Dynamic Person-Independent Facial Expression Recognition

Mohamed Kas[1]([✉]), Yassine Ruichek[1], Youssef EL-Merabet[2], and Rochdi Messoussi[2]

[1] UTBM, CIAD UMR 7533, 90010 Belfort, France
{mohamed.kas,yassine.ruichek}@utbm.fr
[2] Laboratoire SETIME, Département de Physique, Faculte des Sciences, Université Ibn Tofail, BP 133, Kénitra 14000, Morocco
{youssef.el-merabet,rochdi.messoussi}@uit.ac.ma

Abstract. The facial expression recognition (FER) task is widely considered in the modern human-machine platforms (human support robots) and the self-service ones. The important attention given to the FER application is translated by the various architectures and datasets proposed to develop efficient automatic FER frameworks. This paper proposes a new, yet efficient appearance-based deep framework for dynamic FER referred to as Dedicated Encoding-streams based Spatio-Temporal FER (DEST-FER). It considers four input frames where the last presents the peak of the emotion and each input is encoded through a CNN streams. The four streams are joined using LSTM units that perform the temporal processing and the prediction of the dominant facial expression. We considered the challenging FER protocol, which is the person-independent one. To make the DEST-FER more robust to this constraint, we preprocessed the input frames by highlighting 49 landmarks characterizing the emotion' regions of interest, and applying an edge-based filter. We evaluated 12 CNN architectures for the appearance-based encoders on three benchmarks. The ResNet18 model managed to be the best performing combination with the LSTM units, and led the top FER performance that outperformed the SOTA works.

Keywords: Dynamic person-independent facial expression recognition · deep spatio-temporal image processing · LSTM-based classification

1 Introduction

The automatic facial expression recognition (FER) task is attracting important interest and attention of the machine learning research community regarding its promising applications. Automatic FER can be widely applied to various

H. I. Christensen et al. (Eds.): ICVS 2023, LNCS 14253, pp. 17–30, 2023.
https://doi.org/10.1007/978-3-031-44137-0_2

research areas, such as mental diseases diagnosis and human social/physiological interaction detection [18]. In addition, automatic FER is now applied to assess the e-learning quality by real-time analysis of the students faces [5] as well as effective self-service migration [17]. The facial expressions are expressed either spontaneously or with a posed way. The spontaneous facial expressions' recognition is hard to be learned since each individual is expressing the emotions on its way and differently from another person, leading to high intraclass variance. Therefore, only few studies that are published related to spontaneous FER as stated by the survey in [10]. On the other hand, posed-based is the widely studied FER by the researchers. The individuals are instructed to perform the emotions uniformly increasing the intraclass similarities so the machine can understand and detect the emotion-related patterns.

Two popular approaches have been proposed in the literature for decoding facial expressions. The first is geometric-based feature extraction. This approach relies on encoding geometric information such as the position, distance, and angle of the facial landmark points that a landmark detector should first identify and then extracts the feature vectors. The second approach, which is appearance-based, characterizes the appearance textural information resulting from the emotion classes' facial movements. Therefore, a set of features is extracted and is expected to contain relevant discriminating information to classify the different classes. Moreover, the automatic FER task is further categorized into static and dynamic approaches depending on the input configuration. Static FER relies on using only one image to detect the dominant emotions. On the other hand, a dynamic framework requires many observations (samples) of the same person, representing the evolution of the facial expression.

Through this paper, we contribute to the dynamic person-independent FER task by proposing a new deep architecture referred to as Dedicated Encoding-streams based Spatio-Temporal FER (DEST-FER), merging convolutional-based feature extraction with temporal LSTM classification. The proposed dynamic person-independent FER is based on a Deep LSTM-CNN network to compute discriminant filter responses and encode the temporal information through the LSTM gates. Our network includes a dedicated feature encoder to each input image for extracting emotion-related characteristics. An LSTM block joins the feature encodes and predicts the dominant emotion on the input images. To emphasize the person-independent FER performance, we apply 49 face landmarks on each input sample and compute edge filter before proceeding to the deep feature extraction step. The conducted experiments on three widely used benchmarks show that the proposed approach delivers improved performance as compared to the state-of-the-art works. Moreover, we evaluated 12 deep CNN models as feature encoders and the residual-based architectures proved to be more discriminant and leading to the top results.

The main contributions of this paper can be expressed as follows:

- Dedicated encoding-streams based spatio-temporal framework for person-independent facial expression recognition.

- Landmark-guided deep features extraction technique to increase the person-independent scenario performance.
- Evaluation of 12 deep CNN architectures as stream-encoders on 3 widely used benchmarks.
- Comprehensive 10 folds evaluation protocol with no subjects overlapping between the train and test sets.

To provide the field-interested researchers with an immersive reading experience, this paper is organized as follows. Section 2 reviews the literature of automatic-FER highlighting the different strategies used to handle FER and the available opportunity to increase its performance. Section 3 presents the proposed DEST-FER framework exhibiting the evaluated CNN models as encoders and their combination with the LSTM block to perform the FER classification. Section 4 illustrates comprehensive experimental analysis on three widely used benchmarks alongside a SOTA-based comparison and confusion matrix-based analysis of the achieved FER performance. Section 5 discloses the main conclusions and proposes some openings of the proposed method.

2   Related Works

The appearance pattern relies on characterizing the visual textural information affected by the emotion classes' facial movements. Therefore, a set of features is extracted and is expected to contain relevant discriminating information to distinguish the different classes. The appearance-based approach utilizes many techniques for feature extraction and offers larger options for improving the FER performance. The feature extraction methods are divided into handcrafted ones and learning ones. The handcrafted methods, such as Gabor filters [16] and Local Binary Patterns [19], are based on a defined kernel function taking as input the pixels' intensity and translating them to a more discriminant feature space.

For deep-based dynamic FER, the field's researchers proposed many architectures utilizing CNN as can be found in the comprehensive survey in [14]. To benefit from the temporal correlations of consecutive frames in a sequence, a technique must be implemented defining how the frames are fed to the CNN-feature extractors.

The first technique is frame aggregation, which can be performed on the decision stage or the feature extraction one. The decision-based frame aggregation relies on classifying the dynamic FER after classifying the emotion of each frame individually, as can be found in [12]. The feature aggregation stage consists on computing one input from all the input frames by averaging their pixel values [2] or considering transformation matrix and Gaussian distribution [4].

The second technique relies on processing the peak of the emotion and ignoring the others, these methods are referred to as Peak-piloted networks [20,23]. The peak frame is fed to the classification framework to detect the dominant emotion. Both aggregation methods do not benefit from the emotion evolution present over the frames, since each input is classified without considering the other ones. Therefore, the spatio-temporal processing appears to be the suitable one for dynamic FER. However, the existing spatio-temporal FER frameworks consider a series of frames in a temporal window as an independent input without prior knowledge of the dominant emotion and extract learning-based features to be classified as one features set. The majority of the state-of-art works adopted 3D-CNNs input layer to encode the input frames with dedicated weights for each one [1,22]. The classification step is often based on combining LSTM layers with fully connected ones. 3D-CNNs with LSTM based framework proved to be more efficient than frame aggregation and Peak-piloted ones. However, the 3D-CNN feature extraction still merges the different inputs, which may affect the temporal information since the features are merged at the early layers of the network that are less optimized for semantic purpose. Therefore, we overcome this fact by proposing dedicated CNN streams to extract the features from each input frame and merging them until reaching the LSTM-based decision layers. Instead of feeding the original RGB frames to the CNN layers, we feed landmark-guided edge filter of each input frame. This contribution will help to emphasize the person-independent FER constraint.

3   Proposed Deep CNN-LSTM for Dynamic FER

The dynamic Person-Independent FER relies on processing multiple samples to detect the dominant emotion through its evolution. We propose a deep CNN-LSTM network considering four consecutive samples by extracting the deep features based on dedicated CNN streams, then the use of two LSTM gates to decode the temporal information and predict the facial expression class. As shown in Fig. 1, the proposed architecture incorporates different techniques divided into three main steps.

The preprocessing step of our proposed framework is to keep only the visual features related to the facial expression and ignore those describing the person's identity, which will help fulfill the person-independent constraint. The Dlib package detects with high accuracy 49 landmarks on the human face. These 49 regions are believed to carry enough information to describe the emotional state and less person-related features.

We developed a method to make the CNN encoders focus mainly on these regions by building the attention map of each input image. The attention map is achieved by inserting the landmarks on the input image then computing an Edge Glow filter that suppresses the textural information. Therefore, the CNN dedicated streams are extracting only the facial expression filters. We adopted dedicated CNN streams for the feature extraction step to guarantee an efficient extraction of the deep features from each input attention map. Moreover, dedicated streams offer flexible training by adapting the weights to each input rather than finding one suitable configuration for all of them. Also, the extraction is performed in parallel and not in sequence.

Sequence computing makes the network unable to track the patterns between the inputs and will be influenced by the last input fed. Each stream outputs N-filter$^{3\times3}$ bank that is averaged and pooled into an N sized vector. The four vectors extracted from the four streams are then concatenated to form the input of the classification sub-network, which is the third step of our framework.Moreover, our framework architecture is flexible to all models of deep CNN that can be used for extracting the features. The next step classifies the extracted features through deep LSTM cells and fully connected layers following the configurations mentioned in Figure 1. The flatten filters from the dedicated CNN are firstly scaled by a first fully connected layer $FC1$ that has the exact size of the pooled feature vector. The need for feature adaption comes from the LSTM cell, which will process the outputs of $FC1$ as the values should be normalized, representing a homogeneous sequence. Also, FC1 is motivating the non-linearity, hence discovering more patterns.

The core of our architecture is the Deep-LSTM, which is learning the temporal information across the four concatenated deep features. An LSTM gate processes its corresponding bin from the feature vector, then its output is fed to the next one. In addition, the first LSTM cell takes 256 activations as input, which performs feature reduction with a factor of two, leading to 128 activations that are further processed with a second LSTM cell. The final output computed from the Deep-LSTM is 64 activation neurons that represent the temporal patterns. The activations compression makes the prediction more efficient and avoids gradient loss when the number of classes is low, like in FER that has six or seven classes. Therefore, we used two LSTM layers to compress the activations of $FC1$ efficiently in addition to temporal processing. Moreover, Deep-LSTMs are more stable than one LSTM layer and increase the temporal correlation between the input activations.

The final layer of our network is fully connected for predicting the emotion corresponding to the four input time samples. $FC2$ incorporates $Nclasses$ neurons with softmax classification layer. The 64 activations computed by Deep-LSTMs are discriminant enough to detect the correct emotion, which will be proved through an in-depth experimental analysis.

4   Experimental Analysis

This section is devoted to evaluating our proposed CNN-LSTM for dynamic person-independent facial expressions' recognition. We adopted three benchmarks from the state-the-art that include sequence-based posed facial expressions. We set up a hard LOSO evaluation protocol by selecting one sequence of four samples per emotion, and we divided the individuals into ten folds, which guarantees the person-independent constraint. The conducted experiment considers different CNN deep models as feature extractors to find the ultimate configuration for our framework on the three benchmarks. This section presents the setup of the three benchmarks, the recorded results of the deep CNN, and comparative analysis against state-of-the-art works as well as an ablation highlighting the effect of each introduced contributions constructing the proposed DEST-FER.

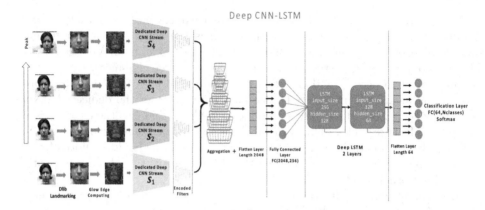

Fig. 1. The overall pipeline of the proposed CNN-LSTM for dynamic FER model. (this figure can be downloaded from here with full resolution)

4.1   Dynamic FER Datasets

We adopted CK+, OuluCasia, and MMI benchmarks for evaluating our developed CNN-LSTM network. These datasets are sequence-based facial expressions. Hence, we present in the following the configuration adopted for each dataset.

– MMI: The MMI database includes a total of 213 sequences from 32 subjects labeled with six basic expressions (excluding "contempt"), where 205 sequences are recorded in frontal view. The sequence starts with a neutral expression and reaches the peak in the middle before returning to the neutral.
– The Oulu-CASIA NIR & VIS expression database is also a sequence based dataset, including 80 subjects (south asian and caucasian) with the six typical expressions. The videos are recorded with two imaging systems, NIR (Near Infrared) and VIS (Visible light).
– Cohn-Kanade v2 database (CK+) is a sequence based database. It contains 593 image sequences from 123 subjects. The first image of each sequence represents the neutral state of the subject, while the peak of the emotion is represented at the end of the sequence.

For the three benchmarks, the first frame (neutral face) and the three peak frames in each frontal sequence are usually selected to perform person-independent 10-fold cross-validation. The 10 folds do not share the same amount of images (subjects); also, we selected only one instance per subject for hard training of our network. Figure 2 shows an example of three individuals performing the same facial expression from the three benchmarks.

Table 1 lists the number of sequences per class (AN: Angry, DI: Disgust, FE: Fear, HA: Happy, SA: Sad, and SU: Surprise) and per dataset that are extracted from the three benchmarks. On CK+, the fear and sad emotion present less samples compared to the rest, which may impact the learning of our approach.

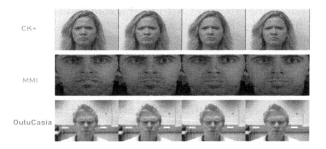

Fig. 2. Examples of the angry sequence from the three datasets

Table 1. Number of samples extracted from the three benchmarks s (AN: Angry, DI: Disgust, FE: Fear, HA: Happy, SA: Sad, SU: Surprise)

Benchmark	AN	DI	FE	HA	SA	SU
CK +	49	65	27	76	30	90
OuluCasia	80	80	80	80	80	80
MMI	137	111	72	155	92	128

4.2   Evaluation of the Proposed CNN-LSTM

This experimental study evaluates the proposed CNN-LSTM network for dynamic person-independent FER regarding different CNN models for dedicated features encoding. We considered 12 well-known CNN models, including AlexNet, VGG16, VGG19, ResNet18, ResNet50, ResNet101, GoogLeNet, Inception.v2, Inception.v3, InceptionResNet.v1, InceptionResNet.v2, and DenseNet200. The comparative analysis relies on calculating the 10 folds average accuracy and the max accuracy that can be achieved. The recorded results are listed in Table 2.

It can be inferred from the recorded results that the achieved overall performance on the three datasets is very satisfying, as the lowest average accuracy is above 81%. This fact proves that the proposed CNN-LSTM architecture is robust to person-independent constraint and grants sustainable recognition performance across the three benchmarks and it works well with all the tested CNN models as feature encoders regarding

On the CK+ dataset, the best-performing configuration is ResNet18, as it reaches 99.41% average accuracy, while the 50 layers ResNet version comes second with 98.72% and the third best-performing model is Inception.v3. The worst-performing model is Inception.v2 with 96.19%, and the rest of the CNN models achieved close results around 97%. According to the max accuracy, all the models reached a 100% rate on at least one fold. The CK+ dataset particularity relies on the uniformity of expressed emotion across all the individuals justifying the high average accuracies. On the other hand, the use of dynamic four samples as inputs improved the performance compared to the static case from 97.53% to 99.41%.

Table 2. Evaluation of the proposed CNN-LSTM according to different CNN models for feature extraction on the three benchmarks

CNN-LSTM	CK+		OuluCasia		MMI	
	Avg	Max	Avg	Max	Avg	Max
AlexNet	97.74	100	84.76	85.94	92.60	96.3
DenseNet200	96.85	100	84.33	85.94	92.17	95.96
GoogLeNet	97.85	100	84.48	85.94	92.32	95.96
Inception.v2	96.19	100	85.02	85.94	91.75	95.96
Inception.v3	98.52	100	84.88	85.94	92.75	95.96
InceptionResNet.v1	96.63	100	81.48	82.81	89.32	92.71
InceptionResNet.v2	97.30	100	81.91	82.81	89.75	92.71
ResNet101	98.36	100	84.91	87.5	93.03	96.3
ResNet18	99.41	100	86.67	89.06	93.42	96.3
ResNet50	98.72	100	85.19	87.5	93.03	96.3
VGG16	97.30	100	82.91	85.94	90.75	92.71
VGG19	97.74	100	84.05	85.94	91.89	92.71
Static FER (peak only)	97.35	100	77.32	85.94	83.12	92.71

On the OuluCasia dataset, ResNet18 and 50 models managed to be the two top-performing by reaching 86.67% and 85.19%, respectively. The third best-performing model is Inception.v2, that controversy outperformed Inception.v3 on the OuluCasia as they scored 85.02% and 84.88%, respectively. The fourth-ranked model is the ResNet101 model by 84.91%. The lowest recorded average accuracy is 81.48% by InceptionResNet.v1, which was also among the worst-models on the CK+. Unlike on the CK+ benchmark, none of the evaluated models could reach 100% as max accuracy. Indeed, only the ResNet18 reached 89.06% and 87.5% for ResNet50, while the rest did not exceed 85.94%. The advantage of using four temporal samples is confirmed once again on the Oulu-Casia as the person-independent recognition rate increased from 77.32% in the static use case to 85.62%.

The MMI benchmarks recorded rates were higher than the OuluCasia ones. The ResNet models successfully ran to be ranked as the three top-performing models and were the only ones that reached above 93% average accuracy. The fourth-ranked model is Inception.v3 with 92.75% average accuracy, followed by the AlexNet model scored with 92.60%. InceptionResnet version 1 and 2 achieved below 90% as the lowest average accuracies (90.75%) on the MMI benchmark, while the rest of the models performed competitively, and their rates ranged between 91% and 92%. In terms of maximum accuracy, only the ResNet and AlexNet architectures reached 96.3%. This fact proves that the MMI benchmark is challenging due to the large interpersonal variation as the facial expressions for the same emotion varies from a subject to another.

4.3   Comparison Against State-of-the-art

Table 3 illustrates the state-of-the-art works that we outperformed on the three considered benchmarks for dynamic person-independent FER based on the FER surveys published in [14].

Table 3. State-of-the-art results on the three benchmarks

Datasets	Methods	Evaluation Protocol	Average Accuracy(%)
CK+	PPDN [23]	10 folds	6 classes: 99.3
	DGIN [15]	10 folds	7 classes: 97.93
	ExpNet [3]	10 folds	6 classes: 97.28
	DTAGN(Weighted Sum) [11]	10 folds	7 classes: 96.94
	DTAGN(Joint) [11]	10 folds	7 classes: 97.25
	Supervised Scoring Ensemble [9]	10 folds	7 classes: 98.47
	PHRNN [21]	10 folds	7 classes: 98.50
	Multi-features DSN-DF [6]	10 folds	6 classes: 98.90
	DEST-FER (ResNet18-LSTM)	10 folds	6 classes: 99.41
MMI	MOSTFR [13]	LOSO	6 classes: 78.61
	DGIN [15]	10 folds	6 classes: 81.53
	3D Inception-ResNet [7]	5 folds	6 classes: 77.50
	CNN-CRF [8]	5 folds	6 classes: 78.68
	PHRNN [21]	10 folds	6 classes: 81.18
	Multi-features DSN-DF [6]	10 folds	6 classes: 71.33
	ExpNet [3]	10 folds	6 classes: 91.46
	DEST-FER (ResNet18-LSTM)	10 folds	6 classes: 93.42
OuluCasia	PPDN [23]	10 folds	6 classes: 84.59
	DCPPN [20]	10 folds	6 classes: 86.23
	DTAGN(Weighted Sum) [11]	10 folds	6 classes: 74.38
	DTAGN(Joint) [11]	10 folds	6 classes: 81.46
	PHRNN [21]	10 folds	6 classes: 86.25
	DEST-FER (ResNet18-LSTM)	10 folds	6 classes: 86.67

It can be inferred from the state-of-the-art comparison that the proposed CNN-LSTM architecture with the ResNet18 configuration successfully outperformed many works in the context of person-independent FER. On the CK+ benchmark, all the methods perform well, reaching more than 90% but only two scored above 99%, including our proposed that reached the best accuracy of 99.41%. The MMI benchmark is more challenging than CK+ as the top state-of-the-art average accuracy, concerning 10 folds cross-validation, is 91.46% reached by ExpNet [3]. Our ResNet18-LSTM managed to outperform it and scored 93.42% with a clear improvement of 2%. The rest literature works were stuck and could not bypass 82% average accuracy. The OuluCasia records highlight a similar performance of many methods, including ours. We underline that only our proposed model, in addition to the PPDN [23] and its deeper version [20] architecture, managed to guarantee an average accuracy above 86%. The Deeper Cascaded Peak-piloted Network [20] slightly outperforms PPDN with 0.02%. The Peak-Piloted Deep Network (PPDN) [23] is one of the competitive works to our approach on the CK+ and OuluCasia benchmarks. The PPDN is based on a special-purpose back-propagation procedure referred to as peak gradient suppression (PGS) for network training. It considers two inputs representing the peak and non-peak samples encoded throw one CNN, and then the extracted features are fed to different classification layers to compare the cross-entropy of the peak and non-peak. ExpNet [3], which is the most competitive model on the MMI dataset, is a 3D approach for FER relying on computing 2D vectors characterizing the facial expression. The classification is done using the nearest neighbor rule with $k = 5$.

4.4   Confusion Matrix-Based Analysis

The confusion matrix analysis allows understanding the behavior of the proposed FER methods emotion-wise and to check if one of the classes is disturbing the others. Figure 3 illustrates the calculated confusion matrices for the adopted datasets CK+, MMI, and OuluCasia.

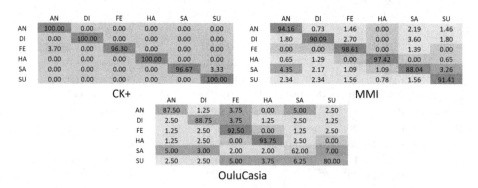

Fig. 3. Confusion matrices computed on three datasets

On CK+ benchmark the proposed framework manages to detect the six classes with a very high accuracy reaching 100% for all of them except Fear and Sad ones and with just two confusion cases on sample of Fear predicted as Angry and one of Sad predicted as Surprise. This fact is a consequence of the fewer samples of both emotions extracted from CK+ as Fear has only 27 samples and 30 for Sad. Close performance is demonstrated on MMI benchmark as the emotions are classified with accuracies above 90% except Sad emotion with 88.04%. The proposed approach suffered from three major confusions related to Sad emotion that was confused with Angry and Surprise. It can be inferred from the confusion matrices of both CK+ and MMI benchmarks that the proposed ResNet18-LSTM approach reaches high recognition rates for the subjected classes. The approach makes fewer confusions between the classes as compared to the OuluCasia benchmark. The challenge of OuluCasia is coming from the ethnicity of the individuals, that most of them are Asians. The main confusion is between Sad and Surprise emotions.

4.5   Ablation Study

In this paper, we proposed a new and efficient framework for person-independent dynamic FER. The framework is referred to as Dedicated Encoding-streams based Spatio-Temporal FER and can be decomposed into three contributions. The first one is the emphasizing the person-independent constraint (PIC) by adopting a landmark guided filter as input to our framework instead of feeding the textural information that characterizes the person more than its emotional state. The second one is how the four frames are fed to the CNN feature encoders. Each frame is fed to an independent CNN stream (ICS) for accurate feature extraction while preserving the frame temporal patterns. The normal scenario is to process the four inputs using only one CNN stream, which treats the four inputs using the same weights and limits the whole framework capability to extract temporal features. The third contribution is the use of deep LSTM block (DLB) for temporal correlation and also for efficient dimensionality reduction just before the classification layer. The LSTM receives $4 \times CNN$ features and maps them into a fully connected layer with 6 neurons (6 classes). Therefore, we decided to perform this LSTM processing and mapping into two stages to avoid information loss between the feature extraction and the classification parts. Table 4 lists the ablation results to highlight in depth the impact of each contribution to the proposed Dedicated Encoding-streams based Spatio-Temporal framework with ResNet 18 as feature encoder. Each time, one component is removed to highlight its effect on the overall performance.

Table 4. Ablation study of the proposed Dedicated Encoding-streams based Spatio-Temporal framework components

Ablation Type			Benchmarks		
PIC	ICS	DLB	CK+	OuluCasia	MMI
X	X		96.16	78.39	87.08
X		X	94.75	80.15	86.75
	X	X	97.35	82.27	87.71
X	X	X	99.41	86.67	93.42

It can be inferred from the ablation recorded results that removing one component dramatically decreases the overall performance. This fact proves that these three contributions are designed to work together, since each one of them deals with a given challenge. The DLB and ICS combination is more contributing compared to PIC with ICS and PIC with DLB ones as it efficiently processes the temporal features right before the classification layer. Moreover, the PIC and ICS combination is outperforming the PIC with DLB on CK+ and MMI benchmarks and not on OuluCasia, which is normal since the detected landmarks with the filtering preprocessing lost their temporal information as the four frames are processed through one CNN stream only and limiting the DLB capabilities. On OuluCasia, the Asian ethnicity is the major challenge faced, that justifies why the PIC and ICS combination is outperformed by the PIC and DLB one.

4.6   Implementation Details and Running Time

The proposed CNN-LSTM framework is developed using the Python3.9 along with PyTorch 1.7 Neural Network Libraries and CUDA GPU Toolkit 11, and performed on Alienware Aurora R11 i9-10900KF Dual RTX2080Ti (22 GB VRAM).

The computational cost is one of the key performance indicators considered in machine learning applications. Therefore, we ran an experiment that calculates the elapsed time required to predict the label of a given input sequence of four images with a pixel resolution of 480×480, highlighting the execution time of each step of the proposed framework averaged on a set of 10 runs:

- Dlib landmark detection: 4×12 ms $= 48$ ms for the four input images.
- Glow Edge computing: 4×8 ms $= 32$ ms for the four input images with inserted landmarks.
- ResNet18-LSTM inference on GPU: 41 ms to predict the emotion represented over the four inputs.

Therefore, the total elapsed time to predict the label is 121 ms, which remains a real-time response for such applications regarding that the emotions are stable states over long periods are switching from one to another takes longer than the recorded inference time.

5   Conclusion

In this paper, we proposed a new deep learning framework for dynamic FER with respect to the person-independent training constraint. The proposed framework is referred to as Dedicated Encoding-streams based Spatio-Temporal FER (DEST-FER), and is based on four dedicated encoding-streams that extract discriminant deep features from the input frames. Then, the four features are fed to the temporal processing units through the LSTM to encode the emotion variations and intensity and predict the dominant facial expression. This paper proved the advantage of considering dynamic FER instead of the static one and the benefits of the LSTM-based temporal processing. Moreover, we disclosed that the ResNet-18 managed to be the best deep encoder among the 12 tested ones while offering a good inference time for FER application. The performance of the 12 CNNs as encoders demonstrated that the proposed spatio-temporal architecture works well with all of them being generic and robust. The evaluation with respect to person-independent protocol challenged our framework and showed the benefits of adopting landmarks overlapping on the input frames, emphasizing the emotion's related appearance than the individual himself. The confusion matrix-based analysis highlighted that the proposed DEST-FER recognizes all the emotions with fewer confusions especially on CK+ and MMI benchmarks while some confusions are faced on OuluCasia regarding its Asian ethnicity challenge. Indeed, this challenge will be addressed with more attention in our future works to find a discriminant appearance feature to characterize the facial expression. Moreover, we are considering deep multi-modal processing coupling visual information with other kind of data (such as speech, writing, pose) to classify the emotional state with higher performance.

References

1. Al Chanti, D.A., Caplier, A.: Deep learning for spatio-temporal modeling of dynamic spontaneous emotions. IEEE Trans. Affect. Comput. **12**(2), 363–376 (2018)
2. Bargal, S.A., Barsoum, E., Ferrer, C.C., Zhang, C.: Emotion recognition in the wild from videos using images. In: Proceedings of the 18th ACM International Conference on Multimodal Interaction, pp. 433–436 (2016)
3. Chang, F.J., Tran, A.T., Hassner, T., Masi, I., Nevatia, R., Medioni, G.: ExpNet: landmark-free, deep, 3D facial expressions. In: 2018 13th IEEE International Conference on Automatic Face & Gesture Recognition (FG 2018), pp. 122–129. IEEE (2018)
4. Ding, W., et al.: Audio and face video emotion recognition in the wild using deep neural networks and small datasets. In: Proceedings of the 18th ACM International Conference on Multimodal Interaction, pp. 506–513 (2016)
5. El Hammoumi, O., Benmarrakchi, F., Ouherrou, N., El Kafi, J., El Hore, A.: Emotion recognition in e-learning systems. In: 2018 6th International Conference on Multimedia Computing and Systems (ICMCS), pp. 1–6 (2018). https://doi.org/10.1109/ICMCS.2018.8525872
6. Gan, C., Yao, J., Ma, S., Zhang, Z., Zhu, L.: The deep spatiotemporal network with dual-flow fusion for video-oriented facial expression recognition. Digit. Commun. Netw. (2022). https://doi.org/10.1016/j.dcan.2022.07.009, https://www.sciencedirect.com/science/article/pii/S2352864822001572
7. Hasani, B., Mahoor, M.H.: Facial expression recognition using enhanced deep 3D convolutional neural networks. In: Proceedings of the IEEE Conference on Computer Vision and Pattern Recognition Workshops, pp. 30–40 (2017)
8. Hasani, B., Mahoor, M.H.: Spatio-temporal facial expression recognition using convolutional neural networks and conditional random fields. In: 2017 12th IEEE International Conference on Automatic Face & Gesture Recognition (FG 2017), pp. 790–795. IEEE (2017)

9. Hu, P., Cai, D., Wang, S., Yao, A., Chen, Y.: Learning supervised scoring ensemble for emotion recognition in the wild. In: Proceedings of the 19th ACM International Conference on Multimodal Interaction, pp. 553–560 (2017)

10. Jia, S., Wang, S., Hu, C., Webster, P.J., Li, X.: Detection of genuine and posed facial expressions of emotion: databases and methods. Front. Psychol. **11**, 580287 (2021)

11. Jung, H., Lee, S., Yim, J., Park, S., Kim, J.: Joint fine-tuning in deep neural networks for facial expression recognition. In: 2015 IEEE International Conference on Computer Vision (ICCV), pp. 2983–2991 (2015). https://doi.org/10.1109/ICCV.2015.341

12. Kahou, S.E., et al.: EmoNets: multimodal deep learning approaches for emotion recognition in video. J. Multimodal User Interfaces **10**(2), 99–111 (2016)

13. Kim, D.H., Baddar, W.J., Jang, J., Ro, Y.M.: Multi-objective based spatio-temporal feature representation learning robust to expression intensity variations for facial expression recognition. IEEE Trans. Affect. Comput. **10**, 223–236 (2019)

14. Li, S., Deng, W.: Deep facial expression recognition: a survey. IEEE Trans. Affect. Comput. 1 (2020). https://doi.org/10.1109/TAFFC.2020.2981446

15. Li, W., Huang, D., Li, H., Wang, Y.: Automatic 4D facial expression recognition using dynamic geometrical image network. In: 2018 13th IEEE International Conference on Automatic Face Gesture Recognition (FG 2018), pp. 24–30 (2018). https://doi.org/10.1109/FG.2018.00014

16. Lyons, M., Akamatsu, S., Kamachi, M., Gyoba, J.: Coding facial expressions with Gabor wavelets. In: Proceedings of the Third IEEE International Conference on Automatic Face and Gesture Recognition, pp. 200–205. IEEE (1998)

17. Martin, C.J., Archibald, J., Ball, L., Carson, L.: Towards an affective self-service agent. In: Kudělka, M., Pokorný, J., Snášel, V., Abraham, A. (eds.) Proceedings of the Third International Conference on Intelligent Human Computer Interaction (IHCI 2011), Prague, Czech Republic, August, 2011. AISC, vol. 179, pp. 3–12. Springer, Heidelberg (2013). https://doi.org/10.1007/978-3-642-31603-6_1

18. Samadiani, N., et al.: A review on automatic facial expression recognition systems assisted by multimodal sensor data. Sensors **19**(8), 1863 (2019)

19. Topi, M., Timo, O., Matti, P., Maricor, S.: Robust texture classification by subsets of local binary patterns. In: Pattern Recognition, 2000. Proceedings. 15th International Conference on, vol. 3, pp. 935–938. IEEE (2000)

20. Yu, Z., Liu, Q., Liu, G.: Deeper cascaded peak-piloted network for weak expression recognition. Vis. Comput. **34**(12), 1691–1699 (2018)

21. Zhang, K., Huang, Y., Du, Y., Wang, L.: Facial expression recognition based on deep evolutional spatial-temporal networks. IEEE Trans. Image Process. **26**(9), 4193–4203 (2017). https://doi.org/10.1109/TIP.2017.2689999

22. Zhao, J., Mao, X., Zhang, J.: Learning deep facial expression features from image and optical flow sequences using 3D CNN. Vis. Comput. **34**(10), 1461–1475 (2018)

23. Zhao, X., et al.: Peak-piloted deep network for facial expression recognition. In: Leibe, B., Matas, J., Sebe, N., Welling, M. (eds.) ECCV 2016. LNCS, vol. 9906, pp. 425–442. Springer, Cham (2016). https://doi.org/10.1007/978-3-319-46475-6_27

Hands, Objects, Action! Egocentric 2D Hand-Based Action Recognition

Wiktor Mucha[✉][ID] and Martin Kampel[ID]

Computer Vision Lab, TU Wien, Favoritenstr. 9/193-1, 1040 Vienna, Austria
{wiktor.mucha,martin.kampel}@tuwien.ac.at

Abstract. Action recognition is at the core of egocentric camera-based assistive technologies, as it enables automatic and continuous monitoring of Activities of Daily Living (ADLs) without any conscious effort on the part of the user. This study explores the feasibility of using 2D hand and object pose information for egocentric action recognition. While current literature focuses on 3D hand pose information, our work shows that using 2D skeleton data is a promising approach for hand-based action classification and potentially allows for reduced computational power. The study implements a state-of-the-art transformer-based method to recognise actions. Our approach achieves an accuracy of 95% in validation and 88% in test subsets on the publicly available benchmark, outperforming other existing solutions by 9% and proving that the presented technique offers a successful alternative to 3D-based approaches. Finally, the ablation study shows the significance of each network input and explores potential ways to improve the presented methodology in future research.

Keywords: egocentric · action recognition · hand pose · AAL

1 Introduction

The popularity of egocentric action recognition has grown in recent years as the quality of wearable cameras improves. The combination of the low costs of the technology and the ease of use results in increasing the number of available egocentric datasets for the research community [5,9,10]. This study focuses on egocentric action recognition employing hand and objects 2D pose for sequence classification using a state-of-the-art transformer-based method. Examples of actions processed in this work from *H2O Dataset* [10] with visualisation of 2D hand and object positions are illustrated in Fig. 1. Research in egocentric action recognition is motivated by its application in lifestyle understanding due to the automatic processing of data from the user perspective that is rich in health-related information, e.g., activity, dietary and social interactions [13]. Besides behaviour modelling, it finds application in Active Assisted Living (AAL) technologies, e.g. assistance for people with vision impairment [18]. In the future, this technology has the potential to lead to health and well-being improvement

© The Author(s), under exclusive license to Springer Nature Switzerland AG 2023
H. I. Christensen et al. (Eds.): ICVS 2023, LNCS 14253, pp. 31–40, 2023.
https://doi.org/10.1007/978-3-031-44137-0_3

Fig. 1. Frames representing the action *take out espresso* (top), and *take out chips* (bottom) from *H2O Dataset* with visualised 2D hand and object positions.

in our society in an automatic manner reducing the burden on the health system. Most of the available literature explores egocentric action recognition based on 3D hand pose information [6,10,14]. However, the market does not offer wearable depth sensors. Therefore, these studies do not employ sensor-acquired depth information, but generate depth estimates from RGB frames, which results in a significant error in pose prediction oscillating around 37 mm [10]. In contrast, exploiting 2D skeleton data is more accurate [19] and demands less computational power. Finally, the market offers several devices, such as the Rayban Stories[1], that are easy to use and lightweight in construction compared with head-mounted cameras or RGB-D sensors [10]. Our study aims to answer the following research questions: How feasible is it to use 2D hand and object pose for egocentric action recognition tasks compared to state-of-the-art methods, including 3D pose-based methods? What is the performance when perfectly accurate 2D poses are employed? How the robustness changes when 2D poses are estimated with current state-of-the-art methods? Finally, which pose (hands or objects) plays the most significant role? Our contribution is listed as: (1) A new methodology for egocentric action recognition using only 2D data about the subject's hand position and object position; (2) An evaluation performed on publicly available benchmark where our model outperforms current state-of-the-art results by 9% in accuracy; (3) Ablation studies showing the significance of various inputs. The code is planned to be released upon publication[2].

The paper is organised as follows: Sect. 2 presents related work in egocentric action recognition, focusing on hand-based methods, and highlighting areas for improvements. Section 3 describes our method and implementation. Evaluation and results are presented in Sect. 4. Section 5 concludes the study and highlights the main findings.

---

[1] https://www.ray-ban.com/usa/ray-ban-stories (Accessed 01.06.2023).
[2] https://github.com/wiktormucha/hand_actions_recognition.

2   Related Work

A recurring strategy for egocentric action recognition is employing hand and object information for action description. Across scientific literature, we observe instances of utilising 2D data as input in the recognition process, like the work of Cartas et al. [4] who propose using an object detector based on a Convolutional Neural Network (CNN) to assess primary region (hands) and secondary region (objects) positions. Sequences of these positions are further processed using a Long Short-Term Memory (LSTM) network. Nguyen et al. [12] go beyond bounding box and exploit 2D hand skeleton information obtained with a CNN. Later, the estimated joints are aggregated using spatial and temporal Gaussian aggregation. To perform action classification, the network learns the SPD matrix. Contrary to approaches based on 2D data, other authors researching hand role in action recognition focus on utilising 3D information [6,10,14]. Tekin et al. [14] use a CNN taking as input a single RGB frame to estimate 3D hand and object poses, which are fed into an LSTM network to output the action class. Das et al. [6] propose an architecture based on a spatiotemporal graph CNN to recognise the action. In their method, they create sub-graphs for the movement description of each finger. Kwon et al. [10] create sub-graphs for each hand and object that are later merged into a multigraph representation, which enables learning about interactions between each of these three interacting parts. In the mentioned studies, 3D hand poses are obtained by performing regression from 2D to 3D using neural networks and intrinsic camera parameters [10,14], and do not employ sensor-acquired depth maps like a stereo camera or a depth sensor. The mean End-Point Error (EPE) of hand pose in *H2O Dataset* oscillates around 37mm, which is far from accurate considering the human hand size with an average length of 18 cm (20.5%). A potential solution is an application based on depth sensors which apart from accurate 3D information enhances privacy [11], but the market lacks wearable depth sensors.

In contrast, our method based on 2D data performs with error in the pose prediction stage equal to 13.4%, and does not require intrinsic camera parameters, therefore permits generalisation to any dataset. Employing 2D data allows processing by networks with fewer parameters, causing computation to be faster. Finally, there are no results of methods employing 2D hand poses on popular egocentric benchmarks like *H2O Dataset* or *Epic-Kitchen* [5].

3   Hand-Based 2D Action Recognition

The proposed method performs action recognition from video or image sequences by processing pose information describing hands and objects in a 2D space. The complete pipeline of our method is presented in Fig. 2 where f_n corresponds to processed frames. It is constructed of three separate blocks performing tasks of object detection, hand pose estimation and finally, action recognition using a transformer encoder block and fully connected layer.

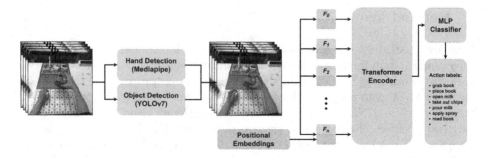

Fig. 2. Our procedure for action recognition. Hand and object poses are extracted from the sequence of frames. With added positional embedding, this information creates input tokens for the transformer encoder, which processes the temporal information. Finally, the multi-layer perceptron predicts the action.

3.1 Object Detection and Its Position

Object detection is the first part of the pipeline and is performed using a state-of-the-art *YOLOv7* [16] network with pre-trained weights. Further, transfer learning is applied for *H2O Dataset* using the given object positions (transforming bounding boxes from 6D to 2D). Each frame f_n includes a representation of the object described as $Po_{bb}^i(x, y)$ where $i \in [1..4]$ corresponds to the corners of bounding box surrounding the object and Po_l is the object label.

3.2 Hand Pose Estimation

Along the object pose information, f_n includes hands pose information of a subject performing action. A separate part of the network estimates the position of hands in 2D space using 21 key points for each hand. These 21 points correspond to wrist and finger joints following the common approach of hand pose description [1]. Each hand pose is represented by $Ph_t^i(x, y)$ where $t \in \{l, r\}$ describes the left or right hand and $i \in [1..21]$ stands for the hand keypoint number. Hand pose detection is done following the *MediaPipe* approach by Zhang et al. [19]. To predict hand skeletons in real-time from RGB images, it first performs a single shot detection on the input frame to determine hand regions. Detected regions are processed to estimate the pose for each hand. Authors report the average precision of detection equal to 96.7%, and Mean-Square-Error (MSE) equal to 13.4% in pose estimation tasks normalised by hand size.

3.3 Action Recognition

Each sequence is represented with frames $f_n, n \in [1..40]$, including hand and object poses. This frame number is chosen heuristically to yield the highest accuracy. Actions represented by less than 40 frames are padded with zeros, and actions longer are sub-sampled. A concatenation of frames f_n creates the input vector V_{seq} described as:

$$f_n = Ph_l^i(x,y) \oplus Ph_r^i(x,y) \oplus Po_{bb}^i(x,y) \oplus Po_l \qquad (1)$$

$$V_{seq} = [f_1, f_2..f_n], n \in [1..40] \qquad (2)$$

This sequence vector V_{seq} is passed to the last stage, which embeds temporal information and performs classification. We employ a model inspired by Visual Transformer by Dosovitskiy et al. [7]. It is constructed from a standard Transformer Encoder block introduced in the work of Vaswani et al. [15]. The input vector V_{seq} representing an action is linearised using a fully connected layer according to the formula $x_{lin} = xA^T + b$. The sequence x_{lin} is merged with a classification token similar to [7], and positional embedding is added. The architecture is found to work best when input is linearised to 42 parameters, the number of encoder layers is equal to 2, and encoder dropout and attention dropout are applied with a probability equal to 0.2.

4   Evaluation

The evaluation of our method is done in *H2O Dataset*. At the time of this analysis, it is the only dataset providing ground truth (GT) to study hand-based actions and object interactions. It features synchronised multi-view RGB-D images along with action labels for 36 classes constructed from verb and object labels, 3D poses for both hands, 6D poses for manipulated objects, GT camera poses, object meshes and scene point clouds. The training, validation and test subsets for action recognition and hand pose estimation tasks are provided. The analysis is conducted in two stages. The first stage aims to determine the robustness of the proposed method based on 2D hand pose and object pose only. The second stage includes a complete model estimating 2D hand and object poses to show how this method places next to the conditions of GT pose utilisation.

4.1   Learning Procedure

Our training strategy includes various augmentation applied to the sequence vectors of keypoints V_{seq}. Overfitting between validation and train subsets is reduced with horizontal flipping, rotations and random cropping employing solutions from Buslaev et al. [2]. Another beneficial augmentation observed is masking one of the hands or objects' positions. It is done by randomly setting corresponding values of hand or object in f_n to a zero. Input sequences are randomly sampled during training, and frames are chosen uniformly for validation and testing. In the beginning, the model is trained using given GT poses. Best results are achieved with batch size equal to 64, AdamW optimiser, cross-entropy loss function and learning rate equal to 0.01.

4.2   Stage I - Preliminary Evaluation

The first stage experiment is based on the given GT poses. The idea is to determine the robustness of action recognition by employing 2D data only in a scenario of poses as close as possible to perfect estimation. The 3D points P_{3D} describing each hand pose and 6D object poses are transformed into a 2D plane P_{2D} using the given camera intrinsic parameters K following the formula:

$$P_{xyz} = (K \cdot P_{3D}^T)^T, P_{2D} = (\frac{P_x}{P_z}, \frac{P_y}{P_z}) \tag{3}$$

The results of our action recognition method on the validation subset are accurate, and they outperform other methods. Our model $OurGT$ yields 95.08% of accuracy for the validation subset. The accuracy on the test subset drops to 88.43% but still outperforms state-of-the-art models which is presented in Table 2. These preliminary results highlight how robust 2D pose-based action recognition is and enhance us for further research. Authors of $H2O\ Dataset$ do not provide labels for test sets, and evaluation is performed using an online system. Due to this fact, deeper analysis using a confusion matrix in Fig. 3 is possible to carry only using a validation subset. Because of the high accuracy of the object prediction module (See Table 2), only verb classes are analysed. It is observed that the model misunderstands the action of opening and closing which are similar but differ in movement direction.

4.3   Stage II -Evaluation of a Complete Pipeline

The complete pipeline includes pose estimation for hands and objects. Fine-tuning of the $YOLOv7$ model results in 0.995 mAP@0.5, causing the object information to be accurate for higher inference. The most challenging part is the hand pose estimation, where are occlusions caused by objects or the appearance of the second hand. The hand estimation model works with significant error, where in the training subset, the detector misses 8757 single hands in frames

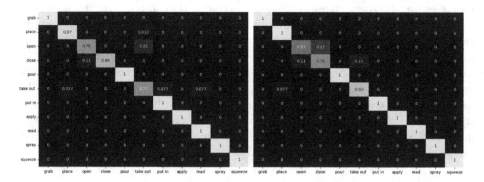

Fig. 3. Confusion matrix for validation subset obtained using GT poses (left), and using *MediaPipe* and *YOLOv7* poses (right).

(a) Ground truth pose   (b) *MediaPipe* pose

Fig. 4. Visualisation of differences in 2D pose prediction between GT pose data from *H2O Dataset* (a) and estimated hand pose using *MediaPipe* (b).

where two hands are visible and 118 complete frames, respectively, in the validation subset 1473 and 24, in the test subset 1442 and 98. The EPE of estimated hand poses is equal to 76.25, 62.31, and 38.78 pixels for training, validation and test subsets in a 1280×720 input image, where missed hands are expressed as vectors of zero pose values (See Table 1). An example error in pose estimation for one of the frames is depicted in Fig. 4 where Fig. 4a represents GT 2D pose and Fig. 4b 2D pose estimated using *MediaPipe* method. In this scenario, our method *Our* performs with accuracy equal to 94.26% for the validation subset and 75.62% for the test placing the above state-of-the-art results in the validation subset only. *OurGTpretrain* shows the model can generalise when trained using GT to predictions with pose estimation in the testing phase, and it performs with the accuracy of 87.70% in validation and 77.68% in test subsets. The confusion matrix is presented in Fig. 3 showing the problem of misunderstanding action *open* with *close* and additionally *take out* with *place*, *put in* and *read*.

Table 1. Results for 2D hand pose estimation with *MediaPipe* in *H2O dataset*. The table provides information regarding the quantity of missed frames, missed pose estimations and EPE in pixels for an image size of 1280×720.

Subset	Train	Validation	Test
Number of frames	55747	11638	23391
Number of actions	569	122	241
Missed frames in hand pose	118	24	98
Missed hands in hand pose	8757	1473	1442
EPE [pixels]	76.25	62.31	40.06

Table 2. Results of various action recognition methods performing on *H2O dataset* expressed in accuracy including our method.

Method:	Validation [%]	Validation Verb [%]	Test [%]
I3D [3] *(None-pose-based)*	85.15	–	75.21
SlowFast [8] *(None-pose-based)*	86.00	–	77.69
H+O [14] *(3D-based)*	80.49	–	68.88
ST-GCN [17] *(3D-based)*	83.47	–	73.86
TA-GCN [10] *(3D-based)*	86.78	–	79.25
OurGT *(2D-based)*	**95.08**	**95.08**	**88.43**
OurGTpretrain *(2D-based)*	87.70	87.70	77.68
Our *(2D-based)*	94.26	94.26	75.62

4.4 Ablation Study

First, ablations are performed to show our estimations' impact on final accuracy. The experiment referenced as *GTHand-OwnObj* connects GT hand poses and object information obtained using *YOLOv7*. It shows robust performance with a drop only in the test subset to 83.88%. *OwnHand-GTObj* combines *MediaPipe* hand poses and GT object information. The drop in accuracy to 89.34% (validation) and 80.99% (test) indicates the importance of accurate pose description. Further ablations determine the importance of each module for the final accuracy of action recognition. *GTPose I* based on GT and *OwnPose I* using own pose estimations do not include object bounding box. This results in 79.50% and 59.09% for validation and test, and respectively 77.05% and 59.09%. It highlights the importance of including object position information. *GTPose II* and *OwnPose II* follow a similar scheme but include only left hand pose and object information. The results are 90.16%, 71.90% and 82.78%, 66.52%. *GTPose III* and *OwnPose III* represent right hand with object information and result in

Table 3. Results of our ablation study depending on inputs: *left hand pose, right hand pose* and *object pose.*

Method:	Left Hand	Right Hand	Obj Pose	Val. [%]	Test [%]
GTHand-OwnObj	✓	✓	✓	95.08	83.88
OwnHand-GTObj	✓	✓	✓	89.34	80.99
GTPose I	✓	✓	✗	79.50	59.09
GTPose II	✓	✗	✓	90.16	71.90
GTPose III	✗	✓	✓	83.60	77.27
OwnPose I	✓	✓	✗	77.05	59.09
OwnPose II	✓	✗	✓	82.78	66.52
OwnPose III	✗	✓	✓	87.70	66.11

83.60%, 77.27% and 87.70%, 66.11% in test. The difference in accuracy for hand type emphasises that one of the hands plays a more significant role in human actions. All of the results are summarised in Table 3.

5 Conclusion

The study implemented an egocentric action recognition method based on hand and object 2D pose. This pose information describes each frame. Input sequences are embedded using a transformer-based network to predict action labels. In the experiments on *H2O Dataset* using ground truth, our method outperformed state of the art by 9%, proving to be a robust approach when pose descriptions are accurate. Further, our method was tested with a state-of-the-art pose estimation and object detector, leading to a drop in accuracy. Results place among other state-of-the-art methods despite the significant error in hand pose estimation. The main reason behind incorrect predictions was a misunderstanding between the actions of *open* and *close* which are similar but differ in movement's direction. The ablation study highlighted the importance of including object pose information in the prediction process and the accuracy of hand pose estimation. In future work, we plan to improve the hand pose description method to boost the final action recognition results and apply it to AAL technologies.

Acknowledgements. This work was supported by VisuAAL ITN H2020 (grant agreement No. 861091) and by KIIS Austrian Research Promotion Agency (grant agreement No. 879744).

References

1. Bandini, A., Zariffa, J.: Analysis of the hands in egocentric vision: a survey. IEEE Trans. Pattern Anal. Mach. Intell. (2020). https://doi.org/10.1109/TPAMI.2020.2986648
2. Buslaev, A., Iglovikov, V.I., Khvedchenya, E., Parinov, A., Druzhinin, M., Kalinin, A.A.: Albumentations: fast and flexible image augmentations. Information **11**(2), 125 (2020). https://doi.org/10.3390/info11020125
3. Carreira, J., Zisserman, A.: Quo Vadis, action recognition? A new model and the kinetics dataset. In: Proceedings of the IEEE Conference on Computer Vision and Pattern Recognition, pp. 6299–6308 (2017). https://doi.org/10.1109/CVPR.2017.502
4. Cartas, A., Radeva, P., Dimiccoli, M.: Contextually driven first-person action recognition from videos. In: Presentation at EPIC@ ICCV2017 Workshop, p. 8 (2017)
5. Damen, D., et al.: Scaling egocentric vision: the dataset. In: Ferrari, V., Hebert, M., Sminchisescu, C., Weiss, Y. (eds.) ECCV 2018. LNCS, vol. 11208, pp. 753–771. Springer, Cham (2018). https://doi.org/10.1007/978-3-030-01225-0_44
6. Das, P., Ortega, A.: Symmetric sub-graph spatio-temporal graph convolution and its application in complex activity recognition. In: ICASSP 2021–2021 IEEE International Conference on Acoustics, Speech and Signal Processing (ICASSP), pp. 3215–3219. IEEE (2021). https://doi.org/10.1109/ICASSP39728.2021.9413833

7. Dosovitskiy, A., et al.: An image is worth 16 × 16 words: transformers for image recognition at scale. In: International Conference on Learning Representations (2021). https://openreview.net/forum?id=YicbFdNTTy
8. Feichtenhofer, C., Fan, H., Malik, J., He, K.: Slowfast networks for video recognition. In: Proceedings of the IEEE/CVF International Conference on Computer Vision, pp. 6202–6211 (2019). https://doi.org/10.1109/ICCV.2019.00630
9. Grauman, K., et al.: Ego4D: around the world in 3,000 hours of egocentric video. In: Proceedings of the IEEE/CVF Conference on Computer Vision and Pattern Recognition, pp. 18995–19012 (2022). https://doi.org/10.1109/CVPR52688.2022.01842
10. Kwon, T., Tekin, B., Stühmer, J., Bogo, F., Pollefeys, M.: H2O: two hands manipulating objects for first person interaction recognition. In: Proceedings of the IEEE/CVF International Conference on Computer Vision (ICCV), pp. 10138–10148, October 2021. https://doi.org/10.1109/ICCV48922.2021.00998
11. Mucha, W., Kampel, M.: Addressing privacy concerns in depth sensors. In: Miesenberger, K., Kouroupetroglou, G., Mavrou, K., Manduchi, R., Covarrubias Rodriguez, M., Penaz, P. (eds.) Computers Helping People with Special Needs. ICCHP-AAATE 2022. LNCS, vol. 13342, pp. 526–533. Springer, Cham (2022). https://doi.org/10.1007/978-3-031-08645-8_62
12. Nguyen, X.S., Brun, L., Lézoray, O., Bougleux, S.: A neural network based on SPD manifold learning for skeleton-based hand gesture recognition. In: Proceedings of the IEEE/CVF Conference on Computer Vision and Pattern Recognition, pp. 12036–12045 (2019). https://doi.org/10.1109/CVPR.2019.01231
13. Núñez-Marcos, A., Azkune, G., Arganda-Carreras, I.: Egocentric vision-based action recognition: a survey. Neurocomputing **472**, 175–197 (2022). https://doi.org/10.1016/j.neucom.2021.11.081
14. Tekin, B., Bogo, F., Pollefeys, M.: H+O: unified egocentric recognition of 3D hand-object poses and interactions. In: Proceedings of the IEEE/CVF Conference on Computer Vision and Pattern Recognition, pp. 4511–4520 (2019). https://doi.org/10.1109/CVPR.2019.00464
15. Vaswani, A., et al..: Attention is all you need. Adv. Neural Inf. Process. Syst. **30** (2017). https://doi.org/10.5555/3295222.3295349
16. Wang, C.Y., Bochkovskiy, A., Liao, H.Y.M.: Yolov7: trainable bag-of-freebies sets new state-of-the-art for real-time object detectors. In: Proceedings of the IEEE/CVF Conference on Computer Vision and Pattern Recognition, pp. 7464–7475 (2023)
17. Yan, S., Xiong, Y., Lin, D.: Spatial temporal graph convolutional networks for skeleton-based action recognition. In: Proceedings of the AAAI Conference on Artificial Intelligence, vol. 32 (2018). https://doi.org/10.5555/3504035.3504947
18. Zhan, K., Faux, S., Ramos, F.: Multi-scale conditional random fields for first-person activity recognition. In: 2014 IEEE International Conference on Pervasive Computing and Communications (PerCom), pp. 51–59. IEEE (2014). https://doi.org/10.1016/j.pmcj.2014.11.004
19. Zhang, F., et al.: Mediapipe hands: on-device real-time hand tracking. arXiv preprint arXiv:2006.10214 (2020)

WiFi CSI-Based Long-Range Through-Wall Human Activity Recognition with the ESP32

Julian Strohmayer$^{(\boxtimes)}$ and Martin Kampel

TU Wien, Computer Vision Lab, Favoritenstr. 9/193-1, 1040 Vienna, Austria
{julian.strohmayer,martin.kampel}@tuwien.ac.at

Abstract. WiFi Channel State Information (CSI)-based human activity recognition (HAR) is an unobtrusive method for contactless, long-range sensing in spatially constrained environments while preserving visual privacy. Despite the presence of numerous WiFi-enabled devices around us, few expose CSI to users, resulting in a lack of sensing hardware options. Recently, variants of the Espressif ESP32 have emerged as potential low-cost, easy-to-deploy solutions for WiFi CSI-based HAR. In this work, we evaluate the ESP32-S3's long-range through-wall HAR capabilities by combining it with a 2.4GHz directional biquad antenna. The experimental setup uses a transmitter-receiver configuration spanning 18.5m across five rooms. We assess line-of-sight (LOS) and non-line-of-sight (NLOS) performance using CNN HAR models trained on CSI spectrograms. CSI HAR datasets used in this work consist of 392 LOS and 384 NLOS spectrograms from three activity classes and are made publicly available. The gathered results clearly demonstrate the feasibility of long-range through-wall presence detection and activity recognition with the proposed setup.

Keywords: human activity recognition (HAR) · channel state information (CSI) · non-line-of-sight (NLOS) · through-wall sensing · ESP32

1 Introduction

WiFi-based Human Activity Recognition (HAR) exploits the measurable signal changes caused by human activities within a WiFi device's electromagnetic field to distinguish and recognize activities [10]. While camera-based approaches dominate the field, WiFi is gaining recognition as a sensing modality. WiFi is cost-effective, unobtrusive, illumination invariant, and protects the visual privacy of monitored individuals by not capturing any color or texture information, a key requirement in privacy-sensitive applications [2]. Additionally, WiFi

---

This work is partially funded by the Vienna Business Agency (Blindsight-grant 4829418) and the Austrian Research Promotion Agency (KIIS-grant 879744).

signals can penetrate walls, enabling contactless long-range activity sensing in spatially constrained environments with operating ranges of up to 35m indoors [19]. This provides an economic advantage over camera-based approaches that require per-room deployment and opens up new possibilities like through-wall HAR [17], the focus of this work. Early WiFi-based HAR relied on the Received Signal Strength Indicator (RSSI) [18], which measures the signal strength of the WiFi channel at the receiver. Current approaches utilize Channel State Information (CSI), which captures amplitude and phase information of WiFi subcarriers [11]. CSI offers higher information density, enabling the recognition of fine-grained activities, and is more robust to environmental effects [12]. While all WiFi devices process CSI internally, most off-the-shelf devices do not expose this information to end users. Consequently, only specific hardware and software combinations allow CSI capture. Examples include the outdated Intel NIC 5300 with the Linux 802.11n CSI Tool[1] and Atheros NIC variants (AR9580, AR9590, AR9344, and QCA9558) with the Atheros CSI Tool[2]. Recently, the Nexmon CSI Tool[3] enabled CSI capture on Raspberry Pi [5]. Another emerging option is the Wi-ESP CSI Tool[4], which leverages the popular ESP32 microcontroller from Espressif Systems [3]. While a handful of works have explored the ESP32's potential in short-range line-of-sight (LOS) scenarios [6] and non-line-of-sight (NLOS) (through-wall) HAR scenarios [1,8], its activity sensing capabilities in long-range NLOS scenarios remain unexplored.

Contributions. In this work, we pair the ESP32-S3 with a 2.4GHz directional biquad antenna to enable long-range through-wall HAR in indoor environments. To the best of our knowledge, this is the first demonstration of such a setup for CSI-based through-wall HAR. We evaluate the proposed setup in long-range LOS and NLOS HAR scenarios, covering a distance of 18.5m across five rooms. A CSI HAR dataset containing 392 LOS and 384 NLOS samples of three activity classes is collected in an office environment and a performance evaluation on the basis of CNN HAR models trained on CSI spectrograms is conducted. The CSI HAR dataset used in this work is made publicly available.

2   Related Work

Through-wall CSI-based HAR has received significant attention, particularly with the Intel NIC 5300 being widely used as a sensing device, as highlighted in the comprehensive survey by Wang et al. [17]. However, due to its discontinuation in 2016, its sustainability for future CSI-based HAR applications is limited. Consequently, researchers have started exploring alternative solutions, such as Espressif ESP32 variants, which could offer a low-cost and easy-to-deploy solution to CSI-based HAR. While the ESP32 has been utilized in LOS scenarios

[1] Linux CSI Tool, https://dhalperi.github.io/, accessed: 05.06.2023.
[2] Atheros CSI Tool, https://wands.sg/, accessed: 05.06.2023.
[3] Nexmon CSI Tool, https://github.com/seemoo-lab/, accessed: 05.06.2023.
[4] Wi-ESP CSI Tool, https://wrlab.github.io/Wi-ESP/, accessed: 05.06.2023.

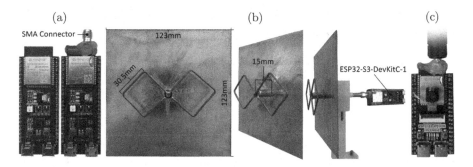

Fig. 1. (a) ESP32-S3-DevKitC-1 boards with built-in PCB antenna and SMA connector, (b) 2.4 GHz directional biquad antenna, and (c) ESP32-S3-WROOM-CAM board.

[3,6,7], there have been limited investigations into NLOS scenarios. To the best of our knowledge, only two works have explored NLOS scenarios to date [1,8]. In the work by Hernandez and Bulut [8], the feasibility of adversarial occupancy monitoring based on CSI is assessed. ESP32 devices are positioned as transmitters and receivers on the external wall of a hallway, successfully sensing the presence and walking direction of humans. Notably, the setup employs aluminum plates as RF shielding to improve signal quality by leveraging the built-in PCB antenna of the ESP32 as a crude directional antenna. Another work addressing NLOS scenarios is presented by Kumar et al. [1], where ESP32 devices are used for presence and fall detection. The conventional transmitter-receiver placement, with activities performed between the devices, is evaluated in a laboratory environment. Experimental results indicate the presence of characteristic CSI patterns induced by activities, even with up to two walls between the transmitter and receiver, demonstrating the feasibility of this approach.

3   Experimental Setup

We now describe the proposed setup, including its hardware components, the characteristics of the recording environment in which LOS and NLOS performance are evaluated, and the procedure for collecting CSI activity samples.

3.1   Hardware

Our hardware setup utilizes two ESP32-S3-DevKitC-1[5] boards equipped with the ESP32-S3-WROOM-1[6] module. The boards are connected using Espressif's ESP-NOW wireless communication protocol. In a transmitter-receiver configuration, CSI packets are sent at a fixed rate of 100 Hz and a Python script running on a notebook captures the incoming CSI packets from the receiver. While the ESP32-S3-WROOM-1 module has a built-in PCB antenna for basic WiFi

---

[5] ESP32-S3-DevKitC-1, https://docs.espressif.com/, accessed: 05.06.2023.

[6] ESP32-S3-WROOM-1, https://www.espressif.com/, accessed: 05.06.2023.

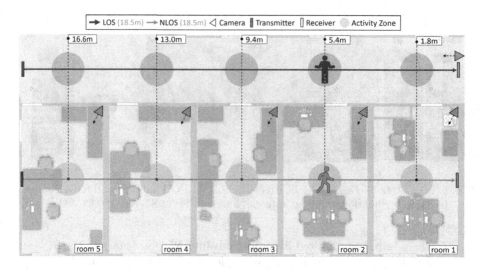

Fig. 2. Overview of the recording environment, showing the placement of hardware components for LOS and NLOS scenarios.

connectivity, we find it unsuitable for long-range through-wall HAR applications due to its low gain and unpredictability observed in preliminary short-range LOS tests. To address this, we replace the built-in PCB antenna with an SMA connector, enabling the use of an external antenna as depicted in Fig. 1a. We evaluate 2.4 GHz antennas, including a commercial omnidirectional dipole antenna with a gain of 8dBi, and a custom directional biquad antenna with a gain of 10–12dBi and a beamwidth of 70° [14], shown in Fig. 1b. To measure signal strength, we place the transmitter and receiver at the outer walls of the outermost rooms in the NLOS scenario (18.5 m across five rooms). The directional biquad antenna achieves the highest RSSI of –67 dB, outperforming the 8dBi omnidirectional dipole antenna with an RSSI of –79 dB. For reference, the built-in PCB antenna fails to establish a connection in this scenario. As a result of this test, we use a directional biquad antenna for both the transmitter and receiver, which not only provides a stable connection in long-range scenarios but also helps to eliminate external noise, which can be problematic with omnidirectional antennas [8]. Considering the relatively high RSSI of –67 dB, the proposed setup is likely to support even larger ranges and a higher through-wall count than evaluated in this work. Finally, for image-based activity labeling in NLOS scenarios, we incorporate an ESP32-S3-WROOM-CAM[7] (camera) board as shown in Fig. 1c, streaming images to the notebook.

3.2 Recording Environment

The evaluation of the proposed setup takes place in an office environment depicted in Fig. 2. It consists of a hallway measuring 18.5 m in length, with

---

[7] ESP32-S3-WROOM-CAM, https://github.com/Freenove/, accessed: 05.06.2023.

five adjacent rooms containing office furniture. These rooms, separated by 25 cm thick brick walls, present a challenging long-range NLOS scenario. The uniform size of the rooms (approximately $3.5\,\text{m} \times 6.0\,\text{m}$) and their arrangement allow for a direct comparison of LOS and NLOS HAR performance at various distances between the transmitter and receiver. For the LOS scenario (purple line in Fig. 2), the transmitter and receiver are positioned at opposite ends of the hallway, facing each other. To capture activity images, the camera is placed next to the transmitter, aligned in its direction. In the NLOS scenario (orange line), the transmitter and receiver are again facing each other, but positioned at the outer walls of rooms 5 and 1, respectively. The alignment of antennas is achieved by fine-adjusting the receiver's horizontal position based on the RSSI. Additionally, to capture activity images in the NLOS scenario, the camera is placed in the room where the activity occurs. The transmitter-receiver spacing remains constant at 18.5 m for both LOS and NLOS scenarios.

3.3   Data Collection and Pre-processing

To assess the feasibility of long-range through-wall HAR with the proposed setup, we collect CSI activity samples in the recording environment. The goal is to detect a person's presence and distinguish between coarse and fine body movements (e.g., walking vs. arm movements). Activities are performed within five circular zones (1.5 m radius) along the LOS and NLOS paths shown in Fig. 2. These zones are located at distances of $\{1.8, 5.4, 9.4, 13.0, 16.6\}$m from the receiver, corresponding to room centers in the NLOS scenario. For both scenarios, we record two minutes of continuous "walking" and "walking + arm-waving" activities in each zone, as well as five minutes of "no activity." Pre-processing involves cleaning the raw CSI recordings using images from the camera and outlier removal with the Hampel filter [13]. The filtered CSI time series data is then converted into time-frequency plots of subcarrier amplitudes over time, i.e. spectrograms. For this, recordings are divided into segments of 400 CSI packets (4-s time intervals @100 Hz sending frequency) and the amplitudes of 52 L-LTF subcarriers are plotted, resulting in a spectrogram size of 400×52. Examples of spectrograms for each activity class are shown in Fig. 3. To evaluate presence detection and activity recognition, the collected spectrograms are labeled. Presence detection labels $\{0, 1, 2, 3, 4, 5\}$ (0 for "no activity") correspond to room numbers, resulting in DP_{LOS} and DP_{NLOS}. Activity recognition labels $\{0, 1, 2\}$ correspond to depicted activities, resulting in DA_{LOS} and DA_{NLOS}. For the evaluation, a 8:1:1 training-validation-test split is used for all datasets. Dataset characteristics are summarized in Table 1. Furthermore, all datasets used in this work are publicly available[8].

---

[8] CSI HAR datasets, https://zenodo.org/record/8021099, accessed: 19.07.2023.

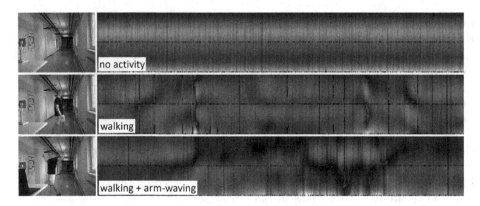

Fig. 3. LOS activity spectrograms of "no activity", "walking", and "walking + arm-waving", captured at a distance of 1.8 m.

Table 1. Characteristics of presence detection and activity recognition datasets.

Dataset	Scenario	Rooms	Persons	Classes	CSI Sampling	Interval	Spectrograms
DP_{LOS}	LOS	1	1	6 rooms	100 Hz	4 s	392
DP_{NLOS}	NLOS	5	1	6 rooms	100 Hz	4 s	384
DA_{LOS}	LOS	1	1	3 activities	100 Hz	4 s	392
DA_{NLOS}	NLOS	5	1	3 activities	100 Hz	4 s	384

4   Evaluation

As shown in [4], CSI spectrograms can be processed using Convolutional Neural Networks (CNNs) for person-centric sensing applications. Following this approach, we train presence detection and activity recognition models on the collected CSI HAR datasets. Separate LOS and NLOS models are trained for both problems to assess the impact of environmental effects, allowing direct comparisons. Generalization between scenarios is explored by training models in one scenario and testing in the other.

4.1   Model Training

To ensure reproducibility, we train presence detection and activity recognition models using the standard *torchvision.models* implementation of the EfficientNetV2 small architecture [15]. Presence detection models, namely P_{LOS} and P_{NLOS}, are trained on DP_{LOS} and DP_{NLOS}, respectively. Additionally, a presence detection model for both scenarios, $P_{LOSNLOS}$, is trained on $DP_{LOS} \cup DP_{NLOS}$. The same approach is used for activity recognition, resulting in models A_{LOS}, A_{NLOS}, and $A_{LOSNLOS}$. All models are trained from scratch and undergo 1k epochs of training using the Adam optimizer with a learning rate of 0.0001 and a batch size of 16. To eliminate class imbalances in the training

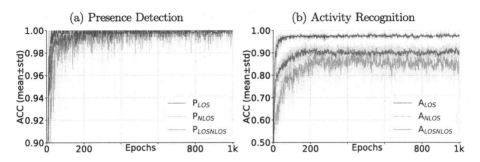

Fig. 4. Validation accuracy (mean±std across ten runs) of (a) presence detection and (b) activity recognition models over 1k training epochs.

Table 2. Performance of presence detection models P_{LOS}, P_{NLOS} and $P_{LOSNLOS}$, reported as mean and standard deviation across ten independent training runs.

Model	Test Dataset	Precision	Recall	F1 Score	ACC
P_{LOS}	DP_{LOS}	98.67 ± 1.8	98.61 ± 1.9	98.64 ± 1.8	98.46 ± 2.1
P_{NLOS}	DP_{NLOS}	98.14 ± 1.6	97.72 ± 2.2	97.93 ± 1.9	97.89 ± 2.0
P_{LOS}	DP_{NLOS}	15.79 ± 8.1	18.49 ± 7.3	16.61 ± 7.1	17.89 ± 7.1
P_{NLOS}	DP_{LOS}	15.71 ± 9.6	21.67 ± 4.5	17.29 ± 7.7	23.59 ± 5.6
$P_{LOSNLOS}$	DP_{LOS}	97.13 ± 2.8	96.57 ± 3.4	96.85 ± 3.1	96.41 ± 3.7
$P_{LOSNLOS}$	DP_{NLOS}	94.71 ± 2.9	91.11 ± 5.7	92.85 ± 4.3	92.37 ± 4.9
$P_{LOSNLOS}$	$DP_{LOS} \cup DP_{NLOS}$	98.33 ± 1.2	98.26 ± 1.6	98.29 ± 1.2	98.31 ± 1.2

dataset, a balanced sampler is employed. Data augmentation includes random circular shifts along the time axis applied to the spectrograms. For each model, ten independent training runs are conducted, and the mean and standard deviation of metrics such as precision, recall, F1-score, and classification accuracy are reported based on the respective test datasets.

4.2 Presence Detection Results

Figure 4a visualizes the training progress of presence detection models P_{LOS} and P_{NLOS}. In the LOS scenario, rapid convergence is observed, with the highest validation performance reached after just 26 epochs. Convergence in the NLOS scenario takes longer, with 118 epochs required. Table 2 presents detailed performance metrics on the corresponding test datasets, DP_{LOS} and DP_{NLOS}. Comparable presence detection accuracies are achieved in both scenarios, with P_{LOS} slightly outperforming P_{NLOS} (98.46 ± 2.1 vs. 97.89 ± 2.0), clearly demonstrating the feasibility of long-range through-wall presence detection with the proposed setup. To explore model generalization between scenarios, we evaluate the performance of P_{LOS} and P_{NLOS} on each other's test datasets, as shown in Table 2. A significant drop in performance, close to random guess-

Table 3. Performance of activity recognition models A_{LOS}, A_{NLOS} and $A_{LOSNLOS}$ reported as mean and standard deviation across ten independent training runs.

Model	Test Dataset	Precision	Recall	F1 Score	ACC
A_{LOS}	DA_{LOS}	97.80 ± 0.9	98.04 ± 0.9	97.92 ± 0.9	97.43 ± 1.1
A_{NLOS}	DA_{NLOS}	90.94 ± 3.8	87.92 ± 4.3	89.39 ± 4.0	88.16 ± 4.6
A_{LOS}	DA_{NLOS}	16.77 ± 5.4	33.60 ± 1.3	22.03 ± 4.5	42.10 ± 1.2
A_{NLOS}	DA_{LOS}	25.73 ± 10.6	32.90 ± 1.5	28.07 ± 5.6	41.79 ± 1.6
$A_{LOSNLOS}$	DA_{LOS}	96.17 ± 2.1	95.98 ± 2.3	96.07 ± 2.2	95.13 ± 2.7
$A_{LOSNLOS}$	DA_{NLOS}	80.35 ± 3.5	78.24 ± 6.2	79.23 ± 4.8	75.53 ± 5.3
$A_{LOSNLOS}$	$DA_{LOS} \cup DA_{NLOS}$	93.42 ± 1.3	92.16 ± 1.2	92.78 ± 1.2	91.95 ± 1.5

ing, is observed for both models. This outcome is expected, as poor generalization to entirely new environments is a well-known problem in WiFi-based HAR [9,16,18]. However, the model trained on both scenarios, $P_{LOSNLOS}$, achieves presence detection accuracies of 96.41 ± 3.7 and 92.37 ± 4.9 on the LOS and NLOS test datasets, respectively. Furthermore, a presence detection accuracy of 98.31 ± 1.2 is achieved on the combined test dataset, demonstrating generalization between LOS and NLOS scenarios.

4.3 Activity Recognition Results

Figure 4b visualizes the training progress of activity recognition models A_{LOS} and A_{NLOS}, highlighting the increased difficulty of the problem. Convergence requires a significantly higher number of training epochs compared to the presence detection problem. A_{LOS} and A_{NLOS} reach their peak validation performance after 349 and 426 epochs, respectively. Detailed performance metrics on the corresponding test datasets, DA_{LOS} and DA_{NLOS}, are provided in Table 3. Unlike presence detection, a larger performance gap between LOS and NLOS scenarios is observed (97.43 ± 1.1 vs. 88.16 ± 4.6). Interestingly, in the NLOS scenario, there is a relatively high standard deviation of 4.6% points, indicating significant run-to-run variance, with individual models occasionally achieving LOS-level performance. These promising results, obtained with a standard CNN architecture and minimal data augmentation, clearly demonstrate the feasibility of WiFi CSI-based long-range through-wall HAR using the proposed setup. As reported in Table 3, we also observe poor model generalization between scenarios in the activity recognition problem. However, both A_{LOS} and A_{NLOS} models achieve activity classification accuracies above random guessing (42.10 ± 1.2 and 41.79 ± 1.6), indicating some level of generalization. Furthermore, the model trained on both scenarios, $A_{LOSNLOS}$, achieves an activity classification accuracy of 91.95 ± 1.5 on the combined test dataset. Interestingly, we see overfitting on the LOS scenario, evidenced by the unbalanced classification accuracies in the individual scenarios (95.13 ± 2.7 and 75.53 ± 5.3). This discrepancy can be attributed to the relative ease of fitting the LOS data, as indicated by the previous results.

5   Conclusion

In this work, we proposed a novel setup for CSI-based HAR, combining the ESP32-S3 with a 2.4 GHz directional biquad antenna, which enables long-range through-wall HAR in spatially constrained environments. To assess performance in LOS and NLOS scenarios, we deployed the setup in a transmitter-receiver configuration within a realistic office environment spanning 18.5 m across five rooms. We collected a dataset of 392 LOS and 384 NLOS activity spectrograms, which is made publicly available. Activity recognition models based on the EfficientNetV2 small architecture, trained on this dataset, achieved accuracies of 97.43 ± 1.1 and 88.16 ± 4.6 in LOS and NLOS scenarios, respectively, clearly demonstrating the potential of the proposed setup for long-range through-wall CSI-based HAR applications.

References

1. Ajit Kumar, S., Akhil, K., Udgata, S.K.: Wi-Fi signal-based through-wall sensing for human presence and fall detection using ESP32 module. In: Udgata, S.K., Sethi, S., Gao, X.Z. (eds.) Intelligent Systems. LNNS, vol. 431, pp. 459–470. Springer, Singapore (2023). https://doi.org/10.1007/978-981-19-0901-6_41

2. Arning, K., Ziefle, M.: Get that camera out of my house! Conjoint measurement of preferences for video-based healthcare monitoring systems in private and public places. In: Geissbühler, A., Demongeot, J., Mokhtari, M., Abdulrazak, B., Aloulou, H. (eds.) ICOST 2015. LNCS, vol. 9102, pp. 152–164. Springer, Cham (2015). https://doi.org/10.1007/978-3-319-19312-0_13

3. Atif, M., Muralidharan, S., Ko, H., Yoo, B.: Wi-ESP–a tool for CSI-based device-free Wi-Fi sensing (DFWS). J. Comput. Des. Eng. **7**(5), 644–656 (2020). https://doi.org/10.1093/jcde/qwaa048

4. Gao, Q., Wang, J., Ma, X., Xueyan, F., Wang, H.: CSI-based device-free wireless localization and activity recognition using radio image features. IEEE Trans. Veh. Technol. 1 (2017). https://doi.org/10.1109/TVT.2017.2737553

5. Gringoli, F., Schulz, M., Link, J., Hollick, M.: Free your CSI: a channel state information extraction platform for modern Wi-Fi chipsets. In: Proceedings of the 13th International Workshop on Wireless Network Testbeds, Experimental Evaluation & Characterization, pp. 21–28. WiNTECH '19, Association for Computing Machinery, New York, NY, USA (2019). https://doi.org/10.1145/3349623.3355477

6. Hao, Z., Wang, G., Dang, X.: Car-sense: vehicle occupant legacy hazard detection method based on DFWs. Appl. Sci. **12**, 11809 (2022). https://doi.org/10.3390/app122211809

7. Hernandez, S.M., Bulut, E.: Performing Wi-Fi sensing with off-the-shelf smartphones. In: 2020 IEEE International Conference on Pervasive Computing and Communications Workshops (PerCom Workshops), pp. 1–3 (2020). https://doi.org/10.1109/PerComWorkshops48775.2020.9156194

8. Hernandez, S.M., Bulut, E.: Adversarial occupancy monitoring using one-sided through-wall WiFi sensing. In: ICC 2021 - IEEE International Conference on Communications, pp. 1–6 (2021). https://doi.org/10.1109/ICC42927.2021.9500267

9. Kosba, A.E., Saeed, A., Youssef, M.: RASID: a robust WLAN device-free passive motion detection system. In: 2012 IEEE International Conference on Pervasive

Computing and Communications, pp. 180–189 (2012). https://doi.org/10.1109/PerCom.2012.6199865

10. Liu, J., Liu, H., Chen, Y., Wang, Y., Wang, C.: Wireless sensing for human activity: a survey. IEEE Commun. Surv. Tutor. **22**(3), 1629–1645 (2020). https://doi.org/10.1109/COMST.2019.2934489

11. Palipana, S., Rojas, D., Agrawal, P., Pesch, D.: Falldefi: ubiquitous fall detection using commodity wi-fi devices. PACM Interact. Mob. Wearable Ubiquitous Technol. (IMWUT) **1** (2018). https://doi.org/10.1145/3161183

12. Parameswaran, A.T., Husain, M.I., Upadhyaya, S., et al.: Is RSSI a reliable parameter in sensor localization algorithms: an experimental study. In: Field Failure Data Analysis Workshop (F2DA09), vol. 5. IEEE Niagara Falls, NY, USA (2009)

13. Pearson, R.K., Neuvo, Y., Astola, J., Gabbouj, M.: Generalized Hampel filters. EURASIP J. Adv. Signal Process. **2016**(1), 1–18 (2016). https://doi.org/10.1186/s13634-016-0383-6

14. Singh, B., Singh, A.: A novel biquad antenna for 2.4 GHZ wireless link application: a proposed design. Int. J. Electron. Commun. Technol. **3**(1), 174–176 (2012)

15. Tan, M., Le, Q.V.: Efficientnetv2: smaller models and faster training (2021)

16. Wang, W., Liu, A.X., Shahzad, M., Ling, K., Lu, S.: Device-free human activity recognition using commercial Wi-Fi devices. IEEE J. Sel. Areas Commun. **35**(5), 1118–1131 (2017). https://doi.org/10.1109/JSAC.2017.2679658

17. Wang, Z., Jiang, K., Hou, Y., Huang, Z., Dou, W., Zhang, C., Guo, Y.: A survey on CSI-based human behavior recognition in through-the-wall scenario. IEEE Access 1 (2019). https://doi.org/10.1109/ACCESS.2019.2922244

18. Youssef, M., Mah, M., Agrawala, A.: Challenges: device-free passive localization for wireless environments. In: Proceedings of the 13th Annual ACM International Conference on Mobile Computing and Networking, pp. 222–229 (2007)

19. Zafari, F., Gkelias, A., Leung, K.: A survey of indoor localization systems and technologies. IEEE Commun. Surv. Tutor. (2017). https://doi.org/10.1109/COMST.2019.2911558

PseudoDepth-SLR: Generating Depth Data for Sign Language Recognition

Noha Sarhan[(✉)], Jan M. Willruth, and Simone Fritnrop

Universität Hamburg, Vogt-Kölln-Str. 30, 22527 Hamburg, Germany
{noha.sarhan,simone.frintrop}@uni-hamburg.de,
jan.willruth@studium.uni-hamburg.de

Abstract. In this paper, we investigate the significance of depth data in Sign Language Recognition (SLR) and propose a novel approach for generating pseudo depth information from RGB data to boost performance and enable generalizability in scenarios where depth data is not available. For the depth generation, we rely on an approach that utilizes vision transformers as a backbone for depth prediction. We examine the effect of pseudo depth data on the performance of automatic SLR systems and conduct a comparative analysis between the generated pseudo depth data and actual depth data to evaluate their effectiveness and demonstrate the value of depth data in accurately recognizing sign language gestures. Our experiments show that our proposed generative depth architecture outperforms an RGB-only counterpart.

Keywords: Sign Language Recognition · Deep Learning · Depth Data · 3D Convolutional Neural Networks

1 Introduction

Sign languages are rich and complex visual languages used by the deaf community for communication. With their own grammar, syntax, and vocabulary, sign languages serve as vital means of expression and facilitate communication among individuals who are deaf or hard of hearing. However, the comprehension and interpretation of sign languages remain a significant challenge for the wider hearing population. Automatic Sign Language Recognition (SLR) has emerged as a promising solution to bridge the communication gap between sign language users and non-signers, aiming to develop systems that can automatically recognize and interpret sign language gestures [6, 12, 20].

SLR can be viewed as a very specific case of human action recognition, a rather challenging one. This is attributed to the unique nature of sign language, which incorporates both overall body motion and intricate arm/hand gestures to convey its meaning. Facial expressions also play a role in conveying emotions [13]. In addition, different signers may perform gestures differently, e.g. in terms of speed, left- or right-handed, etc. Consequently, SLR becomes even more challenging due to the need for diverse data samples from numerous signers, however, sign language data is hard to acquire, owing to several challenges such as privacy and the need for experts to perform and annotate datasets.

© The Author(s), under exclusive license to Springer Nature Switzerland AG 2023
H. I. Christensen et al. (Eds.): ICVS 2023, LNCS 14253, pp. 51–62, 2023.
https://doi.org/10.1007/978-3-031-44137-0_5

RGB

Recorded Depth

Pseudo Depth

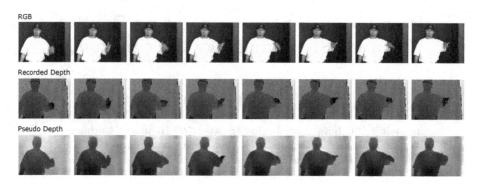

Fig. 1. Example of RGB (top) and recorded depth (middle) and generated pseudo-Depth for the gesture DivingSignal/SomethingWrong.

In order to capture the full dynamics of the gesture, SLR methods rely on the use of several input modalities [3,10,14]. Besides RGB data, one of the key modalities commonly utilized in SLR is depth data, offering rich spatial and depth information that enhance the discrimination of signs that would otherwise seem similar. In addition, the use of depth in conjunction with RGB data can be helpful when distinguishing the signer from a cluttered background, and hands from body, such ensembles lead to improved recognition accuracy and robustness. Consequently, the majority of state-of-the-art SLR systems heavily rely on depth data [8,10,15,16,19]. While depth data has some benefits such as robustness to lighting conditions, some existing sign language dataset lack depth information (e.g. from news broadcasts [12]). In addition, relying on depth data hinders the generalizability of existing models to SLR and vice versa.

Recent research has explored alternative approaches that aim to eliminate the requirement for depth information, proposing the use of solely RGB data [20,21]. These approaches challenge the assumption that depth data is indispensable, suggesting that comparable performance can be achieved without it.

In this paper, we investigate the value of depth data in SLR systems and its impact on overall performance in comparison to RGB-based systems. Additionally, we propose an alternative approach to address the limitations posed by datasets lacking depth information, aiming to bridge the depth gap in SLR. Specifically, we explore the generation of pseudo depth data, which allows for the creation of depth-like information from RGB data. For depth generation, we utilize an architecture, namely DPT (Dense Prediction Transformer) [17] that uses vision transformers [7] as a backbone for the dense depth prediction. Figure 1 shows an example of RGB and depth input modalities and the corresponding generated depth data for a sign language gesture. By comparing the generated depth data with the actual depth data, we validate the efficacy of our method and its potential for enhancing SLR in scenarios where depth data is scarce, or extend it to gesture recognition applications where depth data might be non-existent, e.g. automotive, sports training, etc.

Our main contributions can be summarized as follows:

- We evaluate and analyze the significance of depth data for sign language recognition.
- We propose an alternative approach in case of absence of depth data by the generation of pseudo depth data. We examine its implications on the performance of SLR systems and compare it to the use of actual depth data.
- Our proposed alternative method outperforms methods that disregard depth data completely, while still relying only on RGB modality.

2   Related Work

Significant progress has been made in SLR since the advancements in depth sensing technologies, such as time-of-flight cameras and structured light sensors, have enabled more accurate and detailed depth measurements. Having depth data together with RGB data has helped capture the complex spatial and temporal dynamics of sign language gestures. Since then, depth data has been recognized as a valuable input modality in SLR, and its incorporation has been evident across various methodologies employed over the years. This section provides an overview of related works, highlighting the persistent usage of depth data in SLR, from early hand-crafted feature-based approaches [1,5,19,24] to recent state-of-the-art methods that rely on the advancements in machine learning and computer vision techniques [8,10,20].

Early approaches in SLR primarily relied on handcrafted features, such as shape, motion and appearance descriptors, combined with traditional machine learning algorithms such as support vector machines and hidden Markov Models [1,16,19,24]. This resulted in systems that have very limited generalization capabilities, unable to go beyond applications that lack these extra modalities. However, the introduction of deep learning architectures, such as Convolutional Neural Networks (CNNs) and Recurrent Neural Networks (RNNs), revolutionized SLR by leveraging their ability to automatically learn discriminating features from data [15,20,21].

Automatic SLR(ASLR) has long relied on depth data as a fundamental component for accurate and robust recognition. To date, most deep learning based methods still rely on the depth modality. Wang et al. [23] relied on both RGB and depth information. They utilized full frames to represent the fully body, along with hand crops of both modalities. They fused together a 4-stream ConvNet and 3D ConvLSTMs-based classification to get an average-score fusion. Miao et al. [15] extracted information from RGB and depth input data using and concatenated RGB, flow and depth features using a SVM classifier.

Furthermore, some research rely on extracting even more information from the input depth maps, e.g. depth saliency, depth flow, etc. Jiang et al. [10] propose an ensemble of five 3D CNN streams, two of which rely on depth data. For the first stream, they extract flow information from the input depth maps to feed to the network, for the second stream they extract HHA (Horizontal disparity, Height above the ground, and Angle normal) features from the depth

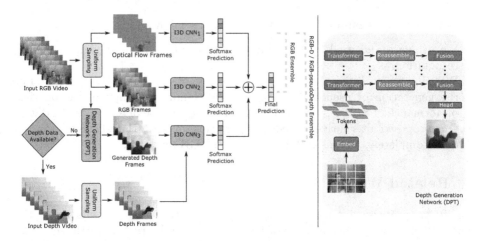

Fig. 2. *Left:* Architecture overview. The RGB ensemble comprises 2 streams of Inflated 3D CNNs (I3D), one is fed RGB frames, and the other optical flow frames. For the inclusion of depth, a third stream is used. It is fed depth frames if depth data is available, otherwise, they are first generated from the RGB frames. For each of the 3 streams, the softmax predictions are averaged together to yield a final label. *Right:* Depth generation network architecture, adapted from [17]. An RGB frame is first transformed into tokens by extracting non-overlapping patches. The tokens are then passed through multiple transformer stages, and reassembled from different stages into an image-like representation at multiple resolutions. Finally, fusion modules progressively fuse and upsample the representations to generate the depth prediction. Details of the Reassemble and Fusion units can be found in [17].

stream, encoding depth information into a 3-channel RGB-like output. Duan *et al.* [8] proposed a two-stream consensus voting network, extracting spatial information from RGB and depth input, and temporal information from RGB and depth flow data. They also aggregated a 3D depth-saliency ConvNet stream in parallel to identify subtle motion characteristics. Late score fusion was adopted for the final recognition.

In attempt to refrain from using depth data, Sarhan and Frintrop [20] proposed a mathod that relies only on RGB data. However, depth data brings about additional information and robustness (e.g. against illumination changes, noise, and background clutter) that RGB alone does not deliver. Therefore, in this work we attempt to bridge the depth gap and propose the generation of pseudo depth data from RGB data for sign language recognition.

3   Methodology

In this section, we first introduce our proposed model, which utilizes depth data along with RGB data. Afterwards, we will explain our method for the generation of pseudo depth data.

3.1   Proposed Architecture

Figure 2 shows our proposed architecture which is made up of 2 ensembles comprising 3 streams in total. The most widely used 3D CNN architectures are Inflated 3D CNNs (I3D) [4], ResNeXt3D-101 [9], and separable 3D CNNs (S3D) [25]. Therefore, for the RGB ensemble, we opted for the I3D CNN-based architecture proposed by Sarhan and Frintrop [20] as I3D CNNs have shown outstanding performance in isolated SLR [10,20,21]. Each stream has one I3D CNN, where the 2D $k \times k$ filters and pooling kernels are inflated into 3D kernels by adding a new dimension t and become cubic through this transformation $t \times k \times k$, spanning t frames. The first stream is fed full-frame RGB sequence as input, while the second stream is fed optical flow data, which are generated from the RGB stream using Dual TV-L1 algorithm [26].

In order to capture features from depth data, we introduced a new third stream, which is fed the recorded depth sequence. Together with the two RGB streams, we present this as the RGB-D ensemble. All input videos are first uniformly sampled to extract a fixed number of frames before being fed to the I3D CNNs.

As a final step, we opt for a late fusion scheme, where the softmax predictions of all three streams are averaged together to yield a final prediction for the signed gesture.

3.2   Pseudo Depth Data Generation

In order to refrain from using recorded depth data while still including depth information, we propose an alternative which is to generate pseudo depth data from the RGB images. In that case, the RGB frames are first used to generate the pseudo depth images, and then fed to the I3D CNN as shown in Fig. 2 (left). Together with the 2 RGB streams, we refer to this as the RGB-pseudoDepth ensemble.

To generate high quality dense depth maps, we tested two different methods for depth prediction: DPT by Ranftl et al. [17], and DenseDepth by Bhat et al. [2]. According to our ablation study in Sect. 6.2, We opted for the encoder-decoder based method by Ranftl et al. [17], namely DPT, since according to our ablation study in Sect. 6.2 it turned out to be better. Their architecture is depicted in Fig. 2 (right). They leverage vision transformers [7] as the backbone for dense prediction, where tokens from various stages of the transformer are assembled into image-like representations at various resolutions and progressively combine them into full-resolution predictions using a convolutional decoder. The transformer backbone processes representations at a constant and relatively high resolution and has a global receptive field at every stage.

4   Experimental Details

In this section, we present the evaluation of our proposed approach on the ChaLearn249 IsoGD dataset [22]. We start by a brief summary about the dataset and how we evaluate our approach on it. Then, we explain how we evaluate the quality of the generated pseudo depth data. Afterwards, we provide more implementation details, that would aid in making this work reproducible.

4.1 Dataset and Evaluation

Evaluation of Proposed Architecture. We evaluate our proposed method on the ChaLearn249 IsoGD dataset [22], a large dataset for isolated SLR. The dataset comprises 47,933 videos, captured by a Microsoft Kinect camera, hence providing RGB and recorded depth images. The dataset is signer-independent, and is one of the mostly used dataset for isolated sign language gestures [8,14,15,23].

For evaluation, we follow the same protocol provided by the dataset. It is split into 35,878 videos for training, 5,784 videos for validation, and 6,271 videos for testing. For all our experiments, we report and compare the accuracy of both the validation and test sets.

Depth Generation Evaluation. To calculate the error between the ground truth recorded depth images and their generated pseudo-depth counterparts, root-mean-square error (RMSE) was calculated as in Eq. 1, where p is an individual pixel, n is the number of pixels in each image, y_p is the ground truth, and $\hat{y}_p$ is the estimated value for pixel y.

$$RMSE = \sqrt{\frac{1}{n}\sum_{p=1}^{n}(y_p - \hat{y}_p)^2} \tag{1}$$

In addition, we also calculate the structural similarity index (SSIM) to determine how structurally similar two images are, in this case how similar the generated depth image is to the recorded equivalent. The SSIM of two images x and y is defined in Eq. 2.

$$SSIM(x,y) = \frac{(2\mu_x\mu_y + C_1)(2\sigma_{xy} + C_2)}{(\mu_x^2 + \mu_y^2 + C_1)(\sigma_x^2 + \sigma_y^2 + C_2)}, \tag{2}$$

where μ_x and μ_y are the average of x and y, respectively, σ_x^2 and σ_y^2 are the variance of x and y, respectively, and σ_{xy} is the covariance of x and y. $C_1 = (K_1L)^2$ and $C_2 = (K_2L)^2$ are variables with K_1, $K_2 << 1$ and $L = 2^{bit\ depth} - 1$. The value of the SSIM lies between –1 and 1, where a score of –1 means the images are complementary, and a score of 1 means that they are identical.

4.2 Implementation Details

Preprocessing. The video sequences are uniformly sampled into a fixed number of frames. The frames are cropped around the center to a spatial size of 224×224. Optical flow frames have been generated from the RGB videos using the Dual-TVL[1] algorithm [26].

Table 1. Accuracy results on the ChaLearn249 dataset using the RGB ensemble, RGB-D ensemble (RGB + recorded depth), and RGB-pseudoDepth (RGB + generated Depth).

Modality	Validation	Test
RGB [20]	61.76%	64.97%
RGB-D	64.54%	70.63%
RGB-pseudoDepth	62.5%	66.02%

Training. For all streams, we adopt the training scheme used by [20]. The I3D CNN was originally trained on ImageNet [18] before inflation into 3D, and then pretrained on Kinetics dataset [4]. The top, randomly initialized layers are first trained for 3 epochs while freezing the pretrained layers, at a learning of 1×10^{-3}. Afterwards, all layers are fine-tuned and the learning rate is lowered to 1×10^{-4}. Here, early-stopping was adopted to halt training once the validation loss has not improved for 3 consecutive epochs. Adam [11] was used as an optimizer in conjunction with a mini-batch size of 4, and categorical cross-entropy as the loss function.

Data Augmentation. Implementing data augmentation in SLR poses challenges despite its significance for small and medium-sized datasets. Common data augmentation techniques such as image flipping or rotation can directly impact the conveyed sign itself. To address this concern, our approaches focuses on data augmentation by shifting images along the x- and y- axes and adjusting brightness levels.

5   Results and Analysis

In this section, we show the results of using depth and generated depth data on the ChaLearn dataset, along with the per-class accuracies. In addition, we compare their performance to state-of-the-art results on this dataset.

5.1   How Significant is Depth Data?

Results on ChaLearn Dataset. In this section, we verify the importance of depth information for SLR. Table 1 shows the validation and test accuracy when using the RGB, RGB-D, and RGB-pseudoDepth ensembles. Recorded depth data (RGB-D) shows the best performance results, 64.54% on the validation set, and 70.63% on the test set. While the use of generated Depth data (RGB-pseudoDepth) achieves lower accuracy in comparison, 62.5% and 66.02% for the validation and test sets respectively, it still outperforms using only RGB data. This shows that generated depth data is indeed valuable, and that the RGB-pseudoDepth ensemble still captures more features, while relying only on RGB input.

Fig. 3. Example of pseudo depth images with best and worst SSIM measure and their RGB and recorded depth counterparts.

Evaluating the Depth Streams Separately. We also evaluate the accuracy of the recorded and generated depth streams on their own, without the RGB ensemble. The recorded depth stream achieved an accuracy of 50.71% and 60.56% on the validation and test sets, while the generated depth stream achieved 38.04% and 44.97% on the validation and test sets. While the generated depth stream does not score a very high recognition rate by itself, they still add valuable information to the RGB input, evident by their higher accuracy in the RGB-pseudoDepth ensemble than the RGB ensemble. To evaluate the quality of the generated depth data, the RMSE was 79.42, while the SSIM was 0.67. In Fig. 3 we show two examples of generated pseudo depth frames with highest and lowest SSIM. It is clear from these images how the quality of RGB image affects the generated depth data.

Per Class Accuracy. In addition to the recognition accuracies, to verify the potential from depth and generated depth information, we compared the RGB-D and RGB-pseudoDepth ensembles by calculating the per class accuracy change with respect to the RGB ensemble. In Fig. 4 we plot these differences. The blue line represents RGB-D ensemble, while the red line represents the RBG-pseudoDepth ensemble. A positive/negative difference means that the inclusion of depth/generated depth brought about a positive/negative effect over the RGB ensemble. A zero means no improvement over the RGB accuracy. As shown in Fig. 4, for the class range c122-c137, using the RGB stream only works well, however in several other classes, such as the range c058-c065 and c192-c197 depth information has resulted in significant improvement. Generally, the higher the positive value of the accuracy difference, the more number of samples there were originally predicted wrong by RGB only, are now predicted correctly. Overall, the average difference in the case of RGB-D ensemble is +3.10, and +0.67 for RGB-pseudoDepth.

5.2   Comparison with State-of-the-Art Results

In Table 2, we compare with top competitors on the leader board and state-of-the-art results on the ChaLearn249 dataset. Our proposed RGB-D architecture that relies on RGB, optical flow and recorded depth data has outperformed the other methods by more than 2.5% on the validation set, and more than 3% on the test set. The use of generated depth was the second best performing method

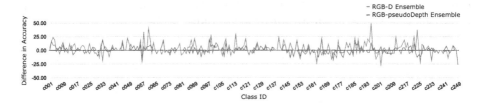

Fig. 4. Differences in class accuracies for RGB-D (blue) and RGB-pseudoDepth (red) ensembles with respect to the RGB ensemble. A positive/negative value means a higher/lower accuracy for that class with respect to the RGB ensemble, a zero means no improvement over the RGB ensemble. (Color figure online)

Table 2. Comparison with state-of-the-art on ChaLearn249 and their modalities. The best results are shown in red and the second best in blue.

Method	Modalities			Accuracy	
	RGB	Depth	pseudoDepth	Validation	Test
XDETVP [27]	✓	✓		58%	60.47%
AMRL [23]	✓	✓		60.81%	65.59%
RGB-pseudoDepth (ours)	✓		✓	62.5%	66.2%
SYSU_ISEE [14]	✓	✓		59.7%	67.02%
2SCVN-3DDSN [8]	✓	✓		49.17%	67.26%
ASU [15][a]	✓	✓		57.88%	–
RGB-D (ours)	✓	✓		64.54%	70.63%

[a] We compare with their averaging fusion scheme, similar to what is used in our method for fair comparison. Test set results for that fusion scheme were not reported.

in comparison to the other methods that also relied on recorded depth, but performed slightly lower on the test set. The results in Tables 1 and 2 demonstrate the effectiveness of generated depth data, they do not only outperform RGB-only methods, but are also comparable with methods that rely on recorded depth data.

6   Ablation Study

In this section, we investigate the use of depth flow data as a fourth stream to our architecture. Additionally, we explore an alternative method for pseudo depth map generation. By conducting this ablation study, we aim to gain insights into the specific contributions and significance of each component within the proposed model.

6.1   Depth Flow Data

Since including RGB and optical flow streams has been successful in several approaches for SLR [10,15,20,21], we experimented with adding a fourth stream

Table 3. Accuracy results on the ChaLearn249 dataset when including depth flow data as a fourth stream to our proposed architecture.

Method	Validation	Test
RGB-D	64.54%	70.63%
RGB-D + Depth flow	61.07%	69.22%
RGB-pseudoDepth	62.5%	66.02%
RGB-pseudoDepth + Depth flow	64.54%	64.84%

to our architecture, where the input was optical flow information extracted from the depth data (depth flow). We performed this experiment for both the recorded depth data, and generated depth data, and report these results in Table 3. The use of depth flow data lowered the recognition accuracy in both cases. One possible reason is that depth data usually suffers form noise and uncertainty, affecting the quality of optical flow estimation. These errors can propagate to the optical flow estimation process due to its inherent recurrence.

6.2   Pseudo Depth Data Generation

As an alternative method for the generation of dense depth maps from a single RGB image, we opted for the deep learning-based method by Bhat *et al.* [2], namely DenseDepth, that utilizes fully convolutional networks. Their architecture is composed of two main components: an encoder-decoder block and an adaptive bin-width estimator block called AdaBins. The used model was pre-trained on NYU Depth V2 dataset [2]. The dataset is composed of images and depth maps for different indoor scenes, and has 120K training samples and 654 testing samples. As a post processing step, all images have been normalized using Min-Max Normalization.

The results are shown in Table 4. The use of visual transforms clearly outperforms the fully convolutional network method. The use of DenseDepth is still outperformed by using RGB-only ensemble. As for the evaluation of the generated depth images, DenseDepth had an RMSE of 146.64 (vs. 92.67 for DPT), and an SSIM of 0.281 (vs. 0.55 for DPT), explaining the poor results achieved by DenseDepth.

Table 4. Comparison of different depth generation methods.

Method	Validation	Test
RGB	61.76%	64.97%
RGB-D	64.54%	70.63%
RGB-pseudoDepth (DPT [17])	62.5%	66.02%
RGB-pseudoDepth (DenseDepth [2])	60.81%	64.34%

7 Conclusion

Depth data has long been recognized as a crucial input modality for SLR systems due to its ability to capture spatial and depth information. However, depth data is not always available, e.g. in news broadcasts, and acquiring it for sign language would be difficult and expensive. In this paper, we aimed to bridge the depth gap and proposed a novel approach for generating pseudo depth data from RGB inputs when recorded depth data is scarce. Our results and analysis further validates the effectiveness of our approach and its potential for improving recognition accuracy in depth-limited scenarios, and open up avenues for SLR research and applications, enabling depth-based insights even when depth data is lacking.

References

1. Badhe, P.C., Kulkarni, V.: Indian sign language translator using gesture recognition algorithm. In: 2015 IEEE International Conference on Computer Graphics, Vision and Information Security (CGVIS), pp. 195–200 (2015)
2. Bhat, S.F., Alhashim, I., Wonka, P.: Adabins: depth estimation using adaptive bins. In: Proceedings of the IEEE/CVF Conference on Computer Vision and Pattern Recognition (CVPR), pp. 4009–4018, June 2021
3. Boháček, M., Hrúz, M.: Sign pose-based transformer for word-level sign language recognition. In: WACV, pp. 182–191 (2022)
4. Carreira, J., Zisserman, A.: Quo vadis, action recognition? A new model and the kinetics dataset. In: CVPR, pp. 6299–6308 (2017)
5. Chai, X., et al.: Sign language recognition and translation with Kinect. In: IEEE Conference on AFGR, vol. 655, p. 4 (2013)
6. Cui, R., Liu, H., Zhang, C.: A deep neural framework for continuous sign language recognition by iterative training. IEEE Trans. Multimed. **21**(7), 1880–1891 (2019)
7. Dosovitskiy, A., et al.: An image is worth 16×16 words: transformers for image recognition at scale. arXiv preprint arXiv:2010.11929 (2020)
8. Duan, J., Wan, J., Zhou, S., Guo, X., Li, S.Z.: A unified framework for multi-modal isolated gesture recognition. TOMM **14**(1s), 1–16 (2018)
9. Hara, K., Kataoka, H., Satoh, Y.: Can spatiotemporal 3D CNNs retrace the history of 2D CNNs and Imagenet? In: CVPR, pp. 6546–6555 (2018)
10. Jiang, S., Sun, B., Wang, L., Bai, Y., Li, K., Fu, Y.: Skeleton aware multi-modal sign language recognition. In: Proceedings of the IEEE/CVF Conference on Computer Vision and Pattern Recognition, pp. 3413–3423 (2021)
11. Kingma, D.P., Ba, J.: Adam: a method for stochastic optimization. arXiv preprint arXiv:1412.6980 (2014)
12. Koller, O., Forster, J., Ney, H.: Continuous sign language recognition: towards large vocabulary statistical recognition systems handling multiple signers. CVIU **141**, 108–125 (2015)
13. Koller, O., Ney, H., Bowden, R.: Deep learning of mouth shapes for sign language. In: Proceedings of the IEEE International Conference on Computer Vision Workshops, pp. 85–91 (2015)
14. Li, B., Li, W., Tang, Y., Hu, J., Zheng, W.: GL-PAM RGB-D gesture recognition. In: 2018 25th IEEE International Conference on Image Processing (ICIP), pp. 3109–3113 (2018)

15. Miao, Q., et al.: Multimodal gesture recognition based on the RESC3D network. In: Proceedings of the IEEE International Cconference on Computer Vision Workshops, pp. 3047–3055 (2017)
16. Pigou, L., Dieleman, S., Kindermans, P.-J., Schrauwen, B.: Sign language recognition using convolutional neural networks. In: Agapito, L., Bronstein, M.M., Rother, C. (eds.) ECCV 2014. LNCS, vol. 8925, pp. 572–578. Springer, Cham (2015). https://doi.org/10.1007/978-3-319-16178-5_40
17. Ranftl, R., Bochkovskiy, A., Koltun, V.: Vision transformers for dense prediction. In: Proceedings of the IEEE/CVF International Conference on Computer Vision, pp. 12179–12188 (2021)
18. Russakovsky, O., et al.: Imagenet large scale visual recognition challenge. Int. J. Comput. Vis. (IJCV) **115**, 211–252 (2015)
19. Sarhan, N., El-Sonbaty, Y., Youssef, S.: HMM-based Arabic sign language recognition using Kinect. In: Tenth International Conference on Digital Information Management (ICDIM), pp. 169–174 (2015)
20. Sarhan, N., Frintrop, S.: Transfer learning for videos: from action recognition to sign language recognition. In: 2020 IEEE International Conference on Image Processing (ICIP), pp. 1811–1815 (2020)
21. Sarhan, N., Frintrop, S.: Sign, attend and tell: spatial attention for sign language recognition. In: 2021 16th IEEE International Conference on Automatic Face and Gesture Recognition (FG 2021), pp. 1–8 (2021)
22. Wan, J., Zhao, Y., Zhou, S., Guyon, I., Escalera, S., Li, S.Z.: Chalearn looking at people RGB-D isolated and continuous datasets for gesture recognition. In: Proceedings of the IEEE conference on Computer Vision and Pattern Recognition Workshops, pp. 56–64 (2016)
23. Wang, H., Wang, P., Song, Z., Li, W.: Large-scale multimodal gesture recognition using heterogeneous networks. In: Proceedings of the IEEE International Conference on Computer Vision Workshops, pp. 3129–3137 (2017)
24. Xiaohan Nie, B., Xiong, C., Zhu, S.C.: Joint action recognition and pose estimation from video. In: Proceedings of the IEEE conference on Computer Vision and Pattern Recognition, pp. 1293–1301 (2015)
25. Xie, S., Sun, C., Huang, J., Tu, Z., Murphy, K.: Rethinking spatiotemporal feature learning: speed-accuracy trade-offs in video classification. In: Proceedings of the European Conference on Computer Vision (ECCV), pp. 305–321 (2018)
26. Zach, C., Pock, T., Bischof, H.: a duality based approach for realtime TV-L^1 optical flow. In: Hamprecht, F.A., Schnörr, C., Jähne, B. (eds.) DAGM 2007. LNCS, vol. 4713, pp. 214–223. Springer, Heidelberg (2007). https://doi.org/10.1007/978-3-540-74936-3_22
27. Zhang, L., Zhu, G., Shen, P., Song, J., Afaq Shah, S., Bennamoun, M.: Learning spatiotemporal features using 3DCNN and convolutional LSTM for gesture recognition. In: Proceedings of the IEEE International Conference on Computer Vision Workshops, pp. 3120–3128 (2017)

Slovo: Russian Sign Language Dataset

Alexander Kapitanov[(✉)], Kvanchiani Karina, Alexander Nagaev,
and Petrova Elizaveta

SaluteDevices, Moscow, Russia
{aakapitanov,kskvanchiani,aonagaev,emikhaylpetrova}@sberbank.ru

Abstract. One of the main challenges of the sign language recognition task is the difficulty of collecting a suitable dataset due to the gap between hard-of-hearing and hearing societies. In addition, the sign language in each country differs significantly, which obliges the creation of new data for each of them. This paper presents the Russian Sign Language (RSL) video dataset Slovo, produced using crowdsourcing platforms. The dataset contains 20,000 FullHD recordings, divided into 1,000 classes of isolated RSL gestures received by 194 signers. We also provide the entire dataset creation pipeline, from data collection to video annotation, with the following demo application. Several neural networks are trained and evaluated on the Slovo to demonstrate its teaching ability. Proposed data and pre-trained models are publicly available[1] (https://github.com/hukenovs/slovo)[2] (https://gitlab.aicloud.sbercloud.ru/rndcv/slovo).

Keywords: Sign Language · Video Dataset · Gesture Recognition · Data Creating Pipeline · Human Computer Interaction

1 Introduction

While the contemporary world is developing rapidly with the advent of high-end technologies, some parts of society are out of their scope. One such part is the hard-of-hearing community, which still struggles in many situations and can be misunderstood in some extreme cases. For example, some hospitals still do not have a sign language interpreter on staff. Therefore the interaction between hard-of-hearing people and healthcare providers is complex, which prevents timely assistance. A similar problem exists in structures such as banks, government institutions, airports, public places, and others, significantly complicating their everyday life. Moreover, many consequences of deaf as social isolation, an education gap with the hearing population, and difficulties in finding employment, also negatively affect the life of this community. Sign Language Recognition (SLR) systems have the potential to simplify these processes by, for example, developing a sign language learning app [3] or embedding a feature in video conferencing apps. Also, such technology can accomplish more transparent communication between people with different hearing and speaking abilities and be integrated into human-computer interaction systems [12], allowing hard-of-hearing individuals access to information and services easier and helping to overcome barriers in education [1] and employment.

Fig. 1. RSL signs "at eight fifteen" (left top), "appetite" (left bottom), "yellow" (right top), and "this" (right bottom). (Color figure online)

SLR is a field of study that should accurately convert sign language gestures from video footage into textual representation. This task is indispensable but daunting due to the tangle and rapid nature of sign language, which entails intricate hand gestures, body postures, and facial expressions. The complexity of data collection is the major problem of SLR due to a gap between hard-of-hearing and hearing communities. Adding to this the need for a different sign language for each country and significant language differences within even one country, Russian SLR system developers face the challenge of data absence. Furthermore, existing RSL datasets have few samples or must be sufficiently diverse across subjects, which is necessary to train a robust model. This paper presents two main contributions to simplify the solution of sign language recognition:

- We provide a pipeline for creating a video dataset consisting of three main steps: video collection, validation, and time interval annotation. Crowdsourcing platforms were used throughout the pipeline to increase the number of signers and improve the dataset's quality. We apply some exam tasks to signers for the most correctly executed gestures and add a quality check to the validation step to extract inappropriate videos. In the third step, all videos were marked by the start and end time of the gesture.
- We release the Russian Sign Language dataset, Slovo, which can become the basis for this area. It consists of 20,000 FullHD videos from 194 signers and is divided into 1,000 classes of glosses from the RSL without words shown by dactyl (finger-spelling) or compound gestures. Figure 1 shows the examples of gestures in our dataset. All signers recorded videos mostly in their homes or office in front of a laptop or smartphone camera. Each video, whose length varies from 1 s to 4, was cropped using two timestamps (start and end), contributing to the production of the "no event" class. Added class corresponds to the video's parts, where the signer is preparing to perform the gesture or has already performed it.

2   Related Work

This paper solely focuses on comparing our findings with the Russian Sign Language. It would be inappropriate to compare RSL datasets with SL datasets in foreign languages as they all differ significantly in structure. However, we provide an overview of datasets in other languages to show the specifics and features of this domain. Table 1 encompasses the prevalent datasets having significant data volumes. Since the collection step is the main problem of SL dataset creation and one of our contributions, we describe the main ways to collect it.

Table 1. The main characteristics of the reviewed SL datasets. Datasets are divided into two categories: isolated datasets, containing individual gestures, and continuous datasets, containing sentences in sign language. In addition, we added a column named "Method" with the collection way information since it says a lot about the videos. "Manually" means that the dataset's authors recorded the video and could influence the scenes, gestures, and recording. "Download" means that the authors downloaded videos from third-party resources that sometimes guarantee the high accuracy of the gestures shown "Crowd" means that the authors used crowdsourcing platforms to collect videos. "Subset" means that RWTH-BOSTON-400 was created from another dataset BU ASL [22].

Dataset	Classes	Videos	Signers	Resolution	Language	Method
Continuous						
GSLC, 2007 [5]	20	840	6	848 × 480	Greek	manually
RWTH-BOSTON-400, 2008 [4]	400	843	5	648 × 484	American	subset
RWTH-PHOENIX-Weather, 2015 [13]	1,066	8,257	9	210 × 260	Germany	download
RSL, 2021 [7]	1,000	35,000	5	FullHD	Russian	manually
Isolated						
LSE-Sign, 2016 [8]	2,400	2,400	2	FullHD	Spanish	manually
LSA64, 2016 [20]	64	3,200	10	FullHD	Argentinian	manually
MS-ASL, 2018 [10]	1,000	25,513	222	varying	American	download
WLASL2000, 2020 [14]	2,000	21,083	8	varying	American	download
AUTSL, 2020 [21]	226	38,336	43	512 × 512	Turkish	manually
TheRuSLan, 2020 [11]	164	13	13	FullHD	Russian	manually
K-RSL, 2020 [9]	600	28,250	10	FullHD	Kazakh-Russian	manually
FluentSigners-50, 2022 [19]	278	43,250	50	varying	Kazakh-Russian	crowd.
Slovo, 2023 (ours)	1,000	20,000	194	HD / FullHD	Russian	crowd.

2.1   Sign Language Datasets in Russian Domain

There are four more widespread RSL datasets. The first, TheRuSLan [11], is composed of a total of 164 gestures, primarily related to the supermarket theme. A group of 13 signers was involved in the video collection, where each signer produced a unique recording with an average duration is 36 min. All signers come from different parts of the country, which generates variability within a class due to various dialects. The authors also proposed subtitles for each sample, which indicate the specific signs class. The second, FluentSigners-50 [19], were created with the help of 6 natives, who chose frequently used signs, produced the templates for them, and wrote the instruction for signers. All signers came from different Kazakhstan regions, making the dataset a high degree of linguistics. Heterogeneity in the signer's age, skin color, clothes, variable background, and lighting make the dataset immensely diverse. The videos are in a total of 43 h of labeled trimmed materials. The third, K-RSL [9], contains 4 subsets of phrases from a linguistic point of view: question-statement pairs, signs of emotion, emotional question-statement pairs, and phonologically similar signs. It was divided into 600 glosses with 28,250 examples in total. Ten signers recorded K-RSL, the first 5 are professional SL interpreters, and the other 5 are deaf native signers. The last, RSL [7], consists of two sets of gestures obtained from an online dictionary. Each gesture was repeated by the signer at least 5 times. All signers are dressed in black suits against a clean background, which makes the dataset visually monotonous. All videos are marked with additional classes named "start gesture" and "end gesture"; suggestions include an additional class named "transition".

The TheRusLan and the FluentSigners-50 datasets are unsuitable for us due to the disuse of Kazakh-Russian Sign Language in Russia since the gestures are outdated. Besides, the TheRusLan dataset was created for only the supermarket domain and cannot be used for everyday life. Also, the two described datasets are not diverse in classes of signs and subjects. The RSL dataset can be used only in limited situations by us because we cannot influence the dataset's update by adding new sign classes. Furthermore, the RSL dataset was recorded by only 5 signers, which do not differ in clothing and background, complicating the training of a stable model. These reasons prompted us to create our dataset with 1,000 frequently used RSL signs received from 194 signers. We plan to extend it with new classes and increase the diversity of subjects.

2.2   Others Sign Language Datasets

Since RSL differs from other sign languages, we describe only notable SL datasets, comparing them according to the main specific features of the domain. Many of reviewed datasets are not diverse in signers: RWTH-BOSTON-400 [4] were recorded by only 5 speakers, LSE-Sign [8] – by two sign language natives, LSA64 [20] – by 10 non-expert signers, and GSLC – by 6 signers. Besides, LSE-Sign was recorded within one week to minimize the diversity of the signer's appearance. Others tried to make more heterogeneous datasets. MS-ASL [10] and WLASL2000 [14] are the most extensive publicly available ASL datasets, and their videos were produced by 222 and 47 signers, respectively. The AUTSL dataset [21] was recorded with 20 backgrounds, including indoor and outdoor scenes and with different angles. The reviewed datasets differ in the goal of creating and choosing the domain of signs. For example, The RWTH-PHOENIXWeather corpus [13] contains SL recordings from the German TV station PHOENIX. The more typical variant to choose a sign basket is to collect it from the frequently daily-used signs like in AUTSL [21].

2.3   Sign Language Dataset Collection

The main problem of dataset creation for SLR is video collection because it is challenging to find sign language experts. The need for diversity in signers makes this task even more problematic. The choice of sign basket is the other significant problem because natural and sign languages are highly different. We reviewed ways to collect sign language videos and divided this overview into three groups by collection methods for convenience.

Manually recorded videos. One of the main ways to collect videos for sign language recognition is to produce them manually with a camera. Kagirov et al. [11] used the MS Kinect 2.0 device to record video in 3D with a depth map to create the TheRusLan dataset. The Turkish Sign Language dataset, AUTSL [21], was collected for real-life scenarios by the same camera. To make the model robust to scenes, 20 different backgrounds, including dynamic, various lighting conditions, from artificial light to sunlight, and different field-of-views were used to create AUTSL. The authors choose the frequently used signs; some are compound signs formed by simultaneously making two consecutive signs. The videos were performed by 43 different signers, where 60% are students of the TSL course, 18% are persons who know TSL (instructors and translators), 15% are trained signers by the AUTSL dataset, and others related. The Argentinian Sign Language dataset, LSA64 [20], was recorded by a Sony HDR-CX240 camera in two different scene conditions: outdoor and indoor. The authors simplified the hand segmentation task with fluorescent-colored gloves. Signers wore black clothes against a white wall's backdrop for more accurate hand extraction.

Downloaded Videos. Another way to collect samples is to download from news or educational video sources. It has the advantage of correctly matching video and signs since sign language experts checked the content. For the WLASL dataset, the authors [14] chose multiple education SL websites as suitable video sources. They filtered samples by signs and leaved videos containing words only. Annotators of sign dialects were not native sign languages: they received training to understand SL specifics and, with a designed interface, compare signs from two videos displayed simultaneously. Samples for the MS-ASL dataset [10] were downloaded from video-sharing platforms to communicate and study ASL. Since videos are recorded and uploaded by ASL students and teachers, they differ by background, lighting, positioning, and dialect. Such platforms accompany the video with subtitles, which authors processed by OCR. Face detection and recognition are integral parts of sample preprocessing in cases where videos were taken from websites, and the authors included them in their dataset creation pipeline.

Kind of Crowdsourcing. Mukushev, Medet, et al. [19] choose a more complicated but effective way to collect videos for SLR. Their dataset, FluentSigners-50, was created with six professional SL interpreters. They developed a sign basket including commonly useful phrases and sentences in the hard-of-hearing community. Other signers were invited by interpreters and use SL daily, and the subsequent distribution of signers by SL use was obtained: 32 deaf, 6 hard of hearing, 3 hearing SODA (Sibling of a Deaf Adult), and 9 hearing CODA (Child of Deaf Adults). They used instructions and templates from interpreters to repeat the KRSL sentences.

3 Dataset Creation

The following part provides details about our data collection pipeline. It consists of 3 main stages: (1) video collection, (2) video validation, and (3) and gesture time interval annotation. We used two crowdsourcing platforms: Yandex Toloka[1] for data mining and ABC Elementary[2] for the validation and the annotation so that different users are involved in recording and verifying videos. In addition, before each stage, crowdworkers must pass a mandatory RSL exam[3] with a score of at least 80% before being granted access to assignments. These two nuances allow us to get a better and unbiased assessment of the correctness of the videos. Figure 2 shows the main part of the dataset creation process.

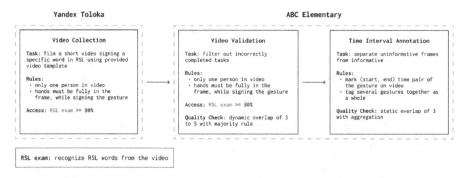

Fig. 2. Crowdsourcing pipeline: collection, validation, and annotation. Each stage used its own rules, but the exam was the same.

1. Video Collection. The essential part of dataset creation started with designing a sign basket. We paid attention to choosing words frequently used in everyday life, and in the end, it turned out to be 1,000 glosses. We chose words related to commonly used topics such as food, animals, emotions, colors. After, we asked the crowdworkers from Yandex Toloka to record a short video of themselves singing a specific word in RSL based on the provided template. Video templates were taken from SpreadTheSign website[4], a project of the European Sign Language Center association. Participants provided informed consent for data processing, ensuring compliance with legal requirements. No discrimination or bias was present in the dataset, promoting fairness and inclusivity.

2. Video Validation. Correctly signing the gesture can be challenging for people not fluent in sign language, so we added the validation stage on the ABC

---

[1] https://platform.toloka.ai/.

[2] https://elementary.activebc.ru.

[3] The RSL exam aims to reveal the knowledge of the language, but it can be passed by language learners too.

[4] https://www.spreadthesign.com/ru.ru/search/.

Elementary platform in our dataset-creating pipeline. Workers were asked to check if the gesture was performed correctly. Each video was checked at least by three different workers. If they disagree, another marker participated in the validation of such a video, so up to 5 markers on the video could be repeated. If most workers mark the video as invalid, it is rejected; otherwise, it is accepted and passed to the next stage. After the validation, we left videos with a short edge of at least 720 pixels and converted them to a 30 fps rate.

3. Time Interval Annotation. Collected videos may contain uninformative frames at the beginning and the end of the video, where workers turn the camera on and off and prepare to show the gesture. Therefore, annotating the gesture's start and end time on the video is necessary. The crowdworkers from ABC Elementary were asked to indicate the time interval with a gesture. Since our dataset contains glosses and phrases, some videos may have several gestures. In this case, workers should tag them together as a full gloss. Each video was annotated by three different crowdworkers.

Figure 3 shows the developed aggregation algorithm to get the average over the responses time interval. After cutting off the gestures, we had the cuts at the beginning and the end of the video where no gesture is shown, and we decided to use them as zero-class objects in training to predict the absence of action.

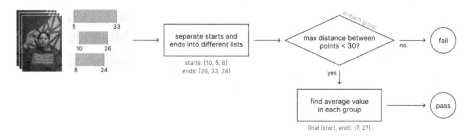

Fig. 3. Time intervals aggregation pipeline. First, we split the beginning and end timestamps into different groups and then independently calculated distances between all points in each group. Then, if the maximum distance is less than 30 frames, we find the average value of each group and assume them to be the final pair (begin, end). Otherwise, video with such annotations was not taken into the dataset.

Dataset Post-processing. While reviewing the collected videos, we noticed that some users show gestures significantly slower than others. This circumstance leads to inhomogeneous video length within the same class: the duration of the same gesture varied by more than five times, complicating the classification of such data. To make our dataset more homogenous, we decided to calculate the distribution of video lengths for each class and speed up those videos that are slower than the average value by more than 30 frames. As a result, 347 videos from 270 classes were sped up by an average of 1.7 times. In addition, we compared two variants – with and without this processing – and ensured that homogenous speed increases the accuracy of RSL recognition.

4 Dataset Description

Dataset Content. Our dataset is approximately 16 GB – it contains 20,000 videos of 1,000 classes representing frequently used glosses and short phrases in Russian Sign Language, including alphabet and numerals. The dataset does not include fingerspelling words, i.e., words spelled letter by letter using dactylology. In addition, we expanded the Slovo by 400 extra samples of a special "no event" class where the subject is not signing any gestures. To the best of our knowledge, 194 crowdworkers participated in the video recording for our dataset, making it the most subject-diverse RSL dataset and the second among all sign language datasets (see Table 1 for more details). The dataset was collected mainly indoors and varied in scenes and lighting conditions.

Video Quality. The videos were recorded primarily in HD and FullHD formats (see Fig. 4d). About 86% of the videos are oriented vertically, 13% are oriented horizontally, and 1% are in square format. The number of frames distribution is also shown in Fig. 4a. The average video length is 1.67 s, and the overall duration of the dataset is about 19.81 h.

Data Splitting. The data was split into training (75%) and test (25%) sets, containing 15 and 5 video samples for each class, respectively. The numbers of subjects in training and test sets are equal 112 and 174, respectively. Note that groups of subjects in these two sets intersect; however, we tried to minimize it by filling out the test set with inactive signers (see Fig. 4b-c - the test set consists mainly of signers who have uploaded a small number of videos). This approach minimizes the intersection of signers in the training and test sets, reducing the risk of model overfitting.

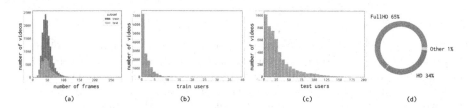

Fig. 4. Video length, resolution and user's splitting analysis. (a) Videos' number of frames distribution divided into sets, (b) distribution of recorded video by users in train, and (c) test, (d) video resolution ratio.

5 Experiments

Models. Addressing the challenge of recognizing sign language necessitates the utilization of formidable and lightweight models endowed with the capacity to analyze video data. Multiscale Vision Transformer (MViT) [6] model was specifically designed for video recognition tasks and provides a significant performance gain over concurrent video transformers that rely on large-scale external pre-training and are several times more costly in computation and parameters. Creating a multiscale pyramid of features, MViT models effectively connect the principles of transformers with multiscale feature hierarchies. An Improved MViT architecture (MViTv2) [15] proves to be a robust general backbone for computer vision tasks in the video domain.

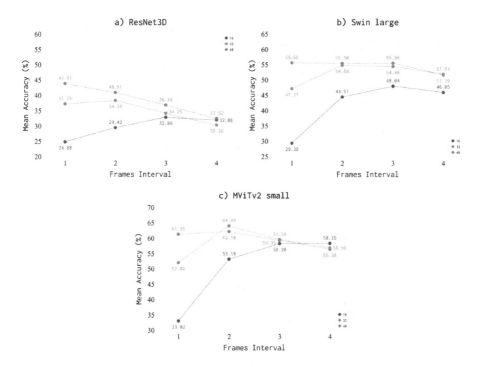

Fig. 5. Mean accuracy is achieved by each model on the Slovo with different sampling strategies. Note that the graphs have various scales depending on the order of the metrics.

The MViTv2 demonstrates state-of-the-art performance in various video recognition benchmarks and can accurately analyze video input. Therefore its small version was chosen as the baseline, we utilized Swin-large [16] and ResNet3D-50 [2], all pre-trained on the Kinetics dataset.

Data Pre-processing. The samples were resized on the maximum side to 300 pixels. MViTv2-small and Swin-large trained with a horizontal flip and sharpness augmentations, whereas ResNet3D-50 – with the same horizontal flip, salt random noise, and color jitter. Horizontal flip augmentation is used to bring the data distribution to the real because RSL signs do not change the meaning of mirror reflection. Finally, the videos were padded to (300, 300) and randomly cropped to 224 pixels.

Implementation Details. Several sampling strategies were tested with a different number of frames from [16, 32, 48] and a frame interval from 1 to 4. We also checked models trained on 64 frames, which generated poor results. Frame intervals are limited to 4 because skipping more frames in the SLR task can miss important information about the sign. We trained all 36 models over 120 epochs with a learning rate 0.001, AdamW [18] optimizer employing betas (0.9, 0.999), and weight decay 0.05. Two schedulers – LinearLR and CosineAnnealingLR [17] – were used to optimize the Swin-large and ResNet3D-50 training processes. Only LinearLR was used for MViTv2-small. The information about their parameters is in the repository.

Results. Since each gesture corresponds to 20 video samples, we validated the models on the test set. Figure 5 shows the results of each chosen model separately with a different number of frames and frame interval. We can observe that MViTv2-small, with 32 frames and an interval of 2, vastly outperforms other models due to its video purpose. We attribute the notably lower metrics of ResNet3D-50 to the superior performance of vision transformers compared to convolutional architectures in the domain of videos.

6   Conclusion

In this paper, we proposed the new Russian Sign Language dataset Slovo and a pipeline for creating diverse video data despite a specific domain. The Slovo is divided into 1,000 classes, each corresponding to 20 videos from 194 signers. It can favorably influence the development of sign language recognition in the Russian domain. Besides, several models were trained and evaluated on Slovo to demonstrate its teaching ability. Shortly, we plan to expand our dataset: increase the number of classes and the number of examples per class and collect not only words but also phrases, n-grams, and sentences. Furthermore, since SL is more expressive than regular ones: not only hand gestures are used to indicate words, but also facial expressions, articulation, and body posture, multimodal models can potentially improve SLR results. The current dataset, pre-trained models, and demo are publicly available in the repository.

References

1. The Importance of Sign Language for Deaf Education and Sign Technology (2012). https://www.academia.edu/2145485
2. Carreira, J., Zisserman, A.: Quo vadis, action recognition? a new model and the kinetics dataset. In: 2017 IEEE Conference on Computer Vision and Pattern Recognition (CVPR), pp. 4724–4733 (2017)
3. Chow, A., Cameron, G., Sherwood, M., Culliton, P., Sam Sepah, S.D., Starner, T.: Google - isolated sign language recognition (2023). https://kaggle.com/competitions/asl-signs
4. Dreuw, P., Neidle, C., Athitsos, V., Sclaroff, S., Ney, H.: Benchmark databases for video-based automatic sign language recognition. In: LREC (2008)

5. Efthimiou, E., Fotinea, S.-E.: GSLC: creation and annotation of a Greek sign language corpus for HCI. In: Stephanidis, C. (ed.) UAHCI 2007. LNCS, vol. 4554, pp. 657–666. Springer, Heidelberg (2007). https://doi.org/10.1007/978-3-540-73279-2_73

6. Fan, H., et al.: Multiscale vision transformers (2021)

7. Grif, M., Elakkiya, R., Prikhodko, A., Bakaev, M., Rajalakshmi, E.: Raspoznavanie recognition of Russian and Indian sign languages based on machine learning. Anal. Data Process. Syst. **3**(83), 53–74 (2021)

8. Gutierrez-Sigut, E., Costello, B., Baus, C., Carreiras, M.: LSE-sign: a lexical database for Spanish sign language. Behav. Res. Methods **48**, 123–137 (2016)

9. Imashev, A., Mukushev, M., Kimmelman, V., Sandygulova, A.: K-RSL: a corpus for linguistic understanding, visual evaluation, and recognition of sign languages. In: Proceedings of the 24th Conference on Computational Natural Language Learning. Association for Computational Linguistics (2020)

10. Joze, H.R.V., Koller, O.: Ms-asl: A large-scale data set and benchmark for understanding American sign language. arXiv preprint arXiv:1812.01053 (2018)

11. Kagirov, I., Ivanko, D., Ryumin, D., Axyonov, A., Karpov, A.: Theruslan: database of Russian sign language. In: Proceedings of the Twelfth Language Resources and Evaluation Conference, pp. 6079–6085 (2020)

12. Kenshimov, C., Buribayev, Z., Amirgaliyev, Y., Ataniyazova, A., Aitimov, A.: Sign language dactyl recognition based on machine learning algorithms. Eastern-Eur. J. Enterp. Technol. **4**(2), 112 (2021)

13. Koller, O., Forster, J., Ney, H.: Continuous sign language recognition: towards large vocabulary statistical recognition systems handling multiple signers. Comput. Vis. Image Underst. **141**, 108–125 (2015)

14. Li, D., Rodriguez, C., Yu, X., Li, H.: Word-level deep sign language recognition from video: a new large-scale dataset and methods comparison. In: Proceedings of the IEEE/CVF Winter Conference on Applications of Computer Vision, pp. 1459–1469 (2020)

15. Li, Y., et al.: Mvitv 2: improved multiscale vision transformers for classification and detection. In: Proceedings of the IEEE/CVF Conference on Computer Vision and Pattern Recognition, pp. 4804–4814 (2022)

16. Liu, Z., et al.: Video swin transformer. In: Proceedings of the IEEE/CVF Conference on Computer Vision and Pattern Recognition, pp. 3202–3211 (2022)

17. Loshchilov, I., Hutter, F.: Sgdr: Stochastic gradient descent with warm restarts (2017)

18. Loshchilov, I., Hutter, F.: Decoupled weight decay regularization (2019)

19. Mukushev, M., Ubingazhibov, A., Kydyrbekova, A., Imashev, A., Kimmelman, V., Sandygulova, A.: Fluentsigners-50: a signer independent benchmark dataset for sign language processing. PLoS ONE **17**(9), e0273649 (2022)

20. Ronchetti, F., Quiroga, F., Estrebou, C.A., Lanzarini, L.C., Rosete, A.: Lsa64: an Argentinian sign language dataset. In: XXII Congreso Argentino de Ciencias de la Computación (CACIC 2016) (2016)

21. Sincan, O.M., Keles, H.Y.: AUTSL: a large scale multi-modal Turkish sign language dataset and baseline methods. IEEE Access **8**, 181340–181355 (2020)

22. Vogler, C., Neidle, C.: A new web interface to facilitate access to corpora: development of the ASLLRP data access interface (2012)

Non-contact Heart Rate Monitoring: A Comparative Study of Computer Vision and Radar Approaches

Gengqian Yang ⓘ, Benjamin Metcalfe ⓘ, Robert Watson ⓘ, and Adrian Evans[✉] ⓘ

Department of Electronic and Electrical Engineering, University of Bath, Bath, UK
{gy299,a.n.evans}@bath.ac.uk

Abstract. The Heart Rate (HR) is a vital sign that is used to assess the physical and mental state of an individual. There is a growing interest in incorporating HR measurement into Driver Monitoring Systems (DMS), providing physiological measurements to help address long-existing road safety issues by minimising human error. In real-world driving scenarios, the HR must be measured using non-contact approaches that avoid distracting or restricting the driver. The most common approaches to non-contact HR measurement use either computer vision (CV) or mm-wave radar, both showing acceptable performances in controlled studies. However, the relative merits of different sensor modalities for real-world scenarios remain unclear, and the potential benefits of a combined approach are unquantified. To address these questions, this paper first proposes and implements non-contact HR measurement architectures for both CV and mm-wave radar systems and characterises their HR estimation performance, using electrocardiography (ECG) to provide ground truth measurements. The effects of distance to sensors and of illumination variations on HR estimation are also studied, showing the relative errors for both modalities to be less than 0.5% for the distances found in practical DMS. These results also highlight the distinctive characteristics of each modality and the benefits of a multi-modality approach for DMS.

Keywords: Non-contact Heart Rate Monitoring · Remote Photoplethysmography · Mm-wave Radar · Driver Monitoring Systems

1 Introduction

Improving road safety remains a major challenge in the automotive sector, with more than one million deaths globally on the road each year and recent studies showing that human factors contributing in more than 90% of road accidents [1]. Two approaches to improving road safety are vehicle automation and driver monitoring using Driver Monitoring Systems (DMS). As the widespread adoption of fully autonomous vehicles

Gengqian Yang is supported by a scholarship from the EPSRC Centre for Doctoral Training in Advanced Automotive Propulsion System (AAPS), under the project EP/S023364/1. The underlying data for this paper is available at: https://github.com/GengqianYang/.

© The Author(s), under exclusive license to Springer Nature Switzerland AG 2023
H. I. Christensen et al. (Eds.): ICVS 2023, LNCS 14253, pp. 74–87, 2023.
https://doi.org/10.1007/978-3-031-44137-0_7

is still many years away, driver behavior will continue to have an important safety role and pressures from both regulatory bodies and industries continue to drive the development of DMS.

As one of the vital signs, the Heart Rate (HR) is critical to the diagnosis of physiological and psychological states and is ubiquitous in medicine. Furthermore, recent studies demonstrating the correlation between HR and fatigue have reinforced the importance of vital signs in DMS [2]. In clinical settings, HR is continuously measured by either electrocardiography (ECG) or photoplethysmography (PPG), both of which are contact methods. However, due to the restrictions and distractions introduced by body-attached sensors, non-contact HR monitoring has gained popularity in applications such as DMS, with many studies using camera-based Computer Vision (CV) or radar-based methods [3].

CV approaches to HR measurement operate in a similar manner to PPG, in which changes in blood flow and blood oxygenation alter the optical absorption and reflection properties of the tissue. From Beer's law, the percentage of light reflected from the skin is inversely proportional to changes in blood volume [4]. This is due to different absorption rates of oxyhemoglobin and deoxyhemoglobin, with the percentage of total hemoglobin varying throughout the cardiac cycle [5]. Alternatively, radar systems monitor chest wall movement with modern mm-wave Doppler radars having the ability to detect mm or even sub-mm motion, enabling the measurement of the small movements of the chest wall caused by cardiac function. Although the effectiveness of both CV and radar non-contact HR estimation has been validated in controlled environments, how the specific characteristics of each modality are influenced by environmental factors such as lighting and movement remains relatively unexplored.

To address this knowledge gap, this paper investigates the characteristics and performance of CV and radar-based non-contact HR monitoring systems. The findings of this work could directly inform the development of DMS and be extended to related fields such as healthcare, aerospace, and navigation. Specifically, the major contributions of this work are as given below:

1. A non-contact HR measurement system for each modality is proposed and implemented using commercially available automotive-grade devices. Performance is validated using a reference ECG device, which is widely used in clinical settings and provides an accurate and reliable reference. The proposed hardware and algorithms for each modality demonstrate good accuracy with relatively low complexity, achieving relative errors of 0.3% and 0.15% for CV and radar-based approaches, respectively.
2. Through a comparative study, the accuracy and robustness of each modality are evaluated in different environments with varying distance and illumination, emphasising the need for a multi-modality approach when designing real-world DMS.

The remainder of this paper is organised as follows. A literature review in Sect. 2 summarises recent work in the field. Section 3 explains the reference non-contact architectures proposed for this study and Sect. 4 details the experimental setting and results discussion, followed by discussion and conclusions in Sect. 5.

2 Non-contact Heart Rate Monitoring

2.1 CV-Based HR Monitoring

Since the concept of remote (non-contact) PPG (rPPG) was first demonstrated [6], it has
been applied across a range of applications, most commonly using the green channel of
an RGB video as this contains the strongest PPG signal due to the corresponding peak
in the absorption spectrum of hemoglobin [6]. A conventional CV-based rPPG pipeline
typically consists of the following main steps: Region of Interest (ROI) selection, signal
extraction, signal processing, and HR estimation.

In the ROI selection phase, face detection algorithms such as HAAR [7], HOG [8], or
deep neural networks are first used to achieve face detection, and then the ROI is selected
for raw signal extraction. Several areas of the face, including the forehead and cheeks
have been used as the ROI [8–11]. Using 68 facial landmarks was shown to enable the
selection of ROI at the locations of large skin areas where the Signal-to-Noise Ratio
(SNR) is higher [12]. However, any inaccuracies found in facial landmarks may also
introduce noise. Alternatively, simply finding a rectangular bounding box of the face,
or part of it, may introduce interference from hair, nose, mouth, and background but
enhance the stability of ROI [7, 13].

The signal extraction phase can directly select the green channel [6] or develop
a new color space from a linear combination of RGB channels, helping to address the
limitations of RGB color space towards motion [14]. A study of the effectiveness of linear
combinations of GB, GR, and GBGR found that GBGR achieved the best performance
[11]. Instead of exploiting the color space, direct averaging can be applied to each
channel and the exploitation task left to the subsequent signal processing stage [7, 13].
A recent work used the near-infrared light spectrum, where the raw signal was shown
to significantly suppress the negative effect of ambient light variation at the cost of a
low SNR [10]. In the signal processing phase, denoising and signal decomposition are
the two most commonly used techniques One of the most significant denoising methods
is the smoothness prior approach [15] which, due to its effectiveness and simplicity,
remains in current use [16, 17].

Advances in Artificial Neural Networks (ANN) have led to the development of
neural-network-based denoising approaches in recent years. Examples include employing an inverse attention mechanism to increase the SNR when the signal of interest is
weak [18] or utilizing Action Units to tackle the noise introduced by facial expressions
[19]. However, the use of ANN raises concerns about the storage and computational
power required for the real-time processing scenarios found in DMS.

The most frequently used signal decomposition technique is Blind Source Separation (BSS), including Independent Component Analysis (ICA) [7, 11, 13, 16] and
Principal Component Analysis (PCA), used in [10] to extract the signal of interest. BSS
assumes that all components are statistically independent and follow a non-Gaussian
distribution. It also introduces two uncertainties: the order of and the magnitude of the
recovered components. The order can be solved by power spectrum analysis or empirical
methods, for example it has been argued that the signal of interest is usually the second
component [11]. Finally, HR estimation is performed by extracting the frequency of the
highest power from the power spectrum or applying peak detection algorithms to the

pre-processed signal. It is worth noting that the accuracy of the power spectrum analysis method is limited by the frequency resolution, determined by the time window length.

Like many other disciplines, deep learning provides a new avenue for research in this field. Qiu et al. proposed the CosTHR architecture, using color space transformation layers to learn the optimal color space and an attention convolutional neural network (CNN) to achieve estimation [20]. Other researchers combined Multi-scale Retinex (MSR) theory with the RGB space and fed the outcome into a CNN for HR estimation [9]. The MSR theory is inspired by the observation that the human vision system is robust to different illumination conditions, thus being used to counter the illumination variation issue of rPPG. Given the inaccuracy of handcrafted features, end-to-end networks were also explored to extract HR directly from the spatiotemporal maps constructed from videos [21, 22].

2.2 Radar-Based HR Monitoring

Since the recent widespread adoption of mm-wave radars in Advanced driver-assistance systems (ADAS), the feasibility of using radar in interior sensing has been studied, especially for HR monitoring. Automotive mm-wave radars operate in the 24–60 GHz range, thus providing the required Doppler resolution to detect the micro-motions caused by heartbeats. However, there are several sources of unwanted artefacts including movements from respiratory function (and harmonics of the same), motion artefacts, background reflection, multi-path interference and noise. To overcome these, typical radar-based HR measurement algorithms employ various filtering techniques and power spectrum analysis. One recent study first employed a 24 GHz Continuous-Wave (CW) Doppler Radar to extract the raw in-phase and quadrature (I/Q) signals and then used spectrum analysis to provide an approximate HR [23]. Finally, a set of more accurate estimations from several narrowband bandpass filters were compared with the previous rough estimation to determine the valid output.

The performance of radar-based sensing is highly dependent on power spectrum analysis – the highest peak may be the HR component but could also be the second respiration harmonic or other interference. To reduce noise, a signal elimination method can be used, for example subtracting the low- and high-frequency noise using two cascaded bandpass filters and feeding the output into a peak detection algorithm [24], though the performance is constrained by the accuracy of the lower and upper bounds of filters which are based on observations. The performances of peak spectrum super resolution techniques, such as the Multiple Signal Classification (MUSIC), and particle filter methods have been compared on both a driving simulator and on-vehicle testing, showing the complex and noisy nature of the driving scenario [25].

Recent radar-based HR monitoring has used a Frequency-modulated Continuous-wave (FMCW) radar to compensate for body motion by introducing the range-azimuth map [26]. This algorithm can estimate and remove large body motion artefacts and background reflection at the cost of more complex signal processing. However, the artefacts caused by micro-body motion such as random body movements and other irregular motions remain a problem because of the restricted range resolution.

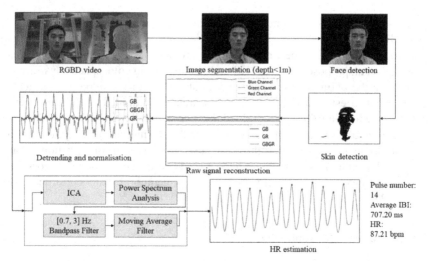

Fig. 1. Processing pipeline of the proposed CV-Based HR monitoring architecture.

3   CV and Radar-Based DMS Testbench Architectures

To summarize the review in Sect. 2, CV-based approaches are mainly influenced by illumination variations and large body motions while radar-based approaches are robust to illumination change but prone to other interference. This observation provides the motivation for further investigation of the failure modes of each sensing modality and the extent to which each may degrade the system performance. To achieve this aim, the CV and radar-based non-contact HR monitoring architectures described below are used to simulate a DMS, enabling the characteristics and robustness of each modality to be investigated. A detailed description of the architectures and the underlying motivations are provided below.

3.1   Proposed CV-Based HR Monitoring Architecture

The proposed CV-based HR monitoring algorithm is based on an RGBD camera [27], which is widely adopted by vehicle manufacturers for interior sensing. The processing pipeline shown in Fig. 1 aims to achieve a trade-off between performance and efficiency and consists of 5 main stages: (1) image segmentation; (2) ROI identification and tracking; (3) raw signal reconstruction; (4) signal processing; and (5) HR estimation from the interbeat intervals (IBI).

The system's input is an RGBD video sequence containing RGB channels and aligned depth information for each pixel and the time index for each frame. To remove the background and exclude passengers each frame is segmented using a simple depth range with a default threshold of 1m, based on the typical distance between the dashboard and the driver, see image in top center of Fig. 1. As an alternative to the depth threshold, image segmentation techniques such as the histogram of depth could be used to provide improved robustness with the cost of greatly increased processing.

Next, a combination of face detection and skin detection algorithms is applied to achieve ROI identification and tracking. The single-shot-detector (SSD) algorithm is significantly faster than most of the widely used deep-learning-based face detectors while outperforming most feature-based methods such as HAAR and HOG, and therefore to locate and track the facial region an SSD is implemented using the DeepFace library [28]. The initial ROI is defined as 80% of the height and width of the given bounding box of the face and, to maintain a stable bounding box, the face coordinates are updated only when the non-overlapping facial area from the previous and the current frames exceeds 3%. However, as the extracted ROI can include hair, nose, mouth, and other interferences in addition to the skin region, a skin detection algorithm based on a YCbCr color space transformation [29] is employed to refine the ROI and enhance the overall SNR. Following [29], The threshold values for the skin detection are:

$$85 \leq Cb \leq 135 \wedge 135 \leq Cr \leq 180, \tag{1}$$

giving a binary mask shown in center right of Fig. 1.

The raw signals are obtained by direct averaging of the values in each RGB channel within the ROI:

$$I(C)_{C \in \{R,G,B\}} = \frac{1}{n} \sum_{i=pixel\ value\ in\ ROI}^{n} i(C)_{C \in \{R,G,B\}}, \tag{2}$$

where $I(C)$ and $i(C)$ are raw signals and ROI pixel values in each channel, respectively. It has been observed that the ratio of these three signals can mitigate the fluctuations in the raw signals caused by light variation and movement, based on the assumption that all channels are equally influenced [11]. Hence, the raw signals used here are reconstructed by $GB = I(G)/I(B)$, $GR = I(G)/I(R)$ and $GBGR = GB + GR$.

In the signal processing stage, a smoothness prior detrending method is employed, which mimics a time-varying FIR high-pass filter [15]. The value of the regularization parameter λ is 50, and the corresponding bandpass frequency is 0.75 Hz when the sampling rate is 30 Hz. After a K-normalization, the three signals are fed into a fast ICA algorithm to recover the HR signal. A power spectrum analysis is performed to select the component within the 0.7–3 Hz frequency band which contains the highest peak. Finally, a 6th-order 0.7–3 Hz Butterworth bandpass filter and a five-point moving average filter are applied to suppress noise. It is worth noting that the 0.7–3 Hz frequency band corresponds to the normal HR range of 40 – 180 beats per minute (bpm).

The HR is then extracted using a prominence-distance-based peak detection algorithm to determine the peak position of each heartbeat, allowing comparison with the ground truth.

3.2 Proposed Radar-Based HR Monitoring Architecture

The radar-based algorithm is developed using the BGT60LTR11AIP from Infineon [30], which is a 60GHz low-power automotive CW Doppler radar. The challenge for a radar-based system is that the amplitude of chest wall motion caused by heartbeats is small when compared to the overall motion of the driver. Moreover, the motion detected is the superposition of cardiac activity and respiration and therefore a set of filtering techniques

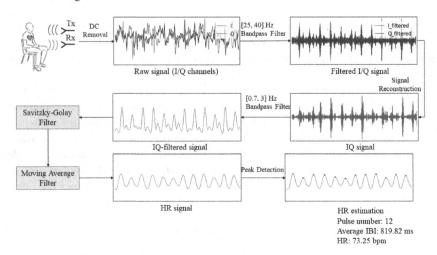

Fig. 2. System flow diagram of the proposed radar-based HR monitoring architecture.

must be employed to recover the signal of interest before any peaks can be recognized. The proposed processing architecture is shown in Fig. 2.

For a CW Doppler radar, the transmitter emits a frequency-modulated signal and the received signal is a motion-modulated signal. By mixing the transmitted and received signals, two baseband signals I and Q are generated, which are the raw signals used. After DC removal, the signals are fed into a 4th-order 25–40 Hz Butterworth bandpass filter to extract the periodic chest wall motion. The 25–40 Hz frequency band has been shown to contain the Doppler frequency range of the heartbeat motion in both synchronized radar signals and ECG ground truth. After complex signal demodulation,

$$IQ(t) = I(t) + jQ(t), \tag{3}$$

the magnitude of $IQ(t)$ is given by the absolute value of the complex number. Although the periodic signal can be visually recognized at this point, interference from other motion sources hinders the use of an automatic peak detection to extract the HR. Hence, a subsequent 2nd-order Butterworth bandpass filter is applied to further suppress interference. The IQ-filtered signal in Fig. 2 shows an interesting phenomenon in which the major peak is always followed by a smaller peak, which is most likely the dicrotic notch, reinforcing the previous observation that smaller regular motions can also be detected. However, these small spikes can sometimes interfere with peak detection, resulting in higher estimations, and to address this problem two further filters are applied. A 10th-order Savitzky-Golay smoothing filter with window size 1/3 of the sampling rate is used to merge the main peak and the dicrotic notch and a moving average filter with a window size 1/4 of the sampling rate is applied to reduce random noise. Finally, the HR estimation is achieved by a prominence-distance-based peak detection algorithm.

4 Experiment Design and Results Analysis

4.1 Performance Validation

A comparative study was designed under different testing environments to expose the performance and characteristics of each modality. Experiments were conducted in a laboratory setting using the CV and radar-based architectures described in Sect. 3 and two subjects with different characteristics (age, weight, and appearance). The RGBD video was captured using an Intel RealSense D435 depth camera [27] at 30 fps and resolution cropped to 640×480. The camera was mounted on a tripod 30 cm from the subject's face and, following a short initial transient period, 30 s of video was recorded. To obtain the ground truth HR, time-synchronized ECG data was collected using a MIKROE ECG 2 Click [31]. To collect the radar data, a BGT60LTR11AIP [30] sensor was mounted on a 3D-printed plastic mount located 30 cm away from the subject's chest and 30 s of data was recorded using a sampling frequency of 2000 Hz, with synchronized ECG again collected.

For each modality, the interbeat intervals (IBI) were found as the time differences between successive peaks and then averaged over the total number of IBIs n to estimate the HR using:

$$ HR = 60 / \left(\frac{1}{n} \sum_{i=1}^{n} IBI_n \right). \tag{4} $$

After investigating the variation of IBI distributions, and hence HR, for each modality, an experimental investigation is used to quantify the sensitivity of the different modalities to distance, illumination and motion.

4.2 Variation of IBI Distribution with Sensor Modality

Due to the different underlying principles of the ECG and non-contact HR monitoring methods, there are variations in the IBI distributions obtained from each sensor type. For example, the ECG measures electrical activity so the timing of the peak with the highest amplitude (the R-peak) does not exactly coincide with the resulting cardiac muscle contraction, and the peaks in radar signals are related to mechanical changes occurring sometime after the muscle contraction. For the CV-based rPPG method, the detected peaks lag the ECG due to the time taken for the blood volume to change. To illustrate the impact of sensor modality on IBI distribution and hence the corresponding HR estimation, Figs. 3 and 4 compare the IBI distributions from the non-contact methods with the ECG ground truth.

The Bland-Altman plots in Fig. 3 show the relationship between the paired non-contact HR estimations and ECG ground truth, with their 95% confidence intervals. It can be seen that no consistent bias exists for either non-contact method. The results from Figs. 3 and 4 show that both the IBIs and the corresponding HR estimations extracted from the CV-based rPPG method are distributed over a wider range than those extracted from the radar method. These results clearly illustrate that the peak of the blood volume change depends on many other factors, including the blood pressure, respiration, etc. However, the overall accuracy of the two methods is comparable, such that when the IBI from the rPPG method is averaged over the 30 s period it has a minimal impact on the final estimation. Hence, the CV-based rPPG method is equally suitable for measurements over a long period while the radar method retains its accuracy over short-time measurements.

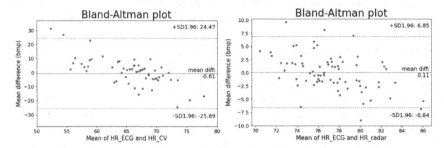

Fig. 3. Bland-Altman plots of the HR distributions of each method.

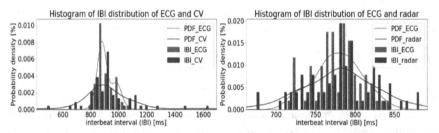

Fig. 4. Histograms of the IBI distributions of each method.

4.3 Impact of Distance on CV and Radar-Based HR Detection

Non-contact sensors are inevitably influenced by the physical distance between the sensor and the subject, often in the form of a lower SNR. Table 1 presents HR estimates for both modalities at distances of 30, 50 and 80 cm, showing that the radar-based method exhibits higher accuracy compared to the CV-based method at short and medium distances. However, the performance of radar diminishes with distance and is almost comparable to the CV-based approach at 80 cm, indicating the radar might be more sensitive to distance than the camera, possibly due to the power loss.

Although the relative error of both methods increases exponentially with distance, implying the existence of thresholds where the algorithms may fail completely, the distance between sensors and the driver in DMS is normally <80 cm and so they operate in the distance range where the proposed architectures for both modalities are effective. The relative errors for this scenario are all below 0.7%.

4.4 Impact of Illumination on CV-Based HR Detection

Illumination is widely recognized as one of the major barriers to CV-based HR monitoring. This contrasts with radar-based monitoring, which is invariant to illumination changes. To investigate the impact of illumination on the CV-based method, the performance of the CV-based architecture was studied under two adverse lighting conditions: low ambient light, where only limited natural sunlight was available, and flickering light conditions where a flash lamp was alternatively on and off for 2 s at a time.

Table 1. Performance of non-contact Heart Rate (HR) estimation modalities with distance.

Sensor type	Distance (cm)	Subject number	Ground truth (bpm)	HR estimation (bpm)	Absolute Error (AE)	Relative Error (RE)
CV-based	30	1	68.62	68.93	0.31	0.45%
		2	63.37	63.28	0.09	0.14%
		Mean			**0.20**	**0.30%**
	50	1	73.29	72.73	0.56	0.76%
		2	63.10	62.71	0.39	0.62%
		Mean			**0.95**	**0.69%**
	80	1	68.65	68.54	0.11	0.16%
		2	69.93	73.59	3.66	5.23%
		Mean			**1.89**	**2.70%**
Radar-based	30	1	78.96	78.95	0.01	0.01%
		2	75.41	75.20	0.21	0.28%
		Mean			**0.11**	**0.15%**
	50	1	72.26	72.06	0.20	0.28%
		2	72.05	71.49	0.56	0.78%
		Mean			**0.38**	**0.53%**
	80	1	72.54	69.84	2.70	3.72%
		2	88.32	86.90	1.42	1.61%
		Mean			**2.06**	**2.67%**

Table 2 summarizes the results, where the distance between sensors and subjects was 50 cm. The results show that, using its raw signal reconstruction technique, the proposed CV-based algorithm is relatively invariant to the adverse illumination conditions and still demonstrates good results. Overall, the low and flickering light conditions only increased the relative error by 0.93% and 1.8%, respectively.

4.5 Impact of Motion on CV and Radar-Based HR Detection

Motion is another significant factor that may degrade the performance of both the CV and radar methods, though in slightly different ways. Typical driving behavior involves motion of the head and body and to fully understand the impact of motion experiments were conducted with different simulated motion types.

Table 2. Performance of CV-based Heart Rate (HR) detection under varying lighting conditions.

Illumination	Subject number	Ground Truth	HR estimation	Absolute Error (AE)	Relative Error (RE)
Low	1	65.91	65.34	0.57	0.86%
	2	64.46	66.00	1.54	2.39%
Mean				**1.06**	**1.62%**
Flickering light	1	67.09	66.78	0.31	0.46%
	2	66.53	69.54	3.01	4.52%
Mean				**1.66**	**2.49%**

Table 3. Performance of each Heart Rate (HR) detection method under different motion types.

Sensor type	Subject number	Ground truth	HR estimation	Absolute Error (AE)	Relative Error (RE)
Camera (motion)	1	71.98	71.60	0.38	0.53%
	2	65.33	62.19	3.14	4.81%
Mean				**1.76**	**2.67%**
Radar (motion)	1	77.07	80.24	3.17	4.11%
	2	80.43	71.07	9.36	11.64%
Mean				**6.27**	**7.88%**

Previous studies have found the CV-based method to be affected by head motion and invariant to body motion, while the radar-based method demonstrates the opposite. Therefore, experiments were conducted using translational movements of the head for the CV-based approach and back-and-forth body vibrations for the radar-based approach. Subjects were asked to repeat the motion every 5 s and the distance to the sensors was kept at 50 cm.

The results presented in Table 3 show that the CV-based method is more robust to head motion than the radar-based method is to body movement, which is in line with expectations given the former measures color variation while the latter detects motion directly.

5   Discussion and Conclusions

In this paper, two non-contact HR monitoring architectures are proposed using CV and radar approaches and implemented using low-cost commercially available products suitable for automotive use. The CV-based system first employs depth information to achieve human background segmentation, followed by a combination of face detection and skin detection algorithms to locate and track the ROI. A raw signal reconstruction technique based on ratios of color channels is employed to reduce the fluctuations caused by illumination variations. A detrending method using smoothness prior is applied to enhance the SNR. Finally, the HR signal is recovered by ICA, bandpass filter, power spectrum analysis, and a moving average filter. Despite employing several techniques to mitigate the problems caused by illumination changes, this system still has a limited capability to handle extreme cases found in real-world deployment, such as drastic changes in brightness, contrast, and shadows. Addressing this robustness is an area of further work.

The radar-based system uses a bandpass filter to extract the chest wall motion from the motion-modulated RF signals, followed by a signal reconstruction process to merge the I and Q channels. Three further filters (bandpass, smoothing and moving average) are then combined to extract the HR signal. Again, real-world factors such as vehicle vibration and drivers' body motions would need to be considered for practical use.

Through the comparison with the ground truth obtained from a reference ECG device, the HR results for both methods were found to demonstrate a high accuracy. A comparative study was performed to investigate the characteristics and failure modes of each method, showing the sensor modality has a significant impact on its performance in different environments and therefore should be carefully selected according to the application scenario.

In the context of DMS, the two modalities each demonstrates different strengths and weaknesses to the illumination changes, vibrations and motion found in real-world driving scenarios. Based on the hypotheses that both modalities will not fail simultaneously and that a temporary loss of data in extremely adverse conditions is acceptable, the development of a multi-modality sensor fusion system has significant potential for future non-contact HR monitoring research and may offer substantial benefits for continuous robust operation as part of a DMS. Further research into the development of a reference-free signal quality index and motion compensation techniques for both sensors are promising areas for future studies.

References

1. Human Error in Road Accidents. https://www.visualexpert.com/Resources/roadaccidents.html. Accessed 18 Apr 2023
2. Jo, S., Kim, J., Kim, D.: Heart rate change while drowsy driving. J. Korean Med. Sci. **34**(8), 56 (2019)
3. Halin, A., Verly, J.G., Van Droogenbroeck, M.: Survey and synthesis of state of the art in driver monitoring. Sensors **21**(16), 5558 (2021)
4. Rovas, G., Bikia, V., Stergiopulos, N.: Quantification of the phenomena affecting reflective arterial photoplethysmography. Bioengineering **10**(4), 460 (2023)
5. Van Kampen, E.J., Zijlstra, W.G.: Determination of hemoglobin and its derivatives. Adv. Clin. Chem. **8**, 141–187 (1966)
6. Verkruysse, W., Svaasand, L.O., Nelson, J.S.: Remote plethysmographic imaging using ambient light. Opt. Express **16**(26), 21434–21445 (2008)
7. Poh, M.Z., McDuff, D.J., Picard, R.W.: Non-contact, automated cardiac pulse measurements using video imaging and blind source separation. Opt. Express **18**(10), 10762–10774 (2010)

8. Muratov, Y., Nikiforov, M., Melnik, O., Loskutov, A.: Heart rate measurements with a web camera based on the facial image moving in the frame. In: 2021 10 th Mediterranean Conference on Embedded Computing (MECO), pp. 1–5. IEEE, Budva, Montenegro (2021)

9. Jaiswal, K.B., Meenpal, T.: rPPG-FuseNet: non-contact heart rate estimation from facial video via RGB/MSR signal fusion. Biomed. Signal Process. Control **78**, 104002 (2022)

10. Magdalena Nowara, E., Marks, T.K., Mansour, H., Veeraraghavan, A.: SparsePPG: towards driver monitoring using camera-based vital signs estimation in near infrared. In: 2018 IEEE/CVF Conference on Computer Vision and Pattern Recognition Workshops (CVPRW), pp. 1353–135309. IEEE, Salt Lake City, USA (2018)

11. Haugg, F., Elgendi, M., Menon, C.: GRGB rPPG: an efficient low-complexity remote photoplethysmography-based algorithm for heart rate estimation. Bioengineering **10**(2), 243 (2023)

12. Asthana, A., Zafeiriou, S., Cheng, S., Pantic, M.: Robust discriminative response map fitting with constrained local models. In: 2013 IEEE Conference on Computer Vision and Pattern Recognition (CVPR), pp. 3444–3451. IEEE, Portland, USA (2013)

13. Poh, M.Z., McDuff, D.J., Picard, R.W.: Advancements in noncontact, multiparameter physiological measurements using a webcam. IEEE Transa. Biomed. Eng. **58**(1), 7–11 (2011)

14. De Haan, G., Jeanne, V.: Robust pulse rate from chrominance-based rPPG. IEEE Trans. Biomed. Eng. **60**(10), 2878–2886 (2013)

15. Tarvainen, M.P., Ranta-Aho, P.O., Karjalainen, P.A.: An advanced detrending method with application to HRV analysis. IEEE Trans. Biomed. Eng. **49**(2), 172–175 (2002)

16. Qiao, D., Zulkernine, F., Masroor, R., Rasool, R., Jaffar, N.: Measuring heart rate and heart rate variability with smartphone camera. In: 2021 22nd IEEE International Conference on Mobile Data Management (MDM), pp. 248–249. IEEE, Toronto, Canada (2021)

17. Krishnamoorthy, A., Bairy, G.M., Siddeshappa, N., Mayrose, H., Sampathila, N., Chadaga, K.: Channel intensity and edge-based estimation of heart rate via smartphone recordings. Computers **12**(2), 43 (2023)

18. Nowara, E.M., McDuff, D., Veeraraghavan, A.: The benefit of distraction: denoising camera-based physiological measurements using inverse attention. In: 2021 IEEE/CVF International Conference on Computer Vision (ICCV), pp. 4935–4944. IEEE, Montreal, Canada (2021)

19. Lokendra, B., Puneet, G.: AND-rPPG: a novel denoising-rPPG network for improving remote heart rate estimation. Comput. Biol. Med. **141**, 105146 (2022)

20. Qiu, Z., Liu, J., Sun, H., Lin, L., Chen, Y.: CoSTHR: a heart rate estimating network with adaptive color space transformation. IEEE Trans. Instrum. Meas. **71**, 1–10 (2022)

21. Yu, Z., Li, X., Zhao, G.: Remote photoplethysmography signal measurement from facial videos using spatial-temporal networks. arXiv: 1905.02419 (2019)

22. Yu, Z., Peng, W., Li, X., Hong, X., Zhao, G.: Remote heart rate measurement from highly compressed facial videos: an end-to-end deep learning solution with video enhancement. In: 2019 Proceedings of the IEEE/CVF International Conference on Computer Vision (ICCV), pp. 151–160. IEEE, Seoul, Korea (2019)

23. Petrović, V.L., Janković, M.M., Lupšić, A.V., Mihajlović, V.R., Popović-Božović, J.S.: High-accuracy real-time monitoring of heart rate variability using 24 GHz continuous-wave Doppler radar. IEEE Access **7**, 74721–74733 (2019)

24. Oh, S.H., Lee, S., Kim, S.M., Jeong, J.H.: Development of a heart rate detection algorithm using a non-contact Doppler radar via signal elimination. Biomed. Signal Process. Control **64**, 102314 (2021)

25. Schwarz, C., Zainab, H., Dasgupta, S., Kahl, J.: Heartbeat measurement with millimeter wave radar in the driving environment. In: 2021 IEEE Radar Conference (RadarConf21), pp. 1–6. IEEE, Atlanta, USA (2021)

26. Wang, F., Zeng, X., Wu, C., Wang, B., Liu, K.J.R.: Driver vital signs monitoring using millimeter wave radio. IEEE Internet Things J. **9**(13), 11283–11298 (2022)

27. Intel RealSense Depth Camera D435. https://www.intelrealsense.com/depth-camera-d435/. Accessed 18 Apr 2023
28. Deepface. https://github.com/serengil/deepface. Accessed 18 Apr 2023
29. Dahmani, D., Cheref, M., Larabi, S.: Zero-sum game theory model for segmenting skin regions. Image Vis. Comput. **99**, 103925 (2020)
30. BGT60LTR11AIP.   https://www.infineon.com/cms/en/product/sensor/radar-sensors/radar-sensors-for-iot/60ghz-radar/bgt60ltr11aip/. Accessed 18 Apr 2023
31. ECG 2 click - board with ADS1194 AD converter from Texas Instruments. https://www.mikroe.com/ecg-2-click. Accessed 18 Apr 2023

Medical and Health Care

CFAB: An Online Data Augmentation to Alleviate the Spuriousness of Classification on Medical Ultrasound Images

Jianhua Huang[1(✉)], Kuan Huang[2(✉)] , Meng Xu[2] , and Feifei Liu[3,4]

[1] School of Computer Science and Technology, Harbin Institute of Technology, Harbin, China
jhhuang@hit.edu.cn
[2] Department of Computer Science and Technology, Kean University, Union, USA
khuang@kean.edu
[3] Department of Ultrasound, Binzhou Medical University Hospital, Binzhou, China
[4] Department of Ultrasound, Peking University People's Hospital, Beijing, China

Abstract. Convolutional neural networks (CNNs) may learn spurious correlations between bias features (*e.g.*, background) and labels in image classification. The spuriousness in CNNs usually occurs in building connections between the background of images and labels. Such spurious correlation limits the generalizability of CNNs in classification tasks. Changing backgrounds and foregrounds of original samples can reduce the spuriousness in natural image classification. However, generating annotations for foreground on medical image datasets is time-consuming and labor-intensive. To solve this problem, we propose an online data augmentation method named Combining Foreground And Background (CFAB), which makes CNNs focus on key causal features without foreground annotations and breaks the correlation between backgrounds and labels by changing different backgrounds for one sample. Furthermore, we propose a framework for collaborative augmenting samples using CFAB and training CNNs. Comprehensive experiments indicate that the proposed method weakens the spuriousness, improves the generalizability of the model, and achieves state-of-the-art results in medical ultrasound dataset classification.

Keywords: Data Augmentation · Classification · Spurious Correlation · Medical Ultrasound Image

1 Introduction

Convolutional neural networks (CNNs) have recently been widely used in various fields, such as the analysis of natural and medical images [5,16]. However, they

The authors acknowledge that this work was supported in part by the National Natural Science Foundation of China (NSFC) No. 82071930.

often use non-causal features to make decisions [4]. For example, Fig. 1 shows two medical ultrasound images along with their corresponding lesion regions and class activation maps (CAMs) for CNN-based classification. Highlighted background regions in CAMs indicate that the CNN relies on these non-causal background regions to predict the classification results. In addition, acquiring a sufficient number of medical images is challenging, which limits the generalizability of CNNs for medical image classification. To solve this problem, data augmentation methods [11,12] are used to expand the data, which can reduce the non-causality and increase the generalizability of CNN models.

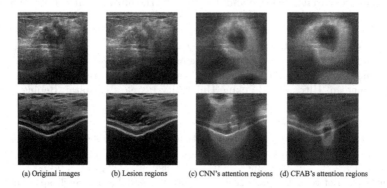

(a) Original images   (b) Lesion regions   (c) CNN's attention regions   (d) CFAB's attention regions

Fig. 1. Visualization of CAMs. The baseline network (c) highlights foreground and non-causal background regions, whereas the proposed method (d) prioritizes only foreground regions.

Data augmentation methods can be divided into offline and online methods. Offline data augmentation is to expand the dataset before training a model. For example, Chen *et al.* [3] propose a Region Confusion Mechanism (RCM) that destroys the context relationship between background features and labels to increase the generalization ability of the model. Online data augmentation is to make various changes to the input samples in each training epoch, such as random inversion and other operations in the PyTorch library. A series of existing online mixup methods [8,9,13,17,18] mix pairs of input samples to improve the generalization of the model. They generate augmented samples by mixing foreground regions from the input pairs. However, these methods do not reduce the non-causal correlation between backgrounds and labels. In fact, foregrounds need enhancement, and backgrounds require weakening as well. In addition, a counterfactual and invariant data generation method [2] changes the foregrounds and backgrounds of original samples in different ways (*i.e.*, grey, random, shuffle, *etc.*) to augment them. However, this approach requires foreground annotations, which is not applicable to datasets with category labels but without foreground annotations, especially medical image datasets. Furthermore, annotating foregrounds to draw lesion boundaries is challenging and costly.

To overcome annotation limitations, many weakly-supervised object localization methods are proposed to determine the approximate object location using image-level labels. These methods often employ attention mechanisms for their implementation [7]. In addition, CAMs, including CAM [19] and Grad-CAM [15], can be used to extract the target region using only image-level labels. However, they generate CAMs from the final convolutional layer of the CNN, resulting in relatively small confidence regions around the object and limited localization capability.

To address the above problems, we propose a novel image augmentation method, named Combining Foreground And Background (CFAB), to alleviate the spurious correlations in CNNs for classification. The CFAB consists of an augmented image generation network and a classification network. Specifically, the proposed augmented image generation network consists of four steps. We first design a weakly supervised foreground generator using Layer-CAM [6] of a pre-trained CNN model to estimate the lesion regions on a pair of input images (*i.e.*, a main sample and a random sample). Second, we pick a threshold for the Layer-CAM to binarize the generated CAMs to obtain two lesion masks for the pair of inputs. Third, two lesion masks are merged to get the final foreground mask of the main sample. Fourth, we generate an augmented image by mixing the foreground of the main sample and the background of the random sample. The augmented image has the same category label as the main sample. Meanwhile, we use the CFAB in a collaborative training framework to train a classification model and augment more images simultaneously using a closed-loop self-feedback strategy. The quality of augmented samples and model performance is gradually improved during the iterative training procedure because the spurious correlation is gradually weakened. Our major contributions are summarized as follows:

- We propose a novel online data augmentation method called Combining Foreground And Background (CFAB). Different from [2], CFAB can approximately identify the lesion's position in an image without requiring foreground annotation. It combines the lesion region with the background from another randomly selected image to create new samples.
- We propose a collaborative training framework to train a classification model and augment images simultaneously. They reinforce each other to enhance the generalizability and credibility of the model.
- We conduct extensive experiments on three medical ultrasound image datasets and use visualizations of CAMs to show the superiority of the proposed CFAB. It reduces the model's attention to non-causal areas while increasing its attention to lesion-like regions in medical ultrasound images. CFAB achieves state-of-the-art (SOTA) performance on three datasets compared to five recent popular augmentation methods.

2   Approach

Figure 2 illustrates the overview of CFAB. It comprises a sample generation network (parameterized by φ) and a classification network (parameterized by θ). Initially, we train the classification network on the original datasets to obtain the initial parameters θ. Then, the generation network, using $\varphi = \theta$, generates class activation maps (CAMs) for image augmentation. These augmented images are then utilized for training the classification network, resulting in updated parameters θ'. For the next iteration, φ is set to θ'. This section provides a detailed explanation of the three steps of CFAB and the training framework.

2.1   Weakly Supervised Lesion Localization

To locate the foreground regions in the input images and avoid foreground anno-tations, a weakly supervised lesion localization method is designed based on Layer-CAM and image-level labels. In the first step, we train the classification network on the original datasets to learn parameters θ. These learned θ values are subsequently assigned to φ of the generation network to generate CAMs for all images in the training set. The generated CAMs are then used to detect the foregrounds in a weakly supervised manner.

Inspired by Layer-CAM [6], our weakly supervised lesion detection method generates CAMs on a specific layer k of the generation network for an input image x. For layer k, the feature map $M_{i,j}^{k\varphi}$ and the gradient map $g_{i,j}^{k\varphi}$ of the classification prediction y^φ with respect to the spatial location (i, j) in the feature map $M_{i,j}^{k\varphi}$ are utilized to calculate the CAMs in this layer, where $g_{i,j}^{k\varphi} = \frac{\partial y^\varphi}{\partial M_{i,j}^{k\varphi}}$. To obtain the CAM of layer k (denoted as $A^{k\varphi}$), we multiply the activation value of each location in the feature map by its weight and linearly combine the values in each channel together, as shown in Eq. (1). The weight is calculated by the gradient map and $ReLU$ activation function.

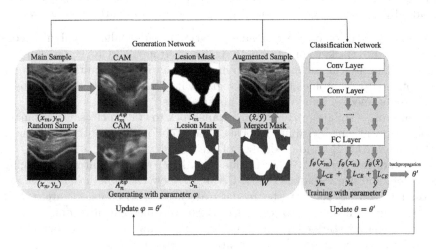

Fig. 2. An overview of the proposed CFAB augmentation method and the collaborative training framework.

In the second step, we binarize the generated CAM with a threshold of $\alpha\%$ of the maximum intensity of the CAM to generate a pixel-level localization mask

S. Values greater than the threshold are set to 1, and others are set to 0, as shown in Eq. (2), where H denotes the unit step function. The optimal value of α depends on the specific properties of the dataset. Experiments for selecting α and convolutional layer index k will be discussed in the experiment section.

$$A^{k\varphi} = ReLU(\sum M^{k\varphi} \cdot ReLU(g^{k\varphi})) \tag{1}$$

$$S = H(A^{k\varphi} - \alpha\% \times \max(A^{k\varphi})) \tag{2}$$

2.2 Mixed Samples Generation

In the third step, we generate augmented images by mixing pairs of images. Given a main sample (x_m, y_m), we randomly select another sample (x_n, y_n) from the training set, where x_m and x_n represents the two images, and y_m and y_n represents their classification labels. Next, the image pair (x_m, y_m) and (x_n, y_n) are fed into the sample generation network. The lesion localization method proposed in Subsect. 2.1 is used to generate the lesion localization masks S_m and S_n for x_m and x_n. Our image augmentation method is to mix the foreground of x_m and the background of x_n to generate an augmented image $\hat{x}$.

The traditional pipeline of the mix-up method includes (1) creating a mask, denoted as W, by resizing S_m to the size of x_m. In this process, the foreground region in x_m is assigned a value of 1, while the background region is assigned a value of 0. (2) generating an augmented sample $\hat{x}$ by:

$$\hat{x} = x_m \odot W + x_n \odot (1 - W) \tag{3}$$

where $\odot$ denotes element-wise multiplication. However, there are several problems: (1) In cases where the lesion locations differ between x_m and x_n, the augmented image will incorporate the lesion from x_n as part of the background. (2) Including the lesion from x_n results in two lesions in the augmented sample. Consequently, the label of the augmented sample is associated with two lesion features from potentially different categories, severely degrading the model's performance. (3) One potential solution to address these issues is to exclude the lesion from x_n and retain only its background. However, it may cause a vacant area in the augmented image when the lesion locations in x_m and x_n differ.

We propose a novel mix-up method to address the above problems. First, S_m and S_n are merged by pixel-wise summation:

$$F = S_m \oplus S_n \tag{4}$$

where $\oplus$ denotes the pixel-wise summation. Then, the mask W is calculated by:

$$W = H(F) \tag{5}$$

where H denotes the unit step function. The bilinear interpolation is utilized to upsample the W back to the original image size. Then, a new augmented image $\hat{x}$ is generated by Eq. (3) with the new mask. As a result, $\hat{x}$ consists of the lesion of x_m, a small part of the background of x_m, and most of the background of x_n. The label for $\hat{x}$, $\hat{y} = y_m$.

2.3 Collaborative Training Framework

In the first iteration, the mixed sample generator locates lesions using the parameters of the initially trained classification network. However, the CAMs for the initial classification network may focus on the backgrounds. Therefore, to get better data augmentation and classification results, the parameters of the classification network (θ) and generation network (φ) are updated with the new classification network parameters θ', which are trained by the augmented data. When the classifier learns more lesion features through augmented samples, we will synchronously update the parameters of the generation network for the next iteration. In this way, the CAMs for data argumentation will be more accurate, and the classifier will pay more attention to the lesion region instead of the background region. We design a closed-loop self-feedback system for training. Specifically, we first freeze the parameters φ of the sample generation network and update the parameters θ of the classification network with the parameters θ' obtained from each epoch of training. We update the parameters φ of the sample generation network with θ' when the classification accuracy with θ' performs better than φ. The loss function used to monitor this process is in Eq. (6). The standard cross entropy loss function is used in the experiment.

$$L = L_{CE}(f_\theta(x_m), y_m) + L_{CE}(f_\theta(x_n), y_n) + L_{CE}(f_\theta(\hat{x}), \hat{y}) \qquad (6)$$

where L_{CE} is cross entropy loss function and f_θ is the classification network.

3 Experiences

Three medical ultrasound image datasets are used in our experiments. The first breast ultrasound image dataset BUSI [1] has 780 images of three categories (benign, malignant, and normal). The second breast ultrasound image dataset BIRADS is collected by various collaborative hospitals, including Peking University People's Hospital, Southeast University Zhongda Hospital, the First Affiliated Hospital of the Guangxi University of Chinese Medicine, and the First Affiliated Hospital of Zhengzhou University and has 2,068 images of six categories (6 BI-RADS [14] categories). The third dataset, ARTHRITIS, is collected by Peking University People's Hospital. It is a cross-section of the inflammatory arthropathic cartilage ultrasound image dataset with 624 images of four categories. Each dataset is split into 70% training, 10% validation, and 20% testing. All images in various sizes are resized to 224 × 224 before being fed into networks.

3.1 Implementation Details

The implementation of the proposed method is based on the public platform PyTorch 1.13.1. All experiments are conducted on a Ubuntu 20.04 system, AMD EPYC 7513 2.60 GHz CPU, and 8 NVIDIA GeForce RTX 3090 graphics cards with 24GB memory. All models are trained using the ADAM optimizer with learning rate 0.0001. The batch size is 32. ResNet-50 is employed as the classification backbone. The initial classification network is trained for 120 epochs using the original non-augmented data. Its parameters are then used in the sample generation network. Other data augmentation methods like resizing and center-cropping are excluded as a form of regularization during training to preserve full-size images and avoid the absence of lesion areas. Our proposed method is applied to the backbone network, training it for 250 epochs until convergence.

3.2 Performance Comparison

We compare our method with the baseline approach, several recent data augmentation methods, including data augmentation implemented by RCM mechanism [3], mixup data augmentation methods [8,17,18], F (Random) and F (Shuffle) [2], and an ultrasound image classification method LTQ [10] which is the SOTA classification model for ultrasound image by reducing the impact of noise and the number of training data. The results are listed in Table 1. The performance of the mixup (α_{mixup}= 0.2) in medical ultrasound datasets is unsatisfactory. Even cut-mixup [17] exhibits a decrease in classification accuracy. In contrast, our proposed method surpasses both the baseline approach and other data augmentation methods, including F(Shuffle) and F(Random), which utilize foreground annotations. The quality of foreground annotations limits the effectiveness of F(Shuffle) and F(Random). However, our CFAB method gradually focuses on crucial causal features, enhancing their attention to the foreground during training, ultimately achieving the best performance.

Table 1. Comparison of the accuracy of data augmentation methods on three medical ultrasound datasets.

Method	Accuracy(%)		
	BUSI	BIRADS	ARTHRITIS
Baseline	91.35%	72.55%	76.35%
DCL-RCM	91.88%	71.54%	73.55%
Mixup (α_{mixup}=0.2)	92.68%	73.68%	77.41%
Cut-mixup	92.96%	73.45%	75.68%
Puzzle-mix	93.12%	73.88%	75.94%
F (Random)	93.55%	75.87%	77.12%
F (Shuffle)	93.67%	78.63%	79.53%
LTQ	94.60%	74.17%	77.58%
CFAB	**94.93%**	**79.34%**	**80.67%**

3.3 Effectiveness of Lesion Localization

To quantify each compared method's attention to the foreground, we use the weakly supervised foreground detection method in Subsect. 2.1 to detect the foreground S. S is resized to match the dimensions of the original image. We evaluate the final result by calculating a δ value, which represents the ratio of overlapping pixels between the weakly detected result and the label, to the total number of pixels in the foreground of the label. This δ value reflects the network's attention toward the foreground region. It also shows the method's capability to reduce the spuriousness of data augmentation methods and the non-causal degree within the classification network. The results are listed in Table 2. Our method significantly enhances the attention of the network to the features that should contribute to classification, that is, the causal features to the foreground.

Table 2. Quantitative evaluation of each method's attention to the foreground.

Method	δ		
	BUSI	BIRADS	ARTHRITIS
Baseline	70.58%	52.93%	56.74%
DCL-RCM	73.64%	47.68%	52.86%
Mixup(α_{mixup}=0.2)	75.89%	58.22%	63.14%
Cut-mixup	77.53%	60.71%	67.98%
Puzzle-mix	79.66%	62.08%	68.56%
F(Random)	86.47%	72.46%	78.63%
F(Shuffle)	88.53%	76.55%	80.02%
LTQ	76.91%	69.73%	73.95%
CFAB	**95.16%**	**83.64%**	**86.71%**

3.4   Ablation Studies

We conduct an ablation study to further verify the effectiveness of the proposed CFAB data augmentation and the collaborative training framework. The results are listed in Table 3. Adding CFAB to the baseline substantially improves the network's classification performance, and the collaborative training framework further enhances performance across all three medical ultrasound image datasets. We also conduct experiments to determine the optimal values of α for each medical ultrasound dataset and the source layer k for the CAMs. For the BIRADS and BUSI, the model performance could be optimized by taking α as 20% and the last convolution layer of Conv4_x as the source of the CAMs. For the Arthrophlogosis dataset, The model performance can be optimized by taking α as 30% and the last convolution layer of Conv5_x as the source of the CAMs.

3.5   Visualization

Figure 3 displays representative ultrasound images and their augmented images (the first and third rows) and their CAMs of all compared data augmentation

Table 3. Ablation studies of the proposed method.

Method	Accuracy(%)		
	BUSI	BIRADS	ARTHRITIS
Baseline	91.35%	72.55%	76.35%
+CFAB	93.72%	78.91%	79.16%
+ CFAB + Collaborative Training	**94.93%**	**79.34%**	**80.67%**

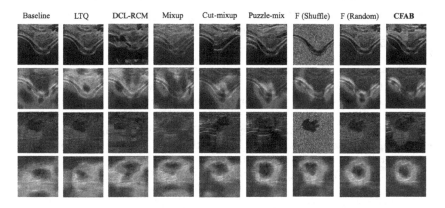

Fig. 3. Visualization of data augmentation results and CAMs.

methods (the second and fourth rows). Original images are shown in the first and second columns because the baseline and LQT methods do not use data augmentation. The baseline method ResNet50 tends to have a high response to the background, and other compared methods also learn spurious correlations to the background. In contrast, the proposed CFAB method distinctly prioritizes the lesion area, demonstrating its credibility and reliability.

4   Conclusion

In this paper, we propose a novel CFAB data argumentation method that can reduce spurious correlations between classification labels and non-causal features. We also design a collaborative training framework to train a classification model using augmented images generated by CFAB. The proposed method consists of three major parts: 1) A weakly supervised lesion localization method based on Layer-CAM. 2) A novel online data augmentation method that can reduce the influence of backgrounds by mixing pairs of images. 3) A simultaneous training framework for data augmentation and classification. The proposed method achieves the best results on the three datasets compared with five recent data augmentation, one baseline network, and one ultrasound image classification method. Our future work includes extending the proposed method to natural image datasets.

References

1. Al-Dhabyani, W., Gomaa, M., Khaled, H., Fahmy, A.: Dataset of breast ultrasound images. Data Brief **28**, 104863 (2020)
2. Chang, C.H., Adam, G.A., Goldenberg, A.: Towards robust classification model by counterfactual and invariant data generation. In: Proceedings of the IEEE/CVF Conference on Computer Vision and Pattern Recognition, pp. 15212–15221 (2021)
3. Chen, Y., Bai, Y., Zhang, W., Mei, T.: Destruction and construction learning for fine-grained image recognition. In: Proceedings of the IEEE/CVF Conference on Computer Vision and Pattern Recognition, pp. 5157–5166 (2019)
4. Geirhos, R., et al.: Shortcut learning in deep neural networks. Nat. Mach. Intell. **2**(11), 665–673 (2020)
5. Grigorescu, S., Trasnea, B., Cocias, T., Macesanu, G.: A survey of deep learning techniques for autonomous driving. J. Field Rob. **37**(3), 362–386 (2020)
6. Jiang, P.T., Zhang, C.B., Hou, Q., Cheng, M.M., Wei, Y.: Layercam: exploring hierarchical class activation maps for localization. IEEE Trans. Image Process. **30**, 5875–5888 (2021)
7. Kim, D., Cho, D., Yoo, D., So Kweon, I.: Two-phase learning for weakly supervised object localization. In: Proceedings of the IEEE International Conference on Computer Vision, pp. 3534–3543 (2017)
8. Kim, J.H., Choo, W., Song, H.O.: Puzzle mix: exploiting saliency and local statistics for optimal mixup. In: International Conference on Machine Learning, pp. 5275–5285. PMLR (2020)
9. Kim, J., Choo, W., Jeong, H., Song, H.O.: Co-mixup: saliency guided joint mixup with supermodular diversity. In: International Conference on Learning Representations (2021). https://openreview.net/forum?id=gvxJzw8kW4b
10. Li, X., Liang, H., Nagala, S., Chen, J.: Improving ultrasound image classification with local texture quantisation. In: IEEE International Conference on Acoustics, Speech and Signal Processing (ICASSP), pp. 1211–1215. IEEE (2022)
11. Moreno-Barea, F.J., Jerez, J.M., Franco, L.: Improving classification accuracy using data augmentation on small data sets. Expert Syst. Appl. **161**, 113696 (2020)
12. Nalepa, J., Myller, M., Kawulok, M.: Hyperspectral data augmentation. arXiv preprint arXiv:1903.05580 (2019)
13. Qin, J., Fang, J., Zhang, Q., Liu, W., Wang, X., Wang, X.: Resizemix: mixing data with preserved object information and true labels. arXiv: Computer Vision and Pattern Recognition (2020)
14. Radiology, A., D'Orsi, C.: ACR BI-RADS Atlas: breast imaging reporting and data system; mammography, ultrasound, magnetic resonance imaging, follow-up and outcome monitoring, data dictionary. ACR, American College of Radiology (2013)
15. Selvaraju, R.R., Cogswell, M., Das, A., Vedantam, R., Parikh, D., Batra, D.: Gradcam: visual explanations from deep networks via gradient-based localization. In: Proceedings of the IEEE International Conference on Computer Vision (ICCV) (2017)
16. Shen, D., Wu, G., Suk, H.I.: Deep learning in medical image analysis. Ann. Review Biomed. Eng. **19**, 221–248 (2017)
17. Yun, S., Han, D., Oh, S.J., Chun, S., Choe, J., Yoo, Y.: Cutmix: regularization strategy to train strong classifiers with localizable features. In: Proceedings of the IEEE/CVF International Conference on Computer Vision, pp. 6023–6032 (2019)

18. Zhang, H., Cisse, M., Dauphin, Y.N., Lopez-Paz, D.: mixup: beyond empirical risk minimization. In: International Conference on Learning Representations (2018). https://openreview.net/forum?id=r1Ddp1-Rb
19. Zhou, B., Khosla, A., Lapedriza, A., Oliva, A., Torralba, A.: Learning deep features for discriminative localization. In: Proceedings of the IEEE Conference on Computer Vision and Pattern Recognition, pp. 2921–2929 (2016)

Towards an Unsupervised GrowCut Algorithm for Mammography Segmentation

Cristiana Moroz-Dubenco$^{(\boxtimes)}$ ⬤, Laura Dioşan ⬤, and Anca Andreica ⬤

Department of Computer Science, Babeş-Bolyai University,
Mihail Kogălniceanu 1, 400084 Cluj-Napoca, Romania
cristiana.moroz@ubbcluj.ro

Abstract. Breast cancer is the most frequent type of malignancy in women, with 2.3 million diagnostics only in 2020. However, as a consequence of early diagnosis and appropriate treatment, more and more women are being cured. Among screening methods, mammography is one of the most used, and segmentation is a crucial step of its analysis. Starting from an enhanced version of the GrowCut segmentation technique, the goal of this paper is to automatically generate the foreground seeds so as to minimize the human expert intervention to the identification of only one pixel. We propose a method that starts with the center of the anomaly and composes the foreground seeds set as a circle inside the anomaly. We test the proposed method on the mini-MIAS dataset for various radius dimensions and two background seeds variants, concluding that the best combination is a circle with a radius of 25 pixels as foreground seeds and the black pixels from the original image as background seeds.

Keywords: Mammography Segmentation · Lesion Detection · Cellular Automaton · GrowCut

1 Introduction

As reported by the World Health Organization, breast cancer is the most frequent type of malignancy in women, with 2.3 million diagnostics and 685000 deaths in 2020. Approximately 50% of the cases develop in women having no other risk factor than gender and age over 40 years [7]. However, since the 1980s, as a consequence of early diagnosis and appropriate treatment, more and more women are being cured. From the existing screening methods, mammography is one of the most used.

Taking into consideration that mammography interpretation depends on both the radiologist's experience and various image quality aspects, such as illumination, noise levels, contrast or the definition of contours [1], we can state that an automated interpretation system can prove to be a real help in improving the

© The Author(s), under exclusive license to Springer Nature Switzerland AG 2023
H. I. Christensen et al. (Eds.): ICVS 2023, LNCS 14253, pp. 102–111, 2023.
https://doi.org/10.1007/978-3-031-44137-0_9

accuracy of the diagnosis. Yet, towards analyzing an abnormality and classifying it as benign or malignant, its contour has to be accurately determined first. It is known that both the contour and the size of a tumor are important factors when it comes to deciding if there is a need for surgery. Therefore, segmentation is a crucial step in the analysis of a mammography.

So far, both supervised and unsupervised mammography segmentation techniques have been proposed. Nonetheless, recent research inclines towards unsupervised methods, due to the fact that ground-truth generation can prove rather challenging. Starting from the GrowCut algorithm [12] - a semi-supervised method for segmentation that starts with initial expert-provided seeds for all the possible classes (i.e. each class corresponds to a different object) and iteratively assigns the pixels to classes -, in our previous work [8], we developed an enhanced method, named Threshold-based GrowCut (TbGC), which aims to reduce not only the demand for human intervention, but also the execution time, and yet preserve a high accuracy. With three different methods of automatically generating initial background seeds, the human intervention is reduced to selecting only the foreground seeds.

Consequently, we address the further improvement of the TbGC algorithm by automatically generating the foreground seeds as well. We propose a technique that starts with the center of the abnormality, provided by the human expert, and constructs the initial foreground seeds as a circle inside the abnormality in an automated manner, thus minimizing the expert intervention to identifying only one pixel. We apply the proposed approach on the mini-MIAS dataset [10] using various radius dimension and two background seeds generation methods and compare the results to one another, aiming to find the best combination towards an unsupervised improved GrowCut algorithm for mammography lesion detection.

This work is organized as follows: Sect. 2 presents the classical GrowCut technique and some of the existing revisions, Sect. 3 describes the proposed method, Sect. 4 advances the experimental qualitative and quantitative results and Sect. 5 tenders our conclusions and ideas for future work.

2   Related Work

The GrowCut algorithm [12] is an image segmentation technique based on a Cellular Automaton (CA), where the image is the space of cells and the pixels are the cells of the automaton. Each cell p is defined by a label (l_p), a "strength" (θ_p), which represents the confidence that p belongs to the class denoted as l_p, and a feature vector (C_p). At first, all the cells have the same state: $(l_p = 0, \theta_p = 0, C_p = I_p)$, with I_p representing the intensity of the pixel p. The user initiates the process of the CA by labeling some cells, called seeds, which then attack the neighboring cells, trying to propagate their labels. Depending on the result of a function based on their intensities, the defender cells can take the attacker's label and their "strength" is updated. This process is repeated as long as at least one cell is updated during an iteration, and stops when the automaton reaches a stable state.

Cordeiro et al. [1] propose a modified GrowCut algorithm, aiming to reduce the effort of seeds selection and increasing the fault tolerance. While the classical GrowCut assigns maximum strength value to all the initial seeds selected by the user, which can lead to the algorithm not being able to recover from wrongfully labeled pixels, their proposed method is based on selecting only foreground seeds. Then, assuming that the center of the mass has a higher chance of being labeled correctly, it is assigned the maximum strength value, while the strengths of all the other cells are initialized with zero. The paper also proposes a modified update rule, such that the attack of cells is based in a region modeled by a Gaussian fuzzy membership function. The proposed method was tested on 57 images from mini-MIAS and the results were compared to various existing methods, obtaining very good results for spiculated and ill-defined lesions, and at least competitive results for circumscribed lesions.

Ghosh et al. [5] introduce an unsupervised method for medical image segmentation, based on the original GrowCut algorithm. In order to overcome the limitation of being dependent on the correctness of the user-labeled pixels, the proposed method identifies the number of classes and the class boundaries in an automated manner, based on the image features. The initial number of seed points and their labels are derived randomly from the space of natural numbers and are assigned a strength value of 1. Moreover, the proposed algorithm constructs equivalence classes for each label, which are updated if two labels merge. The process is iterated until no local label update occurs. The results obtained with this method are comparable to the ones obtained with normalized cut and mean shift methods.

Dafni et al. [2] advance an unsupervised region growing technique for mammogram segmentation that uses a Glowworm Swarm Optimization (GSO) for the selection of initial seed points and threshold values. A collection of glowworm is arbitrarily placed in the solution space and the optimal solution is selected based on the brightness of glowworm. Once the seed points and the threshold values are chosen using this technique, each seed point's region is grown by estimating the distance (in terms of intensity) between the seed point and its neighbors and including all the neighbors in the seed point's region if the computed distance is lower than the threshold value. The proposed segmentation technique is integrated in a complete detection and diagnosis system, which is evaluated on images from the mini-MIAS dataset, reaching a maximum sensitivity of 93.51% and an accuracy score of 86.26%.

Sadad et al. [9] tender another complete computed-aided detection and diagnosis system, which uses cascading of Fuzzy C-Means (FCM) and region-growing techniques, called FCMRG, for anomaly localization. This technique consists of three steps: (1) cascading of Fuzzy C-Means, (2) eliminating of undesired elements through erosion, (3) enlarging the involved objects through dilation and (4) extracting the largest region using the region growing algorithm. The results of the experiments carried on the DDSM database [6] prove that the proposed technique is better than previous approaches when applied to mammographic images.

3   Proposed Method

We previously developed an enhanced variant of the GrowCut technique for mammography lesion detection [8], which aims to reduce not only the demand for human intervention, but also the execution time, while preserving a high accuracy. Our version, named Threshold-based GrowCut (TbGC), tenders three variants of discarding the selection of background seeds: (1) automated generation inside the breast, (2) usage of the black pixels and (3) complete disuse. As a means to conserve qualitative results, we also changed the cell evolution rule, requiring the new "strength" to be higher than an experimentally chosen threshold value in order to change a cell's label. Moreover, TbGC is restricted to a given number of steps, yielding a result whether when the automaton converges or when the maximum number of steps is reached, thus reducing the computational time. The Threshold-based GrowCut method was tested on the mammographies containing abnormalities from the mini-MIAS dataset [10], totaling 119 abnormalities. The dataset also provides, for each mammography that contains at least one abnormality, the coordinates of the center and the radius of its circumscribed circle. Since the background seeds were generated in an automated manner, the input given by the specialist was reduced to the foreground seeds selection. In order to simulate this input, the circle that encloses the mass, as provided with the dataset, was used as foreground seeds. The results were compared to those obtained with the classical GrowCut method, concluding that TbGC yields better results for two out of the three cases: when using background seeds outside the breast and when using only foreground seeds.

The aim of this paper is to reduce the necessity for human intervention even more, by limiting it to the selection of a single foreground pixel. Following the idea presented in [1] - the center of the abnormality has the best chance to be rightly identified by the user - we intend to automatically construct the set of foreground seeds, starting from the center of the tumor. In order for this to happen, we choose the foreground seeds as a circle whose center corresponds to that of the tumor and an experimentally chosen radius. Therefore, we apply the proposed method on the same images from mini-MIAS that were employed in the experiments from the paper which introduces TbGC [8] - all the mammographies that contain abnormalities, with a total of 119 abnormalities -, using the same values for threshold and maximum number of steps - 0.5 and 5, respectively - and then compute and analyze the results obtained using various radius values, so as to find an appropriate one.

The goal of this segmentation technique is to identify the region of interest. However, if the contour of the mass cannot be precisely determined, especially when talking about the mini-MIAS dataset, which does not provide an exact ground truth, but rather an approximation, we consider it better to obtain a result larger than the mass, yet containing it entirely. On the other hand, starting with a radius value too high can lead to the segmentation of the entire breast as region of interest, since the foreground seeds would be outside the mass. Taking all of these into consideration, and also the distribution of abnormality radii in the mini-MIAS dataset, presented in Fig. 1, we employ six radius values in the experiments: 5, 10, 25, 50, 75 and 100.

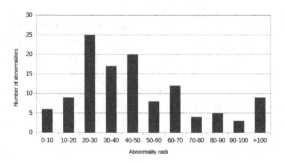

Fig. 1. Distribution of abnormality radii in the mini-MIAS dataset.

Although the TbGC method proposes three variants of generating the background seeds, we now discard the first variant, since it does not longer suit our needs. In order to construct the inner breast background seeds (the first variant), in [8], we used the contour of a rectangle that encloses the ground truth circle. However, in the approach presented in this paper, depending on the radius value, it is possible for the foreground seeds to be entirely inside the mass, leading to the possibility of wrongfully generating the background seeds inside the mass as well (for instance, for a mass having the radius of the ground truth circle higher than 100 and the radius of the foreground seeds circle equal to 10, the background seeds, generated following the first variant, would be entirely inside the mass). Since we aim to find a foreground seeds set that fits any mammography, regardless of the size of the mass, correlating the foreground seeds circle radius and the ground truth circle radius would contradict the goal of our work, thus we are left with the other two variants: employ the black pixels external to the breast as background seeds, and use only foreground seeds.

4   Experimental Results

As a means to finding the most suitable foreground seeds set, we compare the results obtained using a circle whose center corresponds to that of the mass and various radii not only to one another, but also to the results obtained when using the ground truth as foreground seeds, as proposed in [8], and when using the center of the mass as sole foreground seed, as proposed in [1]. The qualitative results, computed for five mammographies from the mini-MIAS dataset, are presented in Fig. 2 for the case when we use background seeds and in Fig. 3 for the case when we use only foreground seeds. For the quantitative results, we compute five metrics for each mammography that contains an abnormality, then compute a mean of the results. The metrics used for evaluation are as follows: *accuracy* - the percent of pixels correctly classified [13], *precision* - the percent of pixels rightly identified as foreground [11], *recall* - the percent of foreground pixels rightly identified [11], *Jaccard index* - the size of the intersection between the segmentation result and the ground truth label sets divided by the size of the union of the two label sets [4] and *Dice coefficient* - two times the area of overlap between the result and the ground truth divided by the total number of pixels in both images [3]. The results are presented in Table 1 for the variant with background seeds and in Table 2 for the variant without background seeds.

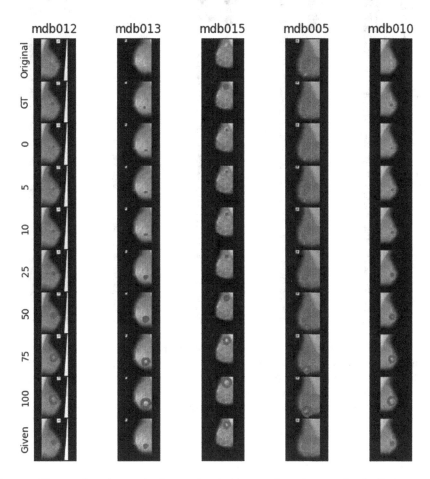

Fig. 2. The results obtained when using background seeds outside the breast, with the first line containing the original images, the second line - the ground-truth images, the following seven lines - the results obtained when using a circle with a radius value of 0, 5, 10, 25, 50, 75 and 100, respectively, as foreground seeds and the tenth line - the results obtained when using a circle with the radius provided with the dataset as foreground seeds.

From Fig. 2 and 3, one can easily notice that the segmented area is increasing proportionally with the radius value. Yet, using a foreground seeds circle with a

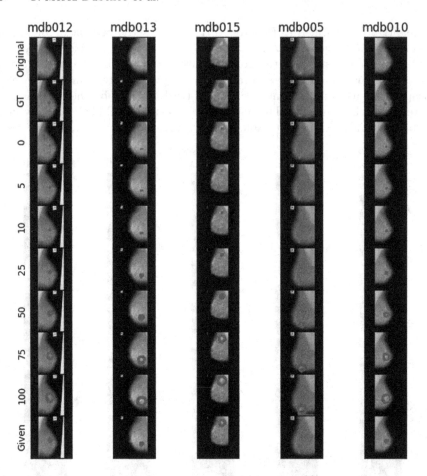

Fig. 3. The results obtained when not using background seeds, with the first line containing the original images, the second line - the ground-truth images, the following seven lines - the results obtained when using a circle with a radius value of 0, 5, 10, 25, 50, 75 and 100, respectively, as foreground seeds and the tenth line - the results obtained when using a circle with the radius provided with the dataset as foreground seeds.

radius higher than 25 leads to the center of the mass not being segmented. If we are to look at the last line in both figures, which contains the results for employing the ground truth as foreground seeds, we can see that the segmented area is much larger than the ground truth. On the other hand, the results obtained when using only the center of the mass as foreground seeds, presented on the third line, are much smaller than the ground truth. As previously stated, we consider better a segmentation result that encloses the entire mass rather than one that leaves out part of the mass, thus, drawing a conclusion from the results presented in Fig. 2 and 3, we consider that the most appropriate radius value is 25.

Tables 1 and 2 hold the mean of the performance metrics computed on 119 images from the mini-MIAS dataset, with background seeds outside the breast and without background seeds, respectively. For this evaluation, the entire segmented area was taken into account. The results in this tables come to support the conclusions drawn from Fig. 2 and 3. The recall, Jaccard index and Dice coefficient values are increasing proportionally with the radius until it reaches the value of 25, then start to decrease. On the other hand, the accuracy and precision values are inversely proportional to the radius. However, the difference in accuracy between the results obtained for a radius equal to 0 and the ones obtained for a radius equal to 25 is of 0.0009 for the variant with background seeds outside the breast and of 0.0040 for the variant without background seeds, thus we can consider the values obtained for a 25-pixel radius good enough. As for the values obtained for precision, in correlation with the ones obtained for recall, we can assume that they are the result of a segmented area a bit larger than the ground truth, but as stated before, we prefer a region of interest that encloses the entire mass to one that does not contain it entirely. Therefore, considering the results obtained from the qualitative and the quantitative experiments, we conclude that the most suitable variant towards an unsupervised TbGC is the combination between background seeds outside the breast and foreground seeds generated as a circle whose center corresponds to that of the mass and a radius equal to 25.

By looking at the results of the experiments and at Fig. 1, one can notice that there is a possible correlation between the foreground seeds circle radius and the distribution of abnormality radii in the mini-MIAS dataset. Taking into consideration that most of the mammographies that were used in the experiments contain an abnormality with a radius between 20 and 30 pixels and only 11% of the abnormalities have a radius lower than 25 pixels, it can be presumed that the value of the foreground seeds circle radius is linked to the abnormality radii distribution of the employed dataset. However, additional experiments are needed to prove this assumption.

Table 1. Mean of performance metrics computed on 119 images using background seeds outside the breast.

Radius	Accuracy	Precision	Recall	Jaccard Index	Dice Coefficient
0	0.9896	0.6675	0.3130	0.2021	0.3277
5	0.9896	0.6319	0.4241	0.2510	0.3827
10	0.9896	0.6044	0.5205	0.2794	0.4233
25	0.9887	0.5128	0.7384	0.3260	0.4668
50	0.9825	0.3372	0.6897	0.2523	0.3596
75	0.9718	0.1873	0.3337	0.1369	0.1993
100	0.9589	0.0987	0.1613	0.0677	0.1025
given	0.9840	0.3030	0.8439	0.2681	0.4107

Table 2. Mean of performance metrics computed on 119 images without using background seeds.

Radius	Accuracy	Precision	Recall	Jaccard Index	Dice Coefficient
0	0.9841	0.6588	0.3154	0.1997	0.3239
5	0.9833	0.6164	0.4274	0.2401	0.3749
10	0.9827	0.5876	0.5253	0.2718	0.4118
25	0.9801	0.4873	0.7525	0.3108	0.4667
50	0.9661	0.3223	0.7275	0.2404	0.3441
75	0.9463	0.1756	0.3805	0.1275	0.1867
100	0.9208	0.0909	0.2091	0.0617	0.0936
given	0.9714	0.2814	0.8562	0.2536	0.3901

5   Conclusions and Future Work

In this paper we propose a novel method of automatically generating foreground seeds for mammography segmentation using the Threshold-based GrowCut algorithm. Starting with the premise that the center of the mass is most likely to be correctly labeled as foreground, we limit the human expert intervention to the selection of a sole foreground seed - the center of the mass - and then construct the foreground seeds set as a circle whose center corresponds to that of the mass and the radius chosen experimentally.

We analyze six different radius values and test the proposed method on images containing 119 abnormalities from the mini-MIAS database, in two manners: using background seeds outside the breast and not using background seeds at all. We compare the results, both qualitatively and quantitatively, to one another and to the results obtained when using only the center of the mass, as proposed in [1], and the ones obtained when employing the ground truth as foreground seeds, as proposed in [8]. Analyzing the results, we conclude that the optimal combination for decreasing the human intervention is the usage of the black pixels from the original image as background seeds and a circle with the center in the center of the mass and a radius of 25 pixels as foreground seeds.

In the future, we aim to analyze to a greater extent the impact that the number and the position of the seed points can have on the results and consider an adaptive foreground seeds circle radius size. Additionally, we intend to remove the need for human intervention completely, with a method for choosing the center of the foreground seeds circle in an automated manner.

References

1. Cordeiro, F.R., Santos, W.P., Silva-Filho, A.G.: An adaptive semi-supervised fuzzy GrowCut algorithm to segment masses of regions of interest of mammographic images. Appl. Soft Comput. **46**, 613–628 (2016)
2. Dafni Rose, J., VijayaKumar, K., Singh, L., Sharma, S.K.: Computer-aided diagnosis for breast cancer detection and classification using optimal region growing segmentation with MobileNet model. Concurr. Eng. **30**(2), 181–189 (2022)
3. Dice, L.R.: Measures of the amount of ecologic association between species. Ecology **26**(3), 297–302 (1945)
4. Ge, F., Wang, S., Liu, T.: New benchmark for image segmentation evaluation. J. Electron. Imaging **16**(3), 033011 (2007)
5. Ghosh, P., Antani, S.K., Long, L.R., Thoma, G.R.: Unsupervised grow-cut: cellular automata-based medical image segmentation. In: 2011 IEEE First International Conference on Healthcare Informatics, Imaging and Systems Biology, pp. 40–47. IEEE (2011)
6. Heath, M., Bowyer, K., Kopans, D., Moore, R., Kegelmeyer, P.: The digital database for screening mammography, iwdm-2000 (2001)
7. International Agency for Research on Cancer: Global cancer observatory: Cancer today (2020). Accessed 20 Apr 2022
8. Moroz-Dubenco, C., Dioşan, L., Andreica, A.: Mammography lesion detection using an improved GrowCut algorithm. Procedia Comput. Sci. **192**, 308–317 (2021)
9. Sadad, T., Munir, A., Saba, T., Hussain, A.: Fuzzy c-means and region growing based classification of tumor from mammograms using hybrid texture feature. J. Comput. Sci. **29**, 34–45 (2018)
10. Suckling J, P.: The mammographic image analysis society digital mammogram database. Digital Mammo, pp. 375–386 (1994)
11. Taha, A.A., Hanbury, A.: Metrics for evaluating 3D medical image segmentation: analysis, selection, and tool. BMC Med. Imaging **15**(1), 1–28 (2015)
12. Vezhnevets, V., Konouchine, V.: GrowCut: interactive multi-label nd image segmentation by cellular automata. In: Proceedings of the Graphicon, vol. 1, pp. 150–156. Citeseer (2005)
13. Zhang, H., Fritts, J.E., Goldman, S.A.: Image segmentation evaluation: a survey of unsupervised methods. Comput. Vis. Image Underst. **110**(2), 260–280 (2008)

DeepLabV3+ Ensemble for Diagnosis of Cardiac Transplant Rejection

Ivan Vykopal[1]([✉]) [iD], Lukas Hudec[1] [iD], Martin Kveton[2] [iD], Ondrej Fabian[2] [iD], Andrea Felsoova[2], and Wanda Benesova[1] [iD]

[1] Faculty of Informatics and Information Technologies, Slovak University of Technology, Ilkovicova 2, Bratislava, Slovakia
{xvykopal,lukas.hudec,vanda_benesova}@stuba.sk
[2] Clinical and Transplant Pathology Centre, Institute for Clinical and Experimental Medicine, Videnska 1958/9, 140 21 Prague 4, Czech Republic
{martin.kveton,fabo,fela}@ikem.cz

Abstract. Heart transplantation is a complex procedure, often joined with complications such as cardiac transplant rejection. Current diagnostic methods include regular invasive and time-consuming biopsies followed by histopathological analysis. Deep learning has the potential to significantly enhance speed and objectivity and introduce new information from the obtained sample to increase the chances of predicting rejection. Our study presents several deep-learning approaches for quantitative analysis of histological scans for acquiring supportive information. The proposed segmentation methods focus on inflammation, endocardium, and blood vessels. The study compares the experimental results of multiple methods evaluated using real data from medical experts. This study lays the groundwork for future research and demonstrates the potential of deep learning applied to the prediction of transplant rejection.

Keywords: Acute Allograft Rejection · Deep Learning · Computer Vision · Semantic Segmentation

1 Introduction

Every patient with a heart transplant undergoes regular medical examinations during which a heart biopsy is taken. A heart biopsy involves extracting a small tissue sample from the heart, which can cause significant stress for patients due to its invasive nature. Considering this reason, doctors want to obtain as much information as possible when evaluating the samples. The analysis is a challenging task requiring the experience and time of pathologists to evaluate the tissue to determine the patient's treatment properly. The entire process, starting from conducting a heart biopsy to the final evaluation of the images, is essential for identifying and potentially preventing any rejection issues following a heart transplant. A major area of doctor's interest is inflammatory regions that

H. I. Christensen et al. (Eds.): ICVS 2023, LNCS 14253, pp. 112–122, 2023.
https://doi.org/10.1007/978-3-031-44137-0_10

pose a high risk of cardiac rejection and blood vessels that may be its gateway to the muscle tissue. The current approaches require manual annotation, cell counting, and area approximation. Deep learning offers enhancement through the automatic segmentation of these regions. Digital pathology evolved over the last decades and now allows doctors to evaluate medical images more efficiently, facilitating quantitative analysis for the doctors. The research presents an opportunity to incorporate artificial intelligence to assess scans and incorporate simultaneous analysis from multiple resolutions and magnifications. The combination of digital pathology and artificial intelligence can enhance the current state-of-the-art and automate the process of analyzing histological scans and provide additional objective information, providing doctors with much more information to state a patient's condition.

In this work, we compare several approaches for segmenting higher morphological structures along with our proposed methods consisting of multiple resolutions, mimicking the image analysis performed by pathologists. We focus on identifying the best approaches for segmenting structures with the most significant impact from a diagnostic point of view. The main objective of our research is to provide complementary objective quantitative data that doctors can use to evaluate and assess individual stages of cardiac transplant rejection rather than completely replacing medical experts with automatic image analysis. The motivation of this work is to enhance the current manual analysis of histological scans obtained after cardiac biopsy with quantitative statistical information that may help predict heart transplant rejection in the early stages.

Our main contributions are:

1. Analysis of several state-of-the-art methods for segmentation of higher morphological structures in histological images.
2. Introduction of custom segmentation models based on the U-Net architecture specialized for multi-magnification histology images.
3. State-of-the-art approach and trained models for combined segmentation of blood vessels, inflammation, and endocardium.

2 Related Work

A significant application of deep learning and, in particular, convolutional neural networks in medicine is in the area of image data detection, classification, and segmentation. Some of the most explored areas using neural networks include identifying brain, breast, and lung diseases.

In the medical image data segmentation, encoder-decoder architectures are very commonly used. Examples of these architectures are the U-Net proposed by Ronneberg et al. [10] and its extension U-Net++ [12]. Other novel segmentation networks used in the medical domain include the Attention U-Net proposed by Oktay et al. [8]. The architecture enhances the U-Net by adding attention gates that aim to filter features propagated through skip connections. Li et al. [6] proposed a Multiscale U-Net for semantic segmentation of histological images, in which they work with three image scales, trying to capture contextual information based on the larger neighborhood of the analyzed patch. The advantage of the wider neighborhood is utilized in DeepLabV3+ architecture [3] and applied for semantic segmentation, for which it performed very well on the PASCAL VOC dataset. It has been later proved that this architecture achieves state-of-the-art results also in the medical domain.

In digital pathology, tools such as QuPath [1] or MONAI Label [4] are widely used to enhance the analysis of histological images. These tools allow pathologists to segment and classify primarily cells, while QuPath uses traditional machine-learning methods for cell segmentation and classification. Some of the shortcomings of the QuPath are addressed by MONAI Label, an open-source framework for the application of neural networks for histological image analysis.

The method proposed by Peyster et al. [9] is designed to classify histological images into a four-level ISHLT scale for acute cellular rejection. This method consists of feature extraction based on the segmentation of nuclei and lymphocyte clusters, and for classification, they use a support vector machine.

Lipkova et al. [7] developed a deep learning-based method for identifying cardiac allograft rejection. The CRANE method processes whole slide images (WSI) stained with hematoxylin and eosin staining. It focuses on important aspects of cardiac rejection diagnosis, including detection of rejection, classification of the level, and detection of Quilty B lesions. F. Giuste et al. [5] proposed a procedure for analyzing histological images and labeling risk regions for possible rejection using semi-supervised learning with a weak teacher.

Our research aims to provide a quantitative analysis of which results could be used as biomarkers to support the possible longitudinal diagnostic process. In collaboration with pathologists, we strive to acquire as much valuable data from invasive biopsy tissue as possible to enhance objectivity and achieve more precise diagnostic outcomes. Our focus is particularly on segmenting and analyzing diagnostically important regions.

3   Our Approach

We experimentally analyze the performance of DeepLabV3+, Stacked U-Net, and mU-Net++ architectures we developed for segmenting higher morphological structures: blood vessels, inflammation, and endocardium.

3.1   Dataset

The research is conducted in cooperation with the Institute for Clinical and Experimental Medicine (IKEM) in Prague. The histologists provided a scanned and annotated dataset of 25 H&E and 20 SRel stained whole slide images obtained via an endomyocardial heart biopsy. Each WSI contains 3–5 1–3 mm long tissue slices obtained from a single patient. In addition to the WSI scans, we have access to a QuPath project with a threshold-based cell detector and a weakly-trained classifier. This provides us with automatically generated cell annotations of three distinct categories: immune, muscle, and other cells.

The doctors from IKEM have manually annotated higher morphological structures that cannot be segmented by methods available in the QuPath tool. The list of annotated structures is in Table 1 with the number of samples and area of each class. The most important from a diagnostic perspective are the blood vessels, inflammation, and endocardium.

Table 1. Number of samples and data distribution in the provided dataset.

Class	Samples	Area [px^2]
Blood vessels	648	16 851 452
Inflammation	596	82 498 898
Endocariums	128	61 270 896
Fat tissue	47	22 660 865
Quilty lesions	5	537 758
Fibrotic tissue	1	14 363

3.2 Data Preprocessing

A crucial step of all our experiments is to preprocess the data. Large-scale WSI scans have to be transformed into smaller patches, an image format legible for the training of neural networks. As part of the initial preprocessing steps, we extracted tissue fragments from all images based on minimal bounding boxes enclosing the identified tissue regions in the WSI scans obtained from the QuPath tool. We stored the tissue fragments from the WSI scans at three magnifications: original, half-size, and quarter-size, providing data for multiple scales we experiment with. Figure 1 shows an example of an extracted fragment from WSI. Along with the generated fragments, we store the patch information needed to train our models, where our stored information represents patches obtained from sliding windows with 50% overlay. The patch sizes for which we created information are 256×256 and 512×512, filtering out 90% patches that do not contain any annotation created by the doctors.

As mentioned, doctors expect blood vessels, inflammation, and endocardium as morphological structures that can contain important information to predict heart transplant rejection correctly. The exports from QuPath are the GeoJSON polygons. The annotations for fibrotic tissue, fat tissue, or quilty lesions were problematic with their small variability and area coverage. Based on the analysis and consultation with the doctors, we simplified the classification problem of quilty lesions by combining it with inflammation. The fat tissue annotations were used as a negative class for blood cells.

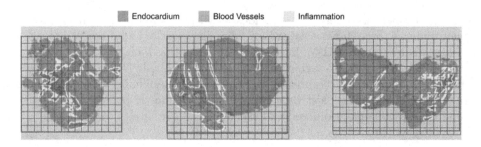

Fig. 1. Preprocessing of data: tissue fragment detection and windowing

We set the resulting area of each class to approximately 50M pixels^2. Increasing the variability of patches with blood vessels, as the smallest class, required horizontal, vertical, and horizontal-vertical flips. We further filtered out images containing the endocardial class, where this class was not located at the tissue edge. As the endocardium is located only on the edge, this would help understand the network of the meta-information. For the inflammation class, some patches were removed randomly to balance the total area for each class. We split our final class-balanced data, approximately 80:20, into training and validation sets.

3.3   DeepLabV3+

The fundamental building block of the DeepLabV3+ architecture is the Atrous Spatial Pyramid Pooling module, which allows each pixel to be classified based on its wider surroundings, which is suitable for histology image analysis. The experiments were conducted as multiclass segmentation, where the order of annotations played a crucial role when the regions overlapped.

The pre-trained ResNet-50 model on the ImageNet dataset was used as the backbone of the DeepLabV3+ architecture, which we employ in the encoder part of the model. We have trained three DeepLabV3+ models, each preferring a different class, making them expert models in the ensemble. The training ran for 25 epochs with a batch size of 4 with the patch size of the processed patches 512×512. The result is the union of the three models' predictions for each class individually to create the final segmentation map.

3.4   Stacked U-Net

We propose a modified version of the U-Net architecture we call Stacked U-net. The input is two images in L*a*b* color space of different resolutions containing local and detailed information, based on which we perform segmentation. We selected the LAB color model due to its implicit ability to distinguish between color shades by definition, making it suitable for histology image analysis. The patches are extracted from the original magnification. The local patch has a resolution of $512 \times 512p$. It is the main input in the first convolutional layer, and the patch with detailed information is 256×256p input to the layer after the first MaxPooling downscale. Another modification of the U-Net architecture consists of our architecture's outputs. In the decoder part, we create output masks from the two decoder levels that correspond to the level of the two input layers. In our architecture (see Fig. 2), we used the CBAM block, proposed by Woo et al. [11], which consists of two modules, channel and spatial attention module, through which the input vector is processed and with the use of this block, the part of the vector that is most relevant for segmentation is identified.

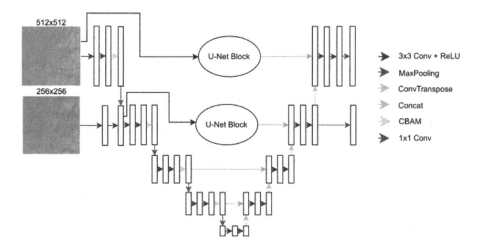

Fig. 2. Stacked U-Net architecture

In our experiments, in addition to the elementary loss functions for each level, we added a combined loss function (see Eq. 2) that worked with the ground truth mask for the detailed image (256×256p). We created a patch from the center of the predicted masks from both levels with size 256×256p, which we combined with the union operation to the final mask. Within the loss function, the predicted mask was optimized with respect to the actual mask for the detailed image. For this combined loss function, we took inspiration from experiments with the DeepLabV3+ architecture using Sparse Categorical CrossEntropy (SCCE), where we adapted the resulting mask union for the combined output to the principle of multiclass segmentation. We used the DiceFocal loss Eq. 1 where additional to TP, FP, FN, $\log(p_t)$ is calculated using the binary cross entropy and p_t as the inverse function of the binary cross entropy.

$$DiceFocal = -(1 - p_t)^\gamma \log(p_t) + (1 - \frac{2TP}{2TP + FP + FN}) \tag{1}$$

The combined loss function is defined as follows:

$$Combined = SCCE(O'_{true}, ((O'_1 + O'_2)/2) > 0.25) \tag{2}$$

where O'_{true} is a true 256×256p detail mask, O'_1 and O'_2 represent the output predictions from the two output branches, where we extracted a 256×256 patch from the center of the output mask.

The final loss function for Stacked U-Net is defined as follows:

$$Loss = (DiceFocal_{O_1} + 0.75 * DiceFocal_{O_2} + 1.25 * Combined)/3 \qquad (3)$$

where we calculated DiceFocal loss for the output for each of the two output branches with the combined loss function.

3.5   mU-Net++

We designed another modified version of U-Net++ architecture, which we called mU-Net++. We use additional information for segmenting high morphological structures in the form of binary segmentation masks of nuclei and the lower resolution patch that represent a downscaling of the original patch. This downscaled patch is added to the second layer of the encoder - similar to a Stacked U-Net. Two 3×3 convolutions are performed over the added slice, which is then input to the original U-Net++ architecture.

During our experiments, we used the original patch size 256×256; for additional information, we used patch size 128×128. We used the DiceFocal loss with the Adam optimizer and the patches' overlay for the training. The training process took over 45 epochs using a batch size of 16.

3.6   Post-processing

To achieve the best segmentation results for each morphological structure, it is possible to apply postprocessing with meta-information about the morphology of classes. This helps to filter incorrect and improve the correct predictions.

These heuristics include the removal of the endocardium inside the tissue, inflammation areas containing less than 10 immune cells, blood vessel predictions outside of the tissue (white background), and the fusion of neighboring endocardium regions. The second part of post-processing focuses on adjusting the shape of the predictions and removing small segmented regions and artifacts using a morphological opening with the horizontal kernel.

4   Results

The experiments were evaluated on a validation dataset selected from annotations provided by pathologists. The experiments were trained on two types of computational resources: one computer with NVIDIA GeForce RTX 2060 with 6 GB GPU RAM and the second with NVIDIA P100 with 16 GB GPU RAM.

4.1   Models Evaluation

The models are evaluated by Intersection over Union (IoU) and Dice score. Both metrics provide information about how much of the true mask the model correctly predicted. Dice score and IoU are calculated over separate WSI images and then averaged across the whole validation scans with annotations.

Table 2. Compared results: proposed architectures, vanilla U-Net and U-Net++

Model	Blood vessels		Inflammation		Endocardium	
	IoU	Dice	IoU	Dice	IoU	Dice
DeepLabV3+	0.31	**0.45**	0.53	**0.68**	0.44	**0.59**
mU-Net++	0.23	0.35	0.46	<u>0.61</u>	0.42	<u>0.57</u>
Stacked U-Net	0.23	0.35	0.41	0.55	0.41	0.56
U-Net++	0.24	0.37	0.41	0.56	0.38	0.53
U-Net	0.29	<u>0.42</u>	0.39	0.54	0.25	0.39

Based on the results in Table 2, the best results were achieved by DeepLabV3+ architecture, where the encoder was pre-trained on the ImageNet dataset, with three expert models in an ensemble that predicted three final classes. The ensemble combination achieved better results compared to the predictions of individual models. Figure 3 shows the DeepLabV3+ models ensemble predictions.

DeepLabV3+, compared to the other models, dealt better with blood vessel regions, which were difficult for all other models to predict. The possible reason could be their heterogeneity and similarity to fatty tissue. The individual models could not generalize and identify blood vessels well from the images, even with the information gained from the larger patches. This difference in blood vessel prediction is around 8% on IoU and 9% on the Dice compared to mU-Net++.

The results for the second-best model for each class are underlined in both tables. As the second-best model, we can consider mU-Net++ with additional information using nuclei masks and the lower resolution. For all models, the best results are achieved for the inflammation class, with the endocardium in second place. For the initial experiments without using post-processing based on defined heuristics, we obtained, on average, 7% worse results for each class.

In most cases, the ensemble of methods using DeepLabV3+ architecture and Stacked U-Net did not identify blood vessels that pathologists annotated. In the case of mU-Net++, many false positive blood vessels in the predictions decreased the overall results. We conducted training using weakly annotated data and attained satisfactory outcomes, which were validated through consultations with doctors, affirming the effectiveness of our approach in the study.

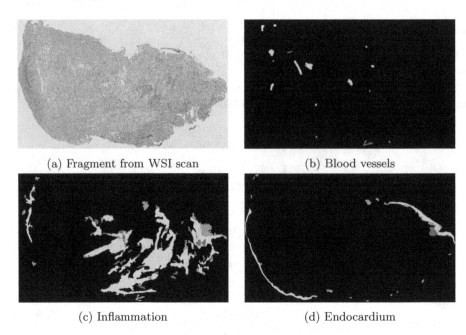

(a) Fragment from WSI scan   (b) Blood vessels

(c) Inflammation   (d) Endocardium

Fig. 3. Predictions made by an ensemble of DeepLabV3+ models. The red color represents the annotation, the green is the prediction, and the yellow is the intersection of correct segmentation. (Color figure online)

5   Conclusions and Discussion

This research presents a novel approach for segmenting higher morphological structures in images obtained after the cardiac biopsy to identify a potential risk of heart transplant rejection. Within the scope of our proposed approaches, we aim to segment three diagnostically important structures found in histological images after cardiac biopsy: blood vessels, inflammation, and endocardium. We present and test our method on H&E, but we also experimented with SRel staining, which better highlights the endocardium. The pathologists concluded that the results are satisfactory and sufficient for further research.

In our work, we experimentally compared three neural network architectures for segmenting higher morphological structures, which we evaluated quantitatively using Intersection over Union and Dice score. Among the approaches we presented, the best results were achieved by the ensemble of methods approach using the DeepLabV3+ architecture, in which we trained three models and combined their predictions into a final one.

This paper introduces new techniques and advanced methods for segmenting heart structures in histological data after cardiac biopsy. To our current knowledge, it is the first work to specifically focus on segmenting blood vessels, inflammation, and endocardium in this type of data. Therefore, we focused mainly on getting the best possible results for cardiac transplant rejection diagnosis, even maybe without introducing a novel state-of-the-art architecture. As there is no prior research specific to our case, we compared our methods to similar ones where we prioritize the segmentation of higher morphological structures.

The paper by Chan et al. [2] focused on segmenting multiple structures found in histological data. One version aims to segment structures into four classes and backgrounds. As a result, they report the average IoU value across all segmented structures, whereas in the case of 4-class segmentation and background, the average IoU value is 55%. Our results using the DeepLabV3+ model achieved an average value of approximately 43% for the three classes we segmented. One of the differences with the work of Chan et al. is their non-overlapping annotations, while in our research, some annotations may overlap.

We see further opportunity to extend our work by segmenting more morphological structures to create a more generic model for structure segmentation that could identify, for instance, fat tissue in addition to blood vessels, inflammation, and endocardium, with a possible extension of the work to identify quilty lesions once sufficient data are available. In future work, there is a possibility of creating and exploring active learning and the Human-in-the-loop method to allow the doctors to gather more data and fine-tune the existing models or to train a more generic model on a larger amount of data.

Our solution is available as an extension for the MONAI Label [4], which can be used within the QuPath tool [1]. The source code of our extension is publicly available on GitHub (https://github.com/ivanvykopal/MONAILabel).

Acknowledgement. This work was partially supported by STU Grant Scheme for supporting excellent teams of young researchers #1344 and Cooperation (Financial support) with Siemens Healthineers Slovakia.

References

1. Bankhead, P., et al.: QuPath: open source software for digital pathology image analysis. Sci. Rep. **7**(1), 1–7 (2017). https://doi.org/10.1038/s41598-017-17204-5
2. Chan, L., Hosseini, M.S., Rowsell, C., Plataniotis, K.N., Damaskinos, S.: HistoSeg-Net: semantic segmentation of histological tissue type in whole slide images. In: Proceedings of the IEEE/CVF International Conference on Computer Vision, pp. 10662–10671 (2019)
3. Chen, L.C., Zhu, Y., Papandreou, G., Schroff, F., Adam, H.: Encoder-decoder with atrous separable convolution for semantic image segmentation. In: Proceedings of the European Conference on Computer Vision (ECCV), pp. 801–818 (2018)
4. Diaz-Pinto, A., et al.: MONAI label: a framework for AI-assisted interactive labeling of 3D medical images. arXiv e-prints (2022)
5. Giuste, F., et al.: Automated classification of acute rejection from endomyocardial biopsies. In: Proceedings of the 11th ACM International Conference on Bioinformatics, Computational Biology and Health Informatics, pp. 1–9. Association for Computing Machinery (2020). https://doi.org/10.1145/3388440.3412430
6. Li, J., et al.: A multi-scale U-net for semantic segmentation of histological images from radical prostatectomies. In: AMIA Annual Symposium Proceedings, vol. 2017, p. 1140. American Medical Informatics Association (2017)

7. Lipkova, J., et al.: Deep learning-enabled assessment of cardiac allograft rejection from endomyocardial biopsies. Nat. Med. **28**(3), 575–582 (2022). https://doi.org/10.1038/s41591-022-01709-2

8. Oktay, O., et al.: Attention U-net: learning where to look for the pancreas (2018). https://doi.org/10.48550/arXiv.1804.03999

9. Peyster, E.G., et al.: An automated computational image analysis pipeline for histological grading of cardiac allograft rejection. Eur. Heart J. **42**(24), 2356–2369 (2021). https://doi.org/10.1093/eurheartj/ehab241

10. Ronneberger, O., Fischer, P., Brox, T.: U-net: convolutional networks for biomedical image segmentation. In: Navab, N., Hornegger, J., Wells, W.M., Frangi, A.F. (eds.) MICCAI 2015. LNCS, vol. 9351, pp. 234–241. Springer, Cham (2015). https://doi.org/10.1007/978-3-319-24574-4_28

11. Woo, S., Park, J., Lee, J.Y., Kweon, I.S.: CBAM: convolutional block attention module. In: Proceedings of the European Conference on Computer Vision (ECCV), pp. 3–19 (2018)

12. Zhou, Z., Siddiquee, M.M.R., Tajbakhsh, N., Liang, J.: UNet++: redesigning skip connections to exploit multiscale features in image segmentation. EEE Trans. Med. Imaging **39**(6), 1856–1867 (2020). https://doi.org/10.1109/TMI.2019.2959609

Farming and Forestry

Of Mice and Pose: 2D Mouse Pose Estimation from Unlabelled Data and Synthetic Prior

Jose Sosa[1]($\boxtimes$) (iD), Sharn Perry[2] (iD), Jane Alty[2,3] (iD), and David Hogg[1] (iD)

[1] School of Computing, University of Leeds, Leeds, UK
{scjasm,d.c.hogg}@leeds.ac.uk
[2] Wicking Dementia Research and Education Centre, College of Health and Medicine, University of Tasmania, Hobart, Australia
{sharn.perry,jane.alty}@utas.edu.au
[3] School of Medicine, College of Health and Medicine, University of Tasmania, Hobart, Australia

Abstract. Numerous fields, such as ecology, biology, and neuroscience, use animal recordings to track and measure animal behaviour. Over time, a significant volume of such data has been produced, but some computer vision techniques cannot explore it due to the lack of annotations. To address this, we propose an approach for estimating 2D mouse body pose from unlabelled images using a synthetically generated empirical pose prior. Our proposal is based on a recent self-supervised method for estimating 2D human pose that uses single images and a set of unpaired typical 2D poses within a GAN framework. We adapt this method to the limb structure of the mouse and generate the empirical prior of 2D poses from a synthetic 3D mouse model, thereby avoiding manual annotation. In experiments on a new mouse video dataset, we evaluate the performance of the approach by comparing pose predictions to a manually obtained ground truth. We also compare predictions with those from a supervised state-of-the-art method for animal pose estimation. The latter evaluation indicates promising results despite the lack of paired training data. Finally, qualitative results using a dataset of horse images show the potential of the setting to adapt to other animal species.

Keywords: Self-Supervised · Pose Estimation · Synthetic · Mouse

1 Introduction

The study of neurodegenerative human diseases, such as Alzheimer's disease [30], Parkinson's disease [14], and Amyotrophic Lateral Sclerosis (ALS) [27], usually involves using animal models. Mice are the preferred and most extensively utilised animals for such studies because of their genomics similarity with humans and the accumulated knowledge on manipulating their DNA [8]. Due to

H. I. Christensen et al. (Eds.): ICVS 2023, LNCS 14253, pp. 125–136, 2023.
https://doi.org/10.1007/978-3-031-44137-0_11

this tight relationship between mice and the ongoing research on neurodegenerative human diseases, developing tools to observe, describe, and measure mouse behaviour has become crucial [20].

Some years ago, prior to the adoption of computer vision techniques, making such measurements meant tons of manual labour [24,25]. For example, if someone wanted to measure the position of the mouse's limbs. It implies recording the animal, looking at each video frame, and manually identifying each required body part. Then, it is evident that manual inspections on large videos can be time-consuming and lead to observation errors. Early computational approaches attempt to minimise human intervention in analysing animal recordings. Some tools involve placing physical markers on the animal's body or require painting the body parts to track [1,33]. Apparent limitations of these techniques are that the physical markers can interfere with the animal's behaviour, and the information that can be extracted is inherently limited by the positioning of the markers or the painted areas. Other approaches use sophisticated and expensive equipment to acquire particular images, which results in costly experiments and problems for deployment and replication [5,13].

Newer computer vision tools for tracking body parts of animals[1] become less dependent on physical markers. Unfortunately, these tools still needed considerable human intervention for pre-processing and post-processing video data. Supervised deep learning approaches have recently become state-of-the-art for pose estimation and tracking of humans and animals [19,26]. Performance of these techniques often depends on the amount and variability of annotated data for training, which is hard to obtain for some animal species.

In this paper we tackle the challenging task of predicting 2D mouse poses from unlabelled images. Different from previous deep learning approaches that generally rely on fully supervised frameworks, we adopt a self-supervised 2D pose estimator from the human domain [10]. This method utilises a GAN architecture to learn 2D human poses. During training, it assumes the availability of unlabelled images and an unpaired prior of 2D pose annotations, generally from the same dataset. Our proposal relaxes much more the assumptions about data by building the needed prior of 2D poses using data generated from a 3D model of a generic mouse [3]. Evidently, incorporating synthetic data also provides more flexibility to train the model with entirely unlabelled datasets, which is common for many animal recordings outside of computer vision. Furthermore, our method shows promising results in generating 2D poses for other types of animals, e.g. horses.

2   Related Work

Deep Learning Methods for Animal Pose Estimation. Analogous to the definition of human pose estimation [16], animal pose estimation refers to the task of estimating the geometrical configuration of body parts of an animal. This problem has gained increasing attention because of research applications

---

[1] https://mousespecifics.com/digigait/.

in many different disciplines, including Biology, Biomechanics [31] and Neuroscience [20]. Compared with human pose estimation, it is still relatively underexplored, principally due to the variability of animal species, and the need for species-specific labelled datasets. Nevertheless, a lot of effort has gone into developing and adapting deep learning models to estimate 2D and 3D animal pose. In particular, for large quadrupeds such as dogs [2,28] and farm animals [6,29] by exploiting similarities between their skeletal forms.

Automatic 2D pose estimation has also been applied successfully on smaller animal species such as mice. As with larger animals, deep learning methods for pose estimation, such as DeepLabCut (DLC) [19], LEAP [26], and DeepPoseKit [9], have been based mostly on supervised methods developed for human pose estimation [23,34,35]. A common feature of these approaches is their reliance on manual annotation of pose in multiple video frames. Even though they normally provide a Graphical User Interface (GUI) for doing the annotation, the process is still time consuming, error prone, and requires specialised knowledge to infer pose correctly. Futhermore, the number of frames to annotate for good generalisation is hard to predict and therefore ultimately determined empirically. In contrast, through adapting a recent self-supervised approach from the human domain, we completely remove the need for manual annotation, making training and testing more straightforward.

Animal Pose Estimation with Synthetic Data. One alternative to avoid manual annotation for training deep learning methods for animal pose estimation is the use of synthetic data. Using an artificial animal model allows producing many synthetic images and their corresponding annotations with less time and effort than manually annotating actual data [3]. In this context, Mu et al. [21] proposes a semi-supervised pose-estimation framework trained in a supervised fashion using synthetically rendered images and ground truth pose annotations from 3D Computer-Aided Design (CAD) models. Then, they perform self-supervised domain adaption with a small portion of actual data to minimise the domain gap. They successfully estimate 2D poses for large animals with similar skeletal structures, such as tigers, horses, and dogs. Some other works relying on synthetic data also focus on the domain adaptation process after learning the animal pose with synthetic data under supervised paradigms [11,15]. We adopt a related approach to [21] by using an existing 3D geometric mouse model [3], except that we do not use rendered images as in supervised settings. We only utilise the synthetically generated 2D poses as a prior for training the method. In particular, we use this prior on 2D poses within a GAN framework that allows our whole model to learn poses not necessarily appearing in the prior, eliminating the need for domain adaptation.

Bolaños [3] has taken inspiration from previous synthetic models of large animals [17,36] to develop a similar model for mice. This 3D CAD model simulates semi-random behavioural patterns from real mice and incorporates the 3D structure of bones and joints. The model has successfully created training data for famous supervised 2D and 3D mouse pose estimation approaches [19,22].

Nevertheless, there is still an unexplored opportunity to utilise the same model to generate data for training pose estimation models with lower levels of supervision. We demonstrate this by relying on a recent self-supervised method that learns to estimate 2D human poses solely from unlabelled images and a prior on unpaired 2D poses. We follow the same idea, but instead of taking the unpaired pose annotations from the dataset to build the prior, we generated them with a 3D mouse model [3]. Note that we do not utilise paired synthetic images and pose annotations like in previous works [3,11,15,21], we discard the synthetic images and only use synthetic 2D poses. This means that our model is trained using actual unlabelled images and a smaller set of artificially generated 2D poses.

3   Method

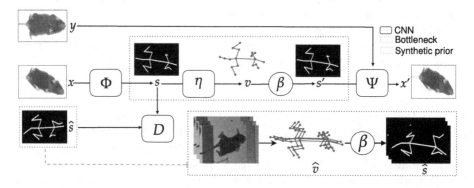

Fig. 1. 2D pose estimator. We use a self-supervised 2D pose estimator from the human domain, which we adapt to work with mice. Differently to the original implementation, we build prior of 2D poses using synthetic data from a 3D model of a generic mouse.

Our method produces a mapping from full body images to the 2D pose of a mouse, as shown in Fig. 1. The pose is represented as an articulated tree structure of 2D line segments corresponding to the parts of the body such as snout, tail, hind limbs, and forelimbs. The method extends the self-supervised approach of [10], which estimates human 2D pose. This 2D pose estimator learns from unlabelled images and uses a set of unpaired 2D poses as a prior. However, for building this prior the method requires a set of manual 2D pose annotations for a subset of images from the dataset, albeit the pairing is discarded. We adapt this approach by changing the pose topology to a mouse model. Most importantly, we generate a prior of 2D poses by projecting from an existing 3D mouse model, which removes the need for manual pose annotation altogether.

The pose-estimator is obtained by training a conditional auto-encoder to map from an image x, depicting a mouse, to a reconstructed image x' that is as similar as possible. The synthesis of the output image is conditioned on an auxiliary mouse image y depicting a fixed pose. The auto-encoder has a bottleneck that encodes the 2D pose as a set of joint positions v. Once trained, our pose predictor is the initial encoder from this network, which maps from an input image to a 2D pose. This mapping is in two steps, consisting of a Convolutional Neural Network (CNN) Φ mapping from the image x to a skeleton image s, followed by a second CNN η mapping from the skeleton image s to the 2D pose v. The decoder mapping from the 2D pose v to the output image x' is also in two steps, consisting of a differentiable function β (same as the one in [10]) which maps the 2D pose v to a skeleton image s'; and a CNN Ψ mapping from the skeleton image s' to the output x'. The second mapping Ψ takes an auxiliary image y as an additional input to compensate for the missing appearance information in s'.

We train the model with a dataset of images $\{x_1 \cdots x_N\}$, depicting mice in different poses, and the prior of synthetic 2D poses. We use a similar loss function as in [10], which contains three terms. The first penalises the difference between the generated image x' and the input x via a perceptual loss. The second term is a regression loss to evaluate the mapping from skeleton image s to the 2D joint positions in v. The third term is an adversarial loss to assess the authenticity of the skeleton images generated in the encoder. In the following sections we provide details on the components of the model, the empirical prior, loss function, and training. The whole pipeline for the conditional auto-encoder is as follows:

$$x = \Psi(\beta(v) \circ \eta(s) \circ \Phi(x), y) \tag{1}$$

We can see the mapping as an autoencoder from input image x to output image x' in which the 2D pose v emerges as an intermediate representation. In training the network, a perceptual loss [12] compares each input image x with the reconstructed image x':

$$\mathcal{L}_{perc} = \frac{1}{N} \sum_{i=1}^{N} \|\Gamma(x_i') - \Gamma(x_i)\|_2^2 \tag{2}$$

where Γ is a pre-trained VGG network [32] with the classification stage removed to utilise the final feature encoding.

A CNN serves as the discriminator network D, which outputs a probability that an input skeleton image comes from the prior distribution of skeleton images. Thus, D measures the extent to which a skeleton image s looks like an authentic skeleton image from the empirical prior distribution. Note that contrary to [10], our prior $\{\hat{v}_j\}_{j=1}^M$ is synthesised by projecting from a 3D mouse model and does not require manual annotation of poses. We obtain the skeleton images $\{\hat{s}_j\}_{j=1}^{j=M}$ via β, i.e. $\{\hat{s}_j = \beta(\hat{v}_j)\}_{j=1}^M$, then we compare this distribution $p_{data}(\hat{s})$ with the distribution $p_{data}(s)$ from the predicted skeleton images $\{s_i = \Phi(x_i)\}_{i=1}^N$ by means of the adversarial loss [18]:

$$\mathcal{L}_D = \frac{1}{M} \sum_{j=1}^{M} D(\hat{s}_j)^2 + \frac{1}{N} \sum_{i=1}^{N} (1 - D(s_i))^2 \tag{3}$$

Finally, we derive a loss from η and β, which combines the two terms as follows:

$$\mathcal{L}_\eta = \|\eta(\hat{s}) - \hat{v}\|^2 + \lambda\|\beta(\eta(s)) - s\|^2 \tag{4}$$

The first term uses unpaired 2D poses from the prior, while the second one utilises the pose on the predicted skeleton image s. The last term ensures that the network learns poses that appear on the training images but not necessarily on the prior. The balancing coefficient λ is set to 0.1 in our experiments.

2D Synthetic Prior. We entirely generate the 2D pose prior required for the discriminator D using synthetic data. In particular, we adopt a synthetic 3D model of a mouse [3]. This animated mouse model simulates synthetic behavioural data using animation and semi-random joint movements. We keep the original joint-constrained movements of the freely moving mouse model. We animate and render the different scenes with the synthetic model and extract the 2D coordinates of 18 joints on the body of the mouse: Snout, Vertebral column base and end (VB and VE), three points located along the tail (TB, TM, and TE), left/right elbows (LE and RE), left/right knees (LK and RK), and two points (tip and top) for each left/right fore and hind limbs (LFP$^{-/+}$, RFP$^{-/+}$, LHP$^{-/+}$, RHP$^{-/+}$). Note that this notation will be used through the paper. Finally, we use those joint positions to create their respective skeleton image, as shown in Fig. 1. Overall, our prior consists of 15,408 different 2D poses transformed into skeleton images.

Training. Following [10] we use a perceptual loss $\mathcal{L}_{perc}$ (2), an adversarial loss $\mathcal{L}_D$ (3), and a regression loss (4) in training the convolutional networks Φ, η, and Ψ. Note that β is not a learnable function. The overall loss $\mathcal{L}$ is given by:

$$\mathcal{L} = \mathcal{L}_D + \mathcal{L}_\eta + \mathcal{L}_{perc} \tag{5}$$

We train the pose estimator using unlabelled images. In particular, each batch is formed by randomly sampling images (x, y), and a random sample $\hat{v}$ from the synthetic 2D poses, which is then transformed to skeleton image $\hat{s}$. The input images x and y were resized to 128×128 pixels. We set the batch size to 32 and use Adam optimiser with a learning rate of 2×10^{-4}. Unlike [10] who use a pretrained η, we train all the neural networks Φ, D, η, and Ψ from scratch by optimising the loss function in Eq. 5. During testing, we only rely on the trained networks Φ and η, to map from an input image to a 2D pose.

4   Experiments

Dataset. Our dataset contains images from 40 videos of rodent models of ALS of different genotypes. Each video has around $13,120$ frames/images, with an original size of 658×190 pixels. We use half of the available videos to get the training images, and reserve the other half for evaluation purposes.

Acquisition Details. The recordings were made using the Digigait^{TM} apparatus, which consists of a transparent treadmill and a camera placed underneath. Mice at both 4 and 16 weeks of age were first acclimatised in the apparatus and then encouraged to run on the treadmill at 10 cm/s, 20 cm/s and 30 cm/s for a minimum of 10 s. The camera captures the mice on video as they move on the treadmill.

Results. Given an unlabelled image depicting a mouse, our trained model produces a 2D representation of the mouse pose composed of 18 joint positions. Figure 2 shows some of those predicted 2D poses. Since our dataset does not contain annotations for the joint positions, we manually annotated 2D poses for some images from the test videos to provide ground truth for a quantitative measure of prediction performance. We compare pose predictions with ground-truth on this test set using the Mean Per Joint Position Error (MPJPE). The first row of Table 1 shows the MPJPE in pixels between the predicted positions for each of the joints composing the mouse pose and their respective ground truth annotations. MPJPE is reported w.r.t to the original image dimensions.

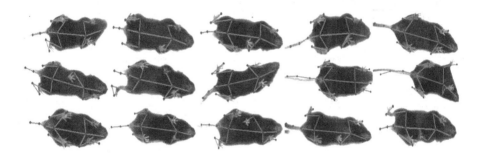

Fig. 2. Estimated 2D poses using our method. During training we use real images and the synthetic pose prior: **RI + SP**.

In addition to the previous experiment, we train and evaluate our model using synthetic images and synthetic unpaired poses (SI + SP). Note that the synthetic 2D poses on the prior are not annotations of the training images. We train the model with different sequences of images synthetically generated from the 3D mouse model and test it using a different set of synthetic images. We use the 2D ground truth annotations for 18 joint positions extracted from the mouse model and compare them with the predicted poses. We report the MPJPE for each joint position in the second row of Table 1.

DLC Comparison. In the absence of a more extensive set of annotated images for evaluating all our predictions, we also report on a quantitative comparison with the predictions from a state-of-the-art supervised method for animal pose

Table 1. MPJPE of predicted poses. **RI + SP** denotes use of the method trained with **R**eal **I**mages and **S**ynthetic **P**rior. **SI + SP** denotes use of the method trained with **S**ynthetic **I**mages and **S**ynthetic **P**rior.

Joints	Snout	VCB	VCE	TB	TM	TE	RE	RFP⁻	RFP⁺	Avg.
	LE	LFP⁻	LFP⁺	RK	RHP⁻	RHP⁺	LK	LHP⁻	LHP⁺	
RI + SP	13.4	8.0	5.6	15.2	17.8	31.8	14.7	15.8	14.8	**14.1**
	12.7	10.5	14.2	7.6	21.1	11.5	14.9	11.7	11.9	
SI + SP	5.9	4.0	3.0	3.7	4.3	6.2	5.9	6.6	7.1	**5.3**
	5.9	6.9	7.0	4.1	5.2	6.0	4.0	5.1	5.0	

estimation: DeepLabCut [19]. The motivation for performing this comparison is to show that our self-supervised approach can work similarly to this supervised method, removing the requirement to annotate 2D poses for training. To build the training set for DLC, we select a subset of 100 consecutive images from one video and label 18 joint positions in each one. We then use these images and their labelled 2D poses to train a DLC model in a supervised fashion. We follow the official implementation of DLC [19]. Using the trained DLC model, we then predict the pose for unseen data.

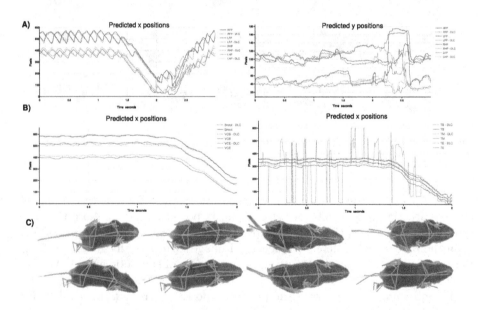

Fig. 3. Comparison of our predicted joint positions against the ones predicted by DLC. **A)** Predictions for RFP, LFP, RHP, and LHP. **B)** Predictions for snout, vertebral column, and tail. **C)**Visual comparison of predicted poses by DLC and our method. Green - ours; pink - DLC. (Color figure online)

We compare the predictions of our method against the ones produced by DLC. Each estimated body joint position is represented as a (x, y) pair of coordinates on the image plane. Figure 3 summarises the results of our comparison. Note that each graph contains our estimated positions (indicated with lines) for a given joint together with the ones estimated by DLC (indicated by dotted lines). In the inset legend, we use the label 'DLC' after the name of the joint to identify the predicted joint positions by DeepLabCut. The predictions of our method simply appear as the name of the joint. Finally, we assess quantitatively the predictions of DLC with the same ground-truth of that we used to evaluate predictions from the self-supervised method. Table 2 shows the MPJPE of DLC predictions and their respective ground truth. As expected, the overall MPJPE is lower for DLC. This may be explained in part by the use of supervision in training DLC, albeit on a limited dataset, and the consistency with which joint positions are manually located in producing ground-truth for the training and testing images.

Table 2. MPJPE of predicted poses with DLC.

Joints	Snout	VCB	VCE	TB	TM	TE	RE	RFP$^-$	RFP$^+$	Avg.
	LE	LFP$^-$	LFP$^+$	RK	RHP$^-$	RHP$^+$	LK	LHP$^-$	LHP$^+$	
DLC	4.7	16.3	18.2	4.0	7.2	20.2	7.8	5.4	5.1	**8.5**
	6.5	5.7	9.8	5.6	5.3	6.1	7.2	9.0	8.3	

Adaptation. We demonstrate that our experimental setting, i.e. using synthetic prior and actual data for training, is adaptable to other animal structures. We build a dataset of horse images using a combination of individual frames from YouTube videos depicting horses in motion and horse images from the TigDog dataset [7]. The 2D poses for the synthetic prior come from the synthetic horse model of [21]. We train the model using our dataset of approximately 30k horse images and a prior of 10k synthetic 2D poses. Once trained, we evaluate it utilising an out-distribution dataset [4] and some horse images from the videos and TigDog [7] that were excluded during training. In addition, we test our model's generalisation capacities using images depicting zebras [37]. Note that we use the same trained model for all the cases; surprisingly, the model still does well on the zebras, although the training set does not contain images of these animals. Figure 4 shows the qualitative results of the 2D poses predicted by our trained model on different data.

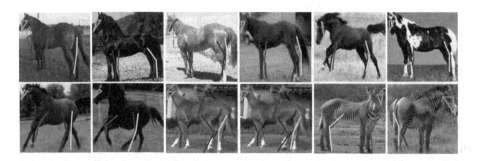

Fig. 4. First row: Pose predictions using images from [4]. **Second row:** Pose predictions using images from [7] and [37].

5   Discussion and Conclusion

Supervised methods learn from annotated poses on the training data, which makes them dependent on the quality of those annotations. Although some joint positions are easy to annotate, others require domain specialists to locate them. Contrary to the supervised methods, our approach is not dependent on the quality of the annotations since it learns from skeleton images generated from synthetic poses. The method produces similar 2D poses to those obtained using DLC (Section C of Fig. 3), and its quantitative performance in terms of MPJPE against ground-truth annotations is not significantly different from DLC.

According to the plots in Fig. 3, despite some visible differences between our method and DLC for specific body parts, most graphs show smooth lines for our predictions. When comparing both methods against ground truth annotations, as expected, the overall performance of DLC is superior. This is probably due in part to the consistency of manual annotation of ground-truth joint locations used in both training and testing of DLC. Our experiment using synthetic images and a synthetic pose prior demonstrates that accurate predictions can be made by matching the pose prior and image domains.

In conclusion, we successfully adapted a self-supervised 2D human pose estimation method to a different animal domain, replacing an empirical prior associated with actual 2D poses with a synthetic prior. We have demonstrated that the approach produces promising results compared to a state-of-the-art supervised approach in the mouse domain. An important motivation for our work has been to explore an approach that can be rapidly deployed to other animal domains without requiring extensive annotation of images. We demonstrate the latter qualitatively using a dataset of horse images. Finally, we plan to use our estimated 2D poses to measure gait on genetically modified mice with different levels of ALS disease. These measures could help to identify and classify patterns related to the development of the disease.

Acknowledgments. Special thanks to Rebecca Stone and Mohammed Alghamdi from the University of Leeds for great discussions and insightful feedback.

References

1. Bender, J.A., Simpson, E.M., Ritzmann, R.E.: Computer-assisted 3D kinematic analysis of all leg joints in walking insects. PLoS ONE **5**(10), e13617 (2010)
2. Biggs, B., Boyne, O., Charles, J., Fitzgibbon, A., Cipolla, R.: Who left the dogs out? 3D animal reconstruction with expectation maximization in the loop. In: Vedaldi, A., Bischof, H., Brox, T., Frahm, J.-M. (eds.) ECCV 2020. LNCS, vol. 12356, pp. 195–211. Springer, Cham (2020). https://doi.org/10.1007/978-3-030-58621-8_12
3. Bolaños, L.A., et al.: A three-dimensional virtual mouse generates synthetic training data for behavioral analysis. Nat. Methods **18**(4), 378–381 (2021)
4. Borenstein, E., Sharon, E., Ullman, S.: Combining top-down and bottom-up segmentation. In: Proceedings of the IEEE/CVF Conference on Computer Vision and Pattern Recognition, p. 46. IEEE (2004)
5. Card, G., Dickinson, M.H.: Visually mediated motor planning in the escape response of drosophila. Curr. Biol. **18**(17), 1300–1307 (2008)
6. Chen, C., Zhu, W., Norton, T.: Behaviour recognition of pigs and cattle: journey from computer vision to deep learning. Comput. Electron. Agric. **187**, 106255 (2021)
7. Del Pero, L., Ricco, S., Sukthankar, R., Ferrari, V.: Articulated motion discovery using pairs of trajectories. In: Proceedings of the IEEE/CVF Conference on Computer Vision and Pattern Recognition, pp. 2151–2160 (2015)
8. Fisher, E.M., Bannerman, D.M.: Mouse models of neurodegeneration: know your question, know your mouse. Sci. Transl. Med. **11**(493), eaaq1818 (2019)
9. Graving, J.M., et al.: DeepPoseKit, a software toolkit for fast and robust animal pose estimation using deep learning. Elife **8**, e47994 (2019)
10. Jakab, T., Gupta, A., Bilen, H., Vedaldi, A.: Self-supervised learning of interpretable keypoints from unlabelled videos. In: Proceedings of the IEEE/CVF Conference on Computer Vision and Pattern Recognition, pp. 8787–8797 (2020)
11. Jiang, L., Liu, S., Bai, X., Ostadabbas, S.: Prior-aware synthetic data to the rescue: animal pose estimation with very limited real data. arXiv preprint arXiv:2208.13944 (2022)
12. Johnson, J., Alahi, A., Fei-Fei, L.: Perceptual losses for real-time style transfer and super-resolution. In: Leibe, B., Matas, J., Sebe, N., Welling, M. (eds.) ECCV 2016. LNCS, vol. 9906, pp. 694–711. Springer, Cham (2016). https://doi.org/10.1007/978-3-319-46475-6_43
13. Kirkpatrick, T., Schneider, C.W., Pavloski, R.: A computerized infrared monitor for following movement in aquatic animals. Behav. Res. Methods Instrum. Comput. **23**(1), 16–22 (1991)
14. Lee, Y., Dawson, V.L., Dawson, T.M.: Animal models of Parkinson's disease: vertebrate genetics. Cold Spring Harb. Perspect. Med. **2**(10), a009324 (2012)
15. Li, C., Lee, G.H.: From synthetic to real: Unsupervised domain adaptation for animal pose estimation. In: Proceedings of the IEEE/CVF Conference on Computer Vision and Pattern Recognition, pp. 1482–1491 (2021)
16. Liu, Z., Zhu, J., Bu, J., Chen, C.: A survey of human pose estimation: the body parts parsing based methods. J. Vis. Commun. Image Represent. **32**, 10–19 (2015)
17. Loper, M., Mahmood, N., Romero, J., Pons-Moll, G., Black, M.J.: SMPL: a skinned multi-person linear model. ACM Trans. Graph. (TOG) **34**(6), 1–16 (2015)
18. Mao, X., Li, Q., Xie, H., Lau, R.Y., Wang, Z., Paul Smolley, S.: Least squares generative adversarial networks. In: Proceedings of the IEEE International Conference on Computer Vision, pp. 2794–2802 (2017)

19. Mathis, A., et al.: DeepLabCut: markerless pose estimation of user-defined body parts with deep learning. Nat. Neurosci. **21**(9), 1281–1289 (2018)
20. Mathis, M.W., Mathis, A.: Deep learning tools for the measurement of animal behavior in neuroscience. Curr. Opin. Neurobiol. **60**, 1–11 (2020)
21. Mu, J., Qiu, W., Hager, G.D., Yuille, A.L.: Learning from synthetic animals. In: Proceedings of the IEEE/CVF Conference on Computer Vision and Pattern Recognition, pp. 12386–12395 (2020)
22. Nath, T., Mathis, A., Chen, A.C., Patel, A., Bethge, M., Mathis, M.W.: Using DeepLabCut for 3D markerless pose estimation across species and behaviors. Nat. Protoc. **14**(7), 2152–2176 (2019)
23. Newell, A., Yang, K., Deng, J.: Stacked hourglass networks for human pose estimation. In: Leibe, B., Matas, J., Sebe, N., Welling, M. (eds.) ECCV 2016. LNCS, vol. 9912, pp. 483–499. Springer, Cham (2016). https://doi.org/10.1007/978-3-319-46484-8_29
24. Noldus, L.P., Trienes, R.J., Hendriksen, A.H., Jansen, H., Jansen, R.G.: The observer video-pro: new software for the collection, management, and presentation of time-structured data from videotapes and digital media files. Behav. Res. Methods Instrum. Comput. **32**, 197–206 (2000)
25. Olivo, R.F., Thompson, M.C.: Monitoring animals' movements using digitized video images. Behav. Res. Methods Instrum. Comput. **20**, 485–490 (1988)
26. Pereira, T.D., et al.: Fast animal pose estimation using deep neural networks. Nat. Methods **16**(1), 117–125 (2019)
27. Philips, T., Rothstein, J.D.: Rodent models of amyotrophic lateral sclerosis. Curr. Protoc. Pharmacol. **69**(1), 5–67 (2015)
28. Rüegg, N., Tripathi, S., Schindler, K., Black, M.J., Zuffi, S.: BITE: beyond priors for improved three-d dog pose estimation. In: Proceedings of the IEEE/CVF Conference on Computer Vision and Pattern Recognition, pp. 8867–8876 (2023)
29. Russello, H., van der Tol, R., Kootstra, G.: T-leap: occlusion-robust pose estimation of walking cows using temporal information. Comput. Electron. Agric. **192**, 106559 (2022)
30. Saito, T., et al.: Single app knock-in mouse models of Alzheimer's disease. Nat. Neurosci. **17**(5), 661–663 (2014)
31. Sheppard, K., et al.: Stride-level analysis of mouse open field behavior using deep-learning-based pose estimation. Cell Rep. **38**(2), 110231 (2022)
32. Simonyan, K., Zisserman, A.: Very deep convolutional networks for large-scale image recognition. arXiv preprint arXiv:1409.1556 (2014)
33. Spink, A., Tegelenbosch, R., Buma, M., Noldus, L.: The ethovision video tracking system-a tool for behavioral phenotyping of transgenic mice. Physiol. Behav. **73**(5), 731–744 (2001)
34. Tompson, J., Goroshin, R., Jain, A., LeCun, Y., Bregler, C.: Efficient object localization using convolutional networks. In: Proceedings of the IEEE/CVF Conference on Computer Vision and Pattern Recognition, pp. 648–656 (2015)
35. Toshev, A., Szegedy, C.: DeepPose: human pose estimation via deep neural networks. In: Proceedings of the IEEE/CVF Conference on Computer Vision and Pattern Recognition, pp. 1653–1660 (2014)
36. Zuffi, S., Kanazawa, A., Black, M.J.: Lions and tigers and bears: capturing nonrigid, 3D, articulated shape from images. In: Proceedings of the IEEE/CVF Conference on Computer Vision and Pattern Recognition, pp. 3955–3963 (2018)
37. Zuffi, S., Kanazawa, A., Jacobs, D.W., Black, M.J.: 3D menagerie: modeling the 3D shape and pose of animals. In: Proceedings of the IEEE/CVF Conference on Computer Vision and Pattern Recognition, pp. 6365–6373 (2017)

SIFT-Guided Saliency-Based Augmentation for Weed Detection in Grassland Images: Fusing Classic Computer Vision with Deep Learning

Patrick Schmidt[✉][iD], Ronja Güldenring[iD], and Lazaros Nalpantidis[iD]

Department of Electrical and Photonics Engineering, Technical University
of Denmark, Lyngby, Denmark
{pasch,ronjag,lanalpa}@dtu.dk
https://electro.dtu.dk/

Abstract. Weed detection is a challenging case within object detection as the weed targets do not generally strike out from the background in terms of color. This paper investigates how the density of structural features can be used to assist the training process of a Deep-Learning-based object detector. SIFT keypoint density is used to create overlay masks to augment images, emphasizing low-density areas—typically corresponding to weed plants. Our method is shown to improve detection $mAP_{.5:.05:.95}$ on the YOLOR-CSP detector by up to 0.0215.

Keywords: Image Augmentation · Weed Detection · YOLO

1 Introduction

With the world's population steadily increasing, the requirements in agriculture regarding productivity and efficiency are becoming stricter. The response to this is increased usage of herbicides, which has more than doubled in the last 30 years [9]. Herbicides seem compelling at first glance, however, there are several risks and shortcomings that come with herbicide usage such as accidentally applying substances to non-target weeds, development of resistances or movement of herbicide particles to undesired areas caused by air turbulence or improperly calibrated equipment [13]. Herbicide usage can be significantly reduced by spot-spraying or manual weed removal, which is a labor- and by that cost-intensive process. Agricultural robots can fill that gap, paving the way toward more sustainable agriculture.

Particularly in grasslands—an environment of interest to e.g. dairy farming—we can observe that weeds, such as Rumex, tend to have a less fine visual structure on their leaves, compared to the surrounding flora, which predominantly consists of grass and clover. Scale-Invariant Feature Transform (SIFT) [18] is a popular candidate when it comes to capturing fine-structured areas in images and

H. I. Christensen et al. (Eds.): ICVS 2023, LNCS 14253, pp. 137–147, 2023.
https://doi.org/10.1007/978-3-031-44137-0_12

has previously been used as a hand-crafted feature descriptor for weed detection in grasslands [14].

In our work, we introduce a novel saliency-based augmentation module leveraging SIFT keypoint density to enhance the training of a Deep Learning model. More focus will be put on spatial areas of lower SIFT keypoint density by lighting up these areas and darken down areas of high keypoint density as demonstrated in Fig. 1. We apply our newly introduced SIFT-guided, saliency-based augmentation module in combination with the detection model YOLOR-CSP [23], and show that it improves the detection $mAP_{.5:.05:.95}$ by up to 0.0215.

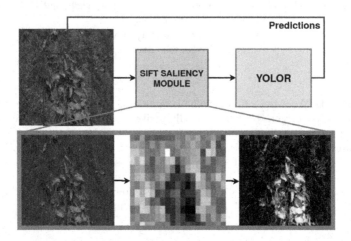

Fig. 1. During the training of the Rumex detector YOLOR [23], we apply a novel SIFT-guided saliency augmentation module to the input image by enlightening areas of low SIFT keypoint density. Low keypoint density can be expected for less structured areas, which corresponds in the majority of cases to plants other than grass or clover.

2   Related Work

2.1   Rumex Detection

The automated detection of *Rumex obtusifolius L.* (broad-leaved dock) has been investigated in agricultural robotics since the early 2000s. This underlines the application's relevance and the need for removing Rumex weed efficiently and robustly at dairy farms. The applied approaches in that field can be assigned to three areas: classic Computer Vision, Machine Learning with hand-crafted feature extraction and Deep Learning.

Using *Classic Computer Vision* techniques, Researchers from Wageningen Research [8,19] applied Fourier Analysis followed by simple thresholding, assuming that Rumex leaves have lower spectral power than grass leaves. [6] use local binary pattern as a feature extractor and apply basic thresholding as well to classify the Rumex weeds. Seatovic and Anken is the only research group so far, that worked with 3D sensor data by applying 3D surface analysis to find Rumex plants with significantly higher leaf surfaces [2,7].

Attempting to use *Machine Learning* with hand-crafted feature extraction, there have been several studies on combining different feature extractors (e.g. Local Binary Pattern, Pyramid Histogram Of Visual Words, Difference of Gaussian, determinant of the Hessian detector) with non-linear and linear Support Vector Machines (SVM) as a final classifier [1,3,14,15,27].

Initial attempts to detect Rumex weeds with *Deep Learning* have been made in recent years. Image classifiers using proven pre-trained Deep Neural Networks, like e.g. AlexNet, have been trained on grassland images [22,27]. Kounalakis et al. [16] keep their SVM classifier from their previous work, but use Deep Neural Networks and transfer learning techniques for automatic feature extraction. Zhang et al. [17] train a VGG16 classifier on grassland images taken with an unmanned aerial vehicle (UAV). They train and evaluate their approach based on semi-automatically annotated data using Image Analysis thresholding techniques and filtering according to object size. While they all apply a sliding window approach to localize the weeds precisely in the image, Güldenring et al. [11] use a recent anchor-based object detector YOLOX and Schori et al. [20] perform pixel-wise predictions of Rumex occurrences using Encoder-Decoder segmentation networks. Furthermore, label efficiency during grassland weed detection training has been addressed using image composition techniques [10] and self-supervised contrastive learning [12].

2.2 Augmentation in Deep Learning

Augmentation methods are commonly used in Deep-Learning-based object detection. These augmentations are usually simple geometric transformations or color space transformations, but there are also more sophisticated augmentations like Mosaic [4], CutMix [25] or Mixup [26].

Uddin et al. [21] and Choi et al. [5] make use of saliency maps to extract visually important image patches which then are pasted on different images. Our approach can be interpreted similarly, we use the density of SIFT keypoints to get a saliency map, but then use the map as an overlay to adjust the contrast in an image. Our method can therefore be seen as a successful attempt to fuse both traditional computer vision techniques with Deep-Learning-based object detection.

3 Method

3.1 YOLOR

You Only Learn One Representation (YOLOR) [23] distinguish between two types of knowledge: explicit, which is directly correlated to a sample X, and implicit, which is not directly linked to a data point but rather to a task. Wang et al. [23] introduce implicit knowledge for the following tasks in the detector [24]:

– **Feature alignment:** Implicit knowledge as a constant tensor is added to the feature maps of each scale of the Feature Pyramid Network (FPN).
– **Prediction refinement:** Implicit knowledge as a constant vector is element-wise-multiplied with each bounding box prediction.

3.2 SIFT-Guided Saliency-Based Augmentation Module

We hypothesize that the density of SIFT features is lower in areas where a Rumex plant is present compared to the rest of the image. Evaluating this on the entire RumexWeeds dataset [11] confirms the hypothesis, Fig. 2 shows the normalized histogram of keypoint densities. Conducting a two-sample Welch's t-test reveals a significant difference between the mean for in-box densities and out-of-box densities.

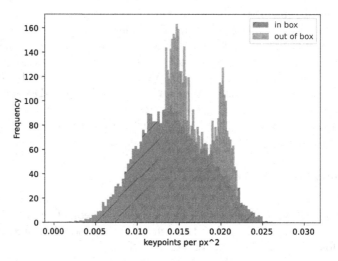

Fig. 2. Normalized histogram of keypoint densities, for keypoints contained within and outside of bounding boxes in blue/orange respectively. Note that the densities for keypoints inside bounding boxes were calculated per box, whereas the out-of-box densities were calculated per image. (Color figure online)

Therefore, the saliency-based augmentation module computes SIFT keypoints for the raw input image. From the SIFT keypoints, a 2D histogram is computed with an arbitrarily chosen bin size of 19×12, marking a down-sampling factor of 10 compared to the original image size of 1900×1200. Finally, the histogram is then used to enlighten areas of low density of SIFT features as shown in Fig. 1.

Note, that computing SIFT features is computationally expensive and reduces the network throughput drastically. Therefore, the SIFT-guided saliency-based augmentation module is only applied during training, and only raw images are used during evaluation (i.e. inference). To overcome this expensive process, we pre-computed the SIFT masks for our experiments and only perform minor operations during training time, so the actual training speed is unaffected. The operations during training time include sampling whether to use the augmentation module and the mask overlay. The methods are described in the following.

We sample from a Bernoulli distribution with $p = p_{\text{sift}}$ to determine whether to use the augmentation module for the current image I or not. Overlaying the SIFT mask and the image is done as follows:

$$D = \alpha I + \beta M \tag{1}$$

where D is the augmented image, I is the original image, M is the SIFT mask, α is the weight of the original image, and β is the weight of the mask. The relationship between the overlay ratio r_{sift} and α as well as β is as follows:

$$\alpha = 1.0 + r_{\text{sift}} \tag{2}$$

$$\beta = -r_{\text{sift}} \tag{3}$$

4 Experimental Setup

4.1 Dataset

RumexWeeds [11] is a grassland dataset, which targets the most problematic grassland weed *Rumex*, while differentiating between two sub-species: *Rumex crispus* and *Rumex obtusifolius*. The data has been collected at four different farms with the Husky robot platform, which is equipped with additional sensors such as RGB camera, wheel encoders, IMU, and GPS. It includes 98 data streams; in total 5,510 images with ground-truth bounding boxes are available. Please refer to Güldenring et al. [11] for a detailed dataset analysis as well as baseline results.

Our experiments use the random split introduced in [11]. Since YOLOR is an anchor-based object detection approach, we have recalculated the anchor boxes based on the training data of the random split using k-means clustering.

4.2 Metrics

We evaluate our experiments with respect to the RumexWeeds **random** test split. To compare our experimental results against the baseline, we mainly make use of COCO $mAP_{.5:.05:.95}$. Wherever reported, we refer to the best $mAP_{.5:.05:.95}$ achieved during training. Since the object detector is deployed on a mobile robotic platform, mean precision and mean recall are further taken into consideration. The higher the recall, the more weed plants are successfully removed. The higher the precision, the fewer non-weed plants are removed. We target a good trade-off between both values; however, higher precision is favored because the process of weed removal is costly, and removing a significant amount of non-weeds would lead to high energy usage and increase the operation time significantly.

4.3 Fixed Training Settings

For our ablation studies and our baseline, we resort to the respective default hyperparameters of each object detector. For YOLOR, these are accumulated in a file in the GitHub repository.[1]. The ablation studies and the respective YOLOR baseline are trained from scratch.

5 Experiments

Our experiments are structured as follows and elaborated in the subsequent sub-chapters.

A. The default YOLOR serves as our baseline, where no SIFT-guided, saliency-based augmentation is applied.
B. We analyze how different augmentation module usage probabilities p_{sift}, i.e. how often pictures get passed through the module, have an effect on the training results.
C. We analyze the effect of different overlay ratios r_{sift} within the augmentation module, i.e. if the ratio is low, the contrast is low, and vice versa.

5.1 Baseline Performance

Baseline performance is achieved, when the module usage probability $p_{\text{sift}} = 0$, as it implies that the original images and default augmentations from YOLOR are used. An overlay ratio of $r_{\text{sift}} = 0$ is also considered to be equal to the baseline performance. Notice that inconsistencies in our data are caused by some randomness between Experiment A and Experiment B and due to a reinstall of the machine and different PyTorch versions. The last rows in Tables 1 and 2 show the training results for the baseline setting. The detector ends up with a validation $mAP_{.5:.05:.95}$ of 0.1995, at a mean recall of 0.6173 and a mean precision of 0.2950. Interpreted onto our use case, the baseline will yield a lot of accidental employments of the weeding mechanism, but won't miss too many weeds in general.

5.2 Ablation Study of Module Usage Probability p_{sift}

We want to examine the relationship between the module usage probability p_{sift} and $mAP_{.5:.05:.95}$, mean precision and mean recall. This study is done with a fixed overlay ratio $r_{\text{sift}} = 0.3$, based on an empirical observation that this overlay ratio keeps the augmentation at a noticeable, but not exaggerated level. Figure 4 illustrates this in the bottom row of the figure. Table 1 summarizes the results of the ablation study.

Compared to the baseline, training YOLOR-CSP with a module usage probability of $p_{\text{sift}} = 0.5$ yields a $mAP_{.5:.05:.95}$ of 0.2191, marking an increase of 0.0196.

---

[1] https://github.com/WongKinYiu/yolor/blob/main/data/hyp.scratch.640.yaml.

This increase in $mAP_{.5:.05:.95}$ comes at the cost of decreasing mean recall, however, the gains in mean precision outweigh this loss. While mean recall decreases by approximately 0.05, mean precision increases by around 0.09. Figure 3 shows the validation $mAP_{.5:.05:.95}$ for different values for p_{sift}, while the dashed lines indicate the best $mAP_{.5:.05:.95}$ for the baseline (purple, $p_{sift} = 0$) and the best performing setup (green, $p_{sift} = 0.5$). It can be observed that both extremes $p_{sift} = 0.0$ and $p_{sift} = 1.0$ perform worse than runs with moderate module usage probabilities.

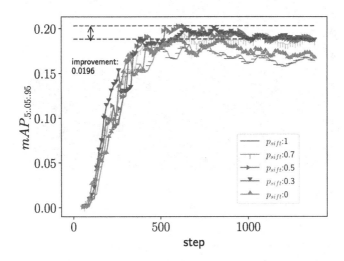

Fig. 3. Validation $mAP_{.5:.05:.95}$ for selected training runs that apply the SIFT-guided, saliency-based augmentation module with a probability of p_{sift}. The best run outperforms the baseline by 0.0137 when considering their best performance over training, which is indicated with the dashed lines accordingly. Note, that the shown curve is smoothed with a rolling mean, window size 5, for readability. Also, note that the given improvement value is based on the non-smoothed data. (Color figure online)⟦⟧

5.3 Ablation Study of Overlay Ratio r_{sift}

Another parameter that can be varied is the overlay ratio between the original image and the SIFT mask, the process is elaborated in Eqs. 1 and 3. In this experiment, we vary r_{sift} from 0.0 to 1.0 in steps of 0.1 while holding p_{sift} fixed at 0.5, which was the best-performing module usage probability in the previous ablation study. Table 2 lists the results of the ablation study. We can observe that when $r_{sift} = 0.7$, we achieve a $mAP_{.5:.05:.95}$ of 0.2132. Compared to the baseline, i.e. $p_{sift} = 0.0$ in Table 1, this marks an increase of 0.0137 in $mAP_{.5:.05:.95}$. However, we can observe another particular effect of higher overlay ratios on the overall training process. Figure 5 illustrates the value of $mAP_{.5:.05:.95}$ for varying r_{sift} with respect to the training step. Note, that the dashed lines indicate the best $mAP_{.5:.05:.95}$ for the baseline (purple, $p_{\text{sift}} = 0$) and the best-performing setup (orange, $r_{\text{sift}} = 0.7$) to stress the improvement. Especially toward the end of the training, we can see that, in general, higher overlay ratios are stabilizing the training process. This is an indicator that the SIFT-guided, saliency-based augmentation module can act as a regularizer.

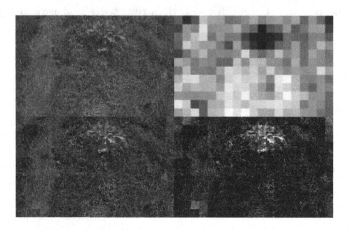

Fig. 4. Visual effect of different overlay ratios. The top left shows the original image and the top right shows the SIFT mask. Bottom left shows image after overlay at $r_{\text{sift}} = 0.3$ and bottom right at $r_{\text{sift}} = 1.0$

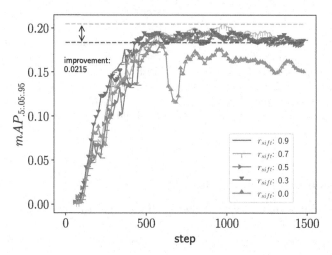

Fig. 5. Plot of $mAP_{.5:.05:.95}$ with respect to training step with different overlay ratios r_{sift} at $p_{\text{sift}} = 0.5$. Note that, the curves are rolling mean smoothed with a window size of 5, and the improvement is reported on the non-smoothed data. (Color figure online)

Table 1. Results of the module usage probability ablation study

p_{sift}	$mAP_{.5:.05:.95}$	mP	mR
1.0	0.1967	0.3362	0.5580
0.9	0.2048	0.3898	0.5201
0.8	0.2042	0.4422	0.5109
0.7	0.2032	**0.4721**	0.4747
0.6	0.2005	0.4283	0.5088
0.5	**0.2191**	0.3809	0.5633
0.4	0.2097	0.4283	0.5392
0.3	0.2044	0.4677	0.4902
0.2	0.2057	0.3716	0.5948
0.1	0.2031	0.4093	0.5340
0.0 (**baseline**)	0.1995	0.2950	**0.6173**

Table 2. Results of the overlay ratio ablation study

r_{sift}	$mAP_{.5:.05:.95}$	mP	mR
1.0	0.2005	0.4104	0.5378
0.9	0.2024	0.4338	0.4977
0.8	0.2088	0.3618	0.5534
0.7	**0.2132**	0.4211	0.5341
0.6	0.2032	0.3311	0.5895
0.5	0.2046	**0.4372**	0.5121
0.4	0.2049	0.3533	0.5633
0.3	0.2068	0.4018	0.5448
0.2	0.2056	0.3131	**0.5945**
0.1	0.2073	0.3631	0.5799
0.0 (**baseline**)	0.1917	0.3516	0.5436

6   Conclusion

Our work showed how traditional computer vision techniques can be combined with Deep-Learning-based techniques. We introduced a saliency-based augmentation guided by SIFT features to increase contrast within images of grasslands to put focus on the plants to be detected. A 2D histogram of SIFT keypoints is used to create a mask, which then is overlaid with the original image to adjust the contrast. It increases the brightness of larger, structure-less areas, which correspond mainly to plant leaves compared to the structure-rich, surrounding areas of grass. We conducted experiments to show the learning-improving capabilities of our augmentations, with an increase of $mAP_{.5:.05:.95}$ of up to 0.0215 points.

Further work could analyze the usage of the module in deeper layers of the network instead of operating directly on RGB images, making it an interesting candidate to act as an attention module.

Acknowledgements. This work has been supported by the European Commission and European GNSS Agency through the project "Galileo-assisted robot to tackle the weed Rumex obtusifolius and increase the profitability and sustainability of dairy farming (GALIRUMI)", H2020-SPACE-EGNSS-2019-870258.

References

1. Ahmed, F., Kabir, M.H., Bhuyan, S., Bari, H., Hossain, E.: Automated weed classification with local pattern-based texture descriptors. Int. Arab J. Inf. Technol. **11**, 87–94 (2014)
2. Anken, T., Šeatović, D., Holpp, M., Venn, W., Kutterer, H.: Automatic detection of broad-leaved dock in grassland (2010)
3. Binch, A., Cooke, N., Fox, C.W.: Rumex and Urtica detection in grassland by UAV. In: 14th International Conference on Precision Agriculture (2018)
4. Bochkovskiy, A., Wang, C.Y., Liao, H.Y.M.: YOLOv4: optimal speed and accuracy of object detection. arXiv:2004.10934 [cs, eess] (2020)
5. Choi, J., Lee, C., Lee, D., Jung, H.: SalfMix: a novel single image-based data augmentation technique using a saliency map. Sensors **21**(24), 8444 (2021). https://doi.org/10.3390/s21248444, https://www.mdpi.com/1424-8220/21/24/8444
6. Dürr, L., Anken, T., Bollhalder, H., Sauter, J., Burri, K.G., Kuhn, D.: Machine vision detection and microwave-based elimination of Rumex obtusifolius L. on grassland (2008)
7. Šeatović, D., Winterthur, Z., Switzerland: 3D-object recognition, localization and treatment of Rumex obtusifolius in its natural environment. In: International Conference on Precision Agriculture (2008)
8. van Evert, F.K., Polder, G., van der Heijden, G.W.A.M., Kempenaar, C., Lotz, L.A.P.: Real-time vision-based detection of Rumex obtusifolius in grassland. Weed Res. **49**(2), 164–174 (2009)
9. FAO: fAO. FAOSTAT Statistical Database. License: CC BY-NC-SA 3.0 IGO (2021). https://www.fao.org/faostat/en/. Accessed 04 July 2022
10. Güldenring, R., Boukas, E., Ravn, O., Nalpantidis, L.: Few-leaf learning: weed segmentation in grasslands. In: 2021 IEEE/RSJ International Conference on Intelligent Robots and Systems (IROS) (2021)
11. Güldenring, R., van Evert, F.K., Nalpantidis, L.: RumexWeeds: a grassland dataset for agricultural robotics. J. Field Robot. (2023). https://doi.org/10.1002/rob.22196, https://onlinelibrary.wiley.com/doi/abs/10.1002/rob.22196
12. Güldenring, R., Nalpantidis, L.: Self-supervised contrastive learning on agricultural images. Comput. Electron. Agric. **191**, 106510 (2021)
13. Johnson, Q., VanGessel, M., Taylor, R.W.: Pasture and hay weed management guide delaware 2015. Technical report, University of Delaware (2015). https://s3.amazonaws.com/udextension/ag/files/2015/01/PHWeedguide.pdf
14. Kounalakis, T., Triantafyllidis, G.A., Nalpantidis, L.: Weed recognition framework for robotic precision farming. In: 2016 IEEE International Conference on Imaging Systems and Techniques (IST), pp. 466–471 (2016). https://doi.org/10.1109/IST.2016.7738271

15. Kounalakis, T., Triantafyllidis, G.A., Nalpantidis, L.: Image-based recognition framework for robotic weed control systems. Multimed. Tools Appl. **77**(8), 9567–9594 (2018)
16. Kounalakis, T., Triantafyllidis, G.A., Nalpantidis, L.: Deep learning-based visual recognition of Rumex for robotic precision farming. Comput. Electron. Agric. **165**, 104973 (2019)
17. Lam, O.H.Y., et al.: An open source workflow for weed mapping in native grassland using unmanned aerial vehicle: using Rumex obtusifolius as a case study. Eur. J. Remote Sens. **54**(sup1), 71–88 (2021)
18. Lowe, D.G.: Object recognition from local scale-invariant features. In: Proceedings of the Seventh IEEE International Conference on Computer Vision, vol. 2, pp. 1150–1157. IEEE (1999)
19. Polder, G., et al.: Weed detection using textural image analysis. in: EFITA/ WCCA Conference (2007)
20. Schori, D., Anken, T., Šeatović, D.: Using fully convolutional networks for Rumex obtusifolius segmentation, a preliminary report. In: 2019 International Symposium ELMAR, pp. 119–122 (2019)
21. Uddin, A.F.M.S., Monira, M.S., Shin, W., Chung, T., Bae, S.H.: SaliencyMix: a saliency guided data augmentation strategy for better regularization (2021). arXiv:2006.01791 [cs, stat]
22. Valente, J., Doldersum, M., Roers, C., Kooistra, L.: Detecting Rumex obtusifolius weed plants in grasslands from UAV RGB imagery using deep learning. ISPRS Ann. Photogram. Remote Sens. Spat. Inf. Sci. **IV-2/W5**, 179–185 (2019)
23. Wang, C.Y., Yeh, I.H., Liao, H.Y.M.: You only learn one representation: unified network for multiple tasks. arXiv preprint arXiv:2105.04206 (2021)
24. Wang, C.Y., Yeh, I.H., Liao, H.Y.M.: You only learn one representation: unified network for multiple tasks. arXiv:2105.04206 [cs] (2021)
25. Yun, S., Han, D., Oh, S.J., Chun, S., Choe, J., Yoo, Y.: CutMix: regularization strategy to train strong classifiers with localizable features (2019)
26. Zhang, H., Cisse, M., Dauphin, Y.N., Lopez-Paz, D.: Mixup: beyond empirical risk minimization (2018)
27. Zhang, W., et al.: Broad-leaf weed detection in pasture. In: 2018 IEEE 3rd International Conference on Image, Vision and Computing (ICIVC), pp. 101–105 (2018)

Key Point-Based Orientation Estimation of Strawberries for Robotic Fruit Picking

Justin Le Louëdec$^{(\boxtimes)}$ ⓘ and Grzegorz Cielniak ⓘ

Lincoln Centre for Autonomous Systems, University of Lincoln, Brayford Way, Brayford Pool,
Lincoln LN6 7TS, UK
{jlelouedec,gcielniak}@lincoln.ac.uk

Abstract. Selective robotic harvesting can help address labour shortages affecting modern global agriculture. For an accurate and efficient picking process, a robotic harvester requires the precise location and orientation of the fruit to effectively plan the trajectory of the end effector. The current methods for estimating fruit orientation employ either complete 3D information registered from multiple views or rely on fully-supervised learning techniques, requiring difficult-to-obtain manual annotation of the reference orientation. In this paper, we introduce a novel key-point-based fruit orientation estimation method for the prediction of 3D orientation from 2D images directly. The proposed technique can work without full 3D orientation annotations but can also exploit such information for improved accuracy. We evaluate our work on two separate datasets of strawberry images obtained from real-world scenarios. Our method achieves state-of-the-art performance with an average error as low as 8°, improving predictions by ∼30% compared to previous work presented in [17]. Furthermore, our method is suited for real-time robotic applications with fast inference times of ∼30 ms.

1 Introduction

Automation through robotisation of the agricultural sector is seen as a promising solution to the socio-economic challenges faced by this industry. A key application is selective crop harvesting which achieves automation through manipulation and grasping of the harvestable crop based on precise information about the location and pose of the crop. Typical approaches for estimating the location and pose of the fruit rely on a combination of 2D images together with 3D information (e.g., [19]) and require additional projection steps and direct operations on point clouds which add significant computation overhead.

In this paper, we present a method that enables precise fruit pose estimation directly from 2D images bypassing computationally expensive transformation and estimation steps. A similar approach has been originally proposed by [17] which estimates the fruit pose by regressing the orientation direction vector directly from an image in a fully supervised manner using a learnt feature extractor and regression layer. The method is characterised by fast inference times but also reduced accuracy caused by occasional failures which are difficult to attribute to any particular part of the architecture. In addition, the supervised approach relies on difficult-to-obtain high-quality orientation annotations making the method impractical for wider use. In contrast, our method employs

H. I. Christensen et al. (Eds.): ICVS 2023, LNCS 14253, pp. 148–158, 2023.
https://doi.org/10.1007/978-3-031-44137-0_13

a two-stage approach first predicting the localisation of two characteristic key points of the strawberry fruit which are then used for pose estimation. This two-stage approach, inspired by prior work in human pose estimation (i.e., [11]), leads to improved accuracy and a simplified training regime thanks to the straightforward annotation of key points. The presented contributions include: 1) a new method for efficient estimation of fruit orientation directly from images based on key-point detectors, 2) an improved roll angle estimation method based on learnt image features and the estimated key point information and 3) evaluation of the proposed system on two real-world datasets of strawberry images without and with a full 3D annotation.

2   Related Work

Early approaches for accurate pose estimation of objects utilised handcrafted image descriptors [10, 12], whilst most recent research focuses on learning approaches exploiting the existing extensive datasets. The examples include work making use of multiple-views for orientation and category estimation [6], through iterative refinement of object's pose using Gated Recurrent Unit (GRU) operators [9] or by employing transformer architectures as in [5]. The state-of-the-art methods rely on difficult-to-obtain annotations and therefore there is a big interest in methods which can reduce that requirement for example through the use of simulation for training as in Sim2Real [20]. When accurate 3D shapes are available, the use of geometric insights can improve orientation prediction across the whole categories of objects [3]. All these techniques, however, do not focus on a specific application and rely on benchmark datasets of non-organic objects exclusively (e.g., YCB-V dataset [18]), making their usefulness for agri-robotics applications difficult to assess.

Object pose estimation for robotic manipulation and grasping has been researched thoroughly over the years. For example, the approach in [2] is proposing the use of simulation and self-supervised training through manipulating objects to identify their pose. There are also methods relying on point cloud data and improved descriptors which were applied to obtain better accuracy of object orientation for robotic bin picking [1]. Crop pose estimation for robotic harvesting has also gained recent interest with various applications in different crops. For example, the approach presented in [8] estimates the pose of guava fruit from point cloud data obtained from an RGBD sensor by segmenting plant components (i.e. fruit and branches) and combining their relative pose. Other methods, such as [4], propose the refinement of the fruit pose by registering a 3D reconstruction of the captured point cloud to offline templates of the identified fruit [4]. The method presented in [7] predicts the crop detection bounding boxes, maturity, pose and precise stem orientation to identify the optimal cutting point for tomatoes, obtaining more accurate and thorough information for harvesting.

For strawberries, recent work introduced a learning-based regression of the orientation vectors of the fruits from a single colour and, optionally, depth image [17]. While achieving state-of-the-art results, the method's accuracy is affected by occasional failures which due to the dimensional difference between the images and the output 3D orientation vector are difficult to analyse. In addition, the fully-supervised nature of the method requires accurate annotation of the fruit orientation in images which are complex to obtain without additional geometrical information about the fruit size and shape.

3 The Approach

The proposed method consists of a learnt key point detector, orientation calculation and an optional, learnt θ component for improved estimation of the orientation. We assume the "roll-pitch-yaw" representation compared to direction vector from [17] and note that the yaw angle is irrelevant in this application due to the relative symmetry the strawberries. Thus, we simplify the definition of the orientation to two angles: pitch ($\phi \in [-180, 180]$) and roll ($\theta \in [0, 90]$). Both angles can be derived numerically from the detected crop key points in 2D, but in addition, we demonstrate that the calculation of θ can be regressed from the image and the key points, leading to improved results when compared to the direct numerical formula. The main advantage of key points is the ease of their annotation in images which involves the marking of a single-pixel location only.

The two "top" and "tip" key points represent projections of the stem attachment point and the extreme point of the fruit, respectively onto the image plane. Due to the fruit growing conditions and typical harvesting robot camera configuration, the tip is always located in space between being parallel to the image plane or pointing towards the camera. At the same time, the top might become obstructed by the crop and invisible in the image. In such a case, its projection on the image plane relative to the centre of mass is a good indication of the fruit's size. The appearance of key point location under different fruit rotations is presented in Fig. 1.

3.1 Key Point Detection

We propose using a method inspired by human pose estimation literature for predicting the position of the key points. For each strawberry image, we estimate two heat maps corresponding to the "top" and "tip" key points. The top and tip key points correspond to the relative position of the stem attachment point and outer part of the berry respectively projected onto the image plane (see Fig. 1). We use the method presented in [11] composed of a stack of S small hourglass networks. For our scenario, we choose experimentally $S = 8$ with one final convolution layer followed by a sigmoid function for each hourglass network. This last activation function forces the network outputs within the range $[0, 1]$ and can be interpreted as the likelihood of the location of the key points. The output of an intermediary hourglass module is combined with its feature map and input for the next module in the stack. Overall, the architecture and building blocks used, do not differ from the original paper which is a standard architecture used in other applications.

During training, we use the average binary cross-entropy as the loss function $L_K = -ylog(f(x)) - (1-y)log(1 - f(x))$, where $f(x)$ is the output of each stacked hourglass and y the ground truth heat map for the key point. During inference, the key point location corresponds to the image coordinates at the maximum value selected from the

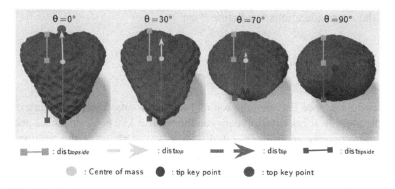

Fig. 1. The location of key points and relative distances used for orientation calculation under changing values of θ.

$S = 8$ predicted heat maps for each key point. The ground truth heatmaps consist of 2D Gaussian kernels ($\sigma = 2.0$) applied to images containing each annotated key point location.

3.2 Key Point-Based Orientation

We define the coordinates of the key points as A and B which correspond to the top and tip of the strawberries respectively. The roll ϕ can be calculated in a straightforward manner: $\phi = \arctan(\frac{y_{BA}}{x_{BA}})$, where $BA = (x_{BA}, y_{BA})$ is a vector between the both key points.

We propose to derive pitch θ from the relative position of the key points to the centre of mass and also to the geometric outline of the strawberry. As the fruit rotates, the two key points get closer/further to each other and it is, therefore, possible to correlate their relative distance to the orientation of the berry. To this end, we define the following four distances with respect to the centre of mass:

- d_{top} and d_{tip} representing the distance to the top and tip key points, respectively;
- $d_{topside}$ and $d_{tipside}$ is the distance to the fruit's contour following the straight line intersecting the top and tip key points, respectively.

We then use these measures to derive normalised distances to the key points as ratios $\hat{d}_{top} = \frac{d_{top}}{d_{topside}}$ and $\hat{d}_{tip} = \frac{d_{tip}}{d_{tipside}}$. The key point locations and corresponding distances relative to the centre of mass for different values of θ are illustrated in Fig. 1. The contour is obtained with [16], using the binary mask from the segmented strawberries.

Due to the specific shape and the skewed centre of mass of strawberries, the 3D rotation of the fruit results in an elliptical trajectory of the key points in the image space which we model using a simple square root model (see Eq. 1). With the changing pitch angle θ, the $\hat{d}_{top}$ decreases fast until a specific value ($\sim\theta = 50°$ in our case), whilst $\hat{d}_{tip}$ is not affected as much (see Fig. 1). The distance $\hat{d}_{tip}$ is, however, a good indicator for θ values above that threshold. Finally, with the image resolution normalised, we can use the length of the berry T as a threshold between the phase of importance for $\hat{d}_{top}$ and

$\hat{d}_{tip}$. With these considerations, we define θ as:

$$\theta = \begin{cases} \sqrt{\hat{d}_{top}}\alpha & \text{if} \quad d_{tt} > T, \\ \sqrt{\hat{d}_{tip}}\omega + \sigma & \text{otherwise,} \end{cases} \tag{1}$$

where d_{tt} is the distance between the top and tip key points. The parameters α, ω and σ define the non-linear relationship between the relative key point distances and θ. The values of these parameters are correlated with a typical shape of the fruit and in our case, for strawberries, these were tuned experimentally using the training set data to $T = 170.0$, $\alpha = 54.0$, $\omega = 50.0$ and $\sigma = 40.0$. For T, as the strawberries instances are cropped from the original image, then centred and resized to 256×256 px, the chosen value is independent from the real fruit size and correlated to the image size and fruit rotation instead.

3.3   Improved Estimation of the Pitch Angle

In general, obtaining the orientation ground truth for images is complex and not always possible. When this ground truth information is available (eg. with simulated data where object orientation is known), however, we propose a supervised method to predict the pitch angle θ from a strawberry image, which results in improved estimation results. Similarly to the previous work presented in [17], we use a pre-trained VGG16 [14] architecture to extract relevant features from a strawberry image. However, the size of the regressor used in our architecture is larger to improve the predictive capabilities of the network. We then combine the extracted feature map with the detected key point locations before using a two-stage classifier to regress θ. The architecture used to predict the θ is presented in Fig. 2. During training the loss is expressed as the mean squared error $L_\theta = (f(x) - y)^2$, where $f(x)$ is the output of the network and y is the ground truth value for θ.

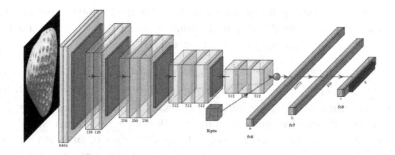

Fig. 2. A network architecture for predicting $\theta \in \left[0, \frac{\pi}{2}\right]$ from the two key points (Kpts) and an input image. The feature extractor (orange) consists of convolutions (light shade) and max-pooling (dark shade) layers whilst the θ regressor (purple) includes fully-connected layers and the sigmoid activation function. (Color figure online)

4   Evaluation Setup

To train and evaluate our method we introduce two datasets: $Straw_{2D}$ with strawberry images collected in-field and annotated with simple key point annotations and $Straw_{3D}$ with images generated from high-quality 3D models of strawberries, which also include the full orientation ground truth.

$Straw_{2D}$ is based on the dataset provided in [13], including high-resolution images of strawberries from 20 different plantations in Spain (see Fig. 3). 600 individual strawberries with minimal occlusion and of different shape, orientation and maturity stage were extracted and preprocessed so that background and calyx were masked out. The cropped square area around each berry was resized to the resolution of $256\,px \times 256\,px$. The top and tip key points were then manually annotated by marking their projected location on the cropped image plane.

Fig. 3. Example original images from [13] (Left) and the annotated instances of individual strawberries from $Straw_{2D}$ together with the annotation of the top (pink) and tip (blue) key points (right). (Color figure online)

$Straw_{3D}$ is a dataset of strawberry images obtained from high-resolution rendered 3D models. In addition to annotated key point locations, full orientation annotation is also available since the models can be rendered at the arbitrary pose. We have used multi-view stereo-photogrammetry which allows for reconstructing 3D shapes from a set of images with unknown poses using the Agisoft Metashape software [15]. Our image capture setup consists of a high-resolution camera mounted on a tripod and a manually rotated table carrying a fixed strawberry (see Fig. 4a). To match the appearance of the models to the field conditions, we capture the dataset outdoors using sunlight (see Fig. 4b). Of the 127 strawberries captured, 36 were from an unknown species bought at the farmer's market, and the rest were a mix between Zara and Katrina. Furthermore, we captured half of the strawberries at the unripe maturity stage and the other half fully ripe for greater variance in shape and appearance.

To create the $Straw_{3D}$ dataset, each 3D berry is rendered in 84 different orientations resulting in 10668 individual views. The images were post-processed in a similar

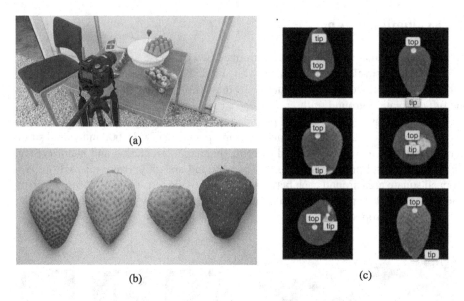

Fig. 4. The photogrammetry setup (a) used for capturing the 3D models of strawberries (b) and selected examples from the $Straw_{3D}$ dataset together with key point annotations.

way as the $Straw_{2D}$ dataset resulting in squared and masked images with the resolution of 256 px × 256 px. The annotation consists of the orientation ground truth and the projected 3D key points (top and tip) on their image locations (see Fig. 4c).

To evaluate the performance of our model for predicting the key point locations, we use the Euclidean distance $e = \sqrt{(x - x_{gt})^2 + (y - y_{gt})^2}$ between the predicted (x, y) and ground truth (x_{gt}, y_{gt}) location expressed in pixels. For evaluating the predicted 3D pose for the strawberries from $Straw_{3D}$, we compute the angular distance between the predicted and ground truth pose. The direction vector $V = RV_{neutral}^{T}$ where $V_{neutral} = [0, -1, 0]$ and R the rotation matrix obtained with ϕ and θ. The angular error ε between the predicted V_{pred} and ground truth V_{gt} direction is then computed as $\varepsilon = acos(V_{pred}V_{gt})$. We use a recent method presented in [17] as the baseline for comparisons on the $Straw_{3D}$ dataset. We use a 10-fold cross-validation evaluation scheme for all datasets, with a dataset split of 90% for training and 10% for testing. For key points prediction, we train with a starting learning rate of 1e−4 for ∼100 epochs for $Straw_{2D}$ and ∼6 epochs for $Straw_{3D}$. We train our baseline [17] and the θ regressor with a starting learning rate of 1e−5 until convergence (∼6 epochs).

5 Results

We first analyse the quality of key point detection, perform comparisons of the direct orientation computation and the supervised approach to the baseline method and present a qualitative analysis of the predictions for the estimated angles.

Table 1 presents the median prediction errors of our key point detector for both datasets. For the in-field dataset $Straw_{2D}$, the results are around 9 px (∼4% image size)

Table 1. Median estimation errors for the top and tip key point locations in $Straw_{2D}$ and $Straw_{3D}$ datasets. As well as ϕ error, when computed from these key points.

dataset	e_{tip} [px]	e_{top} [px]	e_{phi}
$Straw_{2D}$	9.25 ± 4.20	14.91 ± 9.45	$14.53° \pm 39.85$
$Straw_{3D}$	7.61 ± 2.61	8.60 ± 3.21	$12.18° \pm 27.05$

for the tip and 19 px ($\sim$7% image size) for the top but with a high variance, which is still relatively good for imperfect fruit images collected from the field. This higher variance can be attributed to the quality of manual annotation, which was affected by the difficulties in identifying key points and strawberry shape for this dataset. Indeed with atypical shapes, and missing flesh $Straw_{2D}$, presents more challenges for annotation and prediction. With more accurate annotations present in the $Straw_{3D}$ dataset, however, the algorithm identifies the location of the key points more accurately which indicates that this is a critical consideration in training the key point detectors for real applications. Furthermore, the error in ϕ prediction (e_{phi}), shows a clear correlation between keypoints accuracy and angle prediction, with the high-variance coming from difficult cases and ambiguously shaped strawberries.

We further show the correlation between key point localisation error and fruit orientation in Fig. 5a on $Straw_{3D}$. We can see that e_{top} is consistent across different orientations but with a higher variance. e_{tip} spikes mainly when the tip of the fruit points toward the camera and is harder to distinguish precisely ($\sim$70°). Indeed, the top key point aligns with the centre of mass when θ gets close to 90°, while the tip key point is often displaced randomly due to the strawberry shape and growth. It is worth noting that more precise tip point estimation does not improve orientation results at lower values of θ as shown in Fig. 1.

Furthermore, we show in Fig. 5a that the key points are predicted accurately in most of the cases. In $Straw_{2D}$, the errors are primarily due to inaccurate top prediction due to arguable and difficult to annotate precisely. We see in the last example also key points predicted on the centre of mass indicating a value of $\theta = 90°$, probably due to the round shape and missing flesh information. For $Straw_{3D}$, an higher imprecision with the tip prediction for high values of θ can be observed.

The example output from the key point detectors applied to the $Straw_{2D}$ dataset together with numerically calculated angles ϕ and θ is presented in Fig. 6a and Fig. 6b respectively. We indicate the tip key point on the rendered strawberries for θ to compare its localisation with respect to the predicted strawberry. With accurate key points, in Fig. 6a the numerical prediction of ϕ gives a clear indication of the fruit orientation within the image plane. The numerical computation of θ in Fig. 6b shows that using the tip key point and contour of the fruit leads to accurate orientation estimates, with the rendered strawberry meshes precisely aligning with the input images.

The comparison of the predicted poses from our proposed methods including direct numerical estimation and the learnt θ estimator to the baseline from [17] is presented in Fig. 7. The evaluation was performed on the $Straw_{3D}$ dataset which includes the full pose annotation. The supervised orientation method performs significantly better

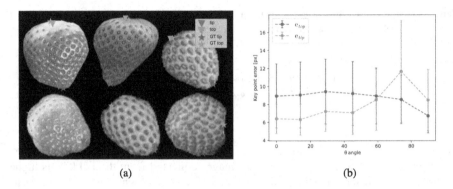

(a)   (b)

Fig. 5. (a) Examples of accurate (top row) and less accurate (bottom row) key point predictions from the $Straw_{2D}$ dataset. (b) Key point prediction error relative to the θ angle for $Straw_{3D}$.

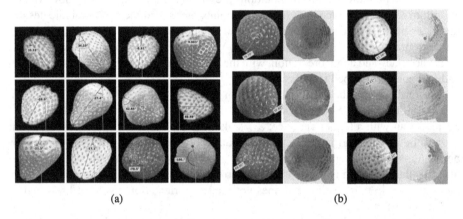

(a)   (b)

Fig. 6. (a) Computed ϕ values for selected strawberry instances. (b) A comparison of estimation accuracy for θ and key point localisation between real strawberries (black background) and 3D renders of similar shaped models (white background). The tip key point is indicated in blue whilst the intersection with the contour is indicated in orange. (Color figure online)

with lower error ($\sim8°$), and less variance than the baseline ($\sim11°$). Furthermore, as displayed in Fig. 7b, the numerical method shows viable results in general with worse performance for the most ambiguous poses $\theta = 0°$ and $\theta = 49°$ only. The latter is due to the ambiguous orientation lying in between the two parts stages of the formula used. This is a limitation of the numerical formula based on 2D images which is difficult to overcome without employing additional 3D shape information. The orientation prediction performs more accurately for all methods as θ gets closer to $90°$. This is coherent with the lack of variation in appearance for values of θ bellow $30°$ as presented in Fig. 1. Our method is computationally very efficient and suitable for real-time robotic applications with inference times of 30.0 ms for the key point detector and 1.4 ms for the supervised regression of θ. The performance is measured on an NVIDIA GeForce GTX 1880 Ti, with Intel(R) Core(TM) i7-7700K CPU and 16 GB memory.

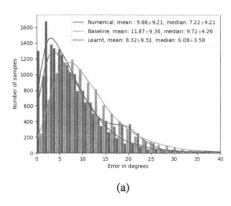
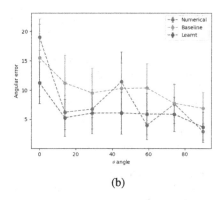

(a)   (b)

Fig. 7. Quantitative evaluation of the different methods on $Straw_{3D}$ with: (a) Distribution of angular errors and median and mean values. (b) Median estimation errors with respect to different values of θ.

6 Conclusions and Future Work

In this paper, we presented a novel approach for predicting the orientation of strawberries from single-view images. Our method exploits the key points and understanding of the fruit's shape, with two different techniques for predicting the rotation angles of the fruit. The experiments indicate that our approach achieves state-of-the-art results with average errors as low as $8°$. In addition, our key point-based method leads to a better understanding of failure cases when compared to the baseline, clearly indicating sources of errors which are directly linked to mislocalised key points. Our method is suited for robotic strawberry harvesting where the fruit's orientation is important for effective end-effector motion planning.

Future work will include further optimisation of the key point prediction network and supervised regression of θ. For example, sharing the weight from the feature extraction layers should reduce the training time and complexity of the models with the number of weights needed. The developed numerical θ computation was developed without considering the possible berry shapes which, if taken into account, should improve the results by improving the correlation between the key point location and orientation. Furthermore, this work can easily be extended to other crops by modifying the numerical formula. Future work would also include considering the external and self-occlusion of the key points, and adding uncertainty measures for hidden key points.

References

1. Cui, X., Yu, M., Wu, L., Wu, S.: A 6D pose estimation for robotic bin-picking using point-pair features with curvature (Cur-PPF). Sensors **22**(5), 1805 (2022)
2. Deng, X., Xiang, Y., Mousavian, A., Eppner, C., Bretl, T., Fox, D.: Self-supervised 6D object pose estimation for robot manipulation. In: 2020 IEEE International Conference on Robotics and Automation (ICRA), pp. 3665–3671. IEEE (2020)

3. Di, Y., et al.: GPV-pose: category-level object pose estimation via geometry-guided point-wise voting. In: Proceedings of the IEEE/CVF Conference on Computer Vision and Pattern Recognition, pp. 6781–6791 (2022)
4. Guo, N., Zhang, B., Zhou, J., Zhan, K., Lai, S.: Pose estimation and adaptable grasp configuration with point cloud registration and geometry understanding for fruit grasp planning. Comput. Electron. Agric. **179**, 105818 (2020)
5. Jantos, T., Hamdad, M., Granig, W., Weiss, S., Steinbrener, J.: PoET: pose estimation transformer for single-view, multi-object 6D pose estimation. In: 6th Annual Conference on Robot Learning (CoRL 2022)
6. Kanezaki, A., Matsushita, Y., Nishida, Y.: RotationNet: joint object categorization and pose estimation using multiviews from unsupervised viewpoints. In: Proceedings of the IEEE Conference on Computer Vision and Pattern Recognition, pp. 5010–5019 (2018)
7. Kim, J., Pyo, H., Jang, I., Kang, J., Ju, B., Ko, K.: Tomato harvesting robotic system based on deep-ToMaToS: deep learning network using transformation loss for 6D pose estimation of maturity classified tomatoes with side-stem. Comput. Electron. Agric. **201**, 107300 (2022)
8. Lin, G., Tang, Y., Zou, X., Xiong, J., Li, J.: Guava detection and pose estimation using a low-cost RGB-D sensor in the field. Sensors **19**(2), 428 (2019)
9. Lipson, L., Teed, Z., Goyal, A., Deng, J.: Coupled iterative refinement for 6D multi-object pose estimation. In: Proceedings of the IEEE/CVF Conference on Computer Vision and Pattern Recognition, pp. 6728–6737 (2022)
10. Muñoz, E., Konishi, Y., Murino, V., Del Bue, A.: Fast 6D pose estimation for texture-less objects from a single RGB image. In: 2016 IEEE International Conference on Robotics and Automation (ICRA), pp. 5623–5630. IEEE (2016)
11. Newell, A., Yang, K., Deng, J.: Stacked hourglass networks for human pose estimation. In: Leibe, B., Matas, J., Sebe, N., Welling, M. (eds.) ECCV 2016. LNCS, vol. 9912, pp. 483–499. Springer, Cham (2016). https://doi.org/10.1007/978-3-319-46484-8_29
12. Park, K., Prankl, J., Vincze, M.: Mutual hypothesis verification for 6D pose estimation of natural objects. In: Proceedings of the IEEE International Conference on Computer Vision Workshops, pp. 2192–2199 (2017)
13. Pérez-Borrero, I., Marín-Santos, D., Gegúndez-Arias, M.E., Cortés-Ancos, E.: A fast and accurate deep learning method for strawberry instance segmentation. Comput. Electron. Agric. **178**, 105736 (2020). https://doi.org/10.1016/j.compag.2020.105736, http://www.sciencedirect.com/science/article/pii/S0168169920300624
14. Simonyan, K., Zisserman, A.: Very deep convolutional networks for large-scale image recognition. In: International Conference on Learning Representations (2015)
15. Software, A.: Agisoft photoscan professional, pp. 1534–4320 (2016). http://www.agisoft.com/downloads/installer/
16. Suzuki, S., be, K.: Topological structural analysis of digitized binary images by border following. Comput. Vision Graph. Image Process. **30**(1), 32–46 (1985). https://doi.org/10.1016/0734-189X(85)90016-7, https://www.sciencedirect.com/science/article/pii/0734189X85900167
17. Wagner, N., Kirk, R., Hanheide, M., Cielniak, G.: Efficient and robust orientation estimation of strawberries for fruit picking applications. In: 2021 IEEE International Conference on Robotics and Automation (ICRA), pp. 13857–13863. IEEE (2021)
18. Xiang, Y., Schmidt, T., Narayanan, V., Fox, D.: PoseCNN: a convolutional neural network for 6D object pose estimation in cluttered scenes (2018)
19. Xiong, Y., Ge, Y., From, P.J.: An improved obstacle separation method using deep learning for object detection and tracking in a hybrid visual control loop for fruit picking in clusters. Comput. Electron. Agric. **191**, 106508 (2021)
20. Zhong, C., et al.: Sim2Real object-centric keypoint detection and description. In: Proceedings of the AAAI Conference on Artificial Intelligence, vol. 36, pp. 5440–5449 (2022)

Residual Cascade CNN for Detection of Spatially Relevant Objects in Agriculture: The Grape-Stem Paradigm

Georgios Zampokas[1,2]([⊠]), Ioannis Mariolis[1], Dimitrios Giakoumis[1], and Dimitrios Tzovaras[1]

[1] Centre for Research and Technology Hellas/Information Technologies Institute, Thessaloniki, Greece
{gzampokas,ymariolis,dgiakoum,dimitrios.tzovaras}@iti.gr
[2] Imperial College London, London, UK

Abstract. Computer vision is becoming increasingly important in agriculture, as it can provide important insights and lead to better informed decisions and reduce costs. However, working on the agriculture domain introduces important challenges, such as adverse conditions, small structures and lack of large datasets, hindering its wide adoption on multiple cases. This work presents an approach to improve the performance of detecting challenging small objects, by exploiting their spatial structure under the hypothesis that they are located close to larger objects, which we define as anchor. This is achieved by providing feature maps from the detections of the anchor class to the network responsible for detecting the secondary class. Thus, the secondary class object detection is formulated as a residual problem on top of the anchor class detection, benefiting from an activation bias close to the anchor object spatial locations. Experiments on the grape-stem and capsicum-peduncle cases, demonstrate increased performance against more computationally expensive baselines, resulting in improved metrics at 37% of baseline FLOPs.

Keywords: instance segmentation · CNN · agriculture · grape · stem

1 Introduction

In the realm of agriculture, where the world's growing population relies heavily on the productivity and sustainability of food systems, the integration of cutting-edge technologies has become imperative. One such technology that has gained significant attention and potential in recent years is computer vision. By enabling machines to "see" and interpret visual data, computer vision has emerged as a reliable solution in the agricultural sector, revolutionizing the way crops are monitored, managed, and optimized, shifting the agricultural landscape towards precision agriculture - an approach that leverages data-driven insights to make informed decisions and optimize resource allocation.

While computer vision holds immense potential in revolutionizing agriculture, it is not without its challenges, which need to be addressed to ensure their

© The Author(s), under exclusive license to Springer Nature Switzerland AG 2023
H. I. Christensen et al. (Eds.): ICVS 2023, LNCS 14253, pp. 159–168, 2023.
https://doi.org/10.1007/978-3-031-44137-0_14

effectiveness and practicality. Agricultural environments often present varying lighting conditions, including shadows, glare, and uneven illumination, affecting the quality and accuracy of images captured by vision systems. Shadows cast by crops or structures can obscure important details, while glare from sunlight or artificial lighting can lead to overexposed areas, making it challenging to extract meaningful information. Agriculture is inherently dependent on weather patterns such as adverse weather conditions such as rain, fog, or dust which can degrade image quality, making it difficult to extract relevant information. Agriculture encompasses vast expanses of land, and the ability to deploy vision systems across these areas is crucial while being able to process large amounts of data, constituting the portability of hardware and the efficiency of algorithms critical. Therefore the development of lightweight, compact, optimized and energy-efficient vision systems that can be easily deployed and operated in various agricultural settings, is necessary for widespread adoption and practical implementation. Moreover, algorithms must be able to adapt and handle plant structures, sizes, colors, and growth stages. To achieve that, computer vision models rely on large and diverse datasets for training, however generating such datasets involves data collection and annotation which is a laborious and costly task.

Towards addressing some of the challenges, this work proposes a methodology to improve the performance and efficiency of detection of small objects, under the assumption that they are located closely to an easier-to-detect anchor class. Our contributions can be summarized as:

- An approach to **increase data efficiency** of relevant data sources from a similar domain which refer to objects with spatial correspondence.
- A novel method to improve the performance of instance segmentation of a secondary class by formulating the detection as a **residual problem** exploiting its spatial correspondence with an anchor class.

2   Related Work

In this section the state of the art in the field of instance segmentation is presented followed by a review of computer vision methods in agricultural scenarios or applications.

2.1   Instance Segmentation

Instance segmentation aims to predict pixel-wise instance masks with class labels for each instance presented in each image. Deep learning approaches rapidly dominated the field with the introduction of Mask R-CNN [8] as a simple and effective system for instance segmentation. It is based on Fast/Faster R-CNN [6,22], using a fully convolutional network (FCN) for mask prediction, along with box regression and classification, constituting a proposal-based approach. To achieve high performance, the feature pyramid network (FPN) [13] is utilized to extract in-network feature hierarchy, where a top-down path with lateral connections is augmented to propagate semantically strong features. More recently, the work of [14] has attempted to shorten the information flow between early and deeper layers by introducing localization signals in early layers by bottom-up path augmentation. Introducing a blender module to combine instance level information and semantic information with lower-level fine granularity [4] can predict dense position-sensitive features resulting in improved efficiency.

Towards achieving higher efficiency, proposal-free or direct approaches have been proposed, which directly predict the segmentation masks for all object instances in the image. The problem of instance segmentation is formulated into a single-shot classification problem [29] by assigning categories to each pixel within an instance according to the instance's location and size. Extending the work in [30], they decouple the mask branch in feature and mask branches, introducing a dynamic learning element to the mask head of the object segmenter to condition the mask head on the location. The popular YOLOv5 [10] has gained popularity due to the ease of use, combined with good accuracy and low execution times. It is based on the YOLOv4 [1] architecture and directly predicts the segmentation masks for all object instances in the image, by using a head network, which predicts the bounding boxes and masks for the objects in the image.

2.2   Object Detection in Agriculture

Deep learning based methods have been widely adopted for the detection of objects of interest in the agriculture domain. Instance segmentation produces objects with binary masks, which is a finer-grained representation compared to the bounding boxes of object detection, making it a suitable solution for fruit and crop detection. The established work of Mask R-CNN is employed for the detection of sweet peppers fruits [7,27] and their peduncles [16] and grapes and their stems [17]. In a similar fashion, the MobileNet SSD detector [15] is used by [20] to produce bounding boxes of sweet peppers and YOLOv5 detector is used by [5] for tomato fruit and peduncle localization.

In [21] a two-step approach for instance segmentation is formulated by introducing a YOLOv5 detector to locate litchi fruit and employ a PSPNet [31] network to perform semantic segmentation inside the bounding boxes of the detected objects. Similarly, [23] adopts a lightweight YOLOv4-Tiny [1] detector to locate the cherry tomato fruit, and a YOLACT++ [2] architecture with a ResNet-101 [9] backbone is selected to split the pixels of fruit and peduncle in the close-up image. Finally, [11] focusing on detected grape fruit boxes, formulates the semantic segmentation as a regression problem by estimating distance maps from the grape stem.

While the approaches above apply deep learning models to detect various objects in images, they mostly perform post-processing steps to enforce spatial constraints or exploit the inherent structure of the targets. Our method departs from the literature, since such **structural information are introduced into the learning process**, which is end-to-end trainable.

3   Motivation

Applying computer vision algorithms in agricultural scenarios introduces important challenges, such as lighting and weather conditions, varying object shape and appearance and occlusion. To tackle such challenges it is important to capture data under varying conditions to ensure reliable learning and robust performance of algorithms. However, capturing data can be a challenging process and includes significant time and cost overheads, since agriculture facilities are often not located close to computer labs and require special equipment for data capture. Moreover, while capturing raw data is beneficial for testing purposes, annotated datasets need to be generated in order to be used in training. This process involves manual annotation of objects of interest in multiple images and is especially laborious. Hence, it is crucial to maximize the potential of computer vision datasets and attempt to re-use information, since generating new datasets for every new case introduces significant overheads. To this end, we attempt to formulate a methodology to leverage data and models trained on a specific class, to improve the performance of detecting a secondary class, under the assumption of spatial correspondence between them.

4   Method

This chapter introduces the proposed methodology by describing the data collection process followed by a description of the proposed architecture based on the YOLOv5 [10] architecture for instance segmentation.

4.1   Data Collection/Annotation

To facilitate the methodology, anchor and secondary classes need to be defined for each case. On the grape-stem case, we define the grape object as anchor and the stem object as secondary class and similarly on the pepper-peduncle case, the pepper fruit is defined as anchor and the peduncle is defined as secondary class. Spatial correspondence is satisfied in both cases since the secondary class is always located close to the anchor class.

Acquiring adequate number of training samples for both classes is important for training robust detectors and avoiding noise-level performance differences. Typically, larger amount of samples are available for the anchor class, since annotation of bounding boxes is much faster compared to mask annotations. To train the models we collected a number of publicly available datasets, while also adding our custom manually annotated datasets for the grape-stem case. The datasets along with the number of samples for train and validation are presented in Table 1 and 2.

4.2   Yolo-V5 Architecture

The YOLOv5 segmentation architecture is based on the YOLOv5 object detection model, but it has been modified to predict pixel-level masks for each object

Table 1. Table presenting the datasets used for training the grape-stem detection.

Dataset	train samples	validation samples
Anchor class: grape		
Embrapa WGISD [26]	240	60
AI4Agriculture Grape Dataset [18]	205	41
wGrapeUNIPD-DL [28]	233	38
ours Grape Dataset	1348	359
Secondary class: stem		
ours Stem Dataset	508	65

Table 2. Table presenting the datasets used for training the capsicum-peduncle detection.

Dataset	train samples	validation samples
Anchor class: capsicum		
Sweet Pepper Detection Dataset [3]	549	200
Deepfruits-capsicum [24]	98	12
deepNIR-capsicum [25]	129	16
Field Capsicum Image Dataset [12]	164	26
Secondary class: peduncle		
Peduncle-roboflow [19]	204	20
Sweet Pepper Detection Dataset [3]	211	96

instance in the image. It consists of the following components: a CSPDarknet53 backbone, which is a modified version of the Darknet53 architecture, a neck module as a pyramid attention network and a head module, responsible for predicting the bounding boxes and masks for the objects in the image. The head used in YOLOv5 segmentation is the YOLOv5 head, which is a modified version of the YOLOv3 head, adding a SPP (Spatial Pyramid Pooling) module to combine features from different scales and a FPN (Feature Pyramid Network) to combine features from multiple layers. The YOLOv5 architecture includes multiple variants ranging from smaller to larger models according to model size.

4.3   Residual Connection of Detectors

The proposed architecture attempts to utilize the features from the anchor class prediction network to improve the performance of the secondary class prediction. To achieve that, we select the output of the YOLOv5 neck module, since this stage contains the richest features at 3 different scales. These features are then added to the outputs of the neck module of the secondary class prediction

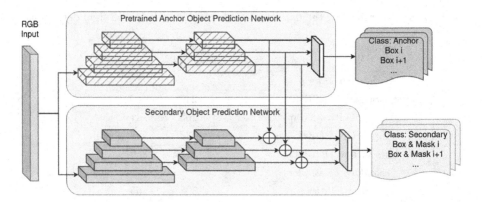

Fig. 1. Architecture diagram of our cascaded residual approach. The top network predicts the locations of the anchor class, while the bottom network predicts the secondary class instances, by fusing its final feature maps with those from the anchor network.

network at each corresponding scale. This generates a bias in the prediction for the secondary class, providing an a-priori strong activation around the estimated anchor class region. Therefore, the secondary class prediction network acts as a residual module on top of an already existing network which localizes the anchor class. The architecture diagram of our proposed connection of detectors is presented in Fig. 1. We start by training the anchor class detection network using the corresponding dataset and freeze its weights. Next, we train the secondary class prediction network using the secondary dataset, while combining its neck features with the anchor network neck features, as described above.

5   Experimental Results

To evaluate our methodology we conducted a set of experiments for the two presented cases, the grape-stem and the capsicum-peduncle, using the datasets of Tables 1 and 2. First, we train YOLOv5 object detection networks for the anchor class (grape and peduncle) to produce anchor detection networks. To serve as a baseline, YOLOv5-seg instance segmentation networks are trained on datasets of the secondary class (stem and peduncle). Finally, our cascaded residual network using a YOLOv5-seg instance segmentation architecture is trained on datasets of the secondary class (stem and peduncle), while using the inference of the pretrained anchor class detectors with frozen weights.

5.1   Evaluation

Results of the proposed models compared with baselines are presented in Fig. 2. In the grape-stem case, the proposed methodology achieved improved metrics for the secondary class compared against the baseline vanilla training of the network. It also predicts stem with increased confidence, demonstrated by the fact that multiple confidence thresholds lead to the same precision-recall point.

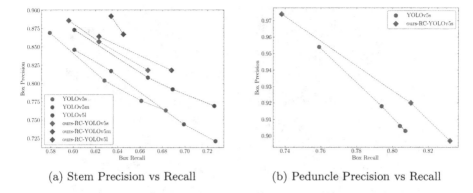

(a) Stem Precision vs Recall   (b) Peduncle Precision vs Recall

Fig. 2. Evaluation metrics for the proposed models and baselines for the instance segmentation of stem (left) and peduncle (right). Precision and Recall are calculated for 0, 0.25, 0.40, 0.70 confidence thresholds during inference.

The behavior remained consistent at any model size, proving the effectiveness of detecting the stem class by introducing the knowledge of where the grape is located. Similar results are demonstrated for the capsicum-peduncle case, where our proposed architecture offers increase in the precision-recall curve, albeit by a smaller margin. We believe that the impact of our proposed methodology between the two cases varies, because the grape-stem case includes larger and more realistic data, whereas the datasets used in the capsicum-peduncle case are less realistic and do not offer diversity. This can be also explained by the metrics, with the capsicum case reaching higher precision and recall metrics than the more challenging grape-stem case.

Table 3. Theoretical computational complexity for baseline and proposed models in FLOPs using 640×640 input image size.

Model	params (M)	GFLOPs	GFLOPs multiplier over YOLOv5s
YOLOv5s	7.6	26.4	1.0×
YOLOv5m	22.0	70.8	2.7×
YOLOv5l	47.9	147.7	5.6×
ours-RC-YOLOv5s	15.2	52.8	2.0×
ours-RC-YOLOv5m	44.0	141.6	5.4×
ours-RC-YOLOv5l	95.8	295.4	11.9×

To evaluate our proposed methodology in terms of efficiency, we also consider the theoretical computational complexity (FLOPs) for the proposed and baseline models from Table 3. Our proposed RC-YOLOv5s outperformed baseline YOLOv5l while using 37% of FLOPs, while RC-YOLOv5m has even better

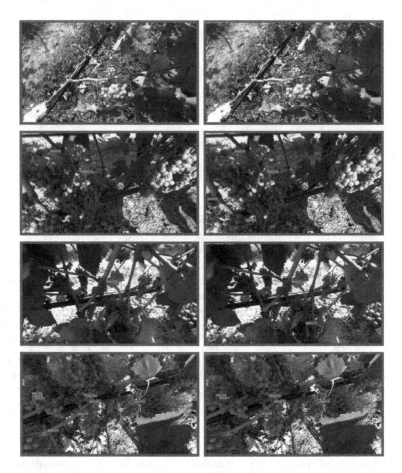

Fig. 3. Qualitative comparison between baseline YOLOv5l (left column) and ours RC-YOLOv5s (right column).

performance while requiring similar flops with YOLOv5l. Our proposed RC-YOLOv5m demonstrated improved performance from baseline YOLOv5l under similar FLOPs requirement, whereas our RC-YOLOv5s outperformed YOLOv5l while requiring 37% of its computations, showcasing the increased efficiency of our proposed method. regarding the number of parameters, our proposed models exhibit more favorable scaling than the baselines, leading to increased parameter efficiency.

Finally, by inspecting the qualitative results from Fig. 3, we observe that both models can identify the most of the stems in the samples Fig. 3 top row. However, our proposed architecture can capture stems that were missed by the baseline model as long as they are close to a grape (Fig. 3 second and third rows), while also not predicting stems that might not belong to a grape, like the bottom left stem in Fig. 3 bottom row.

5.2 Conclusions

In this work we present an approach to maximize the use of hard-to-acquire agricultural computer vision data, by exploiting spatial correspondences of specific objects. In this line, we to created an architecture which leverages strong features from pretrained detectors of an anchor class to improve the performance of segmentation of instances of a more challenging secondary class. Experiments against baselines demonstrate the effectiveness of our methodology in both performance and computational efficiency. In the future, we plan to investigate more cases of spatially relevant objects, even beyond the domain of agriculture and extend the support of the methodology to more network architectures.

References

1. Bochkovskiy, A., Wang, C.Y., Liao, H.: YOLOv4: optimal speed and accuracy of object detection (2020)
2. Bolya, D., Zhou, C., Xiao, F., Lee, Y.J.: YOLACT: real-time instance segmentation. In: Proceedings of the IEEE/CVF International Conference on Computer Vision, pp. 9157–9166 (2019)
3. Cavero, M., Sa, L.E.: Sweet pepper recognition and peduncle pose estimation (2021). https://hdl.handle.net/11285/648430
4. Chen, H., Sun, K., Tian, Z., Shen, C., Huang, Y., Yan, Y.: Blendmask: top-down meets bottom-up for instance segmentation. In: Proceedings of the IEEE/CVF Conference on Computer Vision and Pattern Recognition, pp. 8573–8581 (2020)
5. Giang, T.T.H., Khai, T.Q., Im, D.Y., Ryoo, Y.J.: Fast detection of tomato sucker using semantic segmentation neural networks based on RGB-D images. Sensors **22**(14) (2022)
6. Girshick, R.: Fast R-CNN. In: Proceedings of the IEEE International Conference on Computer Vision, pp. 1440–1448 (2015)
7. Halstead, M., Denman, S., Fookes, C., McCool, C.: Fruit detection in the wild: the impact of varying conditions and cultivar. In: 2020 Digital Image Computing: Techniques and Applications (DICTA), pp. 1–8 (2020)
8. He, K., Gkioxari, G., Dollár, P., Girshick, R.: Mask R-CNN. In: Proceedings of the IEEE International Conference on Computer Vision, pp. 2961–2969 (2017)
9. He, K., Zhang, X., Ren, S., Sun, J.: Deep residual learning for image recognition. In: Proceedings of the IEEE Conference on Computer Vision and Pattern Recognition, pp. 770–778 (2016)
10. Jocher, G., et al.: ultralytics/yolov5: v3.1 - Bug Fixes and Performance Improvements (2020). https://doi.org/10.5281/zenodo.4154370
11. Kalampokas, T., Vrochidou, E., Papakostas, G.A., Pachidis, T., Kaburlasos, V.G.: Grape stem detection using regression convolutional neural networks. Comput. Electron. Agric. **186**, 106220 (2021)
12. Kgp, I.: Field capsicum dataset (2023). https://universe.roboflow.com/iit-kgp-knvbv/field-capsicum
13. Lin, T.Y., Dollar, P., Girshick, R., He, K., Hariharan, B., Belongie, S.: Feature pyramid networks for object detection. In: Proceedings of the IEEE Conference on Computer Vision and Pattern Recognition (CVPR) (2017)

14. Liu, S., Qi, L., Qin, H., Shi, J., Jia, J.: Path aggregation network for instance segmentation. In: Proceedings of the IEEE Conference on Computer Vision and Pattern Recognition, pp. 8759–8768 (2018)
15. Liu, W., et al.: SSD: single shot multibox detector. In: Leibe, B., Matas, J., Sebe, N., Welling, M. (eds.) ECCV 2016. LNCS, vol. 9905, pp. 21–37. Springer, Cham (2016). https://doi.org/10.1007/978-3-319-46448-0_2
16. López-Barrios, J.D., Escobedo Cabello, J.A., Gómez-Espinosa, A., Montoya-Cavero, L.E.: Green sweet pepper fruit and peduncle detection using mask R-CNN in greenhouses. Appl. Sci. **13**(10) (2023)
17. Luo, L., et al.: In-field pose estimation of grape clusters with combined point cloud segmentation and geometric analysis. Comput. Electron. Agric. **200**, 107197 (2022)
18. Morros, J.R., et al.: AI4Agriculture grape dataset (2021). https://doi.org/10.5281/zenodo.5660081
19. People, C.P.: Peduncle segmentation dataset (2023). https://universe.roboflow.com/cmu-pepper-people/peduncle-segmentation
20. Polić, M., Vuletić, J., Orsag, M.: Pepper to fall: a perception method for sweet pepper robotic harvesting. Intell. Serv. Robot. **15** (2022)
21. Qi, X., Dong, J., Lan, Y., Zhu, H.: Method for identifying litchi picking position based on YOLOv5 and PSPNet. Remote Sens. **14**(9) (2022)
22. Ren, S., He, K., Girshick, R., Sun, J.: Faster R-CNN: towards real-time object detection with region proposal networks. In: Advances in Neural Information Processing Systems, vol. 28 (2015)
23. Rong, J., Guanglin, D., Wang, P.: A peduncle detection method of tomato for autonomous harvesting. Complex Intell. Syst. **7** (2021)
24. Sa, I.: Deepfruits capsicum dataset (2021). https://universe.roboflow.com/inkyu-sa-e0c78/deepfruits-capsicum
25. Sa, I., Lim, J.Y., Ahn, H.S., MacDonald, B.: deepNIR: datasets for generating synthetic NIR images and improved fruit detection system using deep learning techniques. Sensors **22**(13) (2022). https://doi.org/10.3390/s22134721
26. Santos, T., de Souza, L., dos Santos, A., Sandra, A.: Embrapa Wine Grape Instance Segmentation Dataset - Embrapa WGISD (2019). https://doi.org/10.5281/zenodo.3361736
27. Smitt, C., Halstead, M., Zaenker, T., Bennewitz, M., McCool, C.: PATHoBot: a robot for glasshouse crop phenotyping and intervention. In: 2021 IEEE International Conference on Robotics and Automation (ICRA), pp. 2324–2330 (2021)
28. Sozzi, M., Cantalamessa, S., Cogato, A., Kayad, A., Marinello, F.: wGrapeUNIPD-DL: an open dataset for white grape bunch detection. Data Brief **43**, 108466 (2022). https://doi.org/10.1016/j.dib.2022.108466
29. Wang, X., Kong, T., Shen, C., Jiang, Y., Li, L.: SOLO: segmenting objects by locations. In: Vedaldi, A., Bischof, H., Brox, T., Frahm, J.-M. (eds.) ECCV 2020. LNCS, vol. 12363, pp. 649–665. Springer, Cham (2020). https://doi.org/10.1007/978-3-030-58523-5_38
30. Wang, X., Zhang, R., Kong, T., Li, L., Shen, C.: SOLOv2: dynamic and fast instance segmentation. In: Advances in Neural Information Processing Systems, vol. 33, pp. 17721–17732 (2020)
31. Zhao, H., Shi, J., Qi, X., Wang, X., Jia, J.: Pyramid scene parsing network. In: Proceedings of the IEEE Conference on Computer Vision and Pattern Recognition, pp. 2881–2890 (2017)

Improving Knot Prediction in Wood Logs with Longitudinal Feature Propagation

Salim Khazem[1,2]([✉]) [ID], Jeremy Fix[2,4] [ID], and Cédric Pradalier[1,3] [ID]

[1] GeorgiaTech-CNRS IRL 2958, Metz, France
[2] Centralesupelec, Metz, France
salim.khazem@centralesupelec.fr
[3] GeorgiaTech Europe, Metz, France
[4] LORIA, CNRS UMR 7503, Metz, France

Abstract. The quality of a wood log in the wood industry depends heavily on the presence of both outer and inner defects, including inner knots that are a result of the growth of tree branches. Today, locating the inner knots require the use of expensive equipment such as X-ray scanners. In this paper, we address the task of predicting the location of inner defects from the outer shape of the logs. The dataset is built by extracting both the contours and the knots with X-ray measurements. We propose to solve this binary segmentation task by leveraging convolutional recurrent neural networks. Once the neural network is trained, inference can be performed from the outer shape measured with cheap devices such as laser profilers. We demonstrate the effectiveness of our approach on fir and spruce tree species and perform ablation on the recurrence to demonstrate its importance.

Keywords: Knot segmentation · Outer-Inter relationship prediction · ConvLSTM

1   Introduction

Distribution of knots within logs is one of the most important factor in wood processing chain since it determines how the log will be sliced and used. A knot is defined as a piece of a branch that is lodged in a stem and often starts at the stem pith. Knots come in various dimensions, shapes and trajectories inside the trunk, these characteristics often depend on tree specie and environmental factors [15]. In wood processing, the knots are considered as defects that affect the quality of logs; hence, detecting their features such as position, size and angle of inclination are relevant and crucial for foresters and sawyers. Knowing these characteristics before the tree processing could generate a relative gain of 15–18% in value of products [2]. Nowadays, internal prediction of tree trunk density from bark observation is a complex and tedious task that requires a lot of human expertise or cannot be performed without expensive X-rays machines. In recent years, with the advent and success of deep learning, convolutional

© The Author(s), under exclusive license to Springer Nature Switzerland AG 2023
H. I. Christensen et al. (Eds.): ICVS 2023, LNCS 14253, pp. 169–180, 2023.
https://doi.org/10.1007/978-3-031-44137-0_15

neural networks have achieved great performances on a variety of tasks such as object detection and image classification due to their strong features extraction capabilities [7,13]. Compared to traditional methods, the data driven deep learning based approaches learn discriminative characteristics from annotated data automatically instead of human engineering. While the era of deep learning led to significant improvements in several areas of computer vision and natural language processing, there are still only a few paper which study the interest of these approaches for forestry and wood processing industry. This is due to the lack of open data, but also due to the lack of transfer of architectures that have demonstrated their efficiency in computer vision to the specific tasks of the forestry and wood processing industry. In this paper, we propose to explore an original task that does not seem to bear resemblance with a task in another domain: predicting the inner structure from the outer appearance of a wood log. The internal knots of a wood log are a consequence of the growth of branches of the tree and there is therefore, at least for some species, a causality between the presence of an inner knot and the growth or scar of an external branch. As we will demonstrate in the paper, the deformation of the outer surface of the tree, which is the consequence of the presence of branches, allows inferring the location and shape of inner knots. Our experiments are carried on conifers for which there is a clear relationship between the growth of branch and the knots. However, for other species such as deciduous trees, this relationship is unclear, and the task remains challenging.

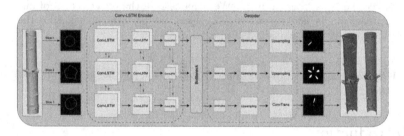

Fig. 1. The recurrent neural network involves a recurrent encoder and feedforward decoder. The context along the slice dimension is propagated with convolutional LSTMs.

To solve the task of predicting the inner knots from the outer contour, we consider convolutional neural networks of the encoder-decoder family, where the encoder extracts features for the contour which are then used to decode the presence of a knot as a binary mask. Regularly spaced contour slices of the tree are provided as input to the network. As the presence of a knot is causally linked with a deformation of the contour due to a branch, inferring a knot needs to integrate features from the contour slices further away up or down the tree. To propagate these features between different slices, we consider convolutional LSTM, which are convolutional bidirectional recurrent neural networks [19]. A convolutional recurrent network keeps the spatial structure of the representation and extracts features along the recurrent paths by applying convolutions rather than dense matrix products. This has the benefit of reducing the cost of the network. In our task, this makes sense because a knot progressively diffuses within the wood as one moves along the longitudinal axis of the tree. That progressive diffusion induces that relevant features can be extracted locally, without having to resort to longer range interactions. Finally, given knots have various shapes and diffuses along a varying number of slices, using LSTMs lets the neural network learn how many slices need to be integrated to properly recover the shape of the knot. In summary, the main contribution of our work lies in two parts:

- we propose to address an original machine learning task that is also valuable for the forestry industry, namely, the prediction of inner defects given observations of the outer deformation of a wood log,
- we demonstrate the efficiency of integrating recurrent connections in the segmentation network to solve this task.

The code used for running all the experiments of this paper are available on the following github repository: https://github.com/jeremyfix/icvs2023.

2   Related Work

Semantic segmentation is a fundamental task in computer vision where the goal is to predict the label of each pixel in an image. Deep learning architectures for this task are typically based on the auto-encoder architecture. An autoencoder consists of an encoder and a decoder. The encoder maps the input data to a lower-dimensional latent space representation, while the decoder maps the latent space back to the original input data dimension [20]. In semantic segmentation, the decoder decodes the target labels instead of reconstructing the input. Fully Convolutional Networks (FCN) [14] is an important approach in semantic segmentation and has influenced the design of modern segmentation network. Other refinements of the encoder-decoder structure, such as U-Net and SegNet, have also been proposed in the literature [1,18].

Recurrent Neural Networks have been introduced to deal with sequence data. They can learn the required size of the temporal window to gather the context required for taking a decision at any given time. The difficulty to integrate and propagate information through time, which is the foundation of the fundamental deep learning problem [10] of the vanishing/exploding gradient, has led authors to design dedicated memory units. Representatives of this family are the Long Short Term Memory networks (LSTMs) [6,8] and Gated Recurrent Units networks (GRUs) [3].

Convolutional LSTM preserves the convolutional nature of the data [19]. Indeed, the recurrent weights in the LSTMs involve dense connections and do not exploit the spatial structure of the data they process. Convolution LSTM, by considering convolutional recurrent ways, do preserve the spatial nature of data and reduces the number of parameters required in the recurrent connections. In the original paper, the convolutional LSTMs have been successfully applied to spatio-temporal sequences for weather forecasting.

In our work, we use an encoder-decoder architecture to predict the knot distribution (binary mask) from the slices of contours of the tree. To propagate encoder features through the slices, the encoder involves recurrent connections. In order to keep the convolutional nature of the representations, the encoder involves convolutional LSTM networks. Alternatively, we could have considered a 3D convolutional encoder, but this would have fixed the size of the slice context necessary to form a prediction. Using LSTMs let the network learn which contour features influence which other contour features.

3   Methodology

3.1   Data Preprocessing

In order to learn to transform the knot distribution from the contour of trees, we need aligned pairs of contours and knot masks. To build the input and target, we considered the pipelines of [11] for segmenting knots and identifying the contours by using X-rays data. Note that even though the pipelines of [11] are used to acquire data from X-rays images. The main objective of our approach is to avoid X-ray scanners and recover the external geometry from other modalities such as vision camera or laser profilers. The dataset is built from 27 fir trees and 15 spruce trees, with slices every 1.25 mm for tree sections of 1 m long in average, which makes a total of 30100 slices. Each image is an 512×512 that is downscaled to 256×256 for the extraction of the contour and knot segmentation, and further downscaled to 192×192 for the sequence models presented in this paper. Every tree is sliced in blocks of 40 consecutive slices. In the following of the paper, the axis along which the slices are stacked will be referred as either the longitudinal axis or the z-axis for short. In the experiments, we used 18 fir tree and 8 spruce tree for the training set, we used 4 fir tree and 2 spruce tree for the validation and 5 tree of each specie for the test set. Note that, each tree is represented with by 800 slices.

3.2   Neural Network Architectures Without Recurrent Connections

We trained two feedforward neural networks based on U-Net [18] and SegNet [1] in order to obtain a baseline to compare with the architecture involving recurrent connections along the z-axis. Although the U-Net and SegNet do not involve recurrent connections, these have been trained on the same data as the recurrent networks, e.g., stacks of slices. This allows to guarantee that training has been performed on the same data and the metrics are computed the same way. The U-Net encoder involves fewer channels than the original network to fit with the input data. The upsampling along the decoder path is performed using a nearest-pixel policy. Along the decoding path, the encoder features are concatenated with the decoder features. The SegNet encoder involves less channels and convolutional layers than the original network. The number of blocks and channels is reduced with respect to the original SegNet because our inputs are smaller.

3.3   Neural Network Architectures with Recurrent Connections

In order to propagate the contextual features of the contours in the encoder, we also consider neural network architectures with recurrent connections along the slice dimension (longitudinal axis of the tree). Recurrent connections are implemented with convolutional LSTMs which allow the network to learn which slice is impacting the features of another slice. We remind that the knots within a log can be causally linked to the presence of a branch. Instead of a fully connected LSTM, the convolutional LSTM involves fewer parameters by exploiting the spatial structure of the input data. In this paper, we consider recurrent connections only in the encoder part and not in the decoder part. The rationale is that introducing recurrent connections in the encoder allows the network to propagate contour features through the slices, and our experiments show that this is already sufficient to get good performances. These recurrent connections are bidirectional to allow information to propagate in both directions along the longitudinal axis. For the decoder, we do not add recurrent connections. That could be helpful but at a higher computational cost, and our experiments already demonstrated good performances with recurrent connections only in the encoder. The neural network architecture is depicted on Fig. 1.

The recurrent encoder is built from 3 consecutive ConvLSTMs bidirectional blocks. Every block has the same number of memory cells than the size of the spatial dimensions times the channel dimension. The input, output, and forget gates compute their values from a convolution with kernel size 3 from the "previous" sequence index (here, previous is to be considered along the longitudinal z-axis and be either following upward or downward directions given we consider bidirectional LSTMs). We use the same representation depth than for the SegNet with 32, 48 and 64 channels and a maxpooling layer is placed after every ConvLSTM layer to downscale spatially the representation by a factor of 2. The decoder is not recurrent and is the same as for our SegNet, namely 3 consecutive blocks with an upsampling (nearest) followed by a $2 \times [Conv2D(3 \times 3) - BatchNorm - ReLU]$ block. The final layer is a $Conv(1 \times 1)$ to output the unnormalized scores for the classification of every pixel.

3.4   Evaluation Metrics

Our experiments use different quantitative metrics to evaluate the quality and the performance of our method. For the segmentation task, the ground truth output is usually very sparse and there are much more negatives than positives. Hence, we need to use evaluation metrics that are not biased due to this class imbalance. We used the Dice similarity coefficient (Dice) [5], which is also known as F1-score as overlap metric, the Hausdorff Distance (HD) [9] as distance-based metric, and the Cohen's Kappa κ [4,17] as counting-based metric to evaluate the segmentation results.

The Hausdorff distance complements the Dice similarity because it indicates if false positives are close to a patch of positives or further away, while the

Cohen's Kappa indicates the agreement between ground truth and the prediction. For each pixel, Cohen's Kappa compares the labels assigned by the model with the ground truth and measures the degree of agreement between them. The Cohen's Kappa ranges from -1 to 1 where a value of 1 indicates perfect agreement between the prediction and ground truth, whereas 0 indicates a prediction which is not better than random guessing and a negative value indicates less agreement than expected by chance. The advantage of using Cohen's Kappa is that it takes into account the possibility of chance agreement and provides a more accurate measure of agreement between prediction and ground truth, this is important in cases where the number of pixels assigned to each class is imbalanced.

For the different equations, we denote FN, FP, TP, TN respectively the number of false negatives, false positives, true positives and true negatives, where $\hat{y}$ is defined as final prediction computed by thresholding the output probability computed by the network (the threshold is set to 0.5 for all the experiments), and y the true value to be predicted (a mask, made of either 1 for a pixel belonging to a knot, or 0 otherwise). The metrics are always evaluated on the whole volume of 40 slices. As mentioned in Sect. 3.2, even the feedforward neural networks (SegNet and UNet) are trained on the volumes. Although these networks do not propagate informations throught the longitudinal axis, training and evaluating these networks on the volume allow to have comparable measures (averaged on the same data). The value of the Hausdorff Distance is reported in millimeters. The metrics reported in the result section are averaged over the total number of volumes in the considered fold.

Table 1. Left) Comparison of the segmentation methods on Dice score and HD using the validation fold. Right) Results of the SegNet and ConvLSTM models for a Fir tree specie. The first row corresponds to the input images, the second row is the associated ground truth and the bottom ones are the predictions. These samples all belong to the validation fold. Every column corresponds to one of 5 slices from different volumes.

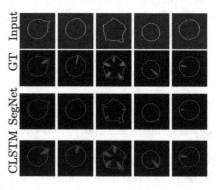

Method	Dice/F1 ↑	HD ↓
SegNet	0.68	26.18
U-Net	0.72	47.80
ConvLSTM	**0.84**	**17.34**

3.5   Other Experimental Hyperparameters

For all the experiments presented in the paper, the optimization followed the same schedule. The networks have been trained for 150 epochs with a batch size of either 10 for U-Nets and ConvLSTMs, reduced to 4 for SegNet. The parameters have been optimized with Adam [12], a base learning rate of 0.0001. The loss is the binary cross entropy. ConvLSTMs trained for one week, the U-Net and SegNet trained for almost 10 days, using two RTX 3090. The experiments were coded either with Tensorflow 2.4[1] or Pytorch 1.9. We used Tensorboard[2] to track the experiments and log the curves (loss and the different metrics). For regularizing the ConvLSTM encoder-decoder, a dropout layer is inserted between the encoder and decoder parts with a probability of 10% to mask a neuron. Following the original papers of U-Net and SegNet, we did not insert dropout layers in these networks. In all the trainings, data augmentation is applied to the input data with a random rotation out of 8 possible angles, and horizontal flip with a probability of 0.5.

4   Results

In this section, we present both quantitatively and qualitatively the performances of the various models on the prediction of knots. The results on the validation fold and test folds are provided respectively in Table 1 and Table 2.

For all the metrics, the ConvLSTM model performs better than the neural networks without recurrent connections. Looking only at the DICE and HD metrics, it seems that even without the recurrent connections, both the SegNet and U-Net perform reasonably well on the task. However, we observed qualitatively that this is not really the case as several knots are not predicted by these models. In that respect, the kappa metric seems to reflect more the difference in performance between the feedforward and recurrent networks.

Including the context with the recurrent connections in the encoder provides a boost in performance. The quality of the segmentation of the recurrent network is better if we look at the Hausdorff distance, which means that the predicted masks with the ConvLSTM are closer in distance to the ground truth than with the non-recurrent segmentation networks. The Hausdorff distance is given in millimeters, and we remind that the slices are 192×192 pixels which correspond to 192mm $\times$ 192mm. Additionally, we computed on the test set the Cohen's Kappa to evaluate the agreement between the predicted masks and the ground truth. The results show that the ConvLSTM achieves a score of 0.41 for fir trees and 0.21 for spruce indicating respectively moderate agreement and fair agreement, while the non-recurrent networks score lower with Kappa values between 0.05 and 0.12 for both species indicating very weak agreement. These findings demonstrate the boost provided by the recurrent networks.

---

[1] https://www.tensorflow.org.

[2] https://www.tensorflow.org/tensorboard.

Table 2. Left) Comparison of the segmentation methods on Dice, HD and Kappa metrics on the test fold. Right) Quantitative results of the ConvLSTM model for the different trees of the test set. These are the same trees than the ones used for table on the left. The metrics are averaged over all the volumes of the same tree. All the trees had almost the same number of slices (from 800 to 810 slices).

Method	Specie	Dice ↑	HD ↓	Kappa ↑
SegNet	Fir	0.68	17.04	0.12
SegNet	Spruce	0.67	33.14	0.06
U-Net	Fir	0.69	37.95	0.10
U-Net	Spruce	0.68	56.62	0.05
ConvLSTM	Fir	**0.74**	**12.68**	**0.41**
ConvLSTM	Spruce	**0.70**	**22.11**	**0.21**

Specie	Tree ID	Dice ↑	HD ↓	Kappa ↑
Fir	4392	0.72	14.6	0.28
	4394	0.75	16.3	0.29
	4396	0.78	8.0	0.52
	5027	0.84	6.5	0.50
	5028	0.78	8.4	0.53
Spruce	4327	0.70	29.0	0.12
	4328	0.72	19.2	0.12
	4329	0.73	9.1	0.25
	4948	0.70	31.0	0.11
	4990	0.73	13.6	0.26

In Table 2, right, we provide the metrics of the ConvLSTM model on the different trees of the test fold, either fir or spruce. The metrics computed on individual trees are consistent with the averaged metrics computed over all the volumes and reported in Table 2, left. However, some spruce trees are particularly challenging. That's the case for example for the trees 4327 and 4948 which have a really unconventional contours, strongly distorted for some reason unknown to the authors. This out-of-distribution contours probably explains why the model fails to correctly predict all the knots. In addition to these averaged metrics, we provide in Fig. 3 the distribution of Cohen's Kappa metric computed on the test fold for both fir and spruce trees, for both the ConvLSTM and SegNet networks. We observe that the ConvLSTM model outperforms the SegNet for all trees for both species, with a clear separation between the distributions. Specifically, the ConvLSTM model achieves nearly a twofold improvement over the SegNet for almost all trees.

As the SegNet performs better on the test set than the U-Net, further comparison will only be made between SegNet and the ConvLSTM network. To better appreciate the difference in segmentation quality between the SegNet and ConvLSTM networks, the prediction masks of both networks on individual slices from different volumes are given in Table 1, right. On this figure, every column is a slice from a different volume of a fir tree and consecutive rows represent the input contour, the ground truth, the prediction of SegNet and the prediction of the ConvLSTM. From these 5 samples, it appears that SegNet usually underestimates knots and sometimes, knots may be even not predicted at all. For the ConvLSTM, most knots are predicted, although the knots might be overestimated in shape.

The predictions on some consecutive slices of the same volume of a tree are shown on Figs. 2 for respectively a fir tree and a spruce tree. On the fir tree

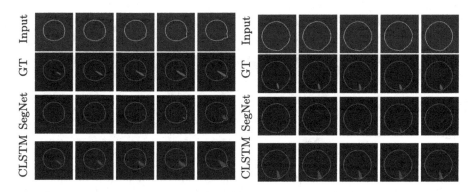

Fig. 2. Results of the SegNet and ConvLSTM models for a fir tree (left) or spruce tree specie (right) on 5 consecutive slices from the same volume. The first row corresponds to the input contours, the second row is the associated ground truth, and the two bottom rows are the predictions. These slices belong to a tree from the test set.

(left), we see part of the branch getting out from the tree, which is the anchor feature from which a network could learn the presence of an inner knot. Indeed, the ConvLSTM seems to be able to propagate information through the slices with its recurrent connections, as it is able to predict the location of a knot on the first of the five slices. It seems unlikely a network could predict the presence of a knot solely based on the first slice, given the deformation of the latter is barely visible on the contour of this first slice.

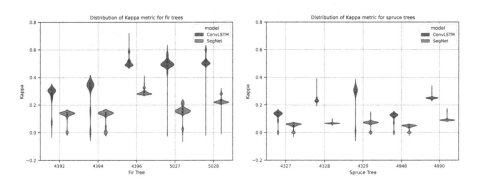

Fig. 3. Distribution of the Kappa metric on the fir and spruce trees of the test fold for both the SegNet and ConvLSTM neural networks. These are the same trees than used in Table 2.

The Fig. 4 shows a 3D representation of the contour of a fir tree from the test set, as well as the ground truth and the prediction produced by the ConvLSTM. The full tree represents a set of 803 slices, and all these slices are processed by sequences of 40 slices, with a stride of 1. From this full tree 3d representation,

Fig. 4. 3D representation of the ground truth (left) and prediction of the ConvLSTM (right) viewed from the side of the tree or the top on both sides. Generated with Paraview.

we observe that every knot present in the ground truth is also predicted by the ConvLSTM. It seems also that some knots may not have been correctly labeled as knots in the ground truth. This 3D representation also highlights the consistency of the knot predictions. From this representation, we also better see that there are various types of branch scars, some being clearly visible while others are more like little bumps on the surface of the tree. The smallest scars are certainly the ones for which it is the most challenging for the network to infer the location of knots, but even in some of these difficult cases, we see that the ConvLSTM model succeeds in predicting knots.

5   Discussion

In this paper, we investigated a machine learning task that is highly valuable for the forestry industry: predicting the location of inner defects, knots, from the outside appearance of the tree. From the machine learning perspective, this task is original. We addressed this problem by training various neural network architectures of the encoder/decoder family and the most promising tested architectures are the convolutional LSTMs which benefit from recurrent connections along the longitudinal axis of the tree to propagate contour features reflecting the scars of a branch to the slices where the knots must be predicted. Although from the averaged metrics (DICE and Hausdorff), the feedforward networks (SegNet, U-Net) seem to perform well, it turns out that their predictions are pretty bad when we observe them qualitatively. This is not the case for the convolutional LSTM model, which have better metrics and clearly better segmentation of the knots when we check them visually. This discrepancy needs further investigation, and it is unclear why good classification metrics would lead to bad segmentation. The performances of the networks appear to be more contrasted by the Cohen's Kappa.

The data used by the proposed machine learning pipeline relies on the work of [11] that extract contour and inner knots of tree logs from X-ray scans. X-ray scans are only essential to produce the targets but are not used by our proposed approach. The required contours for the model can be obtained using laser scanners. We have a work in progress to create a platform with calibrated lasers to extract the contour of a tree log. From a machine learning perspective, the input contours are sparse, but dense representations are used for encoding. There is room for improvement in encoding and decoding methods. Instead of using a binary mask, encoding the contour as a polygon and utilizing graph neural networks for differentiable feature learning could be more efficient. Furthermore, recent research on neural radiance fields [16] suggests the possibility of encoding a 3D volume as a parameterized function, eliminating the need to explicitly construct the 3D volume of knots. Although these ideas require experimentation, a lightweight recurrent encoding of contours that parameterizes a 3D knot density function holds promise.

Acknowledgment. This research was made possible with the support from the French National Research Agency, in the framework of the project WoodSeer, ANR-19-CE10-011.

References

1. Badrinarayanan, V., Kendall, A., Cipolla, R.: SegNet: a deep convolutional encoder-decoder architecture for image segmentation. IEEE Trans. Pattern Anal. Mach. Intell. **39**(12), 2481–2495 (2017)
2. Bhandarkar, S.M., Faust, T.D., Tang, M.: CATALOG: a system for detection and rendering of internal log defects using computer tomography. Mach. Vis. Appl. **11**(4), 171–190 (1999)
3. Cho, K., et al.: Learning phrase representations using RNN encoder-decoder for statistical machine translation. arXiv:1406.1078 [cs, stat] (2014)
4. Cohen, J.: A coefficient of agreement for nominal scales. Educ. Psychol. Measur. **20**(1), 37–46 (1960)
5. Dice, L.R.: Measures of the amount of ecologic association between species. Ecology **26**(3), 297–302 (1945)
6. Gers, F.A., Schmidhuber, J.A., Cummins, F.A.: Learning to forget: continual prediction with LSTM. Neural Comput. **12**(10), 2451–2471 (2000)
7. Goodfellow, I., Bengio, Y., Courville, A.: Deep Learning. MIT Press, Cambridge (2016)
8. Hochreiter, S., Schmidhuber, J.: Long short-term memory. Neural Comput. **9**(8), 1735–1780 (1997)
9. Huttenlocher, D.P., Klanderman, G.A., Rucklidge, W.J.: Comparing images using the Hausdorff distance. IEEE Trans. Pattern Anal. Mach. Intell. **15**(9), 850–863 (1993)
10. Hochreiter, J.: Untersuchungen zu dynamischen neuronalen Netzen. Ph.D. thesis, Technische Universität München (1991)
11. Khazem, S., Richard, A., Fix, J., Pradalier, C.: Deep learning for the detection of semantic features in tree X-ray CT scans. Artif. Intell. Agric. **7**, 13–26 (2023)
12. Kingma, D.P., Ba, J.: Adam: a method for stochastic optimization. arXiv preprint arXiv:1412.6980 (2014)
13. LeCun, Y., Bengio, Y., Hinton, G.: Deep learning. Nature **521**(7553), 436 (2015)
14. Long, J., Shelhamer, E., Darrell, T.: Fully convolutional networks for semantic segmentation. In: Proceedings of the IEEE Conference on Computer Vision and Pattern Recognition, pp. 3431–3440 (2015)
15. Longo, B., Brüchert, F., Becker, G., Sauter, U.: Validation of a CT knot detection algorithm on fresh Douglas-fir (Pseudotsuga menziesii (Mirb.) Franco) logs. Ann. Forest Sci. **76** (2019)

16. Mildenhall, B., Srinivasan, P.P., Tancik, M., Barron, J.T., Ramamoorthi, R., Ng, R.: NeRF: representing scenes as neural radiance fields for view synthesis. In: Vedaldi, A., Bischof, H., Brox, T., Frahm, J.-M. (eds.) ECCV 2020. LNCS, vol. 12346, pp. 405–421. Springer, Cham (2020). https://doi.org/10.1007/978-3-030-58452-8_24

17. Müller, D., Soto-Rey, I., Kramer, F.: Towards a guideline for evaluation metrics in medical image segmentation. BMC. Res. Notes **15**(1), 1–8 (2022)

18. Ronneberger, O., Fischer, P., Brox, T.: U-Net: convolutional networks for biomedical image segmentation. In: Navab, N., Hornegger, J., Wells, W.M., Frangi, A.F. (eds.) MICCAI 2015. LNCS, vol. 9351, pp. 234–241. Springer, Cham (2015). https://doi.org/10.1007/978-3-319-24574-4_28

19. Shi, X., Chen, Z., Wang, H., Yeung, D.Y., Wong, W.K., Woo, W.: Convolutional LSTM network: a machine learning approach for precipitation nowcasting. In: Advances in Neural Information Processing Systems, vol. 28 (2015)

20. Yu, S., Principe, J.C.: Understanding autoencoders with information theoretic concepts. Neural Netw. **117**, 104–123 (2019)

Automation and Manufacturing

Semi-Siamese Network for Robust Change Detection Across Different Domains with Applications to 3D Printing

Yushuo Niu[1] ⓘ, Ethan Chadwick[2] ⓘ, Anson W. K. Ma[2] ⓘ, and Qian Yang[1(✉)] ⓘ

[1] Computer Science and Engineering Department, University of Connecticut, 371 Fairfield Way, Unit 4155, Storrs, CT 06269-4155, USA
{yushuo.niu,qyang}@uconn.edu

[2] Chemical and Biomolecular Engineering Department, University of Connecticut, 97 North Eagleville Road, Unit 3136, Storrs, CT 06269-3136, USA
{ethan.chadwick,anson.ma}@uconn.edu

Abstract. Automatic defect detection for 3D printing processes, which shares many characteristics with change detection problems, is a vital step for quality control of 3D printed products. However, there are some critical challenges in the current state of practice. First, existing methods for computer vision-based process monitoring typically work well only under specific camera viewpoints and lighting situations, requiring expensive pre-processing, alignment, and camera setups. Second, many defect detection techniques are specific to pre-defined defect patterns and/or print schematics. In this work, we approach the defect detection problem using a novel Semi-Siamese deep learning model that directly compares a reference schematic of the desired print and a camera image of the achieved print. The model then solves an image segmentation problem, precisely identifying the locations of defects of different types with respect to the reference schematic. Our model is designed to enable comparison of heterogeneous images from different domains while being robust against perturbations in the imaging setup such as different camera angles and illumination. Crucially, we show that our simple architecture, which is easy to pre-train for enhanced performance on new datasets, outperforms more complex state-of-the-art approaches based on generative adversarial networks and transformers. Using our model, defect localization predictions can be made in less than half a second per layer using a standard MacBook Pro while achieving an F1-score of more than 0.9, demonstrating the efficacy of using our method for *in situ* defect detection in 3D printing.

This work was supported by the National Science Foundation under grant number IIP-1822157 (Phase I IUCRC at University of Connecticut: Center for Science of Heterogeneous Additive Printing of 3D Materials (SHAP3D)). A. W. K. Ma acknowledges support from UConn via the United Technologies Corporation Professorship in Engineering Innovation. Any opinions, findings, and conclusions or recommendations expressed in this material are those of the authors and do not necessarily reflect the views of the National Science Foundation or the sponsors.

H. I. Christensen et al. (Eds.): ICVS 2023, LNCS 14253, pp. 183–196, 2023.
https://doi.org/10.1007/978-3-031-44137-0_16

Keywords: change detection · defect localization · semi-siamese neural network · domain adaptation · 3D printing

1   Introduction

Defect detection methods that can provide feedback in real-time is of significant interest to the additive manufacturing community in order to save on materials cost, printing time, and most importantly, to ensure the quality of printed parts. A key advantage of 3D printing technology that can be leveraged to enable *in situ* defect detection is that 3D objects are printed layer by layer (Fig. 1). Thus, each 2D layer of the object can be imaged and probed for internal defects; unlike traditional manufacturing processes, it is not necessary to wait to analyze the fully printed 3D object, and the interior of the object can be probed as the object is being constructed.

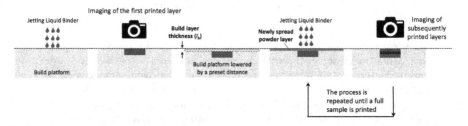

Fig. 1. Schematic diagram of the 3D printing process for binder jet 3D printing with layer-wise imaging during the print.

In this work, we propose a novel defect detection method for 3D printing that poses the problem as one of change detection between a desired reference schematic and a camera image of the printed layer (Fig. 2). In the change detection problem in computer vision, two images such as satellite images of land or surveillance images of streets, are compared for differences. There are several challenges common to both the defect detection and change detection problems: the need to pre-process and pre-align images due to changes in camera angle and lighting, which result in significant and sometimes expensive limitations to the camera setup that must be used, and the data-hungry nature of this complex comparison problem. Additionally, the images we would like to compare for 3D printing are from heterogeneous sources: one is a reference print schematic and the other is a noisy camera image of the actual printed result. In this work, we utilize one-shot learning techniques [11] to develop a novel deep learning architecture that can provide fast and precise localization of defects robust to camera angle and lighting perturbations. A key characteristic of our model is that its relatively lightweight and simple architecture can be easily pre-trained to adapt to new datasets; in fact we show that pre-training enables our simple model to outperform more complex methods based on state-of-the-art techniques such as transformers. The simplicity and flexibility of our model will enable it to be highly transferable to different industrial settings for 3D printing, without requiring careful camera setups and application-specific model customization that is both expensive and time-consuming. Our proposed approach of building on change detection methods from computer vision for tackling the challenges of defect detection is to the best of our knowledge a new direction in the 3D printing field.

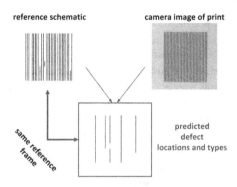

Fig. 2. Our robust defect localization model takes as input a reference print schematic and a camera image of the print, and predicts the precise location and type of defects with respect to the frame of reference of the print schematic. In the predicted image, white corresponds to no defects, red to over-extrusion and green to under-extrusion. This model can be used for *in situ* defect detection: it requires 0.419 s for prediction while printing a single layer on an inkjet-based 3D printer requires tens of seconds or less. (Color figure online)

2   Related Work

Change detection is a fundamental task in computer vision, with many important applications such as analysis of satellite imagery for agricultural monitoring [10], urban planning [17], and disaster assessment [21], among others. A large body of work has thus been built starting from at least the 1980s using methods such as change vector analysis [14]. To handle perturbations such as misalignment and varied lighting, techniques such as incorporating active camera relocation have been proposed [5]. Many state-of-the-art methods today are now based on deep learning, ranging from autoencoders to Siamese neural networks to recurrent neural networks, and various combinations thereof [20]. Recently, several methods based on combining convolutional neural networks (CNN) with Siamese architectures have been proposed. One of the earlier such methods, ChangeNet, uses a combination of ResNet, fully connected, and deconvolution blocks in its Siamese branches [22]. It is designed to handle different lighting and seasonal conditions in the images, but like most existing methods assumes aligned or nearly aligned image pairs. Interestingly, the architecture is different from traditional Siamese architectures in that the deconvolution layers are not required to have the same weights. This is reminiscent of our proposed Semi-Siamese architecture which we will discuss in Sect. 3; however, we will propose the opposite - the deconvolution layers are the portion of our architecture that are required to share the same weights. Another interesting recent approach uses a Siamese pair of autoencoders [15], where the change map is generated based on the learned latent representations. However, this method also assumes coregistered images and can only learn approximate change locations in addition to a classification of whether changes have occurred. A recently proposed architecture that enables fast pixel-level change detection is FC-Siam-diff, a fully convolutional encoder-decoder network with skip connections [3]. In this model, there are two encoders that share the same architecture and weights, while there is only one decoder. However, this model again assumes coregistered images. Finally, the challenge of dealing with images that are not necessarily coregistered, with differences in lighting, camera viewpoint, and zoom, was addressed in Sakurada & Okatani [18] and with CosimNet [6]. The former uses features learned from CNNs trained for large-scale objected recognition in combination with superpixel segmentation to address the problem of change detection in pairs of vehicular, omnidirectional images such as those from Google Street View. The latter, CosimNet, uses the DeeplabV2 model as a backbone and proposes various modifications to the loss function to provide robustness to perturbations [6]. Nevertheless, both of these methods still assume that the images being compared are from the same domain, e.g. they are both camera or satellite images, rather than from different domains such as a camera image versus a schematic. More recently, heterogeneous change detection has been addressed using generative adversarial networks [12] and transformers [2].

Despite its importance for additive manufacturing, defect detection has traditionally been a challenging task. First, there are many different types of defects that may be of interest, including defects caused by missing jets, inconsistent jets, angled jets, and cracks in powder bed material, just to name a few that are relevant to inkjet-based 3D printing; other technologies such as fused deposition modeling have their own set of defects. Many heuristic-based methods such as computing the entropy of depth maps have consequently been developed to address specific defect types [4]. In recent years, both classical machine learning methods such as support vector machines utilizing human-engineered features [8] and deep learning-based methods utilizing convolutional neural networks have begun to be developed to enable more powerful defect detection [9,19]. However, many of these methods require large amounts of labeled experimental data, which is difficult to obtain. They also typically require fixed, high-resolution camera setups, and cannot easily handle differences in camera angle and lighting. For example, one group of methods is based on denoising autoencoders [7], where the idea is that an autoencoder is trained to take as input a "noisy" (defective) image and output its non-defective counterpart. Then, differences between the input and output can be used to identify defects. An advantage of this approach is that it does not require a large amount of labeled experimental data; however, unlike change detection approaches which can handle general differences, this approach can only handle a pre-defined range of defects, since it must be trained to be able to remove them from the output.

3   Semi-Siamese Defect Detection Model

Our proposed model consists of two major components: a novel Semi-Siamese architecture based on U-Net [16] branches, and a fully convolutional network (FCN) to reconstruct the final defect detection mask. The input to the model is a pair of 2D images corresponding to a particular layer during 3D printing: the reference schematic images of the desired print pattern, $I_{ref} \in R^{H \times W \times 3}$, and the camera images of the printed result, $I_{cam} \in R^{H \times W \times 3}$. The image pair (I_{ref}, I_{cam}) is first fed into a Semi-Siamese network to generate a pair of feature maps (F_{ref}, F_{cam}) of the same dimensions as the input. In contrast to standard Siamese networks and existing Semi-Siamese networks which use different decoders, a simple but key innovation of our architecture is that the feature extraction sections of each branch (encoder) do not share the same weights; only the reconstruction section (decoder) share the same weights. This is important for our defect detection problem because the camera image and reference schematic come from different domains. In order to compare them, we first use *different* feature extraction functions to transform them to the same latent feature space, after which we reconstruct them both back into a comparable reference frame using the *same* reconstruction function. Then, their difference is calculated to generate a change map. It is important to calculate the change map from the reconstructed images in a comparable reference frame rather than from the latent feature space in order to enable highly precise pixel-wise defect localization. The final FCN is used to fully transform the change map from this comparable reference frame back to the reference frame of the schematic image.

3.1   Transfer Learning from U-Net Models

As described above, the Semi-Siamese branches of our model are based on the U-Net architecture. This choice is made to leverage the ability of U-nets to produce high resolution outputs [16], enabling precise localization of defects upon comparison of the outputs (F_{ref}, F_{cam}) from each branch. In order to further improve the performance of our model, we first utilize transfer learning from a U-Net model with the same architecture as our Semi-Siamese branches. This U-net model takes as input a perturbed camera image, and outputs a transformation of the image into the same reference frame as its corresponding reference print schematic. When trained on a fixed number of reference schematics, this U-Net can be used for detecting defects by directly comparing a camera image transformed into the reference frame with its corresponding print schematic. However, it is important to note that this architecture cannot handle arbitrary print schematics. Suppose that we would like to detect defects in a print corresponding to a schematic (called "schematic-new") that is similar to a print schematic that the model was previously trained on (called "schematic-old"), but that looks like a perturbed version of it. Then any camera images of a perfect print of "schematic-new" might be erroneously transformed by the model back into the reference frame of "schematic-old". Now when compared with "schematic-new", many defects will be detected, even though no defects occurred in the actual print. Thus, this U-Net architecture cannot be used on its own to handle defect detection for arbitrary desired print schematics. We will instead use this U-Net model pre-trained on a small set of reference schematics to initialize the weights of each branch of our Semi-Siamese model. This allows us the initialize the Semi-Siamese model in such a way that it can offset perturbations for some limited sets of camera images and reference schematics. We then continue training to fine-tune these weights to be able to handle arbitrary reference print schematics and perturbed camera images. As we show in the results, this ability to pre-train the U-Net to initialize our Semi-Siamese model is key to high performance on novel problems. We note that while we have utilized a U-Net backbone for our Semi-Siamese branches, we can replace it with any state-of-the-art encoder-decoder architecture of choice.

3.2 Semi-Siamese Network Architecture

Our deep learning model begins with two U-Net branches sharing an identical architecture. Each U-Net has five fully convolutional blocks to do downsampling (feature extraction) and four convolutional blocks to do upsampling (reconstruction). Each feature extraction block is composed of two 3×3 convolutional layers followed by a batch normalization layer and a rectified linear unit (ReLU) activation. For the first four feature extraction blocks, there is a 2D max pooling layer after each block, where each max pooling layer has pool size 2×2 and strides of 2. For each of the first four feature extraction blocks, the size of the feature maps is thus reduced by half, while the number of channels is doubled. In the last feature extraction block, there is no max pooling layer, so the size of the feature map remains the same and only the number of channels is doubled. For the reconstruction blocks, each block starts with 3×3 convolution layers followed by a batch normalization layer and ReLU activation. Analogous to the feature extraction block, the size is doubled each time but the number of channels is reduced by half. Before each reconstruction layer, there is a 2D transposed convolutional layer for upsampling (upsampling layer). Skip connections link the output from the max pooling layers to the corresponding upsampling layers. From these Semi-Siamese branches, a pair of feature maps are generated and their difference is calculated to get the change map. This change map is then fed into the remaining FCN, which generates the final change mask $\hat{Y}$ giving the predicted probability for each pixel of whether it corresponds to a location with no defect, over-extrusion, or under-extrusion. A full schematic of the proposed architecture is shown in Fig. 3.

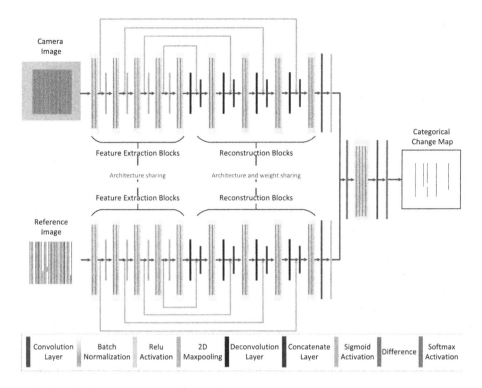

Fig. 3. Full architecture for our model. Different types of layers are labeled by color, as indicated in the legend. The Semi-Siamese branches each consist of an underlying U-Net architecture, with a feature extraction (encoder) section, a reconstruction (decoder) section, and skip connections between corresponding layers. (Color figure online)

3.3   Training Objective

Our model uses focal loss [13] as the loss function in order to address the imbalance in change detection datasets between easy-to-classify background pixels and the smaller number of foreground pixels where changes may occur. We note that this imbalance is more pronounced in datasets from our 3D printing application than in benchmark datasets for change detection typically derived from satellite imagery. The focal loss leverages a modulating term on the cross entropy loss in order to focus learning on hard samples by reducing the contributions to the training loss of samples for which the model is confidently correct (easy samples). The equation for the focal loss is

$$\mathcal{FL}(\mathbf{y}, \mathbf{p}) = -\sum_{i=1}^{N} \alpha_i (1 - p_i)^\gamma \log(p_i) \qquad (1)$$

where p_i is the predicted probability for the true class y_i for pixel i, and $(1 - p_i)^\gamma$ is the modulating term, with tunable focusing parameter $\gamma \geq 0$. The hyperparameters α_i are additional weighting parameters that re-balance the contribution of each pixel to the loss, typically based on its true class. Here we denote **y** as the vector of all y_i and **p** as the vector of all p_i.

4 Experiments

We compare our model against three change detection methods that represent different existing state-of-the-art approaches: ChangeNet [22], which utilizes a ResNet backbone and Semi-Siamese branches with shared encoders; BIT [2], which utilizes transformers; and DTCDN, which utilizes generative adversarial networks [12].

First, we compare our model with existing methods for heterogeneous change detection across different image domains using the benchmark Wuhan dataset [1], which consists of pairs of optical and synthetic aperture radar (SAR) images. Note that this dataset only involves binary classification and does not contain significant perturbations in image alignment and angle; there is no benchmark dataset for heterogeneous change detection in the multi-class case. To test the application of our model to 3D printing with three-class classification (no defect, under-extrusion, and over-extrusion), and also to demonstrate our model's robustness to perturbations in camera angle and lighting, we then created our own experimental dataset consisting of pairs of (1) reference print schematics and (2) top-down camera images of inkjet-based 3D printing on powder bed material, where Dimatix Blue model fluid is used on Visijet core powder. To simplify dataset generation, our set of reference schematic images consist only of images with vertical lines of varying length spaced closely together. The corresponding camera images are taken at various angles, so that a simple template matching approach would not be able to easily achieve pixel-wise accuracy in defect localization. In future work, we will expand to more complex schematic images. However, the efficacy of our model in precisely localizing defects can be sufficiently demonstrated using this dataset.

4.1 Full Dataset Generation Using Data Augmentation

Since generating an experimental dataset is time-consuming, and with a real 3D printer also incurs significant material costs, we start with only a limited dataset of 57 pairs of experimental images. We then use data augmentation to significantly increase our dataset size by adding perturbations in camera angle to existing camera images. Note that lighting perturbations come naturally from the camera images being taken with no special lighting setup. We do not make any changes to the reference schematics. The types of perturbations we use in the data augmentation includes zoom, rotation, shear, and position (width and height) shift. We emphasize that here we use data augmentation to create our initial full dataset, in contrast to the typical setting in computer vision where data augmentation should only be used in training. The perturbations to the camera image given by data augmentation correspond to artificial new "experiments" of different camera setups. To prevent data leakage, we separate the training, validation, and test sets by reference schematic. The final dataset consists of 16400 training, 560 validation, and 560 test images, where 41 underlying schematic images are used in the training data, and 8 schematic images each were used for validation and test.

To create defective image pairs, we match the camera image from one reference image with a different reference schematic. Since all of the images correspond to perfect non-defective prints for their true corresponding schematic, we can precisely localize the "defects" in the defective image pairs by comparing the camera image's true reference schematic with the given new schematic. To generate the training, validation, and test sets, we first randomly select either one underlying schematic for non-defective examples, or two different underlying schematics for defective examples. Then we randomly pick corresponding camera images from among the perturbed variations in our augmented dataset. We note that it is important to balance the dataset between defective and non-defective pairs; otherwise the trained model tends to predict the presence of some defects even for non-defective pairs.

5   Results

Table 1 shows the results of different change detection methods, as well as an ablation study on the Semi-Siamese and transfer learning components of our approach, on our generated vertical line dataset. Note that due to the imbalance between classes in this dataset, the under-extrusion class was the most difficult to correctly identify. We report the F1-score for each class, as well as the averaged macro F1-score. Our Semi-Siamese model with initialization was able to achieve significantly higher performance than the other methods on identifying under-extrusion. Even without initialization, using all of the same hyperparameters for handling the imbalanced dataset, the Semi-Siamese model outperformed

Table 1. Performance comparison on the vertical line dataset. Note that due to the imbalance between classes in this dataset, the under-extrusion class was the most difficult to correctly identify.

Method	Accuracy	macro F1-score	no-defect F1-score	over-extrusion F1-score	under-extrusion F1-score
ChangeNet	0.9842	0.5646	0.9920	0.6431	0.0588
DTCDN	0.9572	0.7613	0.9772	0.6970	0.6097
BIT	0.9957	0.9267	0.9978	0.9555	0.8268
Unet	0.9774	0.7155	0.9884	0.6859	0.4722
Semi-Siam (w/o init)	0.9962	0.9406	0.9981	**0.9709**	0.8529
Siamese (w/init)	0.9658	0.6652	0.9823	0.4629	0.5503
Semi-Siam (w/init)	**0.9972**	**0.9517**	**0.9986**	0.9503	**0.9061**

Table 2. Performance comparison on the Wuhan dataset [1]. DTCDN results are from Ref. [23] since it was difficult to reproduce the high performance without modifications, as also noted in [23].

Method	Precision	Recall	IOU	F1-score
ChangeNet	0.6555	0.6326	0.5232	0.6420
DTCDN*	0.6742	0.6536	0.5492	0.6629
BIT	0.6678	0.6859	0.5564	0.6759
Semi-Siam (w/init)	0.6714	0.7247	0.5659	0.6905
Siamese (w/init)	0.6571	0.6833	0.5476	0.6681
Semi-Siam (w/init)	**0.7306**	**0.7263**	**0.6113**	**0.7284**

Table 3. All training times are based on 200 epochs (not including pre-training the GAN in the case of DTCDN, and pre-training the U-Net in the case of Semi-Siamese with initialization) on the vertical line dataset on a 4-GPU workstation.

Method	Training	Setup	Prediction
ChangeNet	178.14 h	1797.155 ms	423.406 ms
DTCDN	GAN:36.74 h U-Net++:56.28 h	GAN: 1577.17 ms U-Net++:150.958 ms	GAN:10410.228 ms U-Net++:490.128 ms
BIT	105.39 h	569.835 ms	342.935 ms
U-Net	19.34 h	136.563 ms	213.76 ms
Semi-Siam (w/o init)	48.31 h	206.847 ms	419.283 ms
Siamese (w/init)	36.83 h	179.195 ms	408.974 ms
Semi-Siam (w/init)	U-Net:9.34 h Semi-Siam: 48.31 h	206.847 ms	419.283 ms

other methods including BIT. In Fig. 4, we provide both visual and quantitative comparisons of each method on several example pairs of images. Compared to existing methods, in most cases our model is able to capture the defect locations more precisely and with less noise.

Table 2 shows the results of different change detection methods (including an ablation study similar to above) on the benchmark Wuhan dataset, and Fig. 5 provides visual and quantitative comparisons of each method on sample pairs of images. We note that visually, our Semi-Siamese model with initialization is able to better reproduce the smooth shape of the ground truth mask. In the second case where the macro F1-score of DTCDN and BIT outperform our method, the key difference is the detection of a change in a round region in the top left quadrant. While this is not labeled in the ground truth, on close inspection one can see that this is not necessarily inconsistent with the SAR image.

In addition to being more accurate, our method is comparatively simpler and more lightweight. From Table 3, we can see that our model takes significantly less time to train than ChangeNet, DTCDN, and BIT.

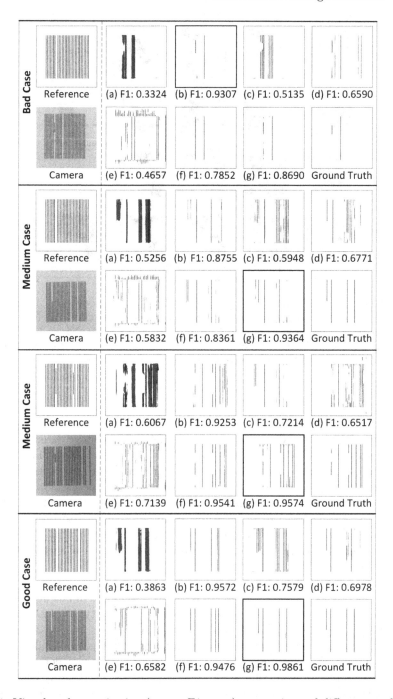

Fig. 4. Visual and quantitative (macro F1-score) comparison of different models on the vertical line dataset. The methods from (a)–(g) are (a) ChangeNet, (b) BIT, (c) DTCDN, (d) U-Net, (e) Siamese model with initialization, (f) Semi-Siamese model without initialization, (g) Semi-Siamese model with initialization. White, red and green correspond to no defects, over-extrusion, and under-extrusion, respectively. (Color figure online)

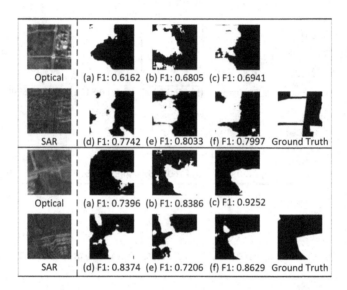

Fig. 5. Visual and quantitative comparison of different models on the Wuhan dataset [1]. The methods from (a)–(f) are (a) ChangeNet, (b) DTCDN, (c) BIT, (d) Siamese model with initialization, (e) Semi-Siamese model without initialization, and (f) Semi-Siamese model with initialization. DTCDN results are from Ref. [23] as it was difficult to reproduce the high performance without modifications, as also noted in [23].

6 Conclusions

We have developed a new deep learning-based method for change detection where (i) a camera image is being compared against a desired schematic rather than another camera image, and (ii) perturbations to the camera angle and lighting do not need to be pre-corrected, and coregistration is not necessary. This novel Semi-Siamese model can be applied to obtain precise *in situ* pixel-wise defect localization for each layer of a 3D print, enabling rapid detection of internal defects, ensuring the quality of 3D printed parts and saving time and material costs. While an acknowledged limitation of this method is that it does not directly handle defects in the z-direction in a *single* layer, due to the ability to observe each printed layer at various perturbed camera angles, large z-direction defects in the top layer will likely project onto the 2D camera image in such a way as to appear as in-plane defects. Robust handling of these types of z-directional defects will be explored in future work.

Defect detection for 3D printing is an important industrial challenge that to the best of our knowledge is being addressed with change detection techniques for the first time in this work. The key benefit of utilizing the change detection framework is that it is not necessary to pre-define the desired print schematic, nor to have a large set of annotated data for each defect type. Our model is capable of detecting defects in a few seconds with more than 90% accuracy, and performs better than many different more complicated state-of-the-art approaches: ResNet-based Semi-Siamese models with shared encoders (ChangeNet), generative adversarial network (GAN)-based models (DTCDN), and transformer-based models (BIT), on not only our custom 3D printing dataset but also on the benchmark heterogeneous change detection Wuhan dataset. The simplicity of our model makes it possible to easily achieve good performance on new problems - it is only necessary to pre-train a U-Net (or other encoder-decoder backbone) and then transfer learn from that onto the Semi-Siamese architecture. The robustness of our algorithm to camera angle and lighting perturbations while enabling domain adaptation, as well as its lower training data requirements, will enable flexibility for utilizing this model in different industrial settings.

References

1. Caltagirone, F., et al.: The Cosmo-Skymed dual use earth observation program: development, qualification, and results of the commissioning of the overall constellation. IEEE J. Sel. Top. Appl. Earth Obs. Remote Sens. **7**(7), 2754–2762 (2014). https://doi.org/10.1109/JSTARS.2014.2317287
2. Chen, H., Qi, Z., Shi, Z.: Remote sensing image change detection with transformers. IEEE Trans. Geosci. Remote Sens. **60**, 1–14 (2021). https://doi.org/10.1109/TGRS.2021.3095166
3. Daudt, R.C., Saux, B.L., Boulch, A.: Fully convolutional Siamese networks for change detection. In: 2018 25th IEEE International Conference on Image Processing (ICIP), pp. 4063–4067 (2018). https://doi.org/10.1109/icip.2018.8451652
4. Fastowicz, J., Grudziński, M., Teclaw, M., Okarma, K.: Objective 3D printed surface quality assessment based on entropy of depth maps. Entropy **21** (2019). https://doi.org/10.3390/e21010097
5. Feng, W., Tian, F., Zhang, Q., Zhang, N., Wan, L., Sun, J.: Fine-grained change detection of misaligned scenes with varied illuminations. In: 2015 IEEE International Conference on Computer Vision (ICCV), pp. 1260–1268 (2015). https://doi.org/10.1109/iccv.2015.149
6. Guo, E., et al.: Learning to measure change: fully convolutional Siamese metric networks for scene change detection. arXiv abs/1810.09111 (2018)
7. Han, Y., Yu, H.: Fabric defect detection system using stacked convolutional denoising auto-encoders trained with synthetic defect data. Appl. Sci. **10**, 2511 (2020). https://doi.org/10.3390/app10072511
8. Jacobsmühlen, J.Z., Kleszczynski, S., Witt, G., Merhof, D.: Detection of elevated regions in surface images from laser beam melting processes. In: 41st Annual Conference of the IEEE Industrial Electronics Society, IECON 2015, pp. 001270–001275 (2015). https://doi.org/10.1109/iecon.2015.7392275
9. Jin, Z., Zhang, Z., Gu, G.: Autonomous in-situ correction of fused deposition modeling printers using computer vision and deep learning. Manuf. Lett. **22**, 11–15 (2019). https://doi.org/10.1016/j.mfglet.2019.09.005
10. Khan, S.H., He, X., Porikli, F., Bennamoun, M.: Forest change detection in incomplete satellite images with deep neural networks. IEEE Trans. Geosci. Remote Sens. **55**(9), 5407–5423 (2017). https://doi.org/10.1109/tgrs.2017.2707528
11. Koch, G.R.: Siamese neural networks for one-shot image recognition. In: ICML Deep Learning Workshop (2015)

12. Li, X., Du, Z., Huang, Y., Tan, Z.: A deep translation (GAN) based change detection network for optical and SAR remote sensing images. ISPRS J. Photogramm. Remote Sens. **179**, 14–34 (2021). https://doi.org/10.1016/j.isprsjprs.2021.07.007

13. Lin, T.Y., Goyal, P., Girshick, R., He, K., Dollár, P.: Focal loss for dense object detection. In: Proceedings of the IEEE International Conference on Computer Vision, pp. 2980–2988 (2017). https://doi.org/10.1109/TPAMI.2018.2858826

14. Malila, W.A.: Change vector analysis: an approach for detecting forest changes with landsat. In: Proceedings of the 6th Annual Symposium on Machine Processing of Remotely Sensed Data (1980)

15. Mesquita, D.B., Santos, R.F.D., Macharet, D., Campos, M., Nascimento, E.R.: Fully convolutional Siamese autoencoder for change detection in UAV aerial images. IEEE Geosci. Remote Sens. Lett. **17**, 1455–1459 (2020). https://doi.org/10.1109/lgrs.2019.2945906

16. Ronneberger, O.: Invited talk: U-Net convolutional networks for biomedical image segmentation. In: Maier-Hein, K.H., Deserno, T.M., Handels, H., Tolxdorff, T. (eds.) Bildverarbeitung für die Medizin 2017. I, p. 3. Springer, Heidelberg (2017). https://doi.org/10.1007/978-3-662-54345-0_3

17. Saha, S., Bovolo, F., Bruzzone, L.: Building change detection in VHR SAR images via unsupervised deep transcoding. IEEE Trans. Geosci. Remote Sens. **59**(3), 1917–1929 (2021). https://doi.org/10.1109/tgrs.2020.3000296

18. Sakurada, K., Okatani, T.: Change detection from a street image pair using CNN features and superpixel segmentation. In: BMVC (2015). https://doi.org/10.5244/c.29.61

19. Scime, L., Siddel, D., Baird, S.T., Paquit, V.: Layer-wise anomaly detection and classification for powder bed additive manufacturing processes: a machine-agnostic algorithm for real-time pixel-wise semantic segmentation. Addit. Manuf. **36**, 101453 (2020). https://doi.org/10.1016/j.addma.2020.101453

20. Shi, W., Zhang, M., Zhang, R., Chen, S., Zhan, Z.: Change detection based on artificial intelligence: state-of-the-art and challenges. Remote Sens. **12**(10) (2020). https://doi.org/10.3390/rs12101688

21. Sublime, J., Kalinicheva, E.: Automatic post-disaster damage mapping using deep-learning techniques for change detection: case study of the Tohoku Tsunami. Remote Sens. **11**(9), 1123 (2019). https://doi.org/10.3390/rs11091123

22. Varghese, A., Gubbi, J., Ramaswamy, A., Balamuralidhar, P.: ChangeNet: a deep learning architecture for visual change detection. In: Leal-Taixé, L., Roth, S. (eds.) ECCV 2018. LNCS, vol. 11130, pp. 129–145. Springer, Cham (2019). https://doi.org/10.1007/978-3-030-11012-3_10

23. Zhang, C., et al.: A domain adaptation neural network for change detection with heterogeneous optical and SAR remote sensing images. Int. J. Appl. Earth Obs. Geoinf. **109**, 102769 (2022). https://doi.org/10.1016/j.jag.2022.102769

Spatial Resolution Metric for Optimal Viewpoints Generation in Visual Inspection Planning

Vanessa Staderini[1,2]([✉]), Tobias Glück[1], Roberto Mecca[1], Philipp Schneider[1], and Andreas Kugi[1,2]

[1] Center for Vision, Automation and Control, AIT Austrian Institute of Technology GmbH, 1210 Vienna, Austria
`vanessa.staderini@ait.ac.at`
[2] Automation and Control Institute, TU Wien, 1040 Vienna, Austria

Abstract. The automation of visual quality inspection is becoming increasingly important in manufacturing industries. The objective is to ensure that manufactured products meet specific quality characteristics. Manual inspection by trained personnel is the preferred method in most industries due to the difficulty of identifying defects of various types and sizes. Sensor placement for 3D automatic visual inspection is a growing computer vision and robotics area. Although some methods have been proposed, they struggle to provide high-speed inspection and complete coverage. A fundamental requirement is to inspect the product with a certain specific resolution to detect all defects of a particular size, which is still an open problem. Therefore, we propose a novel model-based approach to automatically generate optimal viewpoints guaranteeing maximal coverage of the object's surface at a specific spatial resolution that depends on the requirements of the problem. This is done by ray tracing information from the sensor to the object to be inspected once the sensor model and the 3D mesh of the object are known. In contrast to existing algorithms for optimal viewpoints generation, our approach includes the spatial resolution within the viewpoint planning process. We demonstrate that our approach yields optimal viewpoints that achieve complete coverage and a desired spatial resolution at the same time, while the number of optimal viewpoints is kept small, limiting the time required for inspection.

Keywords: Ray tracing · Sampling density matrix · Set coverage problem · Spatial resolution · Viewpoint planning · Visibility matrix

1 Introduction

In the last decades, the automation of industrial production has emerged to play a pivotal role in the manufacturing industries. Companies have made substantial investments toward realizing fully automated processes, driven by optimizing production efficiency. An important process to maximize production performance is visual quality inspection. Automated visual inspection planning can be

H. I. Christensen et al. (Eds.): ICVS 2023, LNCS 14253, pp. 197–207, 2023.
https://doi.org/10.1007/978-3-031-44137-0_17

conceptualized as a Coverage Path Planning Problem, see [1,18], which can be divided into two sub-problems, namely the Viewpoint Planning Problem (VPP) and the Path Planning Problem (PPP). The VPP involves generating a set of viewpoint candidates (VPCs) and selecting the minimum number of viewpoints by solving the Set Coverage Problem (SCP). The optimal solution consists of the smallest number of viewpoints necessary to achieve full coverage. The PPP involves finding a collision-free and time-optimal trajectory for a given mechanical stage or robotic manipulator that connects the optimal viewpoints generated by solving the VPP. In this work, we introduce a novel metric for selecting optimal viewpoints that ensures comprehensive object coverage at a desired spatial resolution. In industrial inspection, it is important to cover an object at a specific spatial resolution for identifying all defects with a minimal size that the user defines. The state of the art in literature for solving the VPP does not take into account any information about how each surface element is covered. Moreover, the object to be inspected is often provided as a non-homogeneous 3D mesh, and all surface elements are treated similarly, regardless of their actual size. To overcome these issues, we define a new matrix to provide maximum coverage and minimum spatial resolution. This is done by considering the area of each surface element and the number of ray intersections. We emphasize that the primary focus of this work is not on generating viewpoint candidates since many methods are already available and offer good performance. Instead, our focus is on selecting optimal viewpoints to achieve complete coverage and provide the desired spatial resolution, given a predefined set of candidates and specific requirements for the inspection task. This paper is organized as follows: In Sect. 2, we introduce the mathematical formulation of the VPP. The state of the art is presented in Sect. 3. Then, in Sect. 4, we describe our novel formulation for viewpoints evaluation and optimal viewpoints selection. In Sect. 5, we show the results obtained when applying our new formulation of the VPP compared to the standard definition. Finally, conclusions are drawn in Sect. 6.

2   Viewpoint Planning Problem Formulation

The VPP consists of a generation and a selection step. We consider a meshed object with $s_i \in \mathcal{S}$, $i = 1, 2, \ldots, M$ surface elements and a set of VPCs defined as $\mathcal{V} = \{\mathbf{v}_1, \mathbf{v}_2, ..., \mathbf{v}_N\}$, with cardinality $N = |\mathcal{V}|$. Each viewpoint is formulated as $\mathbf{v}_j^{\mathrm{T}} = \begin{bmatrix} \mathbf{c}_j^{\mathrm{T}} & \mathbf{g}_j^{\mathrm{T}} \end{bmatrix} \in \mathbb{R}^6$ for $j = 1, \ldots, N$ in world coordinates $\mathcal{W}$ given by the camera position $\mathbf{c}_j$ and the gaze direction $\mathbf{g}_j$. Typically, $M \gg N$ holds. In the context of VPP, see [14], $\mathbf{V} \in \mathbb{R}^{M \times N}$ is the so-called visibility matrix with matrix elements

$$\mathbf{V}_{ij} = \mathbf{V}[i, j] = \begin{cases} 0 & \text{if element } s_i \text{ is not visible from } \mathbf{v}_j, \\ 1 & \text{if element } s_i \text{ is visible from } \mathbf{v}_j. \end{cases} \tag{1}$$

Note that the row $\mathbf{V}[i, \mathcal{V}]$ of the visibility matrix corresponds to the surface element s_i of the mesh, and the column $\mathbf{V}[\mathcal{S}, j]$ to the viewpoint $\mathbf{v}_j$. This is the input of the SCP together with $\mathcal{V}$ that reads as

$$\min_{\mathbf{y}} \sum_{j=1}^{N} w_j y_j \tag{2a}$$

$$\text{s.t.} \sum_{j=1}^{N} \mathbf{V}_{ij} y_j \geq 1, \ i = 1, \ldots, M \tag{2b}$$

$$y_j \in \{0, 1\}, \ j = 1, \ldots, N. \tag{2c}$$

The SCP (2) constitutes a linear integer programming problem that aims to minimize (2a) subject to the constraints of (2b) and (2c). Its optimal solution is the smallest set of viewpoints necessary to fully cover the surface of the object, i.e., $\mathcal{V}^* = \{\mathbf{v}_k, \ldots, \mathbf{v}_l, \ldots, \mathbf{v}_m\}$, with cardinality $K \leq N$ and $\mathcal{J}^* = \{k, \ldots, l, \ldots, m\} \subseteq \{1, 2, \ldots, N\}$. The binary variable y_j is the j-th element of the vector $\mathbf{y}$ and is weighted by the coefficient w_j. Without loss of generality, we assume $w_j = 1$, which means that all viewpoints are of equal cost. Following [13], the coverage of a single viewpoint $\mathbf{v}_j$ is defined as

$$C_j(\mathbf{v}_j) = \frac{1}{M} \sum_{i=1}^{M} \mathbf{V}_{ij}, \tag{3}$$

and the coverage due to all the optimal viewpoints computes as

$$C(\mathbf{v}_j \in \mathcal{V}^*) = \frac{1}{K} \sum_{j \in \mathcal{J}^*} C_j(\mathbf{v}_j). \tag{4}$$

This is the maximum achievable coverage considering all the viewpoint candidates.

3   State of the Art of the VPP

Over more than three decades, extensive research has been conducted on generating optimal viewpoints. Numerous algorithms have been developed for this purpose. Despite these efforts, the problem of generating optimal viewpoints still needs to be solved. No existing method can simultaneously achieve complete coverage of an object, utilize a small set of viewpoints, maintain low computational costs, and provide a high spatial resolution [6,10,15,19]. A comprehensive overview of viewpoint generation methods can be found in [4]. The optimal viewpoint generation methods can be broadly classified into three main groups: space sampling [6,12,19], vertex sampling [3,5,13], and patch sampling [10,11,16]. Space sampling methods are often combined with Next Best View (NBV) approaches, initially introduced in [2]. NBV approaches do not require a detailed model of the object under inspection, but certain information, such as its size, can be beneficial. Various variants of NBV algorithms are documented in [7]. NBV algorithms involve determining a candidate viewpoint as the starting point of the inspection and selecting subsequent viewpoints based on the percentage of the unseen surface area of the object they offer. When the model of the object to be inspected is available, it is advantageous to leverage this knowledge and adopt an alternative approach to NBV. This alternative approach revolves around solving the SCP. The core component of this formulation is the visibility matrix, which we introduced in Sect. 2. The visibility matrix is generated by performing sight ray tracing using the sensor model, viewpoint information, and the 3D model of the object.

In the literature, a surface element is typically considered visible if it satisfies four conditions: (i) it falls within the field of view of the sensor, (ii) it is within the sensor's depth of field, (iii) there are no occlusions along the line of sight between the viewpoint and the surface element, and (iv) the incident angle between the line of sight and the surface's normal is below a certain threshold. This approximation helps to determine if a surface element is intersected by at least one ray originating from a given viewpoint. However, it does not provide information about the surface element's spatial resolution or level of coverage. For an overview of criteria commonly used to evaluate view planning outcomes, we refer to [13]. The author of the aforementioned paper proposes a suitable approach for line-scan range cameras, which considers the precision and sampling density provided by the viewpoints. In this approach, a surface element is deemed visible if it falls within the sensor's frustum, has no occlusions along the line of sight, and the estimated precision and sampling density for that specific surface element and viewpoint meet the problem's requirements. However, one drawback of this approach is that the sampling density is evaluated per surface element from a specific viewpoint. As a result, it may identify optimal viewpoints with excessively high sampling density, leading to an unnecessarily dense representation of surface elements that does not provide significant additional information or contribute to the analysis. Moreover, this high density incurs substantial computational costs. To address these issues, we propose to define a new matrix to replace the visibility matrix to consider the spatial resolution of each surface element in relation to the entire set of VPCs.

4   Sampling Density Matrix

This paper presents a novel formulation to determine optimal viewpoints. We propose a new metric that measures not only visibility but also spatial resolution. In what follows, we will often use the term (spatial) *density*, which is closely related to spatial resolution. We propose a new formulation that aims to achieve high spatial resolution in the sense of a small distance between the rays striking a face and thus a high spatial density. To this end, we introduce a new matrix called the "sampling density" matrix, which serves a similar role as the visibility matrix in the SCP but incorporates additional measurement features. This enables us to resolve the VPP to select optimal viewpoints that maximize coverage while

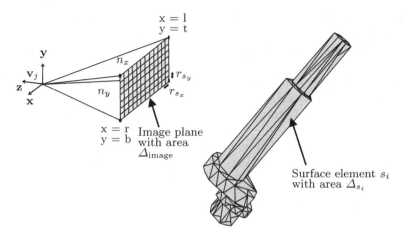

Fig. 1. The visual inspection of an object involves two main components. On the left side, we have the generation of rays in the case of a perspective projection. Each ray originates from a viewpoint $\mathbf{v}_j$ and its direction is determined by the line connecting the viewpoint and the location of a pixel on the image plane denoted as Δ_{image}. The image plane consists of $n_x \times n_y$ pixels, with each pixel separated from one another by distances r_{s_x} and r_{s_y} along the two directions of the image plane. On the right side, we have the representation of the object to be inspected in the form of a 3D mesh with non-homogeneous surface elements s_i, each having an area Δ_{s_i}.

ensuring a minimum spatial resolution $\bar{r}_s$, tailored to the problem's requirements. This is particularly important in visual inspections, where the objective is to detect defects of varying sizes based on the specific use case.

To accurately capture the object's geometry and detect defects, it is necessary to consider the number of rays intersecting each surface element. However, this information is not captured by the visibility matrix. It only distinguishes between visible and non-visible surface elements based on whether at least one ray intersects with a given surface element. One drawback of relying on the visibility matrix is that in the case of a 3D model represented by non-uniform triangular faces (or surface elements), a single ray intersect may be sufficient to identify small faces, especially if they are smaller than the defect of interest. However, this may not hold for larger surface elements since more rays are required to cover larger areas. Moreover if a defect is smaller than the distance between two rays (spatial resolution), it may go undetected. One potential solution to overcome this issue would be to re-mesh the object to have uniform faces, all with a size comparable to the desired spatial resolution. However, this approach introduces geometric changes to the meshed object, negatively impacting viewpoint planning for defect detection.

The objective of this paper is to address the mentioned challenges while avoiding the need for object re-meshing. Additionally, we aim to overcome the lack of information about the achieved spatial resolution, which is influenced by both the surface element's area and the number of rays intersecting it. In order to integrate spatial resolution in the VPP, we consider four crucial factors: (i) the image place with area Δ_{image}, (ii) the surface area Δ_{s_i} of the surface element s_i, (iii) the number of rays R_{ij} associated with $\mathbf{v}_j$ intersecting with s_i, and (iv) the spatial resolution r_{s_x} and r_{s_y} in both directions.

As shown in Fig. 1, we consider an image with $n_x \times n_y$ pixels. This is fitted into a rectangle of size $(r-l) \times (t-b)$ that corresponds to the image plane area Δ_{image} at a reference distance d_r equal to the effective focal length from the viewpoint $\mathbf{v}_j$. Mathematically, this relationship can be expressed as $\Delta_{\text{image}} = (r-l) \times (t-b)$. Furthermore, the spatial resolution of the sensor at the reference distance can be represented as $r_{s_x} = (r-l)/n_x$ and $r_{s_y} = (t-b)/n_y$, as detailed in [8]. For notation purpose, we define the inverse of the spatial resolution at reference distance d as

$$\delta_s|_d = \left.\frac{1}{r_s}\right|_d = \sqrt{\frac{n_x \times n_y}{\Delta_{\text{image}}}}\frac{d_r}{d}, \tag{5}$$

which we refer to as the (spatial) *sampling density*. To determine if a surface element. In the following, we assume the reference distance d to be equal to the working distance of the sensor. To determine if a surface element s_i is intersected by rays originating from viewpoint $\mathbf{v}_j$ and to track the number of rays hitting it, we draw inspiration from Eq. (5). We introduce the *ray matrix* $\mathbf{R}$. Each matrix element $\mathbf{R}_{ij}$ represents the number of rays originating from the viewpoint $\mathbf{v}_j$ that intersect the surface element s_i. In addition, we introduce the *surface element density* as $\delta_{s_{ij}}$, where the index i pertains to the surface element s_i, and the index j pertains to the viewpoint $\mathbf{v}_j$. This variable relates the number of rays $\mathbf{R}_{ij}$ that intersect with a surface element s_i to its surface area Δ_{s_i}. Mathematically, the surface element sampling density due to a single viewpoint $\mathbf{v}_j$ can be expressed as

$$\delta_{s_{ij}} = \sqrt{\frac{\mathbf{R}_{ij}}{\Delta_{s_i}}}. \tag{6}$$

Furthermore, we introduce the *surface element sampling density* δ_{s_i}, which is the cumulative sum of $\delta_{s_{ij}}$ over all viewpoints $\mathbf{v}_j$, with $i = 1, \ldots, N$, i.e.

$$\delta_{s_i} = \sum_{j=1}^{N} \delta_{s_{ij}}. \tag{7}$$

In the problem at hand, we aim not only at full coverage but at a specific minimal sampling density per surface element s_i, i.e. $\delta_{s_i} \geq \bar{\delta}_s$, with *target surface element sampling density* $\bar{\delta}_s$. At this point, we make use of the relations (6) and (7) as well as of the definition of the visibility matrix (1) to introduce the so-called *sampling density matrix* $\mathbf{S} \in \mathbb{R}^{M \times N}$. This reads as

$$\mathbf{S}_{ij} = \mathbf{S}[i,j] = \begin{cases} \delta_{s_{ij}}/\bar{\delta}_s & \text{if } \delta_{s_i} \geq \bar{\delta}_s, \\ \mathbf{V}_{ij} & \text{otherwise.} \end{cases} \tag{8}$$

where $\mathbf{V}_{ij} = \{0, 1\}$ are the elements of the visibility matrix $\mathbf{V}$ introduced in Sect. 2 and $\bar{\delta}_s$ is the target surface element sampling density. In particular, $\mathbf{S}_{ij} = 0$ if there is no ray originating from $\mathbf{v}_j$ intersecting with the surface element s_i and $\mathbf{S}_{ij} = 1$ if the viewpoint $\mathbf{v}_j$ can provide the required spatial density of s_i or if there is no combination of the VPCs that can guarantee $\bar{\delta}_s$. The reason for this is that we want to determine a set of optimal viewpoints which are able to cover all the visible surface elements, even when they cannot be covered with target spatial density. In this case, we use the definition of visible as it is commonly used in the literature and as described in Sect. 3.

In the subsequent steps, we aim to utilize the sampling density matrix to identify the optimal set of viewpoints $\mathcal{V}^*$. These viewpoints should not only maximize coverage but also provide a sampling density that exceeds the target sampling density, i.e., $\delta_{s_i} \geq \bar{\delta}_s$ and therefore offer the required spatial resolution. To achieve this, we replace the visibility matrix with the sampling density matrix in the SCP (2). Additionally, the sampling density per surface element is considered as the sum of the spatial density offered by each viewpoint. This approach helps to avoid excessively high sampling densities that could be computationally expensive.

5   Results and Discussions

The simulation results were conducted using a sensor model with dimensions of 1200×1920 pixels. The sensor has a field of view of $38.7° \times 24.75°$, a depth of field ranging from 300 to 700 mm, and a maximum incidence angle of $75°$. Our evaluation metric considered two objects[1] with distinct geometric characteristics, namely a hirth and a crankshaft. These objects are depicted in Fig. 2. Without loss of generality, in the following we assume a target spatial resolution $\bar{r}_s = 0.18$ mm and a set of 500 viewpoint candidates (VPCs). These were generated with the method proposed in [17] because it achieves a higher coverage than the one achieved with the other methods for VPCs generation. Firstly, our objective is to demonstrate that using our metric allows us to generate candidates starting from a decimated mesh, resulting in higher coverage compared to when the visibility matrix is adopted. In Fig. 3, the coverage is evaluated on

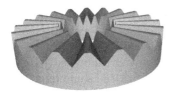 

Fig. 2. Meshed objects used in simulation: (left) Hirth, (right) crankshaft.

---

[1] https://owncloud.fraunhofer.de/index.php/s/H8jV9rwGN84knzP (Accessed August 19, 2023).

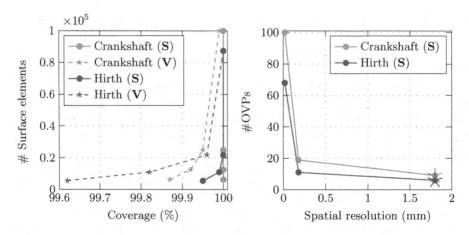

Fig. 3. Evaluation of the sampling density matrix **S**: (left) Achieved coverage with respect to the number of surface elements of the mesh used to generate the viewpoints candidates (VPCs). Coverage is evaluated adopting the visibility matrix **V** (dashed lines) and the novel sampling density matrix (solid lines) as introduced in this work. (right) Relationship between spatial resolution and number of optimal viewpoints (#OVP) when the sampling density matrix is adopted. We indicate with a star the values that have been achieved when the visibility matrix was used.

the original 3D mesh of the target objects, while the VPCs are generated using different decimated meshes. Typically, when decimated mesh models are used for generating VPCs, there are losses in the coverage of the original target object due to geometric differences between the meshes. However, this effect is mitigated when our metric is utilized, as demonstrated in the left subfigure of Fig. 3. The achieved coverage, shown by the solid lines representing the sampling matrix, consistently surpasses the coverage obtained with the visibility matrix (indicated by the dashed lines). Notably, the solid lines are always positioned to the right of their corresponding dashed lines, highlighting the superior coverage achieved when our metric is applied. The difference between the coverage obtained using the two metrics is more pronounced when the VPCs are generated from highly decimated meshes. The number of optimal viewpoints (#OVP) obtained using our metric is relatively small, ranging from 4 to 12 for a higher spatial resolution (smaller values) depending on the mesh model used for generating the viewpoint candidates. The number of viewpoints decreases as the spatial resolution decreases (larger values), eventually reaching a value equivalent to the number of OVPs required when the visibility matrix is employed (indicated by a star in the plots of Fig. 3), as shown in the right subfigure of the same figure. It is important to emphasize that the primary objective of our formulation for the VPP is to provide optimal viewpoints for generating a dense point cloud that satisfies the spatial resolution constraint. This is evident in Fig. 4, where a scalar field representing the number of neighbours within a sphere of radius equal to the target resolution is presented. For both objects, the hirth and crankshaft, the

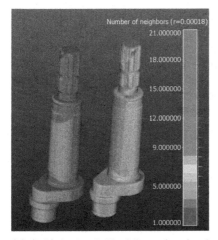

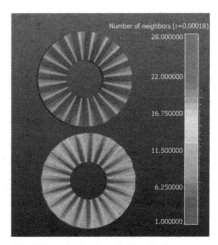

(a) (left) Scalar field of the point cloud generated using the visibility matrix **V**. (right) Scalar field generated using the sampling density matrix **S**.

(b) (above) Scalar field of the point cloud generated using the visibility matrix **V**. (below) Scalar field generated using the sampling density matrix **S**.

Fig. 4. Number of neighbours inside a sphere of radius $R = \bar{r}_s = 0.18$ mm. The number of neighbours is larger (red) when our novel sampling density matrix is used. This means that the achieved spatial resolution is larger and therefore smaller defects can be identified.

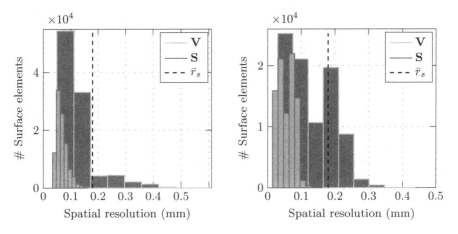

Fig. 5. Histograms showing the resolution per surface element in the case of the crankshaft (left) and hirt (right) when the optimal viewpoints are determined using the visibility matrix **V** and the novel sampling density matrix **S**. The vertical line indicates the target spatial resolution $\bar{r}_s = 0.18$ mm. (Color figure online)

number of neighbours is higher when our formulation is adopted. This indicates that a higher spatial resolution is obtained, enabling the detection of smaller defects. In addition, two histograms are shown in Fig. 5 to compare the spatial resolution achieved with the visibility matrix (blue) and the novel sampling density matrix (red) per surface element. The spatial resolution is larger when our VPP formulation is employed, as shown by the concentration of red bins on the left side of the plots. On the other hand, when the visibility matrix is used, only a few surface elements meet the required spatial resolution (indicated by blue bins between 0 and $\bar{r}_s$), while the majority of surface elements do not meet the requirement (blue bins to the right of $\bar{r}_s$ in Fig. 5).

6   Conclusions and Outlook

In this paper, we introduce a novel metric for evaluating viewpoint candidates by utilizing a new matrix called the sampling density matrix. This replaces the state of the art visibility matrix in the set coverage problem. Our approach takes into account both the surface area of each element of the mesh and the number of rays intersecting it, allowing it to be adapted to homogeneous and non-homogeneous 3D meshes of the target object. The new formulation of the viewpoint planning problem presented in this paper can be integrated into various model-based pipelines that employ sight ray tracing to evaluate viewpoint candidates and solve the SCP. Our method generates optimal viewpoints that ensure desired spatial resolution on a per-surface element basis. The method is versatile and well-suited for different types of visual inspection tasks, including surface and dimensional inspection [9]. The simulation experiments conducted in this study demonstrate that decimated meshes can be used to compute viewpoints for models with a high number of faces, thereby accelerating the computation of optimal viewpoints without sacrificing the achievable coverage. This is in contrast to the standard VPP formulation, where decimated meshes worsen the performance in terms of coverage. Considering that the appearance of the target object can impact visibility during inspection tasks, we propose further research to incorporate photometric information into the viewpoint evaluation process. This would require extending the ray tracing capabilities of our method to account for the reflectivity of the object and to consider the relative positions of the camera and of the illumination points with respect to the position of the object being inspected. By incorporating photometric considerations, a more comprehensive evaluation of viewpoints can be achieved.

References

1. Almadhoun, R., Taha, T., Seneviratne, L., Dias, J., Cai, G.: A survey on inspecting structures using robotic systems. Int. J. Adv. Rob. Syst. **13**(6), 1–18 (2016)
2. Connolly, C.: The determination of next best views. In: IEEE International Conference on Robotics and Automation, vol. 2, pp. 432–435 (1985)
3. Englot, B.J.: Sampling-based coverage path planning for complex 3D structures. Ph.D. thesis, Massachusetts Institute of Technology (2012). http://hdl.handle.net/1721.1/78209
4. Gospodnetić, P., Mosbach, D., Rauhut, M., Hagen, H.: Viewpoint placement for inspection planning. Mach. Vis. Appl. **33**(1), 1–21 (2022)

5. Gronle, M., Osten, W.: View and sensor planning for multi-sensor surface inspection. Surf. Topogr. Metrol. Prop. **4**(2), 777–780 (2016)
6. Jing, W., Polden, J., Lin, W., Shimada, K.: Sampling-based view planning for 3D visual coverage task with unmanned aerial vehicle. In: IEEE/RSJ International Conference on Intelligent Robots and Systems (IROS), pp. 1808–1815 (2016)
7. Karaszewski, M., Adamczyk, M., Sitnik, R.: Assessment of next-best-view algorithms performance with various 3D scanners and manipulator. ISPRS J. Photogramm. Remote Sens. **119**, 320–333 (2016)
8. Marschner, S., Shirley, P.: Fundamentals of Computer Graphics. CRC Press (2018)
9. Mohammadikaji, M.: Simulation-Based Planning of Machine Vision Inspection Systems with an Application to Laser Triangulation, vol. 17. KIT Scientific Publishing (2020)
10. Mosbach, D., Gospodnetić, P., Rauhut, M., Hamann, B., Hagen, H.: Feature-driven viewpoint placement for model-based surface inspection. Mach. Vis. Appl. **32**(1), 1–21 (2021)
11. Prieto, F., Lepage, R., Boulanger, P., Redarce, T.: A CAD-based 3D data acquisition strategy for inspection. Mach. Vis. Appl. **15**(2), 76–91 (2003)
12. Sakane, S., Sato, T.: Automatic planning of light source and camera placement for an active photometric stereo system. In: IEEE International Conference on Robotics and Automation, pp. 1080–1081 (1991)
13. Scott, W.R.: Model-based view planning. Mach. Vis. Appl. **20**(1), 47–69 (2009)
14. Scott, W.R., Roth, G., Rivest, J.F.: Performance-oriented view planning for model acquisition. In: International Symposium on Robotics, pp. 212–219 (2000)
15. Scott, W.R., Roth, G., Rivest, J.F.: View planning for automated three-dimensional object reconstruction and inspection. ACM Comput. Surv. (CSUR) **35**(1), 64–96 (2003)
16. Sheng, W., Xi, N., Tan, J., Song, M., Chen, Y.: Viewpoint reduction in vision sensor planning for dimensional inspection. In: IEEE International Conference on Robotics, Intelligent Systems and Signal Processing, vol. 1, pp. 249–254 (2003)
17. Staderini, V., Glück, T., Schneider, P., Mecca, R., Kugi, A.: Surface sampling for optimal viewpoint generation. In: 2023 IEEE 13th International Conference on Pattern Recognition Systems (ICPRS), pp. 1–7 (2023)
18. Tan, C.S., Mohd-Mokhtar, R., Arshad, M.R.: A comprehensive review of coverage path planning in robotics using classical and heuristic algorithms. IEEE Access **9**, 119310–119342 (2021)
19. Tarbox, G.H., Gottschlich, S.N.: Planning for complete sensor coverage in inspection. Comput. Vis. Image Underst. **61**(1), 84–111 (1995)

A Deep Learning-Based Object Detection Framework for Automatic Asphalt Pavement Patch Detection Using Laser Profiling Images

Ibrahim Hassan Syed[1]([✉]) [ID], Susan McKeever[1] [ID], Kieran Feighan[2], David Power[2], and Dympna O'Sullivan[1] [ID]

[1] School of Computer Science, Technological University, Dublin, Ireland
{ibrahim.syed,susan.mckeever,dympna.osullivan}@tudublin.ie
[2] Pavement Management Services Ltd. Athenry Co, Galway, Ireland

Abstract. Road maintenance and the early detection of road defects rely on routine pavement inspections. While advanced 3D laser profiling systems have the capability to automatically identify certain types of distress such as cracks and ruts, more complex pavement damage, including patches, often require manual identification. To address this limitation, this study proposes an automated patch detection system that employs object detection techniques. The results demonstrate the ability of object detection models to accurately identify patches in laser profiling images, indicating that the proposed approach has the capability to significantly enhance automation in visual inspection processes. This has the potential for significant cost reduction in inspections, improved safety conditions during checks, and acceleration of the current manual inspection processes.

Keywords: Road surface · visual inspection · Object detection · deep learning

1 Introduction

Transportation and road infrastructure departments routinely conduct inspections on pavements to evaluate their surface conditions. Pavement conditions are impacted by traffic, weather, and sunlight, resulting in rutting, cracking, and ravelling that can ultimately lead to the disintegration of the surface layer. Such deterioration may be limited to the surface or indicative of more serious underlying structural issues related to the pavement. The maintenance of pavement surfaces necessitates a substantial number of resources and capital to ensure that optimal maintenance treatment is performed at the appropriate time. These inspections support informed decisions regarding pavement maintenance planning, including cost considerations [1]. In addition, the government can optimize allocation of limited resources for maintenance and consider long-term investment strategies [2]. Therefore, it is highly desirable to conduct pavement inspections in the most cost-effective manner.

Pavement assessment tasks involve a range of activities, from identifying pavement distresses to complete visual inspection of the pavement surface. To minimize maintenance costs, these tasks must align with the objectives of the schemes and the available

budget. According to the survey, the UK, councils allocate 75% of funds for the maintenance of local road conditions and 25% for construction [3]. According to another survey,
in 2008, around \$182 billion was spent on capital improvements and maintenance of
federal highways in the US [4].

Fig. 1. Examples of laser profiling images acquired from asphalt pavement surface. **Note:** For
the interpretation, patches are highlighted in the red boxes.

1.1 Visual Inspection

There are two primary methods for visually inspecting pavements: manual and automatic.
Visual inspection techniques typically involve three main steps: data acquisition, distress
identification, and distress assessment. While the first step of data acquisition is largely
automated using specialized vehicles, distress identification and assessment are typically
performed manually. Manual inspection involves the assessment of pavement surface
conditions by trained pavement engineers or certified inspectors, either through on-site
surveys or by analyzing recorded videos/images. However, the manual visual inspection
process is time-consuming, subjective, prone to errors, and potentially hazardous for
inspectors.

To address these limitations, there is a growing interest in automating the entire
visual inspection process. This can be achieved using advanced technologies such as
machine learning, computer vision, and remote sensing [5].

1.2 Related Work

Several researchers have proposed the use of machine learning and computer vision-
based methods to automate the distress identification step of visual pavement inspection.
Implementing these techniques has the potential to significantly enhance the accuracy
and efficiency of pavement inspections, while reducing the time and cost involved in
manual inspections.

Various methods based on deep learning, particularly convolutional neural networks,
have been suggested for the automatic identification of pavement distress. These methods can be broadly categorized into three main groups based on their approach to the

problem of detecting pavement distress: classification, localization, and segmentation. For instance, Gupta et al. [6] present a pothole detection system using thermal images. The authors employed two object detection models i.e., the ResNet34-single shot multibox detector and the ResNet50-RetinaNet model. The ResNet34-single shot multibox detector yielded an average precision of 74.53%, while the ResNet50-RetinaNet model achieved a precision of 91.15%. Zou et al. [7] proposed a DeepCrack segmentation network that utilizes the encoder-decoder architecture to accurately detect pavement cracks. Through experimentation, the authors demonstrated that the proposed Deep-Crack model achieves an F-measure of over 0.87, highlighting its efficacy in identifying and segmenting pavement image pixels into cracks and background.

Despite extensive research on automatic pavement distress detection, most studies have focused on potholes and cracks, with less attention given to the detection of pavement patches. The detection and localization of patches on pavement surfaces is an essential task for pavement management and maintenance. Patches play a dual role in the pavement maintenance process, offering both temporary and long-term pavement fix solutions and can be made of similar or different materials than the surrounding pavement. They serve various purposes, ranging from covering large areas like utility patching to addressing specific single-pothole distresses. Given the diverse nature of patching, manual intervention by engineers is necessary. They manually label and draw bounding boxes around each patch to aid in the detection process. The manual process is not only time consuming but also cost-intensive. In addition, modern 3D laser profiling technology, such as the LCMS (Laser Crack Measurement System) [8], and Pave3D [9] is now broadly utilized in the pavement inspection process. These systems are equipped with 3D laser profilers that capture range and intensity images of the pavement surface and come with a built-in data processing tool that processes the acquired data and automatically identifies various types of road cracks [10]. Furthermore, 3D laser profiling technology has become a standard technique in pavement inspection companies, where these systems are employed.

Advanced pavement inspection systems like Laser Crack Measurement System (LCMS) have made significant progress in automatically detecting various types of defects such as cracks [8], rutting [11], raveling [12], which can help in the assessment of pavement condition and the planning of maintenance and rehabilitation activities. However, automatic detection of pavement patches presents a significant challenge due to the similarity in color between intact pavement and patched surfaces. As a result, the detection process often involves manual involvement, with engineers manually labeling or drawing bounding boxes around each patch. Therefore, this paper addresses the problem of automatic patch detection on laser profiling images.

2 Methodology

This paper proposes a methodology for the detection and localization of patches using laser profiling images (see Fig. 1). Our approach leverages state-of-the-art object detection techniques based on deep learning algorithms to achieve the detection of patch locations on pavement surfaces. This study aims to address the following research

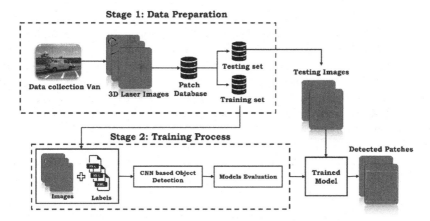

Fig. 2. Proposed pavement patch detection framework.

question: To what extent can an object detection model accurately detect and localize patches on the intact pavement? Fig. 2 illustrates the proposed framework of automatic pavement patch detection system.

To address the above research question, we propose a comprehensive framework for an automatic pavement patch detection system (refer to Fig. 2). Our methodology involves a multi-stage process, which includes pre-processing of the 3D laser profiling images, training and fine-tuning of the object detection model, and post-processing of the detected patches. The pre-processing step involved collecting a dataset of 3D laser profiling images that captured the pavement surface. From this dataset, we selected positive images only (i.e., images that contain one or more patches). These positive images were then manually labeled by an expert by drawing bounding boxes around the patches, indicating their locations in the images. We utilize a state-of-the-art object detection model based on deep learning algorithms, which have been proven to out-perform traditional machine learning and images processing techniques [13]. Once the object detection model identified and localized the patches in the images, in the post-processing step the detected coordinates of the bounding boxes were used to calculate the area of the patched surface on the intact pavement surface. These calculated areas then allowed us to quantify the extent of patching on the normal pavement surface. In addition, given that the patch detection models trained on data obtained from a single country and specific capture settings, Therefore, in order to evaluate the generalizability of the model to road surfaces in different regions with different capture settings, we conducted tests on images acquired from the road network in another country (Ireland).

2.1 Data Collection & Preparation

This study employs asphalt pavement images acquired through 3D laser profiling system LCMS (Laser Crack Measurement System) mounted on the back of a data collection van. This system employs high-speed and high-resolution transverse profiling to capture images of pavement surface. The LCMS takes a transverse profile every 5 mm. That means every 5 mm, there are 4160 laser readings taken across the width of the pavement at 1 mm increments. A transverse profile every 5 mm gives a good profile of the road surface and allows a survey speed of around 90km/h. Each line in the depth image represents 5 mm of road length, 200 lines represents one meter. The rate of transverse profile collection can be adjusted but 5 mm is a good compromise of speed, safety, and data collected. The laser profiling system generates range image output, with sample images shown in Fig. 1. Furthermore, each image has been manually labelled by an engineer at PMS (Pavement Management Services, Ireland) by drawing bounding boxes around the patches in the image.

In this study, 80% of the data was utilized to train the model, while the remaining 20% was reserved for evaluating the model's performance. The dataset details are described in Table 1.

Table 1. Details of the complete training and testing sets.

# Of images	Training set	Testing set
1874	1500	374

2.2 Network Architecture

This study employed two distinct network architectures to obtain comparative results utilizing the specified dataset. Specifically, the state-of-the-art object detection models Faster RCNN [14] and DETR [15] were selected for training and testing using transfer learning technique [16]. The transfer learning technique known as "fine-tuning" was employed to adapt a pre-trained Faster RCNN model to our specific object detection task. Specifically, we utilized a Faster RCNN model pre-trained on a large-scale dataset, such as ImageNet, which had learned general visual features. We then initialized our model with these pre-trained weights and further fine-tuned it on our custom dataset with annotations for the target objects. By fine-tuning, we allowed the model to adapt its learned features to our domain-specific data, enabling it to perform object detection more effectively and efficiently for our specific task. Furthermore, the selection of Faster RCNN and DETR models was motivated by their prior usage in the domain of automatic pavement inspection, including applications such as road marking detection [17], pothole detection [18], and other surface distress identification [19].

2.3 Evaluation Protocol

To assess the effectiveness of the trained model in detecting and localizing patches, its performance was evaluated using the mean Average Precision (mAP) score, specifically for the patch category. Average precision is determined by calculating the area under the Precision-Recall curve for each category, providing a comprehensive understanding of the model's performance across the range of precision and recall values. To achieve the mean average precision score, an IoU threshold of 0.5 was established. This threshold is a widely accepted evaluation metric employed by the PASCAL VOC

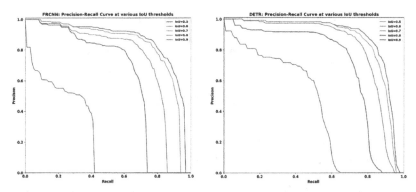

Fig. 3. Precision-recall curve of both models obtained at highest and lowest IoU thresholds.

object detection competition [20]. Furthermore, according to the domain expert for the task of patch detection, a higher IoU threshold is not required, as the exact placement of the patch relative to the predicted area only needs to be enough to say that a patch exists in the intact pavement area [21]. The mean average precision, precision and recall can be calculated as follow:

$$mAP = \frac{1}{N_{classes}} \sum_i AP_i \tag{1}$$

where i is a type of distress and $N_{classes}$ is the total number of distress types, which is 1 in our case.

$$Precision = \frac{TruePositives}{TruePositives + FalsePositives} \tag{2}$$

where True positives + False positives is the total number of detections generated from the model.

$$Recall = \frac{TruePositives}{TruePositives + FalseNegatives} \tag{3}$$

Where True positives + False negatives is the total number of ground truth boxes.

2.4 Experimental Results

The detection performance of the two models is presented in Table 2, while Fig. 3 shows the precision-recall curve obtained at the highest and lowest IoU thresholds. The DETR model outperforms the Faster RCNN model, with a 2% increase in mean average precision.

The analysis of the precision-recall graphs (see Figure-3) revealed that a higher IoU threshold led to a decrease in recall rate. This outcome is because the model only identifies patches as true positives if their overlap is greater than or equal to 0.9. Alternatively, using an IoU of 0.5 would result in an increase in recall rate as shown in Fig. 3 Furthermore, from the precision and recall graphs (Fig. 3) we can easily find the best possible precision

Table 2. Performance of both models on the test set.

Model	Backbone	mAP0.5
Faster RCNN	ResNet50	0.86
DETR	ResNet50	0.88

and recall value. For instance, the blue line on the graph indicates the results obtained at the 0.5 IoU threshold. This line allows us to easily determine where the ideal precision and recall values can be located. For instance, at a recall rate of 0.8, the model's precision will be approximately 0.92. Using this analysis, we can identify the best precision and recall values using different IoU thresholds. It is important to note that if we maintain a tight IoU threshold, the model's precision and recall will gradually decrease. For example, the purple line represents the results achieved at a 0.9 IoU. At a recall rate of 0.4, the precision of the model will be approximately 0.72.

Overall, our results demonstrate the effectiveness of both models in pavement patch detection, in the context of the evaluation performed. However, it is important to note that the choice of evaluation metric and IoU threshold can have a significant impact on the results, and different scenarios may require different models or parameter settings. Additionally, the suitability of deploying such systems in real-world applications largely depends on the task requirements and priorities of the task owner. For instance, if the cost of missing a patch is high, a lower false negative rate may be necessary, even at the cost of an increased false positive rate. Conversely, a false positive rate may be tolerable, provided that the false negative rate remains sufficiently low. In summary, the ideal configuration of object detection models in real-world applications should consider the specific trade-offs between false positives and false negatives that align with the task's objectives and constraints. In addition, as per the insights of domain experts at PMS, it is imperative to consider this trade-off within the specific scope of the patch detection task at hand. To achieve higher recall, the acceptance of false positives may be deemed acceptable.

2.5 Patch Detection on Different Pavement Conditions

The aim of this analysis is to assess the performance of trained models in the context of altered conditions, including variations in pavement surface and image capture.

settings. Our aim is to evaluate the effectiveness of the Faster RCNN and DETR models, which were originally trained on images obtained from the USA road network utilizing a laser profiling system set to acquire images at 5 mm intervals. To achieve this goal, we carried out an experiment on the Ireland road network utilizing the same models, but with the laser profiling system adjusted to capture images at 10 mm intervals (see Fig. 5). Table 3 demonstrates the results achieved by both models on 10 mm interval images.

Our experimental investigation involved the analysis 41 images captured at 10 mm intervals on the Irish road network. The findings indicate that the model performance decreased by 13–15% compared to the results achieved on test set (see Table 2) due to

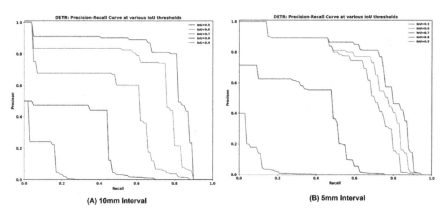

Fig. 4. Precision-recall curves achieved by using best performing model, with two different intervals of images: (A) shows the results achieved using 10 mm interval images, while (B) shows the results achieved using 5 mm interval.

shift in image resolution compared to the images used for model training. Additionally, the shape and composition of the pavement surface may have contributed to a decrease in overall results across both interval images. Table 3 demonstrates the results of further analysis, indicating that there is a slight difference between 10 mm interval images results and 5 mm interval image segments results. The reason for the variance between the 10 mm images and 5 mm image segments is the difference in the number of images. With only 41 images at 10 mm intervals, breaking them down into 5 mm segments results in 82 images, which increases the number of ground truth boxes. This factor may contribute to the observed differences in model performance between the two image types. The overall findings suggest that changes in image quality, patch shape, and pavement surface have a minor impact on model performance, and that additional training or calibration may be necessary for the models to operate effectively in environments with distinct imaging conditions. Moreover, Fig. 4 depicts a precision and recall curve that can aid in identifying the ideal IoU and confidence threshold values for obtaining the desired results in real-world testing scenario. Figure 6 shows in some cases where the model fails to detect the true patch within an image interval of 10 mm, but subsequently identifies it in the corresponding 5 mm interval images.

Figure 7 illustrates the visual results predicted by both models. This can be attributed to the fact that the model was trained on 5 mm images, which makes it easier to detect patches in such images. Secondly, the shift in image resolution also contributes to the model's difficulty in detecting patches on 10 mm interval images.

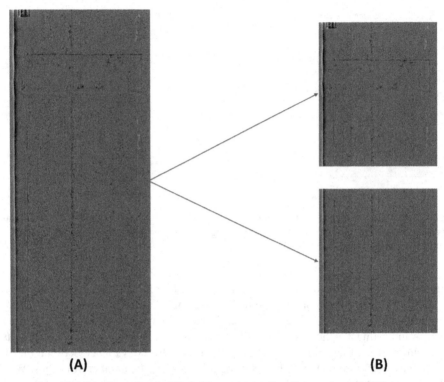

(A)   (B)

Fig. 5. 10 mm image (A) and its corresponding 5 mm segments (B).

Table 3. Comparative analysis of both models on 10 mm & 5 mm interval images.

Model	Interval	# Of images	# Of Patches	mAP
FRCNN	10 mm	41	49	0.72
DETR				0.75
FRCNN	5 mm	82	54	0.7
DETR				0.73

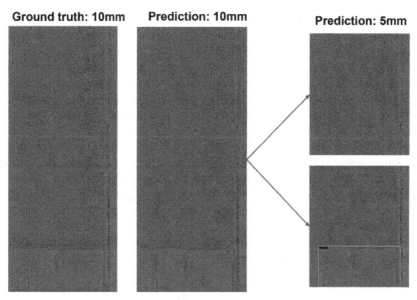

Fig. 6. Visual results of 10 mm interval image: Ground truth, prediction on 10 mm image and its corresponding 5 mm interval images.

Fig. 7. Visual results of 5 mm interval images: Ground truth, DETR prediction and Faster RCNN prediction.

3 Conclusion

This paper addresses automated patch detection, as a step towards an automated system for detecting asphalt pavement patches through the utilization of laser profiling images. Two state-of-the-art object detection models, Faster RCNN and DETR, were trained using a specified dataset. The results indicate that both models achieved higher patch detection accuracy, with a mean average precision of 0.86 and 0.88 for the Faster

RCNN and DETR models, respectively. Compared to the Faster RCNN, the DETR model showed slightly improved performance. Additionally, we assessed the model's generalization capabilities under different road surface and image capture conditions and discovered that the model's performance was slightly affected by the variability in conditions, such as change in the pavement surface, and image capture settings. Furthermore, given consideration to the trade-off between precision and recall is crucial in any object detection task. Different applications may prioritize precision (minimizing false positives) or recall (minimizing false negatives) differently, depending on the specific use case and requirements. The trade-off between precision and recall, as highlighted by industry domain experts at PMS, is crucial to consider within the specific context of patch detection work. For example, in patch detection application scenarios, it is deemed acceptable to tolerate false positives in order to achieve a higher recall rate. This emphasizes the importance of aligning the model's performance with the specific requirements and priorities of the task at hand.

Future work will extend the study to calculate the area of each identified patch and analyse the severity of patched surface.

Acknowledgment. This work was funded by Science Foundation Ireland through the SFI Centre for Research Training in Machine Learning (18/CRT/6183).

References

1. Koch, C., Brilakis, I.: Pothole detection in asphalt pavement images. Adv. Eng. Inform. **25**(3), 507–515 (2011). https://doi.org/10.1016/j.aei.2011.01.002
2. Koch, C., Georgieva, K., Kasireddy, V., Akinci, B., Fieguth, P.: A review on computer vision based defect detection and condition assessment of concrete and asphalt civil infrastructure. Adv. Eng. Inform. **29**(2), 196–210 (2015)
3. Radopoulou, S.C., Brilakis, I.: Patch detection for pavement assessment. Autom. Constr. **53**, 95–104 (2015)
4. Schnebele, E., Tanyu, B.F., Cervone, G., Waters, N.: Review of remote sensing methodologies for pavement management and assessment. Eur. Transp. Res. Rev. **7**(2), 1–19 (2015)
5. Sholevar, N., Golroo, A., Esfahani, S.R.: Machine learning techniques for pavement condition evaluation. Autom. Constr. **136**, 104190 (2022)
6. Gupta, S., Sharma, P., Sharma, D., Gupta, V., Sambyal, N.: Detection and localization of potholes in thermal images using deep neural networks. Multimed. Tools Appl. **79**(35), 26265–26284 (2020)
7. Zou, Q., Zhang, Z., Li, Q., Qi, X., Wang, Q., Wang, S.: Deepcrack: learning hierarchical convolutional features for crack detection. IEEE Trans. Image Process. **28**(3), 1498–1512 (2018)
8. Laurent, J., Fox-Ivey, R., Petitclerc, B.: High resolution multi-lane road surface mapping using 3D laser profilers for 3D paving and milling projects. In: Proceedings of the 7th Eurasphalt and Eurobitume Congress. Brussels, Belgium: European Asphalt Pavement Association (2020)
9. Luo, W., Wang, K.C.P., Li, L., Li, Q.J., Moravec, M.: Surface drainage evaluation for rigid pavements using an inertial measurement unit and 1-mm three-dimensional texture data. Transp. Res. Rec. **2457**(1), 121–128 (2014)

10. Laurent, J., Hébert, J.F., Lefebvre, D., Savard, Y.: Using 3D laser profiling sensors for the automated measurement of road surface conditions. In: 7th RILEM International Conference on Cracking in Pavements: Mechanisms, Modeling, Testing, Detection and Prevention Case Histories, vol. 4, pp. 157–167. Springer, Netherlands (2012). https://doi.org/10.1007/978-94-007-4566-7_16

11. Luo, W., Qin, Y., Zhang, D., Li, L.: Measurement of pavement rutting trajectories on two-lane highway using the 3D line scanning laser system. Int. J. Pavement Eng. 1–16 (2022)

12. Mathavan, S., Rahman, M.M., Stonecliffe-Janes, M., Kamal, K.: Pavement raveling detection and measurement from synchronized intensity and range images. Transp. Res. Rec. **2457**, 3–11. National Research Council (2014). https://doi.org/10.3141/2457-01

13. Qureshi, W.S., et al.: An exploration of recent intelligent image analysis techniques for visual pavement surface condition assessment. Sensors **22**(22), 9019 (2022)

14. Ren, S., He, K., Girshick, R., Sun, J.: Faster R-CNN: towards real-time object detection with region proposal networks. IEEE Trans. Pattern Anal. Mach. Intell. **39**(6), 1137–1149 (2016)

15. Carion, N., Massa, F., Synnaeve, G., Usunier, N., Kirillov, A., Zagoruyko, S.: End-to-end object detection with transformers. In: Vedaldi, A., Bischof, H., Brox, T., Frahm, J.-M. (eds.) ECCV 2020. LNCS, vol. 12346, pp. 213–229. Springer, Cham (2020). https://doi.org/10.1007/978-3-030-58452-8_13

16. Weiss, K., Khoshgoftaar, T.M., Wang, D.: A survey of transfer learning. J. Big data **3**(1), 1–40 (2016)

17. Alzraiee, H., Leal Ruiz, A., Sprotte, R.: Detecting of pavement marking defects using faster R-CNN. J. Perform. Constr. Facil., **35**(4), 4021035 (2021)

18. Hassan, S.I., O'Sullivan, D., Mckeever, S.: Pothole detection under diverse conditions using object detection models. IMPROVE **1**, 128–136 (2021)

19. Wang, J., Xu, G., Yan, F., Wang, J., Wang, Z.: Defect transformer: an efficient hybrid transformer architecture for surface defect detection. Measurement **211**, 112614 (2023)

20. Everingham, M., Van Gool, L., Williams, C.K.I., Winn, J., Zisserman, A.: The pascal visual object classes (VOC) challenge. Int. J. Comput. Vis. **88**(2), 303–338 (2010)

21. Hassan, S.I., O'Sullivan, D., McKeever, S., Power, D., McGowan, R., Feighan, K.: Detecting patches on road pavement images acquired with 3D laser sensors using object detection and deep learning. In: VISIGRAPP (5: VISAPP), pp. 413–420 (2022)

A Flexible Approach to PCB Characterization for Recycling

Alessio Roda, Alessandro Carfì[(✉)] [ID], and Fulvio Mastrogiovanni [ID]

TheEngineRoom, Department of Informatics, Bioengineering, Robotics, and Systems Engineering, University of Genoa, Via Opera Pia 13, 16145 Genoa, Italy
alessandro.carfi@dibris.unige.it.com

Abstract. The rapid growth of electronic waste (e-waste) highlights the need for effective recycling processes. Printed circuit boards (PCBs) are a significant component of e-waste, containing valuable materials and toxic elements. However, the recycling of PCBs faces challenges associated with their diverse materials and components, lack of standardization, and high costs. Current practice involves manual sorting, which is suboptimal, and automation is necessary. This article proposes a novel solution to PCB characterization for recycling, using a simple RGB camera to locate and classify three types of PCBs on a conveyor belt. The approach consists of a modular architecture that combines deep-learning solutions to segment PCBs, identify single components, and classify them. The architecture design considers the requirements of a robotic solution for sorting PCBs, and it has been tested in challenging scenarios.

Keywords: PCB characterization · Classification · Recycling

1 Introduction

The amount of electrical and electronic equipment waste (known as WEEE or e-waste) generated in the EU is one of the fastest-growing waste streams [3]. It includes devices such as monitors, smartphones, and computers discarded as waste. Correct disposal of WEEE is crucial for health and economic reasons, as they contain heavy metals, other toxic elements and valuable materials such as gold, silver, and palladium. Despite recent investments, recycling WEEE still faces challenges because of immature and polluting technologies. The lack of disassembly standardization makes some categories of WEEE challenging to recycle. Furthermore, recycling these components can be unprofitable due to the necessity of high investments, reliance on government incentives, and the need for significant manual labour. As a result, many companies in the industry reject most devices, leading to a global WEEE recycling rate of only 17.4% in 2019 [5].

Printed circuit boards (PCBs) are a significant component of WEEE due to their content of exploitable metal and the toxicity of the substances they contain, such as plastics, resins, and heavy metals, as well as the processes used for their treatment [12]. Furthermore, materials and components can significantly vary

H. I. Christensen et al. (Eds.): ICVS 2023, LNCS 14253, pp. 220–229, 2023.
https://doi.org/10.1007/978-3-031-44137-0_19

when considering different types of PCBs [8]. Therefore, the ability to sort PCBs is fundamental to choosing the best recycling process, minimizing pollution, and increasing investment returns. However, manual sorting, currently adopted as a pre-treatment for WEEE [2], is suboptimal, and industries are investigating new automation solutions.

In the years, there has been growing interest in the automatic sorting of waste, with significant funding towards the introduction of automation in recycling processes to make them more sustainable [7]. Challenges associated with automatic sorting are identifying and categorizing different types of material within a heterogeneous flow of waste while limiting the system's costs to preserve a positive economic balance. When it comes to PCBs, they can be characterized at either the component level or by considering the entire PCB as a whole [11]. At the component level, the process identifies specific components on the PCB, such as integrated circuits, capacitors, and gold connectors, to be recycled. On the other hand, at the whole PCB level, the process involves detecting and classifying a PCB as belonging to a particular class.

Researchers have adopted different approaches to characterize PCBs at the component level. Li et al. [10] utilized synthetic 3D data for training random forest pixel classifiers, which recognized PCB components from RGB-D images obtained from Kinect v2 with an accuracy of 83.64%. Sudharshan et al. [14] employed Regional Convolutional Neural Networks to process RGB and hyperspectral images, enabling the identification of integrated circuits, capacitors, and gold connectors. Polat et al. [13] processed RGB-D and hyperspectral images and classified components on PCB fragments based on a rule-based approach with an accuracy of 98.24%. Finally, Makwana et al. [11] proposed an encoder-decoder architecture that identified eight types of components from PCB images with an accuracy of 95.2%.

However, the promising results in the literature for single-component identification are not directly applicable to automatic sorting. Determining whether a specific PCB is worth processing, or deciding which methodology to adopt, requires an overall characterization of the board. This characterization could use single-component identification but should also consider information from a broader context.

Previous research has been conducted in this area. Fnu et al. [4] used an RGB camera and x-rays to respectively perceive the exterior and interior of a smartphone. By combining these two perception modalities, they were able to use class activation mapping to recognize 10 different smartphones with an accuracy of 98.6%. Similarly, An et al. [1] and Glučina et al. [6] used transformers and the YOLO network, respectively, to recognize PCBs in RGB images, achieving F1 scores over 0.99. Both studies used the same publicly available dataset[1], which contains 8125 images of 13 models of common PCBs, such as Arduino Uno and Raspberry Pi.

From the state-of-the-art analysis, three main observations emerge. First, current studies on overall PCB classification do not build on top of the single-

---

[1] https://www.kaggle.com/datasets/frettapper/micropcb-images.

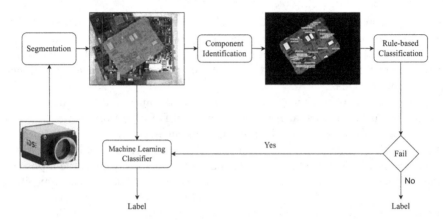

Fig. 1. The graphical description of the proposed approach. An RGB camera, placed over a conveyor belt, captures an image. The system segments a single PCB and identifies its parts. The rule-based classifier processes the list of components. If the classifier can identify one category of PCBs, a label is returned. Otherwise, the machine learning classifier processes the segmented PCB image to determine its class.

component analysis results. Second, PCB classification usually recognizes a specific model of PCB, not types of PCBs. This aspect is a significant limitation for adopting these methods in the recycling field since recycling processes are defined for macro-categories, not for specific models of PCBs. Lastly, while hyperspectral cameras and x-rays are explored, RGB cameras are more popular, probably due to the cost and difficulty of integration in the recycling process of other sensing solutions. This difficulty derives from an additional processing complexity and the necessity for a more structured environment.

In this article, we present a new approach for PCB characterization, functional for automatic sorting and recycling. To simplify the adoption of our solution, we used a simple RGB camera and leveraged single-component analysis to increase flexibility. The rest of the article is organized as follows: Sect. 2 describes the dataset collected in our study and our approach to PCB characterization. Section 3 presents the technical details of the implementation, and Sect. 4 presents the results. Finally, conclusions are drawn.

2   Approach

Our description of the problem generates from a larger project aimed at fully automating the sorting of WEEE and takes into consideration the necessities of a recycling facility. We focus on characterizing PCBs transported on a conveyor belt, and therefore, we need to consider the following problems. First, PCBs are often not precisely aligned on the conveyor belt, leading to overlaps. Second, the orientation of the PCB is unknown, and finally, PCBs could also be upside down.

(a) Class 1   (b) Class 2   (c) Class 3

Fig. 2. Examples of the three classes of PCBs considered in our study.

PCBs can have various compositions of materials and electronic components. Therefore, the PCB classes' description could vary depending on the recycling processes adopted by the specific facility. For these reasons, as previously stated, we decided to approach the problem modularly, leveraging some of the techniques already investigated in the literature. The system will have to:

1. Identify the presence of PCBs and isolate them from the background.
2. Identify the components mounted on the PCBs.
3. Determine the class of each PCB.

The approach to address these problems consists of four main blocks, as presented in Fig. 1. Firstly, images captured by an RGB camera are processed by the segmentation module, which isolates a single PCB from the background. The isolated image is then analyzed to identify parts mounted on the PCB, such as connectors, capacitors, diodes, and resistors. Then the rule-based classifier processes the list of recognized components. This classifier is easy to configure and identifies PCB classes based on the types and distribution of components. However, there may be situations where the rule-based classifier cannot assign a specific label. This situation could be due to errors in the component identification phase or by PCBs with a limited number of visible components. Therefore, to mitigate this problem, our approach also includes a last block. When the rule-based classification is inconclusive, the segmented image is processed by a machine learning (ML) classifier trained to distinguish between all possible PCB types.

2.1 Dataset

Our study addresses a specific problem characterized by three classes of PCBs. These PCBs result from the disassembly process of televisions, and the system should be able to classify them correctly.

1. PCBs for television power supply. They are recognizable by components such as resistors, diodes, capacitors, and inductors (Class 1 see Fig. 2a).

2. PCBs for input signal processing. They are recognizable by components such as processors, HDMI ports, SCART ports, VGA ports, and capacitors (Class 2 see Fig. 2b).
3. PCBs with few or no visible electronic components but containing a high level of gold (Class 3 see Fig. 2c).

To tackle the problem, we collected three custom datasets to train and test all the submodules of our architecture. All the data presented here was collected using an RGB camera with a 2056×1542 pixels resolution.

Dataset A. The first dataset contains 350 pictures of PCBs. We captured these pictures to ensure a diverse dataset. We balanced the representation of PCB classes and considered different PCB orientations. Furthermore, we made sure to include in the dataset all these possible conditions: single PCB, multiple PCBs, overlapping PCBs, PCBs partially outside the camera view, and PCBs upside-down. We used the Roboflow tool to label this dataset twice. Firstly, we created masks for fully visible PCBs in each image. Then, we annotated all visible components. Nine component classes were considered, i.e., capacitors, RCA ports, diodes, inductors, processors, resistors, HDMI ports, SCART ports, and VGA ports.

Dataset B. The second dataset contains isolated images of PCBs. It consists of 411 images with a distribution of 35%, 45%, and 20%, respectively, for classes 1, 2, and 3. Each image is associated with a class label.

Datase C. The final dataset contains images of 71 PCBs used to test the overall approach. These PCBs are new compared to the ones used in datasets A and B but still belong to the three PCB classes. The distribution of these 71 PCBs across classes 1, 2, and 3 are 46, 12, and 13, respectively.

3 Implementation

This section presents the technical solutions we adopted to implement the approach proposed in Sect. 2.

3.1 Segmentation

To solve the PCB segmentation problem, we utilized the Mask R-CNN model from the Detectron2 library [16], which is freely available on Github[2] and can be trained on custom datasets. For our project, we used Dataset A to train and validate the model. Before training, we resized the images to 514×386 pixels while maintaining their original proportions. Additionally, we used the Roboflow tool for data augmentation, which includes 90-degree clockwise and counter-clockwise rotations, image flips, brightness adjustments, and Gaussian noise insertion. The final dataset consisted of approximately 900 images and was split between training (85%) and validation (15%).

---

[2] https://github.com/facebookresearch/detectron2.

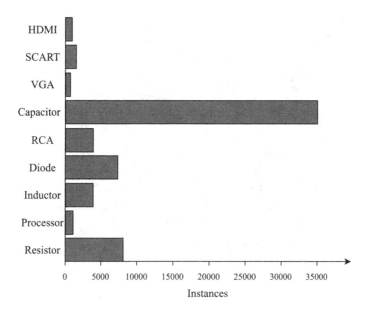

Fig. 3. Distribution of all the different components in the collected dataset.

3.2   Components Identification

After isolating the PCB image from the background, the next step is to detect and recognize the components mounted on it to understand which class the PCB belongs to. We opted for an object detection model and specifically selected YOLOv5 [9], which has been proven effective in solving these problems. Although the model comes pre-trained, we could fine-tune it to our scenario through partial retraining. For training and validating the YOLOv5 model, we used Dataset A. However, to reduce computational complexity, we divided the original 2056×1542 pixel image into 12 sub-images of size 514×514. We discarded the resulting images that did not contain any components and used the Roboflow data augmentation tool, as described for the segmentation problem. The resulting dataset consists of approximately 7300 images divided between training (85%) and validation (15%). We should note that the resulting dataset had an unbalanced distribution of components, as depicted in Fig. 3. The output of YOLOv5 is a list of bounding boxes with the associated label and a level of confidence rating from 0 to 1, and we only considered components recognized with a confidence level higher than 0.7. We introduced this filtering mechanism to avoid considering false recognitions that could significantly influence the rule-based classification.

3.3   Rule-Based Classification

The list of visible components, previously extracted, is then analyzed to determine the class of a specific PCB. The rules adopted in this problem are simple,

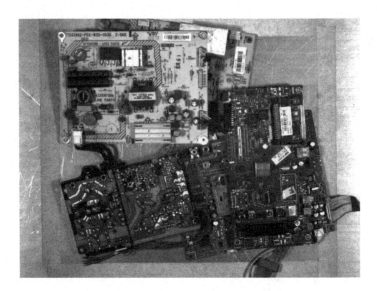

Fig. 4. The images from Dataset C, used during the final test, represent challenging scenarios: including multiple PCBs, variable orientations, and partial overlaps.

as the three classes have distinctive characteristics. We defined a list of components that undoubtedly identify Class 2, such as VGA, SCART, HDMI, and RCA ports. If Class 2 components are in the list, the system classifies the PCB as belonging to Class 2. If no Class 2 components are present, but the PCB contains resistors, diodes, and inductors, then we classify the PCB as Class 1. Since the third class of PCB has no visible components, the rule-based classification fails to assign a label to the PCB only under two conditions: i) the component identification was not accurate; ii) the PCB belongs to Class 3. To distinguish between these two alternatives, we introduced the final module.

3.4   ML Classifier

To solve the classification problem, we used the Inception v3 model to recognize the class of the PCB present in an image [15]. We trained and validated this model using Dataset B and followed the same procedure adopted for the previous neural network models to augment the data. The final dataset result has around 3000 images (with the proportions between classes remaining unchanged). We divided the dataset into training (70%) and validation (30%) sets.

4   Results

To evaluate the overall results of our solution, we adopted images from Dataset C, collected in a realistic and challenging scenario (see Fig. 4). Overall the dataset contains images of 71 PCBs unseen to all the different neural networks adopted

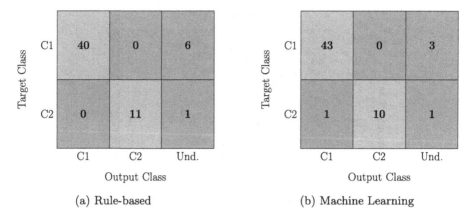

(a) Rule-based   (b) Machine Learning

Fig. 5. The confusion matrix on the left report the classification result relying only on the rule-based classifier, while the one on the right only uses the ML classifier. In both cases, the *Und.* column represents those PCBs that the system was not able to classify.

through our architecture. To provide a more precise evaluation, we carried on two analyses. In the first analysis, we determine if the proposed serialization of a rule-based and ML classifier helps the problem resolution. Then to conclude, we provide results for the overall solution.

4.1 Rule-Based vs ML Classifier

To conduct this analysis, we had to reduce the problem's scope. Specifically, the rule-based classification only works with PCBs from the first and second classes. Therefore, we only used the images from the 58 PCBs belonging to the first two classes. First, all the images were processed by the segmentation module. Then, two classification processes were executed in parallel. In the first one, we performed the rule-based classification based on the component identification results. In the second one, we directly processed the segmentation result with the one-shot classifier. The results are reported in the two confusion matrices shown in Figs. 5a and 5b. Both approaches achieve high levels of accuracy.

The rule-based classifier seems more conservative, with a high percentage of PCBs not classified (12%) but zero misclassification. Conversely, the one-shot classifier has a lower percentage of non-classified PCBs (7%) but misclassified one PCB. By observing the classification results closely, we noticed that the PCBs that the two methods couldn't classify correctly do not coincide. Therefore, combining these two approaches, as proposed by our solution, could improve the system's overall results.

Confusion Matrix

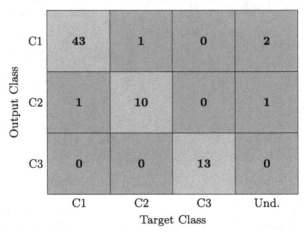

Fig. 6. The confusion matrix reports the result for the overall system. The *Und.* column represents those PCBs that the system was not able to classify.

4.2 PCB Classification

To conclude, we performed the same test, this time considering the entire Dataset C and following the full pipeline introduced in our work. The results are reported in the confusion matrix shown in Fig. 6. Overall, the system produced great results, with a low number of misclassifications (2.8%) and PCBs not classified (4.2%). Furthermore, despite the lower representation of Class 3 in Dataset B, which was used to train the ML classifier, the system recognized these PCBs with 100% accuracy. It is important to note that the ML classifier used for this test was trained to recognize three classes, unlike the one previously tested, which only recognized two classes. Therefore, mismatches in the classification results for Class 1 and Class 2 can be explained by this difference in training.

5   Conclusion

In this article, we present a new solution for categorizing PCBs using a single RGB camera and a composite of data-driven approaches. We tested our approach in a challenging scenario, and the results showed that combining rule-based and machine-learning classifiers helps improve system performance. Furthermore, the system's modular nature allows easy adaptation to new scenarios. If the description of the PCB classes changes, only the two classifiers should be adapted, while the rest of the pipeline remains mostly untouched. Specifically, adapting the rule-based classifier requires defining new rules, while the ML classifier would need partial retraining. Our solution meets the requirements of a real-world recycling facility. Therefore, future studies in this direction should focus on more detailed testing and integration with automatic sorting mechanisms.

Acknowledgements. This research was made, in part, with the Italian government support under the National Recovery and Resilience Plan (NRRP), Mission 4, Component 2 Investment 1.5, funded from the European Union NextGenerationEU and awarded by the Italian Ministry of University and Research.

References

1. An, K., Zhang, Y.: LPViT: a transformer based model for PCB image classification and defect detection. IEEE Access **10**, 42542–42553 (2022)
2. Bigum, M., Brogaard, L., Christensen, T.H.: Metal recovery from high-grade WEEE: a life cycle assessment. J. Hazard. Mater. **207**, 8–14 (2012)
3. European Commission: Waste from electrical and electronic equipment (WEEE) (2019). https://ec.europa.eu/environment/topics/waste-and-recycling/waste-electrical-and-electronic-equipment-weee_en
4. Fnu, A., et al.: RGB-X classification for electronics sorting. In: Proceedings of the 35th IEEE/RSJ International Conference on Intelligent Robots and Systems (IROS), pp. 5973–5980. Kyoto, Japan (2022)
5. Forti, V., Balde, C.P., Kuehr, R., Bel, G.: The global e-waste monitor 2020: quantities, flows and the circular economy potential (2020)
6. Glučina, M., Anđelić, N., Lorencin, I., Car, Z.: Detection and classification of printed circuit boards using YOLO algorithm. Electronics **12**(3), 667 (2023)
7. Gundupalli, S.P., Hait, S., Thakur, A.: A review on automated sorting of source-separated municipal solid waste for recycling. Waste Manage. **60**, 56–74 (2017)
8. Huang, K., Guo, J., Xu, Z.: Recycling of waste printed circuit boards: a review of current technologies and treatment status in china. J. Hazard. Mater. **164**(2–3), 399–408 (2009)
9. Jocher, G.: YOLOv5 by Ultralytics (2020). https://doi.org/10.5281/zenodo.3908559
10. Li, D., Li, C., Chen, C., Zhao, Z.: Semantic segmentation of a printed circuit board for component recognition based on depth images. Sensors **20**(18), 5318 (2020)
11. Makwana, D., Mittal, S., et al.: PCBSegClassNet-a light-weight network for segmentation and classification of PCB component. Expert Syst. Appl. **225**, 120029 (2023)
12. Ning, C., Lin, C.S.K., Hui, D.C.W., McKay, G.: Waste printed circuit board (PCB) recycling techniques. In: Lin, C. (eds.) Chemistry and Chemical Technologies in Waste Valorization. Topics in Current Chemistry Collections, pp. 21–56. Springer, Cham (2018). https://doi.org/10.1007/978-3-319-90653-9_2
13. Polat, S., Tremeau, A., Boochs, F.: Combined use of 3D and HSI for the classification of printed circuit board components. Appl. Sci. **11**(18), 8424 (2021)
14. Sudharshan, V., et al.: Object detection routine for material streams combining RGB and hyperspectral reflectance data based on guided object localization. IEEE Sens. J. **20**(19), 11490–11498 (2020)
15. Szegedy, C., Vanhoucke, V., Ioffe, S., Shlens, J., Wojna, Z.: Rethinking the inception architecture for computer vision. In: Proceedings of the 29th IEEE Conference on Computer Vision and Pattern Recognition (CVPR), pp. 2818–2826. Las Vegas, NV, USA (2016)
16. Wu, Y., Kirillov, A., Massa, F., Lo, W.Y., Girshick, R.: Detectron2 (2019). https://github.com/facebookresearch/detectron2

SynthRetailProduct3D (SyRePro3D): A Pipeline for Synthesis of 3D Retail Product Models with Domain Specific Details Based on Package Class Templates

Jochen Lindermayr[1]([✉])[iD], Cagatay Odabasi[1][iD], Markus Völk[1][iD], Yitian Chen[1][iD], Richard Bormann[1][iD], and Marco F. Huber[2][iD]

[1] Department of Robot and Assistive Systems, Fraunhofer IPA, 70569 Stuttgart, Germany
{jochen.lindermayr,cagatay.odabasi,markus.volk, yitian.chen,richard.bormann}@ipa.fraunhofer.de
[2] Department Cyber Cognitive Intelligence (CCI), Fraunhofer IPA, and Institute of Industrial Manufacturing and Management IFF, University of Stuttgart, 70569 Stuttgart, Germany
marco.huber@ieee.org

Abstract. This research paper presents a novel pipeline for synthesizing high-quality, textured 3D models of retail products, addressing the limitations of existing datasets in the retail automation domain. As retail automation continues to revolutionize various aspects of business operations, there is a growing need for comprehensive and domain-specific datasets to enable the development and evaluation of robust perception systems. However, current datasets lack the necessary variety and size, often containing only a fraction of the products offered by retail companies and failing to capture domain-specific characteristics. To overcome these limitations, we introduce a modular pipeline that focuses on the synthesis of 3D models with high-resolution textures. Unlike previous methods that prioritize visually appealing shapes, our pipeline explicitly incorporates retail domain-specific details, including readable text, logos, codes, and nutrition tables, in the texture of the models. By disentangling the texturing process from shape augmentation, we ensure the visual quality of text areas, providing realistic and readable representations of retail products. In our methodology, we leverage state-of-the-art generative image models to add retail domain-specific details to the 3D models. Our approach enables the synthesis of diverse retail product packages with accurate textures, enhancing the realism and applicability of the generated models for the development and evaluation of perception systems in retail automation and robotics. Experimental results demonstrate the effectiveness and visual quality of models generated by our pipeline.

Keywords: 3D Model · Synthetic · Retail Automation · Robotics

H. I. Christensen et al. (Eds.): ICVS 2023, LNCS 14253, pp. 230–242, 2023.
https://doi.org/10.1007/978-3-031-44137-0_20

Fig. 1. Randomly selected example models from different package categories.

1   Introduction

In recent years, the field of retail automation has emerged as a transformative force, revolutionizing various aspects of business operations. Advancements in technology have made it possible to automate tasks such as vision-only inventory management [3], withdrawal detection in smart vending systems [29], robot-based customer order fulfillment [4], and restocking [7]. These advancements have the potential to enhance efficiency, reduce costs, address labor shortages, and significantly improve the overall shopping experience. The COVID-19 pandemic has further underscored the need for contactless retail experiences like *Click & Collect* or smart vending systems, thus driving the demand for automation and robotics technology to meet these evolving requirements.

To fully exploit the potential of retail automation and enable the development and evaluation of robust perception systems, the availability of high-quality 3D datasets is crucial. Such datasets empower retailers and researchers to explore the diverse applications of retail automation.

During our research, we encountered a significant limitation with the existing datasets as they often do not address the specific aspects and challenges of the retail domain. For instance, while retail companies typically offer thousands of products in their stores, many available 3D model datasets contain only a small fraction, often limited to tens or a few hundred objects [5,6,16]. Moreover, many datasets often lack the typical characteristics specific to the retail domain, such as products from the same brand or objects with similar designs. On the other hand, purely image-based datasets [11,22], while rich in object classes, lack the necessary 3D models required for free-view rendering in custom scenes or comprehensive robot simulations involving manipulation skills like picking, placing, or packing of objects [4,5,7,14,15,25,28].

There are two primary approaches for custom dataset creation to solve the above issues. The first option involves using 3D scanners to capture and model real products [4–6,16,17], but this approach presents challenges in terms of the manual effort required for data collection, potentially limited variance, and potential legal issues related to trademarks and protected shapes or slogans. The second option involves synthesizing 3D models [20], although existing methods often fail to adequately address the domain-specific aspects of the model's texture required for retail applications.

To address these gaps and overcome the limitations of existing datasets, this paper introduces a novel pipeline for synthesizing textured 3D models of retail products. Unlike previous methods that primarily focus on synthesizing visually appealing 3D shapes, our pipeline explicitly incorporates retail domain-specific details in the model's texture like texts, logos, codes, and nutrition tables, including readable text on the models. We improve the visual quality of text areas by disentangling the texturing from the shape augmentation process. By leveraging this innovative pipeline, we aim to provide a comprehensive solution tailored specifically to the challenges and requirements of the retail domain. The synthetic models generated by our solution enable a clean evaluation of downstream tasks like object recognition systems on very large object sets of 10,000 synthetic retail products which would cause high efforts if using real products. Examples of generated 3D models can be seen in Fig.1.

In summary, the main contributions of this work are as follows:

– a modular pipeline[1] approach for the synthesis of multifarious 3D models of retail product packages with high-resolution textures.
– a concept on how to leverage state-of-the-art generative image models for adding retail domain-specific product details on the 3D models of the packages.

In the subsequent sections of this paper, we will elaborate on our methodology, provide experimental results, and discuss their implications.

2   Related Work

The synthetic generation of retail product 3D models is the primary focus of our work, and thus, we specifically address synthesis approaches in our literature review, while neglecting 2D [18] or 3D datasets of real objects [6,16,17], methods that only deform models of scanned real objects, or methods creating synthetic scenes based on models of real objects [8,9].

---

[1] The pipeline is available at http://www.object-twin.ai/SyRePro3D/.

Table 1. Comparison of the most similar approaches to ours.

Criteria	pyclone [21]	DreamFusion [23]	3DGAN [20]	GET3D [10]	**Ours**
retail domain-specific	–	–	–	–	✓
controllable 3d shapes	✓	✓	✓	✓	✓
texture provided	✓	✓	✓	✓	✓
multiple materials per obj	✓	–	✓	✓	✓
guided logo & text placing	–	–	–	–	✓
readable text	–	–	–	–	✓
generative model usage	–	✓	✓	✓	✓

In recent years, there has been a significant increase in the number of approaches for generative 3D content generation [23]. These approaches employ various 3D modalities as their bases, including voxels, point clouds, octrees, and implicit representations, which can subsequently be transformed into 3D mesh models commonly used in rendering engines and physics engines. Earlier methods primarily focused on creating the 3D shape of objects, but more recent works have made significant progress in synthesizing complete textured 3D mesh models [20]. However, even state-of-the-art approaches such as GET3D [10] still face challenges in producing sharp and detailed textures, often resulting in blurry textures. While this may not be a significant concern for objects like houses or fruits [2], where the visual appearance relies less on fine edges, it becomes critical for retail products. Retail products, particularly in their shelf-ready primary packaging, often incorporate a considerable amount of text that needs to be readable to achieve a realistic appearance.

On the other hand, there are also existing works that cover only parts of the retail requirements. Blenderproc or Kubric offer a simple interface to material augmentation of existing 3D models [8,12], but they lack the additional aspect of specific texture creation necessary for retail products. Our solution serves to generate input 3D models to these methods. Besides, methods providing parametric 3D shape object models often lack the retail-specific semantics of parts or even the product model types themselves, as they often focus on other object types. For example, these methods are available for basic shapes like cylinders or cuboids [27] or indoor furniture [21].

To provide a comparative analysis of the existing approaches in the field, we present an aggregated overview in Table 1. This comparison allows us to qualitatively evaluate the approaches based on different attributes.

3   Methodology

Our modular methodology for 3D model synthesis is illustrated in Fig. 2, showcasing the flexibility of our framework. In the upcoming sections, we delve into the intricacies of the base template model (Sect. 3.1) manually crafted with

Blender, and how the template model is used to programmatically create shape-augmented variants from it in Sect. 3.2. In Sect. 3.3 we explain how to automatically generate visually appealing and contextually relevant add-on elements such as backgrounds, logos, text snippets, tables, and barcodes. The augmentation of the base template is followed by an automatic coarse base texturing (Sect. 3.4) and the automatic placing of the above add-on elements for improved realism (Sect. 3.5). Hence, manual effort is only needed for the initial creation of the base template model.

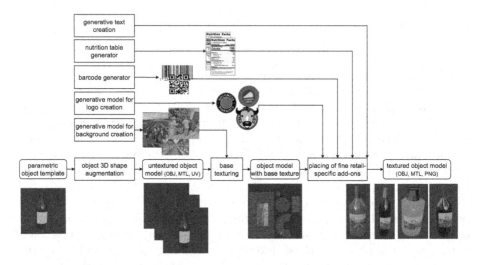

Fig. 2. Architecture of the synthesis pipeline with example artifacts and results.

3.1 Product Package Base Template Model

The synthesis pipeline is primarily based on different parametric template models specifically designed for each package type using Blender. As the number of different package types in the retail domain is limited and rather low, our approach using manually crafted template models seems reasonable. We offer template models for cans, bottles, boxes, and tubes. More can be added easily and are in progress. These template models serve as the foundation for our approach, offering a robust framework for handling various geometric changes and texture creation in the synthesis process. Crucially, the template models are meticulously crafted to incorporate reasonable texture seams, ensuring optimal texture map unwrapping even when faced with complex geometry augmentations.

To enable efficient manipulation of the synthesized models, the template models include both vertex and face groups, which define semantic part volumes and surfaces. This information, specifically the semantic part info within the vertex groups, plays a significant role in the geometric augmentation of the part shapes, as detailed in Sect. 3.2. By leveraging these semantic part groups, our methodology empowers the augmentation process to adapt and modify the shapes of different components accurately.

Moreover, the semantic part information within the face groups also contributes to guiding the placement of add-on elements during the texturing step, as elaborated in Sect. 3.5. Leveraging the insights from these face groups, we ensure the precise positioning and integration of additional domain-specific elements onto the synthesized models. This strategic utilization of the information on semantic parts enhances the overall visual coherence and realism of the synthesized 3D models.

The template models are saved as Blender's ".blend" files. To enable compatibility with other software tools we've implemented a Wavefront OBJ file export. As the default exporter of Blender creates messy face maps, we've created a custom solution using an additional text file.

3.2 Object 3D Shape Augmentation

To implement shape augmentation in our methodology, we leverage the power of Blender and utilize mainly two geometry node modifiers: the *group, boolean math*, and *scale element* nodes. By incorporating these modifiers multiple times in various combinations depending on the base template into our pipeline, we can dynamically manipulate the geometry of the synthesized models, allowing for a wide range of realistic shape variations.

To ensure consistency and control over the augmentation process, we utilize the semantic part information obtained from the vertex groups of the template, as explained in Sect. 3.1. By employing the *boolean math* nodes in conjunction with the semantic part info, we can precisely target specific parts of the template for modification while keeping connected parts unaffected. This approach guarantees a consistent and coherent augmentation of the desired components. For example, the algorithm selects the whole mesh to apply holistic shape augmentation, like changing the size or diameter of the whole bottle. By selecting only semantic parts, like the lid, shoulder, or label of the bottle, we can deform only parts of the shape while sticking to the total size of the bottle. Table 2 shows how the nodes are used to deform the base template model.

Furthermore, to offer flexibility in the augmentation process, we provide a parameter file that defines the range of possible augmentations.

3.3 Generative Models for Domain-Specific Add-Ons

We employ generative image techniques like stable diffusion [26] to automatically generate background images based on a domain-specific text corpus that aligns with the product under consideration. By utilizing a suitable prompt derived from the text corpus, we generate background images that exhibit coherence and relevance to the specific product category. Similarly, we apply the same approach to generate logos, ensuring that they are well-suited to the product's context.

Table 2. Overview of Blender's nodes used for the shape augmentation

Node	Description	Usage
Group	This node enables the grouping of multiple objects or nodes into a single unit, providing organizational and editing benefits.	- Selection of semantic parts defined in the base template (like lid, body, shoulder, or label of a bottle) - Transformations can be applied to the faces of a semantic group as a whole - Simplifies the node architecture.
Boolean math	This node can be used to perform boolean logic operations	- Combine multiple groups of semantic parts to be modified at once.
Scale Elements	This node allows scaling of individual elements within a mesh, such as vertices, edges, or faces.	- Adjusts the size of specific selected semantic parts in a mesh to create variations with differently scaled parts - Controls the proportions of different parts to each other

To create the input text corpus, we offer four different options. The corpus can be manually designed, scraped from the internet, generated using language models like GPT [24], or automatically derived from text reading results on a scanned dataset of retail products. The last three methods can be considered automatic. It is provided as a config file to the software module.

In the creation of the prompt template used for the automatic call of the generative image model, we stack words from the domain-specific text corpus, such as *milk*, with the desired output type, such as *a logo of* or *an image of*, and randomly chosen style attributes like *flat design*, *modern*, or *round*. We have found it beneficial to enhance the prompt by incorporating additional attributes into the domain-specific texts, for example, using *happy cow* instead of just *cow*. This fine-tuning of the prompts contributes to generating more refined and tailored outputs. Example prompts are:

- *"A logo of a milk product, flat design, green, white"*
- *"A logo of a retail brand selling milk products."*
- *"An image of happy cows eating grass on a mountain."*

Moreover, our methodology encompasses the generation of text snippets to be placed on the object. The same text corpus utilized for creating backgrounds and logos can be leveraged for this purpose. We automatically create two types of text snippets, namely product names and marketing slogans, using prompt templates similar to the following:

- *"Synthesize 20 sets of words which advertise a box of oak flakes produced by a brand called SomeCompany. It must not be plagiarism."*
- *"Synthesize 5 fictional company names which would sell milk products. It must not be plagiarism."*

Additionally, we use existing methods or online tools to generate nutrition tables [19] and barcodes [13], incorporating randomly generated but reasonable values encoded within them. If needed, a value range or whitelist set could be provided.

3.4 Base Texturing

First, we import the shape-augmented model and the additional custom file that contains semantic part information about the faces which serves as a crucial guide throughout the subsequent steps. Depending on the type of the part group, we apply different methods. For label areas, we employ background image placement, while untextured homogeneous areas undergo material augmentation.

The information on semantic parts plays a vital role in restricting the areas where the background can be placed. From the generative model, we select the background and carefully crop it to fit within the allowed area, as defined by the semantic part info. To ensure correct and upright texturing of regions like product labels, we calculate world-to-texture space and texture space-to-world coordinate transformations. This process accounts for any potential arbitrary orientations of the faces resulting from shape augmentation in Blender. If needed, we apply rotation to achieve the desired alignment.

For the faces that do not belong to label areas, we focus on augmenting the material properties of the untextured mesh. This augmentation includes adjustments to the specular color and exponent, ambient color, diffuse color, emissive color, optical density, and transparency. The values for these properties can be chosen individually for each part of the object, provided they are properly defined in the base template.

3.5 Placing of Domain-Specific Add-Ons

The semantic part information from the template (Sect. 3.1) plays a crucial role by determining the areas where add-on elements are allowed to be placed. For instance, logos are restricted to label areas that are defined in the base template. To handle the placement of add-on elements, we iterate over all face groups corresponding to semantic parts and utilize alpha blending in the texture space to seamlessly incorporate the generated add-on elements (Sect. 3.3).

During the placement process, add-on elements can either be randomly positioned within the designated texture space area of the corresponding semantic part or placed at specific pre-defined locations, depending on the requirements of the synthesis task. To ensure visually appealing results, we use the same approach as explained in Sect. 3.4, which verifies the correct orientation of the add-on elements. If necessary, rotations are applied to align the elements properly with the target surface. To prevent excessive occlusion between different add-on elements, an Intersection over Union (IoU) check is employed while placing the elements. This check helps to maintain visual clarity and prevents overcrowding or overlap among the elements.

When exporting the final texture image, we also export the positions of the placed add-on elements. These position values serve as ground truth data for the semantic elements and can be utilized for further experiments and evaluation purposes.

4   Results

Fig. 3. Exemplary synthetically generated product models (left) and scanned models of real objects (right).

In order to evaluate the quality and effectiveness of the synthetically generated 3D models of retail products, a three-fold qualitative evaluation approach is employed, as no suitable automatic quantitative method exists for this purpose. It involved:

1. a comparison with models of real objects,
2. a check of domain-specific aspects, and
3. an exemplary usage of the models in a downstream task.

For the first part, to assess how well the synthetically generated models resemble real objects, they are showcased in shelf scenes that represent typical retail-related contexts. This evaluation enables a visual coherence check, examining how seamlessly the models integrate into the given context. Figure 3 illustrates scenes featuring both synthetically created models and scanned models of real objects (scanned by a laser scanner and camera setup and generated by a photogrammetry-based method), demonstrating a subjective retail appearance that is consistent across the two types of models.

The second part focuses on the handling of domain-specific aspects. In this regard, similar-looking objects are generated to evaluate whether the method can capture the specific characteristics of retail products. Figure 4 showcases such objects, demonstrating their visual similarity, including shared features like logos, while also exhibiting minor differences such as variations in size, coloring, or the arrangement of elements on the labels.

Furthermore, the readability of text elements present on the models is assessed. Rendered images of the models are fed into EasyOCR [1], a tool capable of detecting and decoding text. Figure 5 exemplifies the successful application of this method, affirming the ability of the generated models to accurately represent and maintain legible text on the labels.

The assessment of the automatically created 3D models showed that they can be successfully used as replacements for scanned models of real retail products.

Fig. 4. Similar-looking product models in a retail shelf scene.

In order to assess the processing time, we conducted measurements for the synthesis of the 3D models, considering inputs such as backgrounds and logos are already available. On average, the synthesis process for a batch of 50 models took approximately 3.5 min on a desktop PC equipped with an Intel i7-10700k 3.80 GHz CPU and a Nvidia RTX 3090 GPU. The generation and export of augmented models in Blender are remarkably fast, typically ranging from 10 to 25 s. However, the texturing phase accounted for the majority of the processing time. In certain cases, particularly for small texture areas, the texturing process could take up to 9 min for a batch of 50 models. This is primarily due to the need for iterative attempts to correctly position and evaluate the Intersection over Union (IOU) while considering the limited space available for precise texturing. We address improving the handling of these cases in future work.

Fig. 5. Exemplary text reading result on a rendering of a synthetic product.

5 Conclusions

We introduced a pipeline for synthesizing textured 3D models of retail products. Our pipeline addresses the limitations of existing works by incorporating domain-specific details leveraging generative image models. In a qualitative analysis, we compared the synthetic models to real objects in shelf scenes, confirming their contextual integration. We also verified the handling of domain-specific aspects by generating similar-looking objects with subtle variations. The readability of the text on the models was validated using EasyOCR. Our pipeline demonstrates its effectiveness in generating realistic and visually appealing 3D models of retail products, addressing specific challenges in the domain. It provides support for the development and evaluation of perception systems in the field of retail automation and robotics. Future work may involve expanding the pipeline to cover a wider range of product package types and improving speed of the IOU check. The pipeline with its flexible configuration capabilities enables the creation of a retail-specific and diverse dataset of large size. Hence, future work may also cover the evaluation of object detection systems on a set of 10,000 synthetic retail products as a downstream task. It could also address a deep dive into diversity requirements to prevent unfavorable skew in the generative distribution.

Acknowledgement. This work has received funding from the German Ministry of Education and Research (BMBF) under grant agreement No 01IS21061A for the Sim4Dexterity project, the German Federal Ministry for Economic Affairs and Climate Action (BMWK) under grant agreement No 01MK20001G for the Knowledge4Retail project and the Baden-Württemberg Ministry of Economic Affairs, Labour and Tourism for the AI Innovation Center "Learning Systems and Cognitive Robotics".

References

1. Jaided AI: EasyOCR: Ready-to-use OCR with 80+ supported languages and all popular image file formats (2021). https://github.com/JaidedAI/EasyOCR

2. Wu, T., et al.: OmniObject3D: large-vocabulary 3D object dataset for realistic perception, reconstruction and generation. In: IEEE/CVF Conference on Computer Vision and Pattern Recognition (CVPR) (2023)

3. Beetz, M., et al.: Robots collecting data: modelling stores. In: Villani, L., Natale, C., Beetz, M., Siciliano, B. (eds.) Robotics for Intralogistics in Supermarkets and Retail Stores. Springer Tracts in Advanced Robotics, vol. 148, pp. 41–64. Springer, Cham (2022). https://doi.org/10.1007/978-3-031-06078-6_2

4. Bormann, R., de Brito, B.F., Lindermayr, J., Omainska, M., Patel, M.: Towards automated order picking robots for warehouses and retail. In: Tzovaras, D., Giakoumis, D., Vincze, M., Argyros, A. (eds.) ICVS 2019. LNCS, vol. 11754, pp. 185–198. Springer, Cham (2019). https://doi.org/10.1007/978-3-030-34995-0_18

5. Bormann, R., Wang, X., Völk, M., Kleeberger, K., Lindermayr, J.: Real-time instance detection with fast incremental learning. In: 2021 IEEE International Conference on Robotics and Automation (ICRA), pp. 13056–13063 (2021)

6. Calli, B., Singh, A., Walsman, A., Srinivasa, S., Abbeel, P., Dollar, A.M.: The YCB object and Model set: towards common benchmarks for manipulation research. In: 2015 International Conference on Advanced Robotics (ICAR) (2015)

7. Cavallo, A., et al.: Robotic clerks: autonomous shelf refilling. In: Villani, L., Natale, C., Beetz, M., Siciliano, B. (eds.) Robotics for Intralogistics in Supermarkets and Retail Stores. Springer Tracts in Advanced Robotics, vol. 148, pp. 137–170. Springer, Cham (2022). https://doi.org/10.1007/978-3-031-06078-6_6

8. Denninger, M., et al.: BlenderProc. arXiv preprint arXiv:1911.01911 (2019)

9. Fulop, P.: CPGDet-129 (2022). https://github.com/neurolaboratories/reshelf-detection

10. Gao, J., et al.: Get3d: a generative model of high quality 3D textured shapes learned from images. In: Advances In Neural Information Processing Systems (2022)

11. Goldman, E., Herzig, R., Eisenschtat, A., Goldberger, J., Hassner, T.: Precise detection in densely packed scenes. In: Proceedings of the IEEE Conference on Computer Vision and Pattern Recognition (CVPR) (2019)

12. Greff, K., et al.: Kubric: a scalable dataset generator. In: Proceedings of the IEEE/CVF Conference on Computer Vision and Pattern Recognition, pp. 3749–3761 (2022)

13. tec it.com: Barcode generator (2020). https://barcode.tec-it.com/en/EAN13?data=123456789123

14. Khalid, M.U., et al.: Automatic grasp generation for vacuum grippers for random bin picking. In: Weißgraeber, P., Heieck, F., Ackermann, C. (eds.) Advances in Automotive Production Technology – Theory and Application. A, pp. 247–255. Springer, Heidelberg (2021). https://doi.org/10.1007/978-3-662-62962-8_29

15. Kleeberger, K., Roth, F., Bormann, R., Huber, M.F.: Automatic grasp pose generation for parallel jaw grippers. In: Ang Jr, M.H., Asama, H., Lin, W., Foong, S. (eds.) IAS 2021. LNNS, vol. 412, pp. 594–607. Springer, Cham (2022). https://doi.org/10.1007/978-3-030-95892-3_45

16. Lin, Y., Tremblay, J., Tyree, S., Vela, P.A., Birchfield, S.: Multi-view fusion for multi-level robotic scene understanding. In: 2021 IEEE/RSJ International Conference on Intelligent Robots and Systems (IROS), pp. 6817–6824 (2021)

17. Lindermayr, J., et al.: IPA-3D1K: a large retail 3D model dataset for robot picking. In: IEEE/RSJ International Conference on Intelligent Robots and Systems (IROS) (2023)
18. Mata, C., Locascio, N., Sheikh, M.A., Kihara, K., Fischetti, D.: StandardSim: a synthetic dataset for retail environments. In: Sclaroff, S., Distante, C., Leo, M., Farinella, G.M., Tombari, F. (eds.) ICIAP 2022. LNCS, vol. 13232, pp. 65–76. Springer, Cham (2022). https://doi.org/10.1007/978-3-031-06430-2_6
19. onlinelabels: Nutrition table generator (2020). https://www.onlinelabels.com/tools/nutrition-label-generator
20. Pavllo, D., Kohler, J., Hofmann, T., Lucchi, A.: Learning generative models of textured 3d meshes from real-world images. In: IEEE/CVF International Conference on Computer Vision (ICCV) (2021)
21. Peel, A.: Pyclone and homebuilder blender add-on (2020). https://creativedesigner3d.com/2020/09/21/parametric-asset-libraries-in-blender-2-90/
22. Peng, J., Xiao, C., Li, Y.: RP2K: a large-scale retail product dataset for fine-grained image classification. arXiv e-prints pp. arXiv-2006 (2020)
23. Poole, B., Jain, A., Barron, J.T., Mildenhall, B.: Dreamfusion: Text-to-3D using 2D diffusion. arXiv (2022)
24. Radford, A., Wu, J., Child, R., Luan, D., Amodei, D., Sutskever, I.: Language models are unsupervised multitask learners (2019)
25. Riedlinger, M., Voelk, M., Kleeberger, K., Khalid, M.U., Bormann, R.: Model-free grasp learning framework based on physical simulation. In: ISR 2020; 52th International Symposium on Robotics, pp. 1–8 (2020)
26. Rombach, R., Blattmann, A., Lorenz, D., Esser, P., Ommer, B.: High-resolution image synthesis with latent diffusion models. In: Proceedings of the IEEE/CVF Conference on Computer Vision and Pattern Recognition, pp. 10684–10695 (2022)
27. Studio, W.: Wonder mesh (2018). https://blendermarket.com/products/wonder-mesh
28. Villani, L., Natale, C., Beetz, M., Siciliano, B.: Robotics for Intralogistics in Supermarkets and Retail Stores, vol. 148. Springer, Cham (2022). https://doi.org/10.1007/978-3-031-06078-6
29. Wang, K., Shi, F., Wang, W., Nan, Y., Lian, S.: Synthetic data generation and adaption for object detection in smart vending machines. arXiv e-prints pp. arXiv-1904 (2019)

Small, but Important: Traffic Light Proposals for Detecting Small Traffic Lights and Beyond

Tom Sanitz[1,2], Christian Wilms[2(✉)], and Simone Frintrop[2]

[1] Ibeo Automotive Systems GmbH, Hamburg, Germany
[2] Computer Vision Group, University of Hamburg, Hamburg, Germany
{christian.wilms,simone.frintrop}@uni-hamburg.de

Abstract. Traffic light detection is a challenging problem in the context of self-driving cars and driver assistance systems. While most existing systems produce good results on large traffic lights, detecting small and tiny ones is often overlooked. A key problem here is the inherent downsampling in CNNs, leading to low-resolution features for detection. To mitigate this problem, we propose a new traffic light detection system, comprising a novel traffic light proposal generator that utilizes findings from general object proposal generation, fine-grained multi-scale features, and attention for efficient processing. Moreover, we design a new detection head for classifying and refining our proposals. We evaluate our system on three challenging, publicly available datasets and compare it against six methods. The results show substantial improvements of at least 12.6% on small and tiny traffic lights, as well as strong results across all sizes of traffic lights.

1 Introduction

Traffic light detection, which involves locating traffic lights and classifying their state, is an essential task for self-driving cars and driver assistance systems. Due to the complex nature of urban environments with several intersections, heavy traffic, and distracting objects, detecting traffic lights is challenging [14]. Moreover, safe driving in such environments is challenging to humans as well, leading to stress, oversights, and potentially fatal accidents [12]. Hence, support by driver assistance systems is of great importance in such environments.

Several approaches for traffic light detection were proposed, mostly based on standard object detectors [1,3,20,23]. However, the detection of traffic lights appearing small or tiny on the image plane remains a problem. A major reason is the inherent subsampling in CNNs to extract semantically rich features. Moreover, small and tiny traffic lights are much smaller than objects typically annotated in object detection datasets like COCO [17]. Hence, standard object detectors might not be well-suited for the problem of detecting such traffic lights,

---

T. Sanitz and C. Wilms—indicates equal contribution.

H. I. Christensen et al. (Eds.): ICVS 2023, LNCS 14253, pp. 243–254, 2023.
https://doi.org/10.1007/978-3-031-44137-0_21

| Image | TL-SSD [20] | Ours |

Fig. 1. Qualitative results of TL-SSD [20] and our proposed traffic light detection system, which highlight the weak performance of current systems on small and tiny traffic lights. The color indicates the assigned traffic light state. Dark blue denotes the state *off*, while white denotes missed or misclassified traffic lights. Arrows highlight traffic lights for better visibility. (Color figure online)

as visible in the results in Fig. 1. Despite the difficulties, small and tiny traffic lights are essential for safe, efficient, and eco-friendly driving. For instance, detecting traffic lights early, when they are still far away and small or tiny on the image plane, allows a car to slowly approach a traffic light showing a stop signal. This reduces noise emission, fuel consumption, and carbon emission [26,33].

Several directions were proposed to improve the detection of small and tiny objects in computer vision literature [4]. Prominent directions include tiling approaches [2,22,31,32], which process sub-images to increase the objects' relative size. However, this leads to substantially increased runtimes [32]. Another direction is a multi-scale feature representation, combing semantically rich, low-resolution features with high-resolution features lacking high-level semantics [6,16]. A third direction are object proposal generators to discover small objects [10,19,29]. Since the latter two directions do not suffer from substantially increased runtime, we follow them to improve the detection of small and tiny traffic lights.

In this paper, we propose a new traffic light detection system, focusing on small and tiny traffic lights, while also improving the detection across all sizes of traffic lights. First, to better localize small and tiny traffic lights, we propose a new traffic light proposal generator. It utilizes the one-shot paradigm from object proposal generation [9], introduces an improved multi-scale feature representation to create semantically rich features at high resolution, and employs attention for increased efficiency. To classify and refine the proposals, we adapt the Faster R-CNN framework [25] utilizing our high-quality proposals and a new traffic light detection head. Our extensive evaluation on three challenging, publicly available datasets demonstrates the effectiveness of our approach for detecting small and tiny traffic lights, as well as traffic lights of all sizes. Across all three datasets, we outperform all other tested methods and strong baselines.

Overall, our contributions are threefold:

- A novel traffic light detection system focusing on small and tiny traffic lights.
- A new traffic light proposal generator using a multi-scale feature representation and attention.
- An extensive evaluation on three challenging datasets, outperforming all other tested methods and strong baselines across all datasets.

Fig. 2. Overview of our traffic light detection system. First, our novel traffic light proposal generator creates traffic light proposals (pink boxes) covering possible traffic light locations. Subsequently, our detection module refines and classifies each proposal (red/blue boxes). (Color figure online)

2 Related Work

Traffic light detection has attracted considerable attention over the last decade. While early approaches used traditional techniques including color thresholding or extracting shape information, see [12] for a survey, CNNs have been utilized recently. Subsequently, we review the most important and relevant approaches utilizing RGB data only.

Most recent CNN-based traffic light detection approaches extend standard object detectors like SSD [18], YOLO [24], or Faster R-CNN [25]. For instance, [20] and [14] improve SSD's detection quality for small traffic lights by proposing modified anchors or an additional classifier. Various versions of YOLO are also adapted for traffic light detection [3,15,27]. To address the challenge of tiny traffic lights, [3] use a tiling approach, while [27] combine features from various layers of the network for detection. Finally, Faster R-CNN is commonly utilized for traffic light detection with adjustments to the anchor boxes [1], backbones [1, 13], color spaces [13], and the classification head [1,7,23].

Apart from approaches based on standard object detectors, few notable approaches exist. [21] use a fully convolutional approach with a hierarchical per-pixel classifier. [28] propose a heuristics-based proposal generator to improve the detection of small traffic lights. Recently, [34] introduced a detection method for small objects that disentangles the features of different classes and instances, which is also applied to traffic light detection.

Overall, for the challenging detection of small and tiny traffic lights, most approaches use variations of standard object detectors or utilize heuristics-based approaches. In contrast, we propose a new traffic light detection system with a dedicated traffic light proposal generator that introduces an improved multi-scale feature representation to create semantically rich features at high resolution as well as attention for increased efficiency.

3 Method

This section introduces our new traffic light detection system, visualized in Fig. 2. Given an input image, our novel traffic light proposal generator, described in

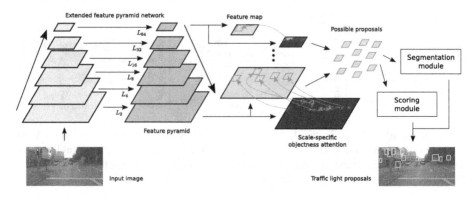

Fig. 3. Detailed view of our traffic light proposal generator. Our extended feature pyramid network (yellow and violet pyramids) extracts semantically rich features across all levels/resolutions (L_2 to L_{64}), yielding a multi-scale feature pyramid (violet pyramid). For each level, we generate a feature map (large cyan boxes) and a scale-specific objectness attention map highlighting possible traffic light locations. Subsequently, we extract windows (possible proposals) at high-attention locations across the feature pyramid. Finally, a segmentation and a score are generated per window to create a ranked list of traffic light proposals. (Color figure online)

Sect. 3.1, extracts possible traffic light locations. The proposal generator explicitly addresses the challenging localization of small traffic lights by improving the resolution of the multi-scale feature representation and utilizes attention for efficient processing. Subsequently, our traffic light detection module refines the proposals and assigns them to a traffic light state based on a new traffic light detection head (see Sect. 3.2). Finally, we discuss the training of our system in Sect. 3.3.

3.1 Traffic Light Proposal Generator

The first stage of our traffic light detection system consists of our novel traffic light proposal generator, visualized in Fig. 3. It is designed to locate all traffic lights and reduce the search space for the subsequent traffic light detection module. Similar to recent object proposal generators [9,29,30], we follow the efficient one-shot approach [9]. Hence, the input image is processed only once by the backbone network, yielding a feature representation that is further subsampled to create a multi-scale feature pyramid. By extracting fixed-size windows from the feature pyramid, proposals for objects of different sizes are generated.

However, simply following this approach is insufficient for traffic light detection with many tiny objects. The additional subsampling to create a feature pyramid on top of the backbone leads to low-resolution feature maps and missing tiny objects. To circumvent this problem, we use the backbone itself as a multi-scale feature pyramid, introducing less subsampling. Yet, two issues arise.

First, the features from early layers of backbones like ResNets [8] are not semantically rich. To generate a feature pyramid that is semantically rich across all levels, we employ and extend the Feature Pyramid Network (FPN) [16] as backbone (yellow and violet pyramids in Fig. 3). The FPN combines a typical CNN-backbone with top-down and lateral connections to create a semantically rich representation across all levels (resolutions) of the feature pyramid (violet pyramid in Fig. 3). In Fig. 3, the levels are denoted by L_n with the downsampling factor n. We further add a new level to the feature pyramid for tiny objects (L_2 in Fig. 3). This multi-scale feature pyramid serves as the base for our proposal generator.

The second issue is the large number of possible locations for extracting windows, i.e., possible traffic light proposals, in our feature pyramid due to the high resolution. To address this issue, we utilize scale-specific objectness attention proposed by [29]. The attention maps are learned per feature pyramid level (scale-specific) and focus the window extraction as well as further processing on the most relevant areas, omitting the background.

Based on the attention maps, we extract all relevant, i.e., high attention, windows of size 10×10 across all levels of our feature pyramid (small cyan boxes in Fig. 3). Subsequently, we use the common head structure of [9] to score the possible proposals and generate a segmentation per proposal. The final result of the traffic light proposal generator are n traffic light proposals with bounding box coordinates and a score to process only the most relevant ones.

3.2 Traffic Light Detection Module

To assign the proposals generated by our traffic light proposal generator to the traffic light states and refine their locations, we apply our traffic light detection module, which is inspired by the Faster R-CNN architecture [25]. First, we extract a feature representation of the image utilizing an FPN backbone. Note that we can share this backbone with the proposal generator.

Given the feature representation of the image and our proposals, we apply region of interest pooling per proposal, leading to a 7×7 feature map per proposal. Subsequently, each proposal is processed by our new traffic light detection head consisting of four fully-connected layers with 2048 neurons each. Based on these features, the detection head refines the traffic light location and assigns a traffic light state or the background label to each proposal.

3.3 Training

This section describes the training of our traffic light detection system. First, we train our traffic light proposal generator utilizing the annotated data of the respective dataset, omitting any state information. We follow [9,29] for defining the respective loss functions of the attention modules and the head for segmenting as well as scoring the traffic light proposals.

After training the traffic light proposal generator, we utilize it to generate positive and negative training samples for our traffic light detection module. A proposal is regarded as a positive sample if it has an Intersection over

Union (IoU) of at least 0.5 with any annotated traffic light, while proposals with an IoU below 0.3 are regarded as negative samples. The rest of the training regime is similar to [25].

4   Experiments

We evaluate our approach on three challenging, publicly available datasets and compare it to six systems across the different datasets. The datasets are the Bosch Small Traffic Lights Dataset (BSTLD) [3], the DriveU Traffic Light Dataset (DTLD) [5], and the recently published dataset Cityscapes TL++ (CS-TL) [11]. They consist of 1978 to 40953 images with an average of 2.4 to 6.6 annotated traffic lights per image. All images show traffic scenes captured from the perspective of the driver and are of high quality. The number of traffic light states differs between the datasets. While all datasets include the states *stop*, *warning*, and *go*, DTLD has *stop/warning* annotated and all datasets include the states *off* or *unknown*. Note that we adapted all systems to the respective number of traffic light states contained in a dataset.

We compare our approach to different methods per dataset due to the limited availability of results and code as well as varying dataset splits. On BSTLD, we compare to [3,23], and the SSD and Faster R-CNN baselines[1] provided by [3]. For DTLD, we generate the results of [20] with their publicly available system[2]. Since no results are publicly available yet on the CS-TL dataset, we compare to a strong baseline using Faster R-CNN [25] with an FPN backbone [16].

To assess the quality of traffic light detection results, we use the mean Average Precision (mAP) with an IoU of 0.5 as the main measure, following [1,15,23,34]. For a more detailed analysis, we report state-specific and size-specific results. While the traffic light states are fixed by the datasets, we define four relative size ranges, based on the ratio of an annotated traffic light's area and the image area. The ranges for relative size a are tiny ($a \leq 0.01\%$), small ($0.01\% < a \leq 0.03\%$), medium ($0.03\% < a \leq 0.05\%$), and large ($0.05\% < a$), denoted as mAP_T, mAP_S, mAP_M, and mAP_L. The ranges are determined such that across all datasets, each class comprises between 20% and 30% of the annotated traffic lights. Finally, we also report $\text{mAP}_{weighted}$ on BSTLD, defined by [3], which incorporates the distribution of traffic light states in the dataset.

The subsequent sections discuss the quantitative results, selected qualitative results, and two ablation studies justifying design choices.

4.1   Quantitative Results

The quantitative results on BSTLD (see Table 1), DTLD (see Table 2), and the CS-TL dataset (see Table 3) all show similar trends. Across all datasets, our proposed system outperforms all other methods and baselines in terms of mAP.

---

[1] Results taken from https://github.com/bosch-ros-pkg/bstld.
[2] https://github.com/julimueller/tl_ssd.

Table 1. Traffic light detection results on the BSTLD test set in terms of mAP, $mAP_{weighted}$, and state-specific mAPs.

System	$mAP_{weighted}$	mAP	mAP_{stop}	$mAP_{warning}$	mAP_{go}	mAP_{off}
YOLO TLD [3]	0.360	–	–	–	–	–
HDA [23]	0.530	–	–	–	–	–
SSD TLD [3]	0.600	0.410	0.550	0.410	0.680	**0.000**
Faster R-CNN NAS [3]	0.650	0.430	0.660	0.330	0.710	**0.000**
Ours	**0.710**	**0.572**	**0.678**	**0.855**	**0.753**	0.000

Table 2. Traffic light detection results on the DTLD test set in terms of mAP and state-specific mAPs.

System	mAP	mAP_{stop}	$mAP_{stop/warning}$	$mAP_{warning}$	mAP_{go}	mAP_{off}
TL-SSD [20]	0.329	0.439	0.283	0.167	0.583	0.010
Ours	**0.552**	**0.699**	**0.564**	**0.564**	**0.789**	**0.142**

Within the datasets, the results for the individual traffic light states vary. One reason is the imbalance of annotations in the datasets. For instance, on DTLD, the states *stop* and *go* amount to almost 85% of the annotations in the dataset. Hence, the results for those states are substantially better than for the other states. Another reason is the intra-class diversity of the states *off* and *unknown*.

On BSTLD, the results in Table 1 show that our proposed traffic light detection system outperforms both SSD TLD and Faster R-CNN NAS [3] based on standard object detectors by 39.5% and 33.0% in terms of mAP. For the state *warning*, the improvement is even up to 159%. Similarly, in terms of $mAP_{weighted}$, our system outperforms all other methods by up to 97.2%.

The results on DTLD in Table 2 comparing TL-SSD [20] based on a standard object detector to our proposed system show again a strong improvement across all traffic light states (+67.8%). On the recently published CS-TL dataset, we compare to the strong Faster R-CNN+FPN [16, 25] baseline (see Table 3). While across all states, i.e. overall, our traffic light detection system outperforms the baseline (+1%), the per-state results favor both systems twice.

Table 3. Traffic light detection results on the CS-TL test set in terms of mAP and state-specific mAPs.

System	mAP	mAP_{stop}	$mAP_{warning}$	mAP_{go}	$mAP_{unknown}$
Faster R-CNN+FPN [16, 25]	0.496	**0.645**	**0.381**	0.626	0.332
Ours	**0.500**	0.638	0.338	**0.650**	**0.375**

Table 4. Size-specific traffic light detection results on the test splits of BSTLD, DTLD, and the CS-TL dataset. T, S, M, and L denote traffic light size ranges tiny, small, medium, and large.

Dataset	System	mAP_T	mAP_S	mAP_M	mAP_L
BSTLD	Ours	0.061	0.508	0.518	0.679
DTLD	TL-SSD [20]	0.079	0.299	0.331	0.530
	Ours	**0.286**	**0.625**	**0.672**	**0.674**
CS-TL	Faster R-CNN+FPN [16, 25]	0.207	0.387	0.385	**0.608**
	Ours	**0.233**	**0.421**	**0.400**	0.531

Image   TL-SSD [20]   Ours

Fig. 4. Qualitative results of TL-SSD [20] and our proposed traffic light detection system on the DTLD test set. The color indicates the assigned traffic light state. Blue denotes the state *off*, while white denotes missed or misclassified traffic lights. Arrows highlight traffic lights for better visibility. (Color figure online)

Analyzing the detection performance in more detail, Table 4 shows the results for different relative sizes of traffic lights. Across all systems and datasets, the results on tiny traffic lights are substantially worse compared to the three other size ranges, with a drop of up to 91%. Note that the traffic light in BSTLD are smaller, resulting in worse results compared to the other datasets. Due to the lack of publicly available results and the novel and custom nature of the evaluation, we can only compare to TL-SSD on DTLD and the Faster R-CNN+FPN baseline on the CS-TL dataset. On both datasets, we outperform the other methods on tiny traffic lights in terms of mAP_T (+262% and +12.6%). This confirms the strong performance of our system on such traffic lights. Across the other size ranges, we also outperform TL-SSD on DTLD by an average of 79.7%. On the CS-TL dataset, we outperform the strong Faster R-CNN+FPN baseline on small and medium traffic lights, with a slight drop on larger ones.

Overall, the quantitative results across three datasets show the strong performance of our traffic light detection system. Particularly, the size-specific results indicate the substantially improved detection of small and tiny traffic lights.

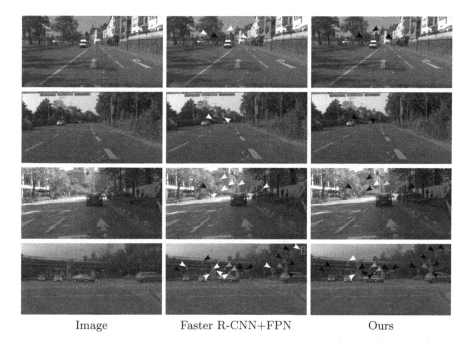

Image   Faster R-CNN+FPN   Ours

Fig. 5. Qualitative results of the Faster R-CNN+FPN [16,25] baseline and our proposed traffic light detection system on the CS-TL test set. The color indicates the assigned traffic light state. Blue denotes the state *unknown*, while white denotes missed or misclassified traffic lights. Arrows highlight traffic lights for better visibility. (Color figure online)

4.2 Qualitative Results

The qualitative results in Fig. 4 on DTLD and in Fig. 5 on the CS-TL dataset support the quantitative results. Comparing the results of TL-SSD and our system on DTLD in Fig. 4, it is clearly visible that both systems detect most larger traffic lights. However, the small and tiny traffic lights are only regularly detected by our system. TL-SSD is only able to detect one smaller traffic light, while our system detects almost all of them in the presented examples.

Switching to the recently published CS-TL dataset, Fig. 5 shows a comparison of our results and the strong Faster R-CNN+FPN baseline. The results across the four images again show a strong performance of both systems on larger traffic lights, with few exceptions like in the complex example in the final row. Investigating the results in the first two rows in more detail, it is visible that despite a rather low scene complexity, only our system is able to consistently detect smaller traffic lights like the two traffic lights with unknown state (blue) in the second row. The lower two rows show more complex scenes with several traffic lights. Despite the complexity, our system again detects most traffic lights and outperforms Faster R-CNN+FPN, especially on smaller instances. Still, some traffic lights are missed by our system due to low contrast (see last row).

252   T. Sanitz et al.

Table 5. Traffic light proposal generation results for three proposal generators on BSTLD in terms of AR for 1000 and 5000 proposals.

Proposal Generator	AR@1000	AR@5000
AttentionMask$_8^{128}$ [29]	0.180	0.180
AttentionMask$_4^{96}$ [29, 32]	**0.390**	0.400
Ours	**0.390**	**0.450**

Table 6. Traffic light detection results for three detection heads on BSTLD in terms of mAP.

Head Structure	mAP
2 × 1024 [25]	0.554
4 × 2048 (ours)	**0.563**
5 × 2048	0.546

Overall, these results correspond well to the findings in Tab. 4. Our system shows a stronger performance on small and tiny traffic lights compared to other systems, while generally accomplishing very good overall results.

4.3   Ablation Studies

This section investigates the choice of the traffic light proposal generator and the detection head. Both ablation studies were conducted on BSTLD.

Proposal Generator. In Sect. 3.1, we proposed a new traffic light proposal generator for locating possible traffic lights. To show the benefit of our proposal generator, which is explicitly designed to discover small and tiny traffic lights, we compare it to two variations of AttentionMask [29]. AttentionMask is a general-purpose object proposal generator designed to discover small objects. The differences between the variations and our system are the spatial resolution of the most fine-grained feature map in the feature pyramid and the usage of an FPN-based backbone (see Sect. 3.1). While the two versions of Attention-Mask utilize a feature map with a downscale factor of 8 (AttentionMask$_8^{128}$ [29]) and 4 (AttentionMask$_4^{96}$ [32]) as the base of the feature pyramid, we use a feature map with downscale factor 2 as a result of the FPN-based backbone. Note that AttentionMask$_8^{128}$ and AttentionMask$_4^{96}$ do not use an FPN-based backbone. The results in Table 5 on BSTLD in terms of Average Recall[3] (AR) for 1000 and 5000 proposals show that we strongly outperform original Attention-Mask with an improvement of 150% on AR@5000. Compared to the variation AttentionMask$_4^{96}$, the improvement is still 12.5%. Therefore, our traffic light proposal generator based on the extended FPN-based feature pyramid outperforms general-purpose object proposal generators on the traffic light localization task.

Detection Head. The detection head in our traffic light detection module refines the traffic light proposals and assigns them a traffic light state. As discussed in Sect. 3.2, our new detection head comprises four fully-connected layers with 2048 neurons each. We compare this design to the detection head of Faster

---
[3] Average Recall assesses how many annotated traffic lights are recalled and how precisely they are located, given a specified number of proposals.

R-CNN [25], which has two layers with 1024 neurons, and a larger detection head with five layers and 2048 neurons each. The results in terms of mAP on BSTLD in Table 6 indicate that our new detection head outperforms Faster R-CNN's detection head (+1.6%) as well as the larger detection head (+3.1%). Hence, our detection head is a good choice for the traffic light detection task.

5   Conclusion

In this paper, we addressed the problem of traffic light detection. We specifically focused on the challenging detection of small and tiny traffic lights, which are important for safe, efficient, and eco-friendly driving. Our approach consists of (i) a novel traffic light proposal generator combining the one-shot approach from object proposal generation with fine-grained multi-scale features as well as attention, and (ii) a detection module featuring a new traffic light detection head. The extensive evaluation across three datasets and six methods clearly shows the strong performance of our novel system on small and tiny traffic lights (at least +12.6%), as well as a strong overall performance on traffic lights of all sizes. Thus, our system can improve safe, efficient, and eco-friendly driving.

References

1. Bach, M., Stumper, D., Dietmayer, K.: Deep convolutional traffic light recognition for automated driving. In: ITSC (2018)
2. Bargoti, S., Underwood, J.: Deep fruit detection in orchards. In: ICRA (2017)
3. Behrendt, K., Novak, L., Botros, R.: A deep learning approach to traffic lights: detection, tracking, and classification. In: ICRA (2017)
4. Chen, G., et al.: A survey of the four pillars for small object detection: multi-scale representation, contextual information, super-resolution, and region proposal. IEEE Trans. Syst. Man Cybern.: Syst. **52**(2), 936–953 (2020)
5. Fregin, A., Muller, J., Krebel, U., Dietmayer, K.: The DriveU traffic light dataset: introduction and comparison with existing datasets. In: ICRA (2018)
6. Gong, Y., Yu, X., Ding, Y., Peng, X., Zhao, J., Han, Z.: Effective fusion factor in FPN for tiny object detection. In: WACV (2021)
7. Gupta, A., Choudhary, A.: A framework for traffic light detection and recognition using deep learning and Grassmann manifolds. In: IV (2019)
8. He, K., Zhang, X., Ren, S., Sun, J.: Deep residual learning for image recognition. In: CVPR (2016)
9. Hu, H., Lan, S., Jiang, Y., Cao, Z., Sha, F.: FastMask: segment multi-scale object candidates in one shot. In: CVPR (2017)
10. Hu, P., Ramanan, D.: Finding tiny faces. In: CVPR (2017)
11. Janosovits, J.: Cityscapes TL++: semantic traffic light annotations for the cityscapes dataset. In: ICRA (2022)
12. Jensen, M.B., Philipsen, M.P., Møgelmose, A., Moeslund, T.B., Trivedi, M.M.: Vision for looking at traffic lights: issues, survey, and perspectives. T-ITS **17**(7), 1800–1815 (2016)
13. Kim, H.K., Park, J.H., Jung, H.Y.: An efficient color space for deep-learning based traffic light recognition. JAT **2018**, 1–12 (2018)

14. Kim, J., Cho, H., Hwangbo, M., Choi, J., Canny, J., Kwon, Y.P.: Deep traffic light detection for self-driving cars from a large-scale dataset. In: ITSC (2018)
15. Lee, E., Kim, D.: Accurate traffic light detection using deep neural network with focal regression loss. IMAVIS **87**, 24–36 (2019)
16. Lin, T.Y., Dollár, P., Girshick, R., He, K., Hariharan, B., Belongie, S.: Feature pyramid networks for object detection. In: CVPR (2017)
17. Lin, T.-Y., et al.: Microsoft COCO: common objects in context. In: Fleet, D., Pajdla, T., Schiele, B., Tuytelaars, T. (eds.) ECCV 2014. LNCS, vol. 8693, pp. 740–755. Springer, Cham (2014). https://doi.org/10.1007/978-3-319-10602-1_48
18. Liu, W., et al.: SSD: single shot multibox detector. In: Leibe, B., Matas, J., Sebe, N., Welling, M. (eds.) ECCV 2016. LNCS, vol. 9905, pp. 21–37. Springer, Cham (2016). https://doi.org/10.1007/978-3-319-46448-0_2
19. Lu, H.F., Du, X., Chang, P.L.: Toward scale-invariance and position-sensitive region proposal networks. In: ECCV (2018)
20. Müller, J., Dietmayer, K.: Detecting traffic lights by single shot detection. In: ITSC (2018)
21. Ouyang, Z., Niu, J., Liu, Y., Guizani, M.: Deep CNN-based real-time traffic light detector for self-driving vehicles. IEEE Trans. Mob. Comput. **19**(2), 300–313 (2019)
22. Ozge Unel, F., Ozkalayci, B.O., Cigla, C.: The power of tiling for small object detection. In: CVPRW (2019)
23. Pon, A., Adrienko, O., Harakeh, A., Waslander, S.L.: A hierarchical deep architecture and mini-batch selection method for joint traffic sign and light detection. In: CRV (2018)
24. Redmon, J., Divvala, S., Girshick, R., Farhadi, A.: You only look once: unified, real-time object detection. In: CVPR (2016)
25. Ren, S., He, K., Girshick, R., Sun, J.: Faster R-CNN: towards real-time object detection with region proposal networks (2015)
26. Rittger, L., Schmidt, G., Maag, C., Kiesel, A.: Driving behaviour at traffic light intersections. Cogn. Technol. Work **17**, 593–605 (2015)
27. Wang, Q., Zhang, Q., Liang, X., Wang, Y., Zhou, C., Mikulovich, V.I.: Traffic lights detection and recognition method based on the improved YOLOv4 algorithm. Sensors **22**(1), 200 (2022)
28. Weber, M., Huber, M., Zöllner, J.M.: HDTLR: a CNN based hierarchical detector for traffic lights. In: ITSC (2018)
29. Wilms, C., Frintrop, S.: AttentionMask: attentive, efficient object proposal generation focusing on small objects. In: Jawahar, C.V., Li, H., Mori, G., Schindler, K. (eds.) ACCV 2018. LNCS, vol. 11362, pp. 678–694. Springer, Cham (2019). https://doi.org/10.1007/978-3-030-20890-5_43
30. Wilms, C., Frintrop, S.: Superpixel-based refinement for object proposal generation. In: ICPR (2021)
31. Wilms, C., Heid, R., Sadeghi, M.A., Ribbrock, A., Frintrop, S.: Which airline is this? Airline logo detection in real-world weather conditions. In: ICPR (2021)
32. Wilms, C., Johanson, R., Frintrop, S.: Localizing small apples in complex apple orchard environments. arXiv preprint arXiv:2202.11372 (2022)
33. Wu, C., Zhao, G., Ou, B.: A fuel economy optimization system with applications in vehicles with human drivers and autonomous vehicles. Transp. Res. D **16**(7), 515–524 (2011)
34. Yang, X., Yan, J., Liao, W., Yang, X., Tang, J., He, T.: SCRDET++: detecting small, cluttered and rotated objects via instance-level feature denoising and rotation loss smoothing. TPAMI **45**(2), 2384–2399 (2022)

MATWI: A Multimodal Automatic Tool Wear Inspection Dataset and Baseline Algorithms

Lars De Pauw[1]([✉]) [ID], Tom Jacobs[2], and Toon Goedemé[1] [ID]

[1] KU Leuven, Sint-Katelijne-Waver, Belgium
lars.depauw@kuleuven.be
[2] Sirris, Diepenbeek, Belgium

Abstract. In this paper, we present MATWI, a new publicly available multimodal dataset for automatic tool wear inspection containing both images and captured sensor data during CNC milling processes. This dataset contains 17 tools ran to failure with 100 measurements over the lifespan, resulting in a large and unique dataset for tool wear estimation. It is also the first dataset that combines accelerometer, microphone and force measurements with image data captured along the tool life. The used setup can be installed on any real production level CNC machine to perform similar data acquisition and advise tool replacements. The size of our dataset allows for artificial neural networks to be trained for wear estimation on the carbide inserts used in milling industry. We present a baseline vision-based regression model based on a ResNet backbone, as well as a novel deep embedding training approach which decreases the prediction error by 37%. Predicting real tool wear with a mean absolute error of 19 μm on wear sizes between 0 and 450 μm, this method can be used in real life production machines to predict tool wear and provide tool replacement advise.

Keywords: Tool Wear · Dataset · Histogram Loss · Deep Embeddings · Multimodal · Time series

1 Introduction

Metal milling techniques are used to produce high precision parts. Machine precision decreases with tool wear over time. Finding a good tool replacement strategy is important to keep production quality high and use tools for its full lifespan. Inspection of these tools is mostly done by visual inspection by a machine operator who spots the wear level and decides for replacement. However, the scale of wear on the inspected tools is between 0 and 450 μm which makes it challenging to evaluate with human eye only.

If a more accurate inspection is needed, this tool is placed under a microscope that allows the flank wear to be measured between the inserts top and bottom of

H. I. Christensen et al. (Eds.): ICVS 2023, LNCS 14253, pp. 255–269, 2023.
https://doi.org/10.1007/978-3-031-44137-0_22

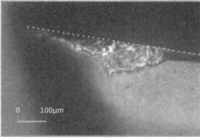

Fig. 1. Carbide insert example from the dataset with measurement method indicated.

the degraded part as shown in Fig. 1. This flank wear is gradually formed during milling process and is often used as indication for the tools state.

Other wear types seen are: crater wear, adhesive wear and chipping. These wear types indicate sub-optimal cutting parameters and provide information on which parameters to tune. This paper focuses on quantizing flank wear to provide an objective measure for insert replacements.

This paper provides a new dataset containing both direct (visual) and indirect (sensor) measurements during real life milling operations. Deep learning is used to provide a first method of tool wear estimation on the direct measured data.

Current state of the art on direct and indirect methods are described in Sect. 2. After this, our newly created multimodal dataset is discussed in Sect. 3 including its measurement setup and the results. In Sect. 4 a baseline wear estimation method for image analysis and a novel method for image time series data is proposed. Section 5 draws conclusions on the dataset and image processing technique. Future work is discussed in Sect. 6.

2   Related Work

Tool wear is a highly researched topic in milling industry. Our application focuses on detecting tool wear of carbide milling inserts.

Direct and indirect measuring setups are found in other tool wear estimation methods. Direct methods are online or offline camera setups that capture images inside or outside of the machine respectively. Indirect measurement setups use a set of sensors (vibration, microphone, force, ...) to estimate wear levels during the milling process. Sensor data is more researched since acquisition of this type of data has very little influence on the milling process, easing the physical implementation in real operational machines and allowing for bigger datasets to be created. We see that sometimes visual inspection using microscope or micro photography is used to obtain ground truth, which indeed indicates the relevance of image data for wear estimation.

Table 1 gives an overview of current available datasets on milling tools in comparison to the proposed MATWI dataset. An earlier overview was given in

[17] where they indicate that very little datasets are publicly available and most of them don't contain images for reference.

Table 1. Comparison of currently available datasets used for tool wear estimation. (Image count incl. augmentations)

Dataset	Public	Sensors	Images	Tool type	Tools	Measur	Sensor samples	Images	Labels
Milling Data Set [1]	Yes	Vibration Acoustic emission spindle current	None	Carbide insert	16	167	167×9000	0	Flank wear
PHM2010 [14]	Yes	Force (x, y, z) Vibration (x, y, z) Acoustic emission	None	End mill	6	1800	1800×220000	0	Flank wear
Garcia-Ordas, M.T. [8]	No	None	Grey	Carbide insert	53×4	212	0	212	2/3 class Flank wear
Wu, X. [19]	No	None	Color	Carbide insert	?	8400	0	8400	Wear type Flank wear
Lutz, B. [16]	No	None	Color	Carbide insert	100	100	0	100	Wear type Segmentation
Bergs, T. [4]	No	None	Color	End mill Carbide insert Drills	8	400	0	400(3000)	Wear type Segmentation
Lutz, B. [15]	No	None	Color	Carbide insert	2	207	0	207	Wear type Segmentation
Brili, N. [6]	No	None	Thermal	Carbide insert	9333	9333	0	9333	4 class Flank wear
NJUST-CCTD [17]	Yes	None	Color	End mill	40	40	0	1600(8000)	2 class Flank wear
Alajmi, S. [2]	No	None	Microscope	Carbide insert	162	162	0	162	Flank wear
MATWI (Ours)	**Yes**	**Force (x, y, z) Vibration Acoustic emission**	**Color**	**Carbide insert**	**17**	**1663**	**1663×94000**	**1663**	**Flank wear Wear type**

2.1 Datasets and Methods with Sensor Data

A commonly used dataset in the Prognostics and Health Management (PHM) for machining purposes is the PHM2010 dataset [7]. This dataset has sensor readings for force in X, Y and Z direction, vibration in X, Y and Z direction and an acoustic emission sensor. These sensors are attached to the workpiece. Goal of this dataset is to predict Remaining Useful Life (RUL) on the used tool. The dataset consists of 6 different tools used for 300 milling passes each. Further detail about the setup is described in [14]. The tools used are ball-nose tungsten carbide milling cutters.

Zhou *et al.* [20] uses graph neural networks to handle small sample sizes for tool condition classification in five classes using sensor data. The data used are C1, C4 and C6 from this PHM2010 dataset. On this small sample size, their proposed method outperforms deep learning techniques such as CNN, AlexNet and ResNet, which are difficult to train on few data. Our proposed dataset contains more data which allows deep learning methods to be used.

Agogino *et al.* [1] created a milling dataset using vibration, accoustic and spindle current measurements for a total of 16 tools with 167 wear measurements for all tools combined.

Bilgili *et al.* [5] proposed a low computationally intensive method for tool wear estimation of a drill using spindle motor current and dynamometer measurements. The used data consists of one run-to-failure experiment of a drill.

2.2   Datasets and Methods with Image Data

Garcia *et al.* [8] used computer vision for wear estimation of carbide inserts on edge milling and generated a dataset of 212 images from 53 different tools with 4 cutting edges each. Methods used are B-ORCHIZ introduced by them to generate descriptors of the worn area, and a SVM to classify descriptors. They achieved 87% accuracy for binary classification on their full dataset, 81% for 3-class classification of the wear. We, on the other hand, focus on regression to have a more gradual estimation of the amount of wear along the milling process.

The same authors [9] later generated a bigger dataset with 254 images of edge profile cutting heads where the top of the insert is inspected. This was the first public dataset large enough for image segmentation by using wear patches. Their method derives the wear level of each patch to determine the overall wear level of the insert, and is based on a trained SVM. However, the method still relies on manually set thresholds for serviceable or worn classification on the wear patches and for the overall evaluation of the cutting edge. In contrast, our method generalizes more by using deep learning on a bigger dataset and performing image regression where one threshold for serviceability can be set after training according to the needs for production (e.g. lower wear threshold for higher quality surface finish).

Bagga *et al.* [3] used more traditional computer vision techniques to achieve a performant wear estimation on carbide inserts. They used image preprocessing, thresholding to segment the image and edge detection to determine flank wear based on images captured at the end of a milling cycle.

Pan *et al.* [17] published a big dataset of end mill tools of 8000 images separated in two classes (wear images and no-wear images). Using this data they obtained an accuracy of 95.375% on the binary prediction of wear. Denoising was used to optimize images before inserting the images into a convolutional neural network. Our dataset focusses on carbide milling inserts from which wear is measured differently than end milling tools.

Wu *et al.* [19] used a large image dataset for tool wear type classification with over 8000 images. Apart from wear type estimation, their tool wear value detection method based on a custom convolutional neural network can detect the wear values at the end of tool usage. This is done with a mean absolute percentage error of 4.7%. However, this dataset was not made publicly available and thus could not be used for comparison.

3   MATWI Dataset

Deep learning is not often used in the field of wear estimation due to the lack of datasets that are large enough. Acquiring a big dataset for this purpose, on real-life machines, is thus needed. In this section we will describe the method we used to automate the generation of such a dataset. This allowed us to generate a unique dataset for tool wear estimation, being both large and multimodal.

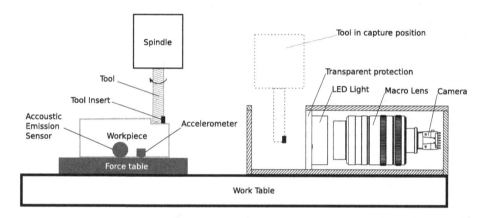

Fig. 2. Machine setup for capturing

3.1   Dataset Acquisition

Our capturing setup is shown in Fig. 2 and consists of two main parts: The CNC machine with location output and a Camera Box we designed containing a camera and controller. All input from camera and controllers is processed on an external computer.

For dataset creation, the CNC mill is programmed to cut one line in the provided workpiece for every run. At the start of a new tool, a zero measurement image is taken after which the milling process is started. During each run we capture sensor measurements starting before the tool enters the workpiece and stops after the tool exits the workpiece. An image of the inserts cutting edge is captured at the end of every run.

The CNC controller has no bidirectional communication so it can only publish spindle locations to the setup controller. Fixed machine positions are thus used to synchronize both controllers. The setup controller constantly monitors the spindle position and will execute functions if a predefined location is reached.

The first predefined position is in front of the camera which is manually set by the operator to ensure the tool edge is in focus. When this position is reached at the start of a new tool or at the end of a run, the setup controller will turn on the LED ring light and capture an image after which the machine continues its operation and wears the tool further.

The second task of the setup controller is capturing sensor data which is coordinated in a similar way. A bounding box in the x and y direction of the spindle is set to span an area larger than the workpiece. The setup controller will start capturing sensor measurements when the spindle enters this box and stops capturing when the spindle exits the bounding box. The three sensors (acceleration, acoustic emission and force) are captured simultaneously and saved to the computer via a DAQ converter.

Human interaction in this process is reduced to a minimum. An operator programs the CNC machine for every new tool used to align the cutting edge with the camera. After this, the setup can work autonomously to generate data until the installed tool is worn. Supervision during this process is only needed to interrupt the process if a hazardous situation would occur.

After generating all data, the dataset is labeled by an expert using the captured images. This is similar to other tool wear datasets where the insert is inspected under a microscope after usage. Using a high resolution camera provides a faster way since the tool doesn't have to be reinstalled for every measurement.

3.2 Data Collection Conditions

The data collection was done under a number of specific conditions. First, we only installed one carbide insert in the multi-insert tool, in order to collect sensor data that only depends on this insert. We also opted to use no cooling fluids, to protect the camera setup and sensors. Moreover, without cooling there are less obstructions on the image output.

As summarized in Table 2, we varied the cutting parameters and workpiece material during data collection. For set 1 the cutting parameters are unknown.

The later milling sets are generated with different parameters where the first three differ a lot with different cutting speed (V_c) and rotation speed (n). Also, the workpiece material changed for set 12 to 17, which could result in other weartypes on the inserts.

3.3 Hardware Setup

The setup as shown on Fig. 2 was used to capture image and sensor data during milling operation. Sensors are programmed to capture when the machine is in operation while the camera image is captured between milling passes when the machine is at a standstill. Our setup uses the machine to position the tool in front of the camera, providing a very accurate positioning of the tool in frame. This makes it possible to crop images to the needed parts as shown in Fig. 5b.

Table 2. Summary of used cutting parameters: cutting speed V_c (m/min), rotation speed n (rev/min), feed f_z (mm), feed rate V_f (mm/min), cutting width A_e (mm), cutting depth A_p (mm), Crop location (left, top, right, bottom).

Set	V_c	n	f_z	V_f	A_e	A_p	Material	Image Crop
1	/	/	/	/	1	1	CK45	(2470, 1000, 3070, 1400)
2	120	2547	0.08	203	1	1	CK45	(1150, 670, 1750, 1070)
3	150	3184	0.05	159	1	1	CK45	(1150, 670, 1750, 1070)
4	174	3705	0.05	185	1	1	CK45	(1150, 670, 1750, 1070)
5	174	3705	0.04	148	1	1	CK45	(1150, 670, 1750, 1070)
6	174	3705	0.04	148	1	1	CK45	(1150, 670, 1750, 1070)
7	174	3705	0.045	170	1	1	CK45	(1150, 670, 1750, 1070)
8	174	3705	0.048	178	1	1	CK45	(1150, 670, 1750, 1070)
9	174	3705	0.048	178	1	0.5	CK45	(1150, 670, 1750, 1070)
10	174	3705	0.05	185	1	0.5	CK45	(1150, 670, 1750, 1070)
11	174	3705	0.043	159	1	1	CK45	(1150, 670, 1750, 1070)
12	120	2547	0.05	127	1	0.5	RVS 304	(1150, 670, 1750, 1070)
13	150	3184	0.05	159	1	0.5	RVS 304	(1150, 670, 1750, 1070)
14	135	2866	0.06	172	1	0.5	RVS 304	(1790, 2030, 2390, 2430)
15	120	2547	0.03	76	1	1	RVS 304	(1790, 2030, 2390, 2430)
16	150	3184	0.03	95	1	1	RVS 304	(1790, 2045, 2390, 2445)
17	150	3184	0.03	191	1	1	RVS 304	(1790, 2045, 2390, 2445)

A firm connection between the camera box and the work table along with the on-line way of creating the dataset makes sure the tool is never reinstalled or re-positioned during the whole capturing process. This provides high quality images that are easier to label and to estimate wear values on as compared to offline datasets.

A white background makes sure to have as little influence possible of the exterior mill. We made our camera case out of white plastic, reflecting light to the side and back of the insert. This way, more light gets into the camera, reducing the time needed to have a well lit image.

Sensors. An acoustic emission sensor and accelerometer are attached to the workpiece table. The accoustic emission sensor is a Vallen CS30-Sic-V2 with a sample range between 25 and 80 kHz. This is set to 1626 HZ to capture the full spectrum expected from the milling machine (rotating at a speed of 2000–4000 revolutions per minute). The accelerometer type is a 333B40 by PCB piezotronics measuring at the same sample rate. Force measurement is done on three axis (x, y and z) by a Kistler force measurement table (type 9255C). All sensors are connected to a National instruments DAQ converter to USB. Combination of the sensors results in five measurements every 0.6 ms throughout the dataset, captured between every image taken during the milling process.

Camera. Small wear sizes require a macroscopic lens to capture inserts, the CA-LMHE0510 from Keyence provided this. The lens was set to a field of view of 17.8 mm by 14.3 mm to capture the insert. The combination of this lens with the Alvium 1800 u-2050 20 MP camera provides a pixel resolution of 3.2 micron per pixel. This is sufficient to label images of worn surfaces with an accuracy high enough for training. A multi-directional LED ring light is installed around the camera lens to provide light on all sides of the worn edge.

3.4   Collected Data

Our resulting dataset contains 17 sets of round 100 images with its captured indirect sensor values. Sets will be seen as indivisible parts of the dataset to prevent data leakage. Figure 3a provides an overview of the distribution of wear levels. Wear values are measured in micrometer, for training purposes these values are divided by 1000 to normalize between 0 and 1. Values range between 0.045 and 0.450 with an outlier at 0.750 mm. Adhesive wear has a higher average value than other wear types since the workpiece cutoffs stick to the insert, resulting in wear levels that could be bigger than the insert size.

All sets contain approximately 100 labeled samples along the cutting process. Exact number of samples can be seen in Fig. 3b. Presence of wear types in each set is visualized in this plot showing an uneven distribution along the different sets. Flank wear is most present and important wear type by which wear levels are determined.

The full dataset is publicly available and can be downloaded online[1].

Sensor Data. The three sensors installed in the setup generate five data values (acceleration, acoustic emission and force in three directions). Figure 4a shows the number of samples captured in every set. On Fig. 4b is an example provided for every sensor modality seen in the dataset. Force measurement in the Z direction stays at zero during full data captation as a result of the spindle only moving in the x and y direction while measuring.

Image Data. All images are captured using the same setup, examples from the middle of the time series for every set are shown in Fig. 5. On Fig. 5a, a raw image result for set 5 is shown. These images are cropped to the marked part on the top left corner of the insert. This is the contact point with the workpiece during operation. Cropped images for selected sets are shown in Fig. 5b. By selecting a high resolution camera setup, the crops still have a resolution of 600 by 400 pixels.

---

[1] MATWI dataset: https://iiw.kuleuven.be/onderzoek/eavise/datasets.

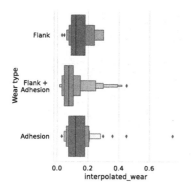

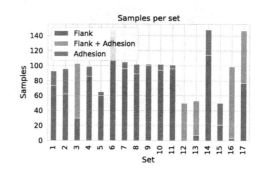

(a) Wear level distribution.   (b) Wear type distribution.

Fig. 3. Dataset characteristics

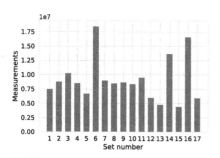

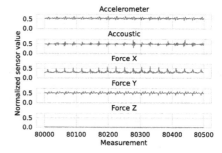

(a) Number of samples captured by the five   (b) Example of captured sensor values at
sensors for every set.   end of set 5.

Fig. 4. Sensor sample distribution and examples for set 5.

The images for the sets show differences in wear types. Set 5 has a much higher wear than other sets, set 12, 16 and 17 visibly have adhesion on the selected images. Other sets appear very similar.

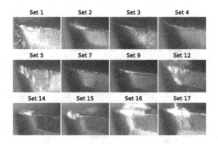

(a) Original resolution image from Set 5.

(b) Examples of selected sets cropped from the original resolution.

Fig. 5. Dataset Image examples.

4   Algorithms for Wear Estimation

In this paper, we present two different neural network approaches for predicting the tool wear using our novel MATWI dataset. For the time being, these benchmark algorithms only use the images from the dataset to predict the wear level (in millimeters) by using image regression. The fusion with the other sensor signals in the multimodal dataset is kept for future work.

We compare both a straightforward ResNet-based regression approach, and a newly introduced histogram-loss based embedding learning for this task in the following subsections.

4.1   Dataset Training/test Split

We performed our baseline experiments on a subset of our dataset, consisting of sets 1 to 13. Sets 1, 2, 5, 7, 8, 10 and 11 are used for training. Set 3, 6 and 12 are used for validation. Testing is done on set 4, 9 and 13. As described in Sect. 3, sets 12 to 17 have been used to mill a different type of material than the one used in all other sets. Due to the properties of this material, there is more adhesive wear in the samples which makes the appearance different from the other sets. Excluding these sets from training provides insight in generalisation of the network on other workpiece materials. Set 3 is also excluded from training and used for testing to get insight in the generalisation for other wear types. As seen in Fig. 3a, only sets 3, 12, 13, 16 and 17 have high levels of the combination of flank wear and adhesive wear.

4.2   Regression Baseline

First, a naive method for image regression is used to set a baseline. This network takes an image as input and provides a direct wear value as output. We adjusted the Resnet50 architecture [11] for a regression task by adjusting the output classifier to output only one class prediction. No activation layer is used to shape the output. This architecture was trained on the 664 images of the training dataset, using a learning rate of 3×10^{-4} for 17 epochs.

Figure 6 displays the test results for this network. Different wear types are highlighted by color. We observe that both flank wear samples and adhesion samples lie very close to the ideal line. The combination of flank wear and adhesive wear has a higher spread and is not following a linear trajectory for the wear values. This shows poor generalisation of the network to an unseen type of wear. (Sets 3, 11 and 12 contain the combination of wear types and are not used for training)

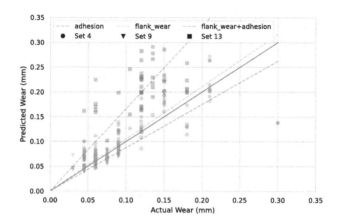

Fig. 6. Regression network output for test data consisting of set 4, 9 and 13. Color specifies wear type. Lines represent linear fit through wear types. Grey line y=x shows ideal prediction. (Color figure online)

4.3   Histogram-Loss Based Embedding Learning

It can be argued that the baseline network presented above is not using the full potential for the time information of the image series provided in the dataset. In each of the series, the wear grows (more or less) gradually over time.

One possible approach to include this time information could be the use of a LSTM [12] on top of the CNN based image processing backbone. However, the full dataset consists only of 17 different time sequences of images. Only using that few sequences would result in very little training data and a fast overfitting LSTM network.

The alternative we propose for this is the following. Learning the difference between images in a sequence would be beneficial for incorporating more of the available information. In a metric learning fashion, we propose the use of a network that converts the input images into an embedding, specifically trained such that the Euclidean distance between embeddings of a pair of images is made equal to the difference in wear (in mm) between these two images.

This is implemented using Resnet101 which is adjusted in a similar way as in the baseline network to output an embedding vector $\boldsymbol{E}$ consisting of 8 values per image. This network can be trained with random pairs of training images using a contrastive loss [10], or with triplets of training images using triplet loss [13]. However, this is only possible for binary classification (in our case, e.g. worn vs. not worn) and adds the additional complexity of hard example mining. Therefore, we chose Histogram loss [18] for training, with the task to shape this embedding space to match the distance between embedding vectors with the difference in wear between images.

To replicate real situations in the testing of the model, the first image is used as reference sample with a known wear value w_{ref}. All other images in the sequence are measured by the distance between this reference sample and the current sample in the embedding space as shown in Eq. 1.

$$\|\boldsymbol{E}_{ref} - \boldsymbol{E}_{curr}\| - w_{ref} = w_{curr} \qquad (1)$$

Figure 7 shows the results of this on the same test sets as before, for different wear types. In contrast to the baseline model, where the combination of wear types was predicted poorly, with the improved embedding model this poses less of a challenge. Indeed, we see that the dashed trend lines of each type lie very close to the ideal line.

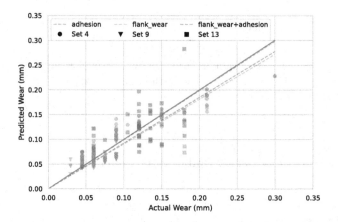

Fig. 7. Histogram network output for test data consisting of set 4, 9 and 13. Color specifies wear type. Lines represent linear fit through wear types. Grey line y=x shows ideal prediction. (Color figure online)

4.4 Quantitative Results

Table 3 specifies quantitative results. We calculated the mean average error (and its standard deviation) on the wear prediction values for each of the wear types for the baseline regression network and the histogram-loss based metric learning approach.

Table 3. Regression network output predictions for test sets.

Category	Regression MAE (μm)	Histogram-loss MAE (μm)
Adhesion	39 ($\pm$ 40)	23 ($\pm$ 16)
Flank Wear	14 ($\pm$ 15)	16 ($\pm$ 15)
Adhesion and Flank Wear	91 ($\pm$ 41)	29 ($\pm$ 24)
Total	30 ($\pm$ 38)	**19 ($\pm$ 18)**

5   Conclusions

In this paper, we presented MATWI, a multimodal dataset for automatic tool wear inspection consisting of 17 labeled time series of both indirect sensor measurements (acceleration, acoustic emmission and force) and direct measurements (micro photography images of the carbide cutting inserts). We detailed the dataset and the set-up built to generate it.

Using the images from this dataset, we trained a naive tool wear regression CNN approach as a baseline. Next to that, a novel embedding-based learning approach is presented that better includes the time information in the training dataset. We demonstrated that using histogram loss for deep embedding enables to generate a tool independent embedding space, yielding high precision wear estimations based on the images.

6   Future Work

In the future, the dataset will be extended to include other types of milling tools with similar cutting edges. This could lead to a more general model that can be widely used in practical applications.

Our current work does not include analysis of the direct sensor measurements yet. Our dataset is especially suited for multimodal sensor fusion for the task of tool wear estimation. Combinations of direct and indirect measurements could improve further on image analysis alone in terms of machine efficiency. Because capturing an image takes several seconds, we can think of ways to reducing the downtime by using first estimations with indirect sensor values after which an image can provide a second opinion for tool replacement advice.

The time aspect of our current dataset is not further explored, there could be potential in this information using theoretical models on the wear curves for the used tools.

Acknowledgements. Funding for this research was provided by VLAIO through the ATWI ICON project.

268   L. De Pauw et al.

References

1. A. Agogino, K.G.: Milling Data Set (2007). https://data.nasa.gov/download/vjv9-9f3x/application%2Fzip. bEST Lab, UC Berkeley
2. Alajmi, M., Almeshal, A.: Estimation and optimization of tool wear in conventional turning of 709M40 alloy steel using support vector machine (SVM) with Bayesian optimization. Materials **14**, 3773 (2021). https://doi.org/10.3390/ma14143773
3. Bagga, P.J., Makhesana, M.A., Patel, K., Patel, K.M.: Tool wear monitoring in turning using image processing techniques. Mater. Today: Proc. **44**, 771–775 (2021). https://doi.org/10.1016/j.matpr.2020.10.680
4. Bergs, T., Holst, C., Gupta, P., Augspurger, T.: Digital image processing with deep learning for automated cutting tool wear detection. Procedia Manuf. **48**, 947–958 (2020). https://doi.org/10.1016/j.promfg.2020.05.134
5. Bilgili, D., et al.: Tool flank wear prediction using high-frequency machine data from industrial edge device (2022). https://doi.org/10.48550/arXiv.2212.13905, arXiv:2212.13905 [cs, eess]
6. Brili, N., Ficko, M., Klančnik, S.: Automatic identification of tool wear based on thermography and a convolutional neural network during the turning process. Sensors **21**(5), 1917 (2021). https://doi.org/10.3390/s21051917, number: 5 Publisher: Multidisciplinary Digital Publishing Institute
7. Chen, Y.C.: 2010 PHM Society Conference Data Challenge (2021). https://ieee-dataport.org/documents/2010-phm-society-conference-data-challenge
8. García-Ordás, M.T., Alegre, E., González-Castro, V., Alaiz-Rodríguez, R.: A computer vision approach to analyze and classify tool wear level in milling processes using shape descriptors and machine learning techniques. Int. J. Adv. Manuf. Technol. **90**(5), 1947–1961 (2017). https://doi.org/10.1007/s00170-016-9541-0
9. García-Ordás, M.T., Alegre-Gutiérrez, E., Alaiz-Rodríguez, R., González-Castro, V.: Tool wear monitoring using an online, automatic and low cost system based on local texture. Mech. Syst. Signal Process. **112**, 98–112 (2018). https://doi.org/10.1016/j.ymssp.2018.04.035
10. Hadsell, R., Chopra, S., LeCun, Y.: Dimensionality reduction by learning an invariant mapping. In: 2006 IEEE Computer Society Conference on Computer Vision and Pattern Recognition (CVPR 2006), vol. 2, pp. 1735–1742 (2006). https://doi.org/10.1109/CVPR.2006.100, iSSN: 1063-6919
11. He, K., Zhang, X., Ren, S., Sun, J.: Deep residual learning for image recognition. In: 2016 IEEE Conference on Computer Vision and Pattern Recognition (CVPR), pp. 770–778 (2016). https://doi.org/10.1109/CVPR.2016.90
12. Hochreiter, S., Schmidhuber, J.: Long short-term memory. Neural Comput. **9**(8), 1735–1780 (1997)
13. Hoffer, E., Ailon, N.: Deep metric learning using triplet network. In: Feragen, A., Pelillo, M., Loog, M. (eds.) SIMBAD 2015. LNCS, vol. 9370, pp. 84–92. Springer, Cham (2015). https://doi.org/10.1007/978-3-319-24261-3_7
14. Li, X., et al.: Fuzzy neural network modelling for tool wear estimation in dry milling operation. In: Annual Conference of the PHM Society, vol. 1, no. 1 (2009). https://papers.phmsociety.org/index.php/phmconf/article/view/1403
15. Lutz, B., et al.: Benchmark of automated machine learning with state-of-the-art image segmentation algorithms for tool condition monitoring. Procedia Manuf. **51**, 215–221 (2020). https://doi.org/10.1016/j.promfg.2020.10.031
16. Lutz, B., Kisskalt, D., Regulin, D., Reisch, R., Schiffler, A., Franke, J.: Evaluation of deep learning for semantic image segmentation in tool condition monitoring. In:

2019 18th IEEE International Conference On Machine Learning And Applications (ICMLA), pp. 2008–2013 (2019). https://doi.org/10.1109/ICMLA.2019.00321

17. Pan, Y., et al.: NJUST-CCTD: an image database for milling tool wear classification with deep learning. Int. J. Adv. Manuf. Technol. **127**, 3681–3698 (2022). https://doi.org/10.21203/rs.3.rs-1953358/v1

18. Ustinova, E., Lempitsky, V.: Learning deep embeddings with histogram loss. In: Advances in Neural Information Processing Systems, vol. 29. Curran Associates, Inc. (2016). https://proceedings.neurips.cc/paper_files/paper/2016/hash/325995af77a0e8b06d1204a171010b3a-Abstract.html

19. Wu, X., Liu, Y., Zhou, X., Mou, A.: Automatic identification of tool wear based on convolutional neural network in face milling process. Sensors **19**, 3817 (2019). https://doi.org/10.3390/s19183817

20. Zhou, Y., et al.: A new tool wear condition monitoring method based on deep learning under small samples. Measurement **189**, 110622 (2022). https://doi.org/10.1016/j.measurement.2021.110622

Mixing Domains for Smartly Picking and Using Limited Datasets in Industrial Object Detection

Chafic Abou Akar[1,2]([✉]), Anthony Semaan[1], Youssef Haddad[1],
Marc Kamradt[1], and Abdallah Makhoul[2]

[1] BMW Group, Munich, Germany
chafic.ac.abou-akar@bmw.de
[2] FEMTO-ST institute, CNRS, Univ. Franche-Comté, Montbéliard, France

Abstract. Object detection is a popular computer vision task that is performed by autonomous industrial robots. However, training a detection model requires a large annotated image dataset that belongs to the camera domain of the robot (the test domain). Acquiring such data in a similar domain or rendering photo-realistic images from a realistic virtual environment composed of accurate 3D models and using powerful hardware, can be expensive, time-consuming, and requires specialized expertise. This article focuses on investigating the growth of average precision (AP) in object detection as we progressively train and test our models using various combinations of acquired and rendered datasets from different domains: real and synthetic. By analyzing the results on industrial load carrier box detection, we discovered that a hybrid dataset comprising 20–30% of images similar to the test domain leads to achieving nearly maximum detection accuracy.

Keywords: Computer Vision · Hybrid Domain · Industry 4.0 · Limited Dataset · Object Detection

1 Introduction

Nowadays, robots are equipped with advanced sensors to understand their environment. For instance, camera sensors are a major input source for inferring computer vision (CV) object recognition and detection tasks [16]. As a result of installing several camera sensors in a factory, various sub-domains arise inside the overall real images domain. To get the best detection accuracy, (1) the model must be trained using images with a small domain gap [26,28] to the robot's camera domain, and (2) a large number of annotated training images must be used [5]. On the first hand, acquiring thousands of real images is hampered by security, safety, privacy, and sophisticated post-processing limitations [10,11]. On another hand, most existing industrial datasets are small and insufficient for CV training. This emphasizes the need to smartly use limited datasets to provide good detection accuracy [22]. According to the state-of-the-art, many researchers advocate employing (1) pre-trained networks [23,29] (2) data augmentation [12] via image transformations [24] or generative models [2,4], and (3) feedforward designs. However, preparing pre-trained model weights, or training a generalized generative model requires real data as well.   Another option is to

(a)   (b)

Fig. 1. (a) Real (b) PBR 3D L-KLT 4147 box model

use domain randomization in virtual settings and 3D engines like Unreal, Unity, or NVIDIA Omniverse to render photo-realistic images with accurate pixel-level annotations [1,5,11]. However, bridging the domain gap - in our case: sim-to-real, and sim-to-sim gaps - remains a priority. While many approaches used a mix of real and synthetic datasets to train their models [3,6,14,15,17,18,20–22], we used this strategy to understand, in general, how mixing multi-domain datasets affect the object detection task. We concentrated on the small load carrier (KLT) box detection (check Fig. 1), a modular and ergonomic industrial asset that is easy to use and store. Despite its effectiveness, this asset is hard to accurately detect since it appears in intricate variations within the industrial context. In this work, we selected different pre-trained models for transfer learning. We gradually mixed datasets from several domains created using NVIDIA Omniverse or real-captured. The models are then examined in different image domains to assess the various combinations. Consequently, we discovered that including 20–30% of images belonging to the testing domain in the training dataset is sufficient to achieve near-maximal detection accuracy.

The rest of this paper is structured as follows: First, in Sect. 3, we propose our use case and therefore, our hybrid strategy before heading to the experimentation in Sect. 4. Then, we analyze the evaluation results in Sect. 4.2 and compare them to the related work presented in Sect. 2. Last but not least, in Sect. 5, we present some visions for expanding this study ahead of concluding.

2   Related Work

Mixing Datasets: Ros *et al.* argues that their synthetic dataset (SYNTHIA) achieves better results in segmenting real images, and using it in combination with real data (real ratio equal to 0.6) can boost a T-NET model's average per class accuracy for outdoor driving scenarios. Yet, it increased FCN's average per-class accuracy for, mainly, individual assets [18]. However, Saleh *et al.*

noticed in [20] that this addition improved the detection of foreground assets only because the model has gained new realistic feature variations despite the background assets that already seemed realistic in SYNTHIA. Therefore, the authors suggested replacing the single segmentation networks with two segmentation models dedicated to the foreground and background assets. On the same side, Richter *et al.* reported in [17] that training on real datasets remarkably outperforms semantic segmentation training on synthetic datasets. But, adding 25% to 33% to 100% of the real data to the synthetic dataset gradually increases the semantic segmentation results. It could also beat the performance of models trained on real datasets only, respectively [22].

Fine-Tuning Models: Gaidon *et al.* trained a model using the ImageNet dataset, the Fast RCNN and VGG-16 architectures, and then fine-tuned it to cars using Pascal VOC 2007 dataset. Afterward, the authors showed that the real dataset (KITTI) outperforms the synthetic dataset (VirtualKITTI) while applying transfer learning to the pre-trained model for a car tracking-by-detection use case. However, the authors proved the usefulness but not the sufficiency of synthetic data: fine-tuning a synthetic-based pre-trained model on real data slightly surpasses the training on real data only [3].

Synthetic Data Over Real Data: Sankaranarayanan *et al.* concluded in [21] that real images are characterized by higher feature variations compared to synthetically generated images. Therefore, a significantly more extensive synthetic dataset (e.g., 50,000 or 200,000) is needed to beat a model that was trained on a small real dataset (e.g., 3,000) [7,19]. Yet, a larger synthetic dataset should include higher domain randomization affecting textures, light, asset positions, camera focal length, and content. Hinterstoisser *et al.* introduced in [6] a novel curriculum strategy for synthetic training dataset generation pipeline to cover 64 completely distinct supermarket assets in all possible poses, conditions, and complexity. To reduce the domain gap, and instead of mixing datasets, they improved their generation quality by (1) using real image backgrounds, (2) 3D scanning all assets to produce realistic textures and rendering them with a curriculum strategy, (3) adding occluders, and (4) setting up the camera settings for a geometrically correct and robust rendering. The authors argue that a model purely trained on their synthetic dataset outperforms object detection models trained on a mixture of real and synthetic data after evaluating on the YCB-Video dataset - a synthetic-based dataset [27].

Generative Models: On a first hand, Ravuri *et al.* showed that despite the high generated image quality of generative adversarial networks (GANs), synthetic GAN images decrease the model Top-1 and Top-5 classification accuracies by 27.9% and 41.6% respectively, compared to models trained on real images only [15]. On another hand, PNVR *et al.* suggested a new GAN (SharinGAN) to reduce the real gap by mapping real and synthetic domains to a single shared domain [14]. Images belonging to the shared domain include shared information from two domains and are indistinguishable by the network performing the primary task. However, SharinGAN was tested for faces' surface normal estimation and outdoor scenes' monocular depth estimation.

Taken all together, when it comes to training with a synthetic dataset, most authors focused on achieving higher accuracy on a specific benchmark real dataset while reducing the domain gap between their synthetic training dataset and the benchmark real evaluation dataset. However, to the best of our knowledge, none of the previously mentioned research studied the different combinations of hybrid datasets or considered evaluating them on other domain datasets like in our proposed study. As previously mentioned, a real image dataset could include many distinct real subdomains (real-to-real gap), and so is the same for synthetic datasets. However, since collecting real images is a difficult task, we considered sim-to-real and sim-to-sim scenarios to understand the behavior of mixing multi-domain datasets in training detection models.

3   Multi-domain Hybrid Datasets

When it comes to industrial AI, we consider deploying the models on a robot knowing all its hardware equipment and executing its functions in a well-defined environment (domain), all through a well-defined industrial chain. Thus, the user can estimate the test domain distribution, and the model is built to satisfy the robot's task. In this paper, we consider detecting a KLT box, one of the most important, yet challenging objects to detect in an industrial environment.

We consider a multi-domain hybrid dataset that combines datasets belonging to different domains into a single dataset. However, a domain is a set of images belonging to the same modality, e.g., all images captured by the same camera settings in similar scenarios or images rendered using the same rendering settings and camera settings in similar environments form distinct domains. Moreover, acquiring large annotated image datasets for the same domain is as complicated and time-consuming as acquiring real global images. We study the efficient mix of images from different domains so-called "domain A" of any related dataset, and "domain B" related to the robot's application domain with the purpose of training an object detection model. We experimented with different combinations of three distinct domain datasets (real R, colored synthetic S, and white synthetic W) and evaluated them on four other evaluation datasets (two real and two synthetic domains) as shown in Fig. 2. The dataset acquisition process is described in the following sections.

3.1   Real Data Acquisition

Data Capture: We recorded 1080p videos for t seconds at a rate of 30 frames per second (fps), while moving around KLT boxes that were placed in different

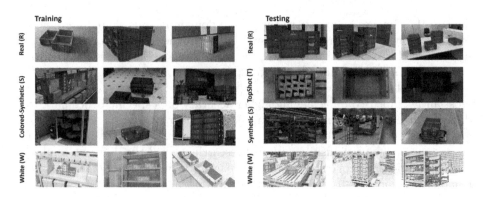

Fig. 2. Different domain KLT box training and testing datasets

rooms, on different surfaces, and in multiple light conditions, e.g., indoor lighting, curtain shadows, backlight, outdoor lighting only, etc. Every video contains low-angle and top-shot viewports taken from far to near distances of the boxes.

Data Cleaning: We extracted the best n frames from the video sequence: we divided the video into equal batches. Then, we selected from each batch the sharpest frame with the lowest Laplacian filter metric.

Downstream Task-Based Annotation: Instead of hand annotating all real images from scratch, we inferred them using existing pre-trained KLT models and fine-tuned the predicted bounding boxes (bbox) manually.

3.2   Synthetic Data Generation

Simulation-Based Generation: We used NVIDIA Omniverse to build our 3D scenes and render photo-realistic synthetic images alongside NVIDIA RTX 3090 GPUs with 24 GB. Omniverse is based on the Universal Scene Description (USD) pipeline and Ray Tracing Texel eXtreme (RTX) technology to guarantee (1) a modular and scalable collaboration between different experts, and (2) a path tracing rendering for fine-quality image production respectively [1]. In this dataset, the asset of interest represents an L-KLT 4147 box 3D model with a realistic Physics-Based Rendering (PBR) material as shown in Fig. 1.

Domain Randomization (DR): Rendering and image content defines the synthetic image's realism level. The first is provided by the quality of the 3D model design and the RTX technology (c.f. Figure 1). However, achieving realistic content consists of replicating real-world environments by spawning the right assets in the right places and a logical aspect. Furthermore, real-world environments are subject to continuous changes, especially concerning KLT boxes as displayed in Fig. 2. Their positions are flexibly adjustable: (1) they are transported over an assembly line, (2) they can be shifted from one rack level to another, (3) a new empty or filled box stacks on top of another one, (4) a larger KLT box combines two aside boxes together, etc. As a solution, domain randomization extends the static scene's synthetic domain into a wider range, covering the real domain and, thus, minimizing the gap. In that case, the model gets used to detect multiple variations, including the realistic combinations, a subset of the whole variation set [25]. In our case, we applied structured DR to avoid physically-invalid distributions such as floating boxes over forming a perfect stack.

In addition, we varied the light's intensity, temperature, direction, etc., and added some rotation randomizations to extend the combinations, bypassing the real world's different light conditions, box surfaces, and viewports.

Image Modalities and Annotations: We used Isaac Sim - an NVIDIA robotics simulation toolkit - to simulate sensor data for ground-truth labeling with bboxes[1].

4   Experimentation and Results

4.1   Experimentation Setup

In this section, we explain how we prepared the datasets, conducted trainings, and assessed the models based on different hybrid datasets:

Dataset Preparation: First, we consider a total of n images for each training dataset divided as follows: For each ratio r of domain A data, we consider $(1-r)$ for domain B data where $r \times n$, and $(1-r) \times n$ images are uniformly selected from both scenarios' domains respectively. Then, we resized all selected images to the same 720p dimension and adjusted all bbox coordinates accordingly. Afterward, we mix and shuffle them all to compose a single hybrid dataset.

Training: We conducted our experiments with a total of $n = 7,500$ training images and gradually combined both domains' images by a step equal to 0.1 from 0 to 1: where 0 indicates a dataset of 7,500 domain B images only while 1 refers to 100% genuine domain A dataset. We selected for transfer learning the TensorFlow2's FRCNN Resnet-50, FRCNN Resnet-101 [16], SSD MobileNet v2 FPNLite, and SSD efficientnet d1 [9] detection models pre-trained on COCO 2017 dataset [8]. We considered the following hybrid datasets: real and plain color synthetic (R+S), real and white color synthetic (R+W), and plain color and white color synthetic (S+W).

---

[1] The real image dataset cannot be shared due to confidential reasons. Only, the rendered synthetic dataset is available upon a valid request from the corresponding author.

Evaluation: We assessed our trained models on approx. 850 new images for each domain dataset:

- Real images with different distributions (R), and top shot images from a different camera (T).
- Synthetic colored (S) and white-shaded (W) images in an industrial scene.

Our use case drops under a binary object detection problem. The adopted evaluation metric concentrates on the average precision (AP) at an intersection over union (IoU) threshold equal to 0.7. The higher the AP@0.7, the more accurate the detection model is.

4.2 Obtained Results and Discussion

Gradual Assessment: In Table 1, we evaluated R+S, R+W, and S+W trained models on R, S, and W datasets. When testing the R+S model on the R dataset (R+S:R), the lowest AP corresponds to a ratio 0.00 (84.77%), i.e., a fully synthetic-based trained model. On the contrary, the maximum AP is achieved with a 0.60 ratio (90.88%). Although, the AP difference between the best model (ratio = 0.60) and the full-real model (r = 1.00) is relatively less than 1.00%. When evaluating R+W:R, we noticed a similar evolution pattern where the full-real model achieves the highest AP (90.93%). In addition, an obvious difference manifests on ratio 0.00 where training using only S (84.77%) outperforms training on W only (18.29%) due to the significant domain gap between both R and W compared to R and S.

For S+R:S, an opposite evolution pattern exists compared to R+S:R. Although, as in all experiments, we can clearly see the boost from 0.00 to 0.10 corresponding to the usage of 10% synthetic images alongside 90% of real images.

Table 1. AP@0.7 gradual evaluation of FRCNN Resnet-50 models trained on mixed domain datasets

Ratio	R+S:R	R+W:R	R+S:T	R+W:T	S+R:S	S+W:S	R+W:W	S+W:W	R+S:R+S
0.00	84.77	18.29	73.24	0.00	5.49	0.59	**45.07**	**44.24**	71.30
0.10	88.68	89.61	87.29	43.97	45.33	53.93	42.49	44.17	73.61
0.20	89.24	89.61	82.75	62.48	50.59	55.82	42.74	44.18	**74.20**
0.30	89.69	89.89	87.07	59.03	52.80	55.87	41.91	43.67	73.29
0.40	89.84	90.71	80.11	71.13	55.14	56.94	40.69	43.04	73.51
0.50	90.78	90.71	87.88	61.83	54.41	56.64	39.69	42.95	72.20
0.60	**90.88**	90.75	86.98	72.96	56.81	57.76	38.66	41.96	72.58
0.70	90.71	90.70	**91.02**	73.37	57.25	57.01	37.73	41.99	70.87
0.80	90.87	90.45	88.23	65.00	**58.60**	58.19	34.91	40.44	70.25
0.90	90.40	90.54	84.23	71.07	58.33	58.04	31.52	37.44	66.79
1.00	90.74	**90.93**	78.42	**75.53**	58.14	**58.85**	1.37	0.00	54.68

Then, the increasing shape slows down to converge around the maximum accuracy.

The inefficiencies of ratio 0.00 in R+S:R and S+R:S are highlighted in R+S:R+S. We evaluated R+S on a mixed dataset equally taken from R and S's evaluation datasets (850 images). We noticed that the best detection accuracy range for R+S hybrid model is not focused on edge ratios but at the middle, which perfectly reflects a hybrid composition for both training and evaluation datasets. However, the range is more shifted to the S domain edge (r = 0.00), since it has previously shown high detection accuracies on R and S distinctly ($AP_{R+S:R}$ = 84.77%, and $AP_{S+R:S}$ = 58.14% at r = 0.00 and r = 1.00 respectively)[2]. Moreover, the boosting effect is perceived at both edges of 10% and 90%.

Additionally, in R+S:T and R+W:T, we evaluated R+S and R+W on T, a new real domain. S and W visualize the same environments with the same domain randomization, but in W, we omit all colors. Analyzing both evaluations reveals the advantage of synthetic data by feeding the network additional variations of the main asset, which on their own are not enough as well.

In R+W:T, a genuine W model is unable to detect any box. Obviously, the maximum AP in R+W is lower than in R+S.

This emphasizes the importance of the synthetic data variations in hybrid datasets, especially when they are combined with rich domain randomization with an appropriate environment setting similar to the evaluation domain.

In S+W:S, S+W:W, and R+W:W, we evaluated S+W and R+W models on S and W domains to endorse previous observations. Taken all together, we found that: (1) Training on data that does not entirely belong to the evaluation domain achieves the worst detection accuracy compared to other combinations. Thus, replacing only 10% of the training dataset with the evaluation domain's images is enough to boost the detection accuracy as clearly visualized in Fig. 3. Successively, after integrating 20–30% of the evaluation domain's images, the detection accuracy could converge around the maximum AP within an average range of 2–4%. Thus, genuine training with the evaluation domain does not always lead to the maximum detection accuracy unless the domain gap is big enough: Thus, the difference between the maximum detection accuracy and the one associated with a 100% evaluation images dataset is, on average, less than 1%. However, this could be interpreted by the additional variations and the generalization ability which the synthetic data can bring to the model. (2) The training domain is strongly boosted by the evaluation domain images. For instance, models trained on white synthetic or colored synthetic images, in R+S:R, and R+W:R respectively, similarly improved while adding real images until they both reach nearly the same maximum detection of a genuine real-based model. (3) Picking the proper domains highly matters when none of the training domains exactly match the evaluation domain: In R+S:T and R+W:T, we evaluated on top-shot images only. Hence, when mixing datasets, it is important to maintain a smaller domain gap between the selected training dataset's domains

---

[2] R has clearly shown better results on R only ($AP_{R+S:R}$ = 90.74% at r = 1.00) compared to its performance on S ($AP_{S+R:S}$ = 5.49% at r = 0.00).

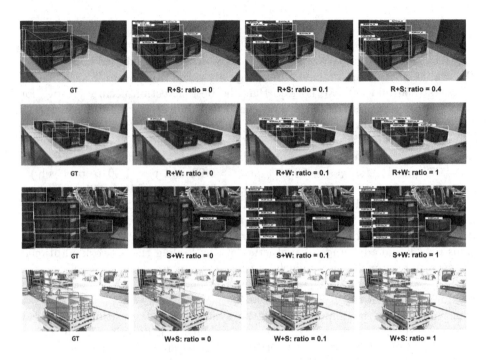

Fig. 3. Bbox predictions using R+S, R+W, and S+W models at different mix ratio

and the evaluation. However, when it comes to synthetic data, a knowledge-based generation [13] increases the data quality of rendered images by specifying the appropriate domain randomization parameters suitable to the evaluation domain.

Training Architectures: Additionally, we noticed the same boosting effect for the R+S mixture (ratio up to 30%) using different architecture as FRCNN Resnet-101, SSD Mobilenet v2 FPNLite, and SSD efficientnet d1. In Fig. 4a, we represent AP@0.7 metrics while gradually evaluating R+S models on R. We remark a more stable AP growth, and faster convergence, when increasing the R domain images in the trainings based on FRCNN compared to SSD's. Additionally, FRCNN has beaten the SSD's predictions.

Dataset Size: From another perspective, in Fig. 4b, we noticed the same pattern, but less accurate, with a smaller training dataset (20%: 1500 R+S images). Nevertheless, this does not confirm that a larger training dataset consistently achieves better results.

Transfer Learning: In Table 2, we examined various combinations of transfer learning using the R, S, and W domains, which were used in previous experiments. The training process involves two stages, i.e., **A→B**: in the first stage,

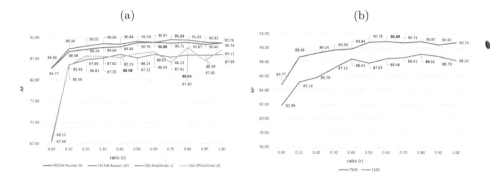

Fig. 4. R+S:R AP@0.9 evaluation trained with (a) FRCNN Resnet-50 and Resnet-101, and SSD Mobilenet v2 and efficientnet d1 architectures (b) with FRCNN Resnet-50 using 1500 and 7500 R+S images

we used the complete domain A dataset (7,500 images) to train the models, as it was previously done. Afterward, in the second stage, we fine-tuned these models using only 30% of the domain B dataset (2,250 images).

We observed that in most evaluation's rows, fine-tuning using R, or S yielded similar results when training on R and S only without any fine-tuning process, e.g., $AP_{R \to S:R} \approx AP_{W \to S:R} \approx AP_{S:R}$ equal to 80.46%, 84.69%, and 84.77% respectively, and $AP_{S \to R:R} \approx AP_{W \to R:R} \approx AP_{R:R}$ equal to 91.25%, 90.56%, and 90.74% respectively. However, when evaluating on S, fine-tuning on R $(AP_{S \to R:S} = 45.94\%, AP_{W \to R:S} = 38.69\%)$ achieved a higher AP than training solely on R $(AP_{R:S} = 5.49\%)$. Similarly, when evaluating on R, and S domains, fine-tunings with W domain (S→W, and R→W) significantly boosted the AP to more than 70% and 30% compared to W's models where the AP was less than 20% and close to 0 respectively. The same remains when evaluating on T. This improvement can be attributed to the shared characteristics between the source and target domains, such as the KLT box size, shape, placement, orientation, etc. Consequently, the model retained its previously learned knowledge, leading to an enhancement in the AP. However, the R→S:W and S→R:W null APs are caused by the training (R and S) and evaluation (W) domains' significant gap.

Table 2. AP@0.7 evaluation of fine-tuned FRCNN Resnet-50 models

	R→S	S→R	W→S	S→W	R→W	W→R	R	S	W
R	84.46	91.25	84.69	72.69	71.64	90.56	90.74	84.77	18.29
S	54.67	45.94	55.62	48.14	31.63	38.69	5.49	58.14	0.59
T	80.00	74.32	62.74	15.98	1.24	69.81	78.42	73.24	0.00
W	0.00	0.00	7.32	41.91	38.74	20.63	1.37	0.00	45.07

5   Conclusion and Future Work

In this paper, we conducted a systematic investigation into the effects of combining datasets from distinct domains. We created hybrid training datasets by merging in-house acquired and rendered image datasets from three different domains. Following transfer learning, we evaluated the performance of our models on various domains. Our findings revealed that integrating 10% of data from the evaluation domain boosts the model accuracy, while ratios of 20–30% yield near maximum detection accuracy. Interestingly, achieving the highest accuracy did not always require training the model exclusively on the evaluation domain but rather at lower ratios: Integrating data from various datasets with significant domain randomization - while still maintaining a smaller domain gap - introduces additional variations that enhanced the model's generalization capability and achieves higher accuracies. This behavior was consistently observed across different dataset sizes and training architectures. The study has been tested on KLT box detection, one of the most critical industrial use cases. This work can be extended to support other challenging logistic assets using additional network architectures for a wider range of industrial applications, e.g., pose estimation, image segmentation, etc. Moreover, it is worth implementing additional significant randomizations such as textures, occlusions, light & camera parameters, post-processing filters, and augmentations, etc. Plus, we can experiment with new formats such as RGB-D images, 3D point clouds, etc. modalities, lossless and lossy image compressions, or data augmentations to optimize the hybrid training pipeline and minimize the dataset size.

References

1. Abou Akar, C., Tekli, J., Jess, D., Khoury, M., Kamradt, M., Guthe, M.: Synthetic object recognition dataset for industries. In: 2022 35th SIBGRAPI Conference on Graphics, Patterns and Images (SIBGRAPI), vol. 1, pp. 150–155. IEEE (2022)
2. Antoniou, A., Storkey, A., Edwards, H.: Data augmentation generative adversarial networks. arXiv preprint arXiv:1711.04340 (2017)
3. Gaidon, A., Wang, Q., Cabon, Y., Vig, E.: Virtual worlds as proxy for multi-object tracking analysis. In: Proceedings of the IEEE Conference on Computer Vision and Pattern Recognition, pp. 4340–4349 (2016)
4. Goodfellow, I., et al.: Generative adversarial nets. In: Advances in Neural Information Processing Systems, vol. 27 (2014)
5. Greff, K., et al.: Kubric: a scalable dataset generator. In: Proceedings of the IEEE/CVF Conference on Computer Vision and Pattern Recognition, pp. 3749–3761 (2022)
6. Hinterstoisser, S., Pauly, O., Heibel, H., Martina, M., Bokeloh, M.: An annotation saved is an annotation earned: Using fully synthetic training for object detection. In: Proceedings of the IEEE/CVF International Conference on Computer Vision Workshops (2019)
7. Johnson-Roberson, M., Barto, C., Mehta, R., Sridhar, S.N., Rosaen, K., Vasudevan, R.: Driving in the matrix: can virtual worlds replace human-generated annotations for real world tasks?. arXiv preprint arXiv:1610.01983 (2016)

8. Lin, T.-Y., et al.: Microsoft COCO: common objects in context. In: Fleet, D., Pajdla, T., Schiele, B., Tuytelaars, T. (eds.) ECCV 2014. LNCS, vol. 8693, pp. 740–755. Springer, Cham (2014). https://doi.org/10.1007/978-3-319-10602-1_48
9. Liu, W., et al.: SSD: single shot multibox detector. In: Leibe, B., Matas, J., Sebe, N., Welling, M. (eds.) ECCV 2016. LNCS, vol. 9905, pp. 21–37. Springer, Cham (2016). https://doi.org/10.1007/978-3-319-46448-0_2
10. Meng, J., et al.: The future of computer vision. APSIPA Trans. Signal Inf. Process. **11**(1) (2022)
11. Morrical, N., et al.: Nvisii: A scriptable tool for photorealistic image generation. arXiv preprint arXiv:2105.13962 (2021)
12. Perez, L., Wang, J.: The effectiveness of data augmentation in image classification using deep learning. arXiv preprint arXiv:1712.04621 (2017)
13. Petrovic, O., Duarte, D.L.D., Storms, S., Herfs, W.: Towards knowledge-based generation of synthetic data by taxonomizing expert knowledge in production. In: Intelligent Human Systems Integration (IHSI 2023): Integrating People and Intelligent Systems, vol. 69, no. 69 (2023)
14. PNVR, K., Zhou, H., Jacobs, D.: Sharingan: combining synthetic and real data for unsupervised geometry estimation. In: Proceedings of the IEEE/CVF Conference on Computer Vision and Pattern Recognition, pp. 13974–13983 (2020)
15. Ravuri, S., Vinyals, O.: Classification accuracy score for conditional generative models. In: Advances in Neural Information Processing Systems, vol. 32 (2019)
16. Ren, S., He, K., Girshick, R., Sun, J.: Faster R-CNN: towards real-time object detection with region proposal networks. In: Advances in Neural Information Processing Systems, vol. 28 (2015)
17. Richter, S.R., Vineet, V., Roth, S., Koltun, V.: Playing for data: ground truth from computer games. In: Leibe, B., Matas, J., Sebe, N., Welling, M. (eds.) ECCV 2016. LNCS, vol. 9906, pp. 102–118. Springer, Cham (2016). https://doi.org/10.1007/978-3-319-46475-6_7
18. Ros, G., Sellart, L., Materzynska, J., Vazquez, D., Lopez, A.M.: The synthia dataset: a large collection of synthetic images for semantic segmentation of urban scenes. In: Proceedings of the IEEE Conference on Computer Vision and Pattern Recognition, pp. 3234–3243 (2016)
19. Seib, V., Lange, B., Wirtz, S.: Mixing real and synthetic data to enhance neural network training–a review of current approaches. arXiv preprint arXiv:2007.08781 (2020)
20. Saleh, F.S., Aliakbarian, M.S., Salzmann, M., Petersson, L., Alvarez, J.M.: Effective use of synthetic data for urban scene semantic segmentation. In: Proceedings of the European Conference on Computer Vision (ECCV), pp. 84–100 (2018)
21. Sankaranarayanan, S., Balaji, Y., Jain, A., Lim, S.N., Chellappa, R.: Learning from synthetic data: addressing domain shift for semantic segmentation. In: Proceedings of the IEEE Conference on Computer Vision and Pattern Recognition, pp. 3752–3761 (2018)
22. Seib, V., Lange, B., Wirtz, S.: Mixing real and synthetic data to enhance neural network training-a review of current approaches. arXiv preprint arXiv:2007.08781 (2020)
23. Shao, S., et al.: Objects365: a large-scale, high-quality dataset for object detection. In: Proceedings of the IEEE/CVF International Conference on Computer Vision, pp. 8430–8439 (2019)
24. Shorten, C., Khoshgoftaar, T.M.: A survey on image data augmentation for deep learning. J. Big Data **6**(1), 1–48 (2019)

25. Tobin, J., Fong, R., Ray, A., Schneider, J., Zaremba, W., Abbeel, P.: Domain randomization for transferring deep neural networks from simulation to the real world. In: 2017 IEEE/RSJ International Conference on Intelligent Robots and Systems (IROS), pp. 23–30. IEEE (2017)
26. Vu, T.H., Jain, H., Bucher, M., Cord, M., Pérez, P.: Advent: adversarial entropy minimization for domain adaptation in semantic segmentation. In: Proceedings of the IEEE/CVF Conference on Computer Vision and Pattern Recognition, pp. 2517–2526 (2019)
27. Xiang, Y., Schmidt, T., Narayanan, V., Fox, D.: Posecnn: a convolutional neural network for 6d object pose estimation in cluttered scenes. arXiv preprint arXiv:1711.00199 (2017)
28. Yao, Y., Zheng, L., Yang, X., Naphade, M., Gedeon, T.: Simulating content consistent vehicle datasets with attribute descent. In: Vedaldi, A., Bischof, H., Brox, T., Frahm, J.-M. (eds.) ECCV 2020. LNCS, vol. 12351, pp. 775–791. Springer, Cham (2020). https://doi.org/10.1007/978-3-030-58539-6_46
29. Zabir, M., Fazira, N., Ibrahim, Z., Sabri, N.: Evaluation of pre-trained convolutional neural network models for object recognition. Int. J. Eng. Technol. **7**(3.15), 95–98 (2018)

Mobile Robotics and Autonomous Systems

Dynamic Vision-Based Satellite Detection: A Time-Based Encoding Approach with Spiking Neural Networks

Nikolaus Salvatore[1]([✉]) and Justin Fletcher[2]

[1] KBR, Inc, Kihei, HI, USA
`nikolaus.salvatore@us.kbr.com`
[2] United States Space Force, Kihei, HI, USA
`justin.fletcher.14.ctr@us.af.mil`

Abstract. The detection of residence space objects (RSOs) is a challenging task due to the lack of distinguishing features and relative dimness of targets compared to the high brightness and high noise of data collection backgrounds. Dynamic vision sensors present a possible solution for ground-based optical detection of RSOs due to their high temporal precision and dynamic range. However, the visual data collected by these sensors is asynchronous, and in the context of high-contrast remote sensing applications, often contains extraneous noise events. We propose a temporally-weighted spike encoding for dynamic vision data which reduces the density of event-based data streams and enables the training of deeper spiking neural networks for classification and object detection applications. The encoding scheme and subsequent spiking neural network architectures are evaluated on available dynamic vision datasets, with competitive classification accuracies on N-MNIST (99.7%), DVS-CIFAR10 (74.0%), and N-Caltech101 (72.8%), as well as showing state-of-the-art object detection performance on event-based RSO data collections.

Keywords: Spiking Neural Networks · Object Detection · Novel Sensors

1 Introduction

Human activity in space is driving a steady increase in the population of resident space objects (RSOs) in low-Earth orbit (LEO) and geosynchronous-Earth orbit (GEO). This growth has motivated increasing interest in technologies and techniques for detecting and tracking these objects using affordable ground-based optical telescopes. However, tracking RSOs like satellites or space debris poses a unique challenge, as they often lack distinguishing features and move too fast to capture clear images. Additionally, these targets are often much dimmer than the surrounding light, which makes it difficult to spot them during daytime viewing or in cis-lunar orbits. Therefore, there is a need for novel hardware sensors and computer vision techniques that can seamlessly integrate with existing ground-based detection methods to overcome these challenges.

Imaging dim or fast-moving resident space objects (RSOs) using conventional sensors presents many challenges, particularly when the background light level is high. Fortunately, dynamic vision sensors, also known as event-based cameras, have emerged as a promising technology to address this problem. Unlike traditional cameras, event-based cameras operate without a global clock, allowing each pixel to emit events asynchronously based on detected changes in illuminance at high frequency. In dynamic vision sensors each pixel exhibits a logarithmic response to illuminance changes thereby producing a sparser data representation compared to conventional sensors sampling at similar rates. These properties make event-based cameras ideal for detecting RSOs that are too challenging for conventional CCD sensors due to their comparative dimness and high velocity. Furthermore, event-based pixels do not saturate, making them an excellent option for imaging RSOs in harsh environments such as near the Moon or in daylight. These features suggest that event-based cameras could be an effective solution for detecting and tracking RSOs.

Object detection in event-based data is challenging due to the asynchronous structure of the captured data stream. One way to approach this problem is to transform the event-based data into a conventional image by integrating it over a defined time window. Since events are generated asynchronously, each event is assigned a timestamp, a polarity flag, and an (x, y) coordinate that corresponds to the location of the event. The polarity flag, which is either +1 or -1, indicates whether the event resulted from an increase or decrease in illuminance. By accumulating these events over a time window Δt at their respective (x, y) coordinates, a conventional image can be produced, which can then be processed using standard object detection techniques. However, this representation suppresses the high-frequency temporal information present in the original event stream, which is disadvantageous.

Ideally, event-based data representations should be derived using a method that preserves high-frequency temporal information while presenting a standard interface to downstream computer visions task models. Spiking neural networks (SNNs) are distinct from conventional neural networks, much like event-based data differs from traditional images. SNNs operate asynchronously, with each neuron in the network emitting spikes only when its inputs reach a predetermined threshold, mimicking the behavior of biological neurons. The sparsity of SNN activation leads to these networks being highly energy-efficient compared to their conventional counterparts of similar size. However, the binary nature of the neuron output and the resulting non-differentiability of their activation make supervised training of SNNs a difficult task. Moreover, SNNs can be susceptible to the vanishing spike propagation issue, where a decrease in spiking activity in subsequent layers leads to significant performance degradation in larger networks [19]. Despite these challenges, the unique properties of SNNs complement the data generated by event-based cameras naturally, and several studies have demonstrated the potential of SNNs for classification and object detection tasks on event-based data.

Our research introduces a new approach to encoding event-based data in which events are weighted in time to reduce the total number of spikes generated while maintaining the spiking behavior and temporal information. This method is shown to reduce the number of time steps required to achieve satisfactory classification and object detection performance in spiking neural networks. Additionally, we propose a pseudo-spiking behavior for conventional convolutional neural networks that eliminates the need for temporal credit assignment, but still preserves some temporal information. This pseudo-spiking behavior can be easily combined with encoded, event-based data and enables us to train deeper models than what is possible with true spiking networks. To validate the effectiveness of our approach we evaluate our method using both simulated and actual space-based data collection. We also demonstrate our method's competitiveness on publicly accessible datasets for event-based classification and object detection. Our method achieves excellent detection performance, which highlights the potential of temporal-weight encoding and pseudo-spiking behavior for handling event-based data.

2   Related Work

The following sections position this work with respect to recent related contributions in space domain awareness, event-based sensor data processing, and spiking neural networks.

2.1   Space Domain Awareness

Detecting dim, high-speed RSOs is a challenging task, which becomes even more difficult under adverse conditions such as daylight, moonlight, and high atmospheric turbulence. Traditionally, specialized radar or laser equipment is used to detect small targets, although ground-based optics have emerged as a cost-effective and power-efficient alternative. However, optical CCD sensors often face challenges such as high levels of background noise and long exposure times, which can complicate the detection of fast-moving objects [12]. As an alternative, event-based cameras have been suggested as an ideal option for replacing or supplementing conventional CCD sensors for RSO detection. Recent research has demonstrated the use of event-based cameras for daytime imaging of LEOs [7], and simulated work has investigated star tracking using event-based data [6]. These successes, together with the successful application of modern object detection models on space imaging datasets [10], have motivated us to investigate space object detection with event-based cameras. Furthermore, recent advances in space scene simulation have enhanced the ability to experiment with high-fidelity, optical space collections. In this work, we use the *SatSim* simulator to generate the large number of samples required for model training [3].

2.2   Event-Based Classification and Object Detection

Due to the asynchronous nature of event-based data, ordinary computer vision techniques are not readily applicable to performing classification or object detection with event-based cameras. In the simplest case, event streams can be accumulated over time into approximated images that can then be used with conventional algorithms, but this eliminates much of the rich, temporal information. Early methods of working with event-based data often relied on updating existing algorithms, such as the Harris corner detector [17] or Hough transform [26], to be compatible with asynchronous data. More sophisticated approaches, such as the HOTS [13] and HATS algorithms [24], use new representations of event-based data (time surfaces), to exploit temporal information for classification and object detection. Newer approaches have begun to modify established machine learning models, such as YOLE or "You Only Look at Events", which adapts the YOLO object detection framework for asynchronous operation [4]. However, one of the chief challenges for algorithm development and model training is the relative lack of event-based data publicly available. While neuromorphic versions of well-known datasets such as N-MNIST, CIFAR10-DVS, and N-Caltech101 exist, all of these datasets are generated using event-based extrapolations of the original datasets rather than actual event-based samples [15,18]. However, the N-Cars and Prophesee Gen1-Automotive datasets are two more recent datasets that include real event-based data collections [24,25].

2.3   Spiking Neural Networks

Given the asynchronous nature of event-based data, SNNs are a natural choice for performing classification and object detection with event-based cameras. Multiple works have already demonstrated effective use of SNNs for performing a wide array of tasks on event-based data, not only limited to classification and object detection [14,23]. Furthermore, the innate compatibility with SNNS have made event-based camera datasets such as CIFAR10-DVS useful for evaluating a range of spiking models and encoding processes [9,27]. However, the greatest challenge to employing SNNs is the method of training used. The behavior of spiking neurons is not differentiable and therefore not immediately trainable using ordinary backpropagation. Also, as previously mentioned, the vanishing spike phenomenon is a further limiting factor on the potential depth of SNN models. As a result, a great deal of research has gone into finding new methods of spike-based backpropagation, surrogate gradients, or entirely new training methods [2,11,28]. Some of the best results in terms of model accuracy have come from converting pre-trained artificial neural networks (ANNs) into spiking models, but this method can incur losses in the efficiency and speed of the resulting SNNs [22]. Despite many possible solutions, training methods for SNNs continues to be an area of great interest.

3   Methods

In the following section, we describe the weighted spike representation used to encode event-based vision streams for use with deep spiking neural networks. We also detail the integration of this encoding process with the spiking neural networks and the truncated, surrogate gradient based learning used to train the large networks used. Finally, we describe the method by which optimal spiking hyperparameters are chosen to maximize both classification and object detection performance.

3.1   Weighted Spike Encoding

Given a dynamic vision sensor of width and height $W \times H$, the stream of events generated by such a sensor would be of the form

$$E_N = e_n|_{n=1}^{N}, e_n = (x_n, y_n, t_n, p_n) \tag{1}$$

where E_N represents the entire stream of N events and each event e_n is of the form (x_n, y_n, t_n, p_n). In this context, x_n and y_n are in the range $[1, W]$ and $[1, H]$ respectively, and represent the pixel location at which the event occurred, while t_n is the timestamp associated with the generated event. p_n is the polarity of the event with a value of $p_n = \in \{-1, 1\}$ indicating that the event is generated by either a increase of luminance, $+1$, or decrease in luminance, -1. In order to use conventional computer vision techniques with event-based data, an event stream can be integrated over either a particular number of events N or a chosen range of time Δt with events accumulated at their respective (x, y) locations.

$$I = \begin{cases} I_{[0, W, H]} = \sum_{n=0}^{N} \delta(x_n, y_n) & p_n = +1 \\ I_{[1, W, H]} = \sum_{n=0}^{N} \delta(x_n, y_n) & p_n = -1 \end{cases} \forall e_n \tag{2}$$

In general, event streams are integrated as described in Eq. 2, where timestamps are ignored and simple counts of events are accumulated at their respective locations (x_n, y_n), with positive and negative polarity events separated into separate channels to produce $2 \times W \times H$ images suitable for image-based models and conventional algorithms. In this work, we use this integration in conjunction with standard object detection and classification models as a baseline for performance comparison.

In order to reduce the possible number of spikes in dense event-based data, while also encoding some of the temporal information into the resulting output, we employ a modified form of event stream integration. While event-based data can be used natively with asynchronous input spiking neural networks, our encoding greatly reduces the timescale over which spikes are presented to the end network and enables the application of conventional convolutional networks through additional pre-processing steps. Our approach to encoding involves a partial integration process that is dependent on whether feature extraction is performed in real-time or on previously recorded event streams. In the real-time case, we choose a time window, Δt, from which events will be accumulated over the event stream until a total of T timesteps, or windows, have been presented to the network. Conversely, with previously recorded event streams, we can choose the number of timesteps, T, and then determine the time window, Δt, required to evenly divide the event stream into the desired number of timesteps.

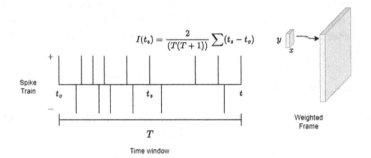

Fig. 1. Generation of a temporally-weighted spike frame from an event stream.

Figure 1 depicts an event stream with a window of events accumulated over a given time range, Δt. In order to capture temporal information in a reduced representation, events at each x-y location added as the time difference of their corresponding timestamp with that of the first timestamp in the associated window, i.e. $t_s - t_o$. Once integrated, temporal weights are normalized over the entire range of possible timestamps within the window and organized into a two-dimensional frame according to their x/y locations. It is also important to note that this integration encoding is applied separately to positive and negative polarity events such that the final frames have two channels similar to ordinary integrated frames. This encoding is formalized in Eq. 3.

$$I(p_n, W, H) = \begin{cases} I_{[0,W,H]} = \frac{2}{\Delta t(\Delta t+1)}[\sum_{n=0}^{N} \delta(x_n, y_n) * (t_n - t_o)] & p_n = +1 \\ I_{[1,W,H]} = \frac{2}{\Delta t(\Delta t+1)}[\sum_{n=0}^{N} \delta(x_n, y_n) * (t_n - t_o)] & p_n = -1 \end{cases} \forall e_n$$

$$(3)$$

Once encoded, the new sequence of temporal weight frames can be used either directly such as in a conventional 3D convolutional network or as modified spikes as in our work. Alternatively, the frames can be unrolled into individual elements with thresholds applied to produce binary spikes for use with non-convolutional spiking neural networks; however, the effectiveness of this approach is not explored in this work.

3.2 Spiking Neural Network Integration

For performing the classification and object detection, we explore two avenues for incorporating spiking event data: a true spiking approach and a pseudo-spiking approach. For our true spiking approach, we use the discretized version of the leaky integrate and fire neuron proposed in [22]. Each layer has an associated membrane potential, $u(t)$, that accumulates with the input of weighted spikes and generates spikes of its own if potential exceeds a voltage threshold, $u^t \geq V_t$. The dynamics are detailed in Eqs. 4 and 5

$$u_i^t = \lambda u_i^{t-1} + \sum_j w_{ij} o_j^t - V_t o_i^{t-1} \tag{4}$$

$$o_i^{t-1} = \begin{cases} 1, u_i^{t-1} > V_t \\ 0, otherwise \end{cases} \tag{5}$$

where t is the current timestep, λ is a potential leak constant, w_{ij} are weights associated with the previous layer, o_j^t are outputs of previous layers, and v is the voltage threshold. Eq. 4 holds for the soft reset case, in which membrane potential is reduced by the voltage threshold upon firing (i.e. the $V_t o_i^{t-1}$ term). Empirically, we found better classification performance on deep networks when using the hard reset alternative, where membrane potential u_i^t is reduced to 0 when $u^t \geq V_t$. We use a similar training process as in [22] by using the membrane potential at the final timestep as the network output needed to calculate the relevant loss metrics: cross-entropy in the classification case and the YOLO loss metrics (box regression, classification, and objectness) in the object detection case. However, since the exact timing of input spikes is altered due to our temporally weighted spike encoding, we opt to use the surrogate gradient

$$\frac{\delta o}{\delta u} = \alpha max\{0, 1 - |u - V_t|\} \tag{6}$$

where o is the layer output, u is membrane potential, and V_t is the voltage threshold for output generation. This surrogate gradient for the spiking neuron output is then used with backpropagation through time (BPTT) in order to perform supervised training with spatial and temporal credit assignment.

Conversely, we posit that, for our purposes, a pseudo-spiking approach that removes the need for temporal credit assignment could still benefit from the temporal information found in the encoded event stream. Removing the need for BPTT should enable much faster convergence and potentially the effective training of much larger models normally too memory intensive for true spiking neural networks. In order to remove the need for temporal assignment, we present the entire spike train to each layer in series, such that membrane potential is accumulated for all timesteps T on each layer before passing output to the succeeding layer. In order to impart some of the temporal information in this pseudo-spiking format, we use the membrane potential directly as the output of active layers. Equation 7 describes the process for the initial layer, which is also depicted fully in Fig. 2, where Eqs. 8 and 9 detail the behavior for all successive layers in the network.

$$U(T) = \sum_T \lambda * I(t_i) \tag{7}$$

$$U_i(T) = \sum_T [\lambda U_i(t) - V_t O(t-1)] + \sum_j w_{ij} O_j(T) \tag{8}$$

$$O_j^T = \begin{cases} U_j(T), U_j(T) > V_t \\ 0, otherwise \end{cases} \tag{9}$$

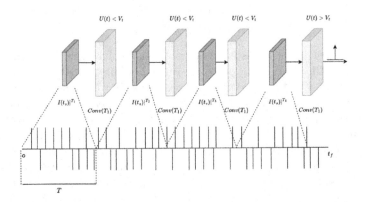

Fig. 2. Accumulation of temporally-weighted spikes on the membrane potential of a pseudo-spiking convolutional layer.

As previously mentioned, the positive and negative polarity events (or ON and OFF events, respectively) of the input stream are encoded separately. After encoding, the positive and negative spikes for a particular time window are accumulated into two-dimensional frames and concatenated to form two-channel spike frames with shape similar to that of an ordinary image.

4   Experiments

4.1   Spiking Hyperparameter Search

We use the hyperparameter optimization package *Optuna* [1] to select spiking behavior hyperparameters. Our hyperparameter optimization considers three network architectures: VGG19, ResNet50, and DarkNet53. While VGG19 and ResNet50 are the feature extraction backbones used for classification tasks, we also optimize hyperparameters for DarkNet53 to increase object detection performance and to investigate the efficacy of training larger networks with the pseudo-spiking behavior and encoding. Each feature extraction backbone is trained on a classification task, using the CIFAR10-DVS dataset, for 10 epochs with hyperparameter search performed for voltage threshold (V_t), leakage (λ), gradient output scaling (α), and total timesteps (T). Hyperparameters are optimized solely for

Table 1. Optimal Spiking Hyperparameters

Architecture	Voltage Thresh. (V_t)	Leakage (λ)	Gradient Scale (α)	Timesteps (T)
sVGG19	3.191	0.325	2.74	185
sResNet50	2.475	0.127	1.73	113
pseudo-VGG19	2.002	0.145	5.58	12
pseudo-ResNet50	2.505	0.07	3.79	39
pseudo-DarkNet53	1.622	0.054	6.51	95

classification accuracy, which will tend to maximize timesteps for the pure spiking case due to the strong positive correlation between spiking timesteps and accuracy. Highest performing parameters are shown in Table 1.

Based on the remaining hyperparameter tuning results, we find that the parameters that correlate most strongly with model size are both the leakage coefficient and the number of spiking timesteps. In general, larger spiking models requiring a greater number of timesteps in order to reach maximum accuracy is expected, and aligns with other previous results with SNN training. However, we observe that the leakage coefficient is small for both ResNet50 and DarkNet53, which suggests that accuracy is maximized when output is generated at nearly every timestep for these larger models. This result may be explained by the overall reduction of input spikes due to the temporal encoding driving the need for neurons to fire more consistently.

4.2   Classification Tasks

While the primary focus of our work is to enhance small object detection, we also include performance on classification tasks as both a means of verification and as a point of comparison with other methods of performing classification on neuromorphic data. Classification results were evaluated for the N-MNIST, CIFAR10-DVS, N-Cars, and N-Caltech101 datasets and compared to some of the most prominent results from literature. Although not widely used as an event-based classification dataset, we chose to include the N-Cars classification dataset due to its relation to the GEN1-Automotive dataset used more prominently for object detection. In all instances, the indicated model architectures for our method use the same layer structure as available in pretrained, PyTorch model zoo [20], albeit with convolutional layer behavior replaced by the pseudo-spiking behavior previously described (Table 2).

In terms of classification accuracy across the general datasets, we see that the VGG19 architecture outperforms the deeper ResNet50 models, but both pseudo-spiking architectures generally outperform their fully spiking counterparts. As intended, the performance gap between the pseudo-spiking and fully spiking methods is greater for the ResNet50 model, suggesting that the pseudo-spiking behavior and temporally-weighted encoding has a positive impact on the training of deeper architectures.

Table 2. Classification Accuracy (Top 2 best classification accuracies per dataset are bolded).

Method	N-MNIST	CIFAR10-DVS	N-Cars	N-Caltech101
sVGG19 + Encoding	0.975	0.7151	0.911	0.689
sResNet50 + Encoding	0.898	0.6119	0.845	0.615
pseudo-VGG19 + Encoding	**0.997**	**0.7404**	0.924	**0.728**
pseudo-ResNet50 + Encoding	0.974	0.6510	0.889	0.662
[24]	0.991	0.524	0.902	0.642
[4]	-	-	**0.927**	0.702
[16]	-	-	**0.944**	**0.745**
[29]	0.9953	0.605	-	-
[23]	**0.996**	0.692	-	-
[27]	-	0.7298	-	-
[9]	**0.996**	**0.748**	-	-

4.3 Object Detection Tasks

For our primary SDA task, we have two RSO detection datasets denoted *Satellite Collect* and *SatSim* in Table 3. As previously mentioned, the *SatSim* space scene simulator is capable of generating high-fidelity, event-based simulations of satellite collections with a degree of tunable conditions and sensor parameters. Given the small size of real data collections available (about 900 samples) in the *Satellite Collect* dataset, we first generate a large collection of simulated samples with approximately equivalent parameters (hardware and collection conditions) using the *SatSim* simulator. To show improvement, we compare results from the pseudo-spiking YOLO model with temporally-weighted encoding to both a conventional YOLO model using an integrated frame and a pseudo-spiking YOLO model using spikes generated from Poisson-encoded integrated images. Poisson-encoding has been used in previous works for generating spike frames from ordinary images [22], and we use this encoding here to gauge the effectiveness of adding the temporally-weighted encoding. Both spiking and non-spiking models are trained and evaluated on this dataset, after which all models are retrained and evaluated on the real dataset to best estimate real-world performance. In the context of the SDA datasets, each dataset has only a single class (satellite) and the goal is to achieve maximal detection. As a result, the metric of greatest interest for the SDA task is the maximum F_1 score, and full precision-recall results are shown for these datasets only. Figure 3 shows an example of real optical, event-based satellite collection and a simulated approximation generated by the *SatSim* simulator.

For general comparison, we also evaluate our method on two publicly available datasets: N-Caltech101 and the Prophesee GEN1-Automotive dataset. As is customary for general object detection, we show the mean average preci-

Fig. 3. Real satellite collection (left) vs. SatSim generated sample (right). Samples are generated as full event streams, but displayed here as integrated frames.

sion (mAP) [8] results for our method and those of other state-of-the-art asynchronous detection methods.

Table 3. Performance results for spiking object detection models and conventional models on equivalent datasets.

Method	Dataset	Precision	Recall	F_1^*	mAP
YOLO+Int. Frame	Satellite Collect	0.43909	0.65570	0.52597	-
pseudo-sYOLO+Int. Frame	Satellite Collect	0.61765	0.88489	0.72750	-
pseudo-sYOLO+Enc.	Satellite Collect	0.67804	0.90103	**0.7740**	-
YOLO+Int. Frame	SatSim	0.65179	0.65710	0.65443	-
pseudo-sYOLO+Int. Frame	SatSim	0.745332	0.739609	0.74246	-
pseudo-sYOLO+Enc.	SatSim	0.77709	0.74871	**0.76264**	-
pseudo-sYOLO+Int. Frame	N–Caltech101	-	-	-	0.331
pseudo-sYOLO+Enc.	N–Caltech101	-	-	-	**0.595**
[4]	N–Caltech101	-	-	-	0.398
[16]	N–Caltech101	-	-	-	**0.643**
pseudo-sYOLO+Int. Frame	GEN1-Auto.	-	-	-	0.124
pseudo-sYOLO+Enc.	GEN1-Auto.	-	-	-	**0.339**
[16]	GEN1-Auto.	-	-	-	0.149
[5]	GEN1-Auto.	-	-	-	0.31
[21]	GEN1-Auto.	-	-	-	**0.40**

Across these object detection results, we see a significant increase in the maximum F_1 score for both real and simulated satellite data collections when using a pseudo-spiking YOLO as compared to a conventional YOLO model on integrated frames. Furthermore, the pseudo-spiking model with temporally-weighted encoding shows a significant increase in performance that appears more pronounced on real collections over simulated equivalents. This may be a result of the less uniform timestamps of generated events in real versus simulated data, which suggests that the temporally-weighted encoding is successfully preserving temporal data lost in the integrated frames. In regards to public datasets, the pseudo-spiking YOLO model with temporally-weighted encoding shows competitive mean average-precision (mAP) on N-Caltech101 and the Prophesee GEN1-Automotive datasets, with its performance only outmatched by the most recent asynchronous methods available. However, given that encoding method presented here improves the performance of spiking, but otherwise typical, object detection architectures, it is possible that the encoding method could be adapted to other current methods with improved performance as well.

In addition to classification and object detection accuracies, we also benchmarked the execution performance of our proposed spiking encoding architecture against a selection of other event-based methods with readily available performance data. Performance data for our models was collected on a single Nvidia A100 GPU evaluated as an average over the SatSim test dataset. In general, our approach showed execution times and complexities that were greater than some of the lighter asynchronous detection schemes, but greatly outperformed these algorithms in terms of accuracy (Table 4).

Table 4. Execution performance comparisons for pseudo-spiking architectures versus a selection of asynchronous methods.

Method	Execution Times	BFLOPS
pseudo-VGG19	375.5 ms	1.40
pseudo-ResNet50	475.2 ms	3.905
pseudo-DarkNet53	413.4 ms	3.810
[5]	202 ms	1.621
[16]	460.2 ms	3.682
[4]	84.3 ms	0.674

5   Conclusion

In this work, we have presented a new temporally-weighted spike encoding for event-based camera streams that greatly reduces the number of spikes required for processing noisy event streams, while preserving useful temporal information. We have additionally demonstrated a pseudo-spiking behavior for convolutional layers that allows us to mimic properties of a spiking network, but allows us to train deep networks with conventional backpropagation. Both object detection and classification results show that the combination of temporally-weighted spike encoding and pseudo-spiking behavior increase accuracy and performance, especially when used on deeper models. This method also demonstrates superior performance on object detection tasks for space-domain awareness, while also generalizing well to publicly available datasets.

In the future, we hope to assess the training of a larger array of models, as well as incorporate the method with newer versions of object detection models and explore the potential of extending this encoding to other event-based object detection algorithms. Furthermore, we have introduced the method by which the temporally-weighted spike encoding could be used to process event streams in real-time, but this potential is as of yet unexplored. Real-time object detection warrants an exhaustive study into the potential energy and memory-saving benefits, and could also highlight the comparative strengths of event-based cameras for SDA tasks.

References

1. Akiba, T., Sano, S., Yanase, T., Ohta, T., Koyama, M.: Optuna: a next-generation hyperparameter optimization framework. In: Proceedings of the 25th ACM SIGKDD International Conference on Knowledge Discovery & Data Mining, pp. 2623–2631 (2019)
2. Bellec, G., Salaj, D., Subramoney, A., Legenstein, R., Maass, W.: Long short-term memory and learning-to-learn in networks of spiking neurons. In: Advances in Neural Information Processing Systems, vol. 31 (2018)
3. Cabello, A., Fletcher, J.: Satsim: a synthetic data generation engine for electro-optical imagery of resident space objects. In: Sensors and Systems for Space Applications XV, vol. 12121, pp. 53–74. SPIE (2022)
4. Cannici, M., Ciccone, M., Romanoni, A., Matteucci, M.: Asynchronous convolutional networks for object detection in neuromorphic cameras. In: Proceedings of the IEEE/CVF Conference on Computer Vision and Pattern Recognition Workshops (2019)
5. Cannici, M., Ciccone, M., Romanoni, A., Matteucci, M.: A differentiable recurrent surface for asynchronous event-based data. In: Vedaldi, A., Bischof, H., Brox, T., Frahm, J.-M. (eds.) ECCV 2020. LNCS, vol. 12365, pp. 136–152. Springer, Cham (2020). https://doi.org/10.1007/978-3-030-58565-5_9
6. Chin, T.J., Bagchi, S., Eriksson, A., Van Schaik, A.: Star tracking using an event camera. In: Proceedings of the IEEE/CVF Conference on Computer Vision and Pattern Recognition Workshops (2019)
7. Cohen, G., et al.: Event-based sensing for space situational awareness. J. Astronaut. Sci. **66**(2), 125–141 (2019)
8. Everingham, M., Van Gool, L., Williams, C.K., Winn, J., Zisserman, A.: The pascal visual object classes (VOC) challenge. Int. J. Comput. Vision **88**(2), 303–338 (2010)
9. Fang, W., Yu, Z., Chen, Y., Masquelier, T., Huang, T., Tian, Y.: Incorporating learnable membrane time constant to enhance learning of spiking neural networks. In: Proceedings of the IEEE/CVF International Conference on Computer Vision, pp. 2661–2671 (2021)
10. Fletcher, J., McQuaid, I., Thomas, P., Sanders, J., Martin, G.: Feature-based satellite detection using convolutional neural networks. In: Proceedings of the Advanced Maui Optical and Space Surveillance Technologies Conference, p. 11 (2019)
11. Huh, D., Sejnowski, T.J.: Gradient descent for spiking neural networks. In: Advances in Neural Information Processing Systems, vol. 31 (2018)
12. Kong, S., Zhou, J., Ma, W.: Effect analysis of optical masking algorithm for geo space debris detection. Int. J. Optics **2019** (2019)
13. Lagorce, X., Meyer, C., Ieng, S.H., Filliat, D., Benosman, R.: Asynchronous event-based multikernel algorithm for high-speed visual features tracking. IEEE Trans. Neural Netw. Learn. Syst. **26**(8), 1710–1720 (2014)

14. Lee, C., Kosta, A.K., Zhu, A.Z., Chaney, K., Daniilidis, K., Roy, K.: Spike-FlowNet: event-based optical flow estimation with energy-efficient hybrid neural networks. In: Vedaldi, A., Bischof, H., Brox, T., Frahm, J.-M. (eds.) ECCV 2020. LNCS, vol. 12374, pp. 366–382. Springer, Cham (2020). https://doi.org/10.1007/978-3-030-58526-6_22

15. Li, H., Liu, H., Ji, X., Li, G., Shi, L.: CIFAR10-DVS: an event-stream dataset for object classification. Front. Neurosci. **11**, 309 (2017)

16. Messikommer, N., Gehrig, D., Loquercio, A., Scaramuzza, D.: Event-based asynchronous sparse convolutional networks. In: Vedaldi, A., Bischof, H., Brox, T., Frahm, J.-M. (eds.) ECCV 2020. LNCS, vol. 12353, pp. 415–431. Springer, Cham (2020). https://doi.org/10.1007/978-3-030-58598-3_25

17. Ni, Z., Pacoret, C., Benosman, R., Ieng, S., RÉGNIER*, S.: Asynchronous event-based high speed vision for microparticle tracking. J. Microsc. **245**(3), 236–244 (2012)

18. Orchard, G., Jayawant, A., Cohen, G.K., Thakor, N.: Converting static image datasets to spiking neuromorphic datasets using saccades. Front. Neurosci. **9**, 437 (2015)

19. Panda, P., Aketi, S.A., Roy, K.: Toward scalable, efficient, and accurate deep spiking neural networks with backward residual connections, stochastic softmax, and hybridization. Front. Neurosci. **14**, 653 (2020)

20. Paszke, A., et al.: Pytorch: an imperative style, high-performance deep learning library. In: Advances in Neural Information Processing Systems, vol. 32 (2019)

21. Perot, E., de Tournemire, P., Nitti, D., Masci, J., Sironi, A.: Learning to detect objects with a 1 megapixel event camera. Adv. Neural. Inf. Process. Syst. **33**, 16639–16652 (2020)

22. Rathi, N., Srinivasan, G., Panda, P., Roy, K.: Enabling deep spiking neural networks with hybrid conversion and spike timing dependent backpropagation. arXiv preprint arXiv:2005.01807 (2020)

23. Samadzadeh, A., Far, F.S.T., Javadi, A., Nickabadi, A., Chehreghani, M.H.: Convolutional spiking neural networks for spatio-temporal feature extraction. arXiv preprint arXiv:2003.12346 (2020)

24. Sironi, A., Brambilla, M., Bourdis, N., Lagorce, X., Benosman, R.: Hats: histograms of averaged time surfaces for robust event-based object classification. In: Proceedings of the IEEE Conference on Computer Vision and Pattern Recognition, pp. 1731–1740 (2018)

25. de Tournemire, P., Nitti, D., Perot, E., Migliore, D., Sironi, A.: A large scale event-based detection dataset for automotive. arXiv preprint arXiv:2001.08499 (2020)

26. Vasco, V., Glover, A., Bartolozzi, C.: Fast event-based Harris corner detection exploiting the advantages of event-driven cameras. In: 2016 IEEE/RSJ International Conference on Intelligent Robots and Systems (IROS), pp. 4144–4149. IEEE (2016)

27. Vicente-Sola, A., Manna, D.L., Kirkland, P., Di Caterina, G., Bihl, T.: Keys to accurate feature extraction using residual spiking neural networks. arXiv preprint arXiv:2111.05955 (2021)

28. Wu, Y., Deng, L., Li, G., Zhu, J., Shi, L.: Spatio-temporal backpropagation for training high-performance spiking neural networks. Front. Neurosci. **12**, 331 (2018)

29. Wu, Y., Deng, L., Li, G., Zhu, J., Xie, Y., Shi, L.: Direct training for spiking neural networks: Faster, larger, better. In: Proceedings of the AAAI Conference on Artificial Intelligence, vol. 33, pp. 1311–1318 (2019)

A Hardware-Aware Sampling Parameter Search for Efficient Probabilistic Object Detection

Julian Hoefer[(✉)] [ID], Tim Hotfilter[ID], Fabian Kreß[ID], Chen Qiu,
Tanja Harbaum[ID], and Juergen Becker[ID]

Karlsruhe Institute of Technology, Karlsruhe, Germany
{julian.hoefer,hotfilter,fabian.kress,harbaum,becker}@kit.edu

Abstract. Recent advancements in Deep Neural Networks (DNNs) have
led to remarkable achievements in object detection, making them increasingly relevant for safety-critical domains like autonomous driving. However, a significant challenge for deploying DNN-based object detection
in safety-critical applications remains the inability of the models to estimate their own uncertainty. To address this issue, Probabilistic Object
Detection has emerged as a solution, allowing for the assessment of both
semantic and spatial uncertainty. Monte-Carlo sampling methods, such
as Dropout and its variants, are commonly used to generate the necessary probability distributions. Nonetheless, determining the appropriate
Dropout variant, sample size, and drop probability for a specific probabilistic model remains a complex task, especially when considering the
importance of balancing algorithmic accuracy and hardware efficiency.
Ensuring hardware efficiency is particularly crucial for deploying these
models in embedded systems. To tackle this challenge, we treat it as
an optimization problem and employ an evolutionary multi-objective
search to identify the best-fitting sampling parameters. In our evaluation using the YOLOv5 model, we demonstrate that Gaussian Dropout
outperforms other Dropout variants. Notably, we achieve a doubling of
the PDQ score with no retraining and an mAP_{50-95} loss of only 1%
on the COCO dataset. Additionally, our study unveils the non-intuitive
trade-offs considering hardware performance.

Keywords: Parameter Optimization · Design Space Exploration ·
Probabilistic Object Detection

1 Introduction

In the past decade, Deep Neural Networks (DNNs) have made their way into our
everyday life, mostly hidden in online services and databases. Now, the importance of DNN-based Object Detection (OD) is growing significantly in specific
fields such as autonomous driving and robot interaction, thanks to advancements in model performance and embedded computing capabilities [7,13]. Most

H. I. Christensen et al. (Eds.): ICVS 2023, LNCS 14253, pp. 299–309, 2023.
https://doi.org/10.1007/978-3-031-44137-0_25

Fig. 1. Example output of a sampling-based probabilistic object detector. Multiple Monte-Carlo sampled bounding boxes are drawn (left) from several inferences on the same input. The coordinates of these samples describe a probability distribution that approximates spatial uncertainty (right).

state-of-the-art object detectors rely on Convolutional Neural Networks (CNNs) for feature extraction. However, traditional CNN-based object detection models tend to be overconfident in familiar scenarios and even worse in unfamiliar or anomalous scenarios such as Out-of-Distribution objects or Dataset Shifts [1]. The emergence of safety-critical systems, guided by new standards like ISO/PAS 21448 (Safety of the intended functionality), now necessitates that DNN-based systems understand their operational domain and their limitations, making uncertainty estimation crucial for their operation.

To address this issue of overconfidence, Probabilistic Object Detection (PDQ) provides a means to not only measure semantic uncertainty (identifying the object) but also spatial uncertainty (locating the object). This involves representing object localization not through traditional bounding boxes with corner points but via probability distributions with a mean and variance, as illustrated in Fig. 1. One approach to approximate these probability distributions is by introducing stochasticity to the CNN, typically through the inclusion of dropout layers during inference [8]. By introducing non-determinism, Monte-Carlo sampling becomes feasible, involving multiple sample inferences on the same input.

However, fine-tuning the Monte-Carlo sampling parameters presents challenges as they are challenging to integrate into the training process. For instance, the dropout function is non-differentiable, making it difficult to update the drop probability during backpropagation, necessitating fixing it before training. Moreover, other critical parameters, such as the type of dropout layer and the sample size (i.e., the number of sample inferences), cannot be trained and have a significant impact on hardware performance. Addressing these challenges and finding the optimal sampling parameters is a complex task, given their non-trainable nature. Balancing the need for accurate uncertainty estimation while considering hardware efficiency requires careful consideration. It is evident that as the sample size increases, hardware performance is compromised due to the need for more inference runs. Moreover, different dropout variants have varying computational complexities, further impacting hardware performance. For instance, Gaussian Dropout is more complex compared to regular Dropout, which simply sets elements to zero with a certain probability. To tackle this challenge, we propose formulating the search for suitable sampling parameters as an optimization problem. Instead of a costly brute-force approach like grid search, we employ a genetic algorithm, allowing different parameter sets to compete after the training phase. Through this process, we identify non-dominated solutions that perform well on a probabilistic metric, a traditional metric and a hardware metric. In summary, with our paper we make the following contributions:

- We present our evolutionary algorithm-based sampling parameter search and show how it is applied to an object detector to enable and optimize probabilistic object detection.
- We perform a proof-of-concept evaluation with an algorithmic objective space on two different YOLOv5 variants using the COCO dataset, showing that Gaussian Dropout dominates the Pareto-front doubling the PDQ score with only a 1% drop in mAP.
- By introducing hardware-awareness into the objective space, we show that Gaussian Dropout is a suitable choice for hardware-constrained systems despite being computationally more expensive due to the smaller sample size needed.

2   Background

2.1   Probabilistic Object Detection

While traditional object detection aims to assign exactly one bounding box to each object, probabilistic object detection represents objects as heatmaps to capture spatial uncertainties. Introduced by Hall et al. [10], probabilistic object detection seeks to accurately quantify both the spatial and semantic uncertainties of the detections. The semantic uncertainty can be estimated by observing each detection's probability distribution across all ground-truth classes. One method to estimate spatial uncertainty involves using probabilistic bounding boxes [10], i.e. bounding boxes that model the top-left and bottom-right corners as normal distributions with mean μ_i and covariance matrix Σ_i:

$$\mathcal{B} = (\mathcal{N}_0, \mathcal{N}_1) = (\mathcal{N}(\mu_0, \Sigma_0), \mathcal{N}(\mu_1, \Sigma_1)) \tag{1}$$

A widely used technique to approximate these probability distributions is to move beyond generating a single detection and instead produce several detections by introducing stochasticity into the inference process. This can be achieved, e.g. by incorporating regulation layers like Dropout into the CNN model, not only during training but also during inference. When the entire model inference or a subset of it is conducted multiple times, generating several sample detections, it is referred to as Monte Carlo dropout [8].

To assess the quality of object detections, Hall et al. introduced the Probability-based Detection Quality Score (PDQ) [10] as a new metric. This metric is designed to combine label quality, capturing the semantic uncertainty, with spatial quality. The spatial quality penalizes detection probabilities outside the ground-truth bounding box and background probabilities inside it. The PDQ score serves as a complementary metric to the widely used mAP score [5]. Ideally, an object detector performs well in both traditional object detection (mAP score) and probabilistic object detection (PDQ score). This co-optimization helps mitigate respective weaknesses of the metrics. For example, the mAP score is known to obscure false positive detections, particularly with a low label threshold, while PDQ penalizes both, false positive and false negative detections [10]. Consequently, achieving an appropriate trade-off that yields high scores in both mAP and PDQ is indicative of a well-balanced object detector.

2.2 Related Work

Gaussian YOLO [3] is a stochastic variant of the YOLOv3 architecture that differs from the traditional Monte-Carlo approach. Instead, the model and loss function are adapted to allow the direct output of coordinates as Gaussian parameters. This sampling-free approach of Gaussian YOLO enables faster inference times while significantly reducing false positive cases. However, the performance of Gaussian YOLO on the PDQ score has not been investigated.

The authors in [1] utilize the PDQ score to evaluate Stochastic-YOLO, a sampling-based probabilistic object detector based on YOLOv3 with Monte-Carlo Dropout. They specifically explore the impact of dataset shifts on probabilistic object detection and demonstrate that Stochastic-YOLO handles various corruptions more effectively than YOLOv3 without the need for retraining. Besides Stochastic-YOLO, other works have also applied Monte-Carlo Dropout to object detectors [11,14,16]. To address some limitations of Dropout in object detection, DropBlock has been proposed as an alternative method for modeling uncertainty estimation in object detection [4]. However, in all these works, the details of the drop probability and sample size are either not provided or set as hyperparameters.

A sampling parameter optimization approach for uncertainty estimation is presented in [6]. The authors use a greedy algorithm to determine the optimal sample size and drop probability, but they focus solely on MC-Dropout and its application to semantic uncertainty in image classification, without addressing probabilistic object detection.

3   GA-Based Sampling Parameter Search

Currently, the manual optimization of the best-fitting sampling parameters for a specific application is a non-trivial task, especially when considering hardware

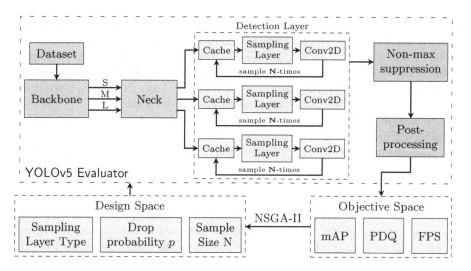

Fig. 2. Overview over the hardware-aware optimization. The NSGA-II picks combinations from the design space and evaluates the probabilistic object detection model to find Pareto-optimal solutions in the objective space.

performance. Therefore we propose a method to automate the process and design space exploration by defining an optimization problem and applying an evolutionary algorithm as depicted in Fig. 2. To demonstrate the effectiveness of our approach, we utilize the YOLOv5 architecture [12] as a baseline in our work.

To transform the YOLOv5 architecture into a probabilistic object detector, we adopt the following concepts from [1]: First, as shown in Fig. 2, we integrate the sampling layer inside the detection module, placed just before the final convolution of the network. Since YOLOv5 consists of three detection heads for small, medium and large objects, three sampling layers are used in total. Second, to minimize sampling overhead, we implement a caching mechanism. Instead of the entire inference, only the last convolutional layer has to be re-executed. Third, we implement the Pre-non-maximum suppression averaging method, originally proposed by [17]. In essence, this method involves averaging the bounding box coordinates of detection samples for a single object before applying non-maximum suppression.

Regarding the possible sampling layers, our search algorithm considers three different regularization options, namely standard Dropout, DropBlock and Gaussian Dropout. *Dropout* is the most commonly used layer for sampling-based uncertainty estimation in various studies [1,8,10]. It sets elements of its input tensor to zero with a predefined *drop probability p*. *DropBlock* follows a more coarse-grained approach by zeroing out entire regions of a tensor with a drop probability p [9]. We include DropBlock as a candidate because it has shown promising results as Monte-Carlo Dropblock for uncertainty estimation in object detection [4], although it has not been tested with probabilistic object detection. For our search, we utilize a block size of 3×3. Another method that is used to add regularization during training is *Gaussian Dropout* [18], where each element is multiplied by a value drawn from a normal distribution with a mean of 1 and a standard deviation of $\sigma = \sqrt{p/(1-p)}$. In our parameter search, we aim to optimize the drop probability parameter p which defines the standard deviation. We include Gaussian Dropout as our third sampling layer candidate, since it has not been previously tested for probabilistic object detection.

The sample size is the last parameter we include in the design space of our sampling parameter search, determining the number of samples drawn in the detection module. Intuitively, a larger sample size improves prediction scores. However, even with the caching mechanism enabled, a large sample size can burden hardware performance, making it a crucial parameter to consider, especially for resource-constrained embedded devices. To measure the hardware performance of the probabilistic object detector, we employ the common metric frames per second (FPS), which we include in our objective space. In addition to the hardware-aware FPS metric, we complete the objective space with the mean Average Precision (mAP), commonly used in traditional object detection, and the previously described PDQ for probabilistic object detection. Our aim is to explore how well the optimized probabilistic object detector performs in both tasks.

Furthermore, alongside defining the design space and search space, it is crucial to specify the problem for the genetic algorithm. We define the problem as a pretrained object detector model that has been made probabilistic through the aforementioned measures. The evaluation process involves conducting inferences on a representative dataset, such as the validation dataset. It is of particular importance to ensure that the evaluation subset is not too small for two main reasons: first, a small number of images may lead to imprecise FPS measurements, and second, a fortuitous selection of evaluation images, where the object detector performs well regardless, could negatively impact the future evolutionary search. After the inference, we then evaluate PDQ using the code provided by [10] and [15] for mAP, respectively. We choose to embed the optimization problem in the NSGA-II algorithm provided by [2], since it is able to find and return a variety of non-dominated solutions to the user.

4   Evaluation

To showcase the advantages of our concept, we conducted three proof-of-concept evaluations using YOLOv5 models. Initially, we focus on an algorithmic objective space, excluding FPS, to expose the trade-off between mAP and PDQ scores while refining the design space. We perform two searches and compare the results for two YOLOv5 variants: the small variant YOLOv5-s and the largest configuration available, YOLOv5-x [12]. YOLOv5-s is tailored for embedded usage and therefore has only 7.2M parameters and 16.5 FLOPS, while YOLOv5-x, with 86.7M parameters and 205.7 FLOPS, is better suited for cloud or server applications. We conduct the inference employing YOLOv5 weights, which were pretrained on the widely used COCO dataset [15]. The evaluation for each parameter combination is performed on the validation subset. In a third search using the YOLOv5-s variant, we emphasize the trade-offs between hardware and algorithmic performance by including frames per second in the objective space. YOLOv5-s is better suited for this evaluation since embedded applications often have stricter computational performance constraints. Considering that we produce numerous bounding boxes with multiple inferences, we set a comparatively high confidence threshold of 0.5 and Intersection over Union (IoU) threshold of 0.6, aligning with the evaluation approach by Azevedo et al. [1].

Table 1. Overview of our defined GA-search parameters for NSGA-II

Category	Search parameter	Value/Constraints
General	Population size	50
	Generations	10 and 5
	Problem	YOLOv5-s, YOLOv5-x
Design space	Sampling layer	{Dropout, Gaussian Dropout, DropBlock}
	Drop probability	[0, 1] and [0, 0.5]
	Sample size	[2, 20]
Objective space	Algorithmic metrics	mAP_{50-95}
		PDQ
	Hardware metric	*FPS*

4.1 YOLOv5-s and YOLOv5-x Evaluation with Algorithmic Objective Space

Our evolutionary search parameters are summarized in Table 1. In the first and second evaluation, the objective space includes the two algorithmic metrics mAP_{50-95} and PDQ. We consider three different sampling layers and, to narrow down the design space within reasonable limits, we constrain the drop probability and the sample size. The drop probability is defined as a floating point number, within the interval [0, 1]. To prevent excessive computational load, we set the maximum sample size to 20.

The first evaluation is performed on the YOLOv5-s model. The results after 10 generations are illustrated in Fig. 3(a) and (b). Our scatter plot presents 32 non-dominated solutions that form the Pareto-front with the best results for PDQ and mAP. For comparison, we include the performance of the original YOLOv5 model, achieving an mAP_{50-95} of 0.277 and PDQ of 0.0933. When applying Gaussian Dropout, the model demonstrates a PDQ improvement of 5% without compromising mAP compared to the original YOLOv5. Furthermore, Gaussian Dropout achieves a maximum PDQ improvement of 13% with less than 1% drop in mAP compared to the original YOLOv5.

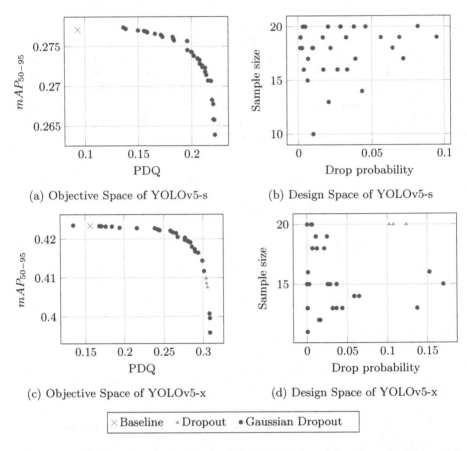

(a) Objective Space of YOLOv5-s

(b) Design Space of YOLOv5-s

(c) Objective Space of YOLOv5-x

(d) Design Space of YOLOv5-x

× Baseline   ▲ Dropout   • Gaussian Dropout

Fig. 3. Results of our searches with algorithmic objective space. Gaussian Dropout is predominant and performs better than the other dropout variants. In both models, Gaussian Dropout is able to significantly improve PDQ with a negligible decline in mAP.

When examining the design space, it becomes evident that Gaussian Dropout outperforms the other sampling layers significantly after 10 generations, as all 32 surviving solutions exclusively consist of models with Gaussian Dropout layers. The distribution of drop probabilities ranges from 0 to 0.1, indicating that Gaussian Dropout with a drop probability under 10% achieves superior performance. In contrast, higher drop probabilities tend to remove too much information from the model inference, leading to diminished detection performance. Moreover, the sample size is predominantly distributed within the interval of 14 to 20, suggesting that a larger number of model samples generally leads to improved performance. In the initial generations, we observed that DropBlock exhibited the weakest performance and was eliminated first, whereas Dropout managed to survive the initial generations.

Based on the experience from the previous search with YOLOv5-s, we slightly adapt the evaluation with YOLOv5-x for faster convergence: We reduce the number of generations to 5, as our initial evaluation showed signs of convergence at this stage. Additionally, we constrain the drop probability to the interval [0, 0.5] since the previous evaluation did not find any solutions with a drop probability greater than 0.1. The results are depicted in Fig. 3(c) and (d). The result of our search consists of 31 surviving non-dominated solutions in total, with 28 of them utilizing Gaussian Dropout and the remaining 3 employing Dropout layers. Gaussian Dropout achieves a notable 9% improvement in PDQ without experiencing a substantial decrease in mAP compared to the baseline YOLOv5-x model.

Similar to the findings in the first evaluation, the majority of the Gaussian Dropout solutions have a drop probability within the range of [0, 0.15], and a sample size within the interval [11, 20]. This indicates that Gaussian Dropout requires a slightly larger sample rate value for the larger YOLOv5-x model. As all the remaining Dropout solutions require 20 samples, it indicates that they generally need more sampling compared to Gaussian Dropout to achieve the same level of accuracy.

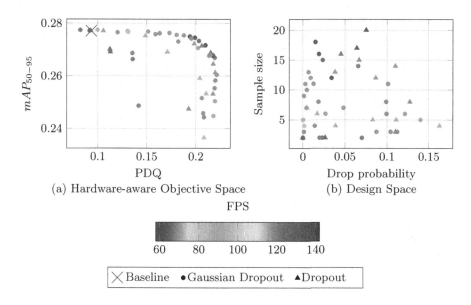

(a) Hardware-aware Objective Space   (b) Design Space

Fig. 4. Results of our hardware-aware search on the YOLOv5-s model. As in the previous evaluations, a significant PDQ improvement can be achieved with minor mAP loss. There are comparably more surviving Dropout solutions, since they tend to have better hardware performance. The most algorithmically accurate solutions (good mAP and PDQ) on the top right corner have the lowest FPS.

4.2   YOLOv5-s Evaluation with Hardware-Aware Objective Space

We run our model on an NVIDIA GeForce RTX 3070 GPU and use a batch size of 4. This configuration provides a performance of ~140 FPS on the unmodified YOLOv5-s model, achieving the highest performance when compared to the same model with sampling involved. After evolving for 10 generations, a significant difference compared to previous evaluations is apparent: there are now more non-dominated solutions built by Dropout, as shown in Fig. 4. Specifically, there are 18 Pareto-optimal Dropout solutions and 32 Pareto-optimal Gaussian Dropout Solutions. Once again, no DropBlock solutions were able to survive. Dropout proves to be the most hardware-friendly function, followed by Gaussian Dropout. Despite its higher computational cost, Gaussian Dropout produces a substantial number of valid solutions that achieve good algorithmic accuracy while maintaining high hardware performance. This is attributed to the fact that Dropout requires more samples, i.e. a higher sample size, to achieve similar algorithmic performance. As expected, the sample size correlates significantly with the achieved FPS. This non-intuitive property emphasizes the importance of our search for the best sampling layer and parameter combination. Although we utilize the caching mechanism in the model, the decrease in FPS cannot be neglected and must be taken into consideration in constrained systems. Nevertheless, it is worth noting that probabilistic OD does not necessarily lead to a significant increase in inference time or a dip in hardware performance. In fact, our results demonstrate that it is still feasible to achieve ~60 FPS with a good algorithmic performance in terms of both mAP and PDQ scores. Solutions with higher hardware performance tend to have either a lower PDQ score or lower mAP score emphasizing the need to carefully balance the trade-offs based on the specific hardware and algorithmic requirements of the OD system.

5   Conclusion

In this paper, we introduced a method to automate the non-trivial task of hardware-aware sampling parameter search for probabilistic object detection. By formulating the search as an optimization problem and employing an evolutionary algorithm to explore the design space, we are able to identify the best sampling parameters tailored to a specific application. To validate our concept, we conducted a proof-of-concept evaluation through three different searches. While performing at 60 FPS, we could achieve a doubling of the PDQ score with only a 1% drop in mAP score. We revealed that Gaussian Dropout outperforms other Dropout variants in an algorithmic objective space and represents the majority of solutions in a hardware-aware objective space, since the smaller sample size needed outweighs the higher computational complexity.

Acknowledgments. This work was funded by the German Federal Ministry of Education and Research (BMBF) under grant number 16ME0096 (ZuSE-KI-mobil). The responsibility for the content of this publication lies with the authors.

References

1. Azevedo, T., de Jong, R., Maji, P.: Stochastic-YOLO: efficient probabilistic object detection under dataset shifts (2020). https://arxiv.org/abs/2009.02967
2. Blank, J., Deb, K.: Pymoo: multi-objective optimization in python. IEEE Access **8**, 89497–89509 (2020)
3. Choi, J., Chun, D., Kim, H., Lee, H.: Gaussian YOLOv3: an accurate and fast object detector using localization uncertainty for autonomous driving (2019). http://arxiv.org/abs/1904.04620
4. Deepshikha, K., Yelleni, S.H., Srijith, P.K., Mohan, C.K.: Monte Carlo dropblock for modelling uncertainty in object detection (2021). https://arxiv.org/abs/2108.03614
5. Everingham, M., Van Gool, L., Williams, C.K.I., Winn, J., Zisserman, A.: The pascal visual object classes (VOC) challenge. Int. J. Comput. Vision **88**(2), 303–338 (2010)
6. Fan, H., et al.: High-performance FPGA-based accelerator for Bayesian neural networks. In: 2021 58th ACM/IEEE Design Automation Conference (DAC) (2021)
7. Fasfous, N., et al.: Binary-LoRAX: low-latency runtime adaptable XNOR classifier for semi-autonomous grasping with prosthetic hands. In: 2021 IEEE International Conference on Robotics and Automation (ICRA), pp. 13430–13437 (2021)
8. Gal, Y., Ghahramani, Z.: Dropout as a Bayesian approximation: representing model uncertainty in deep learning. In: Proceedings of the 33rd International Conference on International Conference on Machine Learning, ICML 2016, vol. 48, pp. 1050–1059. JMLR.org (2016)
9. Ghiasi, G., Lin, T., Le, Q.V.: DropBlock: a regularization method for convolutional networks (2018). http://arxiv.org/abs/1810.12890
10. Hall, D., et al.: Probabilistic object detection: definition and evaluation. In: 2020 IEEE Winter Conference on Applications of Computer Vision (WACV) (2020)
11. Harakeh, A., Smart, M., Waslander, S.L.: BayesOD: a Bayesian approach for uncertainty estimation in deep object detectors (2019). http://arxiv.org/abs/1903.03838
12. Jocher, G.: YOLOv5 by ultralytics (2020). https://doi.org/10.5281/zenodo.3908559,https://github.com/ultralytics/yolov5
13. Kempf, F., et al.: The ZuSE-KI-mobil AI accelerator SOC: overview and a functional safety perspective. In: 2023 Design, Automation & Test in Europe Conference & Exhibition (DATE), pp. 1–6 (2023)
14. Kraus, F., Dietmayer, K.: Uncertainty estimation in one-stage object detection. In: 2019 IEEE Intelligent Transportation Systems Conference (ITSC) (2019)
15. Lin, T.-Y., et al.: Microsoft COCO: common objects in context. In: Fleet, D., Pajdla, T., Schiele, B., Tuytelaars, T. (eds.) ECCV 2014. LNCS, vol. 8693, pp. 740–755. Springer, Cham (2014). https://doi.org/10.1007/978-3-319-10602-1_48
16. Miller, D., Nicholson, L., Dayoub, F., Sünderhauf, N.: Dropout sampling for robust object detection in open-set conditions. In: 2018 IEEE International Conference on Robotics and Automation (ICRA), pp. 3243–3249 (2018)
17. Miller, D., et al.. In: Proceedings of the IEEE/CVF Conference on Computer Vision and Pattern Recognition (CVPR) Workshops (2019)
18. Srivastava, N., et al.: Dropout: a simple way to prevent neural networks from overfitting. J. Mach. Learn. Res. **15**(56), 1929–1958 (2014)

Towards Food Handling Robots for Automated Meal Preparation in Healthcare Facilities

Lukas Knak$^{(\boxtimes)}$, Florian Jordan , Tim Nickel , Werner Kraus ,
and Richard Bormann

Department of Robot and Assistive Systems, Fraunhofer IPA,
70569 Stuttgart, Germany
{lukas.knak,florian.jordan,tim.nickel,
werner.kraus,richard.bormann}@ipa.fraunhofer.de

Abstract. Meal preparation in healthcare facilities is an area of work severely affected by the shortage of qualified personnel. Recent advances in automation technology have enabled the use of picking robots to fill the gaps created by changes in the labor market. Building on these advances, we present a robotic system designed to handle packaged food for automated meal preparation in healthcare facilities. To address the challenge of grasping the large variety of packaged foods, we propose a novel technique for model-free grasping pose detection based on geometric features that is optimized for the given scenario. We provide a comprehensive system overview and conduct evaluations of the grasping success on a real robot. The high grasping success rate of 94% with a processing time of ~280 ms indicates the suitability of the proposed approach for automating meal preparation tasks in healthcare facilities.

Keywords: Robotics · Vision · Grasping · Automation · Meal Preparation

1 Introduction

The search for qualified personnel to prepare meals in healthcare facilities is proving difficult due to the high physical demands of the monotonous work and the shortage of capacity in the labor market caused by demographic change in western countries. The problem is exacerbated in particular by the high hygienic requirements in the workplace and the strict working conditions in the wake of the Corona pandemic. In the meal preparation process, as shown in Fig. 1a, a tray is placed on the conveyor and equipped with dishes, cutlery, and the patient's card. Then, in several stations along the conveyor belt, different types of food are loaded onto the tray. Automating these tasks through the use of robots could be a potential solution to the problem of staff shortages while improving hygiene standards, reducing errors, and ensuring seamless and extensively personalized meal preparation.

As part of the meal preparation task in healthcare facilities, packaged food is picked from various large boxes and placed onto a moving tray on the conveyor

H. I. Christensen et al. (Eds.): ICVS 2023, LNCS 14253, pp. 310–322, 2023.
https://doi.org/10.1007/978-3-031-44137-0_26

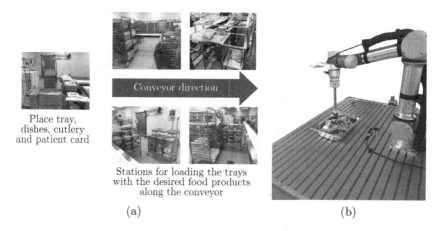

Place tray, dishes, cutlery and patient card

Conveyor direction

Stations for loading the trays with the desired food products along the conveyor

(a)   (b)

Fig. 1. (a) Meal preparation process. (b) Simple robotic setup.

belt. The challenge of grasping objects from the cluttered scenes in such bins for automation purposes has been an active area of research in recent years [4,6,9–13,20]. Approaches for finding robotic grasping poses in cluttered scenes are usually divided into two categories: model-based and model-free techniques [4,5]. In model-based methods, the algorithm is given prior knowledge about the object to be grasped, which enables a precise and robust picking process [2,4,5,19]. However, for applications with a large variety of objects, the use of model-based approaches often requires repeated adjustments due to the inability of the technique to grasp previously unknown objects [3]. To overcome this challenge, model-free methods can be used in these scenarios. Such approaches do not require prior object knowledge and are designed to generalize to novel situations [4,5]. The difficulty of the meal preparation task is further exacerbated as the conveyor target speed and throughput require a strict cycle time of 1 s for grasping the packaged food from the bins (see Fig. 1b) and placing it onto the tray, which limits suitable approaches to techniques with a low processing time and a high grasping success rate.

To address the challenge of handling the large variety of objects encountered in the meal preparation process in healthcare facilities within the cycle time restrictions, this paper presents a novel model-free grasping pose detection algorithm optimized for the picking of packaged food in Sect. 4. The robot and vision system suggested for the task are described in Sect. 3. Finally, the overall system performance is evaluated in Sect. 5.

In summary, the major contributions of this paper are:

- a novel model-free grasping pose detection method optimized for the picking of packaged food,
- a detailed system design description for vision-guided robotic systems for automated meal preparation,
- a comprehensive experimental evaluation of the system performance.

2   Related Work

Grasping packaged food from supply boxes in the meal preparation process requires the detection of robotic grasping poses in cluttered scenes. Such approaches are usually divided into two categories: model-based and model-free techniques [5]. In model-based grasping, algorithms are provided with CAD model knowledge about the target object to be grasped, enabling them to predict the object's location and pose in the scene and to use predefined grasp configurations based on its geometry [2,4,5,19]. Because of their design, they do not generalize to unknown objects [3]. Considering the wide variety of objects to be grasped in the meal preparation process and the frequent changes in shape and appearance of the objects as products are revised or new products are introduced, using a model-based approach here becomes impractical. The solution to this problem are techniques that focus on generic grasping criteria instead of object-specific properties, so-called model-free methods [4].

Before data-driven methods of the machine learning domain started to become a popular choice for model-free grasp detection, analytical methods were used to estimate grasping poses from the RGB-D information of the scene [4]. Analytic methods rely on generic geometric features for grasping objects and often use a template technique to evaluate different scene points [1,6,7]. Due to the computationally intensive calculations in the order of several seconds [16], they are inapplicable to the high-speed meal preparation scenario.

Data-driven machine learning methods, on the other hand, offer the benefit of a fast execution time due to parallelized computations on a GPU. Here, the grasping pose detection techniques can further be distinguished into two categories: discriminative and generative approaches [4,5].

In discriminative approaches, grasp candidates are sampled and ranked using a quality estimation method, which is often implemented using neural networks [4,5]. After ranking, the grasp with the highest score is executed. The advantage of such methods is that an arbitrary amount of grasp poses can be evaluated, although this can become computationally intensive. Several methods are based on a discriminative approach: Levine et al. [10] use a dual servoing method in which the grasping algorithm guides the robot gripper to the grasping pose. Here, the success of grasp candidates in the RGB image of the scene is iteratively predicted using a neural network that was trained on real-world data. Later approaches focus on gathering data in physical simulations, in which huge amounts of grasping scenarios are evaluated and the outcome of the grasps are stored together with the information about the scenes. The most prominent example of such approaches, Dex-Net [11–13], stores the center-aligned cropped image for each grasp candidate and trains a quality prediction convolutional neural network using this cropped image as input and the according grasp success value as output. The authors of Dex-Net further adapted their method to use fully-convolutional neural networks that can predict grasp success values for multiple grasping poses in the scene simultaneously [17].

In contrast to discriminative approaches, generative approaches focus on directly predicting grasping poses for a scene. Lenz et al. [9] proposed a two-stage learning-based system that samples and ranks grasp candidates using a neural network, which can further be improved by using more advanced network architectures [8]. GG-CNN [14,15] is a grasp detection model that utilizes public datasets such as the Cornell grasping dataset [9] for training and outputs grasp configurations and quality estimates for each pixel in the image using a fully convolutional architecture.

In the meal preparation scenario, a high success rate in grasping is required, since failed grasps can cause the conveyor to stop. The aim of optimal generalizability for data-driven model-free methods may conflict with this requirement since it can lead to reduced performance in specific applications, as we show for the picking of packaged food in the meal preparation process in Sect. 5. Thus, an approach optimized for this specific scenario, but flexible enough to generalize to any new objects within the application is required.

Leveraging purely parallelized computations on a GPU along with heuristic grasping pose estimation techniques, we propose an analytical, model-free grasping pose detection method that uses geometric features to find ad hoc grasping poses optimized for the picking of packaged food in the meal preparation scenario. With the computationally efficient implementation, we overcome the problem of long runtimes of existing analytical methods [1,6,7] and enable the application of our approach in high-speed meal preparation.

3   System Overview

As part of the meal preparation task in healthcare facilities, packaged food is picked from various large boxes and placed onto a moving tray on the conveyor (Fig. 2a) according to the patients' menu requests. Each menu is known in advance and contains up to 6 different items that must be gathered within 6 s to match the target conveyor speed and throughput. This results in a cycle time for grasping and placing each item of less than 1 s. To automate this task, we design a robotic system that picks the objects from the boxes using a depth camera. The supply is replenished manually and the task of setting up the tray is not part of this system.

Robot and Vision System. Due to the strict time constraints of less than 1 s for picking and placing each item, a robot with fast acceleration and high terminal velocity is required, which limits the choice of robots to high performance SCARA robots. This meets the requirements for the cylindrical robot workspace, as visualized in Fig. 2a. We choose a vacuum gripper for grasping the packaged food. To ensure that the vision system meets the low cycle time restrictions, a high-speed depth camera is required at the cost of less accuracy. The camera is mounted statically above the robot's supply, so new images of the current scene can be captured while the robot is moving. The details of the hardware used in our setup are provided in Sect. 5.

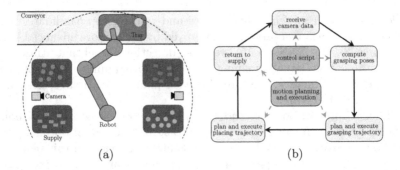

(a)   (b)

Fig. 2. (a) Robot workspace and meal preparation setup. (b) Control chart: the solid arrows mark the higher-level tasks in each cycle; the dashed arrows mark the interaction between the control modules.

Robot Behavior Control. For each tray, a control PC system retrieves information from a server about which items need to be gathered. As soon as a new tray is detected via a sensor on the conveyor belt, the control PC system starts processing the order list, calculating grasping poses using the information from the depth cameras, and commanding the robot to grasp each item from the boxes and to place it onto the tray. The position of the tray for placement is tracked by the speed of the conveyor. The control chart is given in Fig. 2b.

4   Grasping Pose Detection

We propose a new heuristic for model-free grasping pose detection in cluttered scenes that enables the robot to robustly grasp the packaged food objects using a vacuum gripper. The heuristic uses the depth data provided by the vision system to predict the grasping quality at different scene points, based on the idea that the robustness of a suction grasp depends on the regularity of an object's surface. The resulting grasp configurations are then filtered using the properties of the used suction cup. In the following, we present the grasping pose prediction process, as depicted in Fig. 3, that outputs 6 degrees of freedom grasping poses formed by 3D grasping points and the points' surface normal vectors. We provide a detailed ablation study of the components of the method and a hyperparameter study in the Appendix.

Depth Data Acquisition and Preprocessing. We start by receiving the depth data from the vision system and calculating the 3D point cloud of the scene using the intrinsic parameters of the camera. To fill in missing information due to occlusion or reflection, the depth data is preprocessed using the Fast Marching Method inpainting algorithm [18]. The surface normal vector at each point in the scene is computed using the depth image gradients given by a Sobel filter. A segmentation mask for the objects in the point cloud is calculated based on prior knowledge about the fixed position and size of the geometry of the bin, so

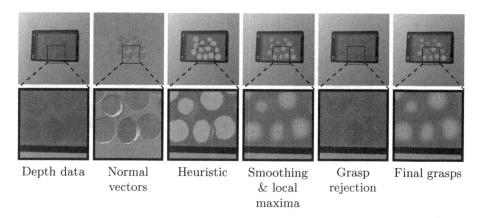

| Depth data | Normal vectors | Heuristic | Smoothing & local maxima | Grasp rejection | Final grasps |

Fig. 3. Heuristic grasp quality estimation process.

non-object pixels are neglected in the following calculations and computational speed is increased.

Grasping Quality Heuristic. After the surface normal vector for each scene point is stored in a tensor $\mathbf{I}_0$, we heuristically estimate grasp quality scores following the steps visualized in Fig. 4a. We start by extracting all pairs of two points $\mathbf{p}_1, \mathbf{p}_2$ in a pixel area A around the center point $\mathbf{p}_c$ for which $\mathbf{p}_1$ and $\mathbf{p}_2$ lie exactly in opposite directions and the same distance from the center. For each pair of points $\mathbf{p}_1, \mathbf{p}_2$, the following calculations are performed: first, the dot product of their surface normal vectors $s_n = \mathbf{n}_1 \cdot \mathbf{n}_2$ is evaluated. This scalar s_n is multiplied by the mean normal vector of the pair, $\mathbf{n}_p = \frac{\mathbf{n}_1 + \mathbf{n}_2}{2}$, to obtain a new vector $\mathbf{v}_p = \mathbf{n}_p \cdot s_n$ whose length is maximal if the two surface normals of the pair are identical, i.e. $\mathbf{n}_1 = \mathbf{n}_2$. Then, the dot product of this resulting vector $\mathbf{v}_p$ with the normal vector of the center point $\mathbf{n}_c$ is calculated. If this scalar $s_c = \mathbf{v}_p \cdot \mathbf{n}_c$ is larger than a threshold value c, the center's normal vector $\mathbf{n}_c$ is appended to an output tensor $\mathbf{T}$. The idea is that if all surface normal vectors inside the area A point in the same direction, the sum over the vectors in the output tensor $\mathbf{T}$ is maximal, so the length of $\mathbf{v}_s = \sum_{\mathbf{v} \in \mathbf{T}} \mathbf{v}$ provides information about the regularity of the local surface. To enforce computational stability, $\mathbf{v}_s$ is divided by the number of pairs N in the area, $\mathbf{v}_r = \frac{\mathbf{v}_s}{N}$, and its norm $||\mathbf{v}_r||_2^2$ is stored as the quality score q for each center point. The resulting averaged vectors $\mathbf{v}_r$ are stored in a new tensor $\mathbf{I}_t$, which is used as the input to the grasping quality heuristic for the next iteration $t + 1$. The heuristic calculations are iteratively reapplied to the output tensors $\mathbf{I}_{t+1}$ for T iterations, summing up the quality scores q along the way. Thus, each entry of the tensor $\mathbf{I}_{t+1}$ aggregates broader information about the local surface with each iteration t and the points at regular surface patches obtain higher scores than those at object edges.

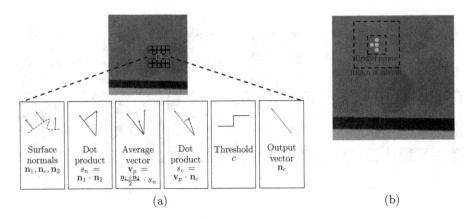

Fig. 4. (a) Grasping quality heuristic calculations. (b) Grasp rejection.

Smoothing and Local Maxima. We post-process the scores by iteratively taking the minimum of the point's score and the average score of the local 3×3 pixel neighborhood, further decreasing the scores towards the object's edges. If the score of a grasping point is greater than or equal to that of all its neighbors, i.e., if we have a local maximum in the score distribution, the point and its surface normal vector, which together form the 6D grasping pose, are added to the set of possible grasping candidates.

Grasp Rejection. To filter out invalid grasps that do not lead to a sealed vacuum at the object's surface with the suction cup of the gripper, an approximated ray-casting procedure for each point is performed in three steps, as depicted in Fig. 4b. First, we create a grid of $N \times N$ points proportional to the suction area of the gripper, where N is proportional to the suction cup diameter. From this square grid, we remove the grid-points whose Euclidean distance from the center is greater than the suction cup radius, leaving $\sim \pi \cdot \left(\frac{N}{2}\right)^2$ valid grid-points that represent the circular suction area of the gripper. This grid is transformed into each grasping pose in camera coordinates, such that the normal vector of the grid is aligned with the normal vector of the surface, and the x-axis of the grid lies in the x-y plane of the camera. Then, a region of interest is extracted from the point cloud that corresponds to the 64×64 pixels around the grasping point in the depth image. Finally, for each grid-point, it is computed whether a point from the region of interest is within a cylindrical volume around the grid-point that is given by the diameter of the suction cup divided by N as the cylinder diameter, an estimated height tolerance of the suction cup as the cylinder length, and the normal vector of the grid as the cylinder axis. The intuition here is that if a point is inside this cylinder, a ray emitted from the suction cup towards the scene would hit the surface of the object at this point. If this is true for all grid-points, the suction cup is assumed to achieve a sealed vacuum and the grasp is added to the list of valid grasps, otherwise it is rejected.

After rejecting grasping poses using the approximated ray-casting process, the remaining grasps are first sorted by their scores in descending order and then the set is further pruned by removing poses whose distance from other candidates is smaller than the suction cup diameter. We start at the point with the highest score and reject points that are too close; then continue at the remaining point with the next highest score until all poses are tested. The final set is returned in descending order of scores.

5   Evaluation

To evaluate the system, two consecutive experiments were conducted.

In the first experiment, we validated the system using a high-speed manipulator as outlined in Fig. 2a. Here, we measure the speed of the grasp execution and placement to estimate the time window for sensor data retrieval and grasp computation. We find a total cycle execution time of ~700 ms for the high-speed robot. Since the camera and robot arm are synchronized, we can retrieve the camera data and perform the calculation of the next grasping pose while the robot is executing the placement for the previous cycle, granting up to half of the execution time, i.e., ~350 ms, until the next grasping pose proposal must be computed.

As the high-speed manipulator scenario was not completely set-up at the time of experimentation, we conducted a second experiment and evaluated the performance of the grasping heuristic on a simpler system. This system consisted of a UR5e robotic manipulator with a Schmalz vacuum gripper and a low-cost RealSense RGB-D camera attached to the robot's wrist, as depicted in Fig. 1b. We provide a supply of different types of packaged food stored inside 2 small bins. We perform a routine of grasping from one bin and dropping the items into another bin. When no more grasps are found, we swap the source and target bins to repeatedly obtain cluttered scenes. We perform a total number of 500 grasping cycles and evaluate the grasping success rate as well as the mean μ and standard deviation σ of the processing time for each cycle, including image retrieval and grasp computation. All calculations for the grasp pose detection are performed on an Nvidia RTX3090 GPU. During each cycle, we first execute the grasp with the highest score. If this is not successful, we try up to two additional grasp attempts without recomputing the grasps to measure both the top-1 and top-3 accuracy. The intuition here is that due to the high-speed robot, we can try a second or third grasp in the scene and still meet the time constraints of 6 items processed in 6 s. We compare the performance of our algorithm with a state-of-the-art model-free grasping pose detection algorithm based on Dex-Net [13]. The results are shown in Table 1. Due to the strict time constraints in the meal preparation scenario, a comparison with other analytical methods is not feasible because they require too much computation time [16].

With a top-1 performance of 94% and a top-3 performance of 99%, the algorithm provides a robust method for grasping and satisfies the time restrictions for the meal preparation task with a total processing time of ~280 ms. We find a

Table 1. Grasping evaluation results for the simple system.

Method	Top-1 success rate	Top-3 success rate	Processing time
Ours	94%	99%	$\mu = 280\,\text{ms}, \sigma = 20\,\text{ms}$
Dex-Net [13]	87%	96%	$\mu = 160\,\text{ms}, \sigma = 10\,\text{ms}$

superior grasping success rate of our heuristic compared to the state-of-the-art algorithm based on Dex-Net [13] that achieves 87% top-1 and 96% top-3 success rates in the same setup. Since the speed of the robot gives ~350 ms of computation time for calculating the next grasping poses, the speed advantage of DexNet does not provide any benefits in the meal preparation scenario. Hence, the main comparative indicator in this context is the grasping success rate.

Due to identical grasp success rates within a small comparative evaluation of the grasping process between the high-speed robot and the simple setup, we assume that the results of the extended experiments with the simple system can be safely transferred to the high-speed setup.

6   Conclusion

In this paper, we described a system for high-speed picking of packaged food for automated meal preparation in healthcare facilities. We proposed a new method for model-free grasping pose detection in cluttered scenes optimized for the picking of packaged food. The method uses depth information provided by a depth camera to recognize suction grasps on the surfaces of the objects and ranks them by heuristically estimating a grasping score based on surface regularity. We evaluated the algorithm on a robotic system and achieved a superior grasp success rate of 94% compared to a state-of-the-art method, within a processing time of ~280 ms. A high-speed robot was used to verify that grasp execution is possible within the specified time restrictions of less than 1 s per grasping and placing cycle for the packaged food. We conclude that the described system is a viable approach for meal preparation and could reduce the high physical demand of workers in healthcare facilities.

Acknowledgments. This work has received funding from the German Ministry of Education and Research (BMBF) under grant agreement No 01IS21061A for the Sim4Dexterity project and the Baden-Württemberg Ministry of Economic Affairs, Labour and Tourism for the AI Innovation Center "Learning Systems and Cognitive Robotics".

Table 2. Grasping evaluation results for the components ablation study.

Method	Top-1 SR	Top-3 SR	Processing time
Dex-Net [13]	87%	96%	$\mu = 160\,\text{ms}, \sigma = 10\,\text{ms}$
Ours	94%	99%	$\mu = 280\,\text{ms}, \sigma = 20\,\text{ms}$
No grasp rejection ray-casting	77%	90%	$\mu = 170\,\text{ms}, \sigma = 10\,\text{ms}$
No grasp set pruning	94%	97%	$\mu = 280\,\text{ms}, \sigma = 20\,\text{ms}$

Appendix

We provide an ablation and hyperparameter study for the components of the grasping pose detection method. The experimental conditions and setup are identical to the evaluations reported in Sect. 5. A reduced number of 100 grasping cycles are performed per experiment, and the grasping success rate as well as the mean μ and standard deviation σ of the processing time for each cycle, including image retrieval and grasp computation, are evaluated. All grasp pose detection calculations are performed on an Nvidia RTX3090 GPU. During each cycle, the grasp with the highest score is executed first. If this is unsuccessful, up to two more grasp attempts are made without recomputing the grasps to measure both the top-1 and top-3 accuracy.

For the component ablation study, the algorithm is evaluated when grasp rejection via the proposed ray-casting approach is not used. In addition, the top-3 success rate is measured when the grasp set is not pruned and all grasping poses whose distance to other candidates is smaller than the suction cup diameter are retained. The results are shown in Table 2.

We observe that the grasping success rate without the ray-casting rejection approach drops to a top-1 performance of 77% with a reduced processing time of ~170 ms. The failed grasps here are attributed to noise in the camera image leading to invalid grasps, which are prevented by checking the local area against the suction cup in the ray-casting process. For the experiment without pruning of the grasp set, we see that the top-3 performance slightly declines to 97% with a negligible processing time difference in the range of microseconds. Thus, the results of the ablation study show the positive impact of the developed algorithm components.

For the hyperparameter study of the grasping detection process, the impact of changes in individual parameters on the success rate and processing time is investigated, with all other parameters remaining unchanged. The optimal hyperparameters used in the results in Sect. 5 are: neighborhood size $A = 5 \times 5$, threshold $c = 0.9$, and iterations $T = 5$. The results for the varied parameters A, c and T are shown in Table 3.

We observe that when varying the neighborhood size A, the grasping results show negligible differences in both success rates and speed, indicating that any of the neighborhood sizes can be chosen for successful grasping. For the threshold parameter c, on the other hand, we find a strong difference in success rates: for

Table 3. Grasping evaluation results for the hyperparameter study.

Method	Top-1 SR	Top-3 SR	Processing time
Dex-Net [13]	87%	96%	$\mu = 160\,\text{ms}, \sigma = 10\,\text{ms}$
Ours	94%	99%	$\mu = 280\,\text{ms}, \sigma = 20\,\text{ms}$
Heuristic hyperparameters:			
Neighborhood size $A = 3 \times 3$	93%	99%	$\mu = 280\,\text{ms}, \sigma = 20\,\text{ms}$
Neighborhood size $A = 7 \times 7$	94%	99%	$\mu = 280\,\text{ms}, \sigma = 20\,\text{ms}$
Threshold value $c = 0.95$	90%	98%	$\mu = 280\,\text{ms}, \sigma = 20\,\text{ms}$
Threshold value $c = 0.7$	83%	90%	$\mu = 280\,\text{ms}, \sigma = 20\,\text{ms}$
Iterations $T = 2$	92%	95%	$\mu = 270\,\text{ms}, \sigma = 20\,\text{ms}$
Iterations $T = 8$	90%	99%	$\mu = 290\,\text{ms}, \sigma = 20\,\text{ms}$

smaller thresholds $c = 0.7$, the top-1 success rate drops to 83%. This is because with smaller thresholds, the object edges are smoothed by the heuristic and the proposed grasps are predicted closer to the edges, leading to more failed grasps. For larger thresholds $c = 0.95$, small irregularities, e.g., on the lid of objects, lead to strongly varying grasp quality values with many local maxima that are not centered on the objects and thus can lead to unstable grasps. Finally, for the number of iterations T the heuristic is applied to the scene, we find that the grasping success declines for both a higher or lower number of iterations. We assume that this hyperparameter, which depends on the object sizes in pixels, must be tuned individually for the given camera intrinsic parameters and distance of the camera from the objects.

References

1. Detry, R., Ek, C.H., Madry, M., Kragic, D.: Learning a dictionary of prototypical grasp-predicting parts from grasping experience. In: 2013 IEEE International Conference on Robotics and Automation (ICRA 2013), pp. 601–608. IEEE (2013). https://doi.org/10.1109/ICRA.2013.6630635
2. Dong, Z., et al.: PPR-Net:point-wise pose regression network for instance segmentation and 6D pose estimation in bin-picking scenarios. In: 2019 IEEE/RSJ International Conference on Intelligent Robots and Systems (IROS). IEEE (2019). https://doi.org/10.1109/iros40897.2019.8967895
3. El-Shamouty, M., Kleeberger, K., Lämmle, A., Huber, M.: Simulation-driven machine learning for robotics and automation. tm - Technisches Messen **86**(11), 673–684 (2019). https://doi.org/10.1515/teme-2019-0072
4. Kleeberger, K., Bormann, R., Kraus, W., Huber, M.F.: A survey on learning-based robotic grasping. Current Robot. Rep. **1**(4), 239–249 (2020). https://doi.org/10.1007/s43154-020-00021-6

5. Kleeberger, K., Huber, M.F.: Single shot 6D object pose estimation. In: 2020 IEEE International Conference on Robotics and Automation (ICRA). IEEE (2020). https://doi.org/10.1109/icra40945.2020.9197207

6. Kopicki, M., Detry, R., Schmidt, F., Borst, C., Stolkin, R., Wyatt, J.L.: Learning dexterous grasps that generalise to novel objects by combining hand and contact models. In: 2014 IEEE International Conference on Robotics and Automation (ICRA 2014), pp. 5358–5365. IEEE (2014). https://doi.org/10.1109/ICRA.2014.6907647

7. Kroemer, O., Ugur, E., Oztop, E., Peters, J.: A kernel-based approach to direct action perception. In: 2012 IEEE International Conference on Robotics and Automation (ICRA 2012), pp. 2605–2610. IEEE (2012). https://doi.org/10.1109/ICRA.2012.6224957

8. Kumra, S., Kanan, C.: Robotic grasp detection using deep convolutional neural networks. In: 2017 IEEE/RSJ International Conference on Intelligent Robots and Systems (IROS). IEEE (2017). https://doi.org/10.1109/iros.2017.8202237

9. Lenz, I., Lee, H., Saxena, A.: Deep learning for detecting robotic grasps. In: Robotics: Science and Systems IX. Robotics: Science and Systems Foundation (2013). https://doi.org/10.15607/rss.2013.ix.012

10. Levine, S., Pastor, P., Krizhevsky, A., Quillen, D.: Learning hand-eye coordination for robotic grasping with large-scale data collection. In: Kulić, D., Nakamura, Y., Khatib, O., Venture, G. (eds.) ISER 2016. SPAR, vol. 1, pp. 173–184. Springer, Cham (2017). https://doi.org/10.1007/978-3-319-50115-4_16

11. Mahler, J., et al.: Dex-Net 2.0: deep learning to plan robust grasps with synthetic point clouds and analytic grasp metrics. In: Amato, N. (ed.) Robotics: Science and System XIII. Robotics, Robotics Science and Systems Foundation (2017). https://doi.org/10.15607/RSS.2017.XIII.058

12. Mahler, J., Matl, M., Liu, X., Li, A., Gealy, D., Goldberg, K.: Dex-Net 3.0: computing robust vacuum suction grasp targets in point clouds using a new analytic model and deep learning. In: 2018 IEEE International Conference on Robotics and Automation (ICRA). IEEE (2018). https://doi.org/10.1109/icra.2018.8460887

13. Mahler, J., et al.: Learning ambidextrous robot grasping policies. Sci. Robot. 4(26) (2019). https://doi.org/10.1126/scirobotics.aau4984

14. Morrison, D., Corke, P., Leitner, J.: Learning robust, real-time, reactive robotic grasping. Int. J. Robot. Res. 39(2–3), 183–201 (2020). https://doi.org/10.1177/0278364919859066

15. Morrison, D., Leitner, J., Corke, P.: Closing the loop for robotic grasping: a real-time, generative grasp synthesis approach. In: Kress-Gazit, H., Srinivasa, S., Atanasov, N. (eds.) Robotics: Science and Systems XIV. Robotics Science and Systems Foundation (2018). https://doi.org/10.15607/RSS.2018.XIV.021

16. ten Pas, A., Gualtieri, M., Saenko, K., Platt, R.: Grasp pose detection in point clouds. Int. J. Robot. Res. 36(13–14), 1455–1473 (2017). https://doi.org/10.1177/0278364917735594

17. Satish, V., Mahler, J., Goldberg, K.: On-policy dataset synthesis for learning robot grasping policies using fully convolutional deep networks. IEEE Robot. Autom. Lett. 4(2), 1357–1364 (2019). https://doi.org/10.1109/lra.2019.2895878

18. Telea, A.: An image inpainting technique based on the fast marching method. J. Graph. Tools **9**(1), 23–34 (2004). https://doi.org/10.1080/10867651.2004.10487596
19. Tremblay, J., To, T., Sundaralingam, B., Xiang, Y., Fox, D., Birchfield, S.: Deep object pose estimation for semantic robotic grasping of household objects. In: Billard, A., Dragan, A., Peters, J., Morimoto, J. (eds.) Proceedings of The 2nd Conference on Robot Learning. Proceedings of Machine Learning Research, vol. 87, pp. 306–316. PMLR (2018)
20. Zeng, A., et al.: Robotic pick-and-place of novel objects in clutter with multi-affordance grasping and cross-domain image matching. In: Lynch, K. (ed.) 2018 IEEE International Conference on Robotics and Automation (ICRA), pp. 3750–3757. IEEE (2018). https://doi.org/10.1109/ICRA.2018.8461044

TrackAgent: 6D Object Tracking via Reinforcement Learning

Konstantin Röhrl[1] , Dominik Bauer[1,2(✉)] , Timothy Patten[3] ,
and Markus Vincze[1]

[1] TU Wien, Vienna, Austria
[2] Columbia University, New York, USA
`dominik.bauer@columbia.edu`
[3] Abyss Solutions Pty Ltd, Sydney, Australia

Abstract. Tracking an object's 6D pose, while either the object itself or
the observing camera is moving, is important for many robotics and augmented reality applications. While exploiting temporal priors eases this
problem, object-specific knowledge is required to recover when tracking
is lost. Under the tight time constraints of the tracking task, RGB(D)-
based methods are often conceptionally complex or rely on heuristic
motion models. In comparison, we propose to simplify object tracking
to a reinforced point cloud (depth only) alignment task. This allows us
to train a streamlined approach from scratch with limited amounts of
sparse 3D point clouds, compared to the large datasets of diverse RGBD
sequences required in previous works. We incorporate temporal frame-to-
frame registration with object-based recovery by frame-to-model refinement using a reinforcement learning (RL) agent that jointly solves for
both objectives. We also show that the RL agent's uncertainty and a
rendering-based mask propagation are effective reinitialization triggers.

Keywords: Object Pose Tracking · 3D Vision · Reinforcement
Learning

1 Introduction

6D object tracking from sequences of images or video streams has broad applications in computer vision systems. For example, knowing the pose of targets in
every frame enables robotic manipulators to grasp objects in dynamic environments [12,16,22] likewise, high-frequency poses of obstacles such as pedestrians
must be known to plan collision free paths in autonomous driving [9,15].

Multi-frame object tracking exploits prior information in the form of previous estimates. Similar to image or point cloud registration, corresponding
information is matched between consecutive frames. However, tracking errors

We gratefully acknowledge the support of the EU-program EC Horizon 2020 for
Research and Innovation under grant agreement No. 101017089, project TraceBot,
the Austrian Science Fund (FWF), project No. J 4683, and Abyss Solutions Pty Ltd.

H. I. Christensen et al. (Eds.): ICVS 2023, LNCS 14253, pp. 323–335, 2023.
https://doi.org/10.1007/978-3-031-44137-0_27

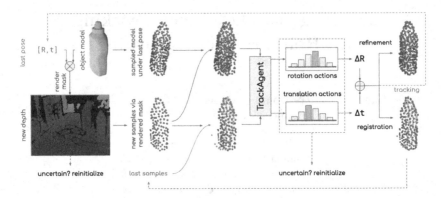

Fig. 1. Given a new depth observation, a point cloud segment is extracted by rendering the tracked object under its last known pose. *TrackAgent* then jointly solves two subtasks, namely registration of the observations and pose refinement with respect to the object model. The predicted alignment action iteratively improves the estimated pose, thus tracking an object over multiple frames. If the agent's uncertainty is large, reinitialization is automatically triggered.

may accumulate and complicate estimation in following frames. In comparison, single-frame object pose estimation may recover from such errors by computing the pose from scratch in every frame. Without leveraging temporal information to constrain the potential object poses, however, this becomes a more difficult and computationally expensive problem to solve. This is further exacerbated by an additional refinement step that aligns an object model in the estimated pose to the current frame, e.g., with the Iterative Closest Point (ICP) algorithm [5].

Both tracking [20,24] and pose estimation [13,23] typically use RGB observations. While textural information allows an object's pose to be accurately determined, RGB features are susceptible to illumination changes and require large volumes of real(istic) training data to learn them. Depth information, on the other hand, is more robust to changes in texture and illumination. Depth-based features are learned data efficiently [4] from low-resolution 3D point clouds. Yet, this robustness is paid for by increased ambiguity between similar geometrical shapes, e.g., of multiple box-like objects. Keeping track of the observed segments that correspond to the moving object is therefore complicated.

We observe the complementary nature of tracking via frame-to-frame registration and frame-to-model refinement, as illustrated in Fig. 1. In our proposed hybrid tracking approach, temporal information is exploited by 1) registration of corresponding segments between frames and 2) refinement of the object's model under its previously predicted pose to the current frame's segment. Both objectives are jointly and efficiently solved by a reinforcement learning (RL) agent as a depth-based, point cloud alignment problem. Using a replay buffer to gather the agent's experience during training, the reward may be considered over multiple steps in a single frame or over long time horizons across multiple frames, gaining flexibility over end-to-end supervision. To deal with the ambiguity in the depth modality, we propagate the segmentation information by rendering the mask of the tracked object under its previously predicted pose. Furthermore, our method identifies when the tracked object is lost by considering the confidence of its own estimated pose and mask predictions.

We demonstrate state-of-the-art (SotA) performance for depth-based object tracking on the YCB-Video dataset [27], closing the gap towards the performance of RGBD-based trackers. We also conduct an ablation study that highlights the efficacy of our hybrid approach over only employing registration and refinement alone as well as alternative subtask fusion methods.

2   Related Work

This section discusses related work of registration, that finds a transformation that aligns two point clouds; object pose refinement, which aims to find such a transformation between a (point cloud) observation and a (3D model of an) object; and tracking, which additionally considers object movement.

2.1   Point Cloud Registration

The Iterative Closest Point algorithm [5] is fundamental to solving the registration task. However, ICP may become stuck in a local optimum and therefore many variants are built around its basic *match-and-update* loop [18,21]. Seminal work by Aoki et al. [2] computes global features per input point cloud using PointNet [17] and proposes a variant of the Lucas-Kanade algorithm to iteratively align the input point clouds. Bauer et al. [3] train an RL agent to predict these pose updates, treating the global features as its state vector.

Compared to these registration approaches, we propose to additionally consider the refinement towards the tracked object's 3D model to increase robustness to low overlap between the registered point clouds.

2.2   Object Pose Refinement

Building upon the RL-based registration in [3], SporeAgent [4] leverages object-related information in the form of symmetries, segmentation labels and physical constraints with respect to multi-object scenes that are jointly refined. Using RGB images as input instead, DeepIM [14] matches an observed and a rendered image of the object under the currently predicted pose to predict refinement transformations. PoseRBPF [8] pairs a Rao-Blackwellized particle filter with an auto-encoder network. Each particle corresponds to a translation hypothesis. Rotation is determined by comparing each hypotheses image crop to precomputed embeddings for the object under discretized rotations.

Our proposed approach achieves temporal consistency by adding a registration objective to the refinement tasks. Compared to RGB-based refinement approaches, depth-based refinement is found to increase data efficiency [4] and we further motivate depth-based tracking by robustness to sensor noise since the registration subtask may align point clouds from the same (noisy) distribution.

2.3 Object Pose Tracking

Refinement approaches are also used in object pose tracking. By initializing DeepIM [14] with the previous frame's pose estimate, tracking performance comparable to dedicated RGBD approaches is achieved. However, since there is no specific means for maintaining object permanence, reinitializations are required when tracking is lost. More adjusted to the tracking task, particles in PoseRBPF [8] are resampled according to a motion model, which exploits temporal consistency between frames. se(3)-TrackNet [24] proposes a novel feature encoding that improves sim-to-real transfer, thus being able to train on large volumes of synthetic data. The Lie algebra is used to better formulate the loss function for learning pose transformations. Recently, ICG [20] tracks textureless objects with a probabilistic model. Colour information derives a region-based probability density function (PDF) that represents the corresponding lines between a model and its contour in the image plane, while depth information formulates a geometric PDF. Optimizing the joint PDF finds the pose that best explains the observation (fundamentally similar to ICP [5]) to track the object.

Rather than attempting to further extend these already complex tracking pipelines, we follow the simpler approach of using the previous frame's poses for initialization [14] and to propagate segmentation information by rendering. However, we only require depth rendering to crop the observed point cloud and track uncertainty, making textureless 3D models sufficient. By casting tracking as a joint registration and refinement task of 3D point clouds, a slim encoder results in more efficient training than in RGB(D)-based approaches.

3 TrackAgent: Reinforced Object Pose Tracking

We consider object pose tracking as a combination of two subtasks. First, the corresponding point cloud observations of an object are aligned between consecutive frames (*registration*). Starting from an initially known pose, the resulting relative transformations yield the object's pose in subsequent time steps. Second, the point cloud observation of an object in each individual frame is aligned to its 3D model (*refinement*). Importantly, this subtask enables tracking even when two point cloud observations do not overlap as the object model serves as a common reference frame. In this work we show that the joint consideration of these two subtasks results in better tracking performance over each in isolation.

Figure 1 gives an overview of our proposed pipeline. In Sect. 3.1, we outline our proposed RL pipeline that solves these two subtasks in a unified manner. In Sect. 3.2 a means to propagate the point cloud observation's segmentation via mask rendering is presented. We moreover discuss heuristics that leverage existing information in our pipeline to automatically trigger a reinitialization when tracking confidence deteriorates.

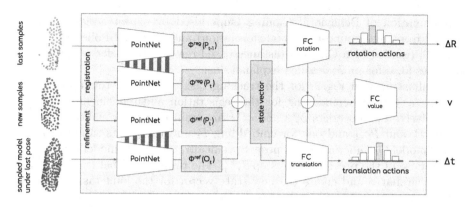

Fig. 2. One iteration of *TrackAgent*. Two separate global feature embeddings are learned, one per subtask. These are concatenated to become the state vector of the policy network, which predicts action distributions for rotation and translation. Its goal is to align the current observation more closely with, both, the previous observation and the model. This is repeated for 10 iterations per frame and the final prediction initializes the tracker in the next frame.

3.1 Keeping Track of the Pose: A Reinforced Agent Architecture for Joint Point Cloud Registration and Refinement

Defining the Subtasks: Let D_t be the depth image at time t and M_t the corresponding segmentation mask for the tracked object. We extract a 3D point cloud P_t from these inputs using the segmented depth and the camera intrinsics. The object is described by its uniformly sampled 3D model O and pose T_t.

The task of registration is to align P_t to P_{t-1} by a rigid transformation T_t^{reg}. Given an initial pose T_0 and by accumulating all relative registration transformations over $t \in (0, T]$, the object's pose T_T is computed for a given time step T. Similarly, we define the task of refinement as finding the alignment by a rigid transformation T_t^{ref} of P_t to the object's model under some initial pose estimate $O_t = T_{t-1} \cdot O_{t-1}$. The combined tracking task that we are aiming to solve is therefore to find a *single* rigid transformation T_t^{tra} that complies with both subtasks' objectives, i.e., $T_t^{reg} = T_t^{ref} = T_t^{tra}$. This may be viewed as aligning the point clouds from two consecutive frames to one another *as well as* to the common reference frame of the tracked object, i.e., its model.

Defining the Agent's Architecture: We base our pipeline on related works that treat point cloud alignment as an RL task, previously applied to the registration [3] and refinement [4] subtasks. To align two point clouds, these approaches first extract a global feature vector per point cloud with a PointNet-like embedding [17]. Both vectors are concatenated to create a state vector for the alignment policy. Using two separate network branches, discrete distributions are predicted that are interpreted as the policy's rotation and translation actions. The highest-probable actions are selected and the combined transformation constitutes the prediction to more closely align the two point clouds. The agent is trained with a combination of Behavioral Cloning (supervised by expert actions that are derived from the ground-truth transformation) and Proximal Policy Optimization [19] (guided by a Chamfer distance based reward). We refer readers to the baselines [3,4] for more detailed explanations.

As illustrated in Fig. 2, for the tracking task, we extend this approach by learning a separate embedding for the registration and refinement objectives, respectively. Two encoders ϕ^{reg} and ϕ^{ref} are trained, one for embedding point clouds P_t and P_{t-1} and one for embedding P_t and the points sampled on the object model O_t under an initial pose. Specifically, the object model is initialized by the pose of the previous time step T_{t-1}^{tra}. The resulting global feature vectors are concatenated and create the new state vector for the joint task. The same policy network as in the baseline approach is used to predict alignment actions based on this state. See Sect. 4.3 for a comparison with alternative early (shared embedding) and late fusion (separate policy networks) of subtask information.

Defining the Agent's Reward: The baseline approaches reward the agent for obtaining a closer alignment over multiple steps i in a single frame with respect to the Chamfer distance d between the two point clouds by the reward

$$r = \begin{cases} +0.5, & d_i < d_{i-1}, \\ -0.1, & d_i = d_{i-1}, \\ -0.6, & d_i > d_{i-1}, \end{cases} \tag{1}$$

that is, reinforcing a closer alignment, giving a small penalty for pausing steps and a large penalty for diverging steps. The authors of [3] suggest that using a larger value for diverging than for alignment should discourage the agent from alternating between the two (as a shortcut to increase its reward).

We want to further reinforce the agent to maintain a close alignment over multiple *frames*, not just steps. The intuition is that an alignment that complicates tracking in subsequent frames should be penalized; conversely, an alignment that serves as useful initialization should be reinforced. A straightforward solution to achieve this is to reuse the multi-step reward in Eq. (1) for the final estimates (i.e., final step) in each frame. We find that combining both timescales works best, as the dense multi-step reward signal simplifies the training as compared to using a sparse multi-frame reward on its own.

3.2   Keeping Track of the Observation and the Agent's Uncertainty: Mask Propagation and Automatic Reinitialization Triggers

Propagating and Refining Mask Information: Based on the agent's prediction, we render the corresponding 3D object model under the estimated pose to create the segmentation mask for the following frame. This keeps track of the point cloud segment that corresponds to the object of interest. A segmentation branch, introduced in [4], refines the resulting point cloud segment by rejecting outlier points from the max pooling operation of the state embedding. See [4] for a more detailed discussion of the branch's architecture.

As an additional benefit of the rendering-based mask propagation, we leverage the rendered depth image to compute tracking uncertainty with respect to the observed depth image. A visibility mask is computed that contains all pixels for which the rendered depth is at most τ behind the observed depth. The number of inlier pixels in the visibility mask is small if there is either a large misalignment (tracking lost) or heavy occlusion (observation lost). In both situations, reinitialization is needed. Relying only on this observed uncertainty, however, results in high sensitivity to heavy occlusion.

Combining Uncertainty-based Reinitialization Triggers: An alternative source for tracking uncertainty stems from the interpretation of the agent's action distribution. Intuitively, the agent learns to classify the misalignment into discrete steps along each axis and in terms of both translation and rotation. Therefore, in the ideal case where the agent eventually aligns the observations, it should predict a *zero-step* action in the final iteration on each frame. We exploit this interpretation by triggering a reinitialization when the predicted misalignment (i.e., alignment stepsize) in the final iteration is consistently large over multiple frames. This is achieved by averaging the predicted stepsizes over multiple frames and selecting the reinitialization threshold such that it is also reached when a large step is predicted for individual frames. Yet, a strategy solely based on the agent's uncertainty may mistrigger reinitializations when either pose or observed points are far from the training distribution, even though the estimated pose might be close to alignment.

We find that, by combining these two strategies, the number of reinitializations is controllably balanced with the achieved tracking performance. In Sect. 4.3, we investigate the effects of varying thresholds of the combined approach.

4   Experiments

In this section, we evaluate TrackAgent with established error metrics for object pose estimation and tracking using the publicly available BOP Toolkit [1] in comparison to other SotA object tracking methods. Additionally, we perform an ablation study to highlight the relevance of individual components.

4.1   Procedure

Data: The YCB-Video (YCB-V) dataset [27] consists of 92 video sequences of 21 YCB objects [6], where a camera moves around a static scene of up to six objects. The official dataset splits this into 80 sequences for training and 12 for testing. In this work, we only use every 7th frame in the 80 sequences for training and evaluate on all of the keyframes in the test set. No synthetic data is used.

Metrics: We consider the Average Distance of Model Points (ADD) and ADD with Indistinguishable Views (ADI) [10] as error metrics. ADD measures the mean distance between corresponding points of the model in the estimated and ground-truth poses, while ADI measures the mean distance between the nearest points. ADI is thus better suited for (geometrically) symmetrical objects.

Table 1. Result on YCB-V [27]. Reported recalls are the AUC (mean recall for equally-spaced thresholds in $(0, 10cm]$) in percent. Results for the RGBD (‡) and two of the depth-only baselines (†) are taken from [20]. All methods are (re)initialized with ground-truth poses. § indicates reinitialization every 30 frames. Best overall AUC per metric is highlighted in **bold**, best depth-based AUC per metric in *italics*.

AUC [%] ↑	se(3)‡ [24]		ICG‡ [20]		POT† [26]		RGF† [11]		ICP§ [5,28]		Reg§ [3]		Ref§ [4]		ours§		ours	
Metric	ADD	ADI	ADD	ADI	ADD	ADI	ADD	ADI	ADD	ADI	ADD	ADI	ADD	ADI	ADD	ADI	ADD	ADI
master chef can	**93.9**	**96.3**	66.4	89.7	55.6	90.7	46.2	90.2	78.7	*94.1*	*84.2*	92.2	80.2	91.6	76.8	92.0	75.0	91.1
cracker box	**96.5**	**97.2**	82.4	92.1	*96.4*	*97.2*	57.0	72.3	78.3	88.4	84.9	91.9	88.6	92.8	93.3	95.7	92.3	95.1
sugar box	**97.6**	98.1	96.1	**98.4**	97.1	97.9	50.4	72.7	81.0	92.2	89.8	94.9	95.7	97.4	95.6	97.0	95.6	97.0
tomato soup can	95.0	97.2	73.2	**97.3**	64.7	89.5	72.4	91.6	75.3	91.4	*92.8*	*95.8*	90.8	94.4	91.0	95.7	87.8	92.6
mustard bottle	95.8	97.4	96.2	**98.4**	*97.1*	98.0	87.7	*98.2*	88.0	94.4	94.3	96.4	96.6	97.7	96.0	97.5	96.1	97.6
tuna fish can	86.5	91.1	73.2	**95.8**	69.1	*93.3*	28.7	52.9	76.4	88.1	*90.4*	93.3	60.0	81.9	64.5	82.6	73.6	91.7
pudding box	**97.9**	**98.4**	73.8	88.9	*96.8*	*97.9*	12.7	18.0	81.5	91.4	93.6	96.1	89.2	94.0	94.4	96.5	94.0	96.4
gelatin box	**97.8**	98.4	97.2	**98.8**	*97.5*	*98.4*	49.1	70.7	81.3	92.0	95.7	97.1	87.6	92.9	96.9	97.7	96.9	97.7
potted meat can	77.8	84.2	**93.3**	**97.3**	*83.7*	86.7	44.1	45.6	81.6	*89.9*	75.5	80.7	77.5	80.1	78.9	82.5	83.4	88.8
banana	94.9	97.2	**95.6**	**98.4**	86.3	96.1	93.3	*97.7*	71.9	87.2	88.8	92.8	*94.8*	97.0	93.6	96.6	93.8	96.7
pitcher base	96.8	97.5	97.0	**98.8**	97.3	97.7	*97.9*	98.2	90.3	96.1	92.9	95.9	94.5	96.9	95.3	97.1	95.4	97.2
bleach cleanser	**95.9**	97.2	92.6	**97.5**	95.2	97.2	*95.9*	*97.3*	71.7	89.2	82.0	91.9	93.2	96.4	91.4	95.5	91.3	95.5
bowl	80.9	94.5	74.4	**98.4**	30.4	*97.2*	24.2	82.4	*78.1*	91.3	72.9	85.7	64.1	87.3	48.7	78.6	63.1	88.1
mug	91.5	96.9	**95.6**	**98.5**	83.2	93.3	60.0	71.2	81.8	93.3	84.0	89.6	93.9	96.6	*94.4*	*96.9*	94.3	96.9
power drill	96.4	97.4	96.7	**98.5**	97.1	97.8	*97.9*	*98.3*	78.1	90.3	90.6	94.1	94.1	96.2	92.4	95.0	94.3	96.5
wood block	95.2	96.7	93.5	**97.2**	*95.5*	*96.9*	45.7	62.5	71.9	90.5	83.6	91.6	89.4	95.6	91.3	95.6	91.4	95.6
scissors	**95.7**	**97.5**	93.5	97.3	35.6	4.2	16.2	20.9	38.6	39.9	73.5	57.3	69.1	70.2	79.5	72.3	80.1	90.0
large marker	**92.2**	96.0	88.5	**97.8**	35.6	53.0	12.2	18.9	51.1	70.5	50.5	66.4	45.6	64.6	54.9	68.4	67.0	*94.2*
large clamp	**94.7**	**96.9**	91.8	96.9	61.2	72.3	62.8	80.1	63.6	77.6	81.0	87.5	*82.1*	88.6	*82.1*	89.0	81.9	89.7
extra large clamp	91.7	95.8	85.9	94.3	*93.7*	*96.6*	67.5	69.7	60.5	80.2	80.7	88.5	78.7	88.2	89.1	94.9	90.8	95.7
foam brick	93.7	96.7	96.2	**98.5**	*96.8*	*98.1*	70.0	86.5	69.6	83.8	94.7	96.4	85.2	90.9	95.3	96.9	95.1	96.9
All Frames	**93.0**	95.7	86.4	**96.5**	78.0	90.2	59.2	74.3	74.9	88.6	84.6	90.6	83.6	90.7	84.9	91.6	*86.8*	*93.6*

Implementation Details: For alignment actions, the stepsizes are set to $[0.00066, 0.002, 0.006, 0.018, 0.054]$, both in the positive and negative directions and with an additional "stop"-action (i.e., stepsize 0). These are set to radians for rotation and to units in the normalized space for translation.

During training, the agent is initialized with the ground-truth pose and learns from trajectories of ten consecutive frames with ten alignment iterations each. We use two separate replay buffers each with a length of 128. The first contains the alignment trajectories in a single frame, while the second replay buffer is used to optimize trajectories over consecutive frames. To simulate inaccurate segmentation, we follow the augmentation strategy introduced in [4], where point clouds are sampled with 80% foreground and 20% background. In each epoch, a new set of trajectories is generated from the training split such that the total number of frames is equal to $1/5^{th}$ of all frames in our already subsampled dataset. This strategy both significantly reduces training time and increases generalization. The model is trained for 60 epochs with the same hyperparameters as in [4].

4.2   Tracking Performance on YCB-V

We report the performance of our proposed hybrid (registration and refinement) approach as well as the two subtasks individually on the YCB-V dataset in Table 1. As can be seen, the hybrid approach achieves higher ADD/ADI recall than agents that consider only one subtask. In comparison to the ICP and two other depth-based baselines [11, 26], all reinforced implementations (registration [3], refinement [4], ours) achieve better tracking performance. Moreover, our proposed reinitialization strategy further improves the AUC recall of our approach (right most column), while reducing the number of reinitializations as compared

Table 2. Ablation study on YCB-V [27] with different state vector fusion-variants.

Reinitialize every nth frame	30		90		120	
AUC [%] ↑	ADD	ADI	ADD	ADI	ADD	ADI
Registration	81.3	88.3	74.3	81.9	73.5	80.3
Refinement	83.6	90.7	78.0	85.0	77.3	85.1
Tracking (early fusion)	74.0	86.0	66.5	77.1	63.0	73.4
Tracking (late fusion)	83.7	90.2	77.2	84.3	76.4	83.3
TrackAgent	**84.9**	**91.6**	**80.0**	**87.3**	**79.3**	**86.6**

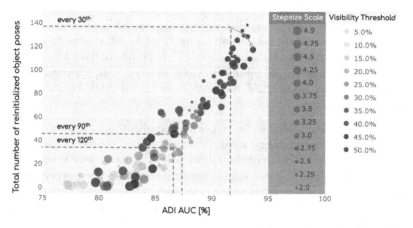

Fig. 3. Reinitialization experiments. Methods are grouped by the visibility threshold with the stepsize threshold indicated by the marker size. Reinitializations are counted and carried out per object. High visibility thresholds correspond to a significantly higher number of reinitializations, while a high threshold for the buffered stepsize reduces the number of reinitializations close to zero. For comparison, static reinitialization every 30/90/120th frame are shown (dashed). For each value we automatically find thresholds that reduce reinitializations while improving recall (gray arrows). Best viewed digitally.

to a fixed time interval (see Fig. 3). The results for SotA RGBD methods taken from [20] demonstrate that our approach is comparable despite only using the depth modality. The results are particularly similar to ICG [20] and we achieve similar performance compared to both se(3)-TrackNet [24] and ICG [20] for some objects. It should be noted that se(3)-TrackNet exploits a large volume of synthetic data in training where as ours and ICG do not.

4.3 Ablation Study

Subtask Fusion Variants: We compare variants of fusing the subtask information at different points in the agent's architecture. To identify the best combination of registration and refinement information, we explore three milestones

in the baseline architecture 1) input point clouds, 2) after state embedding, and
3) after the policy embeddings, resulting in three proposed architectures.

- *Early Fusion:* Merging the input point clouds, the architecture is unchanged
  and only a larger state dimension is used.
- *TrackAgent:* See Sect. 3.1 and Fig. 2.
- *Late Fusion:* Cloning the state embedding and duplicating the policy network,
  registration and refinement actions are separately predicted and merged.

Table 2 presents the results for the different fusion variants. Even though early
fusion is the most lightweight, our experiments show, unsurprisingly, that it is
outperformed by more complex strategies. Late fusion achieves similar results to
the refinement agent, not being able to leverage the additional temporal information of the registration task. Finally, our TrackAgent is able to outperform
agents that consider either subtask alone and both alternative fusion variants.
Depending on the number of reinitializations allowed, our approach is able to
increase the recall by up to 2.0% ADD AUC and 2.3% ADI AUC compared to
the second best variant.

Reinitialization Heuristics: In real-world applications, without annotated
data, a reinitialization strategy must not rely on any source of ground-truth,
but still trigger when tracking of the object is lost. A naive way is to reinitialize
after a certain time has elapsed, e.g., triggering reinitialization every 30 frames.
In comparison, the approach we propose in Sect. 3.2 leverages two measures of
uncertainty that are readily available in our tracking pipeline, namely visibility of the object under the predicted pose and the agent's action distribution.
Figure 3 visualizes an extensive study on how these two correlate and how they
affect the achieved tracking recall. Importantly, we see that, as compared to each
of the fixed reinitialization time steps, our automatic approach achieves a higher
recall using fewer reinitializations. The thresholds for each of the two measures
of uncertainty allow the tradeoff between tracking performance and the number
of required calls to a reinitialization method to be controlled.

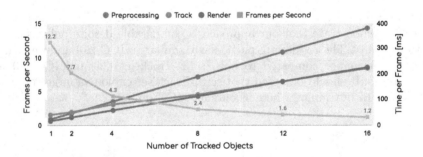

Fig. 4. Runtime of TrackAgent for a varying number of objects. Best viewed digitally.

Runtime: The runtimes shown in Fig. 4 are measured on a system equipped with an Intel i7-8700K and a NVIDIA Geforce RTX 2080 Ti. As shown, for a single object, the most time is spent on the forward pass of the network ("track"). However, parallel processing for multiple objects in a batch scales such that this becomes the fastest part at about 12 objects per frame. Conversely, preprocessing scales linearly and becomes the slowest part at about 4 objects. Optimizing this step, for example the extraction of the point cloud and its transfer to the GPU, has the potential to significantly decrease the runtime. Similarly, for rendering, the bottleneck is reading the rendered image from GPU to CPU memory for preprocessing. While minimal runtime is not the focus for this prototype, we see ample potential for our method in applications with tighter time constraints.

5   Discussion

Our experiments demonstrate that our approach using only depth data closes the gap with SotA RGBD object trackers. Notably, se(3)-TrackNet [24] also leverages a large volume of synthetic data, while we only use a fraction of the real data in the training split. Our ablation study highlights that jointly solving both subtasks of registration and refinement significantly outperforms each strategy on its own. By controlling thresholds on two uncertainty metrics, our proposed automatic reinitialization strategy balances the number of reinitializations with tracking accuracy.

While we exploit temporal information through mask propagation and the registration subtask, we expect the inclusion of a motion model to reduce the number of cases where tracking cannot be recovered. On one hand, this could prevent reinitializations that are far outside the training distribution, while still recovering by solving the refinement subtask. Similarly, we observe failure cases where a tracking error translates into decimated segmentation in the following steps, leading to an eventual loss of tracking. Again, accounting for (continuous) motion by enlarging the rendered mask along the movement direction might avoid losing the tracked object from the segmented point cloud. Finally, this would provide a means to ensure object permanence even under heavy occlusion or when the tracked object is outside the camera frame.

6   Conclusion

We presented TrackAgent: a reinforcement learning-based object tracking approach that combines registration with refinement. We show experimentally that our joint approach outperforms solving each subtask in isolation. We also demonstrate that the RL agent's uncertainty in its action predictions and mask propagation is an effective trigger for reinitialization. Finally, experiments on the YCB-V dataset show that TrackAgent is able to outperform all compared depth-only baselines and closes the gap to state-of-the-art RGBD trackers.

For future work, inspired by BundleSDF [25], a promising direction is to consider the subtask of object reconstruction during tracking. Another avenue for research is the consideration of multiple objects or hand-object interactions in dynamic scenes such as the DexYCB dataset [7], enabling the benefits of our RL-based tracker to be used in complex environments and handover scenarios.

References

1. BOP Toolkit. https://github.com/thodan/bop_toolkit
2. Aoki, Y., Goforth, H., Rangaprasad, A.S., Lucey, S.: PointNetLK: robust & efficient point cloud registration using PointNet. In: IEEE Conference on Computer Vision and Pattern Recognition, pp. 7156–7165 (2019)
3. Bauer, D., Patten, T., Vincze, M.: ReAgent: point cloud registration using imitation and reinforcement learning. In: IEEE Conference on Computer Vision and Pattern Recognition, pp. 14586–14594 (2021)
4. Bauer, D., Patten, T., Vincze, M.: SporeAgent: reinforced scene-level plausibility for object pose refinement. IEEE Winter Conference on Applications of Computer Vision, pp. 654–662 (2022)
5. Besl, P., McKay, N.: A method for registration of 3-D shapes. IEEE Trans. Pattern Anal. Mach. Intell. **14**, 239–256 (1992)
6. Calli, B., Walsman, A., Singh, A., Srinivasa, S.S., Abbeel, P., Dollar, A.M.: Benchmarking in manipulation research: using the Yale-CMU-Berkeley object and model set. IEEE Robot. Autom. Mag. **22**, 36–52 (2015)
7. Chao, Y.W., et al.: DexYCB: a benchmark for capturing hand grasping of objects. In: IEEE Conference on Computer Vision and Pattern Recognition, pp. 9044–9053 (2021)
8. Deng, X., Mousavian, A., Xiang, Y., Xia, F., Bretl, T., Fox, D.: PoseRBPF: a Rao-Blackwellized particle filter for 6D object pose tracking. In: Robotics: Science and Systems (2019)
9. Ess, A., Schindler, K., Leibe, B., Gool, L.V.: Object detection and tracking for autonomous navigation in dynamic environments. Int. J. Robot. Res. **29**(14), 1707–1725 (2010)
10. Hinterstoisser, S., et al.: Model based training, detection and pose estimation of texture-less 3D objects in heavily cluttered scenes. In: Lee, K.M., Matsushita, Y., Rehg, J.M., Hu, Z. (eds.) ACCV 2012. LNCS, vol. 7724, pp. 548–562. Springer, Heidelberg (2013). https://doi.org/10.1007/978-3-642-37331-2_42
11. Issac, J., Wüthrich, M., Cifuentes, C.G., Bohg, J., Trimpe, S., Schaal, S.: Depth-based object tracking using a robust gaussian filter. IEEE International Conference on Robotics and Automation, pp. 608–615 (2016)
12. Kappler, D., et al.: Real-time perception meets reactive motion generation. IEEE Robot. Autom. Lett. **3**(3), 1864–1871 (2018)
13. Labbé, Y., Carpentier, J., Aubry, M., Sivic, J.: CosyPose: consistent multi-view multi-object 6D pose estimation. In: Vedaldi, A., Bischof, H., Brox, T., Frahm, J.-M. (eds.) ECCV 2020. LNCS, vol. 12362, pp. 574–591. Springer, Cham (2020). https://doi.org/10.1007/978-3-030-58520-4_34
14. Li, Y., Wang, G., Ji, X., Xiang, Y., Fox, D.: DeepIM: deep iterative matching for 6D pose estimation. Int. J. Comput. Vis. **128**, 657–678 (2020)
15. Mao, J., Shi, S., Li, H.: 3D object detection for autonomous driving: a comprehensive survey. Int. J. Comput. Vis. 1573–1405 (2023)
16. Marturi, N., et al.: Dynamic grasp and trajectory planning for moving objects. Auton. Robots **43**, 1241–1256 (2019)

17. Qi, C., Su, H., Mo, K., Guibas, L.: PointNet: deep learning on point sets for 3D classification and segmentation. IEEE Conference on Computer Vision and Pattern Recognition, pp. 77–85 (2017)
18. Rusinkiewicz, S., Levoy, M.: Efficient variants of the ICP algorithm. In: International Conference on 3-D Digital Imaging and Modeling, pp. 145–152 (2001)
19. Schulman, J., Wolski, F., Dhariwal, P., Radford, A., Klimov, O.: Proximal policy optimization algorithms. arXiv preprint arXiv:1707.06347 (2017)
20. Stoiber, M., Sundermeyer, M., Triebel, R.: Iterative corresponding geometry: fusing region and depth for highly efficient 3D tracking of textureless objects. IEEE Conference on Computer Vision and Pattern Recognition, pp. 6855–6865 (2022)
21. Tam, G.K.L., et al.: Registration of 3D point clouds and meshes: a survey from rigid to nonrigid. IEEE Trans. Vis. Comput. Graph. **19**, 1199–1217 (2013)
22. Tuscher, M., Hörz, J., Driess, D., Toussaint, M.: Deep 6-DoF tracking of unknown objects for reactive grasping. IEEE International Conference on Robotics and Automation, pp. 14185–14191 (2021)
23. Wang, G., Manhardt, F., Tombari, F., Ji, X.: GDR-Net: geometry-guided direct regression network for monocular 6D object pose estimation. IEEE Conference on Computer Vision and Pattern Recognition, pp. 16611–16621 (2021)
24. Wen, B., Mitash, C., Ren, B., Bekris, K.E.: se(3)-TrackNet: data-driven 6D pose tracking by calibrating image residuals in synthetic domains. IEEE International Conference on Intelligent Robots and Systems, pp. 10367–10373 (2020)
25. Wen, B., et al.: BundleSDF: neural 6-DoF tracking and 3D reconstruction of unknown objects. arXiv preprint arXiv:2303.14158 (2023)
26. Wüthrich, M., Pastor, P., Kalakrishnan, M., Bohg, J., Schaal, S.: Probabilistic object tracking using a range camera. In: IEEE International Conference on Intelligent Robots and Systems, pp. 3195–3202 (2013)
27. Xiang, Y., Schmidt, T., Narayanan, V., Fox, D.: PoseCNN: a convolutional neural network for 6D object pose estimation in cluttered scenes. Robot.: Sci. Syst. (2018)
28. Zhou, Q.Y., Park, J., Koltun, V.: Open3D: a modern library for 3D data processing. arXiv preprint arXiv:1801.09847 (2018)

Improving Generalization of Synthetically Trained Sonar Image Descriptors for Underwater Place Recognition

Ivano Donadi, Emilio Olivastri, Daniel Fusaro, Wanmeng Li,
Daniele Evangelista, and Alberto Pretto

Department of Information Engineering (DEI), University of Padova, Padua, Italy
{donadiivan,olivastrie,fusarodani,liwanmeng,
evangelista,alberto.pretto}@dei.unipd.it

Abstract. Autonomous navigation in underwater environments presents challenges due to factors such as light absorption and water turbidity, limiting the effectiveness of optical sensors. Sonar systems are commonly used for perception in underwater operations as they are unaffected by these limitations. Traditional computer vision algorithms are less effective when applied to sonar-generated acoustic images, while convolutional neural networks (CNNs) typically require large amounts of labeled training data that are often unavailable or difficult to acquire. To this end, we propose a novel compact deep sonar descriptor pipeline that can generalize to real scenarios while being trained exclusively on synthetic data. Our architecture is based on a ResNet18 back-end and a properly parameterized random Gaussian projection layer, whereas input sonar data is enhanced with standard ad-hoc normalization/prefiltering techniques. A customized synthetic data generation procedure is also presented. The proposed method has been evaluated extensively using both synthetic and publicly available real data, demonstrating its effectiveness compared to state-of-the-art methods.

Keywords: Sonar Imaging · Underwater Robotics · Place Recognition

1 Introduction

Autonomous underwater vehicles (AUVs) represent a key enabling technology for carrying out complex and/or heavy but necessary operations in underwater environments in a totally safe way, such as exploration, assembly, and maintenance of underwater plants. AUVs could perform these tasks in a fully autonomous way, without the need for remote piloting and possibly without the need for a support vessel, with undoubted advantages from an economic, environmental, and personnel safety point of view.

However, autonomous navigation in underwater environments poses significant challenges due to factors such as light absorption and water turbidity. These factors severely limit the effectiveness of optical sensors like RGB cameras. Due

H. I. Christensen et al. (Eds.): ICVS 2023, LNCS 14253, pp. 336–349, 2023.
https://doi.org/10.1007/978-3-031-44137-0_28

to their immunity to the aforementioned limitations, the primary sensors used for perception in underwater operations are sonar systems. Sonars operate by emitting acoustic waves that propagate through the water until they encounter an obstacle or are absorbed. Nevertheless, sonar-generated acoustic images (often called *sonar images*) are affected by various sources of noise, including multi-path interference, cross-sensitivity, low signal-to-noise ratio, acoustic shadows, and poor pixel activation. As a result, traditional computer vision algorithms such as handcrafted feature detection and descriptor schemes, which typically perform relatively well on optical images, are less effective when applied to acoustic images. On the other hand, convolutional neural networks are capable of learning highly effective features from acoustic images. However, to effectively generalize, they typically require a large amount of labeled training data, which is often difficult to obtain due to the lack of large publicly available datasets. To address this limitation, simulation has emerged as an invaluable tool. Through synthetically generated data, it is possible to overcome the lack of available datasets and eliminate the need for manual data annotation.

In this work, we address the underwater place recognition problem by using a Forward-Looking Sonar (FLS) sensor, with the goal of improving the autonomous capabilities of underwater vehicles in terms of navigation. Like most place recognition pipelines, our goal is to extract a compact sonar image representation, i.e. an n-dimensional vector. Such compact representation can then be used to quickly match a query image (representing the current place the autonomous vehicle is in) with a database of descriptors (representing places already seen in the past). This process involves techniques such as nearest neighbor search to extract the most probable matching image. We introduce a new deep-features-based global descriptor of acoustic images that is able to generalize in different types of underwater scenarios. Our descriptor is based on a *ResNet18* back-end and a properly parameterized random Gaussian projection layer (RGP). We propose a novel synthetic data generation procedure that enables to make the training procedure extremely efficient and cost-effective when moved to large-scale environments. We also introduce a data normalization/pre-filtering step that helps improve overall performance. Our descriptor is trained to reside in a latent space that maintains as possible a bi-directional mapping with 3D underwater locations. Locally, cosine distances between descriptors aim to encode Euclidean distances between corresponding 3D locations. We provide an exhaustive evaluation of the proposed method on both synthetic and real data. Comparisons with state-of-the-art methods show the effectiveness of our method. As a further contribution, we release with this paper an open-source implementation[1] of our method.

2   Related Work

Visual place recognition is a classical computer vision and robotics task [20], which has been developed mainly in the context of optical images acquired with

---

[1] https://github.com/ivano-donadi/sdpr.

RGB cameras. Initially, traditional vision methods were employed to extract feature descriptors. However, they are limited by the overhead of manual features engineering and are now being gradually supplanted by deep learning-based methods, which on average perform better when properly trained. In this section, we first present previous works focusing on camera-based place recognition, both leveraging traditional and deep learning-based pipelines and then how they have been adapted in the context of underwater sonar images.

2.1 Traditional Methods

Traditional visual place recognition methods can be classified into two categories: global descriptor methods and local descriptor methods. The former approaches primarily focus on the global scene by predefining a set of key points within the image and subsequently converting the local feature descriptors of these key points into a global descriptor during the post-processing stage. For instance, the widely utilized Gist [25] and HoG [7] descriptors are frequently employed for place recognition across various contexts. On the other hand, the latter approaches rely on techniques such as Scale Invariant Feature Transformation (SIFT) [19], Speeded Up Robust Features (SURF) [4], and Vector of Local Aggregated Descriptor (VLAD) [11] to extract local feature descriptors. Since each image may contain a substantial number of local features, direct image matching suffers from efficiency degradation. To address this, some methods employ bag-of-words (BoW) [31] models to partition the feature space (e.g., SIFT and SURF) into a limited number of visual words, thereby enhancing computational efficiency.

2.2 Deep Learning-Based Methods

These methods typically rely on features extracted from a backbone CNN, possibly pre-trained on an image classification dataset [14]. For example, [32] directly uses the convolutional feature maps extracted by an AlexNet backbone as image descriptors. Other methods add a trainable aggregation layer to convert these features into a robust and compact representation. Some studies integrate classical techniques such as BoW and VLAD into deep neural networks to further encode deep features as global descriptors, among others in NetBoW [26], NetVLAD [2], and NetFV [24]. Expanding on this, [12] introduced the Contextual Re-weighting Network (CRN), which estimates the weight of each local feature from the backbone before feeding it into the NetVLAD layer. Additionally, [12] introduced spatial pyramids to incorporate spatial information into NetVLAD. Moreover, several other studies introduced semantic information to enhance the network's effectiveness by integrating segmentation tasks [35] and object detection tasks [33].

2.3 Underwater Place Recognition

Traditional vision methods, such as SURF [3] and BoW technique based on ORB features [9], have been used in underwater camera-based place recognition tasks.

However, these methods face limitations in complex underwater environments that require laborious pre-processing steps [1]. Deep place recognition solutions, such as an attention mechanism that leverages uniform color channels [22] and probabilistic frameworks [17], have been proposed to address these challenges. However, the attenuation of electromagnetic waves in water limits their effectiveness. As a result, underwater sonars have garnered attention from researchers as they are not affected by the aforementioned environmental conditions. For the first time, [18] proposed the use of features learned by convolutional neural networks as descriptors for underwater acoustic images. Building upon this, [5] introduced a siamese CNN architecture to predict underwater sonar image similarity scores. Then, [28] presented a variant of PoseNet that relies on the triplet loss commonly used in face recognition tasks. In particular, an open-source simulator [6] was utilized in this work to synthesize forward-looking sonar (FLS) images, from which the network learns features and ultimately performs well on real-world sonar datasets. Inspired by this, [16] utilized the triplet loss combined with ResNet to learn the latent spatial metric of side-scan sonar images, enabling accurate underwater place recognition. Additionally, [23] employed a fusion voting strategy using convolutional autoencoders to facilitate unsupervised learning of salient underwater landmarks.

3   Method

3.1   Synthetic Dataset Generation

Acquiring and annotating large quantities of sonar images to train and evaluate deep learning models is expensive and time-consuming. Moreover, collecting ground truth pose data can be impractical when the AUV is not close to the water surface since the GPS signal is not available. For this reason, we decided to collect our training data from a simulated environment in which we can freely control sonar parameters and easily retrieve ground truth pose information. In detail, sonar data has been collected using the simulation tool proposed in [40] and the Gazebo simulator[2]. A Tritech Gemini 720i sonar sensor with 30m range and 120° horizontal aperture has been simulated for the acquisitions. The data acquisition pipeline was set up according to the following steps:

- set up a simulated environment in Gazebo, populated by 3 man-made underwater structures (assets) widely separated in space, and an AUV equipped with the sonar sensor described above (Fig. 1);
- define a 2D square grid centered on each object and remove grid cells colliding with the framed object; in our simulations, the grid cell size is 2 m × 2 m and the total grid size is 50 m × 50 m (Fig. 1a, 1b, 1c). The size of the grid was chosen based on both the range of the sonar and the size of the asset. The cell's size parameters, instead, were chosen based on a trade-off that tried to maximize the difference between anchors' sonar images, while ensuring sufficient fine-grained spacing for localization purposes;

---

[2] https://gazebosim.org/home.

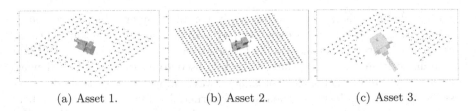

(a) Asset 1.   (b) Asset 2.   (c) Asset 3.

Fig. 1. Pose sampling distribution around each of the three objects in the simulated environment. Asset 2 and 3 were used for training the network and asset 1 was used for validation. Blue points are anchor poses and red points are possible positive/negative samples. (Color figure online)

- move the AUV at the center of each cell, and change its orientation so that it is facing the object at the center of the grid; then acquire a sonar scan and register it as an anchor (see Sect. 3.2);
- sample 5 other sonar scans by adding 0–75 cm of position noise with respect to the center of the cell, and register them all as possible positives/negatives (see Sect. 3.2).

We collect the datasets for the 3 assets separately, obtaining a total of 876 anchors and 4380 possible positives and negatives. With this dataset, we can assess the generalization ability of our method by training it on two assets and validating it on an unseen structure. The underwater assets and pose sampling distribution can be seen in Fig. 1.

It should be remarked that to properly assess the generalization capabilities of the proposed approach, the assets used in our simulated environment have a significantly different geometry than the ones framed in the public datasets used for the final experiments (see Sect. 4.1).

3.2   Triplet Descriptor Learning

In our approach, we follow a basic framework that is typically exploited for deep descriptor computation (e.g., [37]). We compute the descriptor of the sonar reading as the embeddings of a convolutional neural network (CNN) fed with the sonar image. The CNN is trained over a large dataset of sonar images by using a triplet loss. Each data item is composed by a reference sonar image (called anchor), a sonar image with a similar field of view (FOV) to the anchor image (called positive), and an image with a significantly different FOV than the anchor (called negative). Such a strategy has already been applied to sonar images in works such as [5,28]. Let A, P, and N be descriptors for respectively the anchor, positive and negative images; the triplet loss is then defined as:

$$L_T = max\{0, d(A, P) - d(A, N) + m\} \tag{1}$$

where d is a distance metric (usually the Euclidean distance) between descriptors and m is the margin hyper-parameter, representing the desired difference between positive-anchor similarity and negative-anchor similarity. A graphical intuition of the triplet loss is provided in Fig. 2a. In our implementation the distance metric used is based on cosine similarity rather than Euclidean distance: let $C_S(x,y) = \frac{x \cdot y}{||x||_2 \cdot ||y||_2}$ be the cosine similarity between two vectors x and y, then the distance metric between x and y is defined as $d_S(x,y) = 1 - C_S(x,y)$. When vectors are constrained to unit length, the squared Euclidean distance and the cosine distance are proportional, and we chose to use the latter because it provides a more intuitive choice of margin.

3.3 Triplet Generation

The triplet loss requires classifying training samples as positives or negatives with respect the any given anchor. To do so, we employed the metric proposed in [5], in which the similarity between two sonar scans is defined as the relative area overlap between the two sonar FOVs. Given a threshold τ, we classify a sample as negative if its similarity w.r.t the anchor is lower than the threshold, and as positive otherwise. Due to the grid-like nature of our training dataset, additional care is needed when computing sonar similarity scores: in particular, we need to set a maximum allowed orientation difference between the two scans in order to give low similarity to pairs at the opposite ends of the framed object, which share a large amount of area but frame two different object geometries (see Fig. 2a). In order to provide consistently significant samples for each anchor at each epoch, we sample a set of n_{neg} possible negative samples and n_{pos} possible positive samples, and perform batch-hardest negative mining [10] and batch-easiest positive mining [38] inside this sub-set by selecting the negative and positive samples whose descriptors are the closest to the anchor's, speeding up the training process while allowing a certain degree of intra-class variance. The actual values of the parameters we used in our experiment are detailed in Table 1. In particular, n_{pos} was chosen as to include all points sampled close to an anchor, as described in Sect. 3.1, while the choice of n_{neg} was upper-bounded by memory constraints.

3.4 Network Structure

The backbone of our model is a lightweight ResNet18 encoder network, modified to take single-channel inputs, with an output stride of 32 and without the final average pooling and fully connected layers. The network's input is raw sonar images (beams×bins) resized to 256×200. Starting from the input image, we extract, in the final convolutional layer, 512 feature maps of size 25×32, which are then flattened in a single high-dimensional vector descriptor. To reduce the descriptor size, we employ random Gaussian projection (RGP), as in [39], obtaining 128-dimensional image descriptors. Finally, descriptors are normalized to unit length. Our experiments reported no significant advantage when increasing the descriptor size for this task. Overall, our architecture and training strategy are similar to [16], with three key differences: we use cosine distance in place of

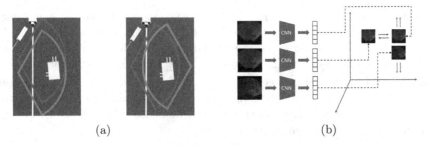

(a)   (b)

Fig. 2. Figure (a) shows two different cases of large sonar FOV overlap: the pair on the left should be classified as framing the same location, while the one on the right shouldn't, since the two objects sides are not symmetrical. Figure (b) provides a graphical intuition of the triplet loss training. This loss is used to learn a descriptor that makes similar images spatially close (e.g., top and middle images) and different images spatially distant (e.g., top and bottom images).

1x256x200   512x32x25   1x409600 409600x128   1x128

Fig. 3. Graphical representation of our descriptor extraction network.

Euclidean distance in the triplet loss, we replace the last fully connected layer with a fixed RGP matrix (resulting in fewer trainable parameters), and we focus on forward-looking sonar and not on side-scan sonar. A graphical representation of this pipeline can be found in Fig. 3. We also developed a different network structure based on NetVLAD descriptors [2], which are extensively used for camera-based place recognition, by keeping the same backbone and substituting the RGP layer with a NetVLAD aggregation layer. The performance of both methods is compared in Sect. 4.

3.5   Image Enhancement

Sonar images taken in a real environment are known to be plagued by a significant amount of additive and multiplicative noise [36]. Furthermore, the sonar emitter might not provide a uniform insonification of the environment, resulting in an intensity bias in some image regions. To mitigate these problems, we enhance real sonar images in three steps: first, we normalize the images to uniform insonification [13,29], then we filter them using discrete wavelet transforms (DWTs) as in [15], and finally we threshold the images with a Constant False Alarm Rate (CFAR) thresholding technique, obtaining binary images [8,34]. In

Table 1. List of parameter values used in our experiments.

Parameter	Value	Parameter	Value
τ	0.7	m	0.5
n_{neg}	10	n_{pos}	5
n_w	40	P_{fa}	0.1

particular, in the first step, the sonar insonification pattern is obtained by averaging a large number of images in the same dataset, and the resulting pattern is used to normalize pixel intensities. In the last step, synthetic images were thresholded using GOCA-CFAR (greatest of cell averaging) and real images using SOCA-CFAR (smallest of cell averaging). Both methods scan each sonar beam independently and select a personalized threshold for each sonar cell in the beam. Let c be the current sonar cell, and let w_l and w_t be windows of n_w cells respectively leading and trailing c in the beam. Let $\overline{w_l}$ and $\overline{w_t}$ be the average intensity in the two windows, then the threshold for SOCA-CFAR is selected as $\min(\overline{w_l}, \overline{w_t})$, while the threshold for GOCA-CFAR is equal to $\max(\overline{w_l}, \overline{w_t})$. Both thresholds are then weighted by a factor dependent on the desired false alarm rate P_{fa}. All CFAR parameters were selected by maximizing the human-perceived quality of the sonar images. Our DWT filtering procedure is identical to [15]. An example of the enhanced image can be seen in Fig. 4.

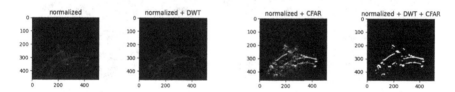

Fig. 4. Example of the proposed image enhancing procedure on a scan from the Wang2022 dataset [34]. Notice how applying CFAR directly on the normalized image is not enough to differentiate between objects of interest and noise.

4   Experiments

4.1   Datasets

We validated our method in three publicly available datasets:

- **Wang2022** [34]: This dataset was collected on a real dock environment to test the sonar-based SLAM approach presented in [34], using a BlueROV AUV equipped with an Oculus M750d imaging sonar, using maximum range equal to 30m and a horizontal aperture of 130°. This dataset has no ground truth pose annotations, so we relied on the author's SLAM implementation to

344   I. Donadi et al.

compute an accurate trajectory for the AUV. Unfortunately, pose annotations extracted with this method are only available for keyframes, resulting in 187 total annotated sonar scans, of which only 87 contain actual structures.

- **Aracati2014** [30]: This dataset was acquired in the Yacht Club of Rio Grande, in Brazil with an underwater robot mounting a Blueview·P900-130 imaging sonar with a maximum range equal to 30m and a horizontal aperture of 130°. Ground truth pose data was acquired by attaching a GPS system to a surfboard connected to the robot. This dataset contains over 10k sonar images, of which 3675 can be synchronized with the position and heading sensors. An additional filter is required to discard sonar scans looking at an empty scene, such as when the AUV is traveling away from any object, so 1895 images are actually usable for testing, similarly to [29]. The AUV's trajectory is displayed in Fig. 5a.
- **Aracati2017** [29]: This dataset was acquired in the same location as Aracati2014, but performed a different trajectory. The sonar sensor and parameters are unchanged except for the maximum range, which was set to 50m. 14350 annotated sonar images are provided, of which 8364 contain some underwater structures. The AUV trajectory can be seen in Fig. 5b.

(a)   (b)

Fig. 5. AUV trajectories for the two Aracati datasets: (a) Aracati2014 [21]. (b) Aracati2017 [29].

4.2   Metrics

Given a trained descriptor extractor D, it is possible to match two sonar images x, y by computing the distance between their descriptors $d_S(D(x), D(y))$ and comparing it against a certain threshold. Image pairs are considered a positive match if their descriptor distance falls below the threshold, and a negative match otherwise. When considering all possible image pairs in a dataset, it is possible to construct a table of all positive and negative matches, which is dependent on the value of the threshold used to classify pairs as positive or negative matches. An analogous table can be computed by considering ground truth matches based on the metric described in Sect. 3.3. Comparing the two tables it is possible to extract true positives (TP), true negatives (TN), false positives (FP), and false negatives (FN) as in any binary classification problem. Based on these values, we evaluated our model using several metrics commonly used in visual/sonar place recognition:

- **Area under the precision/recall curve (AUC)**: given a set of values for the matching threshold, we can compute precision ($\frac{TP}{TP+FP}$) and recall ($\frac{TP}{TP+FN}$) values for each threshold. The precision/recall curve is then obtained by using the precision as the y-axis and the recall as the x-axis. A high area under the curve metric signifies both high precision and high recall. We also report the precision and recall values at the optimal threshold, which is the one maximizing the F1 score.
- **Recall at 95% precision (R@95P)**: if a visual place recognition algorithm is to be used inside a loop detection system for SLAM, it is necessary to have high precision to avoid wrong loop closures. This metric allows to see the percentage of loop closures detected when requiring high precision.
- **Precision over FOV overlap**: In this metric, used by [28], we compute the FOV overlap between the test sonar image and its nearest neighbor - in the descriptors space - in the dataset, and compare it against a set of FOV overlap thresholds (from 10% to 90% in steps of 10%), obtaining the percentage of dataset images whose nearest neighbor share a percentage of FOV over the threshold. As in [28], we also report this metric when removing a window of $s = 3$ seconds, leading and trailing the query image in the trajectory, from the nearest neighbor search: this allows evaluating the ability of the sonar matching method to recognize previously seen locations when circling back to them, rather than in the subsequent trajectory frames.

4.3   Results

In this section, we compare the effectiveness of our model against the NetVLAD-based one on all three real datasets of Sect. 4.1. For the Aracati2014 dataset, we also provide a comparison with another triplet-loss-based sonar place recognition network, introduced in [28], which we will refer to as Ribeiro18 in the remainder of the paper. Results, in this case, are taken directly from [28]. This particular method was trained on the real Aracati2017 dataset and tested on Aracati2014, using 2048-dimensional descriptors. Additionally, we report the performance of our model with randomly initialized weights to assess the contribution of our training strategy to the network's performance. We will refer to this network as Random in the remainder of the paper.

Validation: Our training pipeline, outlined in Sect. 3, aims to establish a mapping between the environment's 3D space and the 128-dimensional latent descriptor space. To evaluate the effectiveness of our approach, we used a validation dataset consisting of regularly spaced anchors in the 3D space (Fig. 1a). We expect this regularity to be reflected in the latent space such that the difference between neighboring anchor descriptors should remain constant across the whole

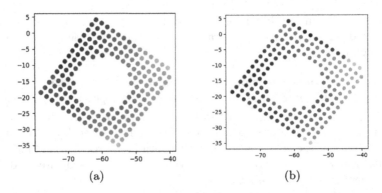

Fig. 6. Descriptor distribution in the Euclidean space: the color of each anchor is obtained by exploiting the 2D t-SNE projection of its descriptor as red and green RBG components, thus, the more smooth is the change in color, the better the descriptor distribution. In Figure (a) the results are obtained using our approach, while in Figure (b) are obtained using the NetVLAD method. (Color figure online)

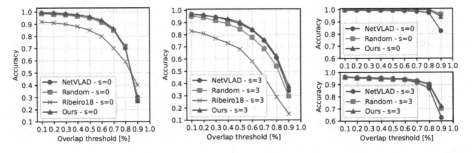

Fig. 7. Evaluation results on both Aracati datasets. In the first two columns we report the results for all methods on the Aracati2014 dataset, while the last column contains the accuracy over FOV overlap on the Aracati2017 dataset.

dataset. The qualitative results reported in Fig. 6 show that our approach successfully achieved this goal, with smoother transitions between nearby locations than NetVLAD.

Real Datasets: Table 2 reports the quantitative evaluation results of both our method and the NetVLAD-based network regarding the area under the precision/recall curve and the recall at 95% precision. We can see that our method is the best-performing one on both Aracati datasets, while NetVLAD performs best on the Wang2022 dataset. It might seem surprising that the non-trained network has a performance so close to the other two methods, especially in the case of $s = 0$, but it is justified by the fact that semi-identical images will provide semi-identical responses to any stable filtering technique, even if random. However, given the huge shift in the domain between training and test datasets, the fact that the trained models still provide superior place recognition abilities proves the effectiveness of the training. In Fig. 7, we report the precision

Table 2. Network performance. P and R columns contain precision and recall values at the optimal matching threshold. Due to the limited size of the Wang2022 dataset, we do not report the results for $s = 3$.

Method		Aracati2014				Aracati2017				Wang2022			
		AUC	P	R	R@95P	AUC	P	R	R@95P	AUC	P	R	R@95P
$s = 0$	Ours	**.86**	**.95**	**.95**	**.93**	.75	**.99**	**.99**	**.99**	.65	.89	.80	**.67**
	NetVLAD	.83	.92	.92	.14	.68	.95	.94	.00	**.79**	**.90**	**.86**	.65
	Random	.85	.94	.93	.78	**.91**	.99	.99	.99	.72	.90	.73	.53
$s = 3$	Ours	**.75**	**.86**	**.84**	.00	.86	**.93**	**.93**	**.83**	–	–	–	–
	NetVLAD	.72	.83	.83	**.01**	.70	.90	.89	.00	–	–	–	–
	Random	.63	.79	.77	.00	**.88**	.92	.92	.80	–	–	–	–

over FOV overlap for both our models and the Random and Ribeiro18 models. The data for the latter method was taken directly from the original paper. It is possible to see how, in the case $s = 0$, even the non-trained network is able to correctly retrieve matching images simply by matching subsequent (almost identical) frames. When setting $s = 3$, instead, the two trained networks show their learned ability to match the same scene from different points of view.

5   Conclusions

In this paper, we proposed a compact sonar image descriptor for underwater place recognition that is computed using deep CNNs trained only on simulated data of underwater scenarios. We demonstrate the effective generalization capabilities of our descriptor through extensive experiments and evaluations. In particular, our sonar descriptor has been validated both on simulated and real data and tested against other recent state-of-the-art approaches, obtaining promising results.

Future developments include the integration of a module capable of determining the distinctiveness of locations, in order to automatically remove sonar images that belong to empty areas, a domain-adaptation strategy to better mimic real data in simulation, and the use of more advanced sonar simulators [27].

Acknowledgements. This work was supported by the University of Padova under Grant UNI-IMPRESA-2020-SubEye.

References

1. Ansari, S.: A review on SIFT and SURF for underwater image feature detection and matching. In: 2019 IEEE International Conference on Electrical, Computer and Communication Technologies (ICECCT) (2019)
2. Arandjelović, R., Gronat, P., Torii, A., Pajdla, T., Sivic, J.: NetVLAD: CNN architecture for weakly supervised place recognition. IEEE Trans. Pattern Anal. Mach. Intell. (2018)
3. Aulinas, J., et al.: Feature extraction for underwater visual SLAM. In: OCEANS 2011 IEEE - Spain (2011)

4. Bay, H., Tuytelaars, T., Van Gool, L.: SURF: speeded up robust features. In: Leonardis, A., Bischof, H., Pinz, A. (eds.) ECCV 2006. LNCS, vol. 3951, pp. 404–417. Springer, Heidelberg (2006). https://doi.org/10.1007/11744023_32

5. Ribeiro, P.O.C.S., dos Santos, M.M., Drews, P.L., Botelho, S.S.: Forward looking sonar scene matching using deep learning. In: 2017 16th IEEE International Conference on Machine Learning and Applications (ICMLA) (2017)

6. Cerqueira, R., Trocoli, T., Neves, G., Oliveira, L., Joyeux, S., Albiez, J.: Custom Shader and 3D rendering for computationally efficient sonar simulation (2016)

7. Dalal, N., Triggs, B.: Histograms of oriented gradients for human detection. In: 2005 IEEE Computer Society Conference on Computer Vision and Pattern Recognition (CVPR'05) (2005)

8. Gandhi, P., Kassam, S.: Analysis of CFAR processors in nonhomogeneous background. IEEE Trans. Aerosp. Electron. Syst. 24, 427–445 (1988)

9. Gaspar, A.R., Nunes, A., Matos, A.: Limit characterization for visual place recognition in underwater scenes. In: Tardioli, D., Matellán, V., Heredia, G., Silva, M.F., Marques, L. (eds.) ROBOT2022: Fifth Iberian Robotics Conference (2023)

10. Hermans, A., Beyer, L., Leibe, B.: In defense of the triplet loss for person re-identification. CoRR (2017)

11. Jégou, H., Douze, M., Schmid, C., Pérez, P.: Aggregating local descriptors into a compact image representation. In: 2010 IEEE Computer Society Conference on Computer Vision and Pattern Recognition (2010)

12. Kim, H.J., Dunn, E., Frahm, J.M.: Learned contextual feature reweighting for image geo-localization. In: 2017 IEEE Conference on Computer Vision and Pattern Recognition (CVPR), pp. 3251–3260 (2017)

13. Kim, K., Neretti, N., Intrator, N.: Mosaicing of acoustic camera images. IEE Proc. Radar, Sonar Navig. 152, 263–270 (2005)

14. Krizhevsky, A., Sutskever, I., Hinton, G.E.: ImageNet classification with deep convolutional neural networks. Commun. ACM 60, 84–90 (2017)

15. Kumudham, R., Dhanalakshmi, Swaminathan, A., Geetha, Rajendran, V.: Comparison of the performance metrics of median filter and wavelet filter when applied on sonar images for denoising. In: 2016 International Conference on Computation of Power, Energy Information and Communication (ICCPEIC) (2016)

16. Larsson, M., Bore, N., Folkesson, J.: Latent space metric learning for sidescan sonar place recognition. In: 2020 IEEE/OES Autonomous Underwater Vehicles Symposium (AUV) (2020)

17. Li, J., Eustice, R.M., Johnson-Roberson, M.: Underwater robot visual place recognition in the presence of dramatic appearance change. In: OCEANS 2015 - MTS/IEEE Washington (2015)

18. Li, J., Ozog, P., Abernethy, J., Eustice, R.M., Johnson-Roberson, M.: Utilizing high-dimensional features for real-time robotic applications: reducing the curse of dimensionality for recursive Bayesian estimation. In: 2016 IEEE/RSJ International Conference on Intelligent Robots and Systems (IROS) (2016)

19. Lowe, D.: Object recognition from local scale-invariant features. In: Proceedings of the Seventh IEEE International Conference on Computer Vision (1999)

20. Lowry, S., et al.: Visual place recognition: a survey. IEEE Trans. Robot. 32, 1–19 (2016)

21. Machado, M., Drews, P., Núñez, P., Botelho, S.: Semantic mapping on underwater environment using sonar data. In: 2016 XIII Latin American Robotics Symposium and IV Brazilian Robotics Symposium (LARS/SBR) (2016)

22. Maldonado-Ramírez, A., Torres-Méndez, L.A.: Robotic visual tracking of relevant cues in underwater environments with poor visibility conditions. Sensors (2016)

23. Maldonado-Ramírez, A., Torres-Mendez, L.A.: Learning ad-hoc compact representations from salient landmarks for visual place recognition in underwater environments. In: 2019 International Conference on Robotics and Automation (ICRA) (2019)

24. Miech, A., Laptev, I., Sivic, J.: Learnable pooling with context gating for video classification (2018)

25. Oliva, A., Torralba, A.: Chapter 2 building the gist of a scene: the role of global image features in recognition. In: Visual Perception. Elsevier (2006)

26. Ong, E.J., Husain, S.S., Bober-Irizar, M., Bober, M.: Deep architectures and ensembles for semantic video classification. IEEE Trans. Circ. Syst. Video Technol. **29**, 3568–3582 (2019)

27. Potokar, E., Ashford, S., Kaess, M., Mangelson, J.: HoloOcean: an underwater robotics simulator. In: Proceedings of IEEE International Conference on Robotics and Automation, ICRA (2022)

28. Ribeiro, P.O.C.S., et al.: Underwater place recognition in unknown environments with triplet based acoustic image retrieval. In: 2018 17th IEEE International Conference on Machine Learning and Applications (ICMLA) (2018)

29. Santos, M.M., Zaffari, G.B., Ribeiro, P.O.C.S., Drews-Jr, P.L.J., Botelho, S.S.C.: Underwater place recognition using forward-looking sonar images: a topological approach. J. Field Robot. **36**(2), 355–369 (2019)

30. Silveira, L., et al.: An open-source bio-inspired solution to underwater SLAM. IFAC-PapersOnLine **48**, 212–217 (2015)

31. Sivic, J., Zisserman, A.: Video Google: a text retrieval approach to object matching in videos. In: IEEE International Conference on Computer Vision, vol. 2, pp. 1470–1477 (2003)

32. Sünderhauf, N., Shirazi, S., Dayoub, F., Upcroft, B., Milford, M.: On the performance of convnet features for place recognition. In: 2015 IEEE/RSJ International Conference on Intelligent Robots and Systems (IROS) (2015)

33. Sünderhauf, N., et al.: Place recognition with convnet landmarks: viewpoint-robust, condition-robust, training-free. In: Robotics: Science and Systems (2015)

34. Wang, J., Chen, F., Huang, Y., McConnell, J., Shan, T., Englot, B.: Virtual maps for autonomous exploration of cluttered underwater environments. IEEE J. Oceanic Eng. **47**, 916–935 (2022)

35. Wang, Y., Qiu, Y., Cheng, P., Duan, X.: Robust loop closure detection integrating visual-spatial-semantic information via topological graphs and CNN features. Remote Sens. **12**(23), 3890 (2020)

36. Wu, D., Du, X., Wang, K.: An effective approach for underwater sonar image denoising based on sparse representation. In: 2018 IEEE 3rd International Conference on Image, Vision and Computing (ICIVC) (2018)

37. Xie, Y., Tang, Y., Tang, G., Hoff, W.: Learning to find good correspondences of multiple objects. In: 2020 25th International Conference on Pattern Recognition (ICPR) (2021)

38. Xuan, H., Stylianou, A., Pless, R.: Improved embeddings with easy positive triplet mining. In: 2020 IEEE Winter Conference on Applications of Computer Vision (WACV) (2020)

39. Zaffar, M., et al.: VPR-bench: an open-source visual place recognition evaluation framework with quantifiable viewpoint and appearance change. Int. J. Comput. Vision **129**, 2136–2174 (2021)

40. Zhang, M.M., et al.: Dave aquatic virtual environment: toward a general underwater robotics simulator (2022)

A Uniform Distribution of Landmarks for Efficient Map Compression

Youssef Bouaziz[1,2]($\boxtimes$), Eric Royer[1], Guillaume Bresson[2], and Michel Dhome[1]

[1] Clermont Auvergne University, Institut Pascal, Clermont-Ferrand, France
{youssef.bouaziz,eric.royer,michel.dhome}@uca.fr
[2] Institut VEDECOM, Versailles, France
guillaume.bresson@vedecom.fr

Abstract. In this paper, we address the challenge of visual-based localization in dynamic outdoor environments characterized by continuous appearance changes. These changes greatly affect the visual information of the scene, resulting in significant performance degradation in visual localization. The issue arises from the difficulty of mapping data between the current image and the landmarks on the map due to environmental variations. One approach to tackle this problem is continuously adding new landmarks to the map to accommodate diverse environmental conditions. However, this leads to map growth, which in turn incurs high costs and resource demands for localization. To address this, we propose a map management approach based on an extension of the state-of-the-art technique called Summary Maps. Our approach employs a scoring policy that assigns scores to landmarks based on their appearance in multiple localization sessions. Consequently, landmarks observed in multiple sessions are assigned higher scores. We demonstrate the necessity of maintaining landmark diversity throughout map compression to ensure reliable long-term localization. To evaluate our approach, we conducted experiments on a dataset comprising over 100 sequences encompassing various environmental conditions. The obtained results were compared with those of the state-of-the-art approach, showcasing the effectiveness and superiority of our proposed method.

Keywords: Visual-Based Navigation · Computer Vision for Transportation · Long-Term SLAM

1 Introduction

Maps play a crucial role in self-driving applications, particularly in the context of high-precision localization using on-board cameras and reconstructed 3D points. However, the computational and memory limitations of mobile computing platforms pose significant challenges for real-time processing of these maps.

This work has been sponsored by the French government research program "Investissements d'Avenir" through the IMobS3 Laboratory of Excellence (ANR-10-LABX-16-01), by the European Union through the Regional Competitiveness and Employment program 2014-2020 (ERDF - AURA region) and by the AURA region.

Therefore, effective map management techniques are essential to optimize processing power and memory usage while maintaining localization accuracy.

While substantial progress has been made in the visual SLAM community for static environments or those with minimal changes, the challenge of localization in dynamic environments with varying conditions has only recently been addressed. Achieving reliable lifelong navigation in such dynamic environments poses a major hurdle for visual SLAM. In this paper, our focus is on real-time visual-based localization in outdoor environments for autonomous shuttles. These shuttles traverse the same path repeatedly but encounter diverse environmental conditions, leading to potential degradation in localization performance, even at familiar locations.

In such scenarios, environmental changes create significant difficulties in associating data between the current image and landmarks in the map. It is imperative for autonomous shuttles to adapt to such changes in order to ensure reliable long-term localization.

One approach to improve localization performance under changing conditions is to build a map that encompasses all environmental variations by continuously adding landmarks. However, this leads to continual map growth, directly proportional to the number of shuttle traversals. Consequently, localization after multiple traversals becomes infeasible due to the excessive memory requirements to store the map and the computational demands to match points between the current image and an extensive landmark database. In essence, achieving long-term real-time localization becomes unattainable after a certain number of localization sessions.

The objective of this paper is to propose a real-time solution that addresses the map growth issue for long-term localization. To this end, we introduce a map management strategy to reduce the map size offline. The proposed strategy focuses on removing redundant data from the map, significantly reducing the computational cost of the SLAM algorithm in long-term scenarios.

Several recent works have also explored the map management problem, including studies by [1], Mühlfellner et al. [14], Dymczyk et al. [7], Burki et al. [5], Krajník et al. [10], Halodová et al. [8], among others. Some of these approaches reduce map size based on a scoring policy that suggests removing landmarks with the lowest observation rate [7,14]. Others eliminate landmarks associated with localization failures [5] or those with a high incorrect matching rate [8].

In this paper, we present an improvement to the Summary Maps approach proposed by Mühlfellner et al. [14]. Their method scores landmarks based on the number of different localization sessions in which they appear and removes landmarks with the lowest scores in an offline process. Our improved version of Summary Maps introduces a new constraint on landmark removal, ensuring a uniform number of landmarks per traversal after map summarization (i.e., compression).

We evaluate our enhanced approach using the publicly available IPLT (Institut Pascal Long-Term) dataset [3]. This dataset comprises 128 sequences recorded over a 16-month period, featuring a vehicle repeatedly following the same path around a parking lot with slight lateral and angular deviations. The IPLT dataset encompasses various environmental conditions, including changes in luminance, weather, seasons, and the presence of parked vehicles. Each sequence spans approximately 200 m in length (see Fig. 1). We utilize this dataset to assess the performance of our approach and compare it against an existing state-of-the-art method.

Fig. 1. Example of 6 sequences recorded in a parking lot.

Our experiments demonstrate that our approach significantly improves localization performance, enabling successful localization even in challenging conditions.

2   Related Work

In most real-world robotic scenarios, the ability to operate in dynamic and ever-changing environments for extended periods is crucial. Simultaneous Localization and Mapping (SLAM) is a fundamental capability required in such scenarios. However, existing SLAM frameworks are often evaluated in static environments or scenes with minimal dynamic objects, such as moving people.

Recently, efforts have been made to extend the performance of localization in dynamic environments. Traditional feature-based comparison techniques in vision-based SLAM are considered unsuitable for long-term operations due to their vulnerability to changing conditions. As an alternative, Murillo and Kosecka proposed an image-based approach using the Gist representation of panoramic images to improve localization in dynamic environments [15]. Unlike local feature descriptors like SIFT and SURF, Gist is a global descriptor calculated using the entire image, representing an abstract scene representation. However, this approach involves an extensive search in the database to find the corresponding image, which becomes computationally expensive in large-scale environments. Milford and Wyeth introduced SeqSLAM, which enhances the performance of global image descriptors by matching sequences of images instead of individual images [13]. Although SeqSLAM demonstrates impressive results on various seasonal datasets, it remains sensitive to viewpoint changes.

Mühlfellner *et al.* proposed Summary Maps (SM) as a map management technique, where landmarks are ranked based on the number of different localization sessions in which they appear, and low-score landmarks are removed in an offline process [14]. However, SM has limitations in that landmarks in rarely visited areas receive low scores and are expected to be removed during map summarization. Dymczyk et al. addressed this bias towards frequently visited regions by designing a scoring policy that considers the expected number of trajectories to observe a landmark [7].

Krajník et al. developed a system that predicts the current state of the environment based on learned temporal patterns, constructing a new independent map in each run and integrating them into a spatio-temporal occupancy grid [10]. Bürki et al. improved appearance-based landmark selection by formulating a new ranking function [5]. They introduced two types of sessions, "rich sessions" and "observation sessions," assuming that the environmental condition of a session performing worse than a predefined threshold is not covered in the map. They added new landmarks to cover the new encountered environmental conditions and employed offline map summarization to produce a reliable map with a fixed size. Halodová et al. extended previous work by presenting an adaptive map update scheme that removes or adds features based on their past influence on localization quality [8]. They introduced an adaptive scoring policy that increments or decrements feature scores based on correct, incorrect, or unmatched matches. This strategy requires an accurate landmark retrieval technique to avoid penalizing incorrectly matched features caused by inaccurate retrievals. Bouaziz et al. proposed a keyframe retrieval technique that employs a ranking function considering factors such as Euclidean distance and underlying environmental conditions to search for keyframes with a higher number of inliers [2].

In this paper, we present an improvement to the Summary Maps (SM) approach proposed by Mühlfellner et al. [14]. Our enhanced version, named Uniform Summary Maps (USM), imposes a new constraint on landmark removal. The objective is to ensure a uniform number of landmarks in each traversal (sequence) after map summarization (compression).

3 Methodology

In this section, we introduce our map management approach, which extends the work proposed by Mühlfellner *et al.* [14] called Summary Maps (SM). We have re-implemented SM on our mapping framework.

Mühlfellner *et al.* [14] defined a landmark scoring policy that assigns scores to landmarks based on the number of different localization sessions in which they appear. Landmarks observed in multiple sessions receive high scores, indicating their value for localization. Conversely, landmarks with low scores are considered irrelevant. The Summary Maps approach utilizes these scores to summarize the map in an offline process conducted after each localization session, removing the least significant landmarks.

Figure 2 illustrates the scoring function strategy proposed by Mühlfellner *et al.*, as described in [14]. It presents an example of localization and showcases the landmarks observed in two different sessions, denoted as i and j.

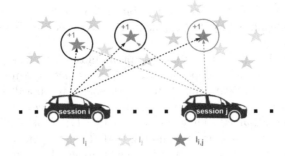

Fig. 2. The landmark scoring policy proposed by Mühlfellner *et al.*. The figure illustrates a localization example where some landmarks ($l_{i,j}$) were observed in two different sessions (session i and session j) and accordingly, their scores were increased by the scoring policy.

An inherent limitation of this approach is that landmarks in rarely visited areas are assigned low scores since they are infrequently observed. Consequently, they are more likely to be removed during the map summarization process. Dymczyk *et al.* [7] referred to this issue as the bias towards regions that were more frequently visited and aimed to address this problem. They enhanced the scoring policy proposed in [14] by considering the expected number of trajectories required to observe a landmark.

However, we have identified another limitation of the Summary Maps approach, which is somewhat similar to the aforementioned bias. This limitation can be defined as a bias towards more experienced environmental conditions. It occurs when a set of sequences with similar environmental conditions is combined with a sequence having a distinct environmental condition in the same map. For example, a collection of daytime sequences incorporated into a map with one nighttime sequence. In such cases, landmarks observed under the odd environmental condition receive low scores from the scoring policy due to their infrequent observations compared to the landmarks from the other sequences. Consequently, these landmarks are filtered out during the map summarization step.

Table 1 presents an example of the bias towards more experienced environmental conditions that arises when summarizing a map containing 10 sequences using the Summary Maps approach. This map was constructed using the 10 sequences depicted in Fig. 4 and includes only one nighttime sequence (the odd sequence). The table demonstrates the compression of the map using different compression ratios (1, 1.5, 2, 3, 5, and 10) with the Summary Maps approach. Compressing the map with a compression ratio r entails sorting all landmarks based on their scores and removing the lowest-scoring landmarks, representing $100 * (1 - 1/r)$ percent of the total (e.g., removing the 50% lowest scored landmarks for r = 2).

Table 1. Bias towards more experienced environmental conditions in Summary Maps.

Traversal	Compression ratio r					
	1 (no compression)	1.5	2	3	5	10
1	140,524	113,922	100,371	75,087	50,304	20,817
2	127,687	93,539	72,205	48,527	28,803	14,071
3	149,065	83,821	52,025	34,912	18,913	9,324
4	140,900	72,955	37,769	26,157	15,868	8,946
5	122,122	97,989	86,896	55,751	29,495	14,022
6	124,643	89,807	76,360	44,106	18,436	9,495
7	72,044	41,333	28,777	16,310	5,092	2,709
8	116,091	67,204	44,438	32,717	24,424	12,825
9	127,972	96,797	78,262	51,610	34,322	16,692
10	143,640	85,758	55,241	36,385	27,280	17,567
total	1,264,688	843,125	632,344	421,562	252,937	126,469

The Table shows the number of landmarks observed in each traversal after compressing the map using the Summary Maps approach at different compression ratios. The second column ($r = 1$) represents the initial map with no compression ($100 * (1 - 1/1) = 0\%$). The last row represents the total number of landmarks on each map.

According to the table, a significant number of landmarks from the 7th traversal (corresponding to the nighttime sequence) were removed after compressing the map. This demonstrates that the Summary Maps approach excludes landmarks observed in rarely experienced environmental conditions. This can pose a serious problem when localizing using nighttime sequences on the compressed map, as most of the nighttime landmarks have been filtered.

Therefore, in this paper, we propose an improvement for the Summary Maps technique called Uniform Summary Maps (USM). The goal of USM is to ensure a uniform distribution of landmarks across all traversals after map summarization. To achieve this, we introduce a constraint that imposes the distribution of a uniform number of landmarks across traversals. The algorithmic procedure for implementing USM is explained in Algorithm 1.

To further illustrate the execution of the algorithm and the effectiveness of our improved version of Summary Maps, we provide an example and compare the results with the original Summary Maps approach. Figure 3 presents an execution example of our algorithm on a map with $N = 4$ traversals. Each traversal l is associated with a specific number of landmarks denoted by n_{land}^{l}. The objective is to remove a total of $n_{tot} = 260$ landmarks from the map while ensuring a uniform distribution across the traversals.

Algorithm 1 Uniform Summary Maps

1: **Parameters:**
2: The total number of landmarks to remove: n_{tot}
3: The number of traversals in the map: N
4: **Steps:**
5: **repeat**
6:    Compute the number of landmarks n_{land}^{l} observed on each traversal l, with $l \in [1, N]$
7:    Sort the n_{land}^{l} landmarks of each traversal l according to the scoring policy
8:    Compute the highest number of landmarks: $n_{\max} \leftarrow \max(\{n_{land}^{1}, \ldots, n_{land}^{N}\})$
9:    Find the set of traversals $\mathcal{S} = \{L_{\max}^{1}, \ldots, L_{\max}^{s}\}$ having $n_{\max}$ landmarks
10:   Find the traversal L_{smax} having the second-highest number of landmarks:
        $n_{\text{smax}} \leftarrow \max(\{n_{land}^{1}, \ldots, n_{land}^{N}\} \setminus \{n_{\max}\})$
11:   Compute $n_{\text{diff}} \leftarrow n_{\max} - n_{\text{smax}}$
12:   Compute the number of landmarks to remove:
        $n_{\text{rem}} \leftarrow \min(n_{\text{diff}} * |\mathcal{S}|, n_{\text{tot}})$ /* the function min is used to make sure that we
                                                           do not remove more than n_{tot} landmarks */
13:   **for each** traversal $L_{\max} \in \mathcal{S}$ **do**
14:      Remove the lowest scored $\dfrac{n_{\text{rem}}}{|\mathcal{S}|}$ landmarks from traversal $L_{\max}$
15:   **end for**
16:   Update the total number of landmarks to remove: $n_{\text{tot}} \leftarrow n_{\text{tot}} - n_{\text{rem}}$
17: **until** $n_{\text{tot}} \leq 0$

In the first iteration, the algorithm computes the number of landmarks n_{rem} to remove from the traversal with the highest number of landmarks, which is the 4th traversal.

In the second iteration, it is observed that there are two traversals, $\mathcal{S} = 2, 4$, with the highest number of landmarks. Consequently, the algorithm calculates the number of landmarks to be removed n_{rem}, and removes $n_{\text{rem}}/|\mathcal{S}|$ landmarks from each traversal in $\mathcal{S}$.

In the third iteration, the set $\mathcal{S}$ contains three traversals. The algorithm calculates the number of landmarks to be removed in this iteration as $n_{\text{diff}} \times |\mathcal{S}| = 150$. However, this value exceeds the total number of landmarks to be removed, which is $n_{\text{tot}} = 120$. To ensure that we do not remove more landmarks than n_{tot}, we use the statement $\min(n_{\text{diff}} \times |\mathcal{S}|, n_{\text{tot}})$.

Table 2 presents the results of compressing the map using our improved version of Summary Maps, while Table 1 displays the results obtained with the original Summary Maps approach.

The comparison in Table 2 reveals that after compressing the map with different compression ratios, the number of landmarks remains uniform across the different traversals. This demonstrates the effectiveness of our proposed technique in achieving a balanced distribution of landmarks while reducing the overall number of landmarks in the map.

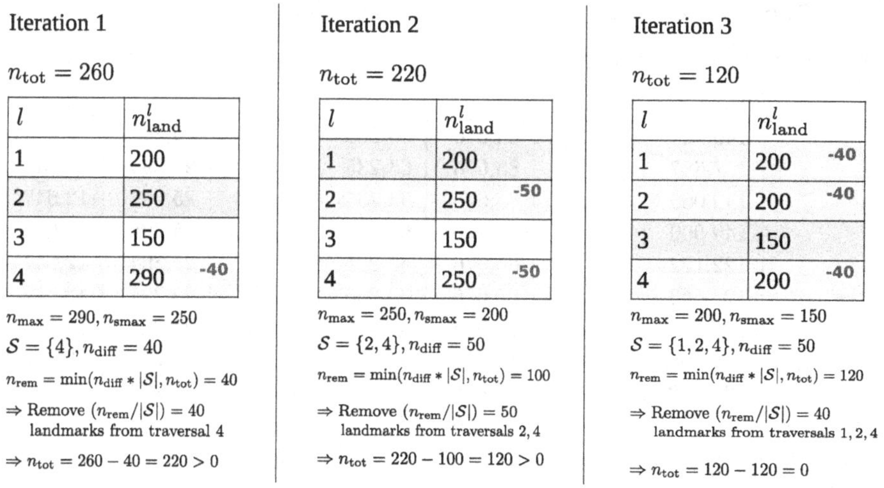

Iteration 1

$n_{\text{tot}} = 260$

l	n^l_{land}
1	200
2	250
3	150
4	290 -40

$n_{\text{max}} = 290, n_{\text{smax}} = 250$

$\mathcal{S} = \{4\}, n_{\text{diff}} = 40$

$n_{\text{rem}} = \min(n_{\text{diff}} * |\mathcal{S}|, n_{\text{tot}}) = 40$

$\Rightarrow$ Remove $(n_{\text{rem}}/|\mathcal{S}|) = 40$ landmarks from traversal 4

$\Rightarrow n_{\text{tot}} = 260 - 40 = 220 > 0$

Iteration 2

$n_{\text{tot}} = 220$

l	n^l_{land}
1	200
2	250 -50
3	150
4	250 -50

$n_{\text{max}} = 250, n_{\text{smax}} = 200$

$\mathcal{S} = \{2, 4\}, n_{\text{diff}} = 50$

$n_{\text{rem}} = \min(n_{\text{diff}} * |\mathcal{S}|, n_{\text{tot}}) = 100$

$\Rightarrow$ Remove $(n_{\text{rem}}/|\mathcal{S}|) = 50$ landmarks from traversals 2, 4

$\Rightarrow n_{\text{tot}} = 220 - 100 = 120 > 0$

Iteration 3

$n_{\text{tot}} = 120$

l	n^l_{land}
1	200 -40
2	200 -40
3	150
4	200 -40

$n_{\text{max}} = 200, n_{\text{smax}} = 150$

$\mathcal{S} = \{1, 2, 4\}, n_{\text{diff}} = 50$

$n_{\text{rem}} = \min(n_{\text{diff}} * |\mathcal{S}|, n_{\text{tot}}) = 120$

$\Rightarrow$ Remove $(n_{\text{rem}}/|\mathcal{S}|) = 40$ landmarks from traversals 1, 2, 4

$\Rightarrow n_{\text{tot}} = 120 - 120 = 0$

Fig. 3. An example illustrating the execution mechanism of our proposed algorithm. The yellow colored rows designate n_{max} and the green colored ones designate n_{smax}. (Color figure online)

4 Experiments and Results

To evaluate the performance of our approach, we conducted experiments using the IPLT dataset [3]. The IPLT dataset is a publicly available dataset that provides a diverse range of sequences for benchmarking visual localization algorithms. The dataset consists of over 100 sequences, each approximately 200 m in length, captured under various environmental conditions including day, night, dusk, rain, and overcast. In all sequences, the vehicle follows a consistent path within a parking lot, as shown in Fig. 1.

Although we acknowledge the importance of evaluating our approach on other widely used datasets such as the Oxford RobotCar dataset [11] or NCLT dataset [6], these datasets do not offer a substantial number of sequences traversing the same path, which is crucial for testing the effectiveness of our work. Therefore, we cannot rely on these datasets for our evaluation.

The IPLT dataset used in our study was generated using recorded images from two grayscale cameras mounted on an experimental vehicle. Each camera has a field of view of 100°. In addition to the image data, there is also wheel odometry information for localization purposes. The dataset includes 103 sequences captured at different times of the day and under various weather conditions, such as rain, sun, and overcast. To introduce additional challenges, some sequences feature lateral and angular deviations. Out of these 103 sequences, we utilized 10 sequences to construct the global map, while the remaining 93 sequences were reserved for evaluation and analysis.

Table 2. Compressing the map with the Uniform Summary Maps.

Traversal	Compression ratio r					
	1 (no compression)	1.5	2	3	5	10
1	140,524	85,676	63,235	42,157	25,294	12,647
2	127,687	85,676	63,235	42,157	25,294	12,647
3	149,065	85,676	63,235	42,157	25,294	12,647
4	140,900	85,676	63,235	42,157	25,294	12,647
5	122,122	85,676	63,235	42,157	25,294	12,647
6	124,643	85,676	63,235	42,157	25,294	12,647
7	72,044	72,044	63,235	42,157	25,294	12,647
8	116,091	85,676	63,235	42,157	25,294	12,647
9	127,972	85,676	63,235	42,157	25,294	12,647
10	143,640	85,676	63,235	42,157	25,294	12,647
total	1,264,688	843,128	632,350	421,570	252,940	126,470

We evaluated our approach on the IPLT dataset using the created global map which incorporates 10 traversals. In Fig. 4, we present an overview of images from the 10 mapping sequences.

We conducted the evaluation using two different compression ratios: $r = 3$ and $r = 2$, where r represents the amount of landmark removal from the map. For instance, for $r = 3$, we removed 2/3 of the landmarks from the map. To assess the performance, we measured the average number of inliers observed in each test sequence, as well as the average number of localization failures per kilometer, which served as evaluation criteria.

We determined that reliable localization could be achieved when at least 30 points were matched between the current image and the database. Below this threshold, we considered it a localization failure. We have set a conservative threshold based on a study conducted by Royer et al. [16] to ensure the safety of the autonomous shuttle. This threshold, which we have adopted, is considered conservative and helps maintain a high level of security during the localization process.

To evaluate the impact of map compression on localization performance, we compared the localization performance on the initial global map, denoted as M_0, which consisted of the 10 traversals, with the performance on two compressed maps: M_{SM} generated using the Summary Maps approach [14], and M_{USM} generated using our improved approach. In Fig. 5, we present the average number of inliers per image and the average number of localization failures per kilometer observed during re-localization on these maps. In our experiments, we use Harris corner detector [9] for extracting key-points which are matched with ZNCC — Zero-mean Normalized Cross-Correlation — computed on 11×11 pixel windows around each key-point. However, our method can still be applied in the same way using other descriptors.

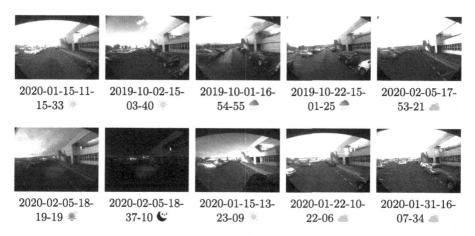

| 2020-01-15-11-
15-33 | 2019-10-02-15-
03-40 | 2019-10-01-16-
54-55 | 2019-10-22-15-
01-25 | 2020-02-05-17-
53-21 |
| 2020-02-05-18-
19-19 | 2020-02-05-18-
37-10 | 2020-01-15-13-
23-09 | 2020-01-22-10-
22-06 | 2020-01-31-16-
07-34 |

Fig. 4. An overview of images from the mapping sequences taken with the front camera. For each sequence, we provide the acquisition date and represent the environmental condition using a small icon.

The test sequences were manually classified into five different classes: "sun," "overcast," "rain," "dusk," and "night," with the "global" class containing all 93 testing sequences.

The Summary Maps approach (M_{SM}) exhibits a notable weakness when it comes to reducing the map size. This weakness is particularly more relevant in night sequences. The limitation arises from the fact that the 10 mapping sequences depicted in Fig. 4 comprise only a single night sequence. As a result, landmarks observed during the night traversal receive a lower score compared to others, making them more likely to be removed during the map summarization process employed by the Summary Maps approach. Consequently, the nocturnal localization performance is adversely affected. This effect is evident in both subfigures (a) and (b) of Fig. 5, where the number of localization failures in the night class is significant (166.6 localization failures/km with $r = 3$ and 49 with $r = 2$).

Conversely, our proposed technique, referred to as USM, effectively addresses this issue by ensuring a balanced representation of landmarks in the map after compression. As depicted in the figure, USM successfully increases the overall number of inliers and reduces the number of localization failures per kilometer, particularly during nighttime scenarios. This improvement in localization performance demonstrates the efficacy of our approach.

4.1   Discussion

Comparing the performance of our approach with existing state-of-the-art techniques poses a significant challenge. The difficulty arises from a fundamental conceptual difference between our approach and other techniques, wherein each state-of-the-art method is designed and applied within a specific mapping frame-

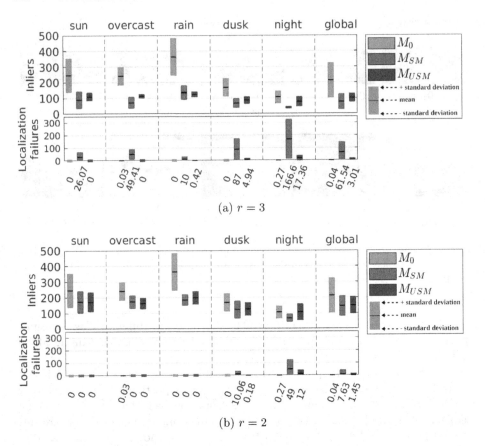

Fig. 5. Localization performance comparison on M_0, M_{SM} and M_{USM}. Each color refers to a map as indicated in the legend, and the boxes represent the mean $+/-$ the standard deviation of inliers or localization failures on all the sequences of the corresponding class. Sub-figures (a) and (b) represent the localization performance when choosing $r = 3$ and $r = 2$ respectively.

work that utilizes distinct feature representations [4,12]. This discrepancy in feature representation makes direct comparisons challenging, especially when comparing approaches applied to different types of SLAM frameworks, such as filter-based SLAM versus keyframe-based SLAM.

The variations in feature representation introduce complexities in evaluating and benchmarking different approaches. Each mapping framework has its own set of assumptions, algorithmic choices, and performance metrics. As a result, the performance evaluation of one approach within a specific framework may not be directly comparable to the evaluation of another approach in a different framework.

While comparing our approach with specific state-of-the-art techniques may be challenging, it is still valuable to highlight the unique aspects and contributions of our approach within the context of our chosen mapping framework. By focusing on the performance and evaluation metrics relevant to our framework, we can assess the effectiveness and efficiency of our approach compared to baseline methods or previous versions of our own approach. Additionally, conducting extensive experiments and providing thorough quantitative and qualitative analyses can help demonstrate the strengths and limitations of our approach in a more comprehensive manner.

In future research, it would be beneficial to establish standardized evaluation frameworks that can facilitate fair comparisons across different mapping approaches and frameworks. Such frameworks could define common datasets, performance metrics, and evaluation protocols, allowing for more direct comparisons between approaches. By adopting standardized evaluation practices, researchers can collectively advance the field and facilitate better understanding and comparison of different SLAM techniques.

5 Conclusions

In this study, we have proposed an enhancement to a state-of-the-art map management approach that leverages landmark observation information. Our improved technique introduces refinements to the scoring policy, allowing for more effective compression of maps while maintaining long-term localization performance. In our experiments, we conducted a comprehensive evaluation of our approach in various environmental conditions.

By comparing our improved technique with the original state-of-the-art approach, we have observed substantial performance gains. Our approach consistently outperformed the baseline method in terms of localization accuracy and robustness, even when operating with compressed maps. This highlights the effectiveness of our proposed enhancements and their positive impact on the overall localization performance.

Looking ahead, our future research endeavors will focus on further refining the scoring policy of our approach. We aim to incorporate additional information, such as past localization successes and failures, into the compression process. By considering a broader range of factors, we expect to enhance the efficiency and effectiveness of our map compression technique, ultimately improving the overall localization capabilities in challenging real-world scenarios.

References

1. Biber, P., Duckett, T., et al.: Dynamic maps for long-term operation of mobile service robots. In: Robotics: Science and Systems, pp. 17–24 (2005)
2. Bouaziz, Y., Royer, E., Bresson, G., Dhome, M.: Keyframes retrieval for robust long-term visual localization in changing conditions. In: 2021 IEEE 19th World Symposium on Applied Machine Intelligence and Informatics (SAMI), pp. 000093–000100. IEEE (2021)

3. Bouaziz, Y., Royer, E., Bresson, G., Dhome, M.: Over two years of challenging environmental conditions for localization: the IPLT dataset. In: Proceedings of the 18th International Conference on Informatics in Control, Automation and Robotics - Volume 1: ICINCO, pp. 383–387. INSTICC, SciTePress (2021). https://doi.org/10.5220/0010518303830387

4. Bürki, M., Cadena, C., Gilitschenski, I., Siegwart, R., Nieto, J.: Appearance-based landmark selection for visual localization. J. Field Robot. **36**(6), 1041–1073 (2019)

5. Bürki, M., Dymczyk, M., Gilitschenski, I., Cadena, C., Siegwart, R., Nieto, J.: Map management for efficient long-term visual localization in outdoor environments. In: 2018 IEEE Intelligent Vehicles Symposium (IV), pp. 682–688. IEEE (2018)

6. Carlevaris-Bianco, N., Ushani, A.K., Eustice, R.M.: University of Michigan North campus long-term vision and lidar dataset. Int. J. Robot. Res. **35**(9), 1023–1035 (2015)

7. Dymczyk, M., Lynen, S., Cieslewski, T., Bosse, M., Siegwart, R., Furgale, P.: The gist of maps-summarizing experience for lifelong localization. In: 2015 IEEE International Conference on Robotics and Automation (ICRA). pp. 2767–2773. IEEE (2015)

8. Halodová, L., et al.: Predictive and adaptive maps for long-term visual navigation in changing environments. In: 2019 IEEE/RSJ International Conference on Intelligent Robots and Systems (IROS), pp. 7033–7039. IEEE (2019)

9. Harris, C.G., Stephens, M., et al.: A combined corner and edge detector. In: Alvey Vision Conference, vol. 15, pp. 10–5244. Citeseer (1988)

10. Krajník, T., Fentanes, J.P., Hanheide, M., Duckett, T.: Persistent localization and life-long mapping in changing environments using the frequency map enhancement. In: 2016 IEEE/RSJ International Conference on Intelligent Robots and Systems (IROS), pp. 4558–4563. IEEE (2016)

11. Maddern, W., Pascoe, G., Linegar, C., Newman, P.: 1 year, 1000 km: the oxford robotcar dataset. Int. J. Robot. Res. (IJRR) **36**(1), 3–15 (2017). https://doi.org/10.1177/0278364916679498

12. Magnago, V., Palopoli, L., Passerone, R., Fontanelli, D., Macii, D.: Effective landmark placement for robot indoor localization with position uncertainty constraints. IEEE Trans. Instrum. Meas. **68**(11), 4443–4455 (2019)

13. Milford, M.J., Wyeth, G.F.: SeqSLAM: visual route-based navigation for sunny summer days and stormy winter nights. In: 2012 IEEE International Conference on Robotics and Automation, pp. 1643–1649. IEEE (2012)

14. Mühlfellner, P., Bürki, M., Bosse, M., Derendarz, W., Philippsen, R., Furgale, P.: Summary maps for lifelong visual localization. J. Field Robot. **33**(5), 561–590 (2016)

15. Murillo, A.C., Kosecka, J.: Experiments in place recognition using gist panoramas. In: 2009 IEEE 12th International Conference on Computer Vision Workshops, ICCV Workshops, pp. 2196–2203. IEEE (2009)

16. Royer, E., et al.: Lessons learned after more than 1000 km in an autonomous shuttle guided by vision. In: 2016 IEEE 19th International Conference on Intelligent Transportation Systems (ITSC), pp. 2248–2253. IEEE (2016)

A Novel Approach: Fourier Series Parameterization and Support Vector Regression for 2D Laser SLAM with Closed Shape Features

Olusesi Ayobami Meadows[1]([✉]) [iD], Ahmed Tijani Salawudeen[2] [iD],
and Oreofe Ajayi[1] [iD]

[1] Ahmadu Bello University, Zaria, Nigeria
oameadows@abu.edu.ng
[2] University of Jos, Jos, Nigeria

Abstract. This paper introduces a novel approach which combines Fourier series-based feature parameterization with support vector regression (FS-SVR) for accurate trajectory estimation in 2D Laser SLAM. By incorporating support vector regression (SVR) into the feature-based SLAM approach, the limitations of the Fourier-only (FS) approach are addressed, allowing for nonlinear estimation, improved robustness against outliers, and enhanced generalization. The proposed hybrid method successfully computes the parametrization states of the features using the FS model and utilizes the trained SVR to predict residuals, resulting in accurate trajectory estimation for closed shape features. Evaluation on artificial and actual data demonstrates the superiority of FS-SVR, achieving lower mean absolute error (MAE) values compared to the sole FS model. The practical experiment further confirms the superiority of the hybrid model in various scenarios, making it a promising method for achieving efficient trajectory accuracy in real-world environments.

Keywords: Support Vector Regression · Fourier series · 2D SLAM

1 Introduction

Simultaneous Localization And Mapping (SLAM), a fundamental research challenge in autonomous robot navigation and map creation, involves estimating the state of robots or sensors and constructing corresponding maps, and recently, planar SLAM using 2D LIDAR or laser rangefinder has gained significant traction in both industry and academia, with a growing number of approaches being developed [1–3].

Presently, there are two commonly used approaches in 2D laser SLAM: scan matching and feature-based approaches. In scan matching, nearby scans are aligned to determine relative poses, followed by pose-graph optimization to refine the poses and construct the map. While scan matching avoids assumptions about the environment, incorporating prior knowledge of geometrical information can enhance accuracy, such as

H. I. Christensen et al. (Eds.): ICVS 2023, LNCS 14253, pp. 363–373, 2023.
https://doi.org/10.1007/978-3-031-44137-0_30

using boundary descriptions provided by manufacturers for objects in industrial settings. Scan matching also faces challenges in accurately integrating information from
consecutive scans. On the other hand, the feature-based approach focuses on estimating
feature parameters in the environment, offering an alternative method for SLAM [4]. A
common approach in feature-based SLAM is point feature SLAM [5], where the position
of the point feature serves as the feature parameter. This method is designed to tackle the
difficulties associated with navigating through large environments that consist of both
feature-rich and featureless regions. In addition to point features [6], feature using vertical lines from an omni-directional camera image and horizontal lines from range sensor
data, which improved accuracy by reducing the effects of illumination and occlusion.
Authors in [7] presented an ellipse feature-based SLAM algorithm by defining a conic
feature parametrization, incorporating conic geometric and odometry information, and
utilizing a factor graph framework.

The application of fitting shapes with Fourier series is commonly used in shape
retrieval within the field of image processing. The process involves sampling shapes
and fitting them using Fast Fourier Transform [8]. Some researchers [9] enhanced the
performance of human iris matching systems by employing a Fourier-based approximation to describe the boundaries of non-circular pupils. Authors in [10] introduced
a Fourier series-based approach for representing and characterizing two-dimensional
general-shape particles. In [11] Fast Fourier Transform (FFT) was employed as a computational tool to analyze scan data. They utilized FFT to extract relevant information,
such as rotation and translation parameters, from the scan data, allowing for accurate
alignment and registration in their research. Authors in [12] formulated the SLAM
problem with Fourier series feature parameterization and introduced a submap joining
process to improve accuracy and reduce dependence on initial guess and computing
time. However, the Fourier series-based parameterization approach assumes a linear
relationship between the parameters and the trajectory. This assumption may not hold
in complex environments or when dealing with nonlinear motion models. By neglecting
the nonlinear aspects of the estimation problem, the method may fail to capture the full
complexity of the trajectory and result in less accurate estimations.

Building upon the previous researches, the contribution of this research lies in the
introduction of a novel hybrid model that combines the Fourier series (FS) and support vector regression (SVR) models, aiming to achieve a robust parameterization of
closed shape features. By integrating the SVR to predict the residuals, the approach
effectively captures the nonlinear associations between the parameterization outcomes
and the actual trajectory. Incorporating the predicted residuals with the parameterization
results produces an enhanced and more precise estimation of the trajectory, ultimately
enhancing the accuracy and dependability of the SLAM algorithm.

2   Theory for Proposed Approach

This section analyzes a brief fundamental theories of Fourier series and support vector
regression.

2.1 Fourier Series Parameterization

For this paper, the semicolon is used to denote vertical vector concatenation. An observed point in the jth frame is defined a $^{(j)}\mathbf{p} \in \mathbb{R}^2$. A 2D point set observed in the jth frame of feature k is represented as $^{(j)}\mathbf{P}_k = [^{(j)}\mathbf{p}_1^k, \ldots, ^{(j)}\mathbf{p}_M^k]$. We also assume that the observed points are subject to zero-mean Gaussian noise $\mathbf{n}_z \in \mathbb{R}^2 \sim N(0, \Sigma_z)$. For an angle $\phi \in [-\pi, \pi)$, let $R(\phi) \in SO(2)$ be the corresponding rotation matrix, denoted as R. The translation is represented by $t = [t_x, t_y]^\top$ indicate the rotation and translation from frame i to frame j. If i is the global frame $\{G\}$, it is often omitted to simplify the formula. Assuming a robot pose $\Xi_j = [t_j; \phi_j]$, we use $T(\Xi_j, ^{(j)}\chi)$ to denote the transformation process of a point/point cloud/feature from frame $\{j\}$ to the global frame $\{G\}$, and $T^{-1}(\Xi_j, ^{(G)}\chi)$ represents the inverse process. Suppose a feature Φ_k has a closed shape, and its boundary point set is denoted by $\mathbf{P}_k$. Details of the parameterization can be found in [12].

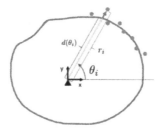

Fig. 1. Demonstration of r_i, (θ_i), $d(\theta_i)$ showing black triangle as the feature center.

Fourier series can be used to represent a periodic function via a sum of sine and cosine functions. The illustration in Fig. 1 depicts r_i, (θ_i), and $d(\theta_i)$ with a black triangle representing the center of the feature. For example, let $f(x)$ be a continuous function with period T, where x is the independent variable. $f(x)$ can be decomposed into triangular functions with different periods as:

$$f(x) = \frac{a_0}{2} + \sum_{n=1}^{\infty} \left(a_n \cos\left(\frac{2\pi nx}{T}\right) + b_n \sin\left(\frac{2\pi nx}{T}\right) \right) \tag{1}$$

where a_n and b_n are the Fourier coefficients.

With the provided collection of boundaries P_k, the determination of Fourier series coefficients a_n and b_n is feasible and well-defined, allowing for their calculation. During the fitting procedure, the recorded points along the feature boundary are arranged in increasing order of angles. Building upon the aforementioned concept, we posit the assumption:

Assumption: There is only one intersection at which any bearing beam intersects the feature's border as it extends from the feature's center to infinity.

The periodic distance function $d(\theta_i)$ of a feature can be expressed as:

$$d(\theta_i) = \sum_{n=0}^{N} [a_n \cos(n\theta_i) + b_n \sin(n\theta_i)] \tag{2}$$

where the period is 2π according to Eq. (1). Here, N can be any positive finite number. A larger value of N results in a fitted boundary that closely matches the observed points.

2.2 Support Vector Regression

Support Vector Regression (SVR) was introduced by [13] as a regression extension of support vector classification. SVR leverages the concept of support vectors and focuses on a subset of training data that lies within the margin. By minimizing the cost function, SVR aims to find the optimal regression model. According to Fig. 2, in support of SVR, the hyperplane separates data classes and predicts the target value, the kernel function maps data points to a higher-dimensional space, boundary lines create a margin around the hyperplane, and support vectors define the hyperplane as extreme data points close to the boundary [14].

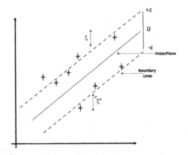

Fig. 2. Regression of support vector

In the context of closed shape features, SVM is employed to explore the intrinsic relationship between the prediction model and the learning capability. By optimizing the model's generalization capability, SVM aims to find the best fit for the given dataset $X \times Y = \{(x_1, y_1), \ldots, (x_i, y_i), \ldots\}_{i=1}^{N} \in R^N \times R$.

The regression task aims to establish a nonlinear function $f : R^N \to R$ that relates the input variable $y = f(x)$. The estimation function and loss function can be defined as follows:

Estimation function:

$$y = f(x) = [\omega \cdot \phi(x)] + b \quad (3)$$

Loss function:

$$minQ = \frac{1}{2}\|\omega\|^2 + C\sum_{i=1}^{N}(\xi_i^* + \xi_i) \quad (4)$$

Subject to:

$$y_i - [\omega \cdot k\phi(x_i)] - b \le \varepsilon + \xi_i^*,$$

$$[\omega \cdot k\phi(x_i)] + b - y = \varepsilon + \xi_i,$$

$$\xi_i^*, \xi_i \geq 0, i = 1, \ldots, N,$$

Here, ω represents the weight vector, $\phi(x)$ is the feature mapping of the input x, b is the bias term, and ε is the loss function to compute prediction accuracy in (4). The convergence speed is modified using the relaxation variables ξ_i^* and ξ_i. The empirical risk and confidence range are calculated using the penalty factor C.

3 Formulation of SLAM Problem Using Fourier Series and Support Vector Regression

The combined approach of Fourier Series (FS) and Support Vector Regression (SVR) combines the capabilities of both methods for improved parameterization and prediction in various applications. FS provides a mathematical framework for representing periodic functions, while SVR utilizes regression techniques to capture nonlinear relationships and make accurate predictions.

The coefficients of the Fourier series are a set of numbers that minimize the difference between the estimated boundary and the observed data. This can be achieved by solving the following cost function [9]:

$$\underset{a_n, b_n}{\arg\min} F = \sum_{i=1}^{M} (d(\theta_i) - r_i)^2 \tag{5}$$

where r_i represents the observed data.

The parameter N is selected to ensure that the truncated Fourier series provides a sufficiently precise estimation of the feature boundary. Increasing N can lead to a more accurate result. In practice, for most smooth closed shape features, N can be set to 5 or 7, while for rectangular features, it can be set to 15 or 17. More information on determining the center can be found in reference [12].

The optimization problem can be formulated as minimizing the following energy function:

$$\underset{\mathbf{X}}{\arg\min} F(\mathbf{X}) = \sum_{\Xi_{j=1}}^{L} \left(E_{o,j} + \sum_{k}^{K} [E_{f,j,k} + E_{c,j,k}] \right) \tag{6}$$

where $E_{o,j}$ represents the energy cost of the odometry, $E_{f,j,k}$ is the distance cost between the estimated boundaries and observed points, and $E_{c,j,k}$ is the energy cost of observed feature centers fitted at each step. Equation (6) can be solved using iterative methods such as Newton's method or the Levenberg-Marquardt algorithm. In this paper, the Levenberg-Marquardt algorithm is employed as the solver for the problem. During each iteration, the covariance matrices $\Sigma_{o,j}$, $\Sigma_{f,j,k}$ and $\Sigma_{c,j,k}$ of the problem will be updated, and these matrices are used as the weights for the three terms in Eq. (6).

The hybrid model proposed in this study leverages its distinctive strengths to detect both linear and nonlinear patterns in closed loop features, applicable in both artificial and real experimental settings. The development process of the hybrid model consists of two main steps. Firstly, a Fourier series (FS) model is utilized to calculate the parameterized states of the features. Subsequently, a support vector regression (SVR) model is employed to accurately estimate the trajectory by predicting the residuals of the FS model. The flow algorithm is presented in Fig. 3. In all available 2,662 datasets, 2,130 are used for training while 532 are used for validation. In this experiment, the Gaussian kernel is employed in 239 iterations. By training the SVR model on representative datasets, it gains the ability to discern the underlying patterns and variations present in the residuals of the parameterization process. The computation of the FS model's state residuals can be expressed as follows:

$$FS_r = GT - FS_{states} \tag{7}$$

where GT is ground truth of the trajectory.

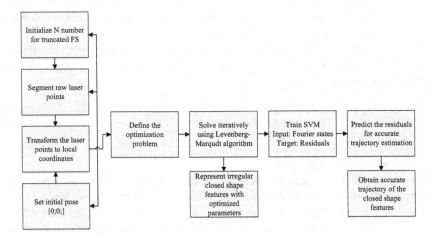

Fig. 3. Algorithm flow

3.1 Error Evaluation Criteria

Mean Absolute Error (MAE) is a commonly used metric in predictive modelling that quantifies the average magnitude of errors between predicted and actual values, providing insight into the overall accuracy of a model.

$$MAE = \frac{\sum_{t=1}^{n} |FS_{rt} - G_{ft}|}{\sqrt{n}S} \tag{8}$$

The MAE is calculated as the average absolute difference between the predicted residuals FS_{rt} and the true values G_{ft} over a given time period. The number of test samples is denoted as n.

4 Experimental Analysis

In this section, a series of simulations and experiments were conducted to assess the effectiveness of the proposed approaches. The Fourier series-based SLAM algorithm was validated and compared against the novel approach that integrates Fourier series with SVR. Subsequently, three experiments were performed, including one in an artificial environment and two in a realistic general environment. The algorithm was tested on a laptop equipped with an Intel i5 processor and 8 GB RAM, and all the code was implemented in MATLAB.

4.1 Artificial Feature Experimentation

The proposed method was evaluated in a real-life scenario depicted in Fig. 4, which involved a lounge area measuring approximately 20 m × 30 m. The environment consisted of manually created irregular features and glass walls. Data collection was performed using a Fetch robot [15]. To filter out outlier laser points that hit or passed through the glass walls, a valid laser range of 4 m was set. Data association was carried out by clustering discrete feature points, and the points were projected back to the initial frame using odometry information. As the number of features was known and sparsely placed, points of each feature were segmented and associated across all time sequences.

(a) Scenario A: a lounge consisting of irregular closed shape features.

(b) Scenario B: underground car park.

Fig. 4. Environment of practical experiments

The comparison of trajectory results between the two methods is illustrated in Fig. 5. The difference between Fig. 5(a) and Fig. 5(b) clearly demonstrates that the FS-SVR method on right side achieved a trajectory with a boundary that closely resembles the real trajectory, while the FS method on left side exhibits a larger dispersion towards the end of the trajectory. Although the FS method's trajectory is similar to the proposed method, it exhibits inconsistency in the lower portion. Since the ground truth for the irregular features is not available, one way to compare trajectories is by evaluating the performance of back-projected laser points using the estimated poses from all methods, which is conducted using the FS method.

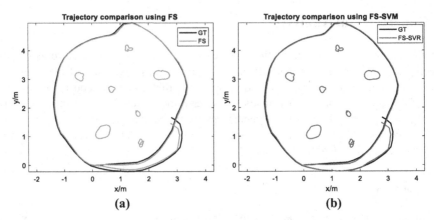

Fig. 5. (a) and (b): Trajectory comparison using artificial features by FS and FS-SVR methods respectively

4.2   Real Feature Experimentation

This section aims to demonstrate the effectiveness of our method in a general environment. Two experiments were carried out to evaluate its performance.

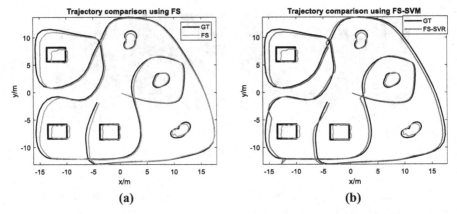

Fig. 6. (a) and (b): Trajectory comparison using real simulated environment by FS and FS-SVR methods respectively

Figure 6(a) and Fig. 6(b) presents the results indicating that the trajectory features achieved with FS-SVR are closer to the ground truth compared to those obtained with FS. While the oscillations at the boundaries of the fitted rectangular, irregular closed shape features, and rectangular room boundary features are estimated by FS alone, as this study focuses solely on trajectory estimation. The example consists of 5 irregular closed shape features, 15 rectangles, and 33 room boundaries.

The second environment used for evaluation is an underground car park, measuring approximately 50 m in width and over 80 m in length, as depicted in Fig. 4(b). The

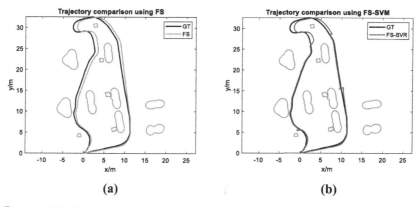

Fig. 7. (a) and (b): Trajectory comparison using car park environment by FS and FS-SVR methods respectively

corresponding result is shown in Fig. 7(a) and Fig. 7(b). As the robot navigated along the aisle and passed through the parking spaces, laser scan messages with a valid range of 20 m and odometry messages were collected. It is evident from the results that the estimated boundary obtained with FS-SVR closely aligns with the actual shape where observations are present. The large jumps in localization for FS-SVR observed in Fig. 7 could be attributed to the interaction between the FS and SVR used for predicting residuals. The FS-SVR hybrid model may not be able to fully capture the complex variations in the dataset due to its limited representativeness of the true underlying function. As a result, the SVR predictions based on residuals could lead to abrupt changes in localization, especially when encountering unseen or challenging scenarios. Table 1 presents the Mean Absolute Error (MAE) between the two methods for the three conducted experiments of Fig. 5, Fig. 6 and Fig. 7. The MAE values provide an indication of the level of accuracy achieved by each method in estimating the parameters and boundaries of the features. The results from the table consistently showed that the FS-SVR method achieved lower MAE values compared to the FS method. This indicates the effectiveness of using SVR to predict residuals in the FS parameterization. The improved performance of FS-SVR demonstrates the capability of SVR in enhancing the accuracy of the overall method.

Table 1. MAE results between the two methods on the three investigated experiments.

Method	First experiment	Second experiment	Third experiment
FS-SVR MAE	0.0272	0.1819	0.1744
FS MAE	0.0524	0.3456	0.301

5 Conclusion

The proposed approach combines Fourier series (FS) and support vector regression (SVR) models in 2D feature-based SLAM, resulting in improved trajectory estimation and accurate parameterization of irregular features. By incorporating SVR to predict residuals, the method captures nonlinear relationships and achieves more accurate trajectory estimation compared to using only FS method. Simulated experiments demonstrated the effectiveness of the FS-SVR model in estimating trajectories and complementing feature boundaries. Real data experiments further confirm the superior performance of the novel method in both trajectory accuracy and feature parameterization. The approach holds potential for general application in various environments. To further enhance its effectiveness, future work can focus on obtaining more diverse and representative training data to improve the SVR model's performance, so as to avoid fitting the training data too closely and not to generalize well to new, unseen data. Additionally, integrating the estimated trajectories with other localization and mapping techniques can be explored as a future research direction.

References

1. Labbé, M., Michaud, F.: RTAB-map as an open-source lidar and visual simultaneous localization and mapping library for large-scale and long-term online operation. J. Field Robot. **36**(2), 416–446 (2019)
2. Ren, R., Fu, H., Wu, M.: Large-scale outdoor slam based on 2D Lidar. Electronics **8**(6), 613 (2019)
3. Wilson, G., et al.: Robot-enabled support of daily activities in smart home environments. Cogn. Syst. Res. **54**, 258–272 (2019)
4. Zhao, J., Zhao, L., Huang, S., Wang, Y.: 2D laser SLAM with general features represented by implicit functions. IEEE Robot. Autom. Lett. **5**(3), 4329–4336 (2020)
5. Guivant, J.E., Masson, F.R., Nebot, E.M.: Simultaneous localization and map building using natural features and absolute information. Robot. Auton. Syst. **40**(2–3), 79–90 (2002)
6. Kim, S., Oh, S.-Y.: SLAM in indoor environments using omni-directional vertical and horizontal line features. J. Intell. Rob. Syst. **51**, 31–43 (2008)
7. Zhao, J., Huang, S., Zhao, L., Chen, Y., Luo, X.: Conic feature based simultaneous localization and mapping in open environment via 2D Lidar. IEEE Access **7**, 173703–173718 (2019)
8. Zhang, D., Lu, G.: A comparison of shape retrieval using Fourier descriptors and short-time Fourier descriptors. In: Shum, H.Y., Liao, M., Chang, S.F. (eds.) PCM 2001. LNCS, vol. 2195, pp. 855–860. Springer, Heidelberg (2001). https://doi.org/10.1007/3-540-45453-5_111
9. Rakshit, S., Monro, D.M.: Pupil shape description using fourier series. In: Pupil Shape Description Using Fourier Series, pp. 1–4. IEEE (2007)
10. Su, D., Xiang, W.: Characterization and regeneration of 2D general-shape particles by a Fourier series-based approach. Constr. Build. Mater. **250**, 118806 (2020)
11. Jiang, G., Yin, L., Liu, G., Xi, W., Ou, Y.: Fft-based scan-matching for slam applications with low-cost laser range finders. Appl. Sci. **9**(1), 41 (2018)
12. Zhao, J., Li, T., Yang, T., Zhao, L., Huang, S.: 2D laser SLAM with closed shape features: Fourier series parameterization and submap joining. IEEE Robot. Autom. Lett. **6**(2), 1527–1534 (2021)
13. Drucker, H., Burges, C.J., Kaufman, L., Smola, A., Vapnik, V.: Support vector regression machines. In: Advances in Neural Information Processing Systems, vol. 9 (1996)

14. https://www.educba.com/support-vector-regression/
15. Wise, M., Ferguson, M., King, D., Diehr, E., Dymesich, D.: Fetch and freight: standard platforms for service robot applications. In: Fetch and Freight: Standard Platforms for Service Robot Applications, pp. 1–6 (2016)

Performance and Robustness

Performance and Failure Cause Estimation for Machine Learning Systems in the Wild

Xiruo Liu[1(✉)], Furqan Khan[1], Yue Niu[2], Pradeep Natarajan[1], Rinat Khaziev[1], Salman Avestimehr[2], and Prateek Singhal[1]

[1] Amazon, Sunnyvale, CA 94089, USA
{xiruoliu,furqankh,natarap,rinatk,prtksngh}@amazon.com
[2] University of Southern California, Los Angeles, CA 90007, USA
{yueniu,avestime}@usc.edu

Abstract. Machine learning systems at the edge may fail as the real world data can be noisy and have different distribution from the training dataset which the machine learning systems were developed on. However, it is very difficult to detect the system failures and identify root cause of the failures for systems on the edge devices due to many factors such as privacy concerns, regulations, constrained computation resources and expensive error labeling. In this work, we propose a flexible and general framework, *PERF*, to estimate the performance of a machine learning system deployed at the edge device and identify the root cause of failure if it fails. *PERF* is similar yet different from the classic teacher-student paradigm. Within *PERF*, a larger performance estimation model $\mathcal{PE}$ is deployed along with the smaller target system $\mathcal{T}$ to be evaluated on the same edge device. While the device is idle, $\mathcal{PE}$ can be activated and predicts $\mathcal{T}$'s performance and the failure causes from $\mathcal{T}$'s internal and outputs features on the device without human intervention. The privacy risk can be avoided as the evaluation is done on the edge device without sending any user data to the backend cloud. We validated *PERF* on two exemplar tasks and showed promising results.

Keywords: Machine learning · Performance evaluation

1 Introduction

Machine learning techniques have gained huge success in recent years and have been widely deployed across a large variety of domains, such as autonomous driving, conversational assistants, face recognition, natural language understanding and fraud detection [1,2,7,12]. A typical development cycle of machine learning systems includes data collection and annotation, model training, model integration, system deployment, and model upgrade or improvement. Ideally, after a system is deployed, feedbacks are collected and analyzed to understand the system performance. Especially, the causes that lead to system failures should be collected and analyzed for future improvements.

However, for a complicated machine learning system deployed at the edge (e.g., Google Home and Amazon Echo Show devices), it is very challenging to

© The Author(s), under exclusive license to Springer Nature Switzerland AG 2023
H. I. Christensen et al. (Eds.): ICVS 2023, LNCS 14253, pp. 377–390, 2023.
https://doi.org/10.1007/978-3-031-44137-0_31

collect feedbacks at a large scale for performance evaluation and pinpointing the cause of failures due to many reasons, such as runtime resource constraints, system complexity, privacy concerns and legal regulations. Due to the privacy concerns and regulations, we do not want to collect raw validation data and send it to the cloud for analysis as it may contain user sensitive information.

Even if it is ever possible to collect raw data on the field, deciding what data to collect for analysis is also not easy due to practical constraints. Specifically, the deployed system itself may either have few clues about its own performance or do not have enough knowledge on how the running statistics at each stage affect the final performance. In addition, considering the limited on-device resources, it is prohibitively costly to run another monitoring system in parallel with the deployed model, to continuously track the target system's performance.

Therefore, we would like to answer the following questions: *Can we design a generic solution that accurately estimates the performance of a deployed target machine learning system without revealing any private user data? Furthermore, can we identify the failure causes without human intervention on spot?*

To answer these questions, we propose a general performance estimation framework *PERF*, as shown in Fig. 1. *PERF* has two major components: a target system T, which is the system to be evaluated and may consist of several cascaded models, and a performance estimation model $\mathcal{PE}$, which is deployed together with T on the same edge device. When the device is idle, $\mathcal{PE}$ accesses both the internal and output features cached by T, and uses it to estimate

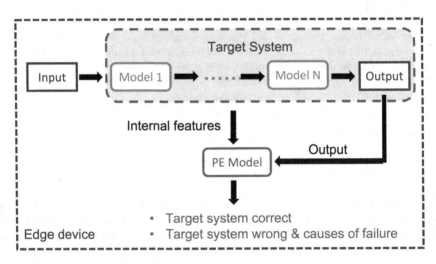

Fig. 1. *PERF* framework for performance estimation and failure cause prediction. A $\mathcal{PE}$ model is deployed aside with the target system T to be evaluated. While T performs its normal operations, it saves its output features and features extracted from selected internal nodes. When the device becomes idle and sufficient compute resources are freed, $\mathcal{PE}$ runs on the saved features from T and estimates if T's final output is correct. If $\mathcal{PE}$ predicts that T failed, it will also estimate the root causes of the failure.

whether $\mathcal{T}$ worked correctly. More importantly, if $\mathcal{T}$ failed, $\mathcal{PE}$ analyzes how anomalies in the input space affect $\mathcal{T}$'s result. It is important to realize the difference between *PERF* and the teacher-student paradigm of knowledge distillation, which will be discussed further in Sect. 2. In *PERF*, the larger model $\mathcal{PE}$ leverages running statistics from the smaller $\mathcal{T}$ to produce its prediction, which is opposite to the teacher-student paradigm where a smaller student model learns from a larger teacher model.

The target system $\mathcal{T}$ often performs real time tasks and hence has tight throughput and latency requirements. Also, an edge device typically has limited compute and storage constraints, which put on resource consumption constraints on $\mathcal{T}$. As a result, individual models in $\mathcal{T}$ are often small and quantized, which limits their representation power. In order to keep the best experience for users, we do not modify $\mathcal{T}$, which is optimized for its designated task. *On the other hand, $\mathcal{PE}$ may run offline on the data saved from $\mathcal{T}$ and does not need to satisfy the same throughput and latency constraints as $\mathcal{T}$.* Therefore, $\mathcal{PE}$ may have larger representation power to perform more complex tasks with better accuracy.

Another important advantage of *PERF* is privacy protection as it neither requires raw user data nor sending any user information to the cloud. Also, compared to conventional methods of analyzing anomalies in inputs [5], our formulation takes a step further and predicts whether certain anomalies in inputs cause failure of the deployed system. To the best of our knowledge, this work comes as the first effort to estimate the deployed machine learning system's performance and *identify the root causes of failures*.

In this paper, we discuss the related work in Sect. 2. Then in Sect. 3, we first introduce the general framework of *PERF* and then elaborate an exemplar design for face directness detection task. Dataset creation and evaluation for the face directness detection task will be presented in Sect. 4 and Sect. 5. Then an additional image classification task will be discussed in Sect. 6 to demonstrate the generalizability and flexibility of *PERF*.

2   Related Work

The problem of interest is related but different from estimating a system's generalization capability. Instead, we aim at obtaining an unbiased empirical performance estimation because commonly used metrics, e.g., precision and recall, are affected by the data distribution in the test set of the development dataset, which may differ from the real deployment environment. Therefore, even if there is no new concept introduced, the empirical performance estimate may differ.

Performance estimation – Performance estimation is an active research area in analyzing machine learning systems, where direct measurements for a system's performance are usually difficult. For instance, in the image captioning task [10,18], it is difficult to provide a quantitative metric evaluating the model's captioning quality. Therefore, [14] proposes an estimation model that probes into the captioning model and collects internal representations. In addition to image captioning, work such as [11] also designed a performance estimation model to examine a conversational assistant system with cascaded neural networks. In [3], a framework was proposed to analyze errors and their impacts on the model performance in object detection and instance segmentation tasks. However, this work does not analyze the root causes of errors and can not apply to other domains. To the best of our knowledge, we have not seen a general framework for automated performance estimation and failure causes analysis.

Anomaly detection – Comparing to identifying the root cause of failures for machine learning models, anomaly detection [5] has been studied for a long time and it aims at identifying outliers that deviate from the majority of the samples. Given an input to a system, anomaly detection does not analyze the causal relationship between the anomalies and the system output, i.e., whether anomalies in the input affect the system's performance.

Knowledge distillation – Our problem formulation is similar yet different from the teacher-student paradigm of knowledge distillation (KD) [9], where a larger teacher model is used to distill knowledge into a smaller student model. The teacher model is expected to perform better than the student model due to its larger representation capacity. The key difference between KD and *PERF* is that in KD the parameters of the smaller student model are learned from the outputs of the larger teacher model, whereas in *PERF* the parameters of the larger $\mathcal{PE}$ model are learned from the smaller $\mathcal{T}$ model and annotations. Note that $\mathcal{PE}$ is only a critic of $\mathcal{T}$ and does not provide any direct feedback to $\mathcal{T}$.

3   PERF Framework

PERF is a general framework that may work with both simple and complex systems. As shown in Fig. 1, there is a target system $\mathcal{T}$ on the edge device that we want to estimate its performance and predict its failure cause if it fails. $\mathcal{T}$ may cache its output and selected internal features during runtime, which will be used as the inputs to a performance estimation model $\mathcal{PE}$. When the device is idle, $\mathcal{PE}$ takes the cached features and predict $\mathcal{T}$'s performance and failure causes.

3.1   Problem Formulation

As the first example of *PERF*, we examine a computer vision task of face directness detection, i.e., determining if a person's face is facing the camera as illustrated in Fig. 2. With a $\mathcal{T}$ model deployed on a device predicting the face directness, our objective is to design a $\mathcal{PE}$ model hat is deployed alongside $\mathcal{T}$ to estimate if its output is correct and error causes if $\mathcal{T}$ fails. To be specific, given intermediate features X and output features Y from $\mathcal{T}$, $\mathcal{PE}$ produces an estimation *est* as $est = \mathcal{PE}(X, Y)$. Note that X may be an ensemble of multiple feature vectors extracted from different internal layers of $\mathcal{T}$. *est* may be either *Correct* (i.e., $\mathcal{T}$ is correct) or at least one of the following errors. Note that errors we consider here are the most commonly observed failure causes in real deployment environments and are not mutually exclusive.

1. *Localization error*: $\mathcal{T}$ fails to localize the person's face correctly at the face detection stage, and hence causes a wrong face directness prediction. For example, this error can be a shifted bounding box detection or a mis-detection.

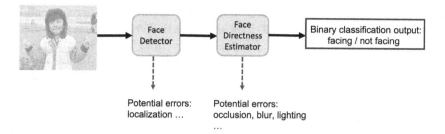

Fig. 2. An example of the target system for the face directness prediction task that includes two cascaded models. An input image (not a customer image, generated for illustration purpose) first passes through a face detection model to generate a face crop, where potential errors such as localization errors may occur. Then the face crop is fed into a face directness estimator to predict whether the face is facing the camera, where causes such as blur, occlusion or poor lighting may cause the estimator to fail.

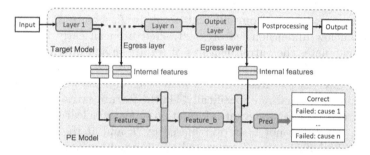

Fig. 3. An example design of *PERF*. Given an input, $\mathcal{PE}$ leverages internal features from $\mathcal{T}$ to predict $\mathcal{T}$'s performance. This exemplar $\mathcal{PE}$ includes three major components: *feature_a* extracts internal features from an early layer of $\mathcal{T}$; *feature_b* combines the output of *feature_a* and features from a middle layer of $\mathcal{T}$ as its input; *pred* combines *feature_b*'s output and features from $\mathcal{T}$'s final layer as its input to produce the performance estimation. $\mathcal{PE}$ outputs the correctness of $\mathcal{T}$ and predicts failure causes.

2. *Occlusion error*: the face is partially occluded by an object (e.g., cup, glasses, mask) that leads to $\mathcal{T}$'s failure.
3. *Blur error*: the image is too blurry, which may happen on a moving subject.
4. *Lighting error*: the lighting condition of the environment is poor (e.g., too dark or too bright) that causes $\mathcal{T}$ failure.

3.2   Model Design

Target System $\mathcal{T}$: As shown in Fig. 2, we chose a face directness prediction system with two stages: face detection and directness prediction. In the first stage, a face detector model finds the bounding box of a face in the image, which is used to crop out the face. In the second stage, a directness prediction model takes the face crop from the previous stage as its input and predicts whether the person is facing the camera. The failure causes considered here extend over both stages. For example, when $\mathcal{T}$ fails, a localization error implies that the face detector failed to produce a good bounding box, and hence affected the final result. If the bounding box has good quality, then the system failure might be due to an error in the second stage. As a result, the capability of identifying failure causes also helps to pinpoint which component fails in a complex $\mathcal{T}$.

Performance Estimation Model $\mathcal{PE}$: Here we elaborate an example instantiation of *PERF* framework as shown in Fig. 3. At a high level, $\mathcal{PE}$ leverages data saved from different stages of $\mathcal{T}$, and learns how different factors in the input space affect $\mathcal{T}$'s outputs. Note that there is no raw or processed user data sent to the cloud and thus the privacy risk is minimized. Also, $\mathcal{PE}$ works on processed data cached by $\mathcal{T}$ and can be activated when device is idle (e.g., during midnight). Therefore $\mathcal{PE}$ may benefit from less compute resource constraints.

Given an input image and $\mathcal{T}$, $\mathcal{PE}$ includes three major components (*feature_a*, *feature_b* and *pred*), which learn how well $\mathcal{T}$ performs from internal representations extracted from different places in $\mathcal{T}$. *feature_a* learns semantic context from low dimension features extracted from an early layer of $\mathcal{T}$; *feature_b* concatenates the output features of *feature_a* and internal features from a middle layer of $\mathcal{T}$ as its input; *pred* concatenates the output features of *feature_b* and internal features from the final layer of $\mathcal{T}$ as its input to produce the performance estimation. Specifically, via the feature extraction and concatenation, $\mathcal{PE}$ learns (1)key relevant information in features learned from the early stage of $\mathcal{T}$, which has not been over biased by $\mathcal{T}$ and at the time reduces privacy risks; (2)what features $\mathcal{T}$ extracted and learned throughout its processing pipeline that lead to its final performance.

Note that $\mathcal{PE}$ does not simply detect specific input characteristics, such as the magnitude of blur or illumination. Instead, it aims at analyzing the causal relationship between patterns in the input data and the performance of the target system. Therefore, $\mathcal{PE}$ includes a set of binary classifiers to generate its output: the first classifier predicts if $\mathcal{T}$ works correctly, while the rest classifiers are error classifiers and estimate the error causes if the first classifier predicts $\mathcal{T}$'s failure. The outputs from the first classifier and the error classifiers are mutually exclusive as $\mathcal{T}$ can not be correct and wrong at the same time. On the other hand, multiple error classifiers may produce positive outputs simultaneously as multiple factors might interweave together and cause $\mathcal{T}$'s failure in the real world scenarios.

4   Augmented Dataset

4.1   Iterative Approach for Continuous Learning

For evaluating the performance of the deployed target model and determining the causes of failures, it would be ideal to have annotated data samples that faithfully reflect $\mathcal{T}$'s failures. However, it is generally very difficult, if possible at all, to collect such type of data from devices deployed on the field due to limitations such as availability, privacy concerns and legal regulations. Not to mention that the real world environment can be dynamic and failure causes may change from time to time. Also there may be a lot of factors, known and unknown, that cause the deployed target system to fail. It is infeasible to exclusively and directly collect data samples of all potential failure causes.

Therefore, one practical approach would be leveraging *PERF* framework to detect $\mathcal{T}$'s failures offline, and extract the embeddings that learn the characteristics of the data causing failures if $\mathcal{T}$ failed. Then the device can send the evaluation results and embeddings to the backend cloud. At the cloud, those collected data can be aggregated and used for further improvements for both $\mathcal{T}$ and $\mathcal{PE}$. Especially for $\mathcal{PE}$'s development, as it is very challenging to collect data from the field at a large scale due to many constraints discussed in Sect. 1, one viable approach is to create a synthetic dataset for the training purpose by using these aggregated embeddings collected from the devices that capture the characteristics of failure causes. This approach has been partially explored by the work in [17], where synthetic images can be generated from a customized GAN [6] to match patterns extracted from provided sketches. This datatset creation method may become an iterative approach for updating $\mathcal{T}$ and $\mathcal{PE}$ whenever needed.

To the best of our knowledge, currently we do not have devices deployed on the field that capture embeddings relevant to the failure causes. Hence, to start with, we created an augmented dataset for developing the $\mathcal{PE}$ model. We envision that after validating the *PERF* approach with the starting synthetic dataset, $\mathcal{PE}$ can be shipped together with $\mathcal{T}$ on devices and then continuously provide feedback and data on the $\mathcal{T}$'s performance to the backend. As a result, an updated synthetic dataset as aforementioned can be created for future improvements and system updates.

4.2 Augmented Dataset Creation

For the face directness prediction task, we created augmented datasets from a real world dataset *ETH-XGaze* [19] by applying augmentation operations to approximate common causes of failures. *ETH-XGaze* dataset includes face crop images of size 224×224 with a large range of head poses. We selected images from 11 random participants in *ETH-XGaze* training set as the base to generate our augmented datasets. Our augmented training set was generated from 7 participants with 69714 images, while both the validation set and the test set used 2 participants' images with 15426 and 17226 images.

The *ETH-XGaze* dataset provides head pose annotations in the form of (*pitch, yaw*) in radian. Therefore, face directness labels can be generated as **facing** if $\cos(yaw) \cdot \cos(pitch) > \theta \cdot \pi/180$; otherwise **not-facing**. Here, θ is an angular threshold for determining face directness, i.e., facing or not facing. We set it to 30 degree when creating the augmented datasets.

We selected four representative failure causes (i.e., *localization error, occlusion error, blur error* and *light error*) and applied data augmentation operations to approximate their effects on images from *ETH-XGaze*. The operations we used to stimulate these commonly observed errors are described below:

1. *Localization error*: to stimulate localization error from a face detector, we randomly changed the size and position of the bounding box of a face in the image within a predefined range.
2. *Occlusion error*: we collected 15 images of occlusion objects, which include mugs, glasses, masks and hands. We randomly picked one occlusion object, scaled it to a proper size and then composite onto the original image to cover the corresponding part of the face. For example, mugs and hands cover the mouth area; glasses cover eyes area; and masks cover the nose and eyes area. The exact position of the occlusion object is determined by the face landmarks from a face mesh estimator.
3. *Blur error*: we used Albumentations library [4] to apply a motion blur operation with a blur convolution kernel to the image.
4. *Lighting error*: we randomly changed the brightness and contrast of an image to simulate different lighting conditions.

The annotations of our augmented dataset include the face directness label and error causes applied on the images. To create a dataset that effectively simulates errors occurring in real environments, we saved 20% original images untouched and applied two operations randomly selected from four aforementioned augmentation operations on each of the rest images. We name this dataset *2-cause dataset*. The purpose of applying multiple augmentations to one image is to approximate the complicated real world environment where multiple factors may coexist and collectively cause the target system to fail. For ablation study purposes, we also created another simpler *1-cause dataset*, where only one randomly chosen augmentation operation was applied to 80% of the images.

5   Evaluations

5.1   Target System Evaluation

Following the system architecture described in Fig. 2, we constructed a face directness estimator by training a head pose estimation model on the original *ETH-XGaze* training dataset, and then applying a postprocessing step to determine the face directness from the predicted head pose vector as described in Sect. 4.2. The head pose estimator uses a MobileNetV2 (with width multiplier 1.0) [16] as its backbone and replaces the original top layer with a fully connected layer for the head pose estimation purpose.

Note that Fig. 2 shows a cascaded target system, which includes a face detector and a face directness estimator. In our experiments, since the images from *ETH-XGaze* are cropped faces already, we skipped the face detector. And the localization error introduced by augmentation operations can still represent one of the potential causes of the face detector failure in the wild.

We compared $\mathcal{T}$'s performance on the original unmodified images as well as on our augmented datasets in Table 1. It shows that $\mathcal{T}$ performs very well on the non-augmented dataset with 98.84% average accuracy. On the *1-cause* dataset, the average accuracy drops to 85.56%. The accuracy drops even further to 80.73% on the *2-cause* dataset as it introduces more complicated perturbations.

Table 1. The average accuracy of T on the non-augmented dataset and two augmented datasets for the face directness detection task. The accuracy on non-augmented is very high (98.84%). It drops to 85.56% on the *1-cause* dataset, and drops even further to 80.73% on the *2-cause* dataset as it introduces more complicated perturbations.

Dataset	Non-aug	1-cause	2-cause
Ave accuracy	98.84%	85.56%	80.73%

Table 2. An example $\mathcal{PE}$ model architecture used for the face directness detection task. The *feature_ a* module includes 2 residual blocks and extracts features from the an early layer (17th) of T. The *feature_ b* module includes 6 residual blocks and combines the features learn by *feature_ a* and the features extracted from a node of in the middle of T as its input. The *pred* module learns from both *feature_ b*'s output and T's output to predict the performance of T and its potential failure causes.

$\mathcal{PE}$	T's Egress Layer	Layer	Layer params	Input	Output
Feature_a	17th	Conv2D	7×7, 64, stride 2	112×112	56×56
		Residual Block	$[3 \times 3, 64]$x2	56×56	26×28
Feature_b	57th	Conv2D	3×3, 256, stride 1	28×28	28×28
		Residual Block	$[3 \times 3, 256] \times 2$	28×28	4×4
			$[3 \times 3, 512] \times 2$		
			$[3 \times 3, 1024] \times 2$		
Pred	Final	Conv2D	$[3 \times 3, 128]$	3	131
		Ave pool	pool size 2		

5.2 Performance Estimation Model Evaluation

We adopted a ResNet-18 [8] based architecture, where both *feature_ a* and *feature_ b* modules use several residual blocks depending on where to extract features from T. Similar to ResNet-18, after every 2 residual blocks, we downsized features by 2. In the classification layer, we used 6 binary classifiers: one classifier is to predict T's correctness; four classifiers are for predictions of aforementioned four error causes; and the last classifier is for other failure causes which are not introduced by augmentation operations. Overall, the computation and memory overhead of $\mathcal{PE}$ is similar to ResNet-18.

As shown in Fig. 3, *feature_ a* and *feature_ b* modules extract features from T. Theoretically, they may extract features from any layers in T. The choice of the extracted internal node may lead to different $\mathcal{PE}$ model architecture and bring impacts on the $\mathcal{PE}$ model performance. Table 2 shows the architecture details of an example $\mathcal{PE}$ model, which extracts features from the 17th and 57th layer of the target model as the inputs for *feature_ a* and *feature_ b* components. In this model, *feature_ a* consists of 2 residual blocks, and *feature_ b* consists of 6 residual blocks. Worth to note that unlike T, which may have limited design choices due to the strict runtime constraints on the latency and memory consumption, the architecture design of the $\mathcal{PE}$ model has more freedom and hence possibly better performance as it typically runs when the device is idle and hence does not have the same constraints as $\mathcal{T}$.

To train the PE model in Table 2, we used a SGD optimizer with momentum 0.9 and weight_decay 0.0004. We adopted a multi-step learning rate decay strategy with initial learning rate 0.1 and decaying it by 0.1 after every 10 epochs. We trained 30 epochs with batch size 64.

We first evaluated the $\mathcal{PE}$ model described in Table 2 and trained on *2-cause* augmented dataset. Table 3 shows the performance of this $\mathcal{PE}$ model. Overall, it performs well on the test set of *2-cause* dataset, and it can predicate if the target model fails with an accuracy of 95.01%. The True Negative Rate (TNR) is 98.18%, which shows that the $\mathcal{PE}$ model predicts correctly most of the time when the target model $\mathcal{T}$ predicts correctly. When $\mathcal{T}$ fails, $\mathcal{PE}$ predicts the failure correctly with a True Positive Rate (TPR) 82.41%. Note that when $\mathcal{T}$ fails, a correct prediction of the $\mathcal{PE}$ model requires that the $\mathcal{PE}$ model predicts both the failure and the causes of the failure correctly. We further analyzed how the $\mathcal{PE}$ model performs on identifying the causes of the failures. The breakdown analysis on the failure causes in Table 3 shows that for the known causes which were introduced to the augmented dataset, the $\mathcal{PE}$ model is able to identify the failure causes with a high accuracy (varying from 89.71% to 92.82%). For unknown causes (i.e., *Other causes*), the accuracy drops to 80%.

Table 3. Performance analysis of a $\mathcal{PE}$ model trained and tested on the *ETH-XGaze 2-cause* dataset for the face directness detection task. The overall accuracy of predicting if the target model predicts correctly is high (95.01%) on the test set. The breakdown analysis shows that the $\mathcal{PE}$ model can predict the failure causes with a high accuracy (varying from 89.71% to 92.82%) for the known causes introduced by augmentation operations. For unknown causes (i.e., *Other causes*), the accuracy drops to 80%.

Accuracy	TNR	TPR
95.01%	98.18%	82.41%
Breakdown accuracy for cause of failure		
Localization	89.71%	
Occlusion	91.25%	
Blur	92.82%	
Lighting	91.71%	
Other causes	80%	

5.3   Ablation Study

We created two augmented datasets with different complexities. A cross-dataset comparison was conducted to understand how models generalize to different sce-

Table 4. Performance comparison of two $\mathcal{PE}$ models trained on *1-cause* and *2-cause* augmented *ETH-XGaze* dataset. Both models perform well on the test set that corresponds to their training set for known causes. However, the model trained on the *1-cause* dataset does not perform well on the *2-cause* test set. On the other hand, the model trained on the *2-cause* has consistent performance on both test sets. This observation indicates that models trained on a dataset with more complex perturbations mixed together generalize well on a simpler dataset, where only a single type of perturbation is applied to the images.

Training set	Test set	Localization	Occlusion	Blur	Lighting	Others
1-cause	1-cause	99.87%	99.73%	93.65%	98.39%	61.54%
	2-cause	68.73%	59.33%	55.02%	50.59%	40%
2-cause	1-cause	96.6%	96.22%	98.99%	96.78%	69.23%
	2-cause	89.71%	91.25%	92.82%	91.71%	80%

Table 5. Performance comparison of different feature extraction choices on *2-cause* dataset in face directness detection task. We compared three choices for the inputs of *feature_a* and *feature_b* modules. In the first choice, *feature_a* takes the original image in the dataset as its input, while *feature_b* extracts the features generated by the 57th layer of $\mathcal{T}$. In the second choice, the inputs of *feature_a* and *feature_b* are extracted from $\mathcal{T}$'s 17th layer and 57th layer respectively. In the last choice, the inputs of *feature_a* and *feature_b* are taken from the later part of $\mathcal{T}$, i.e., 57th and 119th layer. The results show that these three design choices have similar performance, though the first choice is the best and the last choice is the worst. This indicts that without sacrificing privacy, our design may still achieve good performance.

Feature_a input	Feature_b input	Overall Accuracy	TNR	TPR
Image	57th layer	95.41%	98.55%	82.9%
17th layer	57th layer	95.01%	98.18%	82.41%
57th layer	119th layer	94.56%	97.86%	81.46%

narios. As shown in Table 4, we trained two models with the same architecture as described in Table 2 on both *1-cause* and *2-cause* datasets. Both models perform well on the test set that corresponds to their training set as shown in the second row and the last row of Table 4 for known causes (i.e., localization, occlusion, blur and lighting). However, the model trained on the *1-cause* dataset does not perform well on the *2-cause* test set as shown by the third row in Table 4. On the other hand, the model trained on the *2-cause* has consistent performance on both test sets, where the accuracy for known causes are all above 89%. Other models trained on these two datasets with different $\mathcal{PE}$ model architectures also show a similar pattern. This observation indicates that models trained on a dataset with more complex perturbations mixed together generalize well on a simpler dataset, where only a single type of perturbation is applied to one image. This implies that by aggregating features collected from deployed edge devices and using them to create a complex augmented dataset, models trained with this type of datasets may generalize reasonably well on both complex and simple scenarios.

With the flexible *PERF* framework, there may be different design choices, e.g., choices for the positions to extract features from the target system T. Here we explored three choices for the inputs of *feature_a* and *feature_b* modules. In the first experiment, *feature_a* takes the original image in the dataset as its input, while *feature_b* extracts the embeddings generated by the 57th layer of T. This choice may violate privacy considerations. But it is useful to understand if using the raw user data would bring benefits. In the second choice, the inputs of *feature_a* and *feature_b* are extracted from T's 17th layer and 57th layer respectively. In the last choice, the inputs of *feature_a* and *feature_b* are taken from the later part of T, i.e., 57th and 119th layer. The results in Table 5 show that these three design choices have similar performance, with the first choice being slightly better and the last choice being the worst. This indicates that without using the raw user data and sacrificing user privacy, our design may still achieve good performance.

6   PERF on an Image Classification Task

Table 6. Performance of a $\mathcal{PE}$ model trained and tested on the augmented *CIFAR-10* *2-cause* dataset for an image classification task, where T is a 17 layers baseline model. The overall accuracy for predicting T's performance is reasonably well. $\mathcal{PE}$ is able to estimate the error causes with high accuracy from 88.95% to 99.23% for all three introduced causes as well as for unknown causes. This shows that *PERF* framework is a general approach that may be applied to various scenarios.

Accuracy	TNR	TPR
75.18%	62.84%	79.25%
Breakdown accuracy for cause of failure		
Localization	88.65%	
Blur	99.23%	
Lighting	94.99%	
Other causes	98.37%	

To demonstrate the flexibility and generalizability of *PERF* framework, we also validated it on an image classification task using *CIFAR-10* dataset [13]. We used the same approach as discussed in Sect. 4.2 to create an augmented *2-cause* dataset from *CIFAR-10*. The only difference is that we did not introduce occlusion due to the small image size in *CIFAR-10*, which is only 32×32. We trained a simple 17 layers baseline model T (adapted from [15]) on the original *CIFAR-10* dataset to classify 10 image classes. This baseline T model has an accuracy of 78.78% on the test set of the clean dataset and a poor accuracy of 22.09% on the test set of the augmented dataset. We trained a simplified $\mathcal{PE}$

model which learns from the output of $\mathcal{T}$'s first layer and $\mathcal{T}$'s output. As shown in Table 6, this $\mathcal{PE}$'s overall accuracy for predicting $\mathcal{T}$'s performance is reasonably well (75.18%), with better TPR than TNR. $\mathcal{PE}$ model is able to estimate the error causes with high accuracy from 88.95% to 99.23% for all three introduced failure causes as well as for unknown causes. This shows that *PERF* framework is a general approach that may be applied to machine learning systems of different complexity in various scenarios.

7   Conclusions

In this work, we propose a generic performance estimation framework *PERF* to estimate the performance of a machine learning system deployed on the edge and identify the root cause if the system fails. Within *PERF* framework, a performance estimation model leverages both the intermediate features and the output from the target system, and analyzes hidden relations between them. By learning these relations, *PERF* can identify major factors in the input space that affect the target model's performance. We evaluated *PERF* on a face directness detection task and an image classification using *ETH-XGaze* and *CIFAR-10* datasets. The results are promising that *PERF* may achieve good performance on both predicting the target model's performance and identifying failure causes. One limitation of the current work is the predefined causes used to generate the augmented datasets. Therefore, in the future we would like to explore a combination of generative models and unsupervised approaches to augment the training dataset so as to cover more general scenarios.

References

1. Abdallah, A., Maarof, M.A., Zainal, A.: Fraud detection system: a survey. J. Netw. Comput. Appl. **68**, 90–113 (2016)
2. Amazon: Build with amazon's newest devices and services. https://developer. amazon.com/en-US/alexa/devices/connected-devices. Accessed 08 Mar 2023
3. Bolya, D., Foley, S., Hays, J., Hoffman, J.: TIDE: a general toolbox for identifying object detection errors. In: Vedaldi, A., Bischof, H., Brox, T., Frahm, J.-M. (eds.) ECCV 2020. LNCS, vol. 12348, pp. 558–573. Springer, Cham (2020). https://doi. org/10.1007/978-3-030-58580-8_33
4. Buslaev, A., Iglovikov, V.I., Khvedchenya, E., Parinov, A., Druzhinin, M., Kalinin, A.A.: Albumentations: Fast and flexible image augmentations. Information **11**(2), 125 (2020)
5. Chandola, V., Banerjee, A., Kumar, V.: Anomaly detection: a survey. ACM Comput. Surv. (CSUR) **41**(3), 1–58 (2009)
6. Goodfellow, I., et al.: Generative adversarial networks. Commun. ACM **63**(11), 139–144 (2020)
7. Google: Introducing the new google home. https://home.google.com/the-latest/. Accessed 08 Mar 2023
8. He, K., Zhang, X., Ren, S., Sun, J.: Deep residual learning for image recognition. In: Proceedings of the IEEE Conference on Computer Vision and Pattern Recognition, pp. 770–778 (2016)

9. Hinton, G., Vinyals, O., Dean, J., et al.: Distilling the knowledge in a neural network. stat 1050, 9 (2015)
10. Hossain, M.Z., Sohel, F., Shiratuddin, M.F., Laga, H.: A comprehensive survey of deep learning for image captioning. ACM Comput. Surv. (CsUR) **51**(6), 1–36 (2019)
11. Khaziev, R., Shahid, U., Röding, T., Chada, R., Kapanci, E., Natarajan, P.: FPI: Failure point isolation in large-scale conversational assistants. In: Proceedings of the 2022 Conference of the North American Chapter of the Association for Computational Linguistics: Human Language Technologies: Industry Track, pp. 141–148 (2022)
12. Kiran, B.R., et al.: Deep reinforcement learning for autonomous driving: a survey. IEEE Trans. Intell. Transp. Syst. **23**(6), 4909–4926 (2021)
13. Krizhevsky, A., Hinton, G., et al.: Learning multiple layers of features from tiny images (2009)
14. Levinboim, T., Thapliyal, A.V., Sharma, P., Soricut, R.: Quality estimation for image captions based on large-scale human evaluations. In: Proceedings of the 2021 Conference of the North American Chapter of the Association for Computational Linguistics: Human Language Technologies, pp. 3157–3166 (2021)
15. Rahman, F.: CIFAR-10 object classification model. https://www.kaggle.com/code/faizanurrahmann/cifar-10-object-classification-best-model. Accessed 08 Mar 2023
16. Sandler, M., Howard, A., Zhu, M., Zhmoginov, A., Chen, L.C.: MobileNetV2: inverted residuals and linear bottlenecks. In: Proceedings of the IEEE Conference on Computer Vision and Pattern Recognition, pp. 4510–4520 (2018)
17. Wang, S.Y., Bau, D., Zhu, J.Y.: Sketch your own GAN. In: Proceedings of the IEEE International Conference on Computer Vision (2021)
18. You, Q., Jin, H., Wang, Z., Fang, C., Luo, J.: Image captioning with semantic attention. In: Proceedings of the IEEE Conference on Computer Vision and Pattern Recognition, pp. 4651–4659 (2016)
19. Zhang, X., Park, S., Beeler, T., Bradley, D., Tang, S., Hilliges, O.: ETH-XGaze: a large scale dataset for gaze estimation under extreme head pose and gaze variation. In: Vedaldi, A., Bischof, H., Brox, T., Frahm, J.-M. (eds.) ECCV 2020. LNCS, vol. 12350, pp. 365–381. Springer, Cham (2020). https://doi.org/10.1007/978-3-030-58558-7_22

Data-Free Model Extraction Attacks in the Context of Object Detection

Harshit Shah[1,2], G. Aravindhan[1,3], Pavan Kulkarni[1(✉)],
Yuvaraj Govindarajulu[1], and Manojkumar Parmar[1]

[1] AIShield, Bosch Global Software Technologies Pvt. Ltd., Bangalore, India
{pavan.kulkarni,govindarajulu.yuvaraj,manojkumar.parmar}@in.bosch.com
[2] Nirma University, Ahmedabad, India
[3] Coimbatore Institute of Technology, Coimbatore, India
https://www.boschaishield.com/

Abstract. A significant number of machine learning models are vulnerable to model extraction attacks, which focus on stealing the models by using specially curated queries against the target model. This task is well accomplished by using part of the training data or a surrogate dataset to train a new model that mimics a target model in a white-box environment. In pragmatic situations, however, the target models are trained on private datasets that are inaccessible to the adversary. The data-free model extraction technique replaces this problem when it comes to using queries artificially curated by a generator similar to that used in Generative Adversarial Nets. We propose for the first time, to the best of our knowledge, an adversary black box attack extending to a regression problem for predicting bounding box coordinates in object detection. As part of our study, we found that defining a loss function and using a novel generator setup is one of the key aspects in extracting the target model. We find that the proposed model extraction method achieves significant results by using reasonable queries. The discovery of this object detection vulnerability will support future prospects for securing such models.

Keywords: Adversarial attacks · Black-box attacks · Data-free model extraction · Object detection

1 Introduction

The advent of artificial intelligence (AI) has revolutionized the world, bringing numerous benefits by automating various tasks. However, these advancements have also created new opportunities for exploitation and risk. AI models are vulnerable to a wide range of attacks, and one such novel method of attack is adversarial AI. Adversarial attacks can manipulate the model, carefully poison

---

This paper represents the combined and equal contributions of Harshit Shah and Aravindhan during their internship at AIShield.

input data, or use queries to create a copy of the original model. Adversarial attacks on AI models have evolved significantly over the years, and they can be categorized into three different methods: evasion, poisoning, and extraction. Evasion attacks are designed to fool the AI model into making a wrong decision, while poisoning attacks introduce a small number of malicious inputs into the training data to manipulate the model's decision-making process. Extraction attacks, on the other hand, aim to extract the model's information without accessing the original training data.

Object detection is an essential application of AI, with widespread use in various fields, including surveillance, autonomous vehicles, and robotics. Object detection models can detect and locate objects of interest within an image, making it a crucial component in the development of intelligent systems. However, adversarial attacks on object detection models can have severe consequences. For example, an attacker can manipulate the model to ignore or misidentify specific objects, leading to security breaches or accidents in autonomous systems. Previous research has proposed various methods to evade object detection and image segmentation models [25]. Other research has proposed using text generation to mimic a model extraction attack on object detection models [13]. However, to the best of our knowledge, no previous research has explored model extraction attacks in object detection tasks in a black-box environment.

The remainder of the paper is organized as follows: Sect. 2 presents the literature survey. Section 3 presents the concepts of related work, DFME and object detection. Section 4 presents a detailed analysis of our proposed methodology and algorithm. In Sect. 4.5, we describe the dataset used and present the experimental results. Finally, Sect. 5 concludes the paper by discussing its limitations and future research directions.

2   Literature

The vulnerability of AI models has been explored by several researchers who have proposed various methods to secure them. Szegedy et al. demonstrated the susceptibility of deep neural networks to adversarial examples, which are perturbed inputs used in three types of attacks: evasion, poisoning, and extraction [22]. Biggio et al. provided an overview of adversarial machine learning and emphasized the imperceptibility of perturbations used in evasion and poisoning attacks to the human eye [2]. The authors also highlighted the exploitation of Machine Learning as a Service (MLaaS) environments by adversaries.

Multiple attacks have been proposed to steal machine learning or deep learning models from MLaaS platforms, using a prepared dataset to train a clone model from the predictions obtained from the original model [3,23,26,27]. Yu et al. proposed a transfer learning-based approach to minimize the queries required for this process [27], while Yan et al. suggested a cache side-channel attack for stealing the architecture of Deep Neural Networks (DNNs) [26] . These attacks pose a significant threat to the security of machine learning systems, highlighting the need for effective defense mechanisms to mitigate their impact.

The concept of data-free model extraction (DFME) is an extension of knowledge distillation [4,8,11], where knowledge is transferred from a target model to a stolen model without using any dataset. Hinton et al. proposed distillation, which uses teacher logits and ground truth to monitor student learning [11], while Romero et al. and Zagoruyko et al. improved distillation's effectiveness in [19,28]. Truong et al. introduced DFME, which uses zero-order optimization (ZOO) to extract a trained classification model in a black-box setting [24]. Kariyapa et al. emphasized the importance of using loss functions like Kullback-Leibler divergence and l_1 norm loss when using ZOO for model extraction [12]. Miura et al. demonstrated that DFME attacks are possible on gradient-based explainable AI, where explanations are used to train the generative model to reduce the number of queries needed to steal the model [14].

In the object detection domain [7,18], where the output of an object detection model differs significantly from a classification model, attacks on object detection and image segmentation models can be challenging. Xie et al. proposed the Dense Adversary Generation (DAG) technique, which generates adversarial examples for semantic segmentation and object detection [25]. Liang et al. recently proposed an imitation-based model extraction attack on object detection models using dataless model extraction and text-image generation to generate a synthetic dataset [13]. The authors propose using natural scenes and text-image generation to accelerate the generation of a domain-specific synthetic dataset and then train an imitation object detector on this dataset.

In this paper, we introduce a new technique for extracting object detection models in a black box setting. One critical aspect of object detection is the precise labeling of objects and their corresponding bounding box coordinates. Since these coordinates are the outcome of a regression task, any model extraction attack used for the classification task cannot be directly applied to an object detection task. To the best of our knowledge, this is the first time that a model performing a regression task has been successfully extracted in a black box environment. The proposed method is crucial to improving the security of object detection models, which are essential in developing intelligent systems.

3   Methodology

3.1   Data-Free Model Extraction on Object Detection

The proposed attack setup builds on the DFME attack [24] and customizes it to extract object detection models. This attack architecture revolves around three key components: a victim model (V), a student model (S), and a generator (G) as shown in Fig. 1. The victim model is a pre-trained model specialized in object detection tasks, while the student model aims to distill knowledge from the victim. The generator, on the other hand, synthesizes data to maximize the error between the victim and student models. By leveraging this architecture, adversarial queries can be crafted to extract essential information from the victim model, even when the attacker has only black-box access to it.

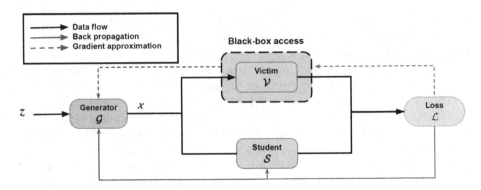

Fig. 1. Adapted Data-free Model Extraction Attack [24] on object detection Framework.

Victim Model: A pre-trained model that is specialized for a task-oriented domain data set D_v. Typically, these victim models are accessible through an application programming interfaces (API) call, providing adversaries with only black box access to the model. For object detection tasks, V is trained on a dataset that includes both the class information (θ_{cls_i}) and the bounding box coordinates (θ_{bb_i}) of the objects in the image. The bounding box coordinates are represented as a set of four real values, denoted as

$$\theta_{bb_i} = (x_{min_i}, y_{min_i}, x_{max_i}, y_{max_i}) \tag{1}$$

Therefore, the V predicts two outputs: *label* for classification and *bbox* for regression, which are combined as

$$\theta_i = \theta_{cls_i} + \theta_{bb_i} \tag{2}$$

Student Model: It is employed to demonstrate knowledge distillation, proving that knowledge from a model can be effectively transferred to another model, even if the latter has a smaller architecture compared to V [1,11]. For this purpose, a pre-trained model is selected as V, and another model is chosen as S. This setup allows the adversary to choose a suitable student model architecture without needing any prior knowledge of the victim model's architecture, thereby maintaining the black box condition. The results are presented for various student-victim model pairs in later sections. The loss function l, based on knowledge distillation, is used to identify disagreement between the predictions of V and S. The student model produces three values: *pre-label* (logits before classification activation), *label* (logits after classification activation), and *bbox* (regression coordinates).

Generator: The traditional architecture of DFME involves a single generative model denoted as G. It is responsible for synthesizing data using random vector points (z) sampled from a Gaussian (Normal) Distribution ($\mathcal{N}$). The goal of the generator is to maximize the error between V and S by generating synthetic data that highlights their discrepancies. Unlike image classification tasks, where models only need to recognize features, object detection tasks require both semantic and spatial information. Thus, the generator's architecture captures both semantics and spatial information to produce synthetic data that mimics the characteristics of the original dataset. The loss functions used for the generator are the same as those for the student model. However, the generator aims to maximize the error between V and S for predictions made on the synthetic data (D_s). This results in a game of minimization and maximization between G and S, represented by Eqs. (3) and (4).

$$\min_{S}\max_{G} \mathbb{E}_z \left[l_{total}(V(G), S(G))\right] \tag{3}$$

$$G = \mathbb{E}_{z \approx \mathcal{N}(0,1)} \tag{4}$$

The process worflow is summarized in Fig. 1 where the random vector points z, sampled from Gaussian and Laplacian distributions, are fed into G, which generates a synthetic image X. This synthetic image X is then passed as input to both V and S models. Predictions made by V and S models combine probabilistic confidence values of different classes $P_{class_i}, \forall class_i \in [0,1]$ with bounding box coordinates of the detected object $B_{box_i}, \forall box_i \in [0,1]$. The classification loss (l_{cls}) and regression loss (l_{reg}) are calculated based on the predictions of the V and S.

The total loss (l_{total}) is computed as the sum of the classification and regression losses, as shown in Eq. (5). During the back-propagation phase, gradients are calculated from the total loss, and they are used to train both S and G by updating their respective weights and biases in each iteration. The aim is to minimize the loss of the S while maximizing the error between V and S on synthetic data.

$$l_{total} = l_{cls} + l_{reg} \tag{5}$$

Algorithm. G and S are trained alternatively at each iteration. To achieve min-max agreement between G and S, G is trained on n_G iterations and S is trained n_S iterations. In this setting, it is important to avoid over-training of G in order for the S to capture the necessary details effectively. Therefore, the value of generator iteration (n_G) is set to 1, while the value of student iteration (n_S) is set to 5. Additionally, several parameters are introduced in the algorithm:

- Q: Query budget, which represents the number of times data generation is performed in one iteration.
- η: Learning rate of the networks, which is used to update the parameters as explained in the subsequent sections.
- d: Latent dimension, indicating the number of random vector points sampled from the distributions.

Algorithm 1: DFME on object detection

Input: Query budget Q, generator iteration n_G, student iteration n_S, learning
    rate η, latent dimension d

Result: Trained student model S

while $Q > 0$ **do**

   for $i \leftarrow 1$ **to** n_G **do**

     $z_d \sim \mathcal{N}(0, 1)$

     $x = G(z_d; w_G, b_G)$

     approximate gradient $\nabla_{(w_G, b_G)} \, l_{total}(x)$

     $w_G, b_G = (w_G, b_G) - \eta \nabla_{(w_G, b_G)} l_{total}(x)$

   end

   for $i \leftarrow 1$ **to** n_S **do**

     $z_d \sim \mathcal{N}(0, 1)$

     $x = G(z_d; w_G, b_G)$

     $X = \text{shuffle}(x)$

     compute $V_X, S_X, l_{total}(X), \nabla_{(w_S, b_S)} \, l_{total}(X)$

     $w_S, b_S = (w_S, b_S) - \eta \nabla_{(w_S, b_S)} l_{total}(X)$

   end

   continue remaining query budget Q

end

3.2 Loss Functions

In this section, we provide an explanation of the loss function utilized in our classification and object detection tasks. Prior research on DFME has discussed two approaches for the loss function. The first approach, called distillation, employs the Kullback-Leibler (KL) Divergence represented as l_{KL} and the l_1 norm loss, as shown in Eq. (6), where N denotes the number of classes. It has been noted by Fang *et al.* that when the student learning approaches the victim's values, the KL Divergence loss function encounters the issue of vanishing gradients [5].

Additionally, the authors of DFME incorporate the forward differences method as presented in [24]. Our work extends the distillation method by defining the classification loss l_{cls} using the l_1 norm loss function, and for object detection, we employ the root mean squared error (MSE).

$$l_{KL} = \sum_{i=1}^{N} V_i(x) log \left(\frac{V_i(x)}{S_i(x)} \right) \tag{6}$$

$$l_1 = \sum_{i=1}^{N} |V_i(x) - S_i(x)| \tag{7}$$

$$l_{mse} = \sum_{i=1}^{K} |V_i(x) - S_i(x)|^2 \tag{8}$$

$$l_{crossentropy} = -\sum_{c=1}^{M} S_i(x) \log(V_i(x)) \tag{9}$$

The total loss for object detection is considered as the sum of these two losses l_{total}

$$l_{total} = l_1 + l_{mse} \tag{10}$$

4   Experimental Analysis

In this section, we discuss the dataset and its preprocessing required, along with the setting of experiments performed. In addition to this, we showcase the final results with evaluation metrics.

4.1   Dataset Description

We showcase results for the **Caltech-101** [6] and the **Oxford-IIIT Pet Dataset** [16]. There were 101 item categories for Caltech-101, however for the experiment, we selected a sample of 1000 images from the original dataset that belonged to 10 classes. Faces, Leopards, aeroplanes, butterflies, cameras, dalmatians, pizza, revolvers, umbrellas, and wheelchairs were among the labels that were given some thought for the experiment. The Pets dataset consisted of 37 classes of different breeds of animals. To reduce the complexity we reduce the classification to a binary classification with one class as dog and other as cat. The datasets ground truth consisted of the class name of the image D_{V_i} and four coordinates corresponding to the object's location. These coordinates were $x_{min}, y_{min}, x_{max}, y_{max}$ along with width W and height H of the image.

4.2   Preprocessing

Initially, the Caltech-101 and Oxford Pets images were in varying shapes, necessitating standardization of the image shapes. Subsequently, pixel values were scaled to the range [0,1].

Furthermore, each starting coordinate value x_{min_i} and y_{min_i} were divided by their respective width W_i and height H_i, and each ending coordinate value x_{max_i} and y_{max_i} were divided by their corresponding width W_i and height H_i.

$$x_{min_i} = \frac{x_{min_i}}{W_i} \qquad\qquad x_{max_i} = \frac{x_{max_i}}{W_i}$$
$$y_{min_i} = \frac{min_i}{H_i} \qquad\qquad y_{max_i} = \frac{y_{max_i}}{H_i} \tag{11}$$

Table 1. DFME results on Oxford Pets and Caltech101 datasets

Dataset	**Oxford Pets**							
Trained Models		Accuracy(%)		Success Rate(%)	IoU(%)		Success Rate(%)	
Victim	Student	Baseline	Attack		Baseline	Attack		
VGG16	VGG16	99	70	70	94	66	70	
Resnet50	VGG16	91	73	80	71	68	95	
Inception V3	InceptionV3	99	**90**	90	90	**68**	75	
Dataset	**Caltech101**							
Trained Models		Accuracy(%)		Success Rate(%)	IoU(%)		Success Rate(%)	
Victim	Student	Baseline	Attack		Baseline	Attack		
VGG16	VGG11	93	**91**	98	88	**82**	93	

4.3 Experimental Setting

To conduct our experiments, we utilize open-source pre-trained models, namely ResNet-50 [10], VGG-16 [20], and InceptionV3 [21]. From these models, we carefully select the architecture for both V and S models.

For the classification task in the victim model, we employ the widely used cross-entropy loss as defined in Eq. (9). On the other hand, for the object detection task, we use the root mean squared logarithmic error (RMSLE) as the loss function. To optimize our models, we choose the adaptive momentum estimator, Adam, as the optimizer. The initial learning rate (η_V) is set to 0.001 and is reduced by a factor of 0.5 after three epochs. The learning rate decay continues until a minimum value of 0.0001 is reached.

To activate the victim's label, we employ the sigmoid function (σ) as the chosen activation function. Likewise, for both the classification branch and the bounding box task, we use the σ as the activation function. This choice is motivated by the need for binary classification, achieved through σ_{cls} for the classification branch. Similarly, for the bounding box values, we require them to be within the range of zero to one, which is achieved by using the sigmoid activation function denoted as σ_{bb}, as shown in equation (12).

$$\sigma(z) = \frac{1}{1 + e^{-V_{y_i}}} \qquad\qquad y_i = G(x)\forall x \in D_v \qquad (12)$$

In the context of data-free model extraction for object detection, we refer to Algorithm 1. In this algorithm, the latent dimension (d) for random vector points (z) is configured to be the same as the batch size, which is 256. These random vector points are utilized to generate synthetic data (D_S), resulting in a total of 256 images for each iteration. The value of Q is set to 5,000,000, and the number of generator iteration (n_G) is set to 1, while the number of student iterator (n_S) is set to 5.

Both S and G are optimized using the Adam optimizer, with the learning rates ($\eta_{S,G}$) decaying exponentially at rates of 0.8 and 0.96, respectively, for 1000 steps. Through our experiments, we determined that the initial values of

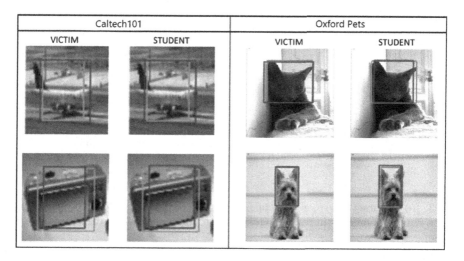

Fig. 2. Comparison of victim and student performance with ground truth on Caltech101 and Oxford Pets datasets. The green box represents the ground truth, and the red box represents the prediction by the victim and student models. (Color figure online)

$\eta_{S,G}$ should be within the range of [0.02–0.0002]. Furthermore, our findings indicate that for improved results, setting the learning rate of the generator (η_G) higher than the learning rate of the student model (η_S) helps achieve min-max disagreement. The loss weights for both V and S in the classification and object detection parts are assigned equally. Each attack is executed for a total of 53 iterations, corresponding to a query complexity of 5 million.

4.4 Evaluation Metrics

In order to evaluate the performance and effectiveness of the attack, we use metrics Accuracy (y_{acc}) for assessing both V and S [24].

For the bounding-box regression problem, the IoU (y_{iou}) metric is used [9,15]. It compares the overlap between the predicted bounding box and the ground truth box.

4.5 Experimental Results

Table 1 shows the comparative performance of student models against the victim models. We experimented with different pretrained backbone models. The Baseline evaluation metrics refer to the performance of victim model. It is named Baseline as we compare our student model to the performance of victim model. Consequently, the evaluation metrics for student is known as Attack.

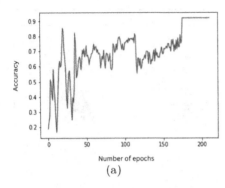 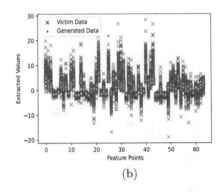

(a)   (b)

Fig. 3. (a) Accuracy curve of Student model on Caltech101 dataset. (b) Scatter plot on the generated images (in red) along with the original images (in green) (Color figure online)

Success Rate percentage is the efficacy of attack, i.e., the performance of student model (Attack Accuracy) to the victim's accuracy (Baseline Accuracy).

$$SuccessRate = Attack(\%)/Baseline(\%) \tag{13}$$

We use the IoU threshold of 0.5 in our experiments [17]. For Oxford Pets dataset, we observe that using a similar backbone model architecture of Inception V3 specifically produces a student model with accuracy of 90% and relative accuracy (between Student and Victim) of 90%. The IoU value for the same student model is 68% and a relative IoU (between Student and Victim) of 75%. For Caltech 101, the victim model, with VGG16 as a backbone architecture, was able to achieve a classification accuracy of 93% and 88% IoU. In comparison to the victim model, the student model underwent the DFME algorithm and did not have access to the original data at all. The student model can attain a classification accuracy of 91% and IoU of 82%.

Sample example outputs from the Caltech 101 and Oxford Pets datasets are shown in Figure 2. The student model is able to make predictions of bounding box coordinates, that is, the regression branch of object detection as well as the victim model. Figure 3(a) depicts the accuracy trend of the student model, illustrating its continuous improvement over multiple epochs as it successfully emulates the victim model. On the other hand, Fig. 3(b) showcases the presence of generated images within the victim domain. This observation validates the generator's capability to identify the victim domain and generate images that serve as attack vectors for model extraction.

The primary objective of our research paper is to demonstrate the process of model extraction. Specifically, we aim to highlight the potential vulnerabilities of object detection models to model extraction attacks. The experimentation setup allows for the possibility of expanding to multiple objects if the feasibility for a single object is established. The models selected for this study will serve as a fundamental reference point. Additionally, the scope of the research can be broadened to include transformer-based techniques by altering the student and victim models while maintaining consistency with the generator model.

5 Conclusion and Future Scope

We proposed a method based on the DFME technique for stealing object detection models. By conducting experiments we have shown the feasibility of our approach and revealed existing vulnerabilities in this task. One potential avenue for future exploration is the extension of our method to encompass multiple object detection tasks. This would involve applying the DFME technique to a broader range of datasets and model architectures, providing substantial evidence of the attack's efficacy and generalizability.

Additionally, given the significant implications of model extraction attacks, it becomes crucial to focus on developing robust defense mechanisms. Building defense models that can effectively counter DFME attacks and enhance the security of object detection systems represents a promising direction for future research. By investigating and implementing countermeasures, we can work towards strengthening the integrity and confidentiality of object detection models, ultimately ensuring the privacy and trustworthiness of such systems.

References

1. Ba, J., Caruana, R.: Do deep nets really need to be deep? In: Advances in Neural Information Processing Systems, vol. 27 (2014)
2. Biggio, B., Roli, F.: Wild patterns: ten years after the rise of adversarial machine learning. Pattern Recogn. **84**, 317–331 (2018)
3. Chandrasekaran, V., Chaudhuri, K., Giacomelli, I., Jha, S., Yan, S.: Exploring connections between active learning and model extraction. In: 29th USENIX Security Symposium (USENIX Security 20), pp. 1309–1326 (2020)
4. Chen, P., Liu, S., Zhao, H., Jia, J.: Distilling knowledge via knowledge review. In: Proceedings of the IEEE/CVF Conference on Computer Vision and Pattern Recognition, pp. 5008–5017 (2021)
5. Fang, G., Song, J., Shen, C., Wang, X., Chen, D., Song, M.: Data-free adversarial distillation. arXiv preprint arXiv:1912.11006 (2019)
6. Fei-Fei, L., Fergus, R., Perona, P.: Learning generative visual models from few training examples: an incremental Bayesian approach tested on 101 object categories. In: 2004 Conference on Computer Vision and Pattern Recognition Workshop, pp. 178–178 (2004). https://doi.org/10.1109/CVPR.2004.383
7. Ge, Z., Liu, S., Wang, F., Li, Z., Sun, J.: YOLOX: exceeding yolo series in 2021. arXiv preprint arXiv:2107.08430 (2021)
8. Gou, J., Yu, B., Maybank, S.J., Tao, D.: Knowledge distillation: a survey. Int. J. Comput. Vision **129**(6), 1789–1819 (2021)
9. Gower, J., Legendre, P.: Metric and Euclidean properties of dissimilarity coefficients. J. Classif. **3**, 5–48 (1986). https://doi.org/10.1007/BF01896809
10. He, K., Zhang, X., Ren, S., Sun, J.: Deep residual learning for image recognition. In: Proceedings of the IEEE Conference on Computer Vision and Pattern Recognition, pp. 770–778 (2016)

11. Hinton, G., Vinyals, O., Dean, J., et al.: Distilling the knowledge in a neural network. arXiv preprint arXiv:1503.02531 2(7) (2015)
12. Kariyappa, S., Prakash, A., Qureshi, M.K.: MAZE: data-free model stealing attack using zeroth-order gradient estimation. In: Proceedings of the IEEE/CVF Conference on Computer Vision and Pattern Recognition, pp. 13814–13823 (2021)
13. Liang, S., Liu, A., Liang, J., Li, L., Bai, Y., Cao, X.: Imitated detectors: stealing knowledge of black-box object detectors. In: Association for Computing Machinery, pp. 4839–4847 (2022)
14. Miura, T., Hasegawa, S., Shibahara, T.: MEGEX: data-free model extraction attack against gradient-based explainable AI. arXiv preprint arXiv:2107.08909 (2021)
15. Padilla, R., Netto, S.L., da Silva, E.A.B.: A survey on performance metrics for object-detection algorithms. In: 2020 International Conference on Systems, Signals and Image Processing (IWSSIP), pp. 237–242 (2020). https://doi.org/10.1109/IWSSIP48289.2020.9145130
16. Parkhi, O.M., Vedaldi, A., Zisserman, A., Jawahar, C.: Cats and dogs. In: 2012 IEEE Conference on Computer Vision and Pattern Recognition, pp. 3498–3505. IEEE (2012)
17. Redmon, J., Farhadi, A.: YOLOv3: an incremental improvement. arXiv (2018)
18. Ren, S., He, K., Girshick, R., Sun, J.: Faster R-CNN: towards real-time object detection with region proposal networks. In: Advances in Neural Information Processing Systems, vol. 28 (2015)
19. Romero, A., Ballas, N., Kahou, S.E., Chassang, A., Gatta, C., Bengio, Y.: FitNets: hints for thin deep nets. arXiv preprint arXiv:1412.6550 (2014)
20. Simonyan, K., Zisserman, A.: Very deep convolutional networks for large-scale image recognition. arXiv preprint arXiv:1409.1556 (2014)
21. Szegedy, C., Vanhoucke, V., Ioffe, S., Shlens, J., Wojna, Z.: Rethinking the inception architecture for computer vision. In: Proceedings of the IEEE Conference on Computer Vision and Pattern Recognition, pp. 2818–2826 (2016)
22. Szegedy, C., et al.: Intriguing properties of neural networks. arXiv preprint arXiv:1312.6199 (2013)
23. Tramèr, F., Zhang, F., Juels, A., Reiter, M.K., Ristenpart, T.: Stealing machine learning models via prediction {APIs}. In: 25th USENIX Security Symposium (USENIX Security 2016), pp. 601–618 (2016)
24. Truong, J.B., Maini, P., Walls, R.J., Papernot, N.: Data-free model extraction. In: Proceedings of the IEEE/CVF Conference on Computer Vision and Pattern Recognition, pp. 4771–4780 (2021)
25. Xie, C., Wang, J., Zhang, Z., Zhou, Y., Xie, L., Yuille, A.: Adversarial examples for semantic segmentation and object detection. In: Proceedings of the IEEE International Conference on Computer Vision, pp. 1369–1378 (2017)
26. Yan, M., Fletcher, C.W., Torrellas, J.: Cache telepathy: leveraging shared resource attacks to learn {DNN} architectures. In: 29th USENIX Security Symposium (USENIX Security 2020), pp. 2003–2020 (2020)
27. Yu, H., Yang, K., Zhang, T., Tsai, Y.Y., Ho, T.Y., Jin, Y.: CloudLeak: Large-scale deep learning models stealing through adversarial examples. In: NDSS (2020)
28. Zagoruyko, S., Komodakis, N.: Paying more attention to attention: improving the performance of convolutional neural networks via attention transfer. arXiv preprint arXiv:1612.03928 (2016)

xAI-CycleGAN, a Cycle-Consistent Generative Assistive Network

Tibor Sloboda$^{(\boxtimes)}$ ⬤, Lukáš Hudec ⬤, and Wanda Benešová ⬤

Vision and Graphics Group, Faculty of Informatics and Information Technology,
Slovak University of Technology, Bratislava, Slovak Republic
xslobodat2@stuba.sk
https://vgg.fiit.stuba.sk/

Abstract. In the domain of unsupervised image-to-image transformation using generative transformative models, CycleGAN [7] has become the architecture of choice. One of the primary downsides of this architecture is its relatively slow rate of convergence. In this work, we use discriminator-driven explainability to speed up the convergence rate of the generative model by using saliency maps from the discriminator that mask the gradients of the generator during backpropagation, based on the work of Nagisetty et al. [3], and also introducing the saliency map on input, added onto a Gaussian noise mask, by using an interpretable latent variable based on Wang M.'s Mask CycleGAN [5]. This allows for an explainability fusion in both directions, and utilizing the noise-added saliency map on input as evidence-based counterfactual filtering [4]. This new architecture has much higher rate of convergence than a baseline CycleGAN architecture while preserving the image quality.

Keywords: CycleGAN · Generative Adversarial Networks · Explainability

1 Introduction

Unsupervised image-to-image transformation using generative transformative models has gained significant attention in recent years. Among the various architectures developed, CycleGAN has emerged as a popular choice due to its ability to learn transformations between unpaired datasets. However, one of the major drawbacks of CycleGAN is its slow convergence rate. In this work, we propose a method to combine the approaches of two authors with unrelated contributions to create a novel approach and architecture that significantly speeds up converge of CycleGAN.

CycleGAN is an autoencoder-like architecture consisting of two pairs of generators and discriminators. The generators aim to generate realistic images, while the discriminators try to distinguish between real and fake images. The cyclic nature of the network allows for unsupervised learning by passing the generated images through the other generator to ensure consistency with the original input.

© The Author(s), under exclusive license to Springer Nature Switzerland AG 2023
H. I. Christensen et al. (Eds.): ICVS 2023, LNCS 14253, pp. 403–411, 2023.
https://doi.org/10.1007/978-3-031-44137-0_33

Building upon CycleGAN, we incorporate the concepts from two existing approaches: Mask CycleGAN and discriminator-driven explainability. Mask CycleGAN introduces an interpretable latent variable using hard masks on the input [5], allowing for selective image transformation. However, it warns against using soft masks due to potential information leakage, which we actually take advantage of in our work.

We combine this approach with discriminator-driven explainability, inspired by Nagisetty et al. [3] This approach involves using saliency maps from the discriminator to mask the gradients of the generator during backpropagation, which we also use in the latent interpretable variable as a mask on input.

Our Contribution. In our proposed method, we combine the interpretable latent variable from Mask CycleGAN with the explainability-driven training of the generator. We use a soft mask on the input, which includes Gaussian noise, and apply the saliency maps from the discriminator as a mask on the gradients during backpropagation as well as added to the mask on the input. Additionally, we adjust the saliency maps based on the performance of the discriminator, allowing for adaptive filtering of information.

Our architecture, named xAI-CycleGAN, demonstrates a significantly higher convergence rate compared to the baseline CycleGAN while preserving image quality. We evaluate the performance using the horses and zebras dataset and qualitatively compare the results. The initial experiments show promising results, with xAI-CycleGAN producing high-quality images even at early epochs of training.

2   Related Work

2.1   CycleGAN

Our work is based on CycleGAN, the autoencoder-like architecture that contains two pairs of generator and discriminator, where the generator and discriminator compete in a zero-sum game [7]. The generator attempts to improve by producing continuously more convincing images, while the discriminator attempts to improve by discerning which from a pair of two images is fake, and which one is real.

It is based on classical GAN models [2] which have shown impressive results in both generative and image editing tasks [1,6,7].

The cyclic nature of the network that makes it possible to use it in unsupervised, unpaired scenarios comes in with the cycle pass of the fake image through the other generator. Given an image of domain X and the generator $X \rightarrow Y$, we produce a fake image Y' and then use the $Y \rightarrow X$ generator to translate Y' back to X', the cycled image, which needs to be consistent with the original image X.

2.2 Mask CycleGAN

Mask CycleGAN introduces an interpretable latent variable using hard masks on the input and fusing them together, using a 1×1 2D convolutional layer, and then adds the inverse of the mask to the output, which produces our resulting image.

The method introduces new hyperparameters that balance the importance of the mask on input as well as the effect of a new mask discriminator's loss on the total loss. This allows the author to isolate which parts of the image are to be converted, while the rest remains untouched on the basis of the hard masks. The mask discriminator is introduced to prevent the boundaries of the hard mask to be used as evidence of the image being fake.

The author warns against the use of soft masks as they may cause features to leak into the encoder, and they have therefore avoided those.

2.3 Discriminator-Driven Explainability Assisted Training

Nagisetty et al. proposes a new approach where the discriminator provides a richer information to the generator for it to learn faster and need less data to achieve similar results [3]. The authors achieved this by generative explanation matrices based on the generated image, the discriminator's prediction, and the discriminator model itself.

The explanation matrix is used to mask the gradient of the generator output with respect to the loss $\nabla_{G(z)}$, before the gradient is backpropagated, hence changing how the generator learns, and filtering out unimportant information:

$$\nabla'_{G(z)} = \nabla_{G(z)} + \alpha \nabla_{G(z)} \odot M \qquad (1)$$

Here $\nabla_{G(z)}$ represents the generator gradient based on the discriminator classification, M is the explanation matrix and α is a hyperparameter with a small value to dampen the magnitudes of the gradient before a Hadamard product is computed between the gradients and the explanation matrix, in order to modify the resulting gradient only by small increments.

This method was originally only designed for classical GANs [2] but can be expanded to any such architecture based off of them.

3 Proposed Method

Beginning with a base CycleGAN, we first introduce the interpretable latent variable using a soft mask to distill semantically significant features into the encoder layer for the mask. Wang M. [5] in the original paper Mask CycleGAN warns that a soft mask may cause unwanted information leaking from the gradient during backpropagation into the mask encoder.

3.1 Explanation Map Application

While this was considered a downside in the original paper, we exploit the soft mask leakage feature by introducing Lambda-adaptive explainability assisted training based on Nagisetty et al. [3] which masks the gradients during backpropagation with explanation or saliency maps from the discriminator. We combine this with a soft mask on input that contains Gaussian noise, with a mean equal to 1.0 and with a standard deviation of 0.02, to excessively express this denoted downside of the approach and distill these explanations or saliency maps through the learned parameters of the network into the mask encoder, but otherwise keep the mask mostly transparent to the network, and remove the need for a mask during inference.

For our explainability approach to produce explanation maps from the discriminator, we use saliency as it has shown to be the most effective based on the rate of convergence. The explanation maps are adjusted by a new pair of hyperparameters, λ_a and λ_b which are based on the performance of the discriminator:

$$\lambda_{a,b} = min(1, 4(min(0.5, x) - 0.5)^{\gamma}) \tag{2}$$

The x represents the loss of the discriminator, and γ adjusts the slope of the function. The function has a maximum value of 1.0 when the loss of the discriminator equals to 0.0, or a minimal value of 0.0 when the loss of the discriminator is equal to 0.5, because that in our case represents a discriminator that cannot distinguish between a fake and real image, so it cannot be trusted.

We use explanation maps from the primary discriminator to mask the gradients and explanation maps from the mask-discriminator, identical to the one in Mask CycleGAN, to add to the input mask.

In the cases where the explanation map becomes significantly dampened by λ_b, due to the mask on input being Gaussian noise, it becomes mostly indistinguishable from the noise itself and therefore no longer has any impact on the generator, which also additionally serves as a means of augmenting the data by adding random noise.

3.2 Generative Assistive Network

Just like in the original paper, the mask is concatenated with our image, before being reduced back to 3 channels like the input image using a 1×1 Conv2D layer. In addition, however, we run the generative process in two passes, where weights are only being updated in the second pass, due to us adding the explanation mask from the mask discriminator network to the mask on input, produced by the first pass, adjusted by a new hyperparameter λ_b.

The idea behind this approach is that the explanation map from the mask discriminator contains insight on which part of the image contributes to the correct identification of the true class of the generated image, and which parts are detrimental. Normally, this information is backpropagated through the network, and weights are adjusted based on the error. Here, we take a two-sided approach of counterfactual-suppression or prefactual-suppression using the mask to either reduce the initial errors made by the generator, or to exaggerate them for the discriminator to then provide better guidance to the generator.

Both approaches need to be tested for feasibility, but in either case, this re-defines the idea of a generative adversarial network to a generative assistive network, as the explanations from the discriminator are helping the generator learn, and promote the generator into tricking the discriminator, rather than the typical competition analogy.

The idea is supported by an already existing well-developed method of counterfactual suppression in image classification networks, where removing, masking or hiding parts of the image helps correct the predicted image class [4]. This, however, can also be used to produce adversarial examples, which would in turn cause a misclassification of an otherwise correctly classified image. It is possible that the generator may learn to use this advantage to generate examples where the discriminator will always be tricked into thinking the generator is producing good images.

3.3 Architecture Technical Parameters

The initial setup of the neural network before adjustments were made based on the results contains several hyperparameters. The model was implemented in PyTorch and based on the original CycleGAN implementation with added skip-connections and modified discriminators and activation functions.

The generator network consists of two initial mask encoder layers for the mask and inverted mask to be combined with the image, followed by an initial feature extraction convolution layer that maintains the shape of the encoded image, but results in **ngf** filters, where **ngf** is the hyperparameter that represents the initial filter count before downconvolution.

Following are three downconvolution steps that half the size using a kernel size 3 with stride 2 and padding 1, while doubling the amount of filters.

Next, we have our latent feature maps, which are transformed with residual blocks that maintain the feature map dimensions. The number of residual blocks can be adjusted using the **num_resnet** hyperparameters.

Finally, we have three upconvolution steps which use transposed convolution layers to achieve dimensions equal to the downconvolution steps at a given level, which allows us to add the downconvolution step to the upconvolution as a skip connection. At the end, we have a convolution layer that reduces the number of filters from **ngf** to 3 as a standard 3-channel image, which can then be visualized.

The discriminators use an alternating set of downconvolution layers with kernel size 4 and stride 2 for halving the dimensions with batch norm disabled, and kernel size 7 while preserving dimensions for feature extraction at various levels of downconvolution. The initial filter size is determined by the hyperparameter **ndf** and doubles with each halving of the spatial dimensions, where the error is the evaluated based on mean square error. The complete architecture is depicted in Fig. 1.

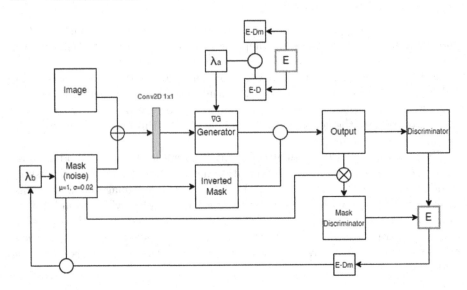

Fig. 1. The custom xAI enhanced CycleGAN architecture—xAI-CycleGAN; The 'E' blocks represent our produced explanation maps that are used to mask the generator gradients after being dampened by λ_a and also added to the input, dampened by λ_b.

The adversarial loss in our method is identical to the one used in CycleGAN which is the basis of our comparison used in Fig. 4:

$$\mathcal{L}_{GAN}(G, D_Y, X, Y) = \mathbb{E}_{x \sim p_{data}(x)} \left[\log(1 - D_Y(G(x)))\right] \\ + \mathbb{E}_{y \sim p_{data}(y)} \left[\log D_Y(y)\right] \tag{3}$$

4   Results

We used the classical horses and zebras dataset along with the apples to oranges dataset to evaluate the new architecture and approach qualitatively, by comparing the quality of the images at the same training step between baseline CycleGAN and our improved architecture, the results of which can be seen in Fig. 2 and Fig. 3. It is clearly visible that our network produces much higher quality and more accurate results at after seeing the same amount of training samples.

These results show great promise, where translations from **domain A (horse)** to **domain B (zebra)** as well as **domain A (apple)** to **domain B (orange)** produce excellent quality images even as early as the 6th epoch of training after approximately 7200 seen training samples. This highly exceeds the capabilities of an unmodified original CycleGAN.

The loss graphs also reveal that xAI-CycleGAN is able to learn much faster and better initially as opposed to the classic CycleGAN which further supports the qualitative assessment, seen in Fig. 4.

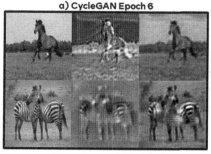

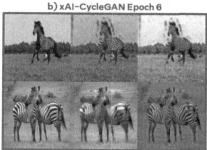

Fig. 2. a) The results of ordinary unmodified CycleGAN with the same hyperparameters as b) xAI-CycleGAN results with added mask and explanation assisted training, and other minor modifications. Both images taken after 7200 seen training data samples with batch size 1.

There are still some issues with the approach, and the generator managed to sometimes produce counterfactual examples. If we investigate the results later in the training, we start to see that the generator has learned to take advantage of the explanation maps in order to produce adversarial examples which trick the discriminator, as seen in Fig. 5.

This is likely due to the initial choice of explanation maps, which are currently using the saliency map approach, where the activations from the output layer of the discriminator, based on the loss, backpropagate to the input where we are able to produce a saliency map of importance values to pixels.

5   Discussion

This approach introduces a new possibility and method of training an unsupervised transformative generative model, in this case CycleGAN, significantly boosting the convergence rate and the speed at which it produces good quality transformations, albeit at the cost of some issues that still need to be addressed such as the presence and possibility of the generator producing counterfactuals later during training.

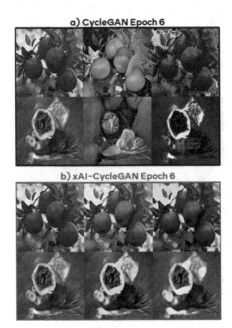

Fig. 3. a) Additional results of ordinary unmodified CycleGAN with the same hyper-parameters as b) xAI-CycleGAN results with added mask and explanation assisted training, and other minor modifications. Both images taken after 7200 seen training data samples with batch size 1. Dataset is the Apples to Oranges dataset from Cycle-GAN [7].

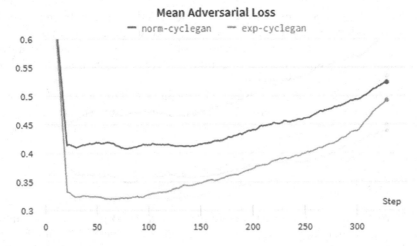

Fig. 4. Comparison of mean adversarial losses of an ordinary CycleGAN architecture (norm-cyclegan) against xAI-CycleGAN (exp-cyclegan).

We believe that with additional specifically-tailored loss function, it is possible to entirely eliminate these counterfactual examples and make the approach completely reliable.

Fig. 5. Sample of a produced image where the generator created a patch of zebra-like texture to trick the discriminator, likely due to feeding of saliency maps to input as well as gradients, where a more complex explanation map could yield better results.

With concerns over the energy use of training networks, especially with a large amount of data and parameters, this is a positive step forward to increasing the training efficiency in one domain of deep learning.

References

1. Denton, E.L., Chintala, S., Fergus, R., et al.: Deep generative image models using a Laplacian pyramid of adversarial networks. In: Advances in Neural Information Processing Systems, vol. 28 (2015)
2. Goodfellow, I., et al.: Generative adversarial networks. Commun. ACM **63**(11), 139–144 (2020)
3. Nagisetty, V., Graves, L., Scott, J., Ganesh, V.: xAI-GAN: enhancing generative adversarial networks via explainable AI systems (2020). https://doi.org/10.48550/arxiv.2002.10438. https://arxiv.org/abs/2002.10438v3
4. Vermeire, T., Brughmans, D., Goethals, S., de Oliveira, R.M.B., Martens, D.: Explainable image classification with evidence counterfactual. Pattern Anal. Appl. **25**(2), 315–335 (2022). https://doi.org/10.1007/S10044-021-01055-Y/TABLES/5
5. Wang, M.: Mask CycleGAN: unpaired multi-modal domain translation with interpretable latent variable (2022). https://doi.org/10.48550/arxiv.2205.06969. https://arxiv.org/abs/2205.06969v1
6. Zhu, J.-Y., Krähenbühl, P., Shechtman, E., Efros, A.A.: Generative visual manipulation on the natural image manifold. In: Leibe, B., Matas, J., Sebe, N., Welling, M. (eds.) ECCV 2016. LNCS, vol. 9909, pp. 597–613. Springer, Cham (2016). https://doi.org/10.1007/978-3-319-46454-1_36
7. Zhu, J.Y., Park, T., Isola, P., Efros, A.A., Research, B.A.: Unpaired image-to-image translation using cycle-consistent adversarial networks (2017). https://github.com/junyanz/CycleGAN

Improving 3D Inline Computational Imaging of Textureless Objects Using Pattern Illumination

Nicholas Baraghini[1]([envelope]) [iD], Pablo Eugui[2]([envelope]) [iD], Laurin Ginner[2]([envelope]) [iD], and Nicole Brosch[2]([envelope]) [iD]

[1] Alma Mater Studiorum - Università di Bologna, Bologna, Italy
baraghini.nicholas@gmail.com
[2] AIT Austrian Institute of Technology, Giefinggasse 4, 1210 Vienna, Austria
{pablo.eugui,laurin.ginner,nicole.brosch}@ait.ac.at

Abstract. Feature-based 3D reconstruction methods only work reliably for images with enough features (i.e., texture) that can be identified and matched to infer a depth map. Contradicting the core assumption of such methods, the 3D reconstruction of textureless objects remains challenging. This paper explores a simple solution to this problem, i.e., adding artificial texture to such objects. In particular, we equipped a multi-view stereo based inline computational imaging system with a pattern illumination module to compensate for the absence of texture. Comparisons of 3D reconstructions from acquisitions with and without projected patterns show an increase in accuracy when using the pattern illumination.

Keywords: 3D reconstruction · textureless objects · Inline Computational Imaging · pattern illumination

1 Introduction

In this paper, we equip an optical 3D quality inspection system with a static pattern illumination module and investigate its effects on the reconstructions of textureless objects. Industrial quality inspection often relies on non-destructive imaging systems and optical methods to detect defects during the production [14,15]. Depending on the application, this may involve detecting deviations from a specified geometry for uniform or textureless objects - a challenging task for feature-based 3D reconstruction methods. One particular example are 3D printed ceramics for medical applications (e.g., blood pumps). They are uniform in color and cannot be altered, e.g., painted on, leaving the used 3D reconstruction method to deal with its textureless surfaces. The *Inline Computational*

This work is funded by the Austrian Research Promotion Agency (FFG) within the project OptiFlow3D (Projectnr. FO999891239). We also thank Abhijeet Lale (Lithoz) for providing the ceramic test samples and their ground truth and Christoph Nowak (AIT) for supporting the pattern projector design and assembly.

H. I. Christensen et al. (Eds.): ICVS 2023, LNCS 14253, pp. 412–421, 2023.
https://doi.org/10.1007/978-3-031-44137-0_34

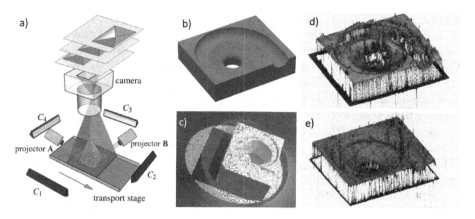

Fig. 1. *a)* Inline computational imaging (ICI) setup with new pattern illumination module (projector *A* and *B*). Standard ICI comprises of a camera, transport stage and the illuminations $C1$–$C4$. *b)* Ground truth 3D model of ceramic print. *c)* Photo of the ceramic print illuminated with projector *A* (red) and *B* (green). *d)* Standard ICI 3D reconstruction without pattern projector. *e)* New ICI 3D reconstruction with pattern projector. (Color figure online)

Imaging (ICI) concept [3,18] (Fig. 1, *a)*), which is the focus of this paper, is one of various 3D computer vision techniques [10] that is used for automatic inspection. The ICI system uses a single stationary camera to efficiently acquire multiple images of a moving object. Due to the motion relative to the camera, these images capture several object views. Thus, a multi-view stereo approach can be used to calculate depth. Stationary high-power LED lights illuminate the object from different angles, increasing the system's robustness and enabling ICI to refine the depth maps based on photometric surface information. In [18], the ICI system achieves excellent results, when being compared to other 3D measurement systems, i.e., a structured light sensor, a laser triangulation sensor and a stereo sensor. However, as all feature-based 3D reconstruction approaches, it shows weaknesses in the case of textureless surfaces (e.g., Fig. 1, *d)*). Its algorithm relies on the availability of corresponding features in the images. Without them (e.g., for uniformly coloured objects), the ambiguity in the corresponding search range increases and, thus, the 3D reconstruction quality decreases.

This paper explores a simple solution to this problem, i.e., adding missing texture by equipping the ICI setup with a pattern illumination module (Fig. 1, *a)*). Its projectors move with the scanned object and "paint" it with a light pattern in a non-destructive way. This improves the 3D reconstruction quality without altering its imaging method or reconstruction algorithm. This approach was previously explored in context of stereo systems (e.g., [7,8]). In [7], Konolige designed a stereo setup for 3 m indoor scenes, that is equipped with a pattern projector. The pattern designs were determined in an optimization procedure that takes the self-dissimilarity and the specific setup (resolution, blur, ...) into account. In some similarity to these approaches, 3D scanners commonly pretreat the scanned object [11,12], e.g., spray paint it to avoid reflections. Baker et al. [2] use texture paint during the acquisition of image sequences that enables a subsequent correspondence analysis which computes high-accurate motion vectors. While spray paint can greatly increase the features available in the acquired images, it also alters the object surface and, in the context of high-resolution 3D scanning, might add depth (i.e., paint particles). Feature-based 3D imaging methods have addressed the problem of reconstructing textureless objects algorithmicaly. Typically they apply regularizers that propagate information from more confident regions to less confident ones, such as textureless regions. It was additionally proposed to improve visual image features (e.g., [1,9]) or introduce segmentation into the 3D reconstruction process (e.g., [17]).

Alternatively, different imaging techniques that rely on depth cues that are independent of the object's surface texture can be applied. Structured illumination methods [6] project specific intensity patterns and extract the depth from observed object geometry-caused changes in the patterns. To this end, individual patterns have to be identified in the images. This is, for example, done by projecting not only a single, but a sequence of different patterns on the scene, so that image regions have an unique binary encoding. This process is time consuming and, thus, not suitable for industrial inline inspection tasks. While in this paper we also project patterns into the scene, a different 3D reconstruction approach is taken on. Unlike structured light methods, we simply use fixed projected patterns to "paint" untextured surfaces. This facilitates the feature matching between the views, which applied to infer depth. Contrary, structured illumination methods identify and analyse several alternating patterns to infer depth. Another alternate technology is laser scanning, which can be used to effectively collect spatial data. Industrial laser scanners apply one of three main techniques, i.e., time of flight, phase shifting or triangulation [5], from which laser triangulation systems are most commonly used in industrial applications. When laser stripe detection is used in an industrial setting, the center of mass approach has been found to produce the best results [4]. However, similar limitations as for pattern projectors apply. Those methods usually only read out a single depth profile consecutively, what ultimately limits the 3D scanning speed.

In this paper, we show that the 3D reconstruction quality of a feature-based 3D reconstruction system, i.e., the ICI system [3], can be improved for textureless objects by adding a pattern illumination module (Fig. 1). Section 2 describes the standard ICI system and our added pattern illumination module. In Sect. 3, we evaluate the proposed approach by comparing 3D reconstructions from acquisitions with and without projected patterns with corresponding ground truth.

2 Methods

We implemented and tested a new pattern illumination module for the Inline Computational Imaging System (ICI) [3,18]. The initial ICI setup and the newly added pattern illumination are described below.

Initial setup. The initial ICI setup (Fig. 1, *a)*) comprises a transport stage, a stationary camera and a stationary photometric illumination module. It acquires multiple views of a moving object which is illuminated from different directions. The ICI setup can be tailored to different applications according to their respective requirements (e.g., resolution and field-of-view) by exchanging basic components and adjusting its configuration parameters. For our experiments, we used a Mikrotron EoSens-25MCX6-FM camera with $25MP$ (i.e., 5120×5120 pixel) with a pixel size of $4.5 \times 4.5\,\mu m$ and a macro-lens (Sigma 105 mm $f/2.8$). The objective has a focal length of 105mm, and the aperture was set to approx. $f/8$. The setup has a lateral sampling of $10\,\mu m$, imaging an field-of-view of 51.2×51.2 mm.

ICI's high-precision transport stage uses a Parker High Performance DC Servo Motor - RS Series | RS330ER1100 able to run at $3000RPM$ as rated speed and dispensing a nominal torque of 0.78 Nm. The scanned object is placed on this transport stage, which ensures uniform linear motion during the acquisition. In this manner, the camera captures the object every 0.5 mm.

ICI's photometric illumination module has four high-power light sources, which are sequentially activated, to capture four images that illuminate the scanned object from four different directions. The intensity of these light bars and the camera exposure were adjusted to ensure the visibility of the pattern which is projected with our added pattern illumination module.

The result of the acquisition process is an image sequence that captures the scanned object from different viewpoints and illuminates it from different angles. The 3D reconstruction algorithm is described in [3]. In a nutshell, images are analysed with a multi-view stereo matching algorithm. Each location in one image, i.e., a center pixel and its neighborhood, is correlated with nearby locations in the same scan line, but in another image. The position shift between found correspondences is used to infer depth. This results in multiple depth maps and their confidences which are subsequently merged. They are the input for a final regularization and denoising step, which takes photometric surface information into account.

Pattern illumination module. The new illumination module consists of two custom-made laser projectors (Fig. 2, *a)*), each with a high power LED (red or green wavelength)[1] and a 17.5 mm/F8 lens (Edmund Optics Inc.) optimized for close working distances. The power of each projector was adjusted individually to compensate for the camera sensor's different sensitivities to each wavelength. This was done to achieve the same intensity for both colors. Due to mechanical restrictions of the ICI setup, the designed projectors have a rather compact size of $5 \times 3 \times 3$ cm. The projectors are mounted on the transport stage illuminating the object from two distinct directions (Fig. 1, *a)*). Thus, a larger area (focus, occlusions, ...) can be covered than with a single projector. By having the projectors fixed on the same moving stage as the object, we can maintain a static texture projected onto the sample through-

---

[1] Different colored LEDs could be used to increase the visibility of a pattern for a certain sample (e.g., red sample vs. red pattern).

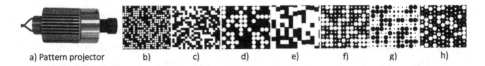

Fig. 2. *a)* Pattern projector. *b–h)* Pattern designs (cropped), which were engraved in a wafer and can be placed in front of a projector's LED to apply an artificial texture onto previously textureless surfaces. *b)* 25 pixel diameter dots, *c)* 25 pixel squares, *d)* 50 pixel dots, *e)* 50 pixel squares, *f)* combination of 50 and 25 pixel dots, *g)* 50, 25 and 12 pixel dots inverted, *h)* 50, 25 and 12 pixel dots.

out the acquisition. Before scanning an object, the position and focus of the projectors must be adjusted to cover the entire object's surface.

Pattern design. The patterns were engraved on a wafer using a lithography technique and cut into 10 × 10 mm slides, which are mounted between the LED and the focusing lens of the projector. Since that ICI relies on multi-view stereo matching, which is performed within a certain size range and related to the optical resolution, the patterns are not required to be unique over the entire image, but only distinguishable within their search range. Hence, we created patterns with randomly dispersed dots or squares of varying sizes to also analyze which feature size was optimal for our feature matching algorithms, spanning from 12 to 50 pixels. The size of each pixel was approximately 2 µm. The used pattern designs are shown in Fig. 2, *b)–h)*.

3 Experimental Results

The evaluation study investigates the impact of the introduced pattern illumination module applied in the context of the ICI system [3]. To this end, we compare 3D reconstructions without and with seven different patterns (Fig. 2, *b)–h)*) and of five different test samples with uniformly colored surfaces, i.e., (i) two *plane samples* (Fig. 3, *a)* and *b)*) and (ii) three *printed ceramic samples* (Fig. 3, *c)–e)*). For each sample, all seven patterns were tested and are compared to their initial 3D reconstruction results without the pattern illumination. Throughout our experiments, we used constant acquisition and reconstruction parameters. Only the focus and the position of the projectors were adjusted to maintain the sharpness of the projected feature for samples of different size.

The plane samples (Fig. 3, *a)* and *b)*) are white plastic sheets with the size of 17.7 × 17.7 cm. One of the samples is placed flat on the ICI's transport stage, while the second one is 14 degrees inclined. Due to the setups smaller field-of-view only a part of the samples is acquired. For these samples, no ground truth data is available. Here, a quantitative analysis is performed by comparing the 3D reconstruction result with a plane fitted through the points of the reconstruction result. When using the pattern illumination, the plane fitting and the comparison only considers points that are also covered by the pattern illumination.

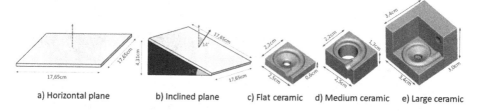

a) Horizontal plane   b) Inclined plane   c) Flat ceramic   d) Medium ceramic   e) Large ceramic

Fig. 3. Textureless test samples used in evaluation. Horizontal *a)* and inclined *b) plane samples*, i.e., white plastic sheets. Ground truth 3D models of printed *ceramic samples* with different sizes *c)–e)*.

Table 1. Evaluation results, i.e., 3D accuracy of reconstruction from acquisitions without pattern (*np*) and with different patterns: 25 pixel diameter dots (*25d*), 25 pixel squares (*25s*), 50 pixel dots (*50d*), 50 pixel squares (*50s*), combination of 50 and 25 pixel dots (*25, 25d*), 50, 25 and 12 pixel dots inverted (*50 ,25, 12di*), and 50, 25 and 12 pixel dots (*50, 25, 12d*). More accurate 3D reconstructions have higher 3D accuracy values. The used patterns are shown in Fig. 2, *b)–h)*.

3D accuracy [%]	*np*	*25d*	*25s*	*50d*	*50s*	*50, 25d*	*50, 25, 12di*	*50, 25, 12d*
Horizontal plane	71.56	**92.05**	86.00	82.16	32.73	74.24	85.81	63.16
Inclined plane	13.42	44.49	**69.69**	54.60	51.08	62.83	59.24	62.61
Flat ceramic	29.66	50.02	41.71	51.89	**52.78**	44.90	45.67	48.61
Medium ceramic	8.41	41.98	45.10	41.74	33.21	44.62	**46.82**	46.49
Large ceramic	4.94	27.93	25.01	17.90	10.75	33.05	**33.10**	28.04

For the three printed ceramic samples (Fig. 3, *c)–e)*) corresponding ground truth, i.e., their 3D model input to the ceramic printer, enable further comparisons. Here, the evaluation is carried out by comparing 3D reconstructions from acquisitions with and without the support of the pattern illumination, with the given ground truth. To this end, each 3D reconstruction result was segmented manually, registered with the ground truth using an Iterative Closest Point [16] algorithm and their alignment refined with the algorithm described in [13].

Figure 1 and Fig. 4, *c)–e)* visually compare the ICI 3D reconstruction results obtained with and without the new pattern illumination, and show their respective reference solutions. For the plane samples, the colored reference plane is overlaid with the gray ICI points that were determined from acquisitions without a pattern (i.e., Fig. 4, *a)–b)*, first column). Example results for the same plane, but acquired when using the pattern projector are shown next to them (i.e., Fig. 4, *a)–b)*, second column, red and blue points due to projectors LED colors). Figure 4, *c)–e)* show example results for the ceramic samples, where the blue points belong to the ground truth 3D model and the red points are ICI reconstructions determined without (first column) and with (second column) using the pattern illumination module. With projected patterns the algorithm computes overall more dense 3D reconstructions that are closer to the reference

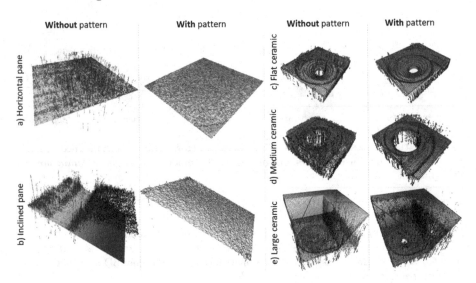

Fig. 4. Qualitative evaluation results, i.e., 3D reconstructions with and without additional pattern illumination for textureless *plane samples* in *a)* and *b)*, and for *ceramic samples c)–e)*. The 3D reconstruction results of the pattern with the highest accuracy are shown. In *a)* and *b)*, the gray points form the ICI 3D reconstruction without pattern clearly deviate from the reference solution that was obtained via plane fitting, i.e., colored plane in *a)*. The 3D reconstructions from data that used the pattern projector (green, red points) are significantly less noisy. This can also be observed for *c)–e)*, where the obtained ICI 3D reconstruction (red) are, closer to the available ground truth 3D model (blue). (Color figure online)

solution. Since low confident points (i.e., a constant confidence threshold) are excluded from ICI's 3D reconstructions, they might be incomplete for textureless surfaces. Thus, the increased density in 3D reconstructions with projected patterns indicates a more confident reconstruction. We observe a visual improvement, which is especially striking for the plane samples shown in Fig. 4 *a)* and *b)*. The introduced pattern removes large outlines caused by the ambiguity in the textureless regions. Similarly, the ceramic samples in Fig. 4 *c)* and *e)* contain less outliers, especially in the spiral area. We observe some limitations for the largest ceramic sample (Fig. 4, *e)*), where the height exceeds the field of focus of the camera, leading to generally less accurate results. However, when comparing the reconstruction results for these samples, a visually better estimation is achieved when using the pattern projector during acquisition. In particular, the vertical walls of the ceramic sample are only found when using the pattern projector.

Table 1 and Table 2 list the quantitative evaluation results that enable us to compare the 3D reconstruction quality achieved with and without the pattern illumination module. To this end, in Table 1 the reconstruction results of the test samples are compared to their corresponding ground truth, i.e., fitted planes for the plane samples and aligned 3D models for the ceramic samples. Our *3D accuracy measure* is derived from the distance of the resulting 3D reconstruction's

Table 2. Evaluation results, i.e., mean reconstruction confidence from acquisitions without pattern (*np*) and with different patterns: 25 pixel diameter dots (*25d*), 25 pixel squares (*25s*), 50 pixel dots (*50d*), 50 pixel squares (*50s*), combination of 50 and 25 pixel dots (*25,25d*), 50, 25 and 12 pixel dots inverted (*50, 25, 12di*), and 50, 25 and 12 pixel dots (*50, 25, 12d*). More confident 3D reconstructions have higher values. The used patterns are shown in Fig. 2, *b)–h)*.

3D confidence	*np*	*25d*	*25s*	*50d*	*50s*	*50, 25d*	*50, 25, 12di*	*50, 25, 12d*
Horizontal plane	0.007	0.046	0.080	0.041	0.008	**0.123**	0.068	0.018
Inclined plane	0.010	0.031	**0.063**	0.022	0.013	0.026	0.034	0.039
Flat ceramic	0.025	0.051	0.026	0.036	0.041	**0.085**	0.029	0.033
Medium ceramic	0.010	0.037	0.035	0.017	0.015	**0.119**	0.038	0.033
Large ceramic	0.004	0.024	0.015	0.010	0.004	**0.033**	0.010	0.021

points to their corresponding points in its reference solution. In particular, we provide the percentage of points with a distance below a certain threshold (i.e., $0.05mm$). Thus, larger 3D accuracy measures indicate less large outliers.

Table 2 lists the mean confidence value for each 3D reconstruction. The used confidence value of each point is given by the ICI 3D reconstruction algorithm [3]. It is calculated based on the consistency of the depths determined form different pairs of views and feature channels. In case of contradictory depth estimates, the overall fused depth has a lower confidence value.

We observe (Table 1) an accuracy increase with almost all tested patterns. On average, the 3D accuracy obtained without pattern illumination (i.e., 25.6%) significantly increases when using the pattern illumination (i.e., 49.5%). This is in line with evaluation in terms of mean confidence (Table 2), where ICI reconstructions from acquisitions with projected patterns have increased confidences, i.e., on average 0.011 and 0.038, respectively. These observations indicate that the pattern illumination module leads to improved 3D reconstructions when dealing with textureless surfaces. Analogue to the visual comparison in Fig. 4, the largest improvement in terms of 3D accuracy can be observed for the inclined plane sample (Table 1). Despite its seemingly simple geometry, this test sample is challenging. Its uniformly colored surface exhibits different depths and matching corresponding pixel based on color becomes virtually impossible. The projected pattern enables a correspondence analysis and leads to a significantly improved 3D accuracy. In Table 2, large confidence increases can be observed for the horizontal plane. Since this sample is flat, the patterns projected by both projectors are in focus on the entire sample.

When comparing the performance of various types and sizes of projected textures (Table 1, Table 2), we cannot identify a significant best pattern for all samples. On average patterns with smaller features (e.g., 25 pixel squares) perform better than those with only larger features (e.g., 50 pixel squares) in terms of 3D accuracy (Table 1). This is also the case when considering the confidences in Table 2. Patterns with smaller features have larger confidences than their larger counterparts (e.g., 25 vs. 50 pixel dots). Using textures with smaller features in theory increases the edge frequency on the sample surface, which is beneficial for the correspondence analysis performed during ICIs multi-view stereo matching process. However, this consideration does not account for the advantage of even more additionally introduced features due to the overlap of the patterns from our two differently colored projectors. Furthermore, possible position changes of the projectors during the exchange of the patterns or the different amount of light introduced when using different patterns are not considered. This might explain the sometimes better 3D accuracy and mean confidence for patterns with only large features (e.g., 50 squares vs. 25 squares for flat ceramic).

4   Conclusion

With the presented pattern illumination module, we were able to provide additional image features for the 3D reconstruction algorithm used by the Inline Computational Imaging System (ICI) [3]. In particular, we equipped our ICI setup with two pattern projectors that "paint" artificial textures on uniformly colored objects during image acquisitions. Having projected textured patterns enable a successful correspondence analysis and, thus, are vital to feature-based 3D reconstruction methods such as used by ICI. We investigated the impact of the pattern illumination module using five textureless samples and with seven different pattern designs. This evaluation showed that the added texture improves the ICIs reconstructions. When using the pattern projector, we observed fewer outliers, more dense 3D reconstructions and more confident results. While all tested pattern designs lead to an improvement of the 3D reconstructions, we could not identify one specific design that performs best over all samples, but observed a tendency towards patterns with smaller features. The choice of pattern depends on multiple factors including acquisition and reconstruction parameters such as size of the projected features, the system optical resolution or the neighborhood size considered for the matching algorithms.

For our experiments, we analyzed samples with white color, which is commonly used in 3D printing of ceramic components which is one of the fields in which this imaging technique is used. This allowed the use of colored LEDs. For applications involving materials with different colors, appropriate adaptations of the LED colors are necessary to achieve optimal contrast of the texture on the material. The results presented in this paper demonstrate the concept of using projected light from two projectors to enhance the reconstruction of textureless objects. However, it is important to note that more projectors can be added, potentially leading to even greater improvements in reconstructions. This is especially the case in areas prone to occlusions, as observed in our case with only two projectors. The decision to employ two projectors was made due to practical constraints and resource limitations, which allowed for a meaningful proof of concept while still highlighting the potential benefits of incorporating additional projectors for further advancements in textureless object reconstruction.

References

1. Aldeeb, N., Hellwich, O.: Reconstructing textureless objects - image enhancement for 3D reconstruction of weakly-textured surfaces. In: VISAPP 2018: International Conference on Computer Vision Theory and Applications, pp. 572–580 (2018)
2. Baker, S., Roth, S., Scharstein, D., Black, M.J., Lewis, J., Szeliski, R.: A database and evaluation methodology for optical flow. In: ICCV 2007: International Conference on Computer Vision, pp. 1–8 (2007)
3. Blaschitz, B., Breuss, S., Traxler, L., Ginner, L., Stolc, S.: High-speed inline computational imaging for area scan cameras. In: EI 2021: Electronic Imaging, pp. 301–306 (2021)
4. Brosed, F., Aguilar, J., Santolaria, J., Lázaro, R.: Geometrical verification based on a laser triangulation system in industrial environment. Effect of the image noise in the measurement results. Procedia Eng. **132**, 764–771 (2015)
5. Ebrahim, M.: 3D laser scanners' techniques overview. Int. J. Sci. Res. **4**, 323–331 (2015)
6. Geng, J.: Structured-light 3D surface imaging: a tutorial. Adv. Opt. Photon. **3**, 128–160 (2011)
7. Konolige, K.: Projected texture stereo. In: ICRA 2010: International Conference on Robotics and Automation, pp. 148–155 (2010)
8. Lim, J.: Optimized projection pattern supplementing stereo systems. In: ICRA 2009: International Conference on Robotics and Automation, pp. 2823–2829 (2009)
9. Liu, S., et al.: Feature matching for texture-less endoscopy images via superpixel vector field consistency. Biomed. Opt. Express **4**, 2247–2265 (2022)
10. Neethu, N., Anoop, B.: Role of computer vision in automatic inspection system. Int. J. Comput. Appl. **123**(13), 28–31 (2015)
11. Palousek, D., Omasta, M., Koutny, D., Bednar, J., Koutecky, T., Dokoupil, F.: Effect of matte coating on 3D optical measurement accuracy. Opt. Mater. **40**, 1–9 (2015)
12. Pereira, J.R.M., De Lima e Silva Penz, I., Da Silva, F.P.: Effects of different coating materials on three-dimensional optical scanning accuracy. Adv. Mech. Eng. **11**(4), 1–6 (2019)
13. Rusu, R., Blodow, N., Beetz, M.: Fast point feature histograms (FPFH) for 3D registration. In: ROBOT 2009: International Conference on Robotics and Automation, pp. 3212–3217 (2009)
14. Schmitz, V., Kröning, M., Kangenberg, K.: Quantitative NDT by 3D image reconstruction. Acoust. Imaging **22**, 735–744 (1996)
15. Shaloo, M., Schnall, M., Klein, T., Huber, N., Reitinger, B.: A review of nondestructive testing (NDT) techniques for defect detection: application to fusion welding and future wire arc additive manufacturing processes. MDPI Mater. (15), 1–26 (2022)
16. Shi, X., Peng, J., Li, J., Yan, P., Gong, H.: The iterative closest point registration algorithm based on the normal distribution transformation. In: International Conference on Identification, Information, and Knowledge in the Internet of Things, pp. 181–190 (2018)
17. Tao, H., Sawhney, H.: Global matching criterion and color segmentation based stereo. In: Workshop on Applications of Computer Vision, pp. 246–253 (2000)
18. Traxler, L., Ginner, L., Breuss, S., Blaschitz, B.: Experimental comparison of optical inline 3D measurement and inspection systems. IEEE Access **9**, 53952–53963 (2021)

Integrating Visual and Semantic Similarity Using Hierarchies for Image Retrieval

Aishwarya Venkataramanan[1,2,3](✉) ⓘ, Martin Laviale[1,3] ⓘ,
and Cédric Pradalier[2,3] ⓘ

[1] Laboratoire Interdisciplinaire des Environnements Continentaux,
Université de Lorraine, Metz, France
`aishwarya.venkataramanan@univ-lorraine.fr`
[2] GeorgiaTech Lorraine - International Research Lab Georgia Tech - CNRS IRL
2958, Metz, France
[3] LTSER - "Zone Atelier Moselle", Metz, France

Abstract. Most of the research in content-based image retrieval (CBIR) focus on developing robust feature representations that can effectively retrieve instances from a database of images that are visually similar to a query. However, the retrieved images sometimes contain results that are not semantically related to the query. To address this, we propose a method for CBIR that captures both visual and semantic similarity using a visual hierarchy. The hierarchy is constructed by merging classes with overlapping features in the latent space of a deep neural network trained for classification, assuming that overlapping classes share high visual and semantic similarities. Finally, the constructed hierarchy is integrated into the distance calculation metric for similarity search. Experiments on standard datasets: CUB-200-2011 and CIFAR100, and a real-life use case using diatom microscopy images show that our method achieves superior performance compared to the existing methods on image retrieval.

Keywords: Similarity Search · Visual Hierarchy · Content-based image retrieval

1 Introduction

In recent years, the exponential growth of image data has made effective management of such data increasingly important. One way to manage this data is through Content-based Image Retrieval (CBIR), where a query image is used to retrieve images from the database that are visually similar to it [5]. The comparison is performed on the features extracted from the images, represented by a set of numerical descriptors or vectors. The search is performed on these descriptors using a similarity measure such as the Euclidean or cosine distance. The challenge is to extract robust feature representations, such that objects belonging to the same category are close by, despite the changes in view-point, background and

H. I. Christensen et al. (Eds.): ICVS 2023, LNCS 14253, pp. 422–431, 2023.
https://doi.org/10.1007/978-3-031-44137-0_35

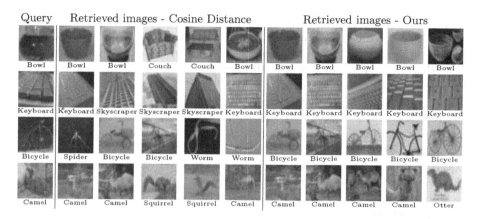

Fig. 1. Examples of top-5 images retrieved using cosine distance and our method on CIFAR100. Our method incorporates hierarchy while ranking image similarity, with retrieves images that are more visually and semantically relevant.

illumination. Recent methods employing Convolutional Neural Network (CNN) for feature extraction have proven to be robust and effective over the classical hand-crafted feature extractors [16]. A commonly adopted approach is to extract feature vectors from the latent space of a trained CNN classifier. Deep classifiers use cross-entropy loss that learns feature representations to group together objects belonging to the same category, while separating them from the rest. Thus, given a query image, the retrieved data from the local neighbourhood in the latent space should ideally consist of images belonging to the same classification category.

Despite the ability of the CNNs to learn discriminative representations, it has been observed that sometimes, images unrelated to the query are retrieved [1,10]. These images are typically visually similar to the query, but semantically very different. Figure 1 illustrates this for the images retrieved using cosine distance on CIFAR100 [8]. While the retrieved images have certain visual similarities with the query, some of them are semantically very different. One way to address this is by incorporating domain knowledge while training, so that the network learns feature representations that are both visually and semantically relevant [1]. The semantic data is obtained from expert domain knowledge or lexical databases such as WordNet [9]. However, incorporating external domain knowledge during training can be challenging since it would require significant changes in the training procedure, and can be detrimental when there are inconsistencies between visual and semantic similarities [3]. Also, it assumes that the specialized domain knowledge is available, which can be hard to obtain or irrelevant in certain situations, such as, querying the images of people or vehicles. In this paper, we demonstrate that the visual hierarchies obtained from the representations learned by the classification network are rich in visual and semantic information, achieving superior retrieval performance. Contrary to other approaches, our method does not require specialized domain knowledge or modifications to the training procedure, making it easy to integrate into an off-the-shelf classification network.

Our method relies on two key aspects for the retrieval: construction of a hierarchy that is visually and semantically meaningful, and integration of hierarchy into the distance calculation metric for similarity search. Our method for hierarchy construction involves identifying the classes in the latent space whose feature representations overlap with one another. This is based on the assumption that the overlapping classes are those that are very similar to each other, both visually and semantically. The clusters of overlapping classes are then grouped together into the same class at a higher hierarchy level. This process is repeated at different levels of the hierarchy until there are no overlaps in the feature representations, resulting in a hierarchical structure that captures both visual and semantic similarities between images. Once the hierarchy is obtained, we combine the cosine distance and a hierarchy-based distance to obtain a metric for ranking the images for retrieval. Experimental results show that our method improves image retrieval performance on two standard benchmarks: CIFAR100 [8] and CUB-200-2011 [15], and a real life diatom image retrieval use case. Additionally, we demonstrate the robustness of our method by evaluating on images subject to perturbations that mimic practical difficulties encountered during acquisition.

Our contributions are as follows: (i) we develop a method to construct a hierarchy that is visually and semantically relevant and show that incorporating this hierarchy in the distance metric enhances the image retrieval performance, (ii) we design the method such that it does not require any additional domain knowledge and introduces no modifications to the model architecture or training procedure. The code is available in https://github.com/vaishwarya96/Hierarchy-image-retrieval.git.

2   Related Works

The role of visual attributes and semantics is crucial in describing images for identification or retrieval. Hierarchies are an intuitive way to express this, and several methods have leveraged it for image categorization and retrieval [11]. This is done by integrating hierarchy obtained from the biological taxonomy or from lexical databases to learn feature representations that capture semantic similarity between the categories. [4] uses WordNet to construct hierarchies and incorporates the domain knowledge obtained from it into a CNN classifier to improve the network's performance. [2] extends the traditional cross-entropy loss used in flat classification to work on hierarchies. To do so, they compute the conditional probability of the nodes at each layer of the hierarchy and calculate the cross-entropy loss at each layer. DeViSE [6] transfers semantic knowledge from text to visual object recognition. It involves pre-training a language model to learn word embeddings and re-training a deep visual model using these embeddings for image label prediction. [1] uses an embedding algorithm that maps images onto a hypersphere. The distances on this hypersphere represent similarities that are derived from the lowest common ancestor height in a given hierarchy tree. One limitation of these methods is their reliance on an existing domain knowledge, which can be difficult to obtain or irrelevant in some contexts.

A line of work relies on the visual features learnt by the network. [18] uses metric loss while training the network for image retrieval. Metric loss tries to pull closer the representations of images belonging to the same class, while pushing apart the inter-class representations. While this reinforces the condition that the intra-class representations are clustered tightly, it does not impact the semantic relationship between the instances. [19] constructs a visual hierarchy from the distance values between the image features and uses it to improve classification. Our method is similar to [10], which uses Ward clustering for constructing the hierarchy and uses it for re-ranking the images retrieved using a distance metric. A drawback of using Ward clustering is that they are sensitive to outliers and can sometimes group classes with low semantic similarities. In contrast, our approach groups classes only when their features overlap, which results in a more meaningful and semantically relevant hierarchy.

3 Method

This section explains the two main steps of our method: the construction of the hierarchy from the learned feature representations, and the calculation of the distance metric for ranking the images.

Notations: Consider a CNN classifier trained on K classes, each class represented as $\{C_1, ..., C_K\}$. The feature vectors are extracted from the penultimate layer of the CNN. We apply dimensionality reduction on these feature vectors using PCA to reduce the redundant features and speed up the computation [17]. We automatically determine the number of principal components required to explain 95% of the original data variance by examining the eigenvalues in decreasing order. Let the feature vectors corresponding to the training images be x_{train}. Assume that the class features follow multivariate Gaussian distributions with mean μ_c and covariance Σ_c, where $c = \{1, .., K\}$. Note that this assumption can be broken when the intra-class variance is large. In such cases, one can constrain the latent space to be Gaussian using the methodology in [13]. Given a query image q, its feature vector is denoted as x_q. Suppose the database consists of N images, their corresponding feature vectors are denoted as $\{x_1, .., x_N\}$.

3.1 Hierarchy Construction

The hierarchy construction involves identifying the classes with overlapping distributions of feature vectors in x_{train}. Inter-class overlapping typically occurs when there are visual and semantic similarities in the class images. To construct the hierarchy, a bottom-up approach is used, where the overlapping classes in the latent space are merged in the higher hierarchy level. The overlapping classes are identified using the Bhattacharya Coefficient (BC), which is a statistical metric to measure the amount of overlap between two statistical populations.

The Bhattacharya distance between two classes C_i and C_j is given by:

$$D_B(C_i, C_j) = \frac{1}{8}(\mu_i - \mu_j)^T \Sigma^{-1}(\mu_i - \mu_j) + \frac{1}{2}\ln\left(\frac{\det \Sigma}{\sqrt{\det \Sigma_i \det \Sigma_j}}\right) \quad (1)$$

where $\Sigma = \frac{\Sigma_i + \Sigma_j}{2}$

The BC is calculated as:

$$BC(C_i, C_j) = e^{-D_B(C_i, C_j)} \quad (2)$$

The value of BC ranges from 0 to 1 inclusive, where a value of 0 signifies no overlap and 1 means full overlap. If the value of the BC between two classes is greater than or equal to a specified threshold t, then they are considered to be overlapping. Every cluster of classes that overlap with each other are identified. All classes within each cluster are merged into a unified class at a higher level of the hierarchy. On the other hand, if the BC is less than t, then these classes are considered to be distinct and are kept separate in the higher hierarchy level. The t value is a hyperparameter that depends on the dataset. The process of BC estimation is repeated at each level on the new set of classes, and the overlapping classes are merged to create a hierarchy structure. This is performed until there are no overlaps between the classes, or all the classes have been merged. At the higher hierarchy levels, some classes include feature vectors from multiple small classes that were merged. At every level, the μ and Σ values are recalculated from the feature vectors of the merged classes.

3.2   Distance Calculation

After constructing the hierarchy, we use it to perform the similarity search for image retrieval. The distances are calculated between the query feature x_q and the image features x_i in the database. Our final distance metric for ranking the images is a weighted sum of two distance values: cosine distance and a hierarchy based distance.

Cosine Distance: The cosine distance is a similarity measure between two feature vectors and is popularly used in image retrieval tasks. The cosine distance between x_q and x_i is given by:

$$D_C(x_q, x_i) = 1 - \frac{x_q \cdot x_i}{\|x_q\|\|x_i\|} \quad (3)$$

where $\cdot$ is the dot product and $\|\ \|$ is the L2 norm.

Hierarchical Distance: The hierarchy is a tree structure $\mathcal{H} = (V, E)$ where V represents the nodes and E, the edges. $\mathcal{H}$ consists of K leaf nodes. We want to identify the position of any database image in the hierarchy, which means finding the leaf closest to each image. To identify the leaf nodes, we calculate the Mahalanobis Distance (MD) between the feature vectors x_i and the feature vectors x_{train} corresponding to each leaf node. The MD between x_i and node c, is given as:

$$MD_c(x_i) = \sqrt{(x_i - \mu_c)^T \Sigma_c^{-1}(x_i - \mu_c)} \tag{4}$$

x_i is assigned to the leaf node n_i corresponding to the smallest MD value.

Similarly, the leaf node n_q corresponding to x_q is identified. The distance calculation uses the height of the lowest common ancestor (LCA), where the LCA of two nodes is the parent node that is an ancestor of both nodes and does not have any child that is also an ancestor of both nodes. The hierarchical distance [1] between x_q and x_i is calculated as:

$$D_H(x_q, x_i) = \frac{\text{height}(\text{LCA}(n_i, n_q))}{\text{height}(\mathcal{H})} \tag{5}$$

The final distance is given as:

$$D = D_C(x_q, x_i) + \alpha D_H(x_q, x_i) \tag{6}$$

where α is a hyperparameter.

The images are sorted in ascending order of D to rank the images based on similarity and retrieve them.

3.3   Robustness Analysis

Robustness analysis demonstrates the ability of the image retrieval methods to maintain accurate and reliable performance even when the images are distorted or corrupted. The distortions introduced during the robustness analysis mimic real-world scenarios where images can be affected by factors like blurring, occlusions, and changes in lighting conditions.

We consider the following scenarios: (i) Blurring – The images are subject to Gaussian blurring, simulating the effect of an out-of-focus camera or a low-quality image (ii) Saturation change – The saturation values of the original images are modified to simulate variations in colour intensity. (iii) Occlusions – Random occlusions are introduced in different parts of the images, simulating objects or regions being partially or completely blocked.

4   Experiments

4.1   Baselines

We compare our method against the following approaches: (i) Image retrieval using Euclidean Distance, (ii) Image retrieval using Cosine Distance, (iii) Our method using hierarchical distance only, (iv) Semantic Embeddings [1], (v) Our method applied on the features extracted from semantic embeddings in (iv), (vi) Distance calculation using the method in Sect. 3.2 on hierarchy constructed using Ward clustering [10], (vii) Distance calculation on semantic hierarchy obtained using domain knowledge.

4.2 Experimental Setup

We perform our experiments on three datasets with fine-grained visual features:

CUB-200-2011 [15]. This is a widely used dataset for image retrieval, consisting of 200 classes of birds and a total of 11,788 images. The train data consists of 5,994 images and the test data consists of 5,794 images. The images were resized to 224 × 224, and random horizontal flipping and rotation (±30°) were used for data augmentation. Following [1], we used ResNet-50 [7] for training with an SGD optimizer. The network was trained for 100 epochs with a batch size of 12. The values of $t = 0.30$ and $\alpha = 3$ are obtained using hyperparameter search.

CIFAR100 [8]. It consists of 60,000 images, of size 32 × 32 belonging to 100 classes of wide range of objects. The training dataset consists of 50,000 images and the remaining are test data. Following [1], we used ResNet-110 [7] for training with an SGD optimizer. The network was trained for 400 epochs with a batch size of 24. The values of $t = 0.20$ and $\alpha = 5$ are obtained using hyperparameter search.

Diatom Dataset. The diatom dataset consists of 9895 individual diatom images belonging to 166 classes [14]. The network was trained using EfficientNet [12]. An SGD optimizer with a learning rate of 0.0002 was used. The images were resized to 256 × 256. This dataset contains high intra-class variance with distinct feature representations per class, and hence the latent space is not Gaussian, making it incompatible for BC calculation. The network was trained using the method in [13], which ensures a Gaussian latent space. The training was performed for 100 epochs with a batch size of 12. The values of $t = 0.25$ and $\alpha = 3$ are obtained using hyperparameter search.

For the CIFAR100 and CUB-200-2011, 80% of the train data was used for training and 20% for validation. For the diatoms, 70% of the dataset was used for training, 10% for validation and 20% for testing. The networks were trained on GeForce RTX 3090 with 24 Gb of RAM. The semantic hierarchy of CUB-200-2011 and CIFAR100 for the baseline experiments were obtained from [1]. The diatom hierarchy was obtained from the taxonomy of the species, consisting of two levels: 'genus' and 'species'. The same model architectures were used for comparing all the baselines.

Setup for Robustness Analysis. The analysis is performed on the CUB-200-2011 dataset with the following settings. (i) A Gaussian Blur with kernel size (11, 11) was applied to all the images, (ii) The saturation of images were adjusted with randomly chosen values in the range [0, 1, 0.5, 1, 2,5] and (iii) A random crop of dimension (70,70) was replaced by black patch in every image. The networks were retrained on the modified images, with the same training parameters.

4.3 Evaluation Metrics

We use MAP@k values for evaluating the image retrieval performance. MAP@k measures the average precision (AP) of the top k retrieved images, and then takes the mean across all queries. A higher value indicates better performance.

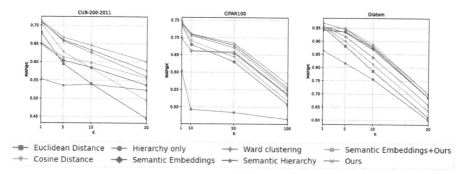

Fig. 2. Retrieval performance on CUB-200-2011, CIFAR100 and Diatom dataset. Our method achieves state-of-the-art performance. The results suggest that incorporating hierarchy into content-based image retrieval is effective in improving the retrieval performance.

5 Results

5.1 Retrieval Results

Figure 2 shows the plots of mAP@k values for different values of k for the three datasets. The results suggest that combining the visual and semantic cues improves the retrieval. Overall, our method achieves the best performance over the other baselines.

Effect of Distances: The cosine distance retrieves images that are visually similar to the query, whereas, the hierarchical distance takes into account the semantic relationships between classes. Both these aspects are important when retrieving the images, and removing one of them deteriorates the performance. There is a significant drop in the MAP values in CIFAR100 when using only the hierarchical distance. One explanation for this is that CIFAR100 contains classes that are visually diverse, and hence, visual cues are more important over the semantic ones here. This could also explain the marginal improvement in the metrics when combining both the visual and semantic attributes than when using only the visual information for CIFAR100 over the other datasets.

Effect of Hierarchy: In the hierarchy-based methods, our approach outperforms the baselines. This is closely followed by our approach of distance calculation using semantic hierarchy. While semantic embeddings [1] also relies on visual and semantic features for the retrieval, its drop in performance could be attributed to the errors introduced due to disagreements between the visual and semantic relationships while training [3]. Our approach of hierarchy construction merges the classes only when there is a correlation between visual and semantic attributes, and thus it is robust against these errors. The Ward hierarchy approach may sometimes group classes that are semantically unrelated, resulting in less effective performance.

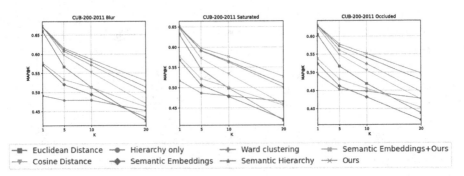

Fig. 3. Robustness analysis on the CUB-200-2011 dataset. Blurring, saturation change and occlusion were applied to test the impact on the retrieval. Results show that our method still achieves the best performance.

Qualitative Analysis: Figure 1 shows some images retrieved using cosine distance and our method. While cosine distance retrieves images that are visually similar, some of them are semantically very different. Whereas, our method retrieves images that are visually and semantically meaningful.

Robustness Analysis: Figure 3 shows the MAP@K plots for the robustness analysis on CUB-200-2011. Compared to the plot in Fig. 2, one can observe a drop in the metrics. However, our method still achieves the best performance over the other baselines, indicating its robustness even in challenging conditions.

6   Discussion and Conclusion

In this paper, we presented a method to tackle the problem of semantically dissimilar images retrieved in CBIR. By leveraging the learned feature representations from a CNN classifier, we construct a meaningful hierarchy that captures both visual and semantic information. This hierarchy is then integrated into the distance metric for similarity search, resulting in superior image retrieval performance, as demonstrated on fine-grained visual datasets. One limitation of our method arises when classes exhibit high variance in their features, resulting in potential overlaps with several or all other classes. Consequently, the network may incorrectly group them all into a single class when constructing the hierarchy. To mitigate this, we only group classes when the degree of overlap is above a threshold. One could also train the network using a metric loss to alleviate this, which we leave for future work.

References

1. Barz, B., Denzler, J.: Hierarchy-based image embeddings for semantic image retrieval. In: 2019 IEEE WACV, pp. 638–647. IEEE (2019)
2. Bertinetto, L., Mueller, R., Tertikas, K., Samangooei, S., Lord, N.A.: Making better mistakes: leveraging class hierarchies with deep networks. In: Proceedings of the IEEE/CVF CVPR, pp. 12506–12515 (2020)
3. Brust, C.-A., Denzler, J.: Not just a matter of semantics: the relationship between visual and semantic similarity. In: Fink, G.A., Frintrop, S., Jiang, X. (eds.) DAGM GCPR 2019. LNCS, vol. 11824, pp. 414–427. Springer, Cham (2019). https://doi.org/10.1007/978-3-030-33676-9_29
4. Brust, C.-A., Denzler, J.: Integrating domain knowledge: using hierarchies to improve deep classifiers. In: Palaiahnakote, S., Sanniti di Baja, G., Wang, L., Yan, W.Q. (eds.) ACPR 2019. LNCS, vol. 12046, pp. 3–16. Springer, Cham (2020). https://doi.org/10.1007/978-3-030-41404-7_1
5. Chen, W., et al.: Deep learning for instance retrieval: a survey. IEEE Trans. Pattern Anal. Mach. Intell. **45**, 7270–7292 (2022)
6. Frome, A., et al.: DeViSE: a deep visual-semantic embedding model. In: Advances in Neural Information Processing Systems, vol. 26 (2013)
7. He, K., Zhang, X., Ren, S., Sun, J.: Deep residual learning for image recognition. In: Proceedings of the IEEE CVPR, pp. 770–778 (2016)
8. Krizhevsky, A., Hinton, G., et al.: Learning multiple layers of features from tiny images (2009)
9. Miller, G.A.: WordNet: a lexical database for English. Commun. ACM **38**(11), 39–41 (1995)
10. Park, G., Baek, Y., Lee, H.-K.: A ranking algorithm using dynamic clustering for content-based image retrieval. In: Lew, M.S., Sebe, N., Eakins, J.P. (eds.) CIVR 2002. LNCS, vol. 2383, pp. 328–337. Springer, Heidelberg (2002). https://doi.org/10.1007/3-540-45479-9_35
11. Silla, C.N., Freitas, A.A.: A survey of hierarchical classification across different application domains. Data Min. Knowl. Disc. **22**, 31–72 (2011)
12. Tan, M., Le, Q.: EfficientNet: rethinking model scaling for convolutional neural networks. In: International Conference on Machine Learning, pp. 6105–6114. PMLR (2019)
13. Venkataramanan, A., Benbihi, A., Laviale, M., Pradalier, C.: Self-supervised gaussian regularization of deep classifiers for mahalanobis-distance-based uncertainty estimation. arXiv preprint arXiv:2305.13849 (2023)
14. Venkataramanan, A., et al.: Usefulness of synthetic datasets for diatom automatic detection using a deep-learning approach. Eng. Appl. Artif. Intell. **117**, 105594 (2023)
15. Wah, C., Branson, S., Welinder, P., Perona, P., Belongie, S.: The Caltech-UCSD birds-200-2011 dataset (2011)
16. Wan, J., et al.: Deep learning for content-based image retrieval: a comprehensive study. In: Proceedings of the 22nd ACM International Conference on Multimedia, pp. 157–166 (2014)
17. Wu, P., Manjunath, B., Shin, H.: Dimensionality reduction for image retrieval. In: Proceedings of ICIP, vol. 3, pp. 726–729. IEEE (2000)
18. Yang, J., She, D., Lai, Y.K., Yang, M.H.: Retrieving and classifying affective images via deep metric learning. In: Proceedings of the AAAI Conference, vol. 32 (2018)
19. Zhang, C., Cheng, J., Tian, Q.: Image-level classification by hierarchical structure learning with visual and semantic similarities. Inf. Sci. **422**, 271–281 (2018)

BEVSeg: Geometry and Data-Driven Based Multi-view Segmentation in Bird's-Eye-View

Qiuxiao Chen[1]([✉])[ID], Hung-Shuo Tai[2][ID], Pengfei Li[3], Ke Wang[2], and Xiaojun Qi[1][ID]

[1] Utah State University, Logan, UT 84322, USA
`chenqiuxiao.ee@gmail.com`
[2] DiDi Labs, Mountain View, CA 94043, USA
[3] University of California, Riverside, Riverside, CA 92521, USA

Abstract. Perception and awareness of the surroundings are significant for autonomous vehicle navigation. To drive safely, autonomous systems must be able to extract spatial information and understand the semantic meaning of the environment. We propose a novel network architecture BEVSeg to generate the perception and semantic information by incorporating geometry-based and data-driven techniques into two respective modules. Specifically, the geometry-based aligned BEV domain data augmentation module addresses overfitting and misalignment issues by augmenting the coherent BEV feature map, aligning the augmented object and segmentation ground truths, and aligning augmented BEV feature map and its augmented ground truths. The data-driven hierarchy double-branch spatial attention module addresses the inflexibility of the BEV feature generation by learning multi-scale BEV features flexibly via the enlarged feature receptive field and learned interest regions. Experimental results on the nuScenes benchmark dataset demonstrate BEVSeg achieves state-of-the-art results with a higher mIoU of 3.6% than the baseline. Code and models will be released.

Keywords: Deep Learning · Semantic Segmentation · Spatial Attention

1 Introduction

The capability to obtain perception and awareness of the surrounding environment is crucial for autonomous vehicles. To drive safely, self-driving cars must be able to obtain semantic understanding in the 3D space, not just from the camera views. Only with such spatial comprehension, can a self-driving vehicle maneuver safely while obeying traffic rules.

Geometry-based and data-driven semantic segmentation techniques are commonly used to generate an understanding of surrounding environments for

H. I. Christensen et al. (Eds.): ICVS 2023, LNCS 14253, pp. 432–443, 2023.
https://doi.org/10.1007/978-3-031-44137-0_36

autonomous vehicle navigation. Specifically, geometry-based techniques [7–9, 12–14, 20] use the geometric relationships across different views to create an intermediate Bird's-Eye-View (BEV) representation, which can be used for object detection and segmentation. However, they tend to have an overfitting issue in the BEV feature domain [8]. They also tend to lack the flexibility to generate BEV features from single-view features. On the other hand, data-driven techniques [19, 21] employ self-attention mechanisms using transformers to directly learn semantic segmentation features from input images. Although effective in many tasks, such a paradigm usually incurs high computation complexity and requires non-trivial architecture designs.

In this paper, we propose a novel network architecture BEVSeg by converting BEVDet [8] (a multi-view 3D object detection network) to a multi-view BEV semantic segmentation model. BEVSeg replaces the detection head with the BEV Segmentation Head (SD). Furthermore, it seamlessly incorporates geometry-based and data-driven techniques into two respective modules to generate a BEV map of input images and extract the semantic information from the BEV map. To address overfitting and misalignment issues, we incorporate Aligned BEV domain data Augmentation (ABA) in the geometry module to augment the coherent BEV map, align the augmented object and segmentation ground truths, and align the augmented BEV map and its augmented ground truths geometrically. To increase the flexibility of the BEV feature generation, we incorporate Hierarchy Double-branch Spatial Attention (HDSA) in the data-driven module to weigh the importance of spatial features. BEVSeg consists of five modules as shown in Fig. 1, where 1) image encoder extracts features from multi-view camera images; 2) image-to-BEV view transform projects multi-view image features into the BEV domain to create unified BEV features; 3) ABA (the geometry module) rotates, flips, and scales unified BEV features and their corresponding ground truths to augment the coherent BEV map, aligns the augmented object and segmentation ground truths, and aligns the augmented BEV map and its augmented ground truths; 4) HDSA & BEV encoder (the data-driven module) selects relevant spatial regions and enlarges the receptive fields in the augmented BEV map; and 5) BEV map SH generates segmentation results for each category.

We evaluate the ground segmentation results of the proposed BEVSeg for six crucial semantic categories on the nuScenes dataset [2]. Our extensive experimental results demonstrate that BEVSeg beats all state-of-the-art methods on the nuScenes dataset. Our contributions are as follows: (1) Proposing a new network architecture BEVSeg to perform semantic segmentation of a scene with multi-view images and achieve state-of-the-art results. (2) Incorporating ABA in the geometry module to augment the coherent BEV map, align the augmented object and segmentation ground truths, and align the augmented BEV map and its augmented ground truths to address overfitting and misalignment issues. (3) Incorporating low-complexity HDSA in the data-driven module to learn multi-scale BEV features flexibly by enlarging the feature receptive field and learning interest regions.

2   Related Work

In this section, we briefly review research work in two directions, namely, semantic segmentation and attention. Some ideas behind these two research directions are explored and integrated into BEVSeg to improve segmentation results.

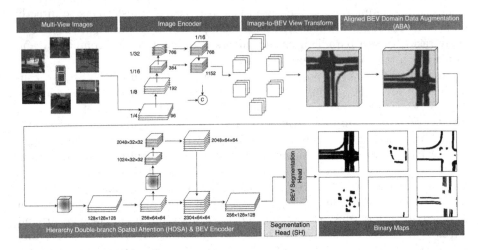

Fig. 1. Illustration of BEVSeg's overall architecture. ABA is the proposed geometry module and HDSA is the proposed data-driven module. The SH is proposed to replace the detection head in BEVDet.

2.1   Semantic Segmentation

Semantic segmentation often constructs a BEV segmentation map and performs BEV segmentation for each category. BEV semantic segmentation is divided into single-view segmentation and multi-view segmentation.

Single-view segmentation [1, 22] often uses high perspective synthetic datasets created by CARLA [4] to construct a BEV semantic understanding since it is challenging to rebuild the whole BEV semantic perception from one monocular image captured by a front-view camera. With the emergence of multi-view datasets [2,16], current multi-view semantic segmentation techniques utilize the additional ground data and intrinsic and extrinsic matrices of the camera to translate multi-view autonomous driving datasets into the BEV semantics.

The transformer-based segmentation [9,21] and the BEV intermediate representation structure [12–15,18] are two representative multi-view segmentation techniques. Cross-View Transformer (CVT) [21] is one representative transformer-based segmentation technique. It uses a camera-aware transformer together with the intrinsic and extrinsic matrices of cameras to obtain BEV segmentation from multi-view monocular images. Specifically, it uses position embeddings to encode camera orders and their intrinsic and extrinsic matrices and allow the transformer to gain implicit cross-view information. However, the absence of explicit geometric information (i.e., intrinsic and extrinsic matrices) leads to its diminished interpretability. LSS [14] is a pioneer work of BEV intermediate representation structure techniques. It builds a BEV transform network to yield better BEV segmentation results. Specifically, it obtains a feature map frustum in each view and combines all frustums into a unified BEV intermediate representation containing the geometric connection of each camera. BEVFusion [12] extends LSS into a multi-sensor framework by combining the camera and LiDAR BEV feature maps to achieve better segmentation results. However, it has a higher computational cost than LSS.

2.2   Attention

Attention mechanisms have recently been widely employed in the Deep Neural Network (DNN) to focus on important parts of the input data to capture sufficient outstanding features. Spatial attention [3,6,17] is one of representative attention mechanisms.

Spatial attention [3,17] usually applies average-pooling and max-pooling operations along the channel axis and concatenates them to generate an efficient feature descriptor across the spatial domain to capture the inter-spatial relationship of features and select the most relevant spatial regions. Some spatial attentions tend to have a high time complexity, which limits their application.

3   Method

We propose a new network architecture BEVSeg, which uses multi-view camera images to produce better segmentation results in a BEV map. BEVSeg projects camera features via ABA in the geometry module to augment the unified BEV map, align the augmented object and segmentation ground truths; and align the augmented BEV map and its augmented ground truths to capture the explicit geometric relationship among multiple cameras. It also learns low-complexity HDSA in the data-drive module to optimize the implicit geometric information in BEV maps and learn multi-scale BEV features flexibly via enlarged feature respective field and learned interest regions. In the following subsections, we provide BEVSeg's overall architecture. We then describe the proposed modules, which are uniquely incorporated in BEVSeg to improve segmentation accuracy.

3.1   Overall Architecture

Figure 1 illustrates the overall architecture of the proposed BEVSeg framework, where image encoder and image-to-BEV view transform modules are directly adopted from the conventional BEV network [8]. The BEV map SH replaces the detection head of the conventional BEV network to obtain segmentation results. ABA (the geometry module) and HDSA (the data-driven module) are proposed modules, which are incorporated in BEVSeg to improve segmentation accuracy.

3.2 Aligned BEV Domain Data Augmentation (ABA)

In order to improve network performance and address the overfitting and mis-alignment problem in the BEV domain, we propose an ABA technique to simultaneously augment and align BEV feature maps and the ground truths, including 3D object and segmentation ground truths. By aligning three augmented counterparts, ABA ensures that most 3D object ground truths are located in the drivable area, which increases the model interpretability. Specifically, we apply rotation, flipping, and scaling operations on the BEV feature maps and their corresponding ground truths to augment the coherent BEV map, align the augmented object and segmentation ground truths, and align the augmented BEV map and its augmented ground truths.

Given 3×3 rotation and flipping transformation matrices T_{Rot} and T_{Flip} and the scaling transformation parameter S, the augmented BEV feature map M_{AugBEV} is generated by:

$$M_{AugBEV} = S \times T_{Flip} \times T_{Rot} \times M_{BEV} \tag{1}$$

where M_{BEV} is the BEV feature map. In order to align the segmentation ground truths with augmented BEV feature maps, the corresponding rotation angle is computed by the Euler angle formula [5]:

$$angle = \arctan\left(\frac{T_{Rot}^{-1}(2,1)}{T_{Rot}^{-1}(1,1)}\right) \tag{2}$$

where $T_{Rot}^{-1}(x,y)$ denotes the element at the coordinate of (x,y) of the inverse rotation matrix. The augmented ground truth segmentation results G_{Aug} are estimated by:

$$G_{Aug} = S \times T_{Flip} \times G(loc, angle, sz) \tag{3}$$

where $G(loc, angle, size)$ is the ground truth segmentation result rotated by $angle$ at location loc with a size of sz, which is a predefined value directly adopted from BEVFusion [12]. We adopt the data augmentation idea in [8] to estimate the augmented 3D object ground truths. We finally align the augmented BEV feature map, augmented segmentation ground truths, and augmented 3D object ground truths.

3.3 Hierarchy Double-Branch Spatial Attention (HDSA)

To improve the flexibility of the BEV feature generation, we propose to incorporate HDSA & BEV encoder (a data-drive module) to automatically choose significant regions of augmented and aligned BEV features. The structure of the double-branch spatial attention in HDSA is shown in Fig. 2, where input features are the augmented and aligned BEV features.

We denote input features by $F \in \mathbb{R}^{C \times H \times W}$, where C, H, and W represent the number of channels, the height, and the width of F. To simplify the complicated matrix calculation and reduce the computational complexity of spatial attention, we replace the matrix multiplication with a two-branch convolution. The spatial attention weight matrix $A_{Spatial}$ is efficiently computed by:

$$A_{Spatial} = \sigma(w_{sum}(w_{11}F + w_{22}w_{21}F)) \qquad (4)$$

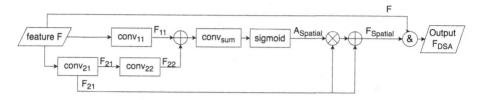

Fig. 2. Structure of double-branch spatial attention.

Specifically, we use two branches of 1×1 convolutions $conv_{11}$ whose weights are w_{11} and $conv_{21}$ whose weights are w_{21} to transform F into two new feature maps F_{11} and F_{21} of the same dimension, respectively. We then employ another $d \times d$ convolution $conv_{22}$ whose weights are w_{22} to transform F_{21} into F_{22} of the same dimensions and enlarge the receptive field at the same time. We combine different receptive field feature maps F_{11} and F_{22} via the elementwise addition and apply another convolution $conv_{sum}$ whose weights are w_{sum} to merge the combined feature map. A sigmoid layer represented by σ is applied to obtain the spatial weight matrix $A_{Spatial}$. The weighted output features F_{DSA} are computed by concatenating input features F and $F_{Spatial}$, which is computed by:

$$F_{Spatial} = F_{21} + A_{Spatial} \times F_{21} \qquad (5)$$

3.4   BEV Map Segmentation Head (SH)

For multi-view images, one category may cross over into another category in the BEV representation. To address the aforementioned overlapping issue, we utilize one binary mask to store segmentation results for one category. Since there are six major semantic categories, we generate six binary masks to store their respective segmentation results.

Specifically, BEV map SH contains eight 3×3 convolutions and one 1×1 convolution due to the unified BEV representation. To further reduce the number of parameters, we reduce output channels by half.

4   Experiments

We organize this section as follows: Subsect. 4.1 presents the architecture of BEVSeg and its parameters used in training. Subsection 4.2 describes the NuScenes dataset. Subsection 4.3 explains the two segmentation metrics used in our evaluation. Subsection 4.4 compares the segmentation results of seven methods on each of six classes and evaluate the overall segmentation performance. Subsection 4.5 presents ablation study results by comparing a few variant systems. Subsection 4.6 demonstrates qualitative segmentation results.

4.1 Network Architecture and Its Parameters

Figure 1 illustrates overall architecture of the proposed BEVSeg network. To achieve higher computational efficiency, we downsample each raw multi-view camera image to a resolution of 256×704. All six multi-view camera images are preprocessed by a pre-trained SwinTransformer [11] to obtain a pyramid of image features in $\frac{1}{4}$, $\frac{1}{8}$, $\frac{1}{16}$, and $\frac{1}{32}$ of the original resolution (256×704), respectively. The neck structure, which combines Feature Pyramid Networks (FPN) [10] and LSS [14], concatenates image features from the last two pyramid layers ($\frac{1}{16}$ and $\frac{1}{32}$ of the original resolution) for further processing. The image-to-BEV view transformer then converts multi-view image features into a single unified BEV feature of 64 channels with a resolution of 128×128. The proposed ABA is applied to the unified BEV features to augment the coherent BEV map, and align the augmented BEV map and its augmented ground truths to address overfitting and misalignment issues. The proposed HDSA & BEV encoder uses ResNet to build the backbone and obtain multi-resolution features of 256, 1024 and 2048 channels to learn multi-scale BEV features flexibly via the enlarged feature receptive field and learned interest regions. Finally, a neck structure [8] is used to merge these features to a $256 \times 128 \times 128$ feature and the BEV map SH produces a mask for each semantic category.

We use the AdamW optimizer to train BEVSeg with an initial learning rate of $2e-4$, a weight decay value of 0.01, and a batch size of eight samples for each GPU. In addition, the learning rate linearly increases in the first 40% of epochs and linearly decreases in the remaining epochs using the cyclic learning rate policy. There are 20 epochs for all experiments. Each experiment takes about 20 h on a workstation with 8 RTX 3090 GPUs.

4.2 Dataset

We use the benchmark dataset nuScenes [2] to evaluate BEVSeg and all compared methods. NuScenes is the most recent and popular benchmark for 3D object detection, tracking, and BEV semantic segmentation in autonomous driving. It is an extensive outdoor dataset consisting of 1,000 driving scenes collected in Boston Seaport and Singapore's One North, Queenstown and Holland Village districts. Each scene is 20 s long and contains a LiDAR scan and RGB images from six horizon monocular cameras. Each scene is also labeled with semantic mask annotations for 11 semantic classes and additional bitmaps. We utilize the ego-motion measurements to produce the fixed-size ground truths of the corresponding area at the same ego-direction. We also use BEVFusion's experimental setup to choose six crucial BEV semantic classes including drivable area, ped crossing, walkway, stop line, carpark area, and divider for all evaluations. The training, validation, and testing splits of the nuScenes dataset contain 700, 150, and 150 scenes, respectively.

4.3   Metrics

Two common segmentation evaluation metrics are used to evaluate the performance of all compared methods. We first calculate different Intersection-over-Union (IoU) scores using thresholds ranging from 0.35 to 0.65 with a stepsize of 0.05. We then report the highest IoU score for each of the six crucial semantic classes. Finally, we use the mean IoU (mIoU) of six semantic classes as the major metric to evaluate the overall segmentation performance of each method [8].

Table 1. Comparison of segmentation results of seven state-of-the-art methods for six classes on nuScenes in terms of IoU and mIoU.

	Driv.	Ped.	Walkway	Stop	Carpark	Divider	Mean
OFT [15]	74.0	35.3	45.9	27.5	35.9	33.9	42.1
LSS [14]	75.4	38.8	46.3	30.3	39.1	36.5	44.4
CVT [21]	74.3	36.8	39.9	25.8	35.0	29.4	40.2
M^2BEV [18]	77.2	–	–	–	–	40.5	–
BEVFormer [9]	80.7	–	–	–	–	21.3	–
BEVFusion [12]	81.7	54.8	58.4	47.4	50.7	46.4	56.6
BEVSeg (Ours)	**81.9**	**57.2**	**60.7**	**52.9**	**54.5**	**54.1**	**60.2**

4.4   Results

We compare the proposed BEVSeg method with six state-of-the-art BEV segmentation methods including Orthographic Feature Transform (OFT) [15], LSS [14], CVT [21], Multi-Camera Joint 3D Detection and Segmentation with Unified Bird's-Eye View Representation (M^2BEV) [18], BEVFormer [9], and BEVFusion [12]. Table 1 lists the IoU scores of all seven compared methods for each of six semantic categories and mIoU for all six categories. Since M^2BEV and BEVFormer only report their segmentation results on drivable road and divider, we only list these results in Table 1. We report segmentation results of the multi-sensor-model-based network (e.g., BEVFusion) using images captured by cameras. We report segmentation results of some early methods like OFT, LSS, and CVT on the nuScene dataset as published in [12]. Table 1 clearly shows that BEVSeg outperforms mIoU of the best segmentation method (e.g., BEV-Fusion) by 3.6% for all six semantic classes. Specifically, it achieves a higher IoU of 0.2%, 2.4%, 2.3%, 5.5%, 3.8%, and 7.7% than BEVFusion on drivable area, ped crossing, walkway, stop line, carpark area, and divider, respectively. We conclude that BEVSeg performs better than the leading method, BEVFusion, when a category contains small and delicate regions. It performs slightly better than BEVFusion on the drivable area, which contains a large section of road and tends to be easily segmented by all methods with the highest accuracy among the other categories. In addition, our proposed BEVSeg is able to perform segmentation at 12.9 frames per second, which is comparable to BEVFusion and makes real-time map segmentation possible.

4.5   Ablation Study

Table 2. Ablation study of the overall performance of BEVSeg (variant E) and its four variants. Here, N-L represents non-local attention [17] and DSA represents the proposed double-branch spatial attention without a hierarchical structure.

Variant	SH	ABA	Att.	Driv.	Ped.	Walkway	Stop	Carpark	Divider	Mean
A	✓			65.8	30.1	34.3	26.7	29.9	28.4	35.9
B	✓	✓		80.6	54.4	58.5	48.1	51.7	51.8	57.5
C	✓	✓	N-L	80.4	53.0	57.8	46.5	52.5	50.6	56.8
D	✓	✓	DSA	81.5	56.2	60.1	51.1	51.5	54.0	59.0
E	✓	✓	HDSA	81.9	57.2	60.7	52.9	54.5	54.1	60.2

Table 2 compares the performance of BEVSeg and its four variants. Variant A is the baseline network, which replaces the BEVDet's detection head by the BEV map SH. Variant B incorporates the proposed ABA module in variant A. Variant C adds a classical spatial attention, non-local attention [17], to variant B. Variant D adds the DSA module to variant B. Variant E is the proposed BEVSeg, which adds the HDSA module to variant B. Table 2 clearly shows that variant B achieves a higher mIoU of 21.6% than variant A, variant D achieves a higher mIoU of 1.5% than variant B, and variant E achieves a higher mIoU of 1.2% than variant D. The significant performance boost of variant B over variant A indicates that ABA is the most contributing module because augmented geometry information increases the variety of ground truth segmentation maps and avoids overfitting and misalignment issues. The performance boost of variant D over variant B indicates that DSA helps to find the inherent structure of augmented geometry information to gather more usable information from highlighted relevant regions and therefore improve segmentation accuracy. The performance boost of variant E over variant D indicates that the hierarchy structure further helps to gather more reliable information at different scales. However, the classical spatial image attention, non-local attention, does not work well on BEV features since variant C drops 0.7% accuracy when compared to variant B. In summary, BEVSeg achieves the best performance by integrating geometry-based and data-driven semantic segmentation techniques (e.g., ABA and HDSA) into its two modules to obtain augmented and aligned geometry information and to find inherent and important information in different receptive fields.

4.6   Qualitative Results

Figure 3 presents four sample scenes along with their segmentation results and ground truth for six categories. Each scene has six multi-view images captured by six cameras. These six images are shown on the left side of Fig. 3 and presented in two rows, where the top row shows input images from the front-left, front,

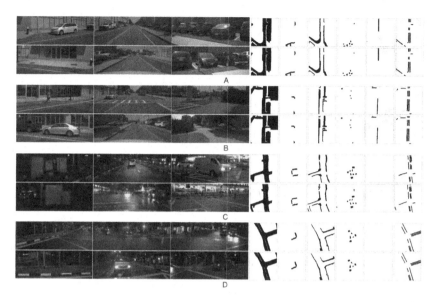

Fig. 3. Illustration of four sample scenes (every two rows on the left side) and their segmentation results (upper row on the right side) and ground truth (lower row on the right side) for six categories.

and front-right view and the bottom row shows input images from the back-left, back, and back-right view. Both segmentation results and the ground truth for six semantic categories are presented on the right side of Fig. 3 with segmentation results shown above the ground truth. The segmentation and ground truth results for drivable area, ped crossing, walkway, stop line, parking area, and divider categories are shown in the order from the left to the right corresponding-ingly. Figure 3(A) and (B) are scene shot in the daytime, while Fig. 3(C) and (D) are scene shot at the night. Figure 3(A), Fig. 3(B), and Fig. 3(D) show the proposed BEVSeg can successfully segment all six semantic classes. Figure 3(C) shows the segmentation results are not perfect since the long-distance obscured regions are more difficult to segment, especially in the night scenes. However, BEVSeg in general can produce segmentation results that match relatively well with ground truths.

Figure 4 demonstrates segmentation results of BEVSeg variant A and BEVSeg for one front-view scene. To facilitate comparison, we show the ground truth of six semantic classes, their corresponding segmentation results of BEVSeg variant A, and their corresponding segmentation results of BEVSeg on the 1st, 2nd, and 3rd rows, respectively. We observe that BEVSeg produces segmentation results that have a higher similarity to the ground truth when compared to its variant A. Its variant A also produces distorted segmentation results. These results show the two proposed modules (ABA and HDSA) improve the segmentation results for six categories.

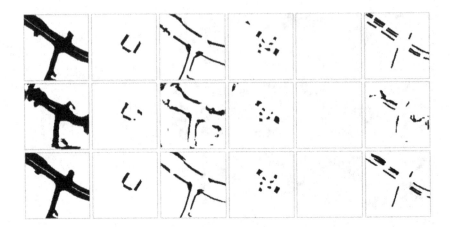

Fig. 4. Illustration of segmentation results of two variants on one scene. From top to bottom: the ground truth and segmentation results of variant A and BEVSeg, respectively.

5 Conclusions

In this paper, we propose a novel network architecture BEVSeg to generate a BEV segmentation map. Unlike other state-of-the-art methods, BEVSeg utilizes the ABA (geometry) and HDSA (data-driven) modules to handle the overfitting and misalignment concerns and resolve the inflexibility issues, respectively. The experimental results on the nuScenes dataset demonstrate that BEVSeg is able to achieve better segmentation accuracy comparing with six state-of-the-art segmentation methods. We hope that future studies in semantic segmentation and autonomous driving will benefit from the proposed efficient modular network architecture BEVSeg.

References

1. Ammar Abbas, S., Zisserman, A.: A geometric approach to obtain a bird's eye view from an image. In: Proceedings of the IEEE/CVF International Conference on Computer Vision Workshops, pp. 4095–4104 (2019)
2. Caesar, H., et al.: nuscenes: A multimodal dataset for autonomous driving. In: Proceedings of the IEEE/CVF Conference on Computer Vision and Pattern Recognition, pp. 11621–11631 (2020)
3. Carion, N., Massa, F., Synnaeve, G., Usunier, N., Kirillov, A., Zagoruyko, S.: End-to-End object detection with transformers. In: Vedaldi, A., Bischof, H., Brox, T., Frahm, J.-M. (eds.) ECCV 2020. LNCS, vol. 12346, pp. 213–229. Springer, Cham (2020). https://doi.org/10.1007/978-3-030-58452-8_13
4. Dosovitskiy, A., Ros, G., Codevilla, F., Lopez, A., Koltun, V.: Carla: an open urban driving simulator. In: Conference on Robot Learning, pp. 1–16. PMLR (2017)
5. Eberly, D.: Euler angle formulas, pp. 1–18. Geometric Tools, LLC, Technical report (2008)

6. Gregor, K., Danihelka, I., Graves, A., Rezende, D., Wierstra, D.: Draw: a recurrent neural network for image generation. In: International Conference on Machine Learning, pp. 1462–1471. PMLR (2015)
7. Hu, A., et al.: Fiery: future instance prediction in bird's-eye view from surround monocular cameras. In: Proceedings of the IEEE/CVF International Conference on Computer Vision, pp. 15273–15282 (2021)
8. Huang, J., Huang, G., Zhu, Z., Du, D.: Bevdet: High-performance multi-camera 3d object detection in bird-eye-view. arXiv preprint arXiv:2112.11790 (2021)
9. Li, Z., et al.: Bevformer: Learning bird's-eye-view representation from multi-camera images via spatiotemporal transformers. arXiv preprint arXiv:2203.17270 (2022)
10. Lin, T.Y., Dollár, P., Girshick, R., He, K., Hariharan, B., Belongie, S.: Feature pyramid networks for object detection. In: Proceedings of the IEEE Conference on Computer Vision and Pattern Recognition, pp. 2117–2125 (2017)
11. Liu, Z., et al.: Swin transformer: hierarchical vision transformer using shifted windows. In: Proceedings of the IEEE/CVF International Conference on Computer Vision, pp. 10012–10022 (2021)
12. Liu, Z., et al.: Bevfusion: Multi-task multi-sensor fusion with unified bird's-eye view representation. arXiv preprint arXiv:2205.13542 (2022)
13. Pan, B., Sun, J., Leung, H.Y.T., Andonian, A., Zhou, B.: Cross-view semantic segmentation for sensing surroundings. IEEE Rob. Autom. Lett. 5(3), 4867–4873 (2020)
14. Philion, J., Fidler, S.: Lift, splat, shoot: encoding images from arbitrary camera rigs by implicitly unprojecting to 3D. In: Vedaldi, A., Bischof, H., Brox, T., Frahm, J.-M. (eds.) ECCV 2020. LNCS, vol. 12359, pp. 194–210. Springer, Cham (2020). https://doi.org/10.1007/978-3-030-58568-6_12
15. Roddick, T., Kendall, A., Cipolla, R.: Orthographic feature transform for monocular 3d object detection. arXiv preprint arXiv:1811.08188 (2018)
16. Sun, P., et al.: Scalability in perception for autonomous driving: Waymo open dataset. In: Proceedings of the IEEE/CVF Conference on Computer Vision and Pattern Recognition, pp. 2446–2454 (2020)
17. Wang, X., Girshick, R., Gupta, A., He, K.: Non-local neural networks. In: Proceedings of the IEEE Conference on Computer Vision and Pattern Recognition, pp. 7794–7803 (2018)
18. Xie, E., et al.: M^2BEV: Multi-camera joint 3d detection and segmentation with unified birds-eye view representation. arXiv preprint arXiv:2204.05088 (2022)
19. Xu, R., Tu, Z., Xiang, H., Shao, W., Zhou, B., Ma, J.: Cobevt: Cooperative bird's eye view semantic segmentation with sparse transformers. arXiv preprint arXiv:2207.02202 (2022)
20. Zhang, Y., et al.: Beverse: Unified perception and prediction in birds-eye-view for vision-centric autonomous driving. arXiv preprint arXiv:2205.09743 (2022)
21. Zhou, B., Krähenbühl, P.: Cross-view transformers for real-time map-view semantic segmentation. In: Proceedings of the IEEE/CVF Conference on Computer Vision and Pattern Recognition, pp. 13760–13769 (2022)
22. Zhu, M., Zhang, S., Zhong, Y., Lu, P., Peng, H., Lenneman, J.: Monocular 3d vehicle detection using uncalibrated traffic cameras through homography. In: 2021 IEEE/RSJ International Conference on Intelligent Robots and Systems (IROS), pp. 3814–3821. IEEE (2021)

Descriptive Attributes for Language-Based Object Keypoint Detection

Jerod Weinman[1]([⊠])[iD], Serge Belongie[2][iD], and Stella Frank[2][iD]

[1] Grinnell College, Grinnell, IA, USA
jerod@acm.org
[2] Department of Computer Science, University of Copenhagen,
Copenhagen, Denmark

Abstract. Multimodal vision and language (VL) models have recently shown strong performance in phrase grounding and object detection for both zero-shot and finetuned cases. We adapt a VL model (GLIP) for keypoint detection and evaluate on NABirds keypoints. Our language-based keypoints-as-objects detector GLIP-KP outperforms baseline top-down keypoint detection models based on heatmaps and allows for zero- and few-shot evaluation. When fully trained, enhancing the keypoint names with descriptive attributes gives a significant performance boost, raising AP by as much as 6.0, compared to models without attribute information. Our model exceeds heatmap-based HRNet's AP by 4.4 overall and 8.4 on keypoints with attributes. With limited data, attributes raise zero-/one-/few-shot test AP by 1.0/3.4/1.6, respectively, on keypoints with attributes.

Keywords: Keypoint detection · Vision & language models · Attributes

1 Introduction

Many computer vision tasks involve finding and identifying things in images, such as objects and their constituent parts. In these settings, the use of multimodal vision and language (VL) models can extend the scope of computer vision models, by replacing a limited set of object classes or part IDs with the ways that people refer to these objects in natural language. These multimodal models support open-world object detection by learning rich representations of the co-occurrences and interactions between words and pixels.

The VL model GLIP [19] was trained for phrase grounding and open-vocabulary object detection. In this paper, we extend GLIP's capabilities to object keypoint detection, *i.e.*, locating the *parts* of particular objects. For example, given an image of a bird and a textual caption containing English part names (*e.g.*, "bill, nape, tail, ..."), our GLIP-KP model detects "objects" corresponding to the parts by grounding the phrases in the query caption to specific regions or points in the image (see Fig. 1). The advantage of this approach is that it allows

© The Author(s), under exclusive license to Springer Nature Switzerland AG 2023
H. I. Christensen et al. (Eds.): ICVS 2023, LNCS 14253, pp. 444–458, 2023.
https://doi.org/10.1007/978-3-031-44137-0_37

us to use not only the part names but also additional adjectival attributes of the part: the model can detect the 'yellow and black crown' of the goldfinch, or the 'long red bill' of an oyster-catcher.

Fig. 1. Example of detecting keypoints with richer descriptions. Attributes are drawn from CUB [35] images and applied to corresponding keypoints of NABird [33] species.

This work explores the following research questions:

RQ1 Architecture: How well does a VL model for object detection perform at keypoint detection?

RQ2 Pretraining: What is the advantage of using the pretrained VL model, along with its image and language encoders?

RQ3 Attributes: How does adding richer descriptive attributes to keypoint names influence detection performance?

We assess these questions in both a small data/few-shot setting, where the multimodal pretraining enables identification of some keypoints, and in a fully finetuned keypoint detection setting. Our system design (Sect. 3) and the supporting experiments (Sect. 5) on a bird keypoint detection task (Sect. 4) demonstrate three primary findings. First, a multimodal vision and language (VL) model designed for object detection offers a compelling, competitive keypoint detector (RQ1). In particular, our model outperforms several top-down pose estimation baselines on the bird keypoint detection task. Second, pretraining the VL model benefits both test performance and train time (RQ2); finetuning pretrained models provides a modest AP improvement, while training VL layers from scratch takes 50% more epochs. Finally, leveraging keypoint descriptions enhances VL model test performance (RQ3), whether in data-limited (zero-/one-/few-shot) or fully finetuned models.

2   Related Work

In this section we situate our work in the context of recent trends in detecting keypoints, leveraging language for object detection and phrase grounding, and using descriptive attributes for transfer to novel prediction tasks.

2.1 Keypoint Detection

Keypoint detection for pose estimation is a core computer vision task commonly performed on human data [1,18,21], but it is also applicable to non-human animals [39,41], including birds [33,35]. Architectures for keypoint detection typically distinguish between two-stage and single-stage models. Two-stage models are top-down, in that first the body is found using an object detector, and then the keypoints are identified [20,32,36]. Single-stage models process bottom-up, with all visible keypoints (e.g., in a crowd) found at once [10,28]. Earlier models depend on convolutions both for the image processing backbone and further processing [32,36]. More recent models factor out the visual backbone, which can either use a convolutional or visual transformer architecture to provide features for the main model [12,20,24,37,38,42].

To predict keypoint locations, many model heads typically use heat-map estimation [36]. More recent works have used direct regression [24] or treat keypoints the same as objects (i.e., as the centers of detected bounding boxes) [25]. Our work extends the latter approach, treating keypoint detection like object detection. Whereas KAPAO [25] trains a keypoint/object detection network from scratch using an architecture based on the YOLO [30] object detector, our work is based on a *pretrained* multimodal VL model, which allows us to easily incorporate few-shot learning and richer keypoint descriptions.

2.2 Open-Vocabulary Object Detection

Open-vocabulary object detection combines language models with object detection to detect objects beyond a limited set of training object classes. Approaches typically leverage pretrained models with vision and language aligned at the image level (e.g., CLIP [29] or ALIGN [13]); a difficulty then lies in how to extract region information, such as bounding boxes, from these image-level models. Early work used VL models to classify regions found by a class-agnostic region-proposal model ViLD [11]. OWL-VIT adds visual-token level classification within a VL encoder to fine-tune these models for object detection with class predictions from the language encoder [26]. Kim et al. [15] perform additional pretraining at the region level (using crops), resulting in a VL model with region understanding. Kuo et al. [16] train only a detector head on top of a large-scale frozen VL model.

2.3 Phrase-Region Grounding

While open-vocabulary object detection aims to find the correct label for novel objects, text grounding models find the most relevant region in an image for a given phrase. mDETR [14] extends the detection transformer DETR [3] with alignment to captions, going beyond object classes to the free text found in natural language captions. GLIP [19,43] continues this line of work, based on the functional equivalence between phrase grounding and object detection. GLIP excelled at these tasks by fusing the vision and language encodings more deeply than mDETR, specifically using a dynamic head [6]. FIBER [8] improves further by fusing the vision and language streams in the backbones. In an orthogonal approach, PEVL [40] interleaves language tokens and positional tokens (bounding box coordinates) in the text, turning text-region grounding into a masked language-modelling task. As noted above, this work applies the GLIP framework to keypoint detection, with keypoint labels (and attributes) being the caption of the detected keypoint "object".

2.4 Descriptive Attributes

Declarative attributes have long been used for few-shot transfer learning to novel categories [17]. Zero-shot performance of pretrained models depends on several factors [4,34]. Vogel *et al.* [34] find that whether attributes aid instance-classification depends on the VL model and the specific way attributes are incorporated. To reduce annotator burden in specialized domains, Mall *et al.* [23] create a method that interactively requests informative attributes for new classification tasks using pretrained models. Forbes *et al.* [9] created birds-to-words, which describes the differences between species in support of a model architecture generating such natural language comparisons.

Although such attributes or descriptions naturally include keypoints among the noun phrases, none of these models localize them. To our knowledge, this work is the first to leverage descriptive attributes for keypoint detection, rather than whole-image classification or object/region grounding.

3 Keypoint Detection System

Our system is based on GLIP [19], which fuses the vision and language representations within the region proposal network. In this section we briefly review that model and then describe how it is adapted to GLIP-KP for keypoint detection.

3.1 GLIP Model

The original GLIP (Guided Language Image Pretraining) model [19] combines a visual backbone with a language backbone, fusing these encodings in an inter-linking multilayer head [6]. The model is trained with a mixture of two losses. Classification loss—a binary focal sigmoid loss—rewards agreement between the fused visual regions and language phrases that are matched in the ground truth. Localization loss rewards bounding box proposals that overlap with *and* are centered closer to the ground truth box.

We base our GLIP-KP experiments on the GLIP-L model, which was pretrained on 27M image-text pairs and uses SWIN-L [22] and BERT-base-uncased [7] as the vision and language backbones, respectively.

3.2   Vision and Language Keypoint Detection

We adapt the GLIP model for keypoint detection by treating each keypoint as an object to be detected, which is similar to what KAPAO [25] does for YOLO [30]. Annotated keypoints are typically only pixel coordinates, but object detectors like GLIP are trained to produce bounding boxes. To address the mismatch, we center a small bounding box around each keypoint. Although our keypoint-detecting GLIP-KP is trained to reproduce these small boxes, only the box center is used for evaluating predictions (see Sect. 5.2). Unlike KAPAO and other keypoint detection models, GLIP-KP uses *language* as the query modality, rather than symbolic class IDs. Thus "red nape. black left wing." can be used as the query caption to locate these two keypoints (cf. Fig. 1).

We arbitrarily chose a fixed 40×40 box size for all keypoints in all experiments. This setting roughly aligns with the sizes found to perform well for KAPAO on human pose estimation [25]. As a feature of the training data (not the model), varying keypoint box size can trivially be incorporated. Although our box size is presently fixed, keypoint bounding boxes could vary with the object size or the precision of a particular keypoint's location. Our evaluation measure (Sect. 5.2) controls for both object size and keypoint annotator precision.

4   Data

The North American Birds (NABirds) data set [33] is our primary training and testing data, due to its higher data quality and larger size compared to the commonly used Caltech-UCSD Birds 200 (CUB-200) [35]. NABirds consists of nearly 50K bird images from 400 different species, organized in a hierarchy. Our model does not directly use species information for keypoint detection, but attributes are applied at a species level (more below). The images in the NABirds data set are annotated with 11 body part keypoints (see Table 1). We use the official test split (24,633 images, each with a single bird), and take 10% of the official training split for validation (2,410 images in validation, 21,519 in training); the validation set roughly preserves class frequency while ensuring at least one example of each leaf class from the hierarchy.

Descriptive Keypoint Attributes. The CUB data set includes fine-grained attributes, annotated at the image level. Most of these attributes correspond to keypoints, for example, the bill shape or wing color of a bird. We obtain species-level attributes by retaining attribute values where the majority of images (over half) for that species are annotated with the attribute value. For most species and attributes, there is only one value per attribute, with the exception of some color attributes (*e.g.*, a magpie has a tail color that is both black and white). In order to match CUB species names with NABird species label, we use a manually-obtained many-to-one mapping. This process results in 341 of 555 NABird classes being linked to attributes; roughly 32% of keypoints are assigned enhanced descriptions through these attributes. This rate is fairly consistent across the eleven bird keypoints (mean 35.8%, std. err. 0.86%).

To convert image attribute values to keypoint descriptions for GLIP-KP captions, we apply a set of simple textual transformations. The relevant image attributes (`has_bill_length`, `has_back_color`) are matched to their corresponding keypoints (bill, back). The color attribute values are preserved, and comparative attributes are minimally edited (*e.g.*, the bill length attribute is changed from `shorter/longer_than_head` to short/long, respectively). We arrange multiple attributes for a single keypoint according to standard English adjectival order [2]: length, pattern, shape, color, in order to match language model expectations. Table 2 gives examples of the resulting descriptive captions.

Table 1. Part keypoints with their hierarchically ordered attributes and annotator standard deviations ×100, relative to the bird bounding box dimensions.

Keypoint Label	σ_X	σ_Y	Attributes
bill	1.998	1.340	length/shape/color
crown	3.255	2.065	color
nape	2.956	3.479	color
left/right eye	1.068	0.927	color
belly	4.810	4.537	pattern/color
breast	3.132	4.340	pattern/color
back	3.934	3.372	pattern/color
tail	4.335	3.972	pattern/shape/(under, upper) colors
left/right wing	6.017	5.097	pattern/shape/color

Table 2. Examples of descriptive attributes for each keypoint (first instance in **bold**).

short all-purpose grey **bill**. long needle black bill. dagger orange and black bill. spatulate yellow bill
black and white **crown**. blue crown. brown and buff crown. yellow and black crown. red crown
black and white **nape**. brown and white nape. brown and black nape. buff nape. blue nape
black and red **left eye**. black **right eye**. red left eye. yellow right eye
striped brown and white **belly**. multi-colored yellow belly. solid belly. spotted brown and white belly
multi-colored yellow and black **breast**. striped yellow and black breast. white breast
olive **back**. striped brown black and buff back. solid blue back. multi-colored grey and yellow back
black and white black and white **tail**. solid notched tail. notched brown tail. white black tail
spotted pointed black and white **left wing**. striped rounded brown black white and buff **right wing**

5 Experiments

We perform experiments training the model on several variants of the data. In this section we describe the general training and evaluation regimes before presenting the experimental results.

GLIP-KP is trained to predict keypoint box locations given a caption containing the keypoint labels. We train with two initial conditions for model weights and three data variants:

Symbols To isolate and impede the semantic contribution of the model's language stream, each keypoint label is replaced by a single character, forcing the deep fusion layers to rely on the visual characteristics and a symbol with little intrinsic meaning. We omit characters that might suggest a description of visual shape (*i.e.*, x, s, or t). Caption: "f. g. h. k. m. n. p. q. r. w. y."

Labels The basic keypoint labels are used in the text prompt encoded by the language model. Caption: "bill. crown. nape. left eye. right eye. belly. breast. back. tail. left wing. right wing."

Labels+Attributes Available descriptive attributes precede the keypoint label. Caption: "short cone buff bill. grey crown. grey nape. ..." (see Table 2).

In a "Finetune" initial condition, we begin training using the GLIP-L pretrained weights. For "Scratch", the deep fusion layers are randomly initialized while the language backbone uses the original BERT-base-uncased model pretrained weights and the vision backbone uses the SWIN-L pretrained weights.

To benchmark our overall approach to keypoint detection (*i.e.*, vision and language with attributes) we also use the MMPose library [27] to train and test three methods that predict keypoints via heatmaps: HRNet [32] and two variants of the Simple Baseline model [36] with ResNet-50 [12] and SWIN-L [22] vision backbones.

5.1   Training Details

The validation metric is mAP (Max Dets = 100); see Sect. 5.2 for details. The base learning rate begins at $1e-5$ and is adjusted by a factor of 0.5 after four epochs with no validation set improvement; we establish a minimum learning rate of $1e-7$. Training is stopped altogether after 10 epochs without improvement. Apart from one-shot learning, all models are trained with a batch size of three images (the maximum afforded by our compute setup). One epoch on the full training set takes four hours using one NVIDIA RTX A6000 GPU.

All the keypoints are included together in a single query caption that is to be encoded by the language model. This allows the complete context of the query (including attributes, if available) to influence the encoding. Importantly, we randomly shuffle the keypoints within the captions for each training batch. The model should thus be forced to learn to use the language embedding, rather than simply relying on a positional encoding of the tokens to represent the part.

Following earlier findings that unfreezing visual backbones during finetuning can improve performance [31], the SWIN-L model visual backbone is frozen at layer 2 (subsequent layers are trainable), and the BERT-base-uncased language backbone is not frozen (all layers are updated).

To randomly augment the training data, images may undergo a horizontal flip (with the necessary alteration to the sagittal wing and eye keypoint labels) or may be resized to between 640 and 1024 pixels (preserving aspect ratio).

For the baseline comparison models, we retain the default parameters: input *object* size (cropped bird) is 256×256 and heatmap size is 64×64. All models train for 210 epochs and the best checkpoint is selected using the validation set.

5.2 Evaluation

Because our system is a hybrid of object and keypoint detection, we hybridize object and keypoint detection evaluation measures for our evaluation. Compared to traditional keypoint detection, there are two main differences in our setup: 1) not all keypoints must be predicted on the image, because the model can decide not to ground a keypoint caption label; 2) multiple detections can be predicted for each label, not just the single best detection. There is also the superficial difference between predicting bounding boxes versus pixel coordinates; we simply take the center of each box as the predicted keypoint location.

Traditional keypoint evaluations are limited because they only measure performance on keypoints annotated as visible. Thus, no false positives result from predicting keypoints that are absent from an object; false positives only occur if a keypoint is matched to the wrong parent object. With only a single instance of the object in each NABirds image (and many other pose estimation data sets), these types of false positives are not possible. This omission makes precision metrics relatively meaningless in the traditional keypoint evaluation scheme.

By definition, recall likewise ignores false positives. When considering only the best-scoring detection for each keypoint, recall is therefore equivalent to accuracy (percentage of correct keypoints, or PCK), another traditional metric.

Ultimately, the traditional evaluation schemes can be misleading when a system is to be applied to images where the keypoint visibility is unknown and false positives are to be minimized (as in cases intended for human training).

Thus, to evaluate keypoint detections, we combine elements of the COCO evaluation frameworks for both keypoints and object detection. Specifically, we replace the COCO object detection intersection-over-union (IoU) calculation for matching bounding boxes with a variant of the COCO keypoint detection challenge's object-keypoint-similarity (OKS) calculation. The COCO OKS utilizes the square root of the object area as a "scale" factor so it can account for size-normalized annotator variation in keypoint locations. Rather than collapse height and width, we retain these scales separately, noting that the annotator variation along the x and y axes is anisotropic (see Table 1).

To classify a detection as correct or incorrect, we must first measure the relative detection difference $\mathbf{d} = \mathbf{p} - \mathbf{t}$ between the prediction $\mathbf{p}$ and the ground truth point $\mathbf{t}$. The "error" $\mathbf{e}$ in this difference is normalized by a factor incorporating both the object size (w, h) and the annotator variation (σ_X, σ_Y),

$$\mathbf{e} = \left[\frac{d_x}{k_x w}, \frac{d_y}{k_y h} \right], \tag{1}$$

where $k = 2\sigma$ is the per-dimension scaling factor. Passing this error through an unnormalized Gaussian,

$$s = \exp\left(-\frac{1}{2}\|\mathbf{e}\|^2\right), \tag{2}$$

produces an interpretable object keypoint similarity (OKS) with $s \in (0, 1]$, like the IoU. This setup "means that 68%, 95%, and 99.7% of human annotated keypoints should have a keypoint similarity of .88, .61, or .32 or higher, respectively" [5], according to the COCO keypoint evaluation description. In summary, we use the traditional COCO evaluation scheme for objects, replacing the IoU criterion with our OKS (2).

We report a subset of the COCO evaluation metrics for all object (bird) sizes:

mAP Mean average precision with OKS=0.50:0.05:0.95
AP$^{0.50}$ Average precision at OKS=0.50 (a "loose" metric)
AP$^{0.75}$ Average precision at OKS=0.75 (a "strict" metric)
AR Average recall with OKS=0.50:0.05:0.95

Except when given for individual keypoint labels (*i.e.*, Fig. 3), these metrics are reported as averages over all the keypoint labels.

While we report AR for some comparability with keypoint detectors designed to optimize PCK, we remain more interested in the AP metrics as sensitive to both recall (the true positive rate), and precision (true positives among *predicted* positives). To capture the overall fidelity of the model, we treat the keypoints as if they were independent objects and evaluate accordingly.

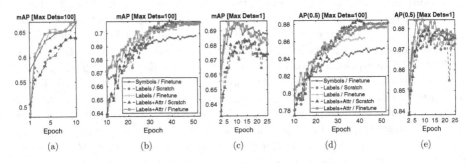

Fig. 2. Training metrics versus train time on validation data. See discussion below.

5.3 Results and Discussion

In this section we present the results of training our GLIP-KP model on the three data variants (Symbols, Labels, Labels+Attributes) with the two initial conditions (Finetune and Scratch).

To gauge the transferability of VL pretraining, we evaluate the "Finetune" models under limited training conditions. From the results in Table 3, we see that in the zero-, one-, and few-shot cases, using labels greatly outperforms the non-semantic "Symbols" variant. In most instances, adding attributes provides a performance boost, particularly among the keypoints that have them. However, "Symbols" surprisingly outperforms all others by a fairly wide margin at one epoch of training on all the data. We hypothesize that at this early stage of training, the symbolic model can focus more directly on the keypoint detection task, while the models using language might be hampered by ambiguous semantics in the keypoint names (*e.g.*, 'crown', 'left wing').

This performance boost evaporates by the second epoch, as can be seen in Fig. 2, which illustrates some of the evaluation metrics on the validation data as training progresses. Aside from epoch 1 (Fig. 2(a)), the "Symbols" model lags by a wide margin, particularly in the 'broad' case (Max Dets = 100—Fig. 2(b, d)), when multiple keypoint detections are considered for each label; this demonstrates the ultimate benefit of involving language in keypoint detection. Models

Table 3. Held-out test data results ("Finetune" initial condition) for zero-, one-, and few-shot training as well as one full epoch of all the training data. One-shot (1 example of each keypoint) and few-shot (10 examples of each keypoint) are both trained for 500 iterations over the limited data, reporting averages and standard errors of ten runs.

	Data	Broad: Max Dets = 100			Narrow: Max Dets = 1			
		mAP	AP(0.5)	AP(0.75)	mAP	AP(0.5)	AP(0.75)	AR
Zero	Symbols	0.20	0.52	0.13	0.13	0.34	0.08	1.95
	Labels	9.46	16.30	9.03	7.36	12.36	7.11	22.70
	Labels+Attr.	**9.74**	**16.63**	**9.33**	**7.58**	**12.83**	**7.29**	**23.64**
One	Symbols	21.40 ±0.38	31.73 ±0.51	21.92 ±0.40	17.79 ±0.36	26.85 ±0.51	18.06 ±0.37	35.65 ±0.45
	Labels	28.97 ±0.18	**43.57** ±0.23	29.68 ±0.20	25.04 ±0.18	39.33 ±0.25	25.20 ±0.20	47.32 ±0.24
	Labels+Attr.	28.74 ±0.22	43.08 ±0.14	29.50 ±0.27	**25.62** ±0.23	**40.17** ±0.15	**25.82** ±0.29	**49.38** ±0.20
Few	Symbols	26.23 ±0.33	36.81 ±0.37	27.35 ±0.36	23.95 ±0.34	36.10 ±0.43	24.42 ±0.36	44.07 ±0.39
	Labels	35.46 ±0.09	48.34 ±0.17	37.19 ±0.10	**33.84** ±0.08	49.86 ±0.11	**34.81** ±0.10	**57.88** ±0.05
	Labels+Attr.	35.43 ±0.13	**49.83** ±0.15	36.96 ±0.15	33.07 ±0.12	49.51 ±0.13	33.93 ±0.14	57.17 ±0.10
Epoch	Symbols	**56.70**	**68.45**	**60.47**	**62.74**	**81.57**	**66.93**	**74.50**
	Labels	48.10	58.36	51.33	51.41	67.76	54.80	73.17
	Labels+Attr.	48.14	58.42	51.35	51.81	68.10	55.23	73.40

Only Data with Attributes

	Data	mAP	AP(0.5)	AP(0.75)	mAP	AP(0.5)	AP(0.75)	AR
Zero	Symbols	0.10	0.25	0.05	0.07	0.17	0.03	1.93
	Labels	4.95	8.44	4.85	4.14	6.88	4.13	22.89
	Labels+Attr.	**6.09**	**9.58**	**6.11**	**5.09**	**8.08**	**5.10**	**25.56**
One	Symbols	14.54 ±0.30	22.50 ±0.44	14.77 ±0.32	12.99 ±0.29	20.32 ±0.44	13.11 ±0.30	37.75 ±0.47
	Labels	19.05 ±0.17	30.80 ±0.24	19.02 ±0.18	17.24 ±0.17	28.70 ±0.25	16.97 ±0.18	49.23 ±0.26
	Labels+Attr.	**21.76** ±0.20	**33.61** ±0.28	**22.15** ±0.21	**20.59** ±0.20	**32.41** ±0.29	**20.81** ±0.21	**52.43** ±0.11
Few	Symbols	18.05 ±0.27	27.36 ±0.34	18.44 ±0.30	17.02 ±0.28	27.24 ±0.39	17.01 ±0.30	46.21 ±0.39
	Labels	23.89 ±0.13	35.90 ±0.23	24.43 ±0.13	23.24 ±0.11	37.10 ±0.20	23.24 ±0.12	**60.09** ±0.07
	Labels+Attr.	**26.22** ±0.22	**40.31** ±0.30	**26.70** ±0.24	**24.88** ±0.22	**39.85** ±0.30	**24.95** ±0.24	58.65 ±0.11
Epoch	Symbols	**48.56**	**64.76**	**51.94**	**53.74**	**75.77**	**57.00**	**75.84**
	Labels	37.37	50.28	39.76	40.33	57.85	42.48	74.78
	Labels+Attr.	39.60	52.23	42.30	42.70	60.07	45.21	75.36

trained from scratch lag behind initially in the 'broad' case, but they do eventually catch up to the finetuned models in later epochs (Fig. 2(b)) and actually excel on the 'loose' metric (Fig. 2(d)). By contrast, finetuned models outperform in the 'narrow' case (Max Dets = 1—Fig. 2(c, e)), which evaluates a single prediction per keypoint. Notably, the narrow metrics peak early before overfitting sets in. However, additional training helps in the broad cases, where the focal loss likely shifts to improving all predictions.

Table 4 shows the test results when training proceeds to completion on all the data. In the narrow case, the attributes provide a modest performance boost in the data overall, but it is more pronounced among the data with attributes. Attributes raise the mAP by about 6 in the broad case and 2.7 in the narrow case. Considering that AR is fairly comparable across most models, it seems the descriptive attributes largely help eliminate false positives and/or improve the prediction confidences.

The HRNet and SimpleBaseline results lag far behind our GLIP-KP model as well, regardless of visual encoder. We hypothesize this may have to do with the use of a heatmap head for prediction, which offers limited location precision. (KAPAO outperforms the SimpleBaseline by a similar degree on human pose estimation.) Since our GLIP-KP uses the SWIN-L visual backbone, we can reasonably compare it to the SimpleBaseline equipped with SWIN-L. Using the "Symbols" data eliminates the model's semantic associations, yet we still find

Table 4. Results for fully-trained models on held-out test data.

Data	VL Weights	Broad: Max Dets = 100				Narrow: Max Dets = 1				
		Epch	mAP	AP(0.5)	AP(0.75)	Epch	mAP	AP(0.5)	AP(0.75)	AR
Symbols	Finetune	51	69.02	84.90	73.71	11	68.79	87.46	73.54	79.70
Labels	Scratch	44	**70.07**	87.63	**74.94**	14	67.64	87.16	72.38	79.21
Labels	Finetune	40	69.57	86.12	74.33	10	68.88	87.51	73.65	**79.92**
Labels+Attr.	Scratch	39	69.95	**87.77**	74.74	14	67.85	87.42	72.64	79.06
Labels+Attr.	Finetune	34	69.75	86.92	74.43	9	**68.92**	**87.69**	**73.80**	79.67
ResNet50 + Heatmap	SimpleBaseline [36]					40	63.58	84.78	68.37	75.67
SWIN-L + Heatmap						180	62.95	84.51	67.52	75.26
HRNet [32]						130	64.53	84.84	69.63	77.71

All Data

Data	VL Weights	Epch	mAP	AP(0.5)	AP(0.75)	Epch	mAP	AP(0.5)	AP(0.75)	AR
Symbols	Finetune	51	57.82	78.69	61.74	11	59.31	81.90	63.38	80.63
Labels	Scratch	44	57.94	80.70	61.65	14	57.40	80.80	61.03	80.03
Labels	Finetune	40	57.87	79.44	61.62	10	59.03	81.66	63.03	**80.72**
Labels+Attr.	Scratch	39	**63.99**	**86.12**	**68.48**	14	60.10	83.30	64.19	79.87
Labels+Attr.	Finetune	34	63.87	85.65	68.30	9	**61.76**	**84.21**	**66.14**	80.70
ResNet50 + Heatmap	SimpleBaseline [36]					40	53.59	77.60	57.09	76.85
SWIN-L + Heatmap						180	52.30	77.07	55.37	76.42
HRNet [32]						130	53.35	76.04	57.18	78.78

Only Data with Attributes

GLIP-KP exceeds the mAP of the SimpleBaseline by 7.0 in this case. This boost confirms the value of formulating keypoint detection as object detection

Tying Table 4's "Epoch" columns to what Fig. 2 shows, finetuning the VL weights requires fewer epochs than training them from scratch, and training with attributes is generally faster than without (for the broad evaluation). The narrow case requires the least time, with validation performance peaking early.

Figure 3 highlights the relative difficulty of the various keypoints and the relative benefits of adding attributes as the amount of training data varies. Higher-performing eyes and bill are well-localized (at the center and tip, respectively) compared to other labels, bearing out lower deviations in Table 1. With a fully-trained model ("All" data), attributes benefit every keypoint label. The crown label benefits significantly from attributes in the one- and few-shot learning cases, perhaps because attributes help resolve semantic ambiguity.

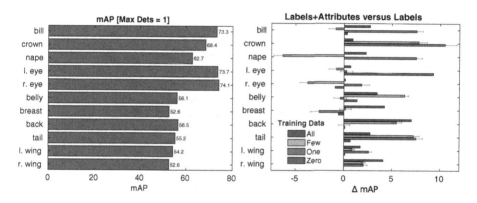

Fig. 3. Per-keypoint test performance on the Finetuned Labels+Attributes model. Absolute mAP on the fully trained model (left) and comparative performance of the Labels+Attributes versus Labels (right) for various training conditions.

6   Conclusion

Vision and language models pretrained for object detection or phrase grounding perform well in a wide-variety of scenarios. This work demonstrates that such models can be adapted for keypoint detection as well. We treat the keypoint detection task as a special case of object detection, albeit with small, fixed-size bounding boxes as the prediction targets. Using GLIP-L as the base model, we demonstrate compelling keypoint detection performance, outperforming comparison models even when the language capabilities are hobbled. Moreover, its language flexibility ultimately allows us to further improve results by incorporating English-language descriptive attributes of the target keypoints.

We also propose an evaluation methodology better-suited to keypoints-as-objects, replacing IoU with a variant of object keypoint similarity (OKS) in the standard COCO object detection framework. We hope the familiarity of the COCO framework and the benefits of considering false positives in keypoint detection will lead to wider adoption of such metrics.

In the future, we hope to investigate not only joint object detection (*i.e.*, the bird bounding box) in the model, but also fine-grained species classification. In addition to the descriptive keypoints, the language-based model may be able to share representations (and better distinguish) among species with similar names and appearances, such as the red-shouldered hawk and the red-tailed hawk.

Acknowledgments. We thank Grant Van Horn for the mapping between NABirds and CUB, Jonathan M. Wells for helpful conversation, Vésteinn Snæbjarnarson for experimental assistance, and the reviewers for important feedback. This work was supported in part by the Pioneer Centre for AI, DNRF grant number P1.

References

1. Andriluka, M., Pishchulin, L., Gehler, P., Schiele, B.: 2D human pose estimation: new benchmark and state of the art analysis. In: Proceedings of the CVPR (2014)
2. Cambridge University Press: Adjectives: order (Cambridge Grammar) (2022). https://dictionary.cambridge.org/us/grammar/british-grammar/adjectives-order
3. Carion, N., Massa, F., Synnaeve, G., Usunier, N., Kirillov, A., Zagoruyko, S.: End-to-end object detection with transformers. In: Vedaldi, A., Bischof, H., Brox, T., Frahm, J.-M. (eds.) ECCV 2020. LNCS, vol. 12346, pp. 213–229. Springer, Cham (2020). https://doi.org/10.1007/978-3-030-58452-8_13
4. Cascante-Bonilla, P., Karlinsky, L., Smith, J.S., Qi, Y., Ordonez, V.: On the transferability of visual features in generalized zero-shot learning (2022). https://doi.org/10.48550/arXiv.2211.12494
5. COCO - Common Objects in Context: Keypoint evaluation (2017). https://cocodataset.org/#keypoints-eval
6. Dai, X., et al.: Dynamic head: unifying object detection heads with attentions. In: Proceedings of the CVPR, pp. 7373–7382 (2021)
7. Devlin, J., Chang, M.W., Lee, K., Toutanova, K.: BERT: pre-training of deep bidirectional transformers for language understanding. In: NAACL-HLT (1), pp. 4171–4186 (2019)
8. Dou, Z.Y., et al.: Coarse-to-fine vision-language pre-training with fusion in the backbone. In: Advances in NeurIPS (2022)
9. Forbes, M., Kaeser-Chen, C., Sharma, P., Belongie, S.: Neural naturalist: generating fine-grained image comparisons. In: Proceedings of the EMNLP-IJCNLP, pp. 708–717 (2019)
10. Geng, Z., Sun, K., Xiao, B., Zhang, Z., Wang, J.: Bottom-up human pose estimation via disentangled keypoint regression (2021). https://doi.org/10.48550/arXiv.2104.02300
11. Gu, X., Lin, T.Y., Kuo, W., Cui, Y.: Open-vocabulary object detection via vision and language knowledge distillation (2022). https://doi.org/10.48550/arXiv.2104.13921
12. He, K., Zhang, X., Ren, S., Sun, J.: Deep residual learning for image recognition. In: Proceedings of the CVPR (2016)
13. Jia, C., et al.: Scaling up visual and vision-language representation learning with noisy text supervision. In: Proceedings of the ICML, pp. 4904–4916 (2021)

14. Kamath, A., Singh, M., LeCun, Y., Misra, I., Synnaeve, G., Carion, N.: MDETR - modulated detection for end-to-end multi-modal understanding. In: Proceedings of the ICCV, pp. 1760–1770 (2021)
15. Kim, D., Angelova, A., Kuo, W.: Region-aware pretraining for open-vocabulary object detection with vision transformers. In: Proceedings of the CVPR, pp. 11144–11154 (2023)
16. Kuo, W., Cui, Y., Gu, X., Piergiovanni, A.J., Angelova, A.: Open-vocabulary object detection upon frozen vision and language models. In: Proceedings of the CoLT (2023)
17. Larochelle, H., Erhan, D., Bengio, Y.: Zero-data learning of new tasks. In: AAAI (2008)
18. Li, J., Wang, C., Zhu, H., Mao, Y., Fang, H.S., Lu, C.: CrowdPose: efficient crowded scenes pose estimation and a new benchmark. In: Proceedings of the CVPR (2019)
19. Li, L.H., et al.: Grounded language-image pre-training. In: Proceedings of the CVPR, pp. 10965–10975 (2022)
20. Li, Y., et al.: TokenPose: learning keypoint tokens for human pose estimation. In: Proceedings of the ICCV (2021)
21. Lin, T.-Y., et al.: Microsoft COCO: common objects in context. In: Fleet, D., Pajdla, T., Schiele, B., Tuytelaars, T. (eds.) ECCV 2014. LNCS, vol. 8693, pp. 740–755. Springer, Cham (2014). https://doi.org/10.1007/978-3-319-10602-1_48
22. Liu, Z., et al.: Swin transformer: hierarchical vision transformer using shifted windows. In: Proceedings of the ICCV, pp. 10012–10022 (2021)
23. Mall, U., Hariharan, B., Bala, K.: Field-guide-inspired zero-shot learning. In: Proceedings of the ICCV, pp. 9546–9555 (2021)
24. Mao, W., et al.: Poseur: direct human pose regression with transformers. In: Avidan, S., Brostow, G., Cissé, M., Farinella, G.M., Hassner, T. (eds.) ECCV 2022. LNCS, vol. 13666, pp. 72–88. Springer, Cham (2022). https://doi.org/10.1007/978-3-031-20068-7_5
25. McNally, W., Vats, K., Wong, A., McPhee, J.: Rethinking keypoint representations: modeling keypoints and poses as objects for multi-person human pose estimation. In: Avidan, S., Brostow, G., Cissé, M., Farinella, G.M., Hassner, T. (eds.) ECCV 2022. LNCS, vol. 13666, pp. 37–54. Springer, Cham (2022). https://doi.org/10.1007/978-3-031-20068-7_3
26. Minderer, M., et al.: Simple open-vocabulary object detection. In: Avidan, S., Brostow, G., Cissé, M., Farinella, G.M., Hassner, T. (eds.) ECCV 2022. LNCS, vol. 13670, pp. 728–755. Springer, Cham (2022). https://doi.org/10.1007/978-3-031-20080-9_42
27. MMPose Contributors: OpenMMLab pose estimation toolbox and benchmark (2020). https://github.com/open-mmlab/mmpose
28. Newell, A., Huang, Z., Deng, J.: Associative embedding: end-to-end learning for joint detection and grouping. In: Advances in NeurIPS, vol. 30 (2017)
29. Radford, A., et al.: Learning transferable visual models from natural language supervision. In: Proceedings of the ICML, vol. 139, pp. 8748–8763 (2021)
30. Redmon, J., Divvala, S., Girshick, R., Farhadi, A.: You only look once: unified, real-time object detection. In: Proceedings of the CVPR (2016)
31. Shen, S., et al.: How much can CLIP benefit vision-and-language tasks? In: Proceedings of the ICLR (2022)
32. Sun, K., Xiao, B., Liu, D., Wang, J.: Deep high-resolution representation learning for human pose estimation. In: Proceedings of the CVPR (2019)

33. Van Horn, G., et al.: Building a bird recognition app and large scale dataset with citizen scientists: the fine print in fine-grained dataset collection. In: Proceedings of the CVPR, pp. 595–604 (2015)

34. Vogel, F., Shvetsova, N., Karlinsky, L., Kuehne, H.: VL-taboo: an analysis of attribute-based zero-shot capabilities of vision-language models (2022). https://doi.org/10.48550/arXiv.2209.06103

35. Welinder, P., et al.: Caltech-UCSD birds 200. Technical report, California Institute of Technology (2010)

36. Xiao, B., Wu, H., Wei, Y.: Simple baselines for human pose estimation and tracking. In: Proceedings of the ECCV (2018)

37. Xu, Y., Zhang, J., Zhang, Q., Tao, D.: ViTPose: simple vision transformer baselines for human pose estimation. In: Advances in NeurIPS (2022)

38. Yang, S., Quan, Z., Nie, M., Yang, W.: Transpose: keypoint localization via transformer. In: Proceedings of the ICCV, pp. 11802–11812 (2021)

39. Yang, Y., Yang, J., Xu, Y., Zhang, J., Lan, L., Tao, D.: APT-36k: a large-scale benchmark for animal pose estimation and tracking. In: Advances in NeurIPS Datasets and Benchmarks Track (2022)

40. Yao, Y., et al.: PEVL: position-enhanced pre-training and prompt tuning for vision-language models. In: Proceedings of the EMNLP, pp. 11104–11117 (2022)

41. Yu, H., Xu, Y., Zhang, J., Zhao, W., Guan, Z., Tao, D.: AP-10K: a benchmark for animal pose estimation in the wild. In: Conference on NeurIPS Datasets and Benchmarks Track (Round 2) (2021)

42. Yuan, Y., et al.: HRFormer: high-resolution vision transformer for dense prediction. In: Advances in NeurIPS (2021)

43. Zhang, H., et al.: GLIPv2: unifying localization and vision-language understanding. In: Advances in NeurIPS, vol. 35, pp. 36067–36080 (2022)

Author Index

Printed in the United States
by Baker & Taylor Publisher Services